# Atlantic Spain and Portugal

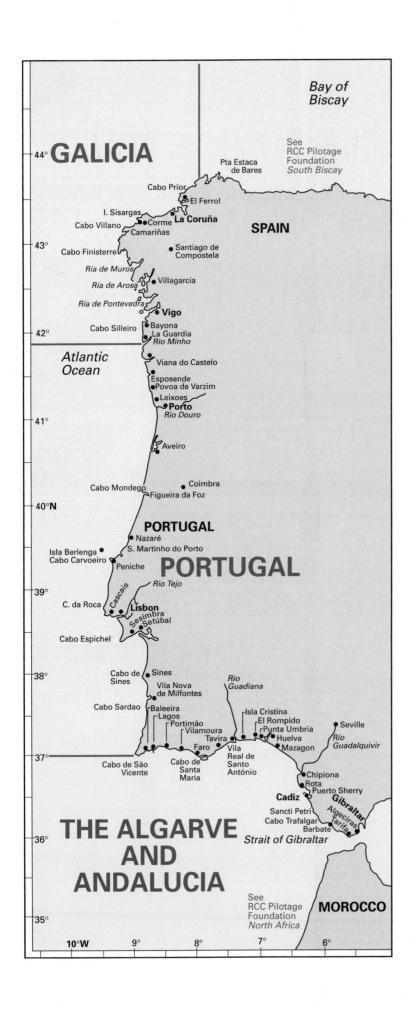

# Atlantic Spain and Portugal

ROYAL CRUISING CLUB
PILOTAGE FOUNDATION

Oz Robinson
Revised by Anne Hammick

**Imray Laurie Norie & Wilson Ltd**
St Ives Cambridgeshire England

Published by
**Imray Laurie Norie & Wilson Ltd**
Wych House St Ives Huntingdon
Cambridgeshire PE27 5BT England
☎ +44 (0) 1480 462114
*Fax* +44 (0) 1480 496109
*E-mail* ilnw@imray.com
*Web* www.imray.com
2000

First edition 1988
Second edition 1990
Third edition 1995
Fourth edition 2000
© Text and photographs: Royal Cruising Club Pilotage Foundation 2000
© Plans: Imray, Laurie, Norie & Wilson Ltd 2000
© Photographs without attribution: Anne Hammick 1999

ISBN 0 85288 405 2

British Library Cataloguing in Publication Data.

A catalogue record for this book is available from the British Library.

This work is correct to March 2000.

## CAUTION

Every effort has been made to ensure the accuracy of this book. It contains selected information and thus is not definitive and does not include all known information on the subject in hand; this is particularly relevant to the plans, which should not be used for navigation. The Pilotage Foundation believes that this selection represents a useful aid to prudent navigation, but the safety of a vessel depends ultimately on the judgement of the navigator who should assess all information, published or unpublished.

## CORRECTIONS

The RCC Pilotage Foundation would be glad to receive any corrections, information or suggestions which readers may consider would improve the book. Letters should be addressed to the Editor, Atlantic Spain and Portugal, care of the publishers.

## CORRECTIONAL SUPPLEMENTS

This pilot book will be amended at intervals by the issue of correctional supplements. These are published on the internet at our web site www.imray.com and may be downloaded free of charge. Printed copies are also available on request from the publishers at the above address.

## PLANS

The plans in this guide are not to be used for navigation – they are designed to support the text and should always be used together with navigational charts. Even so, every effort has been made to locate harbour and anchorage plans adjacent to the relevant text.

It should be bourne in mind that the characteristics of lights may be changed during the life of the book, and that in any case notification of such changes is unlikely to be reported immediately. Each light is identified in both the text and on the plans (where it appears in red) by its international index number, as used in the Admiralty *List of Lights* from which the book may be updated when no longer new.

All bearings are given from seaward and refer to true north. Scales may be taken from the scales of latitude. Symbols are based on those used by the British Admiralty – users are referred to *Symbols and Abbreviations (NP 5011)*.

## Key to symbols used on the plans

|  | **English** | *Spanish* | *Portuguese* |
|---|---|---|---|
| ⚓ | harbourmaster/ port office | *capitán de puerto/capitania* | *diretor do porto/ capitania* |
| ⊖ | customs | *aduana* | *alfândega* |
| 🛢 | fuel (diesel, petrol) | *gasoil, gasolina* | *gasoleo, gasolina* |
| Ⓐ | chandlery shop | *efectos navales* | *fornecedore de barcos* |
| ▣ | travel-lift | *grua firatoria, pórtico elevador* | *e pórtico, pórtico elevador* |
| ⚑ | yacht club | *club náutico* | *clube náutico, clube naval* |
| 🚿 | showers | *duchas* | *duches* |
| ⓘ | information | *información* | *informações* |
| ✉ | post office | *oficina de correos* | *agência do correio* |
| ⚓ | anchorage | *fondeadero* | *fundeadouro* |

See Appendix III, page 264, for further Portuguese and Spanish terms commonly used in a marine context.

Printed in Great Britain by
The Bath Press, Glasgow

# Contents

# Foreword

The Royal Cruising Club Pilotage Foundation was created by members of the RCC to enable them and others to bring their experience of sailing and cruising to a wider public and to encourage the aspiring sailor to cruise further afield with confidence. It was established in 1977 as a registered charity whose object is 'to advance the science and practice of navigation'. Initial funding was provided by a very generous gift by an American member, Dr Fred Ellis, which together with the gift of their copyrights by several other RCC members has allowed the Foundation to fulfill its remit by producing and maintaining pilot books and cruising guides. It now manages the production and updating of over 20 such books.

*Atlantic Spain and Portugal* was the brainchild of Oz Robinson when he was the director of the Pilotage Foundation and has been a bestseller since it was first published in 1988. The need for subsequent editions at frequent intervals has been driven by rapid change in the facilities provided on this coast and by high demand for the book from the ever increasing numbers of yachtsmen cruising or passage making along this coast.

In the course of her research for this edition between July and November 1999, Anne Hammick has visited every harbour to talk to harbourmasters and others to keep abreast of such changes. The Pilotage Foundation is indebted to her for her painstaking efforts to make this book what it is today - the definitive cruising guide for the most westerly coast of Europe.

In order to keep this book up to date during its lifetime, supplements are produced by the Pilotage Foundation and are published on the Imray website. To assist us in doing this we need feedback from users and we ask that you send us (through Imray) updated information and any comments that you feel would benefit others.

Francis Walker
Director
Royal Cruising Pilotage Foundation
March 2000

## Acknowledgements

As the Foreword states, I visited every single harbour described in this book between July and November last year – most for the second or third time, having also researched and written the 1995 edition and meanwhile cruised the Algarve and Andalucían coasts while 'off duty'. Readers might therefore be forgiven for assuming that this left me with little need of input from users of the previous edition. They could not be more wrong.

Not only are letters – and increasingly e-mails – from fellow yachtsmen essential when compiling interim supplements, but they are invaluable in alerting an editor/researcher to harbours where changes are taking place and thus where additional research time – very often a limited resource – should be spent. Perhaps more importantly each individual, be they cruising yachtsman or professional writer, has their visit to any given place coloured by a whole range of factors: the weather, the attitude of local officials, potential language problems, even whether lunch was up to expectations or they meet up with long-lost sailing friends. Input from a wide range of yachtsmen and women overcomes this problem, and more than once an enthusiastic report has caused me to rethink a somewhat negative write-up, or vice versa.

I treat the factual information I receive from different sources as something of a jigsaw, not unlike old-style navigation. If a single piece does not fit, it is my job to crosscheck when possible and start badgering my longsuffering sources for explanations when it is not. In this context I would particularly like to thank (working from north to south) Señor Alfredo Lagos of Astilleros Lagos, Vigo for helping me track down information relating to harbours in his native Galicia; David Lumby, long-term resident of Viana do Castelo, for sharing his considerable knowledge of Portugal and the Algarve; Captain Esteves Cardoso of the Administração do Porto de Lisboa for answering my e-mailed queries promptly, efficiently and with great good humour; José de Sousa Osorio Aragao of the Portuguese Tourist Office for encouraging tardy marina officials to bite the bullet and answer my enquiries; Wolfgang Michalsky, owner of the Varadero Río Piedras in El Rompido, Andalucía for keeping me up to date on the shifting sands of that difficult entrance; and finally Pat & Pippa Purdy of *Ganilly Rose* for agreeing, at a chance meeting in Seville, to check my drafts of Algarve and Andalucía and then doing so with such obvious care.

Closer to home I would like to thank Sara Romero, Gavin Poole and Heidi Smith for assisting with Spanish, Portuguese and German translation respectively; the staff of Newell's Travel, Falmouth for making all my somewhat complicated travel arrangements with expertise and unfailing cheerfulness; Marine Instruments Ltd, Falmouth for technical assistance; and the staff of Ancasta International Boat Sales, Falmouth for the use of their excellent photocopier. Last but far from least I owe a big thank you to the excellent pilot (anonymous at his own request) with whom I took the aerial photographs. That they are not more inspiring – particularly in the early part of the book – sadly reflect the hazy visibility only too typical of Galicia.

I had not realised quite how many cruising yachtsmen and women had taken the trouble to send me feedback until I started to compile an alphabetical list. Some wrote about a single harbour, others sent several pages of useful snippets, but for efforts above and beyond the call of duty I must single out Claire and Jimmy James of *Phœacian*, and Maggie and the late John Hines of *Pushpa*. Claire and John both, but quite independently, compiled pages of notes, suggestions and constructive criticisms. This book would have been much the poorer without them.

It would also have been the poorer without the contributions from: Graham Adam (*Aurora*); Charles & Jacqui Anderson (*Seasoldier*); Colin Barry (*Sundance of Suffolk*); Peter Battley (STS *Lord Portal*); Roger & Penny Bennee (*Soothsaye of Hamble II*); Rasmus, Rillhe and Niels Blixenkrone–Møller (*Nuts*); Sarah Brown & Simon Lee (*Vagabond*); Tony Carey & Lorrie Wood (*Papeche*); Paddy Carr (*Celadus*); Carla & Quenten Cook (*Cassiopeia*); Derek & Jann Dawes (*Great Days*); Jack Edwards (*Thane of Fife*); Paul Fay (*Phase Two*); Nicko Franks (STS *Arethusa*); Tom Geddes (*September Tide*); Mr & Mrs GW Griffin (*Sundancer*); Mike & Sally Hadley (*Pinta's Pilot*); Hollyann Holdsworth (*Riverdancer*); Glory & David van Horn (*Orion*); Bettina & Richard Hutt; Tom & Vicky Jackson (*Sunstone*); Barry & Julia James (*Buster*); Leslie Jones (*Namaqua C*); Bill Keatinge (*Rafiki of Lymington*); Chris Knight (*Globestar*); Henny Kockx-Schipper (*Dutch Brandy*); Guy Lafontaine; Charles-Henri Mangin (*Strella*); John & Sally Melling (*Taraki*); Mary & Guy Morgan (*Mor-ula*); Martin Northney (*Navicula*); Pam & Paul (*Pod*); Niki Perryman & Jamie Morrison (*Siandra*); Matthew Power (*Chinita*); Peter Price (*Lectron*); Annette Ridout (*Nordlys*); Glyn Roberts (*Amity of Peacehaven*); Frank Singleton; Lynne Stothart (*Orlando*); Shirley Strawbridge & Colin Wilkinson (*Sestina of Leune*); Alan J Taylor (*Bellamanda*); David & Pat Teall (*Retreat from Battle II*); Sandy Watson and his daughter Sarah (*Libertà*); John R Wicks (*Dreamtime*), and the skipper of *Godbonden* whose signature I was unable to decipher!

Back at the business end I owe a sincere thank you to Francis Walker, Director of the RCC Pilotage Foundation, for his wise balance of advice, guidance and the freedom to do things my own way; and once again to Willie Wilson and his staff at Imray Laurie Norie & Wilson Ltd – in particular Elaine Sharples for her excellent work in transferring all the old plans into their new and much more legible computer format, and to Julia Knight for her work on the text.

No author would maintain their reputation for very long without the aid of a team of eagle-eyed proof readers, and for the final checking of this book I would like to thank my Mother, Francis Walker, Fay and John Garey, and John Power. It is largely thanks to their efforts that relatively few typing, spelling and grammatical errors should creep through into the finished volume. Any factual errors are my responsibility alone.

Finally, I can do no better than to repeat the final paragraph from the Acknowledgements to the previous edition: 'Much harbour development is currently taking place along the Atlantic coasts of Spain and Portugal. If you, the user, find these pages do not accurately reflect what you encounter, please write to the publishers and bring us up to date'. And thank you once again to all who already have.

Anne Hammick
Yacht *Wrestler of Leigh*
Falmouth, Cornwall
March 2000

## Royal Cruising Club Pilotage Foundation pilots and guides

Published by Imray Laurie Norie & Wilson Ltd
*Atlantic Spain and Portugal*
*Atlantic Islands*
*Islas Baleares*
*Mediterranean Spain – Costas del Sol & Blanca*
*– Costas del Azahar, Dorada & Brava*
*The Baltic Sea*
*North Biscay*
*South Biscay*
*North Brittany*
*Channel Islands*
*Lesser Antilles* – with SHOM
*North Africa*
*Faroe, Iceland & Greenland*
*Chile*

Published by A & C Black Ltd
*Atlantic Crossing Guide*
*Pacific Crossing Guide*

Published by RCC Desktop Publishing Unit
*Cruising Guide to West Africa*
*The Falkland Islands Shores*
*The South Atlantic Coast of South America*

Remembering
JOHN C HINES
1928 – 1999

whose wise and constructive suggestions
led to many of the changes and improvements
incorporated in this new edition

# Introduction

## Atlantic Spain and Portugal

The character of the Atlantic coasts of Spain and Portugal varies widely between the sheer cliffs north of Cabo Finisterre and the flat sandy lagoons of the Faro area. Their attraction for the cruising yachtsman is equally variable. The aim of this book is to indicate both the nature of the cruising grounds and harbours of the regions and how they may be approached. It does not pretend to be a comprehensive guide and should not be used without the appropriate charts. One or more of the many travellers' guides available – see Appendix II – will also justify a place on the bookshelves.

Local place names are used with the exception of Lisbon and Seville, too familiar by now in their anglicised forms. In Galicia the Gallego form of the name may also be given. Gallego, an ancient language which falls somewhere between Castilian Spanish and Portuguese, is still in everyday use and many road signs carry names in both languages. Other non-English words used will be found in the glossary.

Two likely pitfalls for the unwary English speaker in Iberia are the words 'marina' and 'yacht'. In both Spain and Portugal *marina* or *marinha* implies simply 'marine' (as in *marina mercante* – merchant navy) and does not necessarily imply a purpose-built yacht harbour which, unless it is unusually large and has all facilities, is more likely to be designated a *puerto deportivo* in Spain, or either *porto desportivo* or *doca de recreio* in Portugal. Similarly, the description 'yacht' is usually taken to mean a good-sized motorboat, particularly in the south. A sailing boat of whatever size is a *barco de vela* or, in Portugal, a *barco à vela*.

A break has been made with previous editions of this book in that terms for harbour structures have, so far as possible, been translated from the original Spanish or Portuguese into English, so as to indicate of the structure's purpose: *breakwater* – structure of considerable length giving protection to a harbour or anchorage; *mole* – short but solid structure, usually of stone, giving limited protection (possibly in conjunction with an opposing breakwater); *quay* or *wharf* – solid embankment with a sheer face, intended for unloading fish, etc; *jetty* – solid structure raised above the water on metal, concrete or timber supports; *pontoon* – floating structure, usually reached via a sloping walkway.

## Sailing and navigation

### Winds and climate

The northern part of the region is influenced by North Atlantic weather systems. In winter, fronts and occasionally secondary depressions may cross the area. Winds are variable but those between southwest and northwest are more common. In summer, land and sea breezes can be expected inshore but the influence of Azores highs tends to produce winds from the north; this northerly tendency starts about April and as summer progresses and latitude decreases these winds develop into the Portuguese trades. At the height of summer in the south of the region the Portuguese trades remain dominant offshore west of 20°W, while eastwards their influence is felt along the coast from São Vicente towards Faro, often reinforced in the afternoons by the land effect. This influence wanes until, by Cádiz, summer afternoons may produce a westerly sea breeze. Cádiz can also be affected by a *levante* coming out of the Mediterranean. Towards the Strait of Gibraltar the winds tend to be either easterly or westerly, the former more common in summer and the latter in winter.

Gales are uncommon in the summer but may occur. The better known are the *levante* and *poniente*, the easterly and westerly gales of the Strait of Gibraltar, and the *nordeste pardo*, a cloudy northeaster of the Finisterre area. In theory the *vendavale*, a southwesterly blow in Galicia, is unlikely to occur in summer but exceptions do occur, and in 1999 strong to gale force southwesterlies blew at intervals from July onwards.

Galicia is the wet corner of Spain – it has much the same climatic feel as southwest England. To the south, whilst winters may be like June in the English Channel, in summer rainfall decreases and temperatures rise until, around Cádiz, Mediterranean levels are reached.

Sea temperatures in summer range from 17°C in Galicia to 21° at Gibraltar, and in winter from 12° to 14°. The chances of coastal fog along the west coast of the peninsula are greatest in July and August when the incidence may rise as high as one day in ten or twelve, particularly in the *rías bajas* (the larger *rías* of southern Galicia) where in summer it occasionally lasts for a week at a stretch. It is much rarer along the southwest coast.

### Currents and tides

Currents are much affected by recent winds and may set in any direction. The trend along the west coast is from north to south, though north of Finisterre there can be an easterly set into the Bay of Biscay. East of São Vicente the upper layers of the sea re-supply the Mediterranean with water lost through evaporation. The current sets towards the Strait at about 0·5 knot at the western end, increasing to around 2 knots through the Strait itself, to which a tidal element may have to be added – see page 244. However prolonged easterly winds can produce a reverse current, which is said to set into the bays, as far west as São Vicente.

Information on tidal streams is confusing. Off the *rías bajas* the flood is supposed to run north and off Peniche, in Portugal, to the southeast – but no one has identified the nodal point. The only reasonably safe assumption is that the flood tide sets into the Galician *rías* and the ebb drains them. The same is generally true of a Portuguese *rio*, but this is less than a certainty and depends on the amount of water coming down the *rio* itself. The Rio Douro is a particular example of this. In the Strait of Gibraltar, tidal streams can exceed 3 knots at springs.

The standard ports for the area are La Coruña, Lisbon, Cádiz and Gibraltar. The relationship between their times of high water and the time of high water at Dover is not constant from day to day.

Similarly the relationship between the times of high water at standard and secondary ports varies, as does the time lapse between high and low water. Furthermore, times and heights may differ considerably from predictions as a result of wind effects, particularly in the *rías bajas*. Figures given can therefore only be approximate – for more precise data, consult a specialist tide table (though there is no guarantee that predictions will prove more accurate than the approximations used here).

The following is a selection of tidal ranges (in metres):

|  | La Coruña | Vigo | Lisbon | Faro | Cádiz | Gibraltar |
|---|---|---|---|---|---|---|
| Springs | 3·3 | 2·9 | 3·3 | 2·8 | 2·8 | 0·9 |
| Neaps | 1·3 | 1·4 | 1·6 | 1·2 | 1·3 | 0·4 |

# The cruising grounds

In cruising terms, the Atlantic coast of Spain and Portugal falls naturally into three regions: Galicia – the *rías altas* between El Ferrol and Cabo Finisterre and the *rías bajas* from Finisterre to the Portuguese border at the Rio Minho; the Portuguese coast from the Spanish border south to Cabo de São Vicente; and finally the eastward trending coast from Cabo de São Vicente to Gibraltar, which in Portugal is known as the Algarve and in Spain forms part of Andalucía.

## Rías altas

Of all the regions, this is the one most exposed to the Atlantic climate. It also has a dramatic coastline, especially in the west, though the individual *rías* are of a size more suited to day sailing than extended cruising. In fine summer weather the cruise from La Coruña round to Finisterre calling at the Rías de Corme and de Camariñas is an interesting and pleasant sail, but in stormy conditions the coast is one to avoid – not for nothing is it known locally as the *Costa del Morte*. With the exception of La Coruña, which has pretty well everything necessary for the yachtsman plus a long and distinguished history, the small harbours of the *rías altas* have limited facilities for yachts, but they are well set in striking surroundings and relatively free of foreign tourists.

## Rías bajas

Some consider the *rías bajas* to be the best cruising area of all and spend weeks pottering about the ports and anchorages, taking advantage of good communications from such ports as Villagarcía de Arosa or Vigo to explore Galicia (and in particular to visit Santiago de Compostela). Less exposed to the Atlantic weather than the *rías altas*, the great inlets have beaches, interesting towns, and opportunities for rock-hopping for those wishing to test their pilotage. There are many restaurants and hotels.

The region suffers more from fog than the *rías altas*, yet the Azores high pressure system can on occasion produce a clear weather northeasterly blow of force 5–6 which may last for several days – but there is always shelter to be found within a short distance.

### Foz do Minho to Cabo de São Vicente

This coast is not a cruising man's paradise but it includes some remarkable places to visit – notably Porto and Lisbon for their history, and Aveiro and the Rio Sado for their sandbanks and swamps. The coast itself is on the whole low – the hills are inland and in summer may be lost in the haze – and in places there are miles of featureless beach.

The harbours are commercial or fishing in origin, but most are gradually making concessions to yachts. Many have hazards of one sort or another in the approach or entrance – Leixões and Sines are notable exceptions. The most common is a bar which alters with the winter storms and which, although safe enough for freighters, can be dangerous for the smaller vessel if there is a swell running and made worse if it is running across the tidal stream. As the bars are associated with rivers, conditions are usually worst on the ebb.

Another major feature of this region is the Portuguese trade winds, mentioned previously, and many take advantage of the prevailing northerly winds to slide past the whole coast as quickly as possible. The passage northwards is tedious even in early summer, and if it must be made it is worth considering taking a dogleg out as far as the Azores.

### São Vicente to Gibraltar

The southern coasts of Portugal and Spain offer easier cruising than the Portuguese Atlantic margin. Having rounded the corner at Cabo de São Vicente, the influences of the Mediterranean and the Moor begin to show and, despite the tourist overlay on the Algarve, harbours are on the whole more attractive as well as being more frequent. With a couple of exceptions the entrances are easier than those on the west coast.

The Algarve is crowded in summer and its harbours busy. The next stretch of coast, the shallow lagoons of Faro and Olhão, the quiet Guadiana and the relatively busy Guadalquivir, is the best region for wildlife. A peculiar hazard of the Andalucían coast, described in greater detail on page 169, is the tunny net, which can stretch several miles out to sea at right angles to the shoreline and is strong enough to foul the propeller of a small coaster. Currently four or five are set annually, details and locations of which will be found in the text.

# Navigational aids

## Lights and buoyage

All buoys and lights in this area adhere to the IALA A system, based on the direction of the main flood tide. In Portugal and Spain heights of lights are measured from mean sea level. They therefore generally appear in Iberian publications as a metre or so higher than in British Admiralty publications.

The four-figure international numbering system has been used to identify lights in text and on plans. This has the advantage that each number is individual and refers to one light only, wherever it may occur throughout the book. Secondly, it facilitates annual correction from the Admiralty *List of Lights and Fog Signals Volume D (NP 77)* or weekly updating via Admiralty *Notices to Mariners*. Lights are normally listed in the order in which they become relevant upon approach and entry. All bearings are given from seaward and refer to true north.

## Visual harbour signals

Although in theory both Spain and Portugal still use visual signals to indicate whether a harbour is safe to enter, in relatively few cases do they appear to be used. One exception is Figueira da Foz, where danger signals were displayed in September 1999 during strong southwesterlies – see page 133. Further details are given in the text, but it must be remembered that signals indicating the state of a harbour bar are intended for commercial traffic, and that conditions safe for a big ship are not necessarily safe for a yacht.

## Charts

Current British Admiralty information is largely obtained from Spanish and Portuguese sources. The Spanish and Portuguese Hydrographic Offices issue their own charts – often to a much larger scale than Admiralty coverage and corrected by their own *Notices* – but they can be difficult to get hold of outside the peninsula. Both Spanish and Portuguese charts tend to be short on compass roses – carry a chart plotter or rule which incorporates a protractor.

In 1999/2000 the Portuguese *Instituto Hidrográfico* was in the process of reorganising its chart coverage, but since the two series are likely to be running in parallel for some time both numbers are listed under the side headings 'Portuguese (old series)' and 'Portuguese (new series)'. As a general rule, 'old series' charts have a one or two digit number, 'new series' charts a five digit number.

Listing of a chart under both Approach and

Harbour headings in this volume normally implies that a large-scale harbour plan appears as an insert on a smaller-scale approach chart. A full list of charts – Admiralty, Spanish, Portuguese and Imray – will be found in Appendix I, page 259.

*Before departure* Spanish and Portuguese charts (as well as fully corrected Admiralty publications) can be obtained through

**Imray Laurie Norie & Wilson Ltd,**
Wych House, The Broadway, St Ives,
Huntingdon, Cambs PE27 5BT
☎ 01480 462114 *Fax* 01480 496109
*e-mail* ilnw@imray.com, *web site* www.imray.com

*In Spain* – Spanish charts can be ordered from

**Instituto Hidrográfico de la Marina,**
Plaza de San Severiano 3, DP 11007 Cádiz
☎ 956 599409 *Fax* 956 599396

In Galicia there are Spanish chart agents in La Coruña, Villagarcia de Arosa and Vigo; in Andalucía in Huelva, Seville, Cádiz and Algeciras – contact details will be found in the relevant harbour's text. A few marina offices are also willing to order charts for visiting yachts.

*In Portugal* – Portuguese charts can be obtained from

**Instituto Hidrográfico de la Marina,**
Rua des Trinas 49, 1296 Lisboa
☎ 213 955119 *Fax* 213 960515
*e-mail* mail@hidrografico.pt
*web site* www.hidrografico.pt
**J Garraio & Ca Lda,**
Avenida 24 de Julho 2, 1200 Lisboa
☎ 213 473081 *Fax* 213 428950
*e-mail* j.garraio@mail.telepac.pt

Some *capitanias* stock charts of their own areas but this is a matter of private enterprise, while a few marina offices are willing to order charts from Lisbon for visiting yachts.

*In Gibraltar* Though prices are reported to be much higher than in the UK, fully corrected Admiralty charts and other publications are available from

**Gibraltar Chart Agency Ltd,**
11A Block 5 Watergardens
☎ 76293 *Fax* 77293

## Horizontal chart datum and satellite derived positions

Positions given by modern satellite navigation systems are normally expressed in terms of World Geodetic System 1984 (WGS84) Datum unless the receiver is specifically adjusted otherwise. New editions of British Admiralty charts are either based on WGS84 Datum or carry a note giving the correction necessary to comply with it, but charts published by other nations' hydrographic offices may use different datum references when covering the same area. Charts of various scales published by the same national authority may also use different datum references, particularly when the printing of one chart predates another.

In practice, this means that care must be taken when plotting a position expressed in latitude and longitude, or when transferring such a position from one chart to another, particularly when no reference can be made to physical features. For the same reason NO WAYPOINTS are given in this volume – positions of harbours and other features are rounded to the nearest minute of latitude and longitude, and are intended to facilitate location when pre-planning. THEY ARE NOT TO BE USED FOR NAVIGATION – navigators should take their own waypoints from the chart currently in use.

### Magnetic variation

In 2000 magnetic variation at the positions marked on the accompanying plan was:

A.  43°47'N 8°30'W – 5°20'W (8'E)
B.  42°47'N 9°40'W – 5°35'W (8'E)
C.  41°12'N 9°30'W – 5°15'W (9'E)
D.  39°42'N 9°40'W – 5°15'W (8'E)
E.  38°10'N 9°20'W – 5°10'W (8'E)
F.  36°47'N 7°40'W – 3°25'W (11'E)
G.  36°13'N 6°40'W – 3°W (11'E)

In 1999 a magnetic anomaly was reported off southern Galicia and northern Portugal which, unaccountably, appeared to affect GPS receivers. More information on this phenomenon would be welcome.

### Traffic Separation Zones

Traffic Separation Zones exist off Cabo Finisterre, outside Os Farilhões and Ilha Berlenga, off Cabo da Roca, off Cabo de São Vicente and in the Strait of Gibraltar. Each has a wide Inshore Traffic Zone and yachts are strongly advised to avoid crossing the main shipping lanes if at all possible.

# Weather forecasts

### Shoreside weather forecasts

Nearly all marina offices display a weather forecast and synoptic chart/s, usually updated daily, and though often in the local language the vocabulary is limited and can easily be deciphered. At first glance Portuguese synoptic charts seem particularly daunting, giving much more detail of wind strengths and wave heights than is usual in Britain, but again a little study will generally pay off.

For a more general indication of trends try the weather map in a local newspaper – eg. *El País, Voz de Galicia* or *El Correo Galicia* (Spain) or *Jornal de Notícias* or *Público* (Portugal).

### Weather information by telephone

In Spain, recorded marine weather bulletins are provided by the Instituto Nacional de Meteorological for Galicia and the north coast, and Andalúcia and beyond. The service is only available within the country, but can be accessed by vessels equipped with Autolink. The bulletin is read in Spanish.

*Galicia –* ☎ 906 365 372
  *High Seas Bulletin* for Finisterre, etc
  *Coastal Waters Bulletin* for the coasts of Coruña and
  Pontevedra, etc

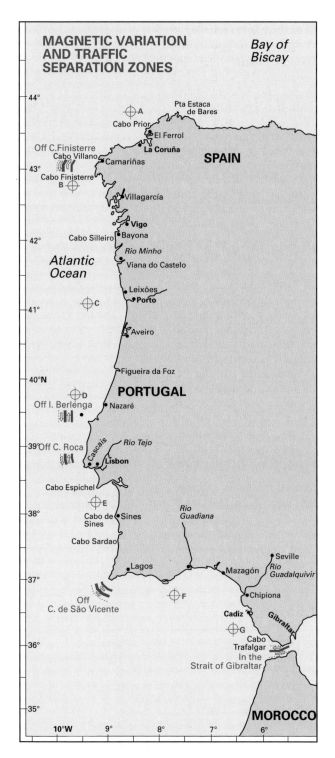

*Andalúcia –* ☎ 906 365 373
  *High Seas Bulletin* for São Vicente, Cádiz, etc
  *Coastal Waters Bulletin* for the coasts of Huelva,
  Cádiz, Cueta, etc

In Portugal, recorded marine weather bulletins are available, in Portuguese, on the following numbers:

*Spanish border to Lisbon* Inshore ☎ 0601 123 123;
  offshore ☎ 0601 123 140
*Lisbon to Cabo de São Vicente* Inshore ☎ 0601 123 124;
  offshore ☎ 0601 123 141
*Cabo de São Vicente to the Spanish border* Inshore ☎ 0601
  123 125; offshore ☎ 0601 123 142.

## Weather forecasts by radio

A variety of weather forecasts are available by radio, though relatively few in English. Details of those broadcast by Coast Radio Stations will be found under the relevant harbour, and can be updated from the *Admiralty List of Radio Signals, Volume 1(1) (NP 281/1)* and *Volume 3(1) (NP 283/1)* as necessary. It should be noted that all times quoted for weather messages, navigational warnings and traffic lists are in Universal Time (UT or, previously, GMT) unless otherwise stated. This contrasts with harbour and marina radio schedules, which are generally governed by office hours and are therefore given in Local Time (LT).

*BBC Radio 4* – shipping forecasts are broadcast on 198kHz (1515m) at 0048, 0535, 1201 and 1754 UK local time (BST in summer, UT in winter). Additional 3 day forecasts are broadcast at 0029 Monday–Friday, 0022 Saturday and 0014 Sunday, with a long range sailing forecast at 0542 on Sunday. While undoubtedly useful, particularly in Galicia, the areas covered are large and forecasts may have little relevance to local conditions. In September 1999 a local radio station, thought to be Portuguese, was interfering with reception of *BBC Radio 4* in southern Galicia and northern Portugal.

*Radio France International* – weather information is broadcast at 1140 UT daily, (timed to fit the vagaries of programming and therefore not always punctual). The following receiving frequencies vary according to location: English Channel and Bay of Biscay 6175kHz; North Atlantic east of 50°W 11700, 15530, 17575kHz. Although in French, the forecast is read clearly and at moderate pace (though non-French speakers may find it helpful to record it for translation). The format is straightforward being gale warnings, synopsis, development and 24 hour area forecasts.

*Radio Nacional de España* – weather information is broadcast at 1000 and 1300 LT via the following stations: La Coruña 639kHz; Seville 684kHz.

*Sociedad España de Radio* – a programme containing information for commercial fishing operations, plus weather forecasts and sea conditions, is broadcast between 0600 and 0700 LT and again in condensed form at 2205 LT simultaneously from the following stations: La Coruña 1080kHz; Vigo 1026kHz; Huelva 100·5MHz; Cádiz 1485kHz; Seville 792kHz.

*Radifusão Portuguesa* – broadcasts a forecast for the coastal waters of Portugal at 1100 daily on the following frequencies, one or more of which may be usable in any particular place: 650kHz, 666kHz, 720kHz, 1287kHz, 94·7MHz, 96·4MHz, 97·6MHz, 97·9MHz.

*Radio Gibraltar (GBC)* and *British Forces Broadcasting Service* – both broadcast weather information regularly in English on 91·3, 92·6, 100·5MHz and 1458kHz *(GBC)* and 93·5 and 97·8MHz *(BFBS)* – see harbour information for schedules, which vary throughout the week.

### Navtex

Four navtex stations cover the waters of the Bay of Biscay and the Iberian coast. Poor reception may be a problem inside the Galician *rías* or in harbours throughout the area. Once at sea, reception appears to be good.

**Corsen (France)** Identification letter 'A'
*Transmits*: 518kHz in English.
*Storm warnings*: 0000, 0400, 0800, 1200, 1600, 2000 for areas North Biscay, South Biscay, Sole and Galicia.
*Weather messages*: 0000, 1200 for areas as above.
*Navigational warnings*: 0000, 0400, 0800, 1200, 1600, 2000 for areas as above.

**La Coruña** Identification letter 'D'
*Transmits*: 518kHz in Spanish and English.
*Weather messages*: 0030, 1230 for areas 1–6.
*Navigational warnings*: 0430, 0830, 1630, 2030 for Navarea II and local waters.

**Monsanto** Identification letter 'R' (located near Lisbon)
*Transmits*: 518kHz in English.
*Storm warnings*: on receipt for coastal waters of Portugal.
*Weather messages/navigational warnings*: 0250, 0650, 1050, 1450, 1850, 2250 for coastal waters of Portugal.

SPANISH FORECAST AREAS

Gran Sol 1
Viscaya 2
Cantábrico 3
Finisterre 4
San Vicente 6
Cádiz 7
Canarias 8
Alborán 10
Palos 11

**Tarifa** Identification letter 'G'

*Transmits*: 518kHz in English.

*Weather messages*: 0900, 2100 gale warnings, synopsis and forecast for areas 6–7.

*Navigational warnings*: 0100, 0500, 1300, 1700 for Navarea II and coastal waters.

### Weatherfax

A number of weatherfax transmissions cover the Iberian pensinsula, including those from *Northwood* and *Bracknell* (UK) and *Offenbach* (Germany). Transmissions from Madrid were discontinued late in 1998 and from Rota in mid 1999.

*Northwood* transmits on 3652, 4307, 6425·5 and 8331·5kHz, with a schedule at 0230 and 1530 and forecasts at 0320, 0650, 0950, 1210, 1500, 1800, 2120 and 2320. The information given at each forecast time varies, but over the 24 hour period forecasts for one, two, three, four and five days are given.

*Bracknell* transmits on 2618·5, 4610, 8040, 14436 and 18261kHz, with general notices at 1622. 24 hour forecasts are transmitted at 0440, 1042, 1641 and 2241; 48 hour forecasts at 0806 and 2222; and 72 hour forecasts at 0812 and 2230.

*Offenbach* transmits on 3855, 7880 and 13882·5kHz, with a schedule at 1111 and surface analyses at 0430, 0525, 0743, 1050, 1600, 1800 and 2200. 24 hour forecasts are transmitted at 0559 and 0612; 48 hour forecasts at 0625 and 0638; and 72 hour forecasts at 0651 and 0704. Coverage varies from transmission to transmission.

Full details are given in the Admiralty *List of Radio Signals, Volume 3(1)*.

### Weather forecasts on the Internet

An ever-increasing amount of weather-related information can be found on the internet, which can be accessed via cybercafés or many public libraries throughout both Spain and Portugal. As of February 2000 the following sites were suggested as useful, though some information is duplicated at least once. Further investigation immediately before departure would pay dividends since other sites are coming on stream all the time.

*Ant Veal's Weather Site*
web.bham.ac.uk/ggy4atv3/weather.htm
  Meteorological links for the UK, Iberian peninsula and Atlantic, with forecast pages, weather charts, climate data, satellite pictures, etc.

*CNN Weather Images*
cnn.com/WEATHER/images.html
  Worldwide weather coverage with charts, satellite imagery and 3 day forecasts for principal cities.

*Nottingham University site*
www.ccc.nottingham.ac.uk/meteosat/
  Meteosat pictures downloaded every 20 minutes (fast graphics are required for the colour images).

*Portuguese Met Office*
www.meteo.pt/
  In Portuguese, but reasonably user-friendly and incorporating animated satellite images, etc.

*Spanish Met Office*
www.inm.es/
  In Spanish but with easily understood colour graphics. Once in the site choose 'Información Meteorológ', and then 'inf.maritima'. Then select first 'salidas de los modelos de prediccion de viento y oleaje' and finally 'ultimos mapas previstos'. This gives a large selection of areas around the Iberian peninsula, Canary Islands and the North Atlantic with a choice of 12, 24 or 48 hour forecasts.

*UK Met Office*
www.meto.govt.uk/
  With satellite photos of Europe, latest UK gale warnings and the text of the latest UK shipping forecast.

*US National Weather Service*
weather.noaa.gov/fax/marine.shtml
  A wide range of surface analysis and forecast charts for both sides of the Atlantic.

*Yahoo! Weather*
http://weather.yahoo.com/
  Easy to navigate site (though with too many irritating advertisements) giving tourist-type weather information worldwide.

## Practicalities

### Entry and regulations

Spain and Portugal are both full members of the European Union, though the latter in particular seems reluctant to abandon form-filling even where EU citizens and their property are concerned. The approach to formalities is much more relaxed in Spain than in Portugal, where foreign yachts are still required to check in at each port visited, though as of 1999 this could generally be done during a single visit to a marina office – local requirements are detailed in the text.

Under EU regulations, EU registered boats arriving in another EU country are not required to fly the Q flag unless they have come directly from a non-EU country (which could be Gibraltar), have non-EU nationals aboard, or are carrying dutiable goods. Yachts registered outside the EU should always fly the Q flag on arrival. All visiting yachts should fly the relevant national courtesy flag – not forgetting to change it at the border.

*Spain* On first arrival in the country check with immigration, most easily done via a yacht club or marina office. Ship's papers, insurance documents (see below) and passports should be to hand. At subsequent ports it is not necessary to seek out officialdom, though one may occasionally be approached for information. This relaxed attitude is more noticeable in Galicia than Andalucía, where smuggling is more common and there is greater public awareness of Gibraltar as a political issue.

*Portugal* As of 1999 it was still obligatory to notify the authorities on arrival at every harbour in Portugal, whether entering the country for the first time or arriving from elsewhere within it – and do so immediately upon coming ashore.

While simply finding the relevant authorities may present problems in more remote anchorages, if berthed in (or anchored off) one of the increasing number of marinas it is relatively simple. Call at the marina office with passports, ship's papers (which should include proof of VAT status – see VAT and temporary import, below) and insurance documents, and complete a single *Movimento de Embarcações de Recreio* form (either on computer or by hand on self-carbonated paper) copies of which are then circulated by the marina to the *capitania* (port control and statistics), *brigada fiscal* and/or *alfândega* (drug control and customs) and *policia maritima* (immigration). There is no charge, and though an intended departure date must be stated, in most harbours there is no need for formal outward clearance. Those marinas not yet following this system almost invariably have the relevant authorities on site, a great improvement on previous years when a tired skipper might have to walk miles in search of the different offices.

Regarding the future, the position is unclear. In September 1999 one marina official (who claimed inside knowledge) stated categorically that the need for clearance in every port would be abolished within a year. Another, also in a senior position, explained that it would always be necessary to keep a eye on the movement of private yachts in order to fight the growing drugs problem. He expected the current system to remain in force until Portugal could afford the sophisticated electronic surveillance systems which, he claimed, were used by other countries. Whatever the situation, it will always be necessary to obtain formal clearance on first arriving in Portugal – take that opportunity to check what is required from then on.

*Gibraltar* Although a British territory, Gibraltar is not part of the EU and for this reason is popular as a long-term base for those from outside the EU. Fly the Q flag on approach and make for the customs quay at Waterport, unless going direct to Queensway Quay Marina. Various forms must be completed and the usual documents required – but at least it all takes place in English. See page 254 for further details.

## Drugs

In recent years drug running has become a serious problem along the entire Iberian coast. Previously confined largely to the south, notably the Algarve (one of the reasons why the Portuguese authorities are reluctant to relax clearance procedures) it is now reported to have spread as far north as Galicia, where hard drugs are brought into some of the smaller harbours in considerable quantities in high speed motorboats.

Yachts may be boarded at any time (day or night, including on passage) though normally this is confined to 'interesting' yachts, with the names of others merely being noted down. It is only sensible to cooperate as required and remember that the authorities have a duty to stop the importation of illegal drugs (and illegal immigrants) into Europe. In both countries yachtsmen are asked to inform the authorities of any yacht in which they believe the authorities should take a particular interest – or presumably of any other goings-on which appear suspicious.

## Third party insurance

In July 1999 Spain introduced a requirement that all vessels of more than 6m using its national waters must carry third party insurance to cover death, personal injury or material damage to third parties, losses which are a direct consequence of the above, and damage to other vessels.

It was stated that the relevant part of the policy must be written in Spanish and must be carried aboard at all times. Failure to do so could be punished with fines or even arrest of the vessel. Those UK insurance companies consulted all confirmed that the cover required was well within that normally provided in their policies and that a suitable letter of confirmation, in Spanish, was available without charge to their policy holders on request.

By the end of the year it appeared that few if any yachts had been asked to present this document, other than in the vicinity of Gibraltar. However evidence of insurance is frequently requested by marina officials in both Spain and Portugal, all of whom appear quite happy for it to be in English (or any other language).

## VAT and temporary import

A boat registered in the EU and on which VAT has been paid in an EU country, or which was launched before 1 January 1985 and is therefore exempt on grounds of age (and has the documents to prove it), can stay indefinitely in any other EU country without further VAT liability. To be totally covered a Single Administrative Document or SAD should be carried, though a full Certificate of Registry gives the date when the vessel was first registered and should therefore be acceptable as evidence of age (in this context it is worth noting that SSR documentation does not state the year of build).

A boat based outside the EU on which VAT has not been paid may be temporarily imported into the EU for a period not exceeding six months in any twelve before VAT is payable, though this period may sometimes be extended by prior agreement with the local customs authorities (for instance, some do not count time laid up – perhaps with the steering mechanism sealed – as part of the six months). While in EU waters the vessel may only be used by its owner, and may not be chartered or even lent to another person, on pain of paying VAT. If kept in the EU longer than six months VAT normally becomes due, unless a 'change of residency' can be established – usually limited to permanent liveaboards. There are marked differences in the way the rules are applied from one harbour to the next, let alone in different European countries.

*Spain* A VAT paid (or exempt) yacht may normally remain in the country almost indefinitely provided a *permiso aduanero* is first obtained, but may not be used commercially (ie. for chartering).

*Portugal* No limitation on length of stay for a VAT paid or exempt yacht. An annual tax is levied on all yachts kept for long periods in Portuguese waters irrespective of their VAT status.

*Gibraltar* As Gibraltar is not a part of the EU, VAT does not apply.

### Laying up

Yachts can safely be left afloat, whether laid up or overwintering, in most of the larger marinas described. It should be clear from the text when this is not the case. Possible places to lay up ashore include:

*Galicia* Sada (Fontan), La Coruña, Portosin, Villagarcía de Arosa, Sangenjo, Vigo and Bayona, with Caramiñal and the new Porto Pedras Negras on the Peninsula del Grove also possible.

*Atlantic Portugal* Leixões, Nazaré, Cascais and Lisbon, with Póvoa de Varzim and Sines likely to be added to the list by 2001.

*The Algarve* Lagos, Vilamoura and Faro, plus Portimão by 2001.

*Andalucia* Isla Cristina, El Rompido, Mazagón, Seville, Chipiona, Rota, Puerto Sherry and Barbate.

*Gibraltar* Though an excellent place to get work done there is little space available for long-term laying up ashore.

### Chandlery and repairs

Well-stocked chandleries are still surprisingly few and far between in both Spain and Portugal, and by no means all marinas have one on site. Amongst the best are those at La Coruña, Villagarcía de Arosa and Bayona (*Galicia*); Viana do Castelo, Leixões and Lisbon (*Atlantic Portugal*); Lagos and Vilamoura (*Algarve*); and El Rompido, Mazagón, Chipiona and Puerto Sherry (*Andalucia*). *Gibraltar*'s chandleries are some of the best in Iberia, as well as being duty-free.

There are numerous boatyards throughout all the regions, mainly geared to fishing and other commercial vessels but able to do basic work on yachts. However for major repairs or other work the best yards – of which details will be found in the text – are currently located at Villagarcía de Arosa and Vigo (*Galicia*); Lisbon (*Atlantic Portugal*); Lagos and Vilamoura (*Algarve*); Isla Cristina, El Rompido, Chipiona, Seville (Puerto Gelves) and Puerto Sherry (*Andalucia*); and, of course, *Gibraltar*. Note that if taking expensive electrical or mechanical equipment ashore for repair, particularly in Portugal, it is wise to first inform the *brigada fiscal*. Possession of a receipt will confirm that the equipment was bought elsewhere.

In this volume, where facilities for yachts are extensive – or at least the best to be found for some distance on either side – they are generally listed under individual side-headings. Where facilities consist of little more than those available in any town or village of similar size details are normally given in paragraph form.

### Fuel

Happily, filling one's fuel tank is no longer the nightmare it was even a decade ago, with diesel now widely available, petrol rather less so. In both countries fishermen have access to diesel at a lower rate of tax than do yachtsmen, but whereas in Spain this invariably means two separate pumps, in Portugal it all comes out of the same pump – simply at a different price. Fuel supplies are generally clean, but it can do no harm to filter all fuel taken aboard as a matter of course. Credit cards are generally – but not always – accepted when paying for fuel and it is essential to confirm the local situation before going ahead.

*Galicia* El Ferrol, Sada, La Coruña, Camariñas (by can), Muros, Portosin, Santa Eugania de Riveira (anticipated), Caramiñal, Villagarcia de Arosa, Porto Pedras Negras, Sangenjo (anticipated), Aguete, Vigo and Bayona.

*Portugal* Viana do Castelo, Póvoa de Varzim (anticipated), Leixões, Figueira da Foz, Nazaré, Peniche, Cascais, Lisbon and the Rio Tejo, Sines, Lagos, Portimão, Vilamoura and Vila Real de Santo António.

*Andalucía* Isla Cristina, El Rompido, Mazagón, Chipiona, Puerto Gelves (Seville – anticipated), Rota, Puerto Sherry, Cádiz, Sancti-Petri and Barbate.

*Gibraltar* At least two sources, at duty-free prices.

Standard grade paraffin (*parafina*) is virtually unobtainable in much of Spain, though the more expensive medicinal grade is stocked by most pharmacies. In Portugal *petróleo para iluminãçao* (lamp oil) is widely available.

### Drinking water

Water is available on all marinas and on many fuelling pontoons. It is usually included in the price of berthing, and if this is not the case this will be indicated in the text. In those harbours where a piped supply is not available for yachts a public tap can generally be found, when a good supply of 5 or 10 litre plastic cans will be useful. Though water quality throughout the peninsula is generally good, bottled water is widely available, not least (chilled) from vending machines.

### Bottled gas

Camping Gaz exchanges are widely available, usually from *ferreterias* (ironmongers), filling stations or supermarkets, in 2·7kg bottles identical to those used in the UK.

Getting other cylinders refilled is much more of a problem. It has been reported (though not confirmed) that EU safety legislation now forbids companies which supply liquid gas from filling any canisters other than their own, and certainly neither Calor Gas in the UK nor REPSOL in Spain will fill other cylinders – in the latter case, not even REPSOL cylinders from Portugal! As of 1999 the situation in Portugal appeared more flexible, with butane refills possible at Viana do Castelo, Lisbon and Vilamoura, though there is no guarantee this situation will continue. A test certificate may be required, particularly if the cylinder is more than five years old.

A simpler option might be to carry the appropriate adaptor so that Camping Gaz can be used while in mainland Europe. In the case of a Calor installation this will normally be part no. 190798, available from most Calor Gas dealers or direct from the company at

> **Southampton Calor Gas Centre Ltd**,
> Third Avenue, Millbrook Trading Estate,
> Southampton SO15 0JX
> ☎ 02380 788155 *Fax* 02380 774768,
> *e-mail* socal@tcp.co.uk.

Also useful is their free leaflet *LPG (Bottled Gas) for Marine Use*, available from

> **Calor Gas Customer Support Centre**,
> ☎ 01926 330088 *Fax* 01926 318706
> *website* www.calorgas.co.uk.

Yachts with propane installations – most frequently those from North America or Scandinavia – will need to fit a different regulator if butane is to be used for any length of time – again, consult the Calor Gas Customer Support Centre.

### Electricity

Mains electricity is 220 volt 50Hz, as is standard throughout Europe, and yachts from elsewhere should note the probable difference in both volts and cycles – certainly American 110 volt 60Hz equipment will require a transformer. Electricity is available on nearly all marina pontoons, often using the same three-pin plugs as in the UK. Shoreside plugs are normally two-pin (ie. no earth) and will require an adapter.

### Marina charges

Since it is obviously not possible to include a full list of rates for each marina, that for a 12m yacht has been chosen as representative. Owners of larger or smaller boats should be able to gain an idea from this as to where any particular marina falls in terms of price range. Some marinas charge double for multihulls, others (including most of those in Portugal) add a 50% surcharge to the monohull rate.

In Galicia and along the Atlantic coast of Portugal the cost of a single night in the high (or sometimes high and medium) season is given; in the Algarve and Andalucía, where northern yachtsmen may wish to winter, the rate for a month in the low (or sometimes medium and low) season is also included. In many cases further reductions are available for longer term berthing.

### Marina office hours

In Spain (both Galicia and Andalucía) it is normal for marina offices to be closed during the siesta period – any time between 1200 and 1700, though seldom for as long as this. In Portugal a shorter lunch break – often from 1230 until 1400 – is the norm. While the majority of marinas have 24 hour security, most offices are closed overnight, sometimes from as early as 1800.

While this latter can cause problems when wishing to leave, a firmly locked office is more likely to disrupt things on first arrival, particularly if an electronic card is needed to open an access gate to the pontoons. More than one hapless crew has been separated from their boat until the officials came back on duty – if in doubt, leave someone on the inside! In Portugal, where marina offices are increasingly handling clearance procedures, it can also frustrate a quick shopping trip into town or a well-deserved meal ashore.

Sometimes security guards have authority to issue pass cards, often they do not. There is not even any guarantee that a guard will re-admit an unknown yachtsman to the marina pontoons, particularly if not carrying the yacht's papers and a passport or other identity document.

### Security

Crime afloat is not a major problem in most areas, and regrettably much of the theft which does occur can be laid at the door of other yachtsmen. It is sensible to take much the same precautions as at home – to lock up if leaving the yacht unattended, to padlock the outboard to the dinghy, and to secure the dinghy (particularly if an inflatable) with chain or wire rather than line, both to the yacht and when left ashore.

For the crew, the situation in the big towns is certainly no worse than in the UK, and providing common sense is applied to such matters as how handbags are carried, where not to venture after dark, etc there are unlikely to be problems.

# General information

### Embassies, consulates and national tourist offices

#### Spanish embassies and consulates
*London* 20 Draycott Place, London SW3 2RZ
  ☎ 020 7581 5921/6 *Fax* 020 7589 5842
*Manchester* Suite 1a, Brook House, 70 Spring Gardens, Manchester M22 2BQ
  ☎ 0161 236 1233
*Washington DC* 2375 Pennsylvania Avenue NW, Washington DC 20009
  ☎ 202 728 2330
*New York* 150 East 58th Street, New York, NY 10155
  ☎ 212 355 4090
Plus many others.

#### Portuguese embassies and consulates
*London* 62 Brompton Road, London SW3 1BJ
  ☎ 020 7581 8722/4
*Washington DC* 2125 Kalorama Road NW, Washington DC 20008
  ☎ 202 328 8610
Plus many others.

## UK and US embassies and consulates
### Spain
*UK – Madrid* Calle Fernando el Santo 16, Madrid
☎ 913 190200
  *Seville* Plaza Nueva 87, 41001 Seville ☎ 954 228875.
*US – Madrid* Calle Serrano 75, 28006 Madrid
☎ 915 774000
  *Seville* Paseo de las Delicias 7, Seville ☎ 954 231883

### Portugal
*UK – Lisbon* Rua São Domingos à Lapa 37, Lisbon
☎ 213 961191
  *Porto* Avenida da Boa Vista 3072, Porto
☎ 226 184789
  *Portimão* Largo Francisco A Mauricio 7, 1st Floor
☎ 282 417800
*US – Lisbon* Avenida das Forças Armadas, Lisbon
☎ 217 266600
  *Porto* Rua Júlio Dinis 826, Third Floor, Porto

## Spanish national tourist offices
*London* 22–23 Manchester Square, London W1M 5AP
☎ 020 7486 8077
*New York* 666 Fifth Avenue, New York, NY 10103
☎ 212 265 8822

## Portuguese national tourist offices
*London* 2nd Floor, 22–25a Sackville Street, London
  W1X 1DE ☎ 020 7494 1441 *Fax* 0171 494 1868
*New York* 590 Fifth Avenue, 4th Floor, New York, NY
  10036 ☎ 212 354 4403 *Fax* 212 764 6137

## Personal documentation
*Spain* Currently EU nationals – including UK
  citizens – may visit for up to 90 days, for which a
  national identity card or passport is required but
  no visa. American, Canadian and New Zealand
  citizens may also stay for up to 90 days without a
  visa, though Australians need one for more than
  30 days. EU citizens wishing to remain in Spain
  may apply for a *permiso de residencia* once in the
  country; non-EU nationals can apply for a single
  90 day extension, or otherwise obtain a long-term
  visa from a Spanish embassy or consulate before
  leaving home.
*Portugal* Currently EU nationals need only a
  national identity card or passport to enter
  Portugal and can then stay indefinitely. American
  and Canadian citizens can remain for up to 60
  days without a visa, Austalians and New
  Zealanders for up to 90 days. Extensions are
  issued by the *Serviço de Estrangeiros* (Foreigner's
  Registration Service) which has a branch in most
  major towns, or failing that, by the local police.
  At least one week's notice is required.

## Time
Spain keeps Standard Euro Time (UT+1),
advanced one hour in summer to UT+2, while
Portugal, after a brief experiment with SET, has
reverted to UT, advanced one hour in summer to
UT+1 (effectively the same as BST). It is
particularly important to allow for this difference
when using tidal data based on Lisbon in the
Spanish *rías bajas*.

All times given in the text are local time (LT)
unless otherwise specified.

## Money
In 2000 the traditional currencies were still in daily
use throughout Iberia – the peseta in Spain and the
escudo in Portugal. However some transactions –
principally those involving credit or debit cards –
could also be made in euros, and it was anticipated
that euro coins would come into general circulation
within two years. The peseta (pta):euro exchange
rate was set at 166·386:1 and the escudo:euro rate
at 200·482:1. Currency conversions can be
confirmed on the internet at www.
moneyworld.co.uk

Cash and travellers' cheques (the latter available
in pesetas, escudos or euros) are readily
exchangeable in banks, though the preferred
method for most foreign visitors must be debit or
credit card. Nearly every town has at least one bank
with an automatic card machine, usually giving
instructions in a choice of languages (including
English) and accepting all the usual credit and direct
debit cards. Banking hours in Spain are normally
0900–1400 Monday to Friday, 0900–1300
Saturday, but many banks remain closed on
Saturday from June until September. In Portugal
they are 0830–1500 Monday to Friday, closed
Saturday.

Most internationally known cards, including
*VISA*, *MasterCard* and *American Express*, appear to
be honoured. The majority of larger supermarkets,
restaurants, car hire firms, etc welcome payment by
plastic, as do most – but not all – marinas. The only
important exceptions are some shoreside filling
stations and a few marina fuel pumps – occasionally
despite the fact that the marina office clearly accepts
payment for berthing by credit card.

## Mail
Nearly all marinas (with the notable exception the
Real Club Náutico at La Coruña) are willing to hold
mail for visiting yachts. Addresses are given in the
text. It goes without saying that all mail should be
clearly labelled with both the name of the recipient
and the yacht, but avoiding honorifics such as Esq,
which may cause confusion and misfiling. In
Portugal it is technically illegal for uncollected mail
to be held for more than five days without being
returned, though most marinas will stretch this
period. Far better to address an outer envelope
directly to the marina office, with a short covering
note asking for the envelope enclosed to be held
pending the yacht's arrival.

Letters also may be sent *poste restante* to any post
office in either country, though again they are likely
to be returned if not collected promptly. In Spain
they should be addressed with the surname of the
recipient followed by *Lista de Correos* and the town
and province. In Portugal *Posta Restante* is used, and
the collection counter labelled *Encomendas*. A
passport is likely to be needed on collection.

## Telephones

*Spain* Telephone kiosks are common, both local and *teléfono internacional*, and most carry instructions in English. The majority use phonecards (available from tobacconists), though coin-operated kiosks can also be found. A BT Chargecard can be used by dialling 900 990044 to access the system and then proceeding as in the UK. American Express and Diners Club cards can also be used in some phone boxes, though oddly enough not VISA or Access. Mobile phones work throughout most of the country, and certainly along the coast.

Calls to the United Kingdom begin with the prefix 0044, followed by the area code (without the initial zero) and number; calls to North America with the prefix 001, plus area code and number. It may be necessary to pause after dialling the initial 00 to await a second dialling tone. Directory Enquiries can be accessed by dialling 1003, the European International Operator on 1008 and the Worldwide International Operator on 1005. The emergency number (fire, police or ambulance is) 900 202 202.

To call a Spanish number from abroad, dial that country's international access code (00 in the UK, 011 in North America) followed by 34, plus area code and number in full. The area code now forms part of the number, so must be included even if dialling locally.

*Portugal* Almost all public telephones (of which there are many) are now card-operated, the latter available from post offices and many bars. Nearly all can handle international calls, and most have instructions posted in several languages. A BT Chargecard can be used by dialling 800 800440 to access the system and then proceeding as in the UK. It may sometimes be necessary to insert some escudos to make the initial connection, but these should be refunded on completion. Mobile phones work throughout most of the country, and certainly along the coast.

Calls to the United Kingdom begin with the prefix 0044, followed by the area code (without the initial zero) and number; calls to North America with the prefix 001, plus area code and number. Unlike in Spain there is no second dialling tone. Directory Enquiries can be accessed by dialling 118, the European International Operator on 099 and the Worldwide International Operator on 098. The emergency number (fire, police or ambulance is) 115.

To call a Portuguese number from abroad, dial that country's international access code (00 in the UK, 011 in North America) followed by 351, plus area code and number in full. The area code now forms part of the number, so must be included even if dialling locally. Dialling codes throughout Portugal were changed at the end of October 1999, the initial '0' being replaced by an initial '2' – eg. Lisbon from 01 to 21, Porto from 02 to 22, etc.

*Gibraltar* As in the UK both card and coin-operated telephones are in use, the latter accepting either local or UK coins. A BT Chargecard can be used by dialling 8400 to access the system and then proceeding as in the UK. Calls to the United Kingdom begin with the prefix 0044, followed by the area code (without the initial zero) and number; calls to North America with the prefix 001, plus area code and number. To call Gibraltar from abroad, dial that country's international access code (00 in the UK, 011 in North America) followed by 350 and the number. There are no area codes.

If telephoning from Spain the access code is 956-7, which must also be included when using a mobile phone in Gibraltar. This is because Gibraltar does not have its own mobile network and the phone will be using one of the Spanish networks (Airtel or Moviestar).

## Fax and e-mail

Nearly all marinas now have fax machines and will send and receive faxes for visiting yachts. A small charge is usually made. Fax numbers will be found in the harbour details, with dialling codes to be added as above.

A growing number of marinas have e-mail addresses, and a few – such as the Monte-Real Club de Yates in Bayona – provide telephone sockets specifically for modem attachment. Probably more yachtsmen rely on cybercafés (which frequently advertise their services at tourist offices) or, in both Portugal and Gibraltar, on the e-mail facility provided at nearly all libraries.

## Public transport

In both Spain and Portugal almost every community has some form of public transport, if only one bus a day. Along the *rías*, and particularly the *rías bajas*, road communications are generally slow though much improved over the past decade. So are the local Portuguese railways. However cruising yachtsmen often have time to spare, in which case local buses and trains can provide a view of the interior not otherwise available without hiring a car. Where particular excursions are suggested – eg. to Santiago de Compostela, easily reached by bus from Portosin or train Vilagarcia de Arosa – details will be found in the text.

There are rail connections to El Ferrol, La Coruña, Pontevedra, Vigo, Porto, Lisbon, Lagos, Faro, Tavira, Vila Real de Santo António, Huelva, Seville, Cádiz and Algeciras. Other towns may be served by branch lines. Long distance coaches are also popular, and on a par with the railways for cost.

International airports serve Santiago de Compostela, Porto, Lisbon, Faro, Seville and Gibraltar. La Coruña, Vigo and Jerez de la Frontera have smaller airports with connections via Madrid.

**Medical**

No inoculations are required for either Spain or Portugal. Minor ailments may best be treated by consulting a *farmacia* (often able to dispense drugs which in most other countries would be on prescription), or by contact with an English-speaking doctor established via the *farmacia*, marina office, tourist office or possibly a hotel. In Spain the emergency telephone number is 091; in Portugal it is 115.

All EU nationals should carry a completed *E111* (see the Department of Health's leaflet *Health Advice for Travellers*, obtainable in most travel agents or by telephoning 0800 555 777), which entitles one to free medical treatment under a reciprocal agreement with the National Health Service. Private medical treatment is likely to be expensive.

**National holidays and *fiestas***

*Fiestas* are extremely popular throughout both Spain and Portugal, often celebrating the local saint's day or some historical event. Where local *fiestas* occur during the sailing season they are normally mentioned in the text.

*Spain*

| | |
|---|---|
| 1 January | New Year's Day |
| 6 January | Epiphany |
| | Good Friday |
| | Easter Monday |
| 1 May | May Day/Labour Day |
| (early/mid June) | Corpus Christi |
| 24 June | *Día de San Juan* (the King's name saint) |
| 25 July | *Día de Santiago* (celebrated throughout Northwest Spain as 'Galicia Day') |
| 15 August | Feast of the Assumption |
| 12 October | National Day |
| 1 November | All Saints Day |
| 6 December | Constitution Day |
| 8 December | Immaculate Conception |
| 25 December | Christmas Day |

When a national holiday falls on a Sunday, the autonomous region may either celebrate it the following day or use it to celebrate a regional festival.

*Portugal*

| | |
|---|---|
| 1 January | New Year's Day |
| | Good Friday |
| 25 April | National or Portugal Day |
| 1 May | Labour Day |
| (early/mid June) | Corpus Christi |
| 10 June | Camões Day |
| 15 August | Feast of the Assumption |
| 5 October | Republic Day |
| 1 November | All Saints' Day |
| 1 December | Restoration of Independence Day |
| 8 December | Immaculate Conception |
| 25 December | Christmas Day |

**Spain and Portugal on the Internet**

Both countries are well represented on the internet, which can be accessed via cybercafés or many public libraries throughout both Spain and Portugal – for preference following some 'general interest' research

before departure. The following sites were operational as of February 2000, most leading to other sites of potential interest:

**Spain**

*City Net Spain*
www.city.net/countries/spain/
  Offers a wide selection (in English) including weather, news, travel, and features on most major cities.

*El País Digital*
www.elpais.es/
  Online version (in Spanish) of one of Spain's leading daily newspapers.

*Si Spain*
www.DocuWeb.ca/SiSpain/
  Masses of fascinating information about Spain past, present and future, including a searchable fiesta directory – and all available in English! Run by the Spanish Ministry of Foreign Affairs.

**Portugal**

*ICEP (Investment, Trade & Tourism Portugal)*
www.portugal.org
  A very well-designed site which exactly reflects the brief of *ICEP* and contains vast amounts of useful information including lists of *fiestas* and even airline schedules. Lots of graphics which take a while to download, but well worth the wait. Choice of languages including English.

*Jornal de Notícias*
www.jnoticias.pt
  Online version of one of Portugal's leading daily newspapers. Mostly, but not entirely, in Portuguese.

*The News*
www.nexus-pt.com/
  Online version of the Algarve's English-language magazine (clearly written by ex-pats for ex-pats, but interesting nonetheless).

*Portugal for Traveller*
http://nervo.com/pt
  A wide range of advice on visiting Portugal, including recent first-hand accounts and links to weather and language sites. The webmaster is a Portuguese citizen with excellent English.

*Público*
www.publico.pt
  Online version (in Portuguese) of one of the country's leading daily newspapers.

# Pilotage

## Galicia – the Rías Altas & Rías Bajas

### El Ferrol to the Portuguese border

The *rías altas* and *rías bajas* offer varied cruising in an attractive setting without, from the British yachtsman's point of view, a prohibitively long passage at either end. Challenging pilotage for those who relish it balanced by secure anchorages to suit most conditions, plus an increasing number of small marinas where fuel and water may conveniently be taken aboard, combine to entice some yachtsmen to return year after year. A vast amount of harbour development has taken place since the mid 1980s, generally benefiting both fishing vessels and yachts – notably, the number of marinas between El Ferrol and Bayona capable of taking visiting yachts of 10m or more has increased from just three in 1984 to seven in 1994 and fourteen by 1999. The aim appears to be at least one marina in each *ría*, with other harbours protected by new or extended breakwaters offering much improved protection.

Perhaps even more importantly, while 15 years ago there were plenty of diesel pumps selling *Gasoleo B* to fishing vessels, it was virtually impossible to buy the more highly taxed *Gasoleo A* required (by law) for a yacht anywhere between La Coruña and Bayona. The chore of carrying diesel in cans from a filling station, and then ferrying it out by dinghy, had very limited appeal. In contrast, by the summer of 2000 there should be at least a dozen places where (clean) *Gasoleo A* can be pumped straight into a yacht's tanks. Once ashore, improvements to the infrastructure – notably the road system – have greatly eased the travel problem for crew arriving or departing by air.

The northern *rías*, the *rías altas*, are generally smaller with longer distances of exposed coastline in between, much of it high. In onshore winds this can become a dangerous lee shore – in fog the lights of the high-sited lighthouses may be entirely lost to view. In general each *ría* contains only one or two harbours.

South of Cabo Finisterre the *rías bajas* provide more sheltered cruising in altogether gentler surroundings. Most contain a series of harbours and, should one wish, it is often possible to visit a different anchorage every night for a week without facing the open sea. Both the *rías altas* and the *rías bajas* have excellent and often almost empty beaches.

With few exceptions the *ría* entrances are wide and deep and the hazards well marked, though this is not always the case further off the beaten track and sometimes even close to the harbours. Lights, buoys and beacons are generally well maintained, with the proviso that minor changes – in particular repainting in fresh new colours – may take months if not years to be officially notified.

### Hazards

There are two principal man-made hazards in the area. The more obvious is the Traffic Separation Zone off Cabo Finisterre – see page 39 – though since this now lies nearly 20M offshore it barely affects the coastal yachtsman.

The other potential hazard encountered in the *rías* is the prevalence of *viveros* – mussel rafts – anchored in great masses wherever there is shelter. The rafts are usually purpose built, though occasionally they may be converted hulks, each with twenty or so booms extending low over the water on either side from which dangle coir ropes. Mussels are grown clinging to the ropes and are harvested by boats fitted with hydraulic grabs. The anchor cables run almost vertically to permit access – it is normally possible to sail through the anchored fleets, and often between them and the shore (5m seems to be their inner limit). Only if sailing at night do *viveros* pose a serious obstacle, when the perils of collision are obvious.

The areas on the plans in this book marked as *viveros* cannot be definitive. During the early and mid 1990s few *viveros* were to be found north of the Ría de Muros, but over the past few years they have been reappearing in the *rías altas* with several as far north as the Rías des Ares y Betanzos. Most (but by no means all) *viveros* are buoyed, usually with spherical yellow buoys with × topmarks, lit Fl.Y if at all.

A final, undeniable hazard is the number of small fishing boats which do not appear to carry lights, either while fishing or when making their way to and from the grounds. Conversely some of the larger boats have such powerful deck lights that an approaching – and correctly lit – yacht is unlikely to be seen. Give all such vessels a wide berth on principal.

*13*

## Swell

The exposed coastline is subject to Atlantic swells from the westerly quadrant, sometimes originating hundreds of miles offshore and building from an apparently flat sea. Swell is often, though not always, the harbinger of an approaching frontal system.

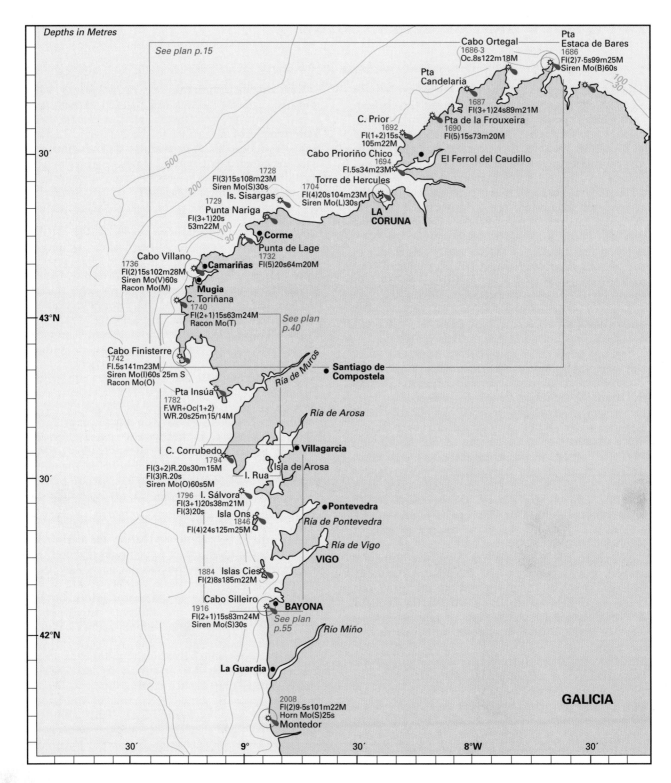

*Depths in Metres*

See plan p.15

Pta
Estaca de Bares
1686
Fl(2)7·5s99m25M
Siren Mo(B)60s

Cabo Ortegal
(1686·3)
Oc.8s122m18M

Pta
Candelaria

1687
Fl(3+1)24s89m21M

C. Prior
1692
Fl(1+2)15s
105m22M

Pta de la Frouxeira
1690
Fl(5)15s73m20M

Cabo Prioriño Chico
1694
Fl.5s34m23M

El Ferrol del Caudillo

1728
Fl(3)15s108m23M
Siren Mo(S)30s

Torre de Hercules
1704
Fl(4)20s104m23M
Siren Mo(L)30s

Is. Sisargas
1729

LA
CORUNA

Punta Nariga
Fl(3+1)20s
53m22M

**Corme**

Punta de Lage
1732
Fl(5)20s64m20M

Cabo Villano
1736
Fl(2)15s102m28M
Siren Mo(V)60s
Racon Mo(M)

**Camariñas**

**Mugia**
C. Toriñana
1740
Fl(2+1)15s63m24M
Racon Mo(T)

See plan
p.40

Cabo Finisterre
1742
Fl.5s141m23M
Siren Mo(I)60s 25m S
Racon Mo(O)

Ría de Muros

**Santiago de
Compostela**

Pta Insúa
1782
F.WR+Oc(1+2)
WR.20s25m15/14M

Ría de Arosa

C. Corrubedo
1794
Fl(3+2)R.20s30m15M
Fl(3)R.20s
Siren Mo(O)60s5M

**Villagarcia**

Isla de Arosa

I. Rua

I. Sálvora
1796
Fl(3+1)20s38m21M
Fl(3)20s

Isla Ons
1846
Fl(4)24s125m25M

**Pontevedra**

*Ría de Pontevedra*

*Ría de Vigo*

**VIGO**

Islas Cies
1884
Fl(2)8s185m22M

Cabo Silleiro
1916
Fl(2+1)15s83m24M
Siren Mo(S)30s

**BAYONA**

See plan
p.55

*Río Miño*

**La Guardia**

**GALICIA**

2008
Fl(2)9·5s101m22M
Horn Mo(S)25s
Montedor

30′

43°N

30′

42°N

30′  9°  30′  8°W  30′

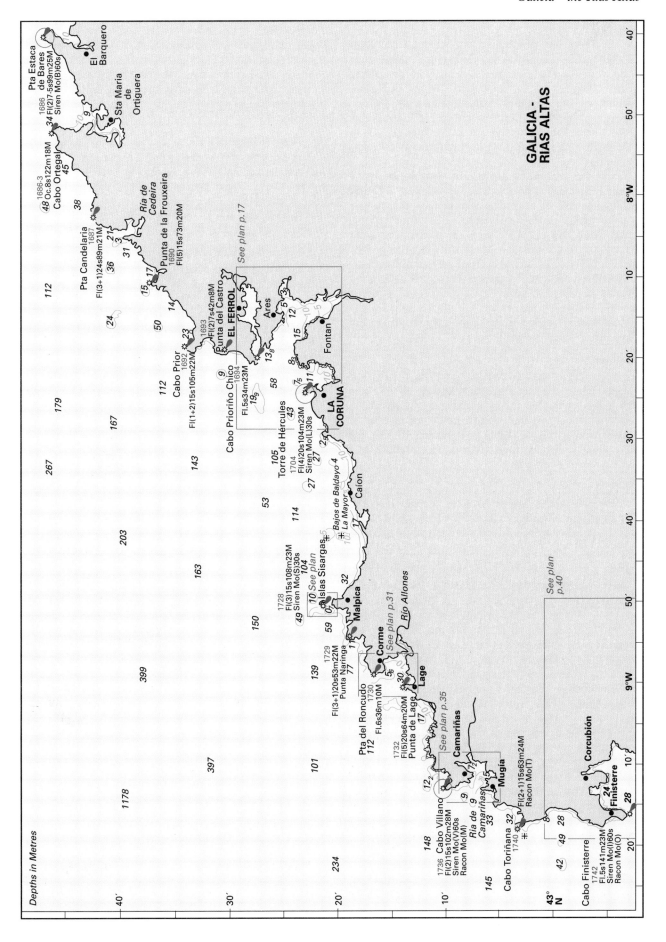

*Depths in Metres*

**GALICIA - RIAS ALTAS**

Pta Estaca
de Bares
1686 Fl(2)7.5s99m25M
34 Fl(2)7.5s99m25M
Siren Mol(B)60s

El
Barquero

Sta Maria
de
Ortiguera

1686·3
48 Oc.8s122m18M
Cabo Ortegal
45

38

*Ría de
Cedeira*

112

Pta Candelaria
1687
Fl(3+1)24s89m21M

21
3
36
31

Punta de la Frouxeira
1690
Fl(5)15s73m20M

15 17

24

50

14

Cabo Prior
1692
Fl(1+2)15s105m22M

1693
Fl(2)7s42m8M
Punta del Castro
**EL FERROL**

Ares

5
12

15

Fontan

*See plan p.17*

112

23

Cabo Priorño Chico
1694
Fl.5s34m23M

9

58

19

13

7
11
19

**LA
CORUÑA**

Torre de Hércules
105
1704
Fl(4)20s104m23M
Siren Mol(L)30s
27

43

2

179

167

112

143

267

203

163

53

114

*Bajos de Baldayo* 4
La Mayor
Caión

27
27

1728
Fl(3)15s108m23M
Siren Mol(S)30s
49

104
*See plan*
*Islas Sisargas*
10

32

150

139

1729
Punta Naringa
77
1

**Malpica**
59

**Corme**
*See plan p.31*

*Río Allones*

399

Pta del Roncudo
1730
112 Fl.6s36m10M

1732
Fl(5)20s64m20M
Punta de Lage
17

6
30
**Lage**

*See plan p.35*

*See plan
p.40*

101

397

234

1178

148

Cabo Villano
1736
Fl(2)15s102m28M
Siren Mol(V)60s
Racon Mol(M)

**Camariñas**

Mugia
Fl(2+1)15s63m24M
Racon Mol(T)

**Corcubión**

12

72
5

1740
*Ría de
Camariñas
33*

Cabo Toriñana 32
1742
Fl.5s141m23M
Siren Mol(I)60s
Racon Mol(O)

9

Cabo Finisterre

24
**Finisterre**
28

42

49 28

145

**43°
N**

15

## Winds

In summer the dominance of the Azores high pressure area, usually combined with low pressure over the Iberian peninsula, leads to prevailing northeasterlies in the northern part of the area, gaining a more northerly component south of Cabo Finisterre. However land or sea breeze effects may dictate conditions locally, sometimes leading to a 180° shift in wind direction during the warmer parts of the day.

Gales are infrequent during the summer but may occur, notably the *nordeste pardo*, a cloudy northeaster of the Finisterre area. In theory the southwesterly *vendavale* is also uncommon at this time of year, though 1999 proved an exception with strong southwesterlies – sometimes reaching gale force – blowing at intervals from July until October.

In winter, Galicia's weather is largely determined by the passage of North Atlantic frontal systems bringing strong southwesterlies, doubtless why the Bay of Biscay gained its fearsome reputation in the days of the square-riggers.

## Visibility

The chances of coastal fog are greatest in July and August when the incidence may rise as high as one day in ten or twelve (many yachtsmen would argue that this is conservative), with many more days of early morning mist which then disperses. In the *rías bajas* visibility of less than 2M may occasionally last for a week at a stretch.

## Currents

Off the *rías altas* currents may set easterly into the Bay of Biscay. South of Cabo Finisterre the general trend is southwards, seldom reaching more than ½ knot.

## Tides

Tidal predictions for the *rías altas* use La Coruña as the Standard Port; those for the *rías bajas* use Lisbon. When calculating Spanish tides using Lisbon data, note that allowance has already been made for the difference in time zone (Spanish time being UT+1, Portuguese time UT, both advanced one hour in summer – see page 10.)

If La Coruña tide tables are not available, as a very rough guide high water occurs at approximately 0510 and 1650 at springs ±20 minutes; and 1045 and 2330 at neaps ±50 minutes. The same figures for Lisbon are approximately 0410 and 1630 ±30 minutes, and 0920 and 2230 ±1hour 10 minutes.

Ranges are near 3m at springs and 1·4m at neaps, but both time and height may be affected by wind, particularly in the *rías bajas*.

The flood stream sets north and northeast around the coast. Unlike some of the *ríos* of Portugal and southern Spain, all Galicia's *rías* are fully tidal, certainly as far as a yacht is likely to penetrate.

Where no tidal data is given for an individual harbour it will be found under the preliminary notes for the *ría* as a whole.

## Climate

Galicia is the wet corner of Spain – it has much the same climatic feel as southwest England, though on average rather warmer. Mean air temperature varies from around 20°C in August to 9°C in January, sea temperature from 17°C in summer to 12°C in winter.

## Coast radio stations

All Coast radio stations in Galicia are remotely controlled from CCR Coruña, ☎ 944 160260 *Fax* 981 183829, and somewhat confusingly all should be addressed as *Coruña Radio*.

Broadcast times are quoted in UT unless otherwise specified.

## Marine weather information by telephone

A recorded marine weather bulletin, ☎ 906 365372 (see also plan page 5), is provided by the Instituto Nacional de Meteorológical for Galica and the north coast. The service is only available within Spain, but can be accessed by vessels equipped with Autolink. The bulletin is read in Spanish.

*High Seas Bulletin* for Finisterre, etc.
*Coastal Waters Bulletin* for the coasts of Coruña and Pontevedra, etc.

# El Ferrol

Ría de El Ferrol
43°29'N 8°15'W

## Tides

*Reference port* La Coruña
*Mean time differences*
HW: +10 minutes ±20; LW: +10 minutes ±15
*Heights in metres*

| MHWS | MHWN | MLWN | MLWS |
|------|------|------|------|
| 3·8 | 3·0 | 1·4 | 0·6 |

*Tidal streams* At springs tidal streams attain a maximum of 3 knots in the narrows and about 2·3 knots off Punta del Vispón. The streams in both directions set towards Punta Leiras off which they cause a rip. The narrows can also be affected by strong squalls.

## Charts

| | Approach | Ría |
|---|---|---|
| Admiralty | *1111* | *1115* |
| Spanish | *929, 412A* | *4122, 4123* |

## Lights

### Approach

1686 **Punta Estaca de Bares** 43°47'·2N 7°41'·1W
  Fl(2)7·5s99m25M Siren Mo(B)60s 150m 345°
  Octagonal tower and building 10m
  Obscd when bearing more than 291°
0925 Radiobeacon *BA* 309·5kHz 100M
1686·3 **Cabo Ortegal** 43°46'·3N 7°52'·2W
  Oc.8s122m18M White round tower, red band 10m
1687 **Punta Candelaria** 43°42'·7N 8°02'·8W
  Fl(3+1)24s89m21M
  Octagonal tower and building 9m
1690 **Punta de la Frouxeira** 43°37'·1N 8°11'·3W
  Fl(5)15s73m20M Angular concrete tower 30m

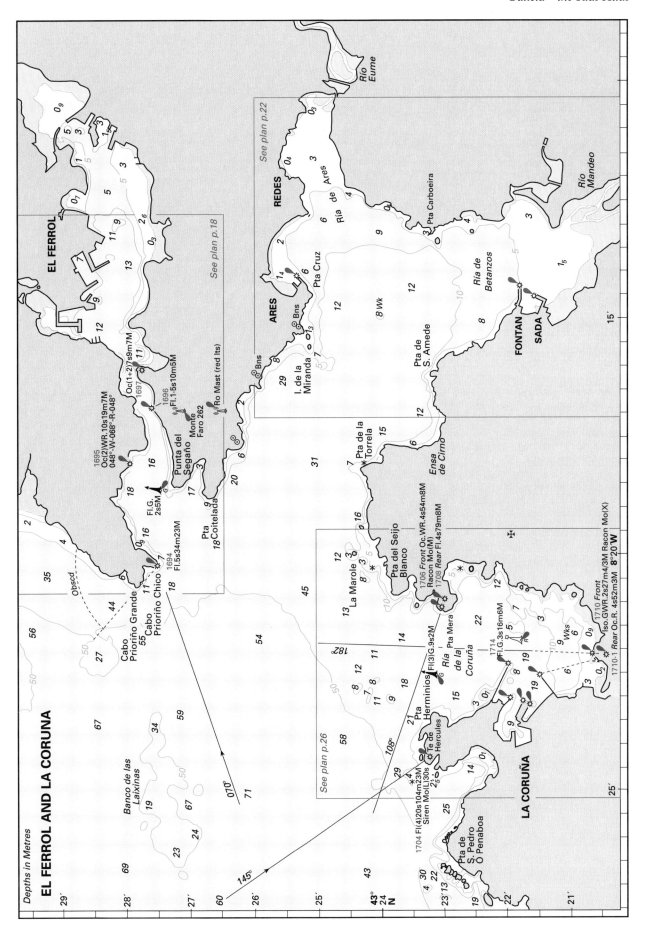

Depths in Metres

# EL FERROL AND LA CORUNA

EL FERROL

See plan p.18

REDES

ARES

Río Eume

Río Mandeo

Ría de Ares

Pta Carboeira

Ría de Betanzos

Pta Cruz

FONTAN

SADA

8 Wk

Pta de S. Amede

Bns

I. de la Miranda

Bns

See plan p.22

Pta de la Torrela

Ensa de Cirno

Cabo Prioriño Grande

Cabo Prioriño Chico

Banco de las Laixinas

Obscd

La Marole

Pta del Seijo Blanco

1706 Front Oc.WR.4s54m8M Racon Mo(M)
1708 Rear Fl.4s79m8M

Ría de la Coruña

Pta Mera

Wks

1710 Front Iso.GWR.2s27m4/3M Racon Mo(X) 8°20'W
1710·1 Rear Oc.R. 4s52m3M

1714
Fl.G.3s16m6M

Pta Herminios
Fl(3)G.9s2M

LA CORUÑA

Te de Hercules

1704 Fl(4)20s104m23M
Siren Mo(L)30s

Pta de S. Pedro O Penaboa

See plan p.26

1695
Ocl(2)WR.10s19m7M
048°-W-068°-R-048°

1697
Oc(1+2)7s9m7M

1696
Fl.1.5s10m5M

Ro Mast (red lts)

Punta del Segaño
Monte Faro 262

Fl.G. 2s5M

1694
Fl.5s34m23M

Pta Coitelada

070°
71

145°
60

29'
28'
27'
26'
25'

43°
24
N

15'

25'

21'
22'

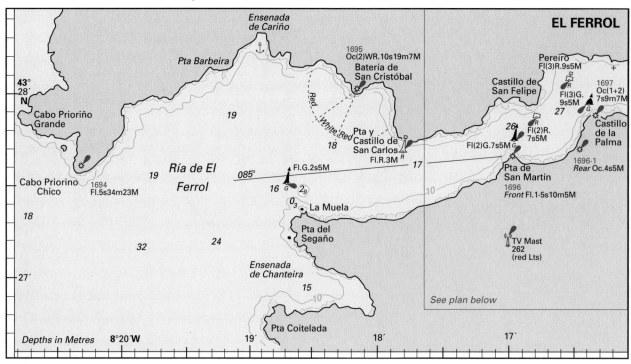

**EL FERROL**

Ensenada de Cariño

Pta Barbeira

1695
Oc(2)WR.10s19m7M

Batería de San Cristóbal

43°
28'
N

Cabo Prioriño Grande

*Red*

*White Red*

Pta y Castillo de San Carlos

Fl.R.3M

Pereiro
Fl(3)R.9s5M

Castillo de San Felipe

1697
Oc(1+2)
7s9m7M

Fl(3)G.
9s5M

27

26

Fl(2)R.
7s5M

Castillo de la Palma

19

18

19

*Ría de El Ferrol*

085°

Fl.G.2s5M

17

Fl(2)G.7s5M

1696-1
*Rear* Oc.4s5M

Cabo Priorino Chico

1694
Fl.5s34m23M

16

2₉

Pta de San Martín

1696
*Front* Fl.1·5s10m5M

18

0₃
La Muela

10

27'

18

32

24

Pta del Segaño

TV Mast
262
(red Lts)

Ensenada de Chanteira

15

10

*See plan below*

*Depths in Metres*   8°20'W

19'

18'

17'

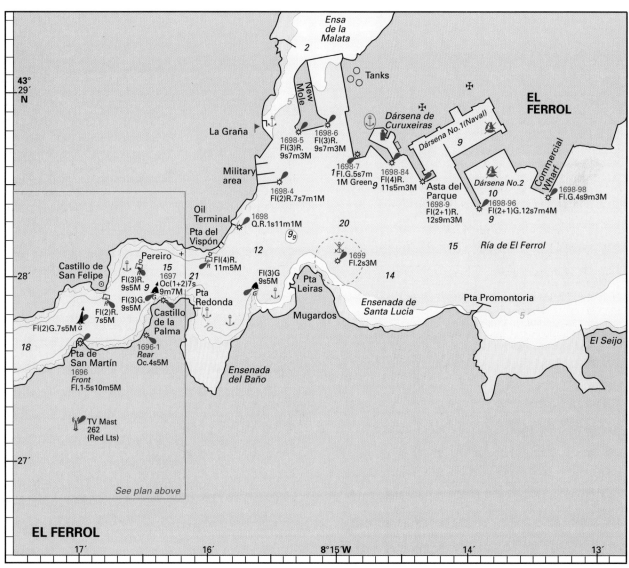

Ensa de la Malata

2

Tanks

43°
29'
N

New Mole

*Dársena de Curuxeiras*

Dársena No.1(Naval)

9

**EL FERROL**

La Graña

1698·6
Fl(3)R.
9s7m3M

1698·5
Fl(3)R.
9s7m3M

Military area

1698·7
Fl.G.5s7m
1M Green

1698·84
Fl(4)R.
11s5m3M

Asta del Parque

Dársena No.2

10

Commercial Wharf

1698·98
Fl.G.4s9m3M

1698·4
Fl(2)R.7s7m1M

Oil Terminal

1698
Q.R.1s11m1M

Pta del Vispón

12

9₉

20

1699
Fl.2s3M

1698·9
Fl(2+1)R.
12s9m3M

1698·96
Fl(2+1)G.12s7m4M

9

15

*Ría de El Ferrol*

Castillo de San Felipe

Pereiro

15

1697
Oc(1+2)7s
9m7M

Fl(3)R.
9s5M

9

Fl(3)G.
9s5M

21

Fl(4)R.
11m5M

Fl(3)G
9s5M

Pta Redonda

Fl(3)G
9s5M

14

Pta Leiras

Pta Promontoria

Fl(2)R.
7s5M

Fl(2)G.7s5M

18

Castillo de la Palma

10

Mugardos

Ensenada de Santa Lucia

5

Pta de San Martín

1696-1
*Rear*
Oc.4s5M

El Seijo

1696
*Front*
Fl.1·5s10m5M

TV Mast
262
(Red Lts)

Ensenada del Baño

27'

*See plan above*

**EL FERROL**

17'                    16'                    8°15'W              14'                    13'

1692 **Cabo Prior** 43°34'·1N 8°18'·9W
Fl(1+2)15s105m22M 055·5°-vis-310°
Dark hexagonal tower on building

1693 **Punta del Castro** 43°30'·2N 8°19'·5W
Fl(2)7s42m8M Octagonal white tower 6m

1704 **Torre de Hércules** 43°23'·2N 8°24'·3W
Fl(4)20s104m23M Siren Mo(L)30s 165m NNW
Square stone tower, octagonal top 49m

*0928* Radiobeacon *L* 301·5kHz 50M

1728 **Islas Sisargas** 43°21'·6N 8°50'·7W
Fl(3)15s108m23M Siren Mo(S)30s
Octagonal granite tower, white cupola, on white
building 11m. On summit of largest island

*Entrance*

1694 **Cabo Prioriño Chico** 43°27'·5N 8°20'·3W
Fl.5s34m23M 129·5°-vis-225°
White octagonal tower and building 5m

buoy **Muela del Segaño** 43°27'·5N 8°18'·7W
Fl.G.2s5M Green pillar buoy, ▲ topmark

*Ria*

1695 **Batería de San Cristóbal** 43°27'·9N 8°18'·3W
Oc(2)WR.10s19m7M 048°-W-068°-R-048°
White conical tower on ruins 6m

1696 **Punta de San Martín Ldg Lts on 085·4°**
43°27'·6N 8°17'W
*Front* Fl.1·5s10m5M White masonry tower 8m
Multiple F.R on two nearby TV antennae

1696·1 *Rear*, 701m from front, 43°27'·7N 8°16'·5W
Oc.4s5M White masonry tower 13m

buoy **San Carlos** 43°27'·7N 8°17'·8W
Fl.R.3M Red pillar buoy, ■ topmark

buoy **San Martín** 43°27'·7N 8°17'W
Fl(2)G.7s5M Green pillar buoy, ▲ topmark

buoy **San Felipe** 43°27'·8N 8°16'·8W
F(2)R.7s5M Red can buoy

1697 **Castillo de la Palma** 43°27'·9N 8°16'·3W
Oc(1+2)7s9m7M Round granite tower on house 7m

buoy **Bajo de la Palma** 43°27'·9N 8°16'·4W
Fl(3)G.9s5M Green conical buoy, ▲ topmark

buoy **Pereiro** 43°28'N 8°16'·5W
Fl(3)R.9s5M Red can buoy, ■ topmark

buoy **Punta del Vispón** 43°28'·1N 8°15'·9W
Fl(4)R.11s5M Red can buoy, ■ topmark

buoy **Punta Piteira** 42°27'·9N 8°15'·6W
Fl(3)G.9s5M Green conical buoy

1698 **La Graña oil pier, SW head** 43°28'·2N 8°15'·7W
Q.R.11m1M Metal post 8m

1699 **Degousing range** 43°28'·1N 8°15'W
Fl.2s3M White pyramid structure

1698·4 **Military area, south jetty** 43°28'·5N 8°15'·4W
Fl(2)R.7s7m1M Red column 4m

1698·5 **New mole, SW corner** 43°28'·8N 8°15'·2W
Fl(3)R.9s7m3M Red metal column 4m

1698·6 **New mole, SE corner** 43°28'·8N 8°15'W
Fl(3)R.9s7m3M Red metal column 4m

1698·7 **Muelle de Concepción Arenal, NW corner**
43°28'·7N 8°14'·8W Fl.G.5s7m1M
Green metal column

1698·84 **Muelle de Concepción Arenal, SE corner
(Dársena de Curuxeiras)** 43°28'·6N 8°14'·6W
Fl(4)R.11s5m3M Red post 5m

1698·9 **Asta del Parque (Basin *No.1*, SW mole)**
43°28'·5N 8°14'·3W Fl(2+1)R.12s9m3M
Round white column 7m

1698·96 **Basin *No.2*, SW mole** 43°28'·4N 8°13'·9W
Fl(2+1)G.12s7m4M Masonry column 5m

1698·98 **Commercial wharf** 43°28'·4N 8°13'·4W
Fl.G.4s9m3M White conical tower 5m

Other lights and buoys in the interior of the harbour.

**Port radio**

*Ferrol Prácticos* VHF Ch 10, 11, 12, 13, 14, 16.

**General**

A commercial port and Spain's largest naval base, El
Ferrol can be entered in almost all conditions and
offers reasonable shelter (though the wind may
squall in the entrance and funnel through the *ria*).
Although the city does not have much attraction for
yachtsmen, other than exceptionally well kept public
gardens, the *ria* is worth a visit for its spectacular
entrance.

Birthplace of Francisco Franco in 1892, for many
years El Ferrol carried the suffix *del Caudillo* (the
Leader), but this was dropped following his death.

**Approach**

In rough weather the sea breaks over two banks
about 1M off the coast north of the *ria* – Bajos
Tarracidos and Cabaleiro – and a third, Banco de
las Laixiñas, some 2–4M west of Prioriño Grande.
The safe approach to both El Ferrol and La Coruña
then lies from the west, between Banco de las
Laixiñas and the Torre de Hércules, and in such
conditions a yacht would probably do better to enter
La Coruña.

If coming from the north intent on making an
approach from the west, a heading of less than 145°
on the Torre de Hércules[1704] will clear the western
edge of Banco de las Laixiñas, after which a heading
of less than 070° on Cabo Prioriño Chico[1694] will
clear its southern edge. If approaching at night, aim
to pass about 0·5M south of Cabo Prioriño Chico to
enter the white sector of the low-power San
Cristóbal light[1695], then turn onto the Punta de San
Martín leading lights[1696]. Cabo Prioriño Chico is
south of Cabo Prioriño Grande and slightly lower;
its light is well below the summit at the very
entrance of the *ria*.

Coming from the north in less than rough
conditions and starting from a point 1M to the west
of Cabo Prior, a course of 185° will lead between the
banks mentioned above and the dangers off Punta
del Castro. Not until Cabo Prioriño Grande is

Looking east-northeast into the Ría de El Ferrol, with Cabo
Prioriño Chico in the foreground and Punta del Segaño on the
right.

abeam will Cabo Prioriño Chico become visible. It can then be rounded close-to, by which time the leading marks of Punta de San Martín will be in view.

Within the entrance the channel is well buoyed and the sides quite steep-to. Once clear of the narrows, if wishing to visit the town make for the Asta del Parque mole[1698·9], identifiable by a pair of two story white buildings with red roofs, in front of which lies the entrance to the Dársena de Curuxeiras.

### Berthing

Yachts are permitted to berth on the east wall of the Dársena de Curuxeiras immediately inside the entrance, where there are two sets of white-painted steps. The area is subject to wash from the ferries and excursion boats which berth around the corner inside the basin proper, and can be slightly noisome at low water springs. The stone wall is rough – use a plank outside the fenders. The three pontoons at the head of the basin, marked Club do Mar Ferrol, are fully occupied by local smallcraft.

### Formalities

Being a naval port visitors are more likely to be asked for their papers than elsewhere, and if berthing in the Dársena de Curuxeiras ship's papers and passports should be taken to the Capitanía in the port area at the head of the basin. This is particularly important if there are non-EU nationals aboard.

### Facilities

El Ferrol does not cater specifically for yachtsmen as does Sada or La Coruña, but there is good provisioning, diesel on the quay at the Dársena de Curuxeiras (available Tuesdays and Thursdays only, 1000–1300) and a chandlery. The fort immediately east of the Dársena houses a club naval, but this is an establishment for naval officers which does not cater for yachtsmen. Also to be found are all the usual facilities of a major city including cafés, restaurants, hotels (one a parador), banks and museums.

The entrance to the Dársena de Curuxeiras (seen here from near the approach line) lies between the timber-laden quay on the left and the long, red-roofed buildings.

The very attractive anchorage close east of the Castillo de San Felipe in the Ría de El Ferrol, looking southwest towards the entrance.

The Nautimar chandlery directly opposite the Club Naval carries a reasonable stock, though heavily fishing orientated and with one department given over entirely to decorative items. There is an excellent produce, fish and general market on the road running northeast from the Dársena, with a small filling station (petrol available by can) just short of the roundabout.

### Communications

Post office and telephones. Trains, buses, taxis, car rental. Ferries to the villages in the *ría* and occasionally to La Coruña.

### Anchorages

1. In the Ensenada de Cariño, on the north side of the ría entrance east of Punta Barbeira, open to the southern quadrant. Holding is poor over rock.
2. In the narrows east of Castillo de San Felipe. Anchor between moored dinghies and Pereiro buoy, well sheltered except from the east when winds tend to be magnified by the funnel effect within the ría. Holding is patchy over mud and stones. The small village offers little beyond a few cafés, though the castle is open to the public.
3. Off the small marina at La Graña and its associated moorings in 4–6m over mud and sand – there is little possibility of a visiting yacht securing to the small pontoon. Water and showers are available by arrangement with the management, plus a small chandlery (though no fuel). There are several telephone kiosks nearby, and the village behind offers cafés, restaurants and basic shopping. Immediately north of the marina is a surprisingly clean beach.
4. Off the town of Mugardos on the southern shore of the ría, where there is a short mole backed by

cafés, restaurants and shops. The bay, which is exposed from west through north to northeast, is fully occupied by moorings – anchor outside them in 5m or more over mud.

5. The Ensenada del Baño, close west of Mugardos and again exposed from northwest to northeast. Anchor off the jetty east of Punta Redonda in 6–8m over mud – the head of the bay is shallow. The shore is largely undeveloped.

The naval basins east of the Dársena de Curuxeiras are prohibited to yachts.

# Ares
Ría de Ares
43°25'N 8°14'W

## Tides
See La Coruña, page 24

## Charts

|  | Approach | Harbour |
| --- | --- | --- |
| Admiralty | 1111 | 1114 |
| Spanish | 929, 412A | 4125 |

## Lights
### Approach
1694 **Cabo Prioriño Chico** 43°27'·5N 8°20'·3W
  Fl.5s34m23M 129·5°-vis-225°
  White octagonal tower and building 5m
1706 **Punta Mera** 43°23'·1N 8°21'·2W
  Oc.WR.4s54m8M
  000°-R-023° 100·5°-R-105·5°-W-114·5°-R-153°
  White octagonal tower and walls 11m
  Racon Mo(M) 020°-196° 18M
1703 **Breakwater** 43°25'·4N 8°14'·2W
  Fl(3)R.9s10m5M Red tower 6m

## General
The Rías Ares and Betanzos are well worth visiting as a change from the noise and dirt of La Coruña or El Ferrol. There are several possible anchorages and the surrounding country is attractive. Ares, which is surrounded by fine sandy beaches, is particularly useful when a north or northeast wind is blowing and La Coruña is unpleasant due to swell.

## Approach and anchorage
The common mouth to the Rías des Ares and Betanzos lies between Punta Coitelada to the north and Punta de la Torrella to the south. The entrance is wide and the approach straightforward, though in any swell the Bajo la Miranda, a 3·7m rocky shoal lying 0·6M southwest of Punta Miranda, should be given generous clearance. Isla de la Miranda itself does not submerge.

In the early 1990s a breakwater with a wide inner quay was built out from Punta de Ares on the southwest corner of the bay, with a short inner mole inside it. However plans to build a marina between the two have not materialised and much of the space is now taken up with moorings. Even so, excellent anchorage is still available in the eastern part of the bay off a sandy beach (very good holding in 2–4m over sand and mud), or further south in 5m or more.

## Facilities
Little specifically for the yachtsman, but reasonable shopping including food stores, pharmacy and hardware, bank with card machine, and the usual cafés, restaurants, etc.

The wide bay at Ares, looking northwest. Despite the many moorings, good anchorage is still to be found at a distance from the breakwater.

Depths in Metres

**Communications**

Post office and telephones. Buses to El Ferrol.

**Alternative anchorage**

Ensenada de Redes, the next bay to the east, offers an attractive anchorage in 2–3m over sand. Pick a spot east or northeast of Punta Modias, off the small quay and outside the many moorings. Though previously full of *viveros*, and with a buoyed area of mussel rafts recently established south of the headland, in 1999 none were to be seen in the bay itself. The small village is surprisingly unspoilt, though the elevated main road built across the *ría* to the east makes the area somewhat noisy.

# Sada (Fontan)

Ría de Betanzos
43°22'N 8°15'W

## Tides

See La Coruña, page 24

## Charts

|  | Approach | Harbour |
|---|---|---|
| Admiralty | 1111 | 1114 |
| Spanish | 929, 412A | 4125 |

## Lights

### Approach

1694 **Cabo Prioriño Chico** 43°27'·5N 8°20'·3W
Fl.5s34m23M 129·5°-vis-225°
White octagonal tower and building 5m

1706 **Punta Mera** 43°23'·1N 8°21'·2W
  Oc.WR.4s54m8M
  000°-R-023° 100·5°-R-105·5°-W-114·5°-R-153°
  White octagonal tower and walls 11m
  Racon Mo(M) 020°-196° 18M
*Harbour*
1700 **North breakwater** 43°21'·8N 8°14'·4W
  Fl(3)G.9s9m4M Green post 6m
1702·6 **South breakwater** 43°21'·6N 8°14'·6W
  Fl(3)R.9s6m5M Red column 5m
1700·5 **Commercial quay** 43°21'·8N 8°14'·7W
  Fl(4)G.11s5m3M Green column 3m
1700·2 **Fishermen's quay** 43°21'·8N 8°14'·8W
  Fl.G.2s5m3M Green column 3m
1701 **Pulgueira rocks** 43°21'·6N 8°14'·7W
  Fl(4)R.11s6m3M Red beacon tower
1702 **Inner mole** 43°21'·6N 8°14'·9W
  Fl.R.2s5m3M 156°-vis-268·5° Red column 3m

## Marina radio

*Marina Sada* VHF Ch 09.

## General

The new marina at Sada off the town of Fontán, begun in 1997 but still being expanded in 1999, is amongst the best in Galicia. It would be an excellent spot from which to visit the attractive old town of Betanzos, which was a port in pre-Roman times and has a number of medieval churches. At high water the trip can by made by dinghy, otherwise buses run regularly. On 16 August boat races and a *fiesta* are held at Sada in honour of San Roque, while Betanzos stages a battle of the flowers.

## Approach

The shoreline between La Coruña and El Ferrol and within the *rías* is fringed with reefs; keep 300m off any visible rock. The Ría de Betanzos shoals gradually.

## Anchorage and berthing

The harbour, which was enlarged in the early 1990s with an angled breakwater on the south side and an extension to the quay to the north, is largely taken up with fishing boat, yacht and smallcraft moorings. However anchorage is possible in the entrance in 4–5m over sand and weed, taking care not to impede access to either the northern quays or the marina. Shelter is good other than from northeast and east.

Alternatively berth in the new Marina Sada, ☎/*Fax* 981 619015 the seven pontoons of which are tucked into the angle of the south breakwater. Though unfinished in 1999, eventually each pontoon should end in a hammerhead to which yachts can secure on arrival, with 3m on the northern pontoons decreasing to 2m further in. Remain close to the pontoon ends while manoeuvring as the Pulgueira rocks extend well east of their identifying beacon.

An angled extension is planned for the end of the south breakwater, to protect the marina from the considerable swell produced by northeasterly winds. Hopefully both this and the hammerheads will be in place by the end of 2000. Unusually for a Galician marina the individual berths all have finger pontoons (of generous length but rather narrow), the whole held in place by numerous piles.

Of the 450 berths some 45 are reserved for visitors, and yachts of up to 15m can be accommodated. In 1999 the high season rate for a visiting yacht of just under 12m was 3,360 ptas

Looking southwest into the entrance of the large harbour at Sada on the Ría de Betanzos with the long north breakwater nearest the camera.

(20·19 euros) per night, with an additional charge of 700 ptas (4·20 euros) per night for electricity and 200 ptas (1·20 euros) per night for water. Visitors were permitted to stay for a maximum of 15 nights only.

## Facilities

*Boatyard* Currently more used to fishing vessels – enquire at the marina office.

*Travel-lift* At the marina, 30 tonne capacity and in excellent condition. Concreted area of hardstanding behind the marina office.

*Engineers, electronic & radio repairs* Enquire at the marina office.

*Sail repairs* Cadenote – ask for directions at the marina office.

*Chandlery* Several – ask for directions at the marina office.

*Charts* In La Coruña (see page 27).

*Water* On the pontoons.

*Showers* In the marina office building.

*Launderette* In the marina office building.

*Electricity* On the pontoons.

*Fuel* Diesel and petrol pumps at the marina, next to the travel-lift. The fuelling berth is provided with a 20–25m floating pontoon.

*Bottled gas* Camping Gaz available in the town.

*Weather forecast* Posted daily at the marina office.

*Banks* In the town, with card machines.

*Shops/provisioning* Good choice in the town.

*Produce market* In the town.

*Cafés, restaurants & hotels* Wide choice in the town.

*Medical services* In the town – ask at the marina office for suggestions.

## Communications

*Post office* In the town.

*Mailing address*
c/o **Marina Sada**, Avda del Puerto s/n, Puerto Deportivo, 15160 Sada, A Coruña, España.
*Fax service* 981 619015

*Public telephones* At the marina office and in the town.

*Car hire/taxis* In the town.

*Buses & trains* Buses to Betanzos, which is on the main line to La Coruña, El Ferrol and beyond.

# La Coruña (A Coruña)

Ría de La Coruña
43°22'N 8°23'W

## Tides

La Coruña is a Standard Port

*Heights in metres*

| MHWS | MHWN | MLWN | MLWS |
|------|------|------|------|
| 3·8  | 2·8  | 1·5  | 0·5  |

## Charts

|           | *Approach*  | *Harbour* |
|-----------|-------------|-----------|
| Admiralty | *1111*      | *1114*    |
| Spanish   | *929, 412A* | *4126*    |
| Imray     | *C18*       | *C18*     |

## Lights

### Approach

1686 **Punta Estaca de Bares** 43°47'·2N 7°41'·1W
  Fl(2)7·5s99m25M Siren Mo(B)60s 150m 345°
  Octagonal tower and building 10m
  Obscd when bearing more than 291°

*0925* Radiobeacon *BA* 309·5kHz 100M

1686·3 Cabo Ortegal 43°46'·3N 7°52'·2W
  Oc.8s122m18M White round tower, red band 10m

1687 **Punta Candelaria** 43°42'·7N 8°02'·8W
  Fl(3+1)24s89m21M
  Octagonal tower and building 9m

The long breakwater which shelters La Coruña, looking northwest. In the centre are the twin white towers of the port authority building, with the venerable Torre de Hércules on the skyline.

1690 **Punta de la Frouxeira** 43°37'·1N 8°11'·3W
Fl(5)15s73m20M Angular concrete tower 30m
1692 **Cabo Prior** 43°34'·1N 8°18'·9W
Fl(1+2)15s105m22M 055·5°-vis-310°
Dark hexagonal tower on building
1694 **Cabo Prioriño Chico** 43°27'·5N 8°20'·3W
Fl.5s34m23M 129·5°-vis-225°
White octagonal tower and building 5m
1704 **Torre de Hércules** 43°23'·2N 8°24'·3W
Fl(4)20s104m23M Siren Mo(L)30s 165m NNW
Square stone tower, octagonal top 49m
*0928* Radiobeacon *L* 301·5kHz 50M
1728 **Islas Sisargas** 43°21'·6N 8°50'·7W
Fl(3)15s108m23M Siren Mo(S)30s
Octagonal granite tower, white cupola, on white
building 11m. On summit of largest island

***Ria entrance***
1706 **Punta Mera Ldg Lts on 108·5°** 43°23'·1N
8°21'·2W
*Front* Oc.WR.4s54m8M
000°-R-023° 100·5°-R-105·5°-W-114·5°-R-153°
White octagonal tower and walls 11m
Racon Mo(M) 020°-196° 18M
1708 *Rear,* 300m from front, Fl.4s79m8M
357·5°-vis-177·5°
White octagonal tower and adjacent walls 14m
1710 **Punta Fiaiteira Ldg Lts on 182°** 43°20'·7N
8°22'·1W
*Front* Iso.GWR.2s28m4-3M
146·4°-G-180°-W-184°-R-217·6°
Square tower on red and white base 10m
Racon Mo(X) 11-21M
1710·1 *Rear,* 380m from front, Oc.R.4s52m3M
Square tower on red and white base 10m
buoy **Bajo Cabanés** 43°23'·1N 8°22'·7W
Fl(3)G.9s2M Green pillar buoy

***Harbour***
1714 **Breakwater** 43°22'N 8°22'·4W
Fl.G.3s16m6M
Conical masonry tower 5m
6 F.R, 975m distant on 296°, mark the roof and
antennae of the Port Control Tower
buoy **Bajo Guisanda** 43°21'·8N 8°21'·8W
Fl.R.5s4M Red pillar buoy
1723 **Oil terminal pierhead** 43°21'·5N 8°22'·6W
Fl(2+1)R.21s3M Red conical tower, green band, 5m
1716 **Castillo de San Antón** 43°22'N 8°23'·1W
Fl(2)G.7s15m6M
Green hexagonal tower 6m
Plus other lights in the interior of the harbour.

## Navtex

**La Coruña** (43°21'N 8°27'W) Identification letter 'D'
*Transmits*: 518kHz in Spanish and English.
*Weather messages*: 0030, 1230 for areas 1–6 (see plan
page 5).
*Navigational warnings*: 0430, 0830, 1630, 2030 for
Navarea II and local waters.
(*Note* This station was reported to be off the air several
times during 1999)

## Coast radio station and weather/navigational services

**La Coruña** (43°22'N 8°27'W) (24 hours) Remotely
controlled from CCR Coruña – call *Coruña Radio*
*Transmits*: 1698, 2182, 2187·5[1], 2806[2]kHz.
*Receives*: 2045, 2048, 2123, 2182, 2187·5[1], 3283[2]kHz
*Traffic lists*: 1698kHz at 0333, 0533, 0733, 0933, 1133,
1333, 1533, 1733, 1933, 2333.

*Weather messages*: 1698kHz at 0833, 1233, 1733, gale
warnings, synopsis and forecast in Spanish for areas
1–9 (see page 5).
*Urgent navigational warnings*: 1698kHz on receipt and at
0003, 0403, 0803, 1203, 1603, 2003 in Spanish and
English.
*Navigational warnings*: 1698kHz on receipt and at 0803,
2003 in Spanish and English for coastal waters from
6°W to Cabo San Adrián.
**VHF** Ch 16[3], 26, 28[2], 70[1].
*Weather messages*: Ch 12, 13, 14 at 0005, 0405, 0805,
1205, 1605, 2005 in Spanish and English for areas
1–6 (see page 5). Ch 26 at 0950, 1150, 2150, 24
hour forecast for coastal waters.
*Navigational warnings*: Ch 13 at 0205, 0605, 1005, 1405,
1805, 2205 local warnings in Spanish and English;
and Ch 26 at 0803, 1503 in Spanish for coastal
waters from Ría de Cedeira to Cabo San Adrián.
1. Digital Selective Calling (DSC) distress and safety traffic.
2. Reserved for Autolink (see Marine weather information by telephone,
page 16).
3. Continuous watch is NOT maintained on VHF Ch 16. Vessels
should call direct on Ch 26.

## Marina and port radio

*Real Club Náutico de Coruña* and *Sporting Club Casino*
VHF Ch 09.
*Dársena Radio Torre Hércules* VHF Ch 12, 13, 16.
*Coruña Prácticos* VHF Ch 12.

## General

La Coruña is the major city of northern Galicia,
with a population nearing 250,000 and still growing
rapidly. The outskirts are modern but parts of the
old city are still picturesque with narrow paved
streets, houses with characteristic glassed-in
balconies, and numerous small restaurants and
cafés. North of the town the Torre de Hércules,
begun by the Romans, is the oldest functioning
lighthouse in the world.

The city's history goes back at least to Phoenician
times, when tin was mined nearby, while its first
charter was granted by the Romans. In 1588 it was
the departure point of the Armada, and though

The Castillo de San Antón in the foreground contrasts with the
modern port authority building, with La Coruña's two marinas
sandwiched between. The semi-submerged breakwater of old
motor tyres can be seen at bottom right.

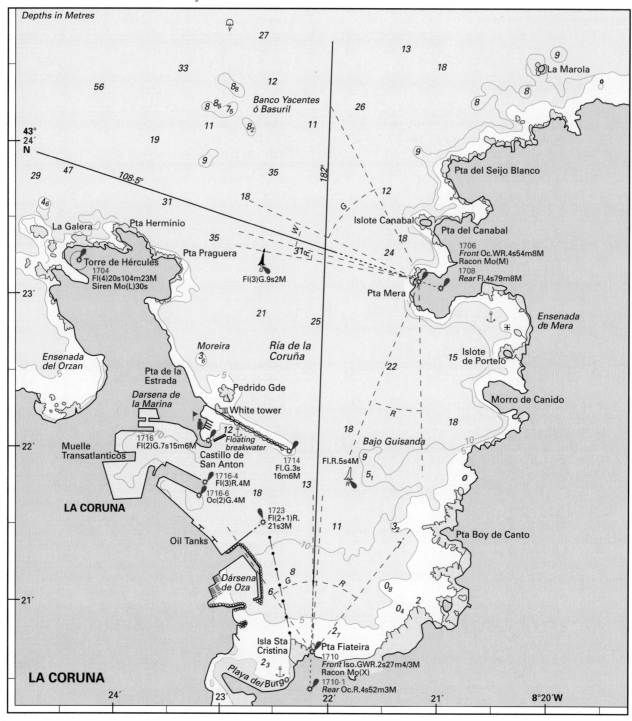

Depths in Metres

LA CORUNA

Drake's attempt to take the city the following year failed, he did sack the harbour area. Later La Coruña played a part in the Peninsula Wars – Sir John Moore is buried in the Jardines de San Carlos close west of the marinas, with a military museum nearby. The Castillo de San Antón (Castelo San Antón), overlooking the harbour houses a museum devoted to archaeology and history and also offers superb views.

La Coruña is also a busy fishing and commercial port, handling mainly tankers and bulk mineral and cereal carriers. The water is noticeably cleaner and less oily since the fishing fleet moved to the purpose-built Dársena de Oza some distance south of the city in 1996.

## Approach

In rough weather the sea breaks over two banks about 1M off the coast north of the *ría* – Bajos Tarracidos and Cabaleiro – and a third, Banco de las Laixiñas, some 2–4M west of Prioriño Grande. The safe approach to La Coruña then lies to the west of Banco de las Laixiñas, and a heading of less than 145° on the Torre de Hércules[1704] will clear its western edge. This line also passes west of Banco Yacentes, slap in the middle of the entrance to La Coruña. In rough weather the sea may break on Banco Yacentes, and also between it and Punta del Seijo Blanco to the east – do not turn east before the line of Punta Mera leading lights[1706], which leads south of Banco Yacentes. Punta Mera rear light[1708] has a wider arc of visibility (180°) than the front[1706] (120°).

Coming from the north in less than rough conditions and starting from a point 1M to the west of Cabo Prior, a course of 185° will lead between the banks mentioned above and the dangers off Punta del Castro, and on into the *ría*, passing between Banco Yacentes and Punta del Seijo Blanco.

On either approach, once in the mouth of the *ría* (and long before if coming from the north), the long grey breakwater can easily be identified, particularly since the advent of a tall white double tower near its root – built to house the port authorities plus a restaurant assured of spectacular views. Six F.R lights mark tower and aerials. Less easy to pick out, particularly in daylight, are the leading marks and lights on Punta Fiaiteira. The white sector of Punta Fiaiteira front light[1710] has a 4° arc centred on 182°.

A floating breakwater (constructed of old motor tyres partially filled with polystyrene) some 200m long and running 065°–245° is moored off Castillo San Antón, placed to protect yachts from wash. It floats low in the water and may be difficult to see, especially at night as it is totally unlit. By day it often serves as a convenient perch for gulls. The harbour is generally clean other than around the *club náutico* fuelling point where diesel sometimes collects.

## Moorings and anchorage

After rounding the breakwater, La Coruña's two yacht clubs with their adjacent small marinas will come into view. To the north is the Sporting Club Casino (also known as the Club Marítimo), to the south the Real Club Náutico de Coruña, ☎ 981 203265 *Fax* 981 203008. Each has moorings in the area between the breakwater and the Castillo de San Antón, where anchoring is forbidden. Buoys belonging to the Sporting Club Casino are labelled 'Casino', those of the Real Club Náutico are painted white – consult the appropriate club boatman if wishing to use one. Space is tight, but it is claimed that yachts of up to 17m can lie to the Real Club Náutico buoys.

It is also possible to anchor outside the mooring area in 10–12m over mud. Holding is patchy. The bottom is littered with wrecks and other detritus and a tripline essential. The Real Club Náutico can arrange for a diver if necessary, but this would not be cheap. No charge is currently made for anchoring.

## Berthing

Each club administers two pontoons, but there is no doubt that those of the Real Club Náutico are the better suited to visiting yachts. Of the 106 berths some 40 are reserved for visiting boats of up to 15m. There is a reception berth on the hammerhead of the northern of the two RCN pontoons, but as of July 1999 this was in poor condition and did not give easy access to the shore. Berthing in the marina itself is bows-on, with a pickup line provided for the stern as well as two bow lines. Space is short, and in crosswinds manoeuvring can be difficult. In 1999 the high season (1/5–30/9) rate for a visiting yacht of any size was 2,600 ptas (15·63 euros) per night on the pontoons or 2,000 ptas (12·02 euros) on a buoy, both inclusive. Discounts were available for stays of a month or more.

There has long been talk of turning the large inner basin known as the Dársena de la Marina into a yacht harbour, but by 1999 this had still to happen. However some 25 berths, five of them reserved for visitors, are available on the two pontoons directly south of the 'old' Real Club Náutico building. These are able to take yachts of up to 17m, and would undoubtedly prove considerably more sheltered if leaving the yacht for any length of time.

## Formalities

Customs and immigration forms are available at the Real Club Náutico, but are normally only required when there are non-EU crewmembers aboard. Officials sometimes visit the club and one may then be asked to produce ship's papers and passport.

## Facilities

*Boatyard* At the RCN, but with minimal security.
*Travel-lift* At the RCN. Claimed to be of 32 tonne capacity, but this appears generous.
*Engineers* Available via the RCN.
  **Motor Siete**, Ronda de Outeiro 10, 15008 A Coruña, ☎ 981 4520221 *Fax* 981 4521337 specialise in Honda, Tohatsu and Volvo Penta.
*Electronic & radio repairs* Available via the RCN.
*Sailmaker/sail repairs* The nearest sailmaker is Cadenote in Sada – arrange via the RCN.
*Chandlery* The small Regata chandlery overlooking the Dársena de la Marina (about five minutes' walk); alternatively a choice of Efectos Navales Pombo, Efectos Navales Coruña Mar, Efectos Navales La Naval or Pombo Náutica all situated close to one another on the Avenida Primo de Rivera opposite the corner of the westernmost basin.
*Charts* Limited stock available from the Real Club Náutico building overlooking the Dársena de la Marina, also from
  **Cartamar**, Paseo de Ronda 39, 15011 A Coruña ☎ 981 255228
  **Producciones Gráficas para Instituciones Públicas SL**, Avda Fernández Latorre 28–30, 15006 A Coruña.
*Water* On the pontoons (no hoses at visitors' berths).
*Showers* At the RCN. A small charge may be made to crews of anchored yachts.
*Launderette* At the RCN.
*Electricity* On the pontoons.
*Fuel* Diesel and petrol at the RCN. The fuel berth,

alongside the wall (with steps) directly astern of the boatyard is awkward of access and carries little more than 1m at low water – inspect before approach, and calculate tidal heights.

*Bottled gas* Camping Gaz exchanges available in the city, but no refills of other makes.

*Club náuticos* The Real Club Náutico, ☎ 981 226880 *Fax* 981 226485, and the Sporting Club Casino, overlooking the marinas and anchorage, as well 'old' Real Club Náutico overlooking the Dársena de la Marina.

Note that the latter is very formal with uniformed doorman, etc, and if intending to visit it would be wise to dress smartly and have the membership card of one's home yacht or sailing club available for inspection.

*Weather forecast* Posted daily at the RCN.

*Banks* Many in the city, nearly all with card facilities.

*Shops/provisioning* Excellent choice, as befits a large city, with a hypermarket on the outskirts (for which a taxi will be necessary).

*Produce market* The San Augustine market, just west of the Plaza de Maria Pita, is particularly good and combines produce and fish market in one building.

*Cafés, restaurants & hotels* Literally hundreds, to suit all tastes and pockets. The RCN has a very pleasant terrace bar/restaurant overlooking the marina.

*Medical services* In the city, with a hospital on the outskirts.

*Tourist office* Very helpful office, ☎ 981 221822, with good English spoken, at the northwest corner of the Dársena de la Marina.

## Communications

*Post offices* Several in the city.

*Mailing address*
c/o *poste restante* at the main post office:
**Oficina de Correos Principal**,
Avenida de la Marina, 15001 A Coruña, España
See also page 10. (There is a separate entrance on the far side of the building for *poste restante* collection.) Most unusually, the Real Club Náutico will NOT hold mail for visiting yachts.

*Public telephones* In the Real Club Náutico and throughout the city.

*Fax service* At the Real Club Náutico, *Fax* 981 203008.

*Car hire/taxis* Wide choice in the city.

*Buses, coaches & trains* Services throughout Galicia and beyond. Enquire at the tourist office for timetables, etc.

*Air services* La Coruña airport does not carry international flights, for which it is necessary to travel the 50km to Santiago de Compostela. The motorway linking the two cities is excellent.

### Alternative anchorages

1. In the Ensenada de Mera, protected from northwest clockwise to south. Beware the unmarked rock some distance from the mole, which only shows near low water. Anchor as moorings and depth permit in 3–4m over sand and weed, surrounded by a crescent of sandy beach (a line of closely spaced yellow buoys may define the swimming area). The village is very much a holiday resort, with restaurants and limited shopping plus a ferry to/from La Coruña.

2. Off the east end of the Playa del Burgo, partly sheltered by the Isla de Santa Cristina, in 2–3m with good holding over sand and weed. Dinghies can be left on the sandy beach. There is a small restaurant ashore and a supermarket one road further back. The ferry to La Coruña departs from the tiny pier every hour, and must not be impeded.

# Malpica
43°19'N 8°48'W

## Tides
See La Coruña, page 24

## Charts
|  | *Approach* |
|---|---|
| Admiralty | *1111, 3633* |
| Spanish | *928, 929* |

## Lights
### *Approach*
1704 **Torre de Hércules** 43°23'·2N 8°24'·3W
  Fl(4)20s104m23M Siren Mo(L)30s 165m NNW
  Square stone tower, octagonal top 49m
*0928* Radiobeacon *L* 301·5kHz 50M
1728 **Islas Sisargas** 43°21'·6N 8°50'·7W
  Fl(3)15s108m23M Siren Mo(S)30s
  Octagonal granite tower, white cupola, on white building 11m. On summit of largest island
### *Harbour*
1726 **Breakwater** 43°19'·4N 8°48'·1W
  Fl.G.3s19m4M Green column 4m

Looking southeast over the Ensenada de Mera on the east side of the Ría de la Coruña.

The busy fishing harbour of Malpica, looking south on a very hazy day.

## General

Malpica is a fishing port and the town has been developed as a tourist outlet for La Coruña. The town is not particularly attractive, but the harbour is colourful and there are good beaches nearby. The mole, backed by a very high wall, is some 420m overall with the entrance looking south of east towards the far side of the bay. There is good protection from south through west and north to northeast, but a northeasterly swell may come some distance round the corner of the mole.

A small inner harbour behind lock gates shelters local craft from winter storms but is not open to yachts. Basic provisions are available in the town, plus restaurants, etc.

Continuous fishing boat activity and wailing sirens on the fish quay may make for disturbed sleep.

The anchorage in the cone between Sisarga Grande and Sisarga Chico, looking north from Cabo de San Adrián. Patches of sand can be made out between the darker rocks and weed.

## Approach

From the east, keep about 5M offshore until northeast of Malpica in order to clear the extensive and unmarked Bajos de Baldayo (unless intent on using the inside passage, which can be passed by following the coast from Caión at a distance of about 0·7M offshore). Malpica stands on an isthmus to the south of a distinctive headland 77m in height, the Atalaya de Malpica.

From the west, once past Islas Sisargas there are no offshore hazards. From either direction the final approach needs to be made with care as there are unmarked rocks near the entrance.

## Anchorage

Anchor in the entrance, clear of the fishing boats which lie on fore-and-aft moorings between the mole and the shore. Around 7m should be found over rock and weed, with sand patches near the breakwater itself (though take care not impede the passage of fishing boats approaching the quays). It may be possible to lie alongside briefly while the fishing boats are away.

Caión, seen here from the northwest, is one of those places which should only be approached in perfect, offshore weather.

## Alternative anchorages

Depending on conditions there are five other possible anchorages in this area:

1. In the entrance to the tiny harbour of Caión (Cayón), about 9M along the coast towards La Coruña by Punta de las Olas. Something of a Malpica in miniature, the harbour faces east with a high stone breakwater offering protection from north through west to south. Strictly a fair-weather spot which, although lit (Fl(3)G.7s5m3M+Ldg Lts), should not be approached in darkness. As in Malpica, it may be possible to lie alongside for a short period if the fishing boats are out and there is no swell.
2. Off the beach west of Malpica, sheltered from the south.
3. Off the Playa de Seaya southeast of Punta del Castro, itself east of Cabo de San Adrián, in 5m over sand. Sheltered from south and west.

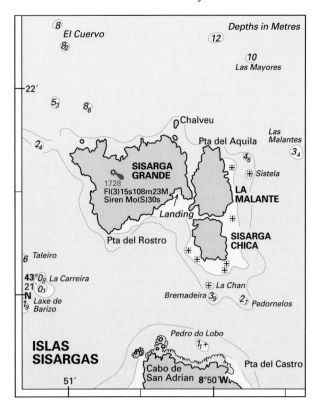

**ISLAS SISARGAS**

4. The Islas Sisargas, in the cone between Sisarga Grande and Sisarga Chico (sometimes referred to as Sisarga Pequeña), sheltered from the north. The gap between the two islands is very narrow, and virtually non-existent at low water. Anchor southeast of the stone quay in 3–4m – holding is variable over sand and rock. There are steps at the quay, and a track leading up to the lighthouse on the island's summit. The islands are a seabird reserve, as is audible from a considerable distance.

The Sisargas channel is hazardous. Both east and west winds can produce breakers and there are strong tidal streams. The approaches, which should not be attempted without large-scale charts (e.g. inset to Spanish 928), are as follows:

a. From the northwest, keeping the prominent headland of Atalaya de Malpica in line with Punta del Castro on 133°.

b. From the southwest, keeping to the south of La Carreira and Laxe de Barizo.

c. From the east, either by following a leading bearing of 265° towards the rock Pedro de Lobo and changing towards Punta del Rostro when this bears 309°, or by eye. The channel is about 400m wide and closer to Punta del Castro than Isla Sisargas Chica (which has a rock, La Chan, awash some 250m to the south).

5. The Ensenada de Barizo, overlooked by cliffs and the Punta Nariga windfarm, about 3M southwest of Sisargas lighthouse and close east of that on Punta Nariga. A ledge runs out from the eastern headland leaving a usable width of about 250m in the entrance. The bay, which is open to the

northwest and subject to swell from that quarter, opens out inside and provides sufficient shelter for small fishing vessels to lie to summer moorings, with more craned out ashore. A short concrete mole, slipway and small quay lie in the southwest corner (as of February 2000 the green light structure on the former remained unlit).

There is a fine sandy beach at the head of the bay, but otherwise the bottom is of rock and sand. There are no facilities other than a couple of restaurants some distance to the east.

# Ría de Corme y Lage

## Tides

*Reference port* La Coruña
*Mean time differences*
HW: +45 minutes; LW: +45 minutes
*Heights in metres*

| MHWS | MHWN | MLWN | MLWS |
|------|------|------|------|
| 3·7 | 2·8 | 1·5 | 0·5 |

## Charts

|  | *Approach* | *Ría* |
|--|-----------|-------|
| Admiralty | *1111, 3633* | *1113* |
| Spanish | *41B, 928* | *9280* |

## Lights

*Approach*

1728 **Islas Sisargas** 43°21'·6N 8°50'·7W
Fl(3)15s108m23M Siren Mo(S)30s
Octagonal granite tower, white cupola, on white building 11m. On summit of largest island

1729 **Punta Nariga** 43°19'·3N 8°54'·5W
Fl(3+1)20s53m22M White round tower 39m

1736 **Cabo Villano** 43°09'·6N 9°12'·7W
Fl(2)15s102m28M 031·5°-vis-228·5°
Siren Mo(V)60s
Buff octagonal tower, white cupola 25m
Racon Mo(M) 360° 35M

0929 Radiobeacon *VI* 290·5kHz 100M

*Entrance*

1730 **Punta del Roncudo** 43°16'·5N 8°59'·5W
Fl.6s36m10M White tower 11m

1732 **Punta de Lage** 43°13'·9N 9°00'·7W
Fl(5)20s64m20M
White conical tower 11m

## General

For many, the Ría de Corme y Lage offers a welcome anchorage following the 35M coastal passage west from La Coruña. The two could hardly be more different, and after making landfall at the latter with its excellent city facilities, the chance to walk in the countryside and – for the hardy – swim from the boat in clear if chilly water, is a contrasting pleasure. If forced to head north into northwesterly winds, departure from Lage or Corme rather than La Coruña avoids giving away considerable ground to windward.

Not only is the local walking excellent, but a dinghy with reliable outboard would permit exploration of the surrounding *ría*, including a visit to the picturesque old bridge at Ponteceso some 5M distant up the shallow and winding Río Allones.

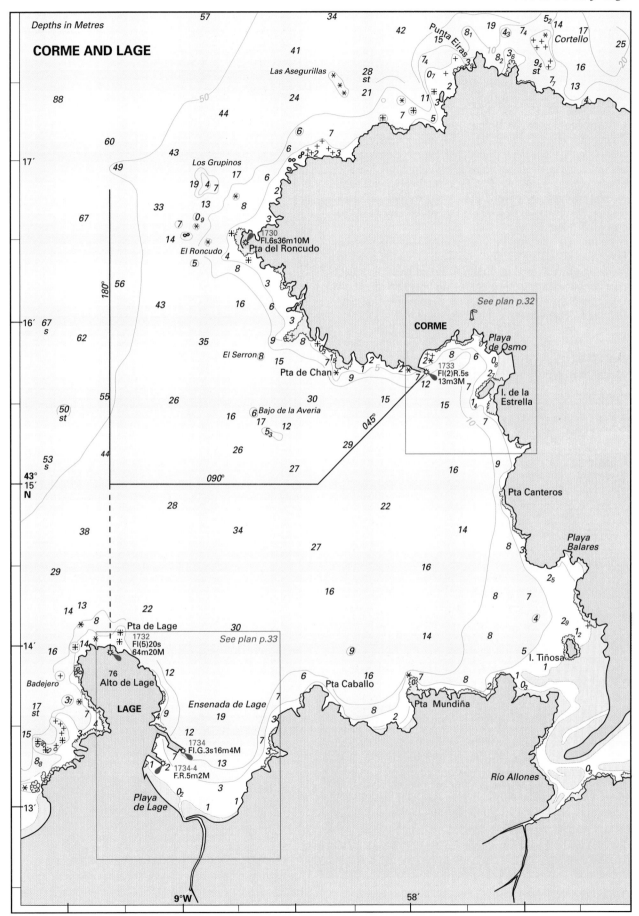

Depths in Metres

# CORME AND LAGE

57
34
42
Punta Eiras
8₁  19  4₃  7₄  5₂ 14  17
Cortello  25

41
15
7₄  0₇  3  8₂  3₆  9₄ st  16
7₇  13

Las Asegurillas  28 st
24  21
11  2
3  4

88
44
6  7  5
7
88
21
6

60
43
6  6  7  +2 +3
49  17
Los Grupinos
19  4  7  6  2
33  13  8  3
0₉
7  14  8
El Roncudo  4  8
5  3  1730
Fl.6s36m10M
Pta del Roncudo

17′

180°
56
43  16  6
67  8  3
62  35  9  8
El Serron 8  15  7  1½ 2 1  2  2
Pta de Chan  9  5

See plan p.32

CORME
Playa de Osmo
8  0₈
2₁
1733
Fl(2)R.5s
13m3M  2₇
12  I. de la
15  1₄  Estrella
7

16′
67 s

55
50 st
26  Bajo de la Averia
16  17  12
5₃
26  30  15
29  045°
15
9
16

44
53 s
27  090°  28
22

**43°
15′
N**

38  34  27
29  14
16
16

14  13  22
8  Pta de Lage  30
16  14  See plan p.33
1732
Fl(5)20s
64m20M
76
Alto de Lage  12
Badejero
LAGE
17 st
3₇  7  4
15  8  9
8₈  19
12
1734
Fl.G.3s16m4M
7  13
1  2  1734-4
F.R.5m2M
Playa
de Lage  0₂
1

Pta Canteros

Playa
Balares
8  3
2₅
8  7
8  2₉
4  1₂
5  I. Tiñosa
1

6  16
Pta Caballo  8
7  8  2
Pta Mundiña  1  0₃
2

Río Allones
0₃

## Approach

In heavy weather the seas break on all the banks in this area and it is advisable to pass west and south of the Bajo de la Averia (5·6m) in the entrance to the *ría*. In calm weather it is possible to sail over the bank.

From the north, round Punta Roncudo[1730] with an offing of at least 1M before turning south towards Punta de Lage[1732]. If making for Corme, continue south until about 1M north of Punta de Lage in order to clear the *bajo*, then head east until Corme breakwater[1733] bears 045°. The northerly approach to Lage is straightforward, always providing at least 500m clearance is allowed off Punta de Lage itself to clear off-lying rocks.

From the southwest, keep 1M off the coast northeast of Cabo Villano[1736] with its attendant wind farm. Round Punta de Lage at 500m or more, and then either head east until Corme breakwater bears 045°, or follow the coast around to starboard to pick up Lage breakwater.

# Corme

43°16'N 8°58'W

## Charts

|  | *Harbour* |
|---|---|
| Admiralty | *1113* |
| Spanish | *9280* |

## Lights

**Harbour**
1733 **Breakwater** 43°15'·7N 8°57'·9W
  Fl(2)R.5s13m3M Red column 6m

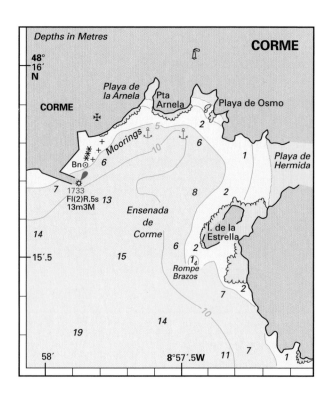

The harbour and anchorage at Corme, looking east of north. Both town and waterfront have changed remarkably little over the past decade.

## General

Once a small and picturesque fishing village with good beaches in a pleasant setting, Corme gained some unattractive apartment blocks during the late 1980s and early 1990s. However little has changed since that time, and Corme remains one of the very few harbours Galicia which has not changed visibly over the past decade. There are limited facilities and none specifically for yachts, though the anchorage is well sheltered other than from the south and southwest when Lage (see opposite) would be preferable.

Energetic crews will enjoy the walk amidst wild granite scenery out to the lighthouse on Punta del Roncudo. Access is via the tunnel behind the harbour.

## Approach

See under Ría approaches, above.

## Anchorage

Fishing boats use the inside of the breakwater, while the small area to the northeast is filled with moorings. There are rocks inshore of the moorings, marked by an unlit green beacon on a grey base.

Anchor east of the town off a small sandy beach, in 10m or less over sand. A few smallcraft moorings fringe the foreshore but there is plenty of room outside them. Dinghies – particularly inflatables – are reported to be less safe from local children than in many places, and at least one crew has returned to find that the valves have been unscrewed.

## Facilities

Reasonable shopping, restaurants, hotels and a bank. There is a freshwater tap immediately inland from the main slipway, but no yacht fuel.

Unlike its neighbour across the *ría*, Lage has moved with the times and now handles sizeable cargo ships against its immaculate quay. Yachts find good anchorage off the beach to the south.

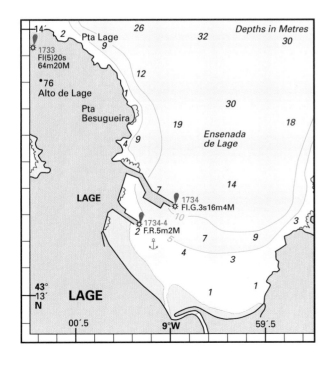

# Lage (Laxe)

43°13'N 9°00'W

## Charts

| | Harbour |
|---|---|
| Admiralty | *1113* |
| Spanish | *9280* |

## Lights

### Harbour

1734 **Breakwater** 43°13'·3N 9°00'W
    Fl.G.3s16m4M Green column 6m

1734·4 **South mole** 43°13'·3N 9°00'·2W
    F.R.5m2M Red column 4m

## General

A typical Galician fishing village fast expanding into a good-sized holiday resort, Lage has a fine, long, sandy beach to the south and attractive walks in the nearby hills. The 14th century church of Santiago de Lage overlooking the harbour is worth a visit, though sadly often locked. There is a street market (*mercadillo*) every Friday.

## Approach

See under Ría approaches, above.

## Anchorage

The 300m breakwater offers good shelter in most conditions, though swell may work in. Anchor off the beach near the south mole, clear of the harbour approach, in 5m or less over sand and weed. Fishing vessels enter day and night – display a riding light – and cargo ships of considerable size berth alongside the outer breakwater quay.

There are many smallcraft moorings within the harbour, some of which trail floating lines. Manoeuvre with care.

## Facilities

Water on the quay, shops (including hardware stores but no chandlery), banks, restaurants and bars. There is a marine railway – though no longer a boatyard – on the south mole, but its cradle would not suit a keel yacht's hull.

## Communications

Infrequent buses to La Coruña.

# Ría de Camariñas

## Tides

*Reference port* La Coruña
*Mean time differences*
HW: +05 minutes; LW: −05 minutes

*Heights in metres*

| MHWS | MHWN | MLWN | MLWS |
|------|------|------|------|
| 3·8 | 2·8 | 1·5 | 0·5 |

## Charts

|  | Approach | Ría |
|------|----------|------|
| Admiralty | 1111, 3633 | 1113 |
| Spanish | 41B, 927 | 9272 |

## Lights

*Approach*
1736 **Cabo Villano** 43°09'·6N 9°12'·7W
   Fl(2)15s102m28M 031·5°-vis-228·5°
   Siren Mo(V)60s
   Buff octagonal tower, white cupola 25m
   Racon Mo(M) 360° 35M
*0929* Radiobeacon *VI* 290·5kHz 100M
1740 **Cabo Toriñana** 43°03'·2N 9°17'·9W
   Fl(2+1)15s63m24M 340·5°-vis-235·5°
   White round tower 11m
   Racon Mo(T) 35M

Looking northeast up the attractive Ría de Camariñas, the harbour and town sheltered by the long breakwater. The two pontoons of the Club Náutico Camariñas can be seen beyond the wide expanse of quay.

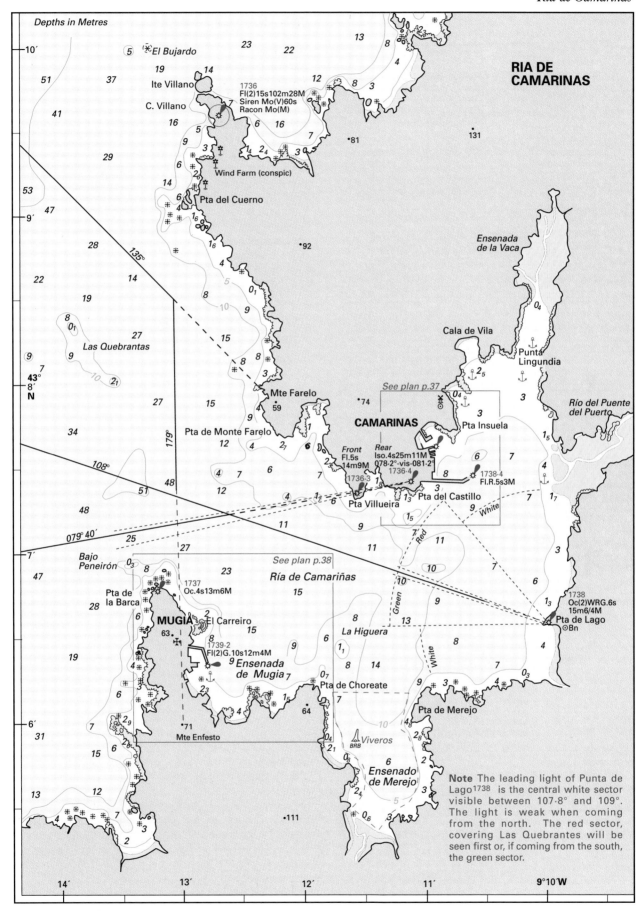

Depths in Metres

RIA DE
CAMARINAS

10′

5  El Bujardo

51    37    19    14
Ite Villano

41    C. Villano    16    5    1736
Fl(2)15s102m28M
Siren Mo(V)60s
Racon Mo(M)

23    22    13    8    4

12    8    3

•81    131

29    9    3
6    14    Wind Farm (conspic)
Pta del Cuerno

53    6    Ensenada
47    de la Vaca

9′    28    14    16

22    14    •92    5    Cala de Vila    0₄    Punta
Lingundia

19    Río del Puente
del Puerto

8  0₁    27    15    8    Mte Farelo    •74    0₄    2₅
9  Las Quebrantas    •59    CAMARINAS    3    Pta Insuela    3

9    7    27    15    Pta de Monte Farelo    3
43°    2₁    12    Front    Rear    1₃
8′    34    Fl.5s    Iso.4s25m11M    1₅
N    14m9M    078.2°-vis-081.2°
1736·3    1736·4    1738·4
48    51    12    4    7    6    Fl.R.5s3M
108°    Pta Villueira    8    Pta del Castillo    7    1₇
079° 40′    25    11    9    White
Bajo    27    See plan p.38    Red    11    10    6
Peneirón    0₃    8    23    Ría de Camariñas
Pta de    1737    15    13    1₃    1738
la Barca    Oc.4s13m6M    Oc(2)WRG.6s
28    MUGIA    El Carreiro    15    La Higuera    Pta de Lago
63    8    1739·2    15    8    6    1₁    ⊙Bn    4
19    Fl(2)G.10s12m4M    9    Ensenada    8    14    White    7    0₃
de Mugia    Pta de Choreate    9    3
6    2₃    1₅    64    7    Pta de Merejo
31    2₉    Mte Enfesto    Viveros
•71    BRB    2₈
15    6    6    Ensenado
de Merejo    Note The leading light of Punta de
13    12    •111    0₆    Lago¹⁷³⁸ is the central white sector
2    3    visible between 107·8° and 109°.
The light is weak when coming
from the north. The red sector,
covering Las Quebrantes will be
seen first or, if coming from the south,
the green sector.

14′    13′    12′    11′    9°10′W

### Entrance

1736·3 **Punta Villueira Ldg Lts on 079·7°** 43°07'·4N
9°11'·6W
*Front* Fl.5s14m9M
White round concrete tower, red diamond 7m
1736·4 *Rear* **Punta del Castillo**, 610m from front,
Iso.4s25m11M 078·2°-vis-081·2°
Round white tower, red bands 7m
1738 **Punta de Lago** 43°06'·6N 9°10'W
Oc(2)WRG.6s15m6/4M
029·5°-W-093°-G-107·8°-W-109·1°-R-139·3°-W-
213·5°
Round white concrete tower 9m
1737 **Punta de la Barca** 43°06'·8N 9°13'·2W
Oc.4s13m6M
Buff conical tower 11m
The nearby church is floodlit at night
*Note* The only sound signal in the area is on Cabo
Villano[1736].

## General

Many would consider the Ría de Camariñas amongst Galicia's loveliest, with the added advantage that it contains anchorages protected from almost every direction – albeit some remote from any habitation – while its two small towns can meet the daily needs of the cruising yachtsman without undue effort. As throughout the area, the possibilities for long walks through unspoilt countryside are endless.

## Approach

There are various isolated dangers in the approach to the Ría de Camariñas, notably El Bujardo, a pinnacle rock awash at low water, lying 0·3M northwest of Islote Villano de Fuera and 0·6M off Cabo Villano lighthouse and Las Quebrantas lying about 1·2M off the Punta de Monte Farelo. Use a large-scale chart and approach by means of the leading marks.

Coming from the north in daylight, round Cabo Villano with its highly visible wind farm inside or outside El Bujardo and steer southwest until the white hermitage on Monte Farelo, a rounded hill, bears east and the middle of the *ría* entrance is open on 108°, the line of the Punta de Lago leading marks. These two white towers (the front one carrying the sectored light) stand on a small promontory on the eastern shore of the *ría* and, though painted a bright white, can be difficult to spot on hazy days. In these conditions take particular care not to confuse the more conspicuous white tower on Punta Villueira[1736·3] with that on Punta de Lago.

Alternatively, pass inshore of Las Quebrantas by heading 135° towards the hermitage on Monte Farelo until about 0·7M from the shore. Then make a broad sweep towards Punta de la Barca (Las Quebrantas are usually marked by broken water) and use the leading marks of Punta de Lago as described above.

On either approach, continue on the Punta de Lago leading marks until Camariñas breakwater bears 020°, or Mugia breakwater bears 200°, before shaping a course for either harbour.

By night from the north, pass at least 1·5M northwest of Cabo Villano light to clear El Bujardo, then turn onto a bearing of not less than 200° (to clear Las Quebrantas) until the white, narrow beam of the Punta de Lago[1738] sector light becomes visible between its broad red and green sectors. If Punta de Lago cannot be seen but Punta de la Barca[1737] can, steer for it as soon as it bears less than 140° (to keep off Las Quebrantas) until the powerful leading lights on Punta Villueira[1736·3] and Punta del Castillo[1736·4] come into transit. If followed, these will lead back across the line of Punta de Lago. Either way, get onto the line of Punta de Lago and follow it until Camariñas breakwater[1738·4] bears 020°, or Mugia breakwater[1739·2] bears 200°, before shaping a course for either harbour.

Approaching from the southwest, steer to pass about 0·5M northwest of Punta de la Barca to clear the off-lying shoal of Bajo Peneirón. Then for Camariñas follow the leading marks on Puntas Villueira and del Castillo, followed by those on Punta de Lago, as described above, or for Mugia follow the shore around to starboard keeping at least 400m off.

# Camariñas
43°08'N 9°11'W

## Charts

| | Harbour |
|---|---|
| Admiralty | 1113 |
| Spanish | 9272 |

## Lights

*Harbour*
1738·4 **Breakwater** 43°07'·5N 9°10'·7W
Fl.R.5s3M Red concrete tower 3m
(*Note* Reported at different times in 1999 to be Fl.R.2s
and Fl.R.3s)
1739 **Inner mole** 43°07'·6N 9°10'·9W
Fl(3)R.8s9m4M Red over white concrete column 6m
**Club Náutico pontoons** 43°07'·6N 9°10'·9W
**South pontoon** F.R. White post 1·5m
**North pontoon** F.G. White post 1·5m

## Marina radio

*Club Náutico Camariñas* VHF Ch 09.

## General

An attractive harbour enclosed by a long breakwater which gives excellent shelter from all directions other than east and northeast, with alternative shelter from these winds to be found across the *ría*. The small Club Náutico Camariñas has a well-deserved reputation for being particularly welcoming to all yachtsmen, whether berthed on their pontoons or not, and in 1999 the manageress spoke good English. However fish landing can make the area noisy at night, with hooters blaring at intervals. The village is a local lace-making centre and has the usual shops, restaurants and hotels.

The surrounding countryside is wild but attractive, and the energetic will enjoy the walk along the Sendeiro da Costa do Morte out past the

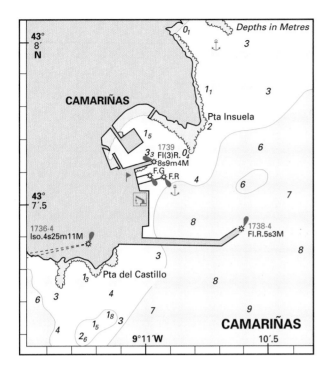

wind farm to Cabo Villano. The lighthouse (and foghorn) are open to the public.

## Approach

See under Ría approaches, opposite.

## Anchorage and berthing

Anchor off the Club Náutico Camariñas, ☎ 981 737130, and its two pontoons in the shelter of the south mole, in 4–5m over mud and sand. Holding is reported to be excellent. However note that the quay south of the *club náutico* (with the large white crane) is used to unload fishing boats, which should not be impeded. Dinghies can be left on the pontoons, and the club facilities used by those anchored off.

Alternatively arrange a pontoon berth (bow or stern-to, with a pick-up line attached to the pontoon but no buoy), a manoeuvre which can be tricky in strong northeasterly (beam) winds, particularly if short-handed. Visiting yachts are generally berthed at the outer end of the southern (longer) pontoon, where there are depths of 4·5–6m.

In 1999 the high season rate for a visiting yacht of just under 12m was 1,450 ptas (8·71 euros) per night inclusive.

## Formalities

Visitors may be asked to complete customs forms at the *club náutico*.

## Facilities

*Travel-lift* Not as such, but the fish landing crane near south of the *club náutico* might be made available in an emergency. Alternatively there are several convenient walls in the old harbour against which it might be possible to dry out.
*Engineers/metalwork* Can be arranged via the *club náutico*.
*Water* On the pontoons.

*Showers* At the *club náutico*. A small charge is made, whether on the marina pontoons or anchored off.
*Launderette* Not as such, but laundry can be arranged via the *club náutico* staff.
*Electricity* On the pontoons.
*Fuel* Diesel available at the *club náutico*, though as of 1999 by can rather than pump. No petrol – and the nearest filling station is 9km up the road!
*Bottled gas* Camping Gaz available in the town.
*Ice* From the ice factory on the fish-landing quay.
*Club Náutico* The Club Náutico Camariñas, ☎ 981 737130, is particularly friendly and welcoming, as mentioned above. Office hours are normally 1000–1300, 1700–2200.
*Banks* In the town (with card facilities)
*Shops/provisioning* Several small supermarkets in the town, plus bakery, etc.
*Produce market* In the town.
*Cafés, restaurants & hotels* Many in the town, as well as a very pleasant bar serving light snacks at the *club náutico*.
*Medical services* In the town.

### Communications

*Post office* In the town.
*Mailing address*
c/o **Club Náutico Camariñas**, Peirao novo s/n, 15123 Camariñas, A Coruña, España.
*Fax service* 981 737130 (faxes should be clearly marked with the yacht's name c/o Club Náutico Camariñas).
*Public telephones* At the *club náutico* as well as in town.
*Car hire/taxis* Available in the town, or the latter via the *club náutico* office.
*Buses* Infrequent bus service, including one to La Coruña.

### Alternative anchorages

1. In the bay off Cala Caldeira (the old fish cannery) northeast of Punta Insuela, in 2m over mud. There is a landing slip ending in a 2m drop immediately north of Punta Insuela which is convenient for the town, but it has foul ground some 150m to the east. Not recommended in westerly winds, when smells from the fishing canning factory (marked 'BOYA' in large letters) pervade the area.
2. In the entrance to Cala de Vila in 2–3m over mud and shells, well sheltered from the strong northwesterlies typical of the area. The inner part of the cala is buoyed off.
3. In the small cove between Punta Lingundia and the unnamed headland to the west, off a small sandy beach.
4. West of Punta Lingundia, towards the head of the *ría*, in 2m over mud and weed.
5. Off the mouth of the Río de Puente de Puerto, on the east side of the *ría*, in 3–5m. It is possible to take a dinghy some 2M up the Río del Puente del Puerto to the town of the same name, where there are shops, restaurants, banks, etc.

# Mugia (Muxia)

43°06'N 9°13'W

## Charts

|            | Harbour |
|------------|---------|
| Admiralty  | *1113*  |
| Spanish    | *9272*  |

## Lights

*Harbour*

1739·2 **Breakwater** 43°06'·4N 9°12'·8W
 Fl(2)G.10s12m4M Grey tower 5m

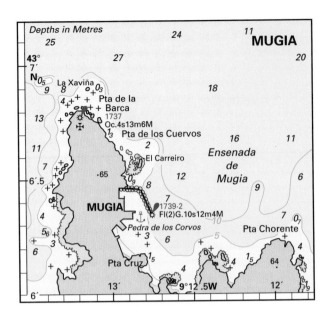

## General

Although falling short of picturesque the village is relaxed and pleasant, with flashes of beauty in individual older buildings and an attractive setting of hills, woods and seascapes. The 17th century church of La Virgen de la Barca on the northern point has ship models suspended from its arches (not surprisingly the church is nearly always locked, but a glimpse can be had through the iron grille), and there are fine views from Punta de la Barca over the *ría* and out to Cabo Villano. There is a clean sandy beach just south of the harbour.

## Approach

See under Ría approaches, above.

## Anchorage

Anchor in 3–4m over sand south of the end of the breakwater, but beware the Pedra de los Corvos rock off the beach to the south. It remains unlit, but is marked by a somewhat flimsy white post. There is another, smaller, rock (totally unmarked) about 50m to the southeast of Pedra de los Corvos, and others further in.

## Facilities

Several small supermarkets, restaurants, bars, banks (with card facility), hardware store, etc.

## Communications

Post office and telephones. Early morning bus daily to La Coruña.

The angled breakwater at Mugia seen from the southeast, with Punta de la Barca behind.

Looking north from the rocks of Punta de la Barca towards Cabo Villano lighthouse and its neighbouring wind farm.

# Finisterre (Fisterra)

42°54'N 9°15'W

## Tides

See Ría de Corcubión, page 43
*Note* A considerable inshore set may be encountered south of Cabo Finisterre with a westerly wind and flood tide.

## Charts

|  | Approach | Harbour |
|---|---|---|
| Admiralty | *1111, 3633* | *3764* |
| Spanish | *41B, 927, 9270* | *9271* |

## Lights

*Approach*
1742 **Cabo Finisterre** 42°52'·9N 9°16'·3W
   Fl.5s141m23M Siren Mo(I)60s 25m S
   Octagonal granite tower and building 17m
   Obscd when bearing more than 149°
   Racon Mo(O) 360° 35M
*0931* Radiobeacon *FI* 288·5kHz 100M
1756 **Islote Lobeira Grande** 42°52'·8N 9°11'·1W
   Fl(3)15s16m9M
   White octagonal tower and building 10m
1782 **Punta Insúa** 42°46'·3N 9°07'·6W
   F.WR+Oc(1+2)WR.20s25m15/14M
   Hexagonal tower and adjacent building 14m
   308°-F.R-012·5° (Leixões to Bajos Los Bruyos)
   012·5°-Oc.R-044·5° (over Bajos Los Bruyos)
   044·5°-Oc.W-093° (over Bajos Los Meixidos)
   093°-F.W-172·5° (Bajos Los Meixidos to coast)
   but obscd by Cabo Finisterre from 145°-172·5°
*Harbour*
1744 **Breakwater** 42°54'·6N 9°15'·4W
   Fl.R.4s12m4M Red concrete tower 5m
1744·4 **Breakwater inner spur** 42°54'·5N 9°15'·5W
   F.R.7m1M Grey concrete tower 5m

## Coast radio station and weather/navigational services

**Finisterre** (42°54'N 9°16'W) (24 hours) Remotely controlled from CCR Coruña – see page 25 – call *Coruña Radio*
*Transmits*: **1764**, 2182, 2187·5[1], 2596[2]kHz.
*Receives*: 2045, 2048, 2108, 2182, 2187·5[1], 3280[2]kHz.

*Traffic lists*: 1764kHz at 0333, 0533, 0733, 0933, 1133, 1333, 1533, 1733, 1933, 2333.
*Weather messages*: 1764kHz at 0803, 1203, 1703, gale warnings, synopsis and forecast in Spanish for areas 1–9 (see page 5).
*Urgent navigational warnings*: 1764kHz on receipt and at 0033, 0433, 0833, 1233, 1633, 2033 in Spanish and English.
*Navigational warnings*: 1764kHz on receipt and at 0833, 2033 in Spanish and English for coastal waters from Cabo San Adrián to the Portuguese border.
**VHF** Ch 16[3], 22, 27[2], 70[1].
*Weather messages*: Ch 11 at 0233, 0633, 1033, 1433, 1833, 2233, in Spanish and English. Ch 22 at 0950, 1150, 2150, 24 hour forecast for coastal waters.
*Navigational warnings*: Ch 22 on receipt and at 0903 1633, in Spanish for coastal waters from Cabo San Adrián to Cabo Corrubedo; and Ch 11 at 0033, 0433, 0833, 1233, 1633, 2033 in Spanish and English.
1. Digital Selective Calling (DSC) distress and safety traffic.
2. Reserved for Autolink (see *Marine weather information by telephone*, page 16).
3. Continuous watch is NOT maintained on VHF Ch 16. Vessels should call direct on Ch 22.

## Traffic Separation Zone

A major Traffic Separation Zone lies off Cabo Finisterre (marked on Admiralty charts *1111* and *3633* amongst others), the north-going lane running from the vicinity of 42°53'N 9°47'W to 43°22'N 9°40'W and the south-going lane from 43°26'N 9°49'W to 42°53'N 9°57'W. (See also plan page 4.) Shipping passes in a steady stream and yachts are very strongly advised to avoid crossing the lanes if at all possible. The Inshore Traffic Zone now has a minimum width of 19M.

The Servicio de Tráfico Marítimo (42°42'N 8°59'W) monitors VHF Ch 11 and 16 as well as 2182 and 2187·5kHz continuously in case of emergencies, and all vessels are advised to maintain a listening watch whilst in the area. Those of more than 50m LOA are required to report on entering and leaving the area – call Finisterre Tráfico, who can also be contacted on ☎ 981 767320/767738.

An unusual view of Cabo Finisterre – looking northwest into the Atlantic Ocean with the tiny island of Centolo de Finisterre visible just above the lighthouse.

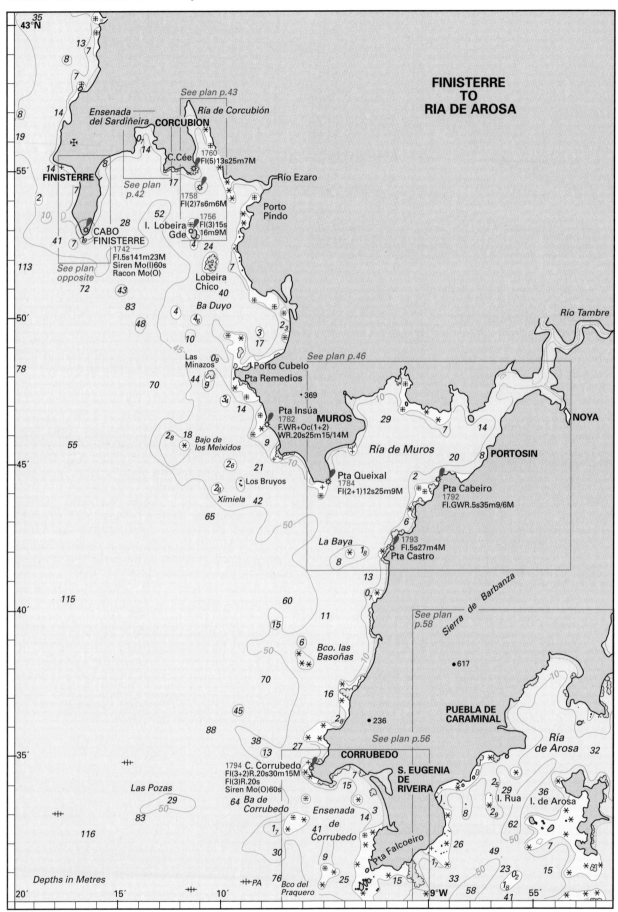

FINISTERRE
TO
RIA DE AROSA

43°N  35
13  7
8
7

8  14

19

Ensenada
del Sardiñeira  Ría de Corcubión
CORCUBIÓN
55′  14  8
FINISTERRE  See plan
p.42  17  C.Cée
1760
Fl(5)13s25m7M
Río Ezaro

2  7
10  14  0₇  1758
Fl(2)7s6m6M  Porto
Pindo
52  1756
28  I. Lobeira  Fl(3)15s
41  Gde  16m9M
CABO  4  24
7  1₉  FINISTERRE
1742  7
Fl.5s141m23M  Lobeira
Siren Mo(I)60s  Chico  40
113  Racon Mo(O)  Ba Duyo
See plan  72  43  4
opposite  83  4₆  3
48  10  17

Las  0₉
78  Minazos
44  9  Porto Cubelo
Pta Remedios  See plan p.46
• 369

3₄  Pta Insúa  7  14  NOYA
14  1782  MUROS
55  2₈  18  Bajo de  F.WR+Oc(1+2)  29
los Meixidos  9  WR.20s25m15/14M  Ría de Muros
45′  2₆  21  Pta Queixal  20  8  PORTOSIN
Los Bruyos  1784  2
2₈  Fl(2+1)12s25m9M  Pta Cabeiro
Xímiela  42  1792
65  6  Fl.GWR.5s35m9/6M
50  1793
La Baya  1₈  Fl.5s27m4M
8  Pta Castro
13  Sierra de Barbanza

0₇
115  60  See plan
40′  p.58
15  11  • 617

50  6  Bco. las
Basoñas  PUEBLA DE
70  CARAMINAL  Río Tambre

16  Ría
45  de Arosa  32
2₈  • 236
88  See plan p.56
38  27  32
35′  13  CORRUBEDO
1794 C. Corrubedo  7  S. EUGENIA  2₅  29  36
Fl(3+2)R.20s30m15M  15  DE  I. Rua  I. de Arosa
Las Pozas  Fl(3)R.20s  RIVEIRA
29  Siren Mo(O)60s  3  8  2₉
64  Ba de  14  62
83  Corrubedo  Ensenada
116  de  49  7
Corrubedo  26
1₇  41
30  9  23  0₂
20′  Depths in Metres  76  Bco del  25  Pta Falcoeiro  33  1₈  15
20′  15′  10′  PA  Praquero  9°W  58  41  55′

40

Finisterre harbour is crowded with moorings leaving little space to anchor and even less to lie alongside.

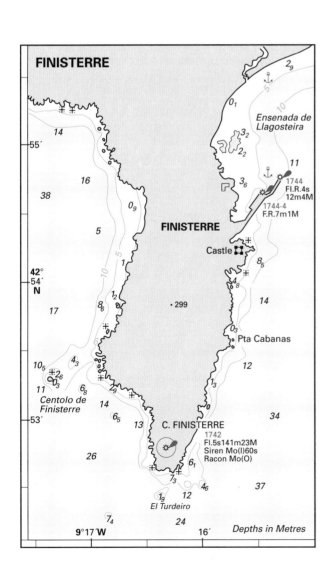

Weather and navigational information is broadcast on VHF Ch 11 every 2 hours at 15 minutes past the hour, and radar assistance is available on request. However it should be noted that the transmitter is situated not at Cabo Finisterre but some 17M to the southeast.

### General

A picturesque and busy town with a resident population of about 2,000, Finisterre can become crowded with tourists during the summer. There are shops, restaurants and banks but no facilities specifically for yachts. The harbour gives good shelter from west and south, but is crowded with moored fishing boats and open to the northeast.

There is a pleasant 3km walk to the lighthouse (141m) from which, being high up as many Spanish lighthouses are, the awesome character of the seascape is well shown. The energetic can obtain even more striking views by climbing the winding road to the Vista Monte do Facho.

The town has two interesting churches, one 12th century and the other baroque.

### Approach

Coming from the north, the main options are either to keep 2M off and avoid the 2m patch La Carraca and, 1M to the southeast, Centolo de Finisterre (an island some 20m high), or to come inside both – much will depend upon the weather. At the point there is a similar option: either pass more than 0·5M off or about 200m off in order to avoid El Turdeiro shoal – a large-scale chart is needed for the latter passage. Once round, keep at least 300m off until reaching Finisterre breakwater[1744].

From the south, give Punta Insúa[1782] a 5M offing to clear Bajo de los Meixidos and head straight for

Finisterre mole. On a night approach, take the outside passages and keep at least 300m away from the east coast.

## Anchorage

Anchor in 7m or so off the harbour mouth, outside the many moorings. Holding is good in sand, but the anchorage may be uncomfortable in north or northeasterly winds, when better shelter can be found in the northern part of Ensenada de Llagosteira (the southwest end of the beach is foul). Space is unlikely to be available alongside the breakwater, which in any case is extremely high.

## Facilities

Water by can from the quay, but no yacht fuel. Adequate shopping, hotels, restaurants, banks.

## Communications

Post office and telephones. Buses to Corcubión, Cée and beyond.

# Ensenada del Sardiñeiro

42°56'N 9°13'W

## Tides

See Ría de Corcubión, opposite

## Charts

|  | Approach | Anchorage |
|---|---|---|
| Admiralty | *1111, 3633* | *3764* |
| Spanish | *41B, 927, 9270* | *9271* |

## Lights

### Approach
1742 **Cabo Finisterre** 42°52'·9N 9°16'·3W
  Fl.5s141m23M Siren Mo(I)60s 25m S
  Octagonal granite tower and building 17m
  Obscd when bearing more than 149°
  Racon Mo(O) 360° 35M
*0931* Radiobeacon *FI* 288·5kHz 100M
1760 **Cabo Cée** 42°55'N 9°11'W
  Fl(5)13s25m7M Octagonal granite tower 8m

Yachts at anchor in the Ensenada del Sardineiro, with Punta Arnela behind them and Playa Estordi on the right.

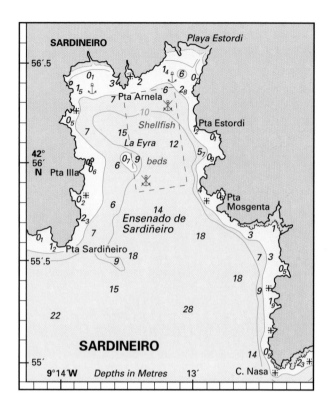

1758 **Carrumeiro Chico** 42°54'·4N 9°10'·8W
  Fl(2)7s6m6M
  Beacon tower with ‡ topmark (isolated danger)
1756 **Islote Lobeira Grande** 42°52'·8N 9°11'·1W
  Fl(3)15s16m9M
  White octagonal tower and building 10m

## General

A relatively unspoilt anchorage open to the south but well sheltered from west through north to east. Both Playa Sardiñeiro and Playa Estordi are good bathing beaches, the latter tending to be crowded with visitors from the nearby campsite, and there are pleasant walks nearby.

## Approach

As for Finisterre before continuing northeast. There is a shoal patch, La Eyra, with only 0·7m on the west side of the bay.

## Anchorage

Playa Sardiñeiro offers shelter from west through north to northeast (behind a small headland), Playa Estordi from east to southeast. Both offer good holding in sand, though Playa Sardiñeiro generally has the least swell.

  If opting for Playa Estordi, pick a spot well inside the shellfish beds where, for obvious reasons, anchoring is prohibited – depths of 4m or less should ensure compliance.

## Facilities

Supermarket, bakery and restaurants in Sardiñeiro. Water by can from cafés or the campsite behind Playa Estordi.

## Communications

Post office and telephones. Bus service to Corcubión and Finisterre, etc.

# Ría de Corcubión

42°57'N 9°11'W

## Tides

*Reference port* Lisbon
*Mean time differences*
HW: +65 minutes ±10; LW: +90 minutes ±10
(the above allows for the difference in time zones)
*Heights in metres*

| MHWS | MHWN | MLWN | MLWS |
|------|------|------|------|
| 3·3 | 2·6 | 1·2 | 0·5 |

## Charts

| | Approach | Ría |
|---|---|---|
| Admiralty | *1111, 3633* | *3764* |
| Spanish | *41B, 927, 9270* | *9271* |

## Lights

### Approach

1742 **Cabo Finisterre** 42°52'·9N 9°16'·3W
  Fl.5s141m23M Siren Mo(I)60s 25m S
  Octagonal granite tower and building 17m
  Obscd when bearing more than 149°
  Racon Mo(O) 360° 35M
*0931* Radiobeacon *FI* 288·5kHz 100M
1782 **Punta Insúa** 42°46'·3N 9°07'·6W
  F.WR+Oc(1+2)WR.20s26m15/14M
  Hexagonal tower and adjacent building 14m
  308°-F.R-012·5° (Leixões to Bajos Los Bruyos)
  012·5°-Oc.R-044·5° (over Bajos Los Bruyos)
  044·5°-Oc.W-093° (over Bajos Los Meixidos)
  093°-F.W-172·5° (Bajos Los Meixidos to coast)
  but obscd by Cabo Finisterre from 145°-172·5°

### Ría entrance

1760 **Cabo Cée** 42°55'N 9°11'W
  Fl(5)13s25m7M Octagonal granite tower 8m
1758 **Carrumeiro Chico** 42°54'·4N 9°10'·8W
  Fl(2)7s6m6M
  Beacon tower with ⁑ topmark (isolated danger)
1756 **Islote Lobeira Grande** 42°52'·8N 9°11'·1W
  Fl(3)15s16m9M
  White octagonal tower and building 10m

### Harbour

1763 **Cée molehead** 42°56'·6N 9°10'·8W
  F.R.8m3M Round red tower on white base 6m
1762 **Corcubión molehead** 42°56'·7N 9°11'·4W
  Fl(2)R.8s9m4M Round red tower on white base 7m

## Port radio

*Corcubion Prácticos* VHF 14, 16.

## General

The Ría de Corcubión is probably the least appealing of all the *rías*, and now that all the more sheltered spots are occupied by smallcraft moorings also one of the least viable for visiting yachts, certainly in winds out of the southern sector. However in the past it enjoyed considerable importance, not least because its relatively narrow entrance overlooked by the twin forts of Fuerte del Príncipe and Fuerte del Cardenal (both now converted into private houses), allowed it to be defended in a way not possible in most of the other *rías*.

The small town of Corcubión, on the west bank of the *ría*, is a summer holiday resort with banks, shops, restaurants and bars. In contrast, there is a large industrial plant on the east side of the *ría* polluting the atmosphere with coal dust.

Waterborne processions mark the *fiesta* of the Virgen del Carmen on 16 July (also at Muros and in many other harbours). Cée, a larger town at the head of the estuary, can be reached on foot or by bus.

## Approach

Coming from the north, round Cabo Finisterre[1742] with an offing of at least 0·5M, and from a point due south of the lighthouse steer 060° to arrive at the mouth of the Ría de Corcubión. This course leads between Carrumeiro Chico[1758] and the point at Cabo Cée[1760].

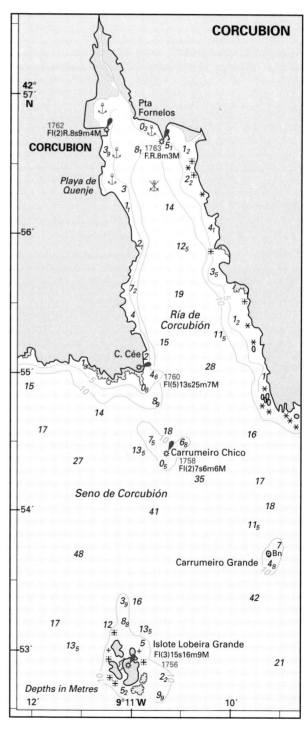

The small, unnamed bay north of Punta de Quenje on the west side of the Ría de Corcubión, backed by its fine sandy beach.

Coming from the south, give Punta Insúa[1782] an offing of at least 5M to clear Bajo de los Meixidos. When past Los Meixidos go north to pass between Finisterre and Islote Lobeira Grande[1756] and then head northeast to pass west of Carrumeiro Chico[1758]. In daylight, with a fair wind and large-scale charts, the passage inside Bajo Los Meixidos is not difficult.

Once round Cabo Cée the *ría* trends 354°. Corcubión is on the western shore about 2M from the entrance. Beyond Corcubión the *ría* shoals rapidly.

### Anchorages

There are four possible anchorages in the *ría*, none of which offer shelter from southerly winds:

1. In the small bay between Punta de Quenje and the tiny (and obviously very old) harbour to the north. Inshore is occupied by moorings, but some shelter will still be gained outside them – even so it would be uncomfortable in winds from south through east to north. There is a restaurant on the beach fringing the bay, and considerable recent development to the south.
2. Southeast of the main quay in 8–10m – probably the best bet, as it has yet to be filled with moorings.
3. North of the main quay in 3–4m, between the many smallcraft moorings and the shoal water to the north. Holding is poor. If not busy it might be possible to lie alongside briefly.
4. In the northeast corner of the *ría* between the commercial quay and Punta Fornelos. Depths shoal rapidly once within the 5m line. This anchorage provides shelter in strong north winds.

The bottom in all these anchorages is a mixture of rock and sand and the holding is variable.

### Facilities

There is a shipyard in Cée geared to fishing and commercial vessels. Water is available, by negotiation and in own containers, from the restaurant mentioned in 3. above. Corcubión has the usual shops, a bakery and banks, plus many restaurants and bars.

### Communications

Post office and telephones. Buses and taxis.

### Alternative anchorages

In settled weather, and with reference to a large-scale chart, there are several possible anchorages on the coast stretching south towards the Ría de Muros:

1. *Ensenada de Ezaro* (42°54'N 9·08'W) – a beautiful bay with fine bathing beaches, but totally exposed to the westerly quadrant. Winds from these directions would probably make it necessary to clear out, which could be tricky at night as there are two rocky shoals – Los Bois and El Asno – in the entrance. Limited shopping is available in the villages of Ezaro and Pindo. Possible anchorages include:
   a. Off Playa de Gures on the north side the bay, east of Punta Caneliñas. Anchor as close inshore as depth permits over sand, avoiding the weed patches. The bay is sheltered from the north but in strong winds the hills may make it very squally.
   b. At the entrance to the little harbour of Porto del Pindo on the south side of the bay in 3–5m over sand, rock and weed – the harbour itself is full of moorings. Most of the rocks off Punta Casel have been incorporated into a short breakwater (Fl(3)G.16s7m9M Green column on white base 6m), but there are two more about 80m northwest of its end. Though unmarked, in a flat sea and good overhead sun – the only safe conditions for approach – these appear a greenish-brown due to weed growth. An approach from due north leads clear of all dangers.

   This anchorage offers some shelter from south or southwest winds but would become an uncomfortable lee shore in a northerly. If there is no swell it may be possible to lie for a short period alongside the steps at the end of the breakwater – the inner part is taken up by stern lines to dinghies. A distinctive single-span concrete bridge almost on the shoreline just northeast of the harbour, with a stretch of pale sandy beach beyond, may aid in identification.

2. *Porto Cubelo* (42°48'N 9°08'W), 6M south of Ensenada de Ezaro on the south side of Ensenada de Carnota, has a breakwater with an angled end (Fl.G.2s8m4M 174°-vis-067° Green column 6m). There are many off-lying dangers, none of

Smallcraft crowded into Porto Cubelo, an attractive spot which belies its difficult approach.

them marked – like Porto del Pindo a case for careful eyeball navigation. Visit only in calm weather with good overhead light and a large-scale chart. Basic shopping is available in the village.

# Ría de Muros

## Tides
*Reference port* Lisbon
*Mean time differences* (at Muros)
HW: +60 minutes ±10; LW: +85 minutes ±10
(the above allows for the difference in time zones)
*Heights in metres*

| MHWS | MHWN | MLWN | MLWS |
|------|------|------|------|
| 3·5  | 2·7  | 1·3  | 0·5  |

## Charts

|           | Approach        | Ría  |
|-----------|-----------------|------|
| Admiralty | 3633            | 1756 |
| Spanish   | 41B, 926,9260   | 9264 |

## Lights
### Approach
1782 **Punta Insúa** 42°46'·3N 9°07'·6W
  F.WR+Oc(1+2)WR.20s26m15/14M
  Hexagonal tower and adjacent building 14m
  308°-F.R-012·5° (Leixões to Bajos Los Bruyos)
  012·5°-Oc.R-044·5° (over Bajos Los Bruyos)
  044·5°-Oc.W-093° (over Bajos Los Meixidos)
  093°-F.W-172·5° (Bajos Los Meixidos to coast)
  but obscd by Cabo Finisterre from 145°-172·5°
1794 **Cabo Corrubedo** 42°34'·6N 9°05'·4W
  Fl(3+2)R.20s30m15M 089·4°-clear-200°
  Fl(3)R.20s 332°-dangerous-089·4°
  Siren Mo(O)60s5M 80m SW Grey round tower
### Entrance
1784 **Punta Queixal (Monte Louro)** 42°44'·4N
  9°04'·8W
  Fl(2+1)12s25m9M
  Obscd 081°-180° by Monte Louro
  Hexagonal granite tower and building, white lantern
  7m
1793 **Punta Castro (Punta Sofocho)** 42°42'N
  9°01'·6W
  Fl.5s27m4M
  White tower on round building 5m
1792 **Punta Cabeiro** 42°44'·4N 8°59'·4W
  Fl.GWR.5s35m9-6M
  054·4°-R-058·5°-G-099·5°-W-189·5°
  Squat tower on white base 4m

## General
Although not the largest, this is perhaps the most scenic and the least spoiled of the *rías* with some good beaches. The old towns of Muros and Noya are both worth visiting (the final stages towards Noya by dinghy, unless able to take the ground) and there are pleasant anchorages. At Portosin, the *club náutico* runs a large marina with good shelter and security and reasonable charges.

Since 1998 the number of *viveros* in the ría appears to have been increasing. However they are generally moored in rows, with sufficient space for a yacht to work its way through to an inner anchorage – the rafts are seldom moored in less than 5m – see page 13.

## Approach
From the north, keep 5M off Punta Insúa[1782] to avoid Bajos de los Meixidos and Los Bruyos (neither marked). Give Puntas Carreiro and Queixal[1784] an offing of 0·7M to clear Leixões. The inshore passage through the Canal de los Meixidos may be taken with care, good weather and the large-scale chart.

From the south, pass 3M west of Cabo Corrubedo[1794] whence a heading of 020° on Pta Queixal or Monte Louro will clear the Banco de las Basoñas and Bajos de la Baya. In daylight the passage inside these banks presents no difficulties. Having entered the *ría* between Leixões and La Baya the deep water extends to the northeast.

# Muros
42°47'N 9°03'W

## Charts

|           | Harbour |
|-----------|---------|
| Admiralty | 1756    |
| Spanish   | 9264    |

## Lights
### Approach
1784 **Punta Queixal (Monte Louro)** 42°44'·4N
  9°04'·8W
  Fl(2+1)12s25m9M
  Obscd 081°-180° by Monte Louro
  Hexagonal granite tower and building, white lantern
  7m
1786 **Cabo Reburdiño** 42°46'·2N 9°02'·9W
  Fl(2)R.6s16m7M 168°-vis-019°
  White round metal tower and building 8m
### Harbour
1788·5 **East breakwater** 42°46'·6N 9°03'·1W
  Fl.R.1·5s3m2M Metal tripod 4m
1788 **North breakwater** 42°46'·7N 9°03'·3W
  Fl(4)R.13s8m4M Red column on white base 6m
1789 **Northwest mole** 42°46'·6N 9°03'·4W
  F.G.8m4M Green column on white base 6m
  Only visible within the harbour
1790 **Inner mole** 42°46'·6N 9°03'·4W
  F.R.8m4M Red column on white base 6m
  Only visible within the harbour

## General
A picturesque old fishing town with colonnaded pavements, narrow streets, covered and open-air markets, a Romanesque church and a number of bars and restaurants. It has long been popular with cruising yachtsmen due to both its atmosphere and its facilities. Waterborne processions mark the *fiesta* of the Virgen del Carmen on 16 July, a practice which has spread throughout the area.

## Approach
Head northeast from the mouth of the *ría* until Cabo Reburdiño lighthouse[1786] comes into view, then steer to clear it by 200m or so. A new eastern spur has been under construction from the angle of the outer breakwater for at least five years, but it remains unsurfaced and low-lying and is marked

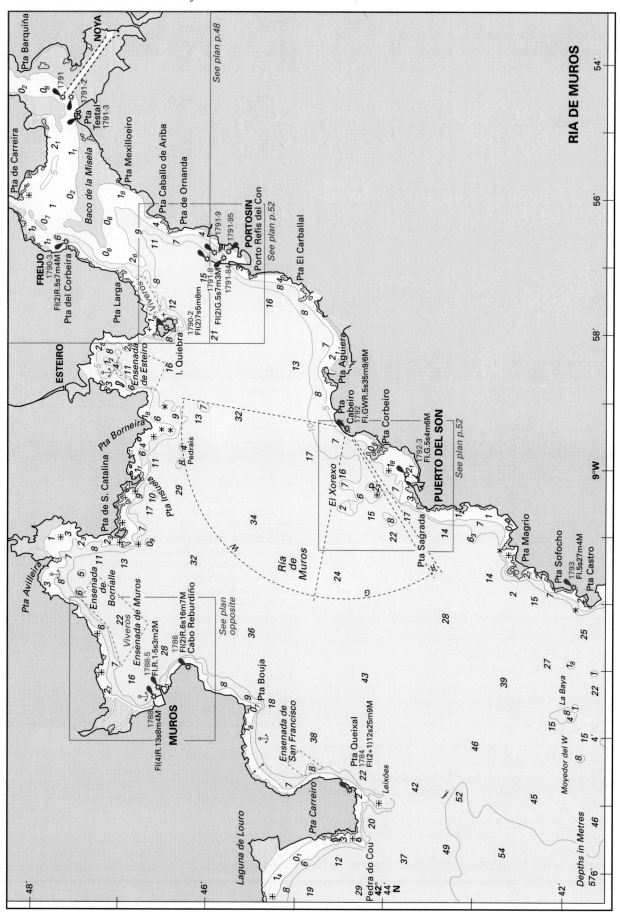

RIA DE MUROS

The harbour at Muros looking northwest, with the yacht anchorage on the right. The wide breakwater at bottom right has retained its distinctly 'unfinished' look since the early 1990s.

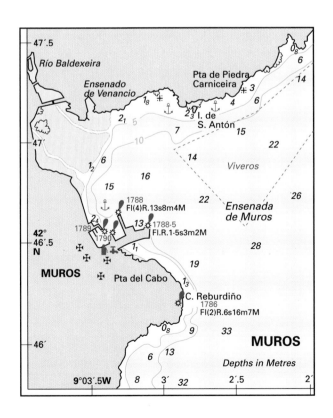

only by a temporary (and reportedly unreliable) light[1788.5]. If approaching at night it would be wise not to close the anchorage until the light on the north breakwater[1788] bears due west.

### Anchorage and berthing

Anchor north of the harbour – for convenience, the nearer the harbour the better. There is rubbish on the bottom which may come up with the anchor, and even though a serious snag is unlikely a tripline may be a wise precaution. The bottom drops off sharply between the 3m and 10m contours, and a few trial circuits with an eye to the echo-sounder may save unnecessary toil. There is a single white mooring buoy near the harbour mouth, but this appears to be privately owned.

The two yacht pontoons in the northwestern part of the inner harbour, introduced in 1995, have been almost entirely colonised by local smallcraft – and a few not so small. Only one area remains against which a few yachts of up to 12m or so may raft alongside. Depths are reportedly less than 2m at low tide, and no facilities whatsoever are provided.

Alternatively it may be possible to secure, at least temporarily, to the north breakwater, which has a short stub near its outer end for additional protection from swell. However the wall is high, with bollards and ladders at intervals of 15m or more.

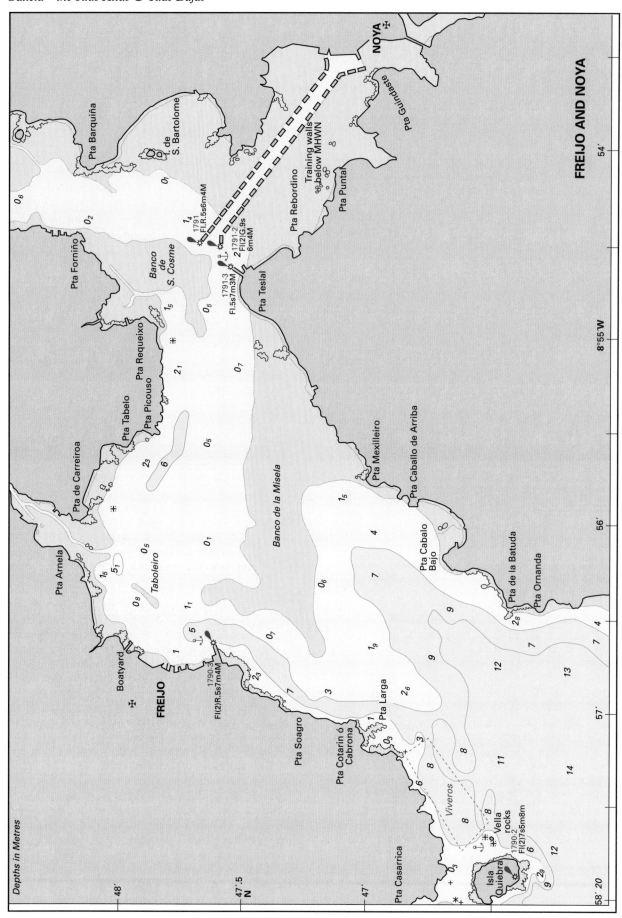

Depths in Metres

FREIJO AND NOYA

NOYA

Pta Barquiña

. de
S. Bartolome

1791
Fl.R.5s6m4M

2 1791.2
Fl(2)G.9s
6m4M

Training walls
below MHWN

Pta Guinpaste

Pta Rebordino

Pta Puntal

Pta Forniño

Banco
de
S. Cosme

1791.3
Fl.5s7m3M

Pta Teslal

8°55'W

Pta Requeixo

Pta Tabelo

Pta Picouso

Pta de Carreiroa

Banco de la Misela

Pta Mexilleiro

Pta Caballo de Arriba

Taboleiro

Pta Arnela

Pta Cabalo
Bajo

Pta de la Batuda

56'

Pta Ornanda

Boatyard

FREIJO

1790.3
Fl(2)R.5s7m4M

Pta Soagro

Pta Larga

Pta Cotarin ó
Cabrona

57'

Pta Casarrica

Viveros

Vella
rocks

1790.2
Fl(2)7s5m8m

Isla
Quiebra

58' 20

48'

47'.5
N

47'

54'

NOYA

## Facilities

Diesel and water from the CEPSA pump on the inner mole, where there is reportedly less than 1m at low tide. The water, from a manhole, is metered. The attendant is usually on duty from 1000–1300, weekdays only, but in contrast to many fishing harbours there is no apparent problem in selling fuel to yachts. There is also a filling station on the road which skirts the head of the bay.

There is a small, fishing-orientated chandlery at the end of one of the buildings on the quay. Repairs would undoubtedly be possible in an emergency, but work is geared generally to fishing boats. There is a tidal scrubbing berth at a quay some 600m north of the harbour, on hard sand with about 2·5m at high water springs. It is well sheltered other than from southwesterly swell.

The town is well provided with shops of all kinds, banks (with card facility), hotels, restaurants and pavement cafés. There is a good produce market, plus a fish market on the quay where the catch is sold retail as well as wholesale. Supermarkets and a good hardware store will be found near the north end of the town, some distance away from the harbour.

## Communications

Post office and telephones. Taxis and a frequent bus service via Freijo and Noya to Santiago de Compostela and Vigo.

## Alternative anchorages

1. In strong northerly winds, the Ensenada de San Francisco 1·5M southwest of Muros provides good shelter. Anchor in the northern part of the bay in 7m or less with excellent holding over sand. Land on the beach, where there are shops and cafés. Viveros now occupy the southern part of the area.

   In 1999 it was reported that a pipe of some kind ran out into the bay from a point near the 'lollipop' lights on the road, terminating near the 10m line – see plan page 46. No more is known of its position or purpose, but it was sufficient to entrap an anchor.
2. Either side of Isla de San Antón, itself 0·7M northeast of Muros, in 3–5m. In 1999 *viveros* were no longer moored to the south of the island – really an island at high water only – though there were plenty further east. A stony reef, culminating in a single rock which breaks at low water, projects from a minute beach a short distance west of the isla, but the water is normally clear enough to see it.
3. In the northwest corner of the Ensenada de Bornalle, nearly 2M northeast of Muros, in 5m or less. There is a good bathing beach and a freshwater stream, but holding is variable due to large patches of very dense weed. The massed ranks of *viveros* in the entrance to the bay give some protection from southwesterly swell.
4. In the Ensenada de Esteiro about 4M east of Muros, well protected from west through north to east. The bay is effectively divided into two by a central rocky promontory (with shallow off-liers) and anchorage can be had on either side in 3–4m over sand and weed, avoiding the rock patches. There is a private quay on the west shore of the western arm and the entire surroundings are somewhat built up. Both arms of the bay shelter small but attractive beaches and there are normally some *viveros* moored in the entrance.
5. Close northeast of Isla Quiebra (Cebra), now lit at its southerly extreme (Fl(2)7s5m8M Metal post 3m) and easily identified by the red-roofed building on its summit. Anchor north of the Vella rocks and clear of the *viveros* in 2–4m, sheltered from southwest to north. This is the most isolated anchorage in the *ría*, with no facilities and notices forbidding landing.

# Freijo (Freixo)

42°48'N 8°57'W

### Tides

West winds may increase tidal heights in the upper parts of the *ría* by up to 0·6m, but tidal flow in general is weak.

### Charts

|  |  | *Harbour* |
|---|---|---|
| Admiralty |  | *1756* |
| Spanish |  | *9264* |

### Lights

**Approach**
1790·2 **Isla Quiebra** 42°46'·4N 8°57'·8W
Fl(2)7s5m8m Metal post 3m
**Harbour**
1790·3 **Molehead** 42°47'·6N 8°56'·6W
Fl(2)R.5s7m4M
Red and white column on white base 6m

The mole at Freijo from the south, with the shipbuilding and repair yard – complete with two large cranes – behind.

## General

An undistinguished, straggling, working village which exists mainly for its busy fishing boat yard and supporting industries. However there is a sheltered anchorage and easy landing. It makes a good base for a dinghy visit to the attractive old town of Noya, about 2·5M to the east.

## Approach

Shape a course up the middle of the *ría* until, about 6M from the entrance, Isla Quiebra, easily identified by a single red-roofed building on its summit, is reached. Pass south of it and turn onto 040° to clear Punta Larga, a reef covered at high water. From Punta Larga to Freijo the deep water (5m) follows the west bank but the edge of the channel shifts – consult the large-scale chart and watch the depth gauge closely.

## Anchorage

Anchor north of the mole, outside the moorings, in 2–6m over mud. It may be possible to lie alongside the inside of the wall for a limited time.

## Facilities

A busy but somewhat ramshackle shipbuilding and repair yard just north of the harbour, with slipways, cranes, etc. In 1999 the gates were guarded by an extremely large (though chained) alsatian dog – enter with care! Diesel in cans from the garage on the quay.

Freijo offers the usual food and other shops, restaurants, hotel and banks.

## Communications

Buses to Noya, and thence to Santiago de Compostela and Vigo. Taxis.

# Puerto de Noya (Noia)

42°47'N 8°54'W

## Tides

West winds may increase tidal heights in the upper parts of the *ría* by up to 0·6m, but tidal flow in general is weak.

## Charts

|  | Harbour |
|---|---|
| Admiralty | 1756 |
| Spanish | 9264 |

## Lights

*Harbour*
1791·3 **Punta Testal** 42°47'·6N 8°54'·7W
   Fl.5s7m3M Green over white tower 6m
1791 **North training wall** 42°47'·7N 8°54'·5W
   Fl.R.5s6m4M Grey concrete tower 6m
1791·2 **South training wall** 42°47'·6N 8°54'·5W
   Fl(2)G.9s6m4M Grey contrete tower 6m

## General

The harbour and approaches to Noya are now severely silted but at high water it is still possible for a yacht drawing less than 2m to get within 1M of the town. Then continue by dinghy, or land at the quay

The heads of Noya's two training walls, looking northeast from Punta Testal.

at Punta Testal and walk into town, a distance of about 2·5km (taxis are available in the main square for the return journey). Punta Testal is fringed by clear sandy beach, where a yacht able to take the ground could dry out in total shelter.

Noya, nicknamed 'Little Florence', was an important port in the 15th century and its picturesque, narrow streets and many old buildings and churches reflect its history. A *fiesta* is held on 24 August.

## Approach

Leave Freijo after half flood or as draught allows. From the 5m patch north of the Freijo molehead head for Punta Tabelo until the 5–6m trench is reached. Follow the trench past Punta Picouso. When it starts to shoal, head just south of the tip of the Punta Testal sand. Borrow to the south if necessary off the tail of the South Cosme bank, then head for Punta Testal molehead[1791·3]. Anchor and continue by dinghy between the training walls, which are clearly marked with stakes. Off Noya quay the water is very shallow.

## Anchorage

Anchor between Punta Testal molehead and the south training wall light[1791·2], in sand. In 1999 there was believed to be a least depth of 2m between these points.

## Facilities

All the facilities to be expected of a modern town.

## Communications

Post office and telephones. Taxis. Buses to Vigo and Santiago de Compostela.

# Portosin

42°46'N 8°57'W

## Charts

|  | Harbour |
|---|---|
| Admiralty | 1756 |
| Spanish | 9260, 9264 |

## Lights

*Harbour*
1791·8 **Breakwater** 42°45'·9N 8°56'·9W
   Fl(2)G.5s7m3M Green over white column 6m

1791·9 **East (marina) mole** 42°45'·9N 8°56'·8W
   Fl.R.2s7m3M Red over white column 6m
   Only visible inside port
1791·84 **Breakwater quay, NE corner** 42°45'·8N
   8°56'·9W
   Q.G.6m1M Green over white column 5m
1791·95 **Bajo A Miñateria** 42°45'·8N 8°56'·8W
   Fl.Y.4m2M Red over black beacon tower

## Marina radio

*Club Náutico Portosin* VHF Ch 09.

## General

Once a small but busy fishing village, the large harbour now houses an established marina and *club náutico* which has received unanimous praise from visiting yachtsmen since it opened in the early 1990s. The town is without any great charm, but the marina has an attractive setting backed by wooded hills and with a good beach nearby. It is also one of the relatively few Galician harbours where a yacht can be left afloat in total safety, whether visiting Santiago de Compostela for the day to view the cathedral (see page 67), or catching an aeroplane to the UK – or other distant parts – for a month or more.

## Approach

Make a course up the middle of the *ría*. About 6M from the entrance Isla Quiebra will be seen against the north shore and Portosin opposite it to the south. Entrance is straightforward with no off-lying hazards.

## Berthing

The Club Náutico Portosin, ☎ 981 766583 *Fax* 981 766389, runs a well-maintained marina in the northeast corner of the harbour. Shelter is good though some surge may be experienced in northeasterlies.

In July 1999 a fourth pontoon was about to be added south of the existing three, bringing the total number of berths up to 240, of which 35 are reserved for visitors – though more can be squeezed in if necessary. On arrival, unless a berth has been pre-arranged by VHF, visitors should secure to the third (hammerhead) pontoon from the harbour entrance where there is a minimum depth of some 5m. Office hours, during which VHF is monitored, are 1000–1330 and 1530–2000 on weekdays, 1030–1330 on Saturday, closed Sunday. The staff are notably welcoming and helpful and a range of European languages spoken.

Berthing is bows-on with a mooring line provided astern, and yachts of up to 20m can be accommodated in depths of 2–5m (the new southern pontoon is intended to take larger boats, which are currently berthed alongside on the end of the central pontoon). Charges are calculated on a length x breadth basis, with the 1999 summer rate for a beamy monohull of just under 12m being around 2,880 ptas (17·31 euros) per night inclusive. There are discounts for long-term or winter berthing.

## Anchorage

Immediately north of the east mole in 5–6m, sheltered from northeast through to south or southwest. Holding is good over sand and the marina make no objections to leaving a dinghy at their pontoons.

Portosin, a favourite with visiting yachtsmen since the marina opened in the early 1990s, looking east.

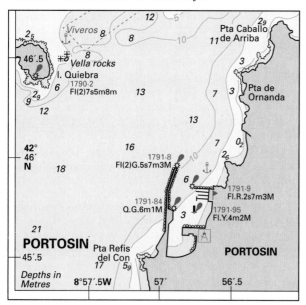

## Facilities

*Boatyard* At the marina plus the nearby Racomar, ☎ 919 969847, where motorboats are moulded in GRP and repairs would certainly be possible.

*Travel-lift* 32 tonne capacity at the marina, with additional hardstanding being created at the root of the new south pontoon.

*Engineers* Racomar and others.

*Sail repairs* Enquire at the marina/*club náutico* office.

*Chandlery* Due to be fully operational for the 2000 season. Otherwise the marina office will order straightforward items from Villagarcía de Arosa.

*Water* On the pontoons.

*Showers* In the *club náutico* building. A small charge may be made to crews of yachts anchored off.

*Launderette* In a separate block behind the *club náutico* building.

*Electricity* On the pontoons.

*Fuel* Diesel pump at the marina, petrol from a filling station in the town. The fuelling berth may not be accessible at dead low water – check beforehand.

*Club náutico* Excellent – in addition to a very pleasant bar and restaurant overlooking the marina, the Club Náutico Portosin boasts a tennis court, a play area for young children, a comfortable TV lounge, and even current foreign (including UK) sailing magazines in the bar!

*Weather forecast* Posted daily in the *club náutico*.

*Banks* In the town, with card facilitiies.

*Shops/provisioning* Supermarkets, etc in the town with a produce market on Saturday.

*Cafés, restaurants & hotels* In the town, as well as the *club náutico*'s own restaurant referred to above.

*Medical services* In the town.

## Communications

*Post office* In the town.

*Mailing address*
c/o **Club Náutico Portosin**, Puerto Deportivo, s/n, 15999 Portosin, A Coruña, España.
*Fax service* 981 766389

*Public telephones* In the *club náutico* building.

*Car hire/taxis* In the town.
*Buses* To Santiago de Compostela and elsewhere.
*Air services* International airport at Santiago de Compostela.

### Alternative anchorage

The bay east of Punta Aguieira (southwest of Portosin) offers an attractive anchorage when the wind is in the southern quadrant. Depths are said to be greater than shown on Admiralty *1756* (shoaling to 2m some way off the beach), and it may be possible to tuck in behind the isthmus running out to the almost-islet of Punta Aguiera and thus avoid any swell running into the *ría*. Holding is good over sand off an inviting sandy beach. There is a short mole running out from Punta Aguiera but it is almost certainly private.

## Puerto del Son (El Son)
42°44'N 9°00'W

### Charts

| | Harbour |
|---|---|
| Admiralty | *1756* |
| Spanish | *9264* |

### Lights

**Approach**
1792 **Punta Cabeiro** 42°44'·4N 8°59'·4W
Fl.GWR.5s35m9-6M
054·4°-R-058·5°-G-099·5°-W-189·5°
Squat tower on white base 4m

**Harbour**
1792·3 **North breakwater** 42°43'·7N 9°00'·1W
Fl.G.5s4m6M Green over white concrete tower 4m

### General

Yet another small Galician harbour which has been expanded almost beyond recognition by the addition of a long outer breakwater – though in 1999 it appeared that parts of the shallow inner

basin were being filled in. The village has little for the yachtsman but there are good beaches nearby.

## Approach

The bay between Puerto del Son and Punta Cabeiro is shallow and largely foul. It is possible to approach along the coast from the west, with Punta Cabeiro[1792] bearing 056·5° (the narrow-beam red sector of the light) until the end of Puerto del Son breakwater[1792·3] bears 170°.

From the north, a bearing of 180° on the breakwater leads inside both Islote Filgueira and El Xorexo shoal 0·4M to its northwest (both covered by the green sector of Punta Cabeiro light[1792]).

In either case, round the breakwater approximately 100m off in order to avoid rocks some 200m to the northeast. Strong nerves, settled weather and a current large-scale chart are essential.

## Anchorage

The old inner basin is small, crowded, and dries out. Anchor in the outer harbour, clear of the approach channel to the fishermen's quay and the many moorings, in 2–4m over mud. In quiet periods it might be possible to lie alongside the quay for an hour or two, astern of the distinctive orange lifeboat.

## Facilities

Water on the quay, shopping, cafés, post office and telephones in the town, but little else. The fuel pump supplies *Gasoleo B* to the fishing fleet but is not licensed to sell to yachts – see page 8.

# Corrubedo

42°34'N 9°04'W

## Tides

See Ría de Muros, page 45

## Charts

| | Approach | Harbour |
|---|---|---|
| Admiralty | 3633 | 1768 |
| Spanish | 41B, 925, 926, 9260 | 9262, 415B |

## Lights

### Approach
1794 **Cabo Corrubedo** 42°34'·6N 9°05'·4W
  Fl(3+2)R.20s30m15M 089·4°-clear-200°
  Fl(3)R.20s 332°-dangerous-089·4°
  Siren Mo(O)60s5M 80m SW Grey round tower
1799·5 **Isla Sagres** 42°30'·5N 9°02'·9W
  Fl.5s23m8M Round metal column 3m
1796 **Isla Sálvora** 42°27'·9N 9°00'·8W
  Fl(3+1)20s38m21M 217°-vlear-126°
  Fl(3)20s 126°-dangerous-160°
  White octagonal tower, red band 16m

### Harbour
1795 **Breakwater** 42°34'·3N 9°04'·2W
  Iso.GWR.3s10m3-6M 000°-R-016°-G-352°-W-000°
  Fat white tower 5m
  Racon Mo(K) 325°-200° 8-17M
*Note* The sound signal is on Cabo Corrubedo[1794]

## General

A small, rock-strewn fishing harbour backed by a well kept village, Corrubedo has little room for

Although undeniably scenic, Corrubedo – seen here from the southwest – has little room for visitors, let alone deep-keeled yachts.

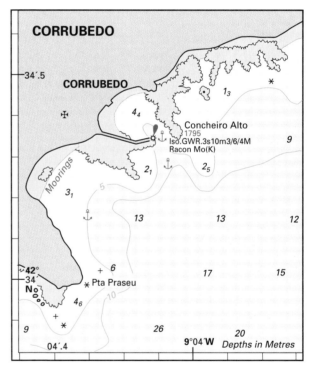

visitors. The long, fine sandy beaches of Playa Ferraira and Playa del Castro running down to the southeast are the product of southwesterly swells against which the harbour offers little protection, and seas may break over the mole even when only the smallest of wavelets are to be seen.

The approaches are intricate and should only be attempted in calm weather by daylight. If a southerly develops it would be necessary to clear out, an operation which, because of the numerous unlit off-lying reefs, would be hazardous at night.

## Approach

From the north, keep outside Bajo de los Meixidos (some 4M off Punta Insúa) and Banco de las Basoñas, heading to pass close to Cabo Corrubedo.

From the Ría de Muros, the Canal de las Basoñas leads inside the Bajos de la Baya and Banco de las Basoñas (both dangers, it should be noted, within the clear sector of Corrubedo light). The passage inside Bajos de la Baya has an unmarked 1·8m patch.

Cabo Corrubedo itself has rocks awash up to 600m offshore and there is an isolated reef, La Marosa, 1M south of the lighthouse and about 0·7M off the shoreline. The passage between is feasible, keeping 0·4M (750m) offshore to avoid the covering reefs off Punta Posalgueiro, but demands care. Continue on this line until Corrubedo breakwater bears 350°.

Coming from the south, either keep 4M offshore until Cabo Corrubedo bears at least 050° and then pass between La Marosa and the shore as described above, or take the inshore passage. For this route, take a departure from the westernmost rock of the Islas Sagres[1799·5], the Laxe Negra which has deep water on the seaward side, from which a course of 350° for 4M leads to Corrubedo between the various dangers in the bay.

Should night departure become essential, a back bearing of 356° (the centre of the narrow white sector of Corrubedo breakwater[1795]) will ensure safe passage through the numerous shoals. Remain on this bearing for 5M until Isla Sálvora[1796] bears 126° (the junction between its 'clear' and 'dangerous' sectors) before standing west or southwest for searoom.

## Anchorage

The harbour, which is small, shallow and largely occupied by smallcraft moorings, lies between the breakwater and a reef to the northeast. There is a launching ramp on the northwest side of the harbour, with shallow rocky ledges between it and the breakwater. Anchoring is possible between the end of the breakwater and the visible rock, Concheiro Alto, on the reef to the east, or in the bay to the southwest, but the anchorage off Playa Ferraira to the east may be preferable. All are fully open to the south.

## Facilities

Basic shopping, bars and cafés.

# Ría de Arosa (Ría de Arousa)

## Tides

*Reference port* Lisbon
*Mean time differences* (at Villargarcía)
HW: +50 minutes ±15; LW: +75 minutes ±5
(the above allows for the difference in time zones)

*Heights in metres*

| MHWS | MHWN | MLWN | MLWS |
|------|------|------|------|
| 3·5 | 2·8 | 1·3 | 0·5 |

## Charts

|  | Approach | Ria |
|--|----------|-----|
| Admiralty | 3633 | 1768 |
| Spanish | 41B, 925, 926 | 415B, 415C, 9261, 9263 |

## Lights

*Approach*

1794 **Cabo Corrubedo** 42°34'·6N 9°05'·4W
　Fl(3+2)R.20s30m15M 089·4°-clear-200°
　Fl(3)R.20s 332°-dangerous-089·4°
　Siren Mo(O)60s5M 80m SW Grey round tower

1846 **Isla Ons** 42°22'·9N 8°56'·2W
　Fl(4)24s125m25M Octagonal tower 12m

*Ría (Canal Principal)*

1799·5 **Isla Sagres** 42°30'·5N 9°02'·9W
　Fl.5s23m8M Round metal column 3m

1796 **Isla Sálvora** 42°27'·9N 9°00'·8W
　Fl(3+1)20s38m21M 217°-clear-126°
　Fl(3)20s 126°-dangerous-160°
　White octagonal tower, red band 16m

1800 **Bajo Pombeiriño** 42°28'·9N 8°56'·8W
　Fl(2)G.12s13m8M
　White conical tower, green band 14m

buoy **Starboard hand** 42°29'·6N 8°56'·1W
　Fl(3)G.10s5M Green pillar buoy, ▲ topmark

1798 **Piedras del Sargo** 42°30'·3N 9°00'·5W
　Q.G.11m6M
　White conical tower, green band 12m

buoy **Bajo Sinal del Castro** 42°31'·2N 8°58'·8W
　Fl.R.3s4M Red pillar buoy

1819 **Punta del Castro (Castiñeiras)** 42°31'·8N 8°59'·7W
　Oc.WR.2s9m3M 263°-W-270°-R-263°
　Round masonry tower 6m

buoy **Bajo Los Esqueiros** 42°30'·7N 8°56'·4W
　Fl(4)G.9s4M Green conical buoy

buoy **Bajo Los Mexos** 42°30'·9N 8°55'·7W
　Fl(4+1)15s6M Red and black can buoy

1816 **Bajo La Loba** 42°31'·8N 8°55'W
　Q.G.8m3M
　Grey conical beacon tower, green top

1818 **Isla Rúa** 42°32'·9N 8°56'·4W
　Fl(2+1)WR.21s24m13M
　121·5°-R-211·5°-W-121·5°
　Round granite tower and building 14m
　Racon Mo(G) 211°-121° 10-20M

1824 **Bajo Piedra Seca** 42°32'·9N 8°55'·2W
　Fl(3)G.15s10m8M
　White conical tower, green band

buoy **Sinal del Maño** 42°34'·3N 8°55'·4W
　Fl.R.5s5M Red can buoy

buoy **Bajo Ter** 42°34'·5N 8°53'·8W
　Fl.G.3s5M Green pillar buoy

1826 **Punta del Caballo**, Isla Arosa 42°34'·3N 8°53'·1W
　Fl(4)11s11m10M
　Grey octagonal tower and white building 5m

1828 **Bajo Sinal de Ostreira** 42°35'·7N 8°54'·8W
　Fl(3)R.15s8m3M
　White conical tower, red top 10m

buoy **Bajo Moscardiño (Findlay)** 42°35'·7N 8°52'·4W
　Fl(2)R.7s6M Red can buoy

buoy **El Seijo** 42°35'·2N 8°50'·6W
　Fl(3)G.10s5M Green pillar buoy

buoy **Bajo Aurora** 42°36'·2N 8°48'·3W
　Fl(4)R.11s5M Red can buoy

In addition to the above, a number of buoys with yellow lights and × topmarks indicate the limits of the *viveros* (mussels rafts) which are to be found throughout the *ría*.

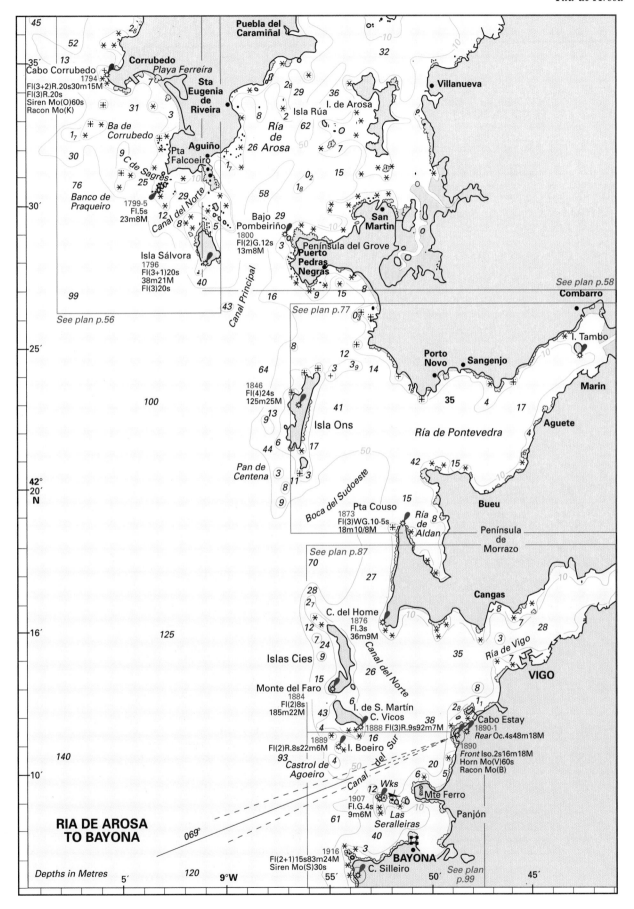

45

52

35′ 13
Cabo Corrubedo +
1794
Fl(3+2)R.20s30m15M
Fl(3)R.20s
Siren Mo(O)60s
Racon Mo(K)

**Corrubedo**
*Playa Ferreíra*

**Sta
Eugenia
de
Riveira**

Puebla del
Caramiñal

32

2₈

29
36
Isla Rúa
I. de Arosa

Villanueva

**Ría
de
Arosa** 26

31

3

**Aguiño**
Pta
Falcoeiro

Ba de
Corrubedo

1₇

30

9 C de Sagres

25

76
Banco de
Praqueiro

1799·5
Fl.5s
23m8M

12

29

5

1₇

1₇

62

2₈

8

50

7

0₂

15

1₈

58

San
Martin

Bajo 29
Pombeiriño
1800
Fl(2)G.12s
13m8M 3

**Puerto
Pedras
Negras**

Península del Grove

Isla Sálvora
1796
Fl(3+1)20s
38m21M
Fl(3)20s

40

30′

99

43

16

9
15

8

See plan p.58

Combarro

See plan p.56

25′

*Canal Principal*

See plan p.77

0₃

8

12

I. Tambo

**Porto
Novo**
**Sangenjo**

64

3
3₉
14

**Marin**

42°
20′
N

1846
Fl(4)24s
125m25M

13
9

41

1₈

**35**
4

17

**Aguete**

100

Isla Ons

*Ría de Pontevedra*

4

44
6

17

Pan de
Centena

3

42

15

8
11
3

50

**Bueu**

9

*Boca del Sudoeste*

Pta Couso 15
1873
Fl(3)WG.10·5s
18m10/8M

*Ría
de
Aldan* 8

Península
de
Morrazo

See plan p.87
70

27

16′

125

28

2₇

**Cangas**

7

28

C. del Home
1876
Fl.3s
36m9M

10

12

7 24

3

*Ría de Vigo*

9

**35**

**Islas Cies**

15

26

*Canal del Norte*

8

**VIGO**

Monte del Faro
1884
Fl(2)8s
185m22M

6

I. de S. Martín
C. Vicos

43

1888 Fl(3)R.9s92m7M

2₈
1₁

Cabo Estay
1890·1
*Rear* Oc.4s48m18M

38

4

16

1889
Fl(2)R.8s22m6M

I. Boeiro

20

1890
*Front* Iso.2s16m18M
Horn Mo(V)60s
Racon Mo(B)

140

93 *Castrol de
Agoeiro*

4

6

5

**RIA DE AROSA
TO BAYONA**

069°

12 *Wks*

Mte Ferro

1907
Fl.G.4s
9m6M

*Las
Seralleiras*

**Panjón**

61

40

1916
Fl(2+1)15s83m24M
Siren Mo(S)30s

3
**BAYONA**

C. Silleiro

See plan
p.99

*Depths in Metres* 5′

120

**9°W**

55′

50′

45′

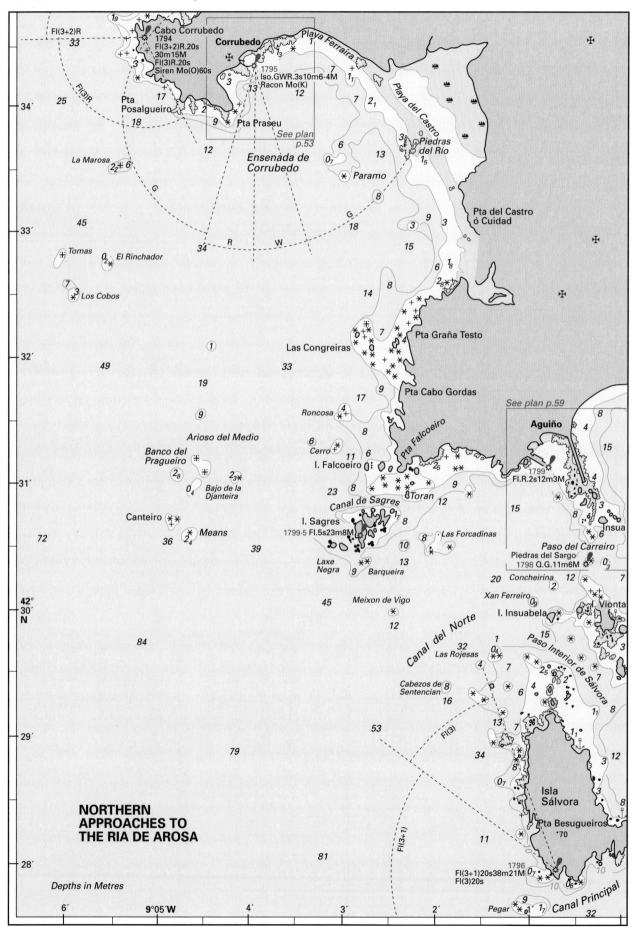

Fl(3+2)R
*33*

Cabo Corrubedo
1794
Fl(3+2)R.20s
.30m15M
Fl(3)R.20s
Siren Mo(O)60s

**Corrubedo**

1795
Iso.GWR.3s10m6-4M
Racon Mo(K)

*Playa Ferraira*

*Playa del Castro*

Pta
Posalgueiro

Pta Praseu

*See plan
p.53*

*Ensenada de
Corrubedo*

Piedras
del Río

Paramo

Pta del Castro
ó Cuidad

La Marosa

Tomas

El Rinchador

Los Cobos

Las Congreiras

Pta Graña Testo

Pta Cabo Gordas

*See plan p.59*

**Aguiño**

Roncosa

Pta Falcoeiro

*Arioso del Medio*

Banco del
Pragueiro

Cerro

I. Falcoeiro

1799
Fl.R.2s12m3M

*Bajo de la
Djanteira*

Toran

Canal de Sagres

Insua

Canteiro

Means

I. Sagres
1799·5 Fl.5s23m8M

Las Forcadinas

**Paso del Carreiro**
Piedras del Sargo
1798 Q.G.11m6M

Laxe
Negra

Barqueira

Concheirina

*I. Vionta*

Meixon de Vigo

Xan Ferreiro

I. Insuabela

*Canal del Norte*

*Paso Interior de Sálvora*

Las Rojesas

Cabezos de
Sentencian

Fl(3)

Isla
Sálvora

Pta Besugueiros
·70

1796
Fl(3+1)20s38m21M
Fl(3)20s

Fl(3+1)

**NORTHERN
APPROACHES TO
THE RIA DE AROSA**

*Depths in Metres*

Pegar

*Canal Principal*

**42°
30´
N**

9°05´W

## General

The largest of the Galician *rías* and perhaps the most attractive for cruising, Ría de Arosa has many pleasant anchorages to explore and some interesting challenges in the way of pilotage. Not surprisingly it is also very popular with the Spanish, both afloat and on the many beaches. Food and other basics may be obtained in most of the small harbours on its shores, though the widest choice is undoubtedly to be had at Villagarcía de Arosa, an otherwise unappealing town.

The variety of anchorages is such that shelter from any wind direction can be found relatively easily. The simplest harbours to enter in darkness are Santa Eugenia de Riveira, Puebla del Caramiñal and Villagarcía de Arosa – night approaches to other places should not be made without local knowledge, not least because of the dangers posed by unlit *viveros*, of which the Ría Arosa is particularly full.

In addition to the harbours detailed in the following pages, a number of nominal *puertos* exist, usually consisting of a short breakwater (sometimes lit) behind which small fishing vessels lie on moorings. Few can be approached by a keel yacht at all states of the tide. Similarly, not all the possible anchorages in this large *ría* can be described, though an attempt has been made to include those most popular.

Finally a word of warning: over the past few years a major trade in hard drugs has developed in Galicia, much of it apparently centred in the Ría de Arosa. At least some of the contraband undoubtedly comes in by sea, and should unexplained movements be witnessed it would be most unwise to become involved. Far better contact the authorities at the first opportunity.

## Approach

The easiest and safest approach to the *ría*, particularly at night or in poor conditions, is from the southwest through the Canal Principal. This leads between Isla Sálvora[1796] and Pombeiriño[1800], at the northwest point of the Península del Grove. Isla Rúa light[1818] can be seen from well out to sea, and from offshore is safe to approach on a bearing of between 010° and 025°.

Coming from the north on passage, clear Cabo Corrubedo by 5M to avoid the dangers of Bajos de Corrubedo. When past them, steer to round Isla Sálvora giving the lighthouse a berth of 1M to avoid the Pegar rock group and enter by the Canal Principal.

The alternative inshore route passes close round Cabo Corrubedo between the offshore rocks and La Marosa, then continues eastwards until Corrubedo breakwater bears 350°. Then turn south onto 170°, towards Laxe Negra, the low-lying, westernmost rock of the Sagres group, generally with surf breaking on it. Approaching the Islas Sagres, either turn into the more difficult Canal de Sagres before reaching Laxe Negra or continue south and round Isla Sálvora.

The Canal de Sagres is narrow and has a submerged rock, Laxes de Falcoeiro, on the north side; on the south side the rocks are visible. If the canal is unfamiliar, identify the lighthouse on Piedras del Sargo[1798] before entering and steer for it on 106°. The course passes about 150m south of Falcoeiro and 80m north of the visible Mayador group. When clear of Mayador and the drying Las Forcadiñas, aim to pass north of Piedras del Sargo (which has two off-lying rocks) by 150m. This channel, the Paso del Carreiro, is no more than 250m wide and bounded on the north side by yet more rocks which dry. A heading of 075° after passing Piedras del Sargo clears off-lying dangers to the east and leads into the *ría* proper.

Strong and unpredictable currents can run strongly through both these channels, which should not be attempted in less than perfect weather, when they provide an interesting exercise in pilotage.

Another approach is from the southwest towards Aguiño breakwater[1799] on 030°, turning into the Paso del Carreiro to pass north of Piedras del Sargo. This channel, sometimes confusingly labelled the Canal del Norte, is used by fisherman but is flanked by rocks awash, many well offshore.

Once clear of Isla Sálvora or Piedras del Sargo, head for Isla Rúa[1818], a distinctive clump of rocks with a prominent lighthouse. Pass between Isla Rúa and Bajo Piedra Seca[1824] on 030° but do not turn further east until Punta Caballo[1826] is south of east and the starboard hand Bajo Ter buoy, which marks ground off Isla de Arosa, has been passed. Equally, do not turn north until Sinal de Ostreira[1828] bears west of north, in order to clear Sinal del Maño bank (now lit) and the dangers south and west of Ostreira itself. See the entries for Villagarcía de Arosa and Puebla del Caramiñal, pages 67 and 62 respectively.

The numerous *viveros* moored near to and sometimes infringing on the channel north of Isla Rúa make it inadvisable to beat up the channel at night or in poor visibility.

# Aguiño

42°31'N 9°01'W

## Charts

|  | Harbour |
|---|---|
| Admiralty | 1768 |
| Spanish | 415B |

## Lights

### Approach
1798 **Piedras del Sargo** 42°30'·3N 9°00'·5W
  Q.G.11m6M
  White conical tower, green band 12m

### Harbour
1799 **Breakwater** 42°31'·1N 9°00'·9W
  Fl.R.2s12m3M Red column 2m

## General

In spite of claims that the harbour dates back to Phoenician times, neither it nor the village can claim to be particularly attractive. However there are good

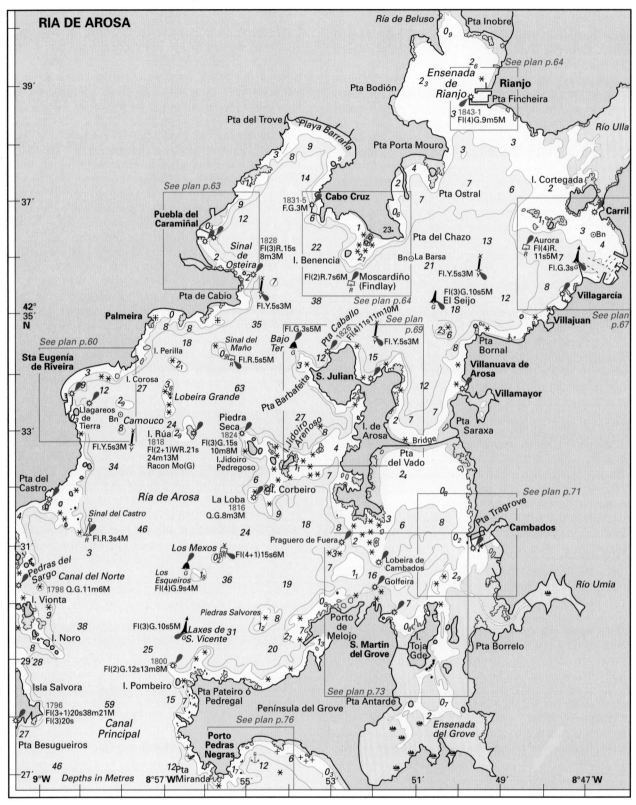

**RIA DE AROSA**

*Ría de Beluso* — Pta Inobre

0₉

Ensenada de Rianjo
2₆ — See plan p.64
Pta Bodión — 2₃ — **Rianjo**
Pta Fincheira
3 1843·1 Fl(4)G.9m5M

Pta del Trove — Playa Barralla — Pta Porta Mouro — *Río Ulla*
3 8 9 — 3
14 — Pta Ostral — I. Cortegada
9 — 2 — 4 — 1 — 5 7 — 6 — 2 — **Carril**

See plan p.63
9 — 1831·5 F.G.3M — **Cabo Cruz** — 1 — Bn
**Puebla del Caramiñal** — 6 — 23 — Pta del Chazo — 13 — **Aurora** Fl(4)R. 11s5M 7
03 — 12 — 1828 Fl(3)R.15s 8m3M — La Barsa — Fl.G.3s
Sinal de Osteira — 2 — 22 — I. Benencia — Bn 21 — Fl.Y.5s3M — 8 — **Villagarcía**
2 — Fl(2)R.7s6M — Moscardiño (Findlay) — Fl(3)G.10s5M El Seijo — 12
Pta de Cabio — 38 — See plan p.64 — 18 — **Villajuan** — See plan p.67
Fl.Y.5s3M

**Palmeira** — 0 — 8 8 — 35 — Fl.G.3s5M — Pta Caballo — See plan p.69 — 2₃6
See plan p.60 — 18 — I. Perilla — Sinal del Maño — Bajo Ter — 1826 Fl(4)11s11m10M — Fl.Y.5s3M — 8 — Pta Bornal
**Sta Eugenía de Riveira** — 09 Fl.R.5s5M — 3 — 12 — 15 — **Villanuava de Arosa**
3 — I. Corosa — **S. Julian** — 12 — **Villamayor**
9 — 12 — 27 — 3 6 — Lobeira Grande — 63 — 27 — 2 — Pta Saraxa
Llagareos de Tierra — Bn Camouco — 24 — Piedra Seca — Arenoso — I. de Arosa — Pta del Vado
3 — 8 — I. Rúa 2₉ — 1824 Fl(3)G.15s 10m8M — 8 — Bridge
Fl.Y.5s3M — 1818 Fl(2+1)WR.21s 24m13M Racon Mo(G) — I.Jidoiro Pedregoso — 4 — 2₄
34 — 1₁ — 7
Pta del Castro — *Ría de Arosa* — 6 — I. Corbeiro — See plan p.71
4 — Sinal del Castro — La Loba 1816 Q.G.8m3M — 9 — 18 — 6 — 8 — Pta Tragrove — **Cambados**
Fl.R.3s4M — 46 — 24 — Praguero de Fuera — 2 — 0₂
31 — 3 — Los Mexos — 3 — 6 — Lobeira de Cambados
Pedras del Sargo — 0₂ Fl(4+1)15s6M — 7 — 1₁ — 16 — Golfeira — 2₉
Canal del Norte — Los Esqueiros Fl(4)G.9s4M — 36 — 19 — *Río Umia*
1798 Q.G.11m6M — Piedras Salvores — 0 — 7
I. Vionta — 38 — Fl(3)G.10s5M — 31 — Porto de Melojo — 0₈
9 — I. Noro — Laxes de S. Vicente — 20 — **S. Martin del Grove** — I. Toja Gde — Pta Borrelo
8 — 25 — 2₇ — 1₃
29 28 — 1800 Fl(2)G.12s13m8M
**Isla Salvora** — I. Pombeiro — Pta Pateiro ó Pedregal — Pta Antarde — 0₇
1796 Fl(3+1)20s38m21M Fl(3)20s — 15 — Península del Grove — 2 — Ensenada del Grove
27 — *Canal Principal* — See plan p.76
Pta Besugueiros — **Porto Pedras Negras** — 6
46 — 12 — 12
27' 9°W — *Depths in Metres* — 8°57'W Miranda — 17 — 55' — 0₃ 53' — 51' — 49' — 8°47'W

white sand beaches nearby and for some the main appeal will be in the intricacies of the approach. A shellfish processing factory is situated close west of the harbour.

## Approach

The three approaches to Aguiño are described in the introduction to the Ría de Arosa, page 57. The easiest is from the east, taking the Paso del Carreiro past Piedras del Sargo[1798] and continuing until Aguiño breakwater[1799] bears 010° to clear the submerged reefs off Las Centolleiras and Duriceira rock. The channel past Piedras del Sargo is only about 250m wide, with two rocks off the light itself and others awash to the north. To clear the foul ground due east of the light, do not approach it on a bearing of more than 255°.

From the northwest, the most direct route is through the Canal de Sagres – again see page 57.

The approach from the southwest through the Canal del Norte is the one usually used by fishermen, but calls either for local knowledge or clear visibility to the Aguiño breakwater bearing 030°. This line clears the rocks awash on either side of the channel which are at some distance from easily identifiable land.

The devoted rock-hopper with a large-scale chart might also try the Paso Interior de Sálvora between Islas Sálvora and Vionta.

## Anchorage

The Las Centolleiras reef has been filled in to form a causeway protecting the harbour from the east. As a result the harbour is reasonably sheltered, though the entrance is exposed to the southwest. Much of it is shallow and the best anchorage occupied by smallcraft moorings. Anchor about 150m north or northeast of the breakwater as space allows in 2–4m over sand, keeping clear of the approach to the fishermen's quay on the inside of the breakwater.

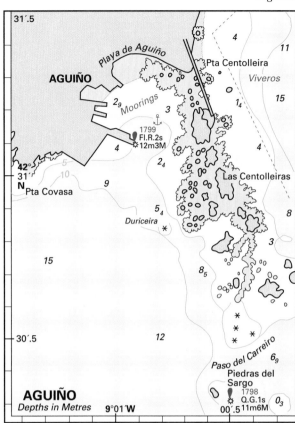

## Facilities

Some repair facilities, including a slipway geared to the needs of fishing trawlers and a fishermen's chandlery. A few shops, cafés and bars, but little else.

## Alternative anchorages

The following isolated anchorages offer interesting daytime exploring in settled weather, but have intricate approaches and in an easterly (not uncommon in the *rías*) would be difficult to leave. None are recommended for an overnight stop.

1. *Isla Vionta*, (northeast coast – 42°30'N 9°00'W). Off the small beach over sand, rock and weed.
2. *Isla Sálvora*. The island is a military area and landing is discouraged, though there appears to be no objection to picnicking on Playa dos Bois. A polite approach to the guards may result in an invitation to visit the *castillo* and other places of interest.
   a. Playa dos Bois (northeast coast – 42°28'·9N 9°00'·4W). Off the beach over sand and weed.
   b. Playa del Castillo (east coast – 42°28'·4N 9°00'W). Off a short stone mole at the southern end of a pair of small sandy beaches, in 4–5m over sand, rock and weed. The *castillo* which gives the bay its name is a low stone affair with a tiled roof.

Looking west over the spacious harbour of Aguiño at the mouth of the Ría de Arosa, with the Las Centolleiras reef in the foreground.

# Santa Eugenia de Riveira (Santa Uxia de Ribeira)

42°34'N 8°59'W

## Charts

|  | *Harbour* |
|---|---|
| Admiralty | *1768* |
| Spanish | *415C, 4152, 9263* |

## Lights

### *Approach (from within the ría)*

buoy **Riveira** C 42°33'N 8°57'·6W
  Fl.Y.5s3M Yellow spar buoy, × topmark
1822 **Bajo Llagareos de Tierra** 42°33'·4N 8°59'W
  Q.R.6m4M Grey conical tower, red top 7m

### *Harbour*

1820 **East breakwater** 42°33'·6N 8°59'·2W
  Fl(2)R.7s7m4M Red round tower on white base 6m
1820·5 **Northwest (marina) breakwater** 42°33'·8N
  8°59'·2W
  Fl.R.2s7m3M Round red over white tower 5m
**Marina north pontoon** 42°33'·8N 8°59'·3W
  F.R. Post 1m

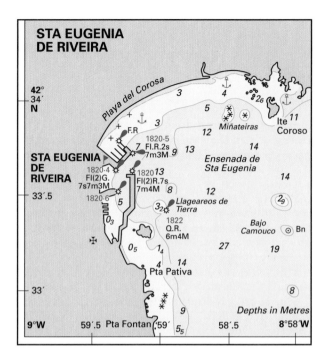

The large commercial and fishing harbour of Santa Eugenia de Riveira, seen from a little east of south. The new marina is at upper right.

1820·4 **Northwest breakwater elbow** 42°33'·7N
8°59'·3W
Fl(2)G.7s7m3M Round green over white tower 5m
1820·6 **Inner mole** 42°33'·5N 8°59'·3W
Fl.G.2s7m3M Round green over white tower 5m

## Marina radio

*Club Náutico Deportivo de Riveira* VHF Ch 09.

## General

Long a large sheltered fishing port used also by medium-sized coasters, where yachts were discouraged, Santa Eugenia – often referred to locally as either 'Riveira' or 'Ribeira' – now has a small, relatively well-sheltered marina where visiting yachts are made welcome, though it is still possible to anchor off. The town claims to be the centre of the sardine trade and it is still sometimes possible to buy freshly cooked fish by the harbourside, grilled in the open over a bed of charcoal, a culinary experience not to be passed by!

## Approach

Enter the Ensenada de Santa Eugenia de Riveira midway between the Isla Rúa[1818], a distinctive lighthouse on a rocky island, and the coastline to the west. Steer to pass west of buoy Riveira *C*, which marks the southwestern limit of the *viveros*, and Bajo Camouco, marked by an unlit green beacon, and east of Llagareos de Tierra[1822], before shaping a course to round the marina breakwater. Remain near the breakwater and pontoons as there is at least one isolated rock between them and the beach, as well as other dangers elsewhere in the bay.

At night, steer for Llagareos de Tierra[1822] on a heading of between 300° and 335°, leaving it about 100m to port before closing the marina breakwater[1820·5].

## Anchorage

Anchor north of the marina off the Playa del Coroso in 3–5m over sand and mud, or further east towards the Islote Coroso – see Alternative anchorages, below.

## Berthing

The marina is administered by the Club Náutico Deportivo de Riveira, ☎/*Fax* 981 873801, and has some 220 berths on four pontoons, of which 40 are nominally reserved for visitors. Most of these can take a maximum length of 12m but a few yachts of up to 16m can be accommodated on the northernmost pontoon. Minimum depths in the northern part of the marina, where visitors are normally berthed, are at least 5m. There is no formal arrivals berth – visitors should secure near the end of the second pontoon in, preferably having contacted the *club náutico* previously on VHF Ch 09. Berthing is bow or stern-to, with haul-off lines tailed to the pontoon. In 1999 the high season (1/6–31/8) rate for a visiting yacht of just under 12m was 2,000 ptas (12·02 euros) per night inclusive of water, electricity and tax.

In September 1999 two new buildings were taking shape near the root of the marina breakwater, one to house offices, showers, etc (currently in a portacabin), with a café and supermarket above; the other to provide premises for workshops, a chandlery, boutiques, etc. Other local facilities include dinghy sailing and diving schools.

## Facilities

*Travel-lift* Not as of 1999, though the characteristic 'jaws' are in place.

*Engineers, electronic & radio repairs* To be established in the new marina buildings (see above), but in the meantime nearly all skills are available in the commercial harbour.

*Chandlery* Planned for the new marina buildings.

*Water* On the pontoons.

*Showers* Currently portacabin, but planned for the new buildings.

*Launderette* In the town.

*Electricity* On the pontoons.

*Fuel* Promised for the 2000 season. In the meantime both diesel and petrol can be ordered for delivery by can.

*Bottled gas* Camping Gaz available in the town.

*Club náutico* The small Club Náutico Deportivo de Riveira is due to move into the new marina buildings on completion. The officials are friendly and helpful, but in 1999 very little English was spoken.

*Banks* In the town (with card facilities).

*Shops/provisioning* Good supermarket a short distance away, plus produce and fish markets, with general shopping in the town. A supermarket is planned for the new building.

*Cafés, restaurants & hotels* Wide choice in the town, plus marina café (planned).

*Medical services* In the town.

## Communications

*Post office* In the town.

*Mailing address*
c/o **Club Náutico Deportivo de Riveira**,
Praza da Lonxa s/n, Apartado 111, 15960 Riveira, A Coruña, España.
*Fax service* 981 873801

*Public telephones* At the marina and elsewhere.

*Car hire/taxis* In the town.

*Buses* Around the *ría* and beyond.

## Alternative anchorages

1. Inside the Miñateiras rocks (which show at low water) west of Isote Coroso, in 3–4m over sand.
2. Tucked in northeast of Islote Coroso, again in 3–4m over sand, surrounded by smooth, pinkish boulders. However there are various rocks in the approach, as well as one in the anchorage itself, making calm water and good light essential.
3. In the Ensenada de Palmeira, northeast of Riveira, either east or west of the reef extending from Punta Cornas, using eyeball navigation and a large-scale chart.

# Puebla del Caramiñal
# (A Pobra do Caramiñal)

42°36'N 8°56'W

## Charts

|  | *Harbour* |
|---|---|
| Admiralty | *1768* |
| Spanish | *415C, 4152, 9263* |

## Lights

### *Approach (from within the ría)*
buoy **Caramiñal G** 42°35'·6N 8°54'·6W
  Fl.Y.5s3M Yellow spar buoy, × topmark
1828 **Bajo Sinal de Ostreira** 42°35'·7N 8°54'·8W
  Fl(3)R.15s8m3M
  White conical tower, red top 10m

### *Harbour*
1830·4 **Outer breakwater** 42°36'·3N 8°55'·9W
  Oc.G.2s8m4M Green and white round column 6m
1830 **Inner molehead** 42°36'·3N 8°56'W
  Fl(2)R.6s7m6M Red and white round column 7m

## Marina radio

*Club Náutico Caramiñal* VHF Ch 09.

## General

Sadly the pleasant and picturesque old town with its narrow streets and squares, well kept public gardens, old church, and various other buildings of interest has been largely submerged by new construction and is no longer the universal favourite with cruising yachtsmen that it once was. The marina – which still has an unfinished feel, despite having been built in the early 1990s – is uncomfortable in winds out of the eastern quadrant, and its associated facilities are currently some distance away at the *club náutico*. The town in often referred to locally as simply 'Pobra'.

## Approach

From the southwest, after passing between Isla Rúa[1818] and Piedra Seca[1824] remain on 030° to clear the Sinal del Maño shoal and the foul ground off Isla Arosa, both buoyed. The red-topped white tower of Sinal de Ostreira[1828] stands out well, as does the outer mole at Caramiñal[1830·4], with the buoy Caraminal *C* closer at hand and marking the easterly limit of the *viveros*. If entering at night it is essential to leave the latter well to port.

## Anchorage

Off the beach south of the marina in 3–4m (though beware shallower patches) over sand and some weed. Both fishing vessels and sizeable coasters use the main harbour, the latter turning in the entrance with the aid of tugs, and anchoring in the harbour or its approaches is to be avoided.

The somewhat exposed pontoons at Puebla del Caramiñal, looking west-northwest over the outer breakwater. One of the Ría de Arosa's many *viveros* can be seen at bottom right.

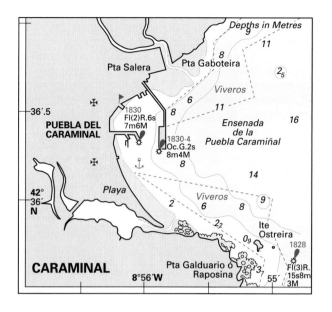

## Berthing

The marina extends south from the central spur of the inner mole, overlooked by a small office manned by a security guard. More permanent premises were under construction in 1999. Of the 150 berths around 30 are reserved for visitors, who are normally berthed at the end of the outer finger where there is a minimum depth of 2·5m. If given the choice, the inner side of the pontoon is a great deal more sheltered than the outside, which is exposed to constant wash from fishing boats as well as any chop. Double hauling-off lines, tailed to the pontoon, are provided and in theory yachts of up to 17m can be accommodated.

The pontoons are administered by the Club Náutico Caramiñal, ☎/*Fax* 981 830970, with a second telephone at the marina itself, ☎ 981 877317. In 1999 the high season rate for a visiting yacht of just under 12m was 1,500 ptas (9·02 euros) per night, inclusive of water and electricity.

## Facilities

*Travel-lift* At the *club náutico*, where minor repairs can also be carried out, with no shortage of hardstanding.
*Water* On the pontoons.
*Showers* Currently at the *club náutico*, though planned to share the new marina office building.
*Launderette* At the *club náutico*.
*Electricity* On the pontoons.
*Fuel* At the marina, following pre-payment to the *club náutico*.
*Club náutico* The Club Náutico Caramiñal have premises next to the slipway in the main harbour.
*Banks* In the town (with card facilities).
*Shops/provisioning* Several supermarkets in the town, together with other shops.
*Produce market* Fish and produce market close to the southern slipway, with additional stalls on Wednesdays.
*Cafés, restaurants & hotels* The usual variety, including several tempting pavement cafés.

*Medical services* In the town.

## Communications

*Post office and telephones* In the town.
*Taxis* In the town.
*Buses* Around the *ría* and beyond.

## Alternative anchorage

Southeast of Caramiñal towards Islote Ostreira, inside the *viveros* (of which there were very few in either 1998 or 1999). The island almost covers at high water and is therefore inconspicuous for much of the time.

# Puerto de Cruz/Cabo Cruz

42°37'N 8°53'W

## Charts

| | *Harbour* |
|---|---|
| Admiralty | *1768* |
| Spanish | *415C, 9263* |

## Lights

### Approach
buoy **Bajo Moscardiño (Findlay)** 42°35'·7N 8°52'·4W
  Fl(2)R.7s6M Red can buoy

### Harbour
1831·5 **Breakwater** 42°36'·9N 8°53'·4W
  F.G.3M Green and white round tower 6m
1831·6 **Old mole** 42°36'·9N 8°53'·3W
  F.R.2M Metal post

## General

A fishing village in an attractive setting, where wooden vessels are hauled out on the quay for painting and repair, but too modest for its variety of names – the harbour is Puerto de Cruz, the village Cabo Cruz (or sometimes Pesqueira), and the anchorage east of the *cabo* itself known to yachtsmen as South Bay.

The harbour gives shelter from all winds other than north, while the open bays to the south provide shelter from west through north to east. The village depends for its livelihood on the cultivation and canning of mussels, and there are many *viveros* close offshore.

## Approach

There is much foul ground to the southeast of Cabo Cruz, and the safe approach lies west of the distinctive humped Isla Benencia (about 0·7M southeast of Cabo Cruz), 16m high with a rocky ridge and a reef extending south-southwest from its southern tip. The port hand channel buoy (labelled 'Findlay or Moscardiño' on Admiralty *1768*) marks the southern end of the foul ground and is on the limit of the *viveros*, but they may extend further to the southwest.

Head for the end of Cabo Cruz peninsula either outside or through the *viveros* – the headland is marked by a stone cross on a cairn. Beyond will be seen the breakwater extending west from the village.

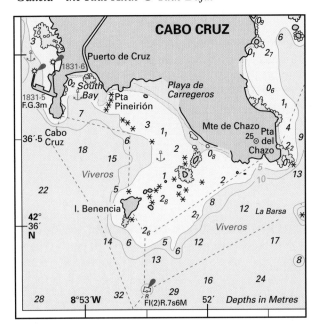

## Anchorages

1. Puerto de Cruz – the harbour offers shelter from the south, but would be untenable in strong northerly winds. It is not possible to lie alongside – fishing boats moor bow-to the breakwater but a yacht would find this difficult. Anchor northwest of the breakwater as space allows.

2. Northwest of the harbour in the Ensenada de Barraña, inside the many *viveros* but otherwise exposed from southeast through to southwest. Holding is good in 3–5m over mud and sand. The short breakwater at Escarbote would be one possible place to land, otherwise use the clean sandy beach.

3. South Bay – anchor in the centre of the bay clear of the fishing boat moorings in 5m over sand and weed, exposed to southeast round to southwest. There are rocks in the eastern part of the bay off Punta Pineirón.

4. Playa de Carregeros – anchor in the angle between the southeast end of the beach and Isla Benencia with its associated reef, in 2–3m over sand. There is reasonable clearance between the island and an isolated half-tide rock to the northeast, but approach should only be made in flat conditions and good light. Protection is excellent from north to east, while both the reef (largely exposed at low tide) and the closely-packed *viveros* give some shelter from the south.

### Facilities

The village of Cabo Cruz has a small supermarket and other shops, cafés, bars and a bank.

# Rianjo (Rianxo)

42°39'N 8°49'W

### Charts

| | Harbour |
|---|---|
| Admiralty | 1768 |
| Spanish | 415C, 9263 |

### Lights

*Approach*
buoy **Villagarcía A** 42°36'N 8°49'·7W
  Fl.Y.5s3M Yellow spar buoy, × topmark

*Harbour*
1843·1 **South breakwater** 42°38'·9N 8°49'·5W
  Fl(4)G.9m5M Green over white post 5m
1843·2 **North breakwater** 42°38'·9N 8°49'·5W
  Fl(4)R.9m3M Red over white post 5m
1843·4 **North breakwater spur** 42°39'·1N 8°49'·5W
  Fl.G.3s9m5M Green over white column 6m

### Marina radio

*Club Náutico de Rianjo* VHF Ch 09.

### General

The harbour at Rianjo has been expanding gradually over some years, with more developments promised for the future. Previously a fair weather anchorage in the attractive setting of the Ensenada de Rianjo with dinghy landing at a short fishermen's mole, there is now a large expanse of water enclosed between the north and south breakwaters, both of which have right-angled ends to create a west-facing entrance some 150m in width. Most of the harbour is occupied by moored fishing vessels, with a single yacht pontoon in the extreme south. Plans exist – as they did five years ago – to build a full service marina to the south of the existing harbour (see plan), but it is not known when work is likely to start.

A sardine festival is celebrated in June, while in September the week-long *fiesta* of Santa Maria de Guadaloupe takes place, with entertainment every evening culminating in an all-night event.

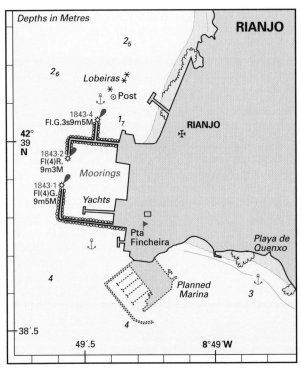

The historic town of Padrón lies 16km away by road. Called Iris Flavia by the Romans, it was important in the middle ages and still displays the stone post to which, legend claims, the boat bearing the remains of St James the Great was moored in the headwaters of the *ría*. The relics were subsequently lost and rediscovered before coming to rest at what is now Santiago de Compostela.

## Approach

Coming up from the southwest, the approach to the Ensenada de Rianjo is straightforward other than the need to avoid the large numbers of *viveros* – the southern end of the gap between the two banks is indicated by buoy Villagarcía *A*. Enter the bay between Punta Porto Mouro to the west and Punta Fincheira to the east, the latter a low cliff surmounted by trees and a stone cross, with a large grey concrete structure and a low tan building with a tan roof in front. Land has already been reclaimed on the west side of the point and the new marina is to be built to the south.

## Anchorage

Anchoring in the harbour is no longer permitted, so a spot must be chosen in light of current wind direction.

In southerlies anchor as near as draught permits to a line between the spur of the north mole and the Lobeiras rocks, marked by a post 200m to the northeast, in a scant 2m over mud. There are steps for landing by dinghy but a long painter is necessary as the securing points are on the top of the wall.

In northerlies, flat water will be found south of the south breakwater where there are a few pontoons belonging to a sailing school (not suitable for berthing), but little protection will be had from the wind. In stronger conditions it would be wise to seek shelter further east off the Playa de Quenxo in 3–4m over mud and sand. This wide, tree-lined bay is perhaps the best anchorage in the *ría* in northerlies and is linked to the town by an attractive clifftop walk.

## Berthing

The yacht pontoon is administered by the Club Náutico de Rianxo, ☎ 981 866107 *Fax* 981 860620, as the projected marina will be. There are 83 berths on the existing pontoon, of which ten are nominally reserved for visitors, but only eight of the total number can accommodate yachts of more than 10m LOA. Depths are said to be 4m near the end of the pontoon shoaling to 2m near its centre (where half of the larger berths are situated). It is well sheltered other than from the northwest and – unusually for the area – all berths are alongside with finger pontoons. Yacht fuel is not available, though promised for the new marina. In 1999 the high season rate for a visiting yacht of just under 12m was 1,320 ptas (7·93 euros) per night inclusive, with discounts for stays of more than 15 nights.

Rianjo's large, square harbour seen from almost due south, with the single yacht pontoon just beyond the nearer breakwater. The long-promised marina has yet to materialise.

## Facilities

*Boatyard & engineers* On the north breakwater overlooking the fishing harbour, accustomed to working in wood or GRP and to fishing boat engines.

*Water* On the pontoon.

*Showers* Next to the small *club náutico* building.

*Launderette* In the town.

*Electricity* On the pontoon.

*Club náutico* The Club Náutico de Rianxo is small, friendly and very helpful, even though no English was spoken in 1999. It is almost certain to expand to new premises when (if) the planned marina takes shape.

*Banks* In the town.

*Shops/provisioning* Reasonable shopping in the town, plus a good fish market.

*Cafés, restaurants & hotels* In the town, plus a bar at the *club náutico*.

*Medical services* In the town.

## Communications

*Post office* In the town.

*Mailing address*
c/o **Club Náutico de Rianxo**, Puerto Deportivo, 15920 Rianxo, A Coruña, España.
*Fax service* 981 860620
Although there is a permanent security guard, at present the office is manned mornings only.

*Public telephones* At the *club náutico* and elsewhere.

*Car hire/taxis* In the town.

*Buses* Bus service to Padrón and thence to Santiago de Compostela or Villagarcía de Arosa.

# Villagarcía de Arosa (Vilagarcía de Arousa)

42°36'N 8°46'W

## Charts

| | Harbour |
|---|---|
| Admiralty | 1768, 1757 |
| Spanish | 415C, 9263 |

## Lights

*Approach (from within the ría)*
buoy **Cambados A** 42°34'·9N 8°51'·9W
Fl.Y.5s3M Yellow spar buoy, × topmark
buoy **El Seijo** 42°35'·2N 8°50'·6W
Fl(3)G.10s5M Green pillar buoy
buoy **Villagarcía A** 42°36'N 8°49'·7W
Fl.Y.5s3M Yellow spar buoy, × topmark
buoy **Bajo Aurora** 42°36'·2N 8°48'·3W
Fl(4)R.11s5M Red can buoy

*Harbour*
buoy **South breakwater** 42°36'·1N 8°47'·1W
Fl.G.3s Green pillar buoy, ▲ topmark
1840·5 **North breakwater** 42°36'·2N 8°46'·3W
Iso.2s2m10M Round masonry tower 3m
1840·2 **Marina entrance, N side** 42°36'N 8°46'·2W
Q.R.6m3M Triangular red tower 3m
1840 **Marina entrance, S side
(Hammerhead mole, N end)** 42°36'N 8°46'·2W
Q.G.6m3M Triangular green tower 3m
1839·7 **Hammerhead mole, S end** 42°35'·9N 8°46'·2W
Fl.R.5s5m5M Round grey concrete tower 3m
1839·6 **Inner mole** 42°35'·9N 8°46'·2W
Fl(2)G.7s6m3M Green post on green and white building 3m
1839·5 **Commercial mole** 42°35'·9N 8°46'·4W
Q(2+1)G.11·5s8m5M Round red tower
*Note* No trace of structure or light in September 1999

Villagarcía de Arosa, the main commercial harbour of the *ría,* looking southeast. A yacht has just passed through the narrow marina entrance.

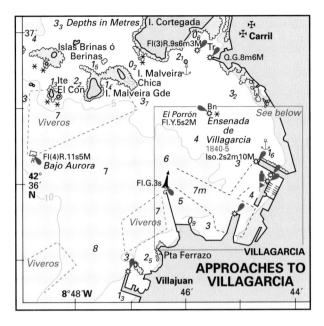

## Port radio

*Marina Villagarcía* VHF Ch 09.
*Villagarcía Prácticos* VHF Ch 12, 16.

## General

Villagarcía is a quiet commercial port and a minor naval base, used by substantial cargo ships and the occasional cruise ship. There is a pleasant Club de Mar and the marina, although apparently full, can generally find space for visiting yachts. The marina, which is run by the Port Authority rather than the Club de Mar, is one of the relatively few places in Galicia where a yacht could safely be left for an extended period, perhaps while returning home. While not particularly attractive, the town is a useful port of call with reliable communications for crew changes and good provisioning. The *fiesta* of Santa Rita takes place on 22 May.

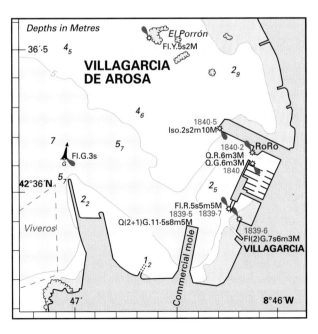

Villagarcía de Arosa is one of the more secure places in the *rías* in which to leave a yacht unattended while visiting Santiago de Compostela, less than an hour's bus ride inland. Santiago has been attracting visitors – medieval pilgrims and modern tourists – for the best part of a thousand years and should not be missed. The old city, containing the cathedral as well as dozens of other historic buildings, is compact within its walls and much can be seen on foot in a few hours. The *fiesta* of Saint James – now celebrated throughout the province as Galicia Day – takes place on 25 July with associated cultural events for a week or so on either side. When this date falls on a Sunday, as it did in 1999, the entire year is declared a 'Holy Year' and the *fiesta* celebrated with even greater enthusiasm.

The north door of Santiago de Compostela's superb cathedral, only one of the many unforgettable buildings in this unique city – well worth the bus or train journey even for those not 'into culture'.

## Approach

When coming up from the entrance of the *ría*, pass between Isla Rúa[1818] and Piedra Seca[1824] heading 030° but do not turn further east until Punta Caballo[1826] is south of east and the starboard hand Bajo Ter marking foul ground off Punta Barbafeita on Isla de Arosa has been passed. Continue east-northeast leaving Cambados *A* and El Seijo buoys to starboard, and Villagarcía *A* and Bajo Aurora buoys to port, until the starboard hand buoy close off the end of the south breakwater is reached. Both the north and commercial breakwaters can be picked out from a considerable distance due to their giant green cargo cranes.

## Anchorage

The harbour is too busy to permit anchoring, other than north of the north breakwater, between it and a mass of stakes marking shellfish beds and exposed from southwest round to north.

## Berthing

The marina is entered to the north of the hammerhead mole[1840], and contains some 460 berths of which 60 are reserved for visitors. Nearly all are bow or stern-to with a haul-off line tailed to the pontoon, and depths generous at 4–5m. There is 24 hour security from a small office on the hammerhead (though see below), and new arrivals will be directed where to moor and given assistance to berth if necessary.

Visitors are normally berthed on the outside of the northeast pontoon, which suffers from the prevailing northeast wind and any swell which may work its way in, and if leaving a yacht for any length of time it would be worth asking if a more sheltered spot is available. Charges are calculated on a length x breadth basis, with the 1999 high season rate for a visiting yacht of 12m LOA x 3·5m beam set at 1,950 ptas (11·72 euros) inclusive.

In 1999 new marina offices were under construction on a platform near the root of the central mole, and eventually should contain the usual restaurant, showers, launderette, etc. Proposals had also been put forward to extend the

The attractive anchorage at Carril, north of Villagarcía, looking northwest towards Isla Cortegada.

marina into the adjoining – and virtually unused – south basin, in which case the pontoon layout in the north basin might well be rearranged.

## Formalities

Customs forms can be completed at the Club de Mar and details may be requested, though this is only likely if the crew includes non–EU nationals.

## Facilities

*Boatyard, engineers, electronic & radio repairs* Astilleros Villagarcía SA, ☎ 986 51136 *Fax* 986 511723, and Nautica Ramon Morel, ☎ 986 508592, have extensive premises on the Rampa del Cavadelo south of the marina where there is a wide slipway. The former advertises hull repairs in GRP, wood and steel, engineering, osmosis treatment, guardinage and painting, as well as spares and accessories. There are yet more engineering workshops at the root of the commercial breakwater.

*Travel-lift* Astilleros Villagarcía SA operate a 50 tonne capacity lift on the Rampa del Cavadelo, with no shortage of either hardstanding or cradles suitable for yachts of all sizes. A mobile crane is also on hand for lifting masts.

*Chandlery* Several chandleries in the town, mostly slanted towards sport fishing, or Astilleros Villagarcía SA on the Rampa del Cavadelo if parts need to be ordered in. A chandlery is planned for the marina building.

*Charts*
   **Libreria Anton**, Calle Alcalde Rey Daviña 11
   ☎ 986 510154 *Fax* 986 510154
   are official suppliers of Spanish charts.

*Water* On the pontoons.

*Showers* At the marina.

*Launderette* At the marina plus several in the town.

*Electricity* On the pontoons.

*Fuel* Diesel and petrol at the marina.

*Bottled gas* Camping Gaz available in the town.

*Club náutico* The Club de Mar appears to be an offshoot of the marina rather than vice versa, but has a pleasant restaurant with an excellent view. The more formal Real Club de Regatas Galicia will be found on the road overlooking the public gardens opposite the marina.

*Banks* In the town (with card facilities).

*Shops/provisioning* Supermarket close to the marina's road exit, with plenty more good shops in the town's pedestrian precinct.

*Produce and fish markets* Produce market Tuesday and Saturday plus large fish market.

*Cafés, restaurants & hotels* Reasonable variety, with two cafés on the hammerhead itself.

*Medical services* In the town.

## Communications

*Post office* In the town.

*Mailing address*
   c/o **Marina Villagarcía**, Muelle de Pasajeros – Puerto Deportivo, 36600 Vilagarcía de Arousa, Pontevedra, España.

*Fax service* 981 130749

*Public telephones* At the marina and elsewhere.

*Car hire/taxis* In the town.

*Buses & trains* Frequent services to Santiago de Compostela, La Coruña, Vigo, etc.

*Air services* International airport at Santiago de Compostela.

## Alternative anchorages

1. Southwest of Carril mole (Q.G.8m6M Square tower 6m) and the nearby Bahia de Tierra beacon (Fl(3)R.9s6m3M, White tower, red band), and northwest of El Porrón beacon (Fl.Y.5s2M Yellow lattice metal tower), well clear of the lines of stakes which mark the shellfish beds in 3–4m over mud. Shelter is good from northwest through north to east, with more distant protection from southeast and south.

   A right-angled extension has recently been added to the short mole to protect four dinghy pontoons (convenient for landing), but there is certainly no room for a yacht. The surroundings are attractive, particularly to the north and west, and the town has the usual shops, cafés and restaurants.

2. At Villajuan (Vilaxoán), a small fishing harbour close southwest of Villagarcía breakwater. It may be possible to anchor in the shelter of the breakwater, or more probably outside, but it has no obvious charm or appeal.

3. At Villanueva de Arosa (Vilanova de Arousa), a somewhat larger harbour about 3M southwest of Villagarcía and opposite the Isla Arosa. Again Villanueva is very much a working harbour with little space for visitors, although the addition of a new outer end to the north breakwater has created a little more sheltered water.

   Approach leaving El Seijo buoy and the unlit beacon south of it to port, and pass south down the channel between the two banks of *viveros* until Villanueva mole can be approached from the west. Either anchor west of the south mole, which extends from Punta Nauxida, or explore possibilities within the harbour (avoiding the inner basin which dries out). An octopus festival is held on 29 July.

Villanueva de Arosa, seen here looking southeast, is a busy fishing harbour with little space for visitors.

## Isla de Arosa

42°34'N 8°52'W

### Charts

|  | *Island* |
|---|---|
| Admiralty | *1768* |
| Spanish | *415C, 4152, 9263* |

### Lights

buoy **Bajo Ter** 42°34'·5N 8°53'·8W
  Fl.G.3s5M Green pillar buoy

buoy **Cambados *A*** 42°34'·9N 8°51'·9W
  Fl.Y.5s3M Yellow spar buoy, × topmark

1826 **Punta del Caballo** 42°34'·3N 8°53'·1W
  Fl(4)11s11m10M
  Grey octagonal tower and white building 5m
  *Note* Reported in 1999 to be Fl(4)7s

1827 **San Julian molehead** 42°34'N 8°52'·2W
  F.R.7m1M Red masonry column 6m

### General

The Isla de Arosa comprises two lumps of land connected by an isthmus on which the village of San Julian sits. It is connected to the mainland by the O Vado bridge which is conspicuous when approaching from the north. The west coast of the island has a number of islets and numerous isolated rocks, but the approach from the north is clear.

San Julian is a working fishing village with a mussel cannery and anchorages on both sides of the isthmus. The northern one, known locally as Porto O Xufre, has more space and better depths. The most attractive prettiest anchorage is in the northwest, off the Playa Arena da Secada west of Punta Caballo, where there is a good beach.

### Approaches and anchorages

1. Porto O Xufre – from the entrance of the *ria*, pass between Isla Rúa[1818] and Piedra Seca[1824] heading 030° but do not turn further east until Punta Caballo[1826] is south of east and the starboard hand Bajo Ter buoy, marking foul ground off Punta Barbafeita, has been passed. Round Punta

Campelo (which has an off-lying rock) and enter Porto O Xufre through the many *viveros*. From the northeast, leave El Seijo buoy to port, after which the entrance to Porto O Xufre has no obstructions apart from the *viveros*.

Anchor anywhere in the bay where space can be found between the moored fishing boats and the many *viveros* (in 1999 this would have implied the western part), exposed to north and northeast. The bottom is a mixture of sand, mud and stones. More hazardous rocks fringe the extreme western shore.

2. Off the Playa Arena de la Secada, between Pta Barbafeita and Punta Caballo[1826]. The approach poses no particular problems once Bajo Ter buoy has been left to starboard.

Anchor inshore of the *viveros* at any point along the beach, which is split into two unequal parts by a central rocky promontory. The entire anchorage is exposed to the northern sector (though the *viveros* will reduce the fetch should the wind shift) with holding variable over sand and weed with some rock patches. Ashore there is a sailing school and a small bar/restaurant, but little else without walking into San Julian.

3. In the unnamed south bay, a tight anchorage beset with unmarked rocks. Approach and entry calls for good overhead light, careful visual pilotage and a current large-scale chart. From Piedra Seca[1824] shape a course for Punta Testas, skirting the headland at about 250m off in order to pass north of the dangerous Touza rock, before working as far north into the bay as space and confidence permit. Once inside, shelter is good from all directions other than southwest.

### Facilities

San Julian has a large supermarket, pharmacy and other shops, as well as restaurants, cafés and bars.

### Communications

Buses to Villagarcía and beyond.

The anchorage at Playa Arena da Secada, Isla de Arosa seen from the southwest. Orderly rows of *viveros* stretch away into the mist.

The unnamed south bay at Isla de Arosa, looking southwest. Although attractive, the approach is intricate and space very limited.

Porto O Xufre on the north side of the Isla de Arosa, looking northwest towards Punta Campelo.

# Cambados

42°31'N 8°49'W

## Charts

|  | Harbour |
| --- | --- |
| Admiralty | 1768 |
| Spanish | 415B, 4152, 9261 |

## Lights

*Approach (from within the ría)*

1816 **Bajo La Loba** 42°31'·8N 8°55'W
Q.G.8m3M
Grey conical beacon tower, green top

1806 **Praguero de Fuera** 42°31'N 8°52'·8W
Fl.G.3s8m4M White conical tower, green band

1808 **Lobeira de Cambados**
42°30'·7N 8°51'·9W Fl(4)R.12s9m5M
White conical tower, red top 10m

1810 **Bajo Golfeira** 42°30'·3N 8°52'W
Fl(3)G.12s9m4M
White conical tower, green top 10m

*Harbour*

1815 **Northwest breakwater** 42°31'N 8°49'·5W
Fl(2)R.7s9m3M Red tower on white base 7m

1815·2 **South breakwater** 42°31'N 8°49'·5W
Q.G. Green post 6m

1814 **Inner mole, south head** 42°30'·9N 8°49'·1W
Fl.R.4·5s7m8M Red and which square column 6m

## General

Cambados is a small town with an attractive and historic central square, the Praza de Fefiñanes, surrounded by imposing buildings but rendered dangerous to the unwary pedestrian by speeding traffic. It is the home of O Albariño, considered by many to be Galicia's best wine. A *sardinada* (sardine festival) is held on 25 July (Galicia Day), followed by a wine festival on the first Sunday in August.

The large north harbour would provide protection if caught by a blow whilst inside the Isla de Arosa, but has no specific provision for yachts.

## Approach

The outer approach to Cambados is shared by Isla Toja Grande and San Martín. It needs good charts and careful pilotage as there are many unmarked shoals and isolated rocks.

Starting from a position about 0·8M south of Isla Rúa[1818], get the two towers Praguero de Fuera[1806] and Lobeira de Cambados[1808] in line on 110°. The closest tower in that direction, Bajo La Loba[1816], then lies 350m northeast of the line and a fourth tower, Bajo Golfeira[1810], about 750m to the south.

Whether or not Lobeira de Cambados has been identified, head for Praguero de Fuera on a bearing of 110°, passing southwest of La Loba at a distance of at least 300m. Pass 50–100m north of Praguero, and then some 100–150m south of Lobeira. A host of *viveros* then awaits. A fairway through them on 078° leads to Cambados, at about halfway passing the unlit Orido buoy which marks a 1·5m patch. A covered rock, depth unknown, has been reported close off the harbour entrance.

The large fishing harbour at Cambados, looking northeast.

## Alternative approaches

The following approaches are also possible, though intricate, and require a current, large-scale chart:

1. *From southwest* North of the Península del Grove, either inside or outside Piedras Sálvores, thence through the *viveros* to Bajo Golfeira tower (which may have two yellow buoys, both with × topmarks, about 200m northwest and 500m due east respectively) and on to Cambados.

2. *From northwest* Between the two Islotes Jidoiros (*pedregoso* = rocky, *arenoso* = sandy) inside Bajo Piedra Seca[1824], then between Jidoiro Arenoso and Islote Corbeiro to Praguero de Fuera.

3. *From northwest* Between Islote Camallón and the Isla de Arosa to Praguero de Fuera, taking care to avoid the Laxe de Camallón rock.

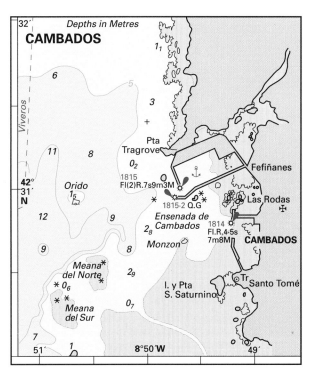

## Anchorage

Anchor in the north harbour – a trip line would be a wise precaution – or secure alongside either the quay or (temporarily) to a fishing boat. The outer angle of the breakwater is rough, and though fishing vessels lie bows-to this would not be feasible for a yacht. Much of the harbour carries little more than 2m at low water. Do not attempt to enter the basin to the south, immediately in front of the village of Cambados, as this dries out and is suitable only for very small craft.

## Facilities

Nothing specifically for the yachtsman, but shops, banks and the usual restaurants and cafés. It would be a long and dusty walk into town from the suggested anchorage, a dinghy and outboard proving their worth.

## Communications

Post office and telephones. Buses to Villagarcía and Pontevedra.

## Alternative anchorage

The large bay to the north, between the Isla de Arosa and the mainland, shoals gradually towards the shores and the bridge. It has fine beaches which, having anchored offshore in 2–4m, can be reached by dinghy.

# Isla Toja Grande (Illa de a Toxa)

42°29'N 8°50'W

## Charts

|  | *Island* |
| --- | --- |
| Admiralty | *1768* |
| Spanish | *415B, 4152* |

## Lights

### *Approach (from within the ría)*

1806 **Praguero de Fuera** 42°31'N 8°52'·8W
Fl.G.3s8m4M White conical tower, green band

1808 **Lobeira de Cambados** 42°30'·7N 8°51'·9W
Fl(4)R.12s9m5M White conical tower, red top 10m

1810 **Bajo Golfeira** 42°30'·3N 8°52'W
Fl(3)G.12s9m4M
White conical tower, green top 10m

## General

Isla Toja Grande is touted as the Galician people's favourite holiday destination, a fact borne out by the mixture of extremely wealthy homes, well-kept public gardens and vendors of second-rate souvenirs. However little of this is visible from offshore where there are attractive anchorages in the channel on the east side of the island, well sheltered except from a strong blow from due north or south. Two large hotels and a casino dominate much of the coastline but could provide an alternative to shipboard life.

Looking north between Isla Toja Grande (left) and Isla Toja Pequeña (right), with the short club náutico jetty at centre left.

## Approach

There are several approaches to Isla Toja Grande. All call for careful pilotage and good charts as there are numerous unmarked shoals and isolated rocks. Approach and departure should only be made on a rising tide as all routes must cross shifting sandbanks of uncertain depths.

1. From Bajo Golfeira tower[1810] (which may have two yellow buoys, both with × topmarks, about 200m northwest and 500m due east respectively) head towards Punta Cabreíron (the northeast corner of Toja Grande) on a bearing of approximately 103°, crossing the bank north of Isla Toja Grande at least 100m offshore and turning to 175° when deep water is reached again. On no account attempt to pass inside the rock off Punta Cabreíron.

2. Approach Punta Cabreíron on a bearing of approximately 122° from Lobeira de Cambados[1808].

3. Follow the northern approach to Cambados as far as the Orido buoy (see page 71), timing it so that departure from Orido is halfway through the rising tide. From Orido, there are two routes and the one which has the more water depends (amongst other things) on the events of the previous winter. Both have a nominal depth of 0·5m and banks on either side with rocks:

    a. Head for the middle of the gap between Toja Grande and Toja Pequeña on 175°.

    b. Continue on 078° almost to Cambados before turning onto 210° towards Punta Cabreíron and then onto 175° shortly before reaching Punta Cabreíron.

Approaches to Lobeira de Cambados and Bajo Golfeira are described on page 71.

The two prominent hotels at the southern end of Isla Toja Grande, with the bridge to the Peninsula del Grove in the background. The reef which extends from the shore between the two buildings shows clearly.

## Anchorages

1. Off the bay on the northeast side of the island in 3–5m, but kelp may be a problem.

2. South of the small *club náutico* jetty and floating pontoon – where the security guard may permit landing by dinghy – and northeast of the largest hotel in 3m or so over sand. There are moorings close inshore.

3. Between Islote Beiró (low-lying and not easy to identify against the land behind) and the southeast corner of Isla Toja Grande, where the other large hotel is situated. It should possible to find a quiet spot in 3–4m over sand north of the *viveros*.

## Facilities

Little on Isla Toja Grande other than the hotels mentioned previously, but the Peninsula del Grove is not far away.

## Communications

Taxis at the hotels, plus occasional buses.

# San Martín del Grove (San Martino del O Grove)

42°30'N 8°51'W

## Charts

|  | Harbour |
|---|---|
| Admiralty | *1768* |
| Spanish | *415B, 4152* |

## Lights

### Approach (from within the ría)
1806 **Praguero de Fuera** 42°31'N 8°52'·8W
Fl.G.3s8m4M White conical tower, green band
1808 **Lobeira de Cambados**
42°30'·7N 8°51'·9W Fl(4)R.12s9m5M
White conical tower, red top 10m
1810 **Bajo Golfeira** 42°30'·3N 8°52'W
Fl(3)G.12s9m4M
White conical tower, green top 10m
buoy **O Grove** *R* 42°30'·3N 8°51'·6W Fl(4)Y.11s3M
Yellow spar buoy, × topmark

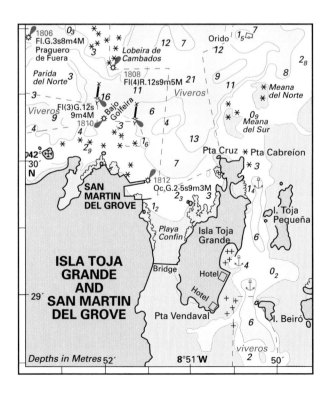

Like many of Galicia's working harbours, San Martín del Grove – seen here from a little north of east – has very limited space for visitors.

### Harbour
1812 **Breakwater** 42°29'·8N 8°51'·5W
   Oc.G.2·5s9m3M Green column on white base 8m

### General
A former fishing village with reasonable shopping and other facilities, the harbour of San Martín del Grove was improved in the early 1990s by the addition of a south mole. The peninsula as a whole is a popular holiday area, and a seafood festival takes place at El Grove on 14 September.

### Approach
From Lobeira de Cambados[1808], head towards Punta Cabreíron (the northeast corner of Toja Grande) on a bearing of approximately 122° until San Martín breakwater[1812] bears west of south, then steer a course to round its end.

Alternatively, from Bajo Golfeira tower[1810] (which may have two yellow buoys, both with × topmarks, about 200m northwest and 500m due east respectively) shape a course of approximately 103° towards Punta Cabreíron, again steering for the breakwater when it bears west of south. Do not cut the corner as foul ground projects northeast of the line from Bajo Golfeira to the breakwater end.

Approaches to Lobeira de Cambados and Bajo Golfeira are described on page 71.

### Anchorage and berthing
San Martín del Grove is a busy fishing harbour to which it is no longer possible to pay more than a brief visit, since the combination of moorings and *viveros* leaves little space to anchor and none with 360° swinging room. In addition depths are shoal at no more than 2–3m over mud and weed. Securing alongside a fishing boat might be possible for an hour or two, but the yacht should not be left unattended.

### Facilities
Water on the quayside. Several grocery stores, and many restaurants, cafés and bars.

### Communications
Post office and telephones. Buses to the mainland.

### Alternative anchorage
In the entrance to Porto de Melojo (42°29'N 8°53'W), a bay on the northwest side of the peninsula almost totally filled by moored fishing boats. It is open to the west though the inner part is protected by a northwestern mole with a red light tower. There is a mussel processing factory near the root of the mole, and a growing village on the shores of the bay with cafés, restaurants and a few shops.

Porto de Melojo, on the northwest coast of the Peninsula del Grove, looking east-southeast.

Brand new Porto Pedras Negras, seen here from the northeast, is the first 'marina village' development in Galicia and a complete contrast to the vast majority of harbours.

# Porto Pedras Negras
## (San Vicente do Mar)

42°27·5'N 8°55'W

## Tides

See Ría de Arosa, page 54

## Charts

|  | *Harbour* |
|---|---|
| Admiralty | *1758, 1768* |
| Spanish | *415B* |

## Lights

### *Approach*

**Bajo Lobeiras de Fuera** 42°27'N 8°54'·8W
  Fl(6)+LFl.15s3M Yellow post, ⍖ topmark
**Bajo Pedra Seca** 42°27'N 8°54'·7W
  Fl(3)R.9s5M Red post, ■ topmark
**Bajo Sinal de Balea** 42°27'·1N 8°54'·2W
  Fl(3)G.9s5M Green post, ▲ topmark

### *Harbour*

**Breakwater** 42°27'·5N 8°54'·9W
  Fl(4)WR.11s4/3M 305°-W-315°-R-305°
  Red column 7m

**Starboard hand beacon** 42°27'·6N 8°54'·9W
  Fl.5s1M Dark green post, ▲ topmark

## Marina radio

*Porto Pedras Negras* VHF Ch 09.

## General

In 1994 Pedras Negras was no more than a small, rocky cove where plans for a marina and associated holiday accommodation were displayed, but when revisited five years later construction appeared to be almost complete. Situated near the western end of the large Ensenada de la Lanzada on the south side of the Peninsula del Grove, the Porto Pedras Negras, ☎ 986 738430 – sometimes referred to as the Porto Deportivo San Vicente do Mar – occupies the east-facing hook formed by Punta Espiño. A small, sleepy, well-designed marina with a distinctly Mediterranean atmosphere, Porto Pedras Negras seems rather out of place on the rocky Atlantic coast of Galicia.

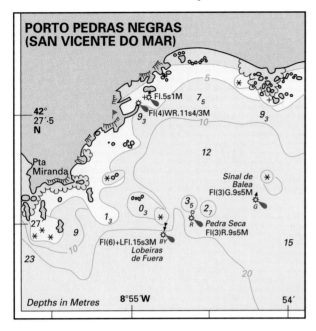

**PORTO PEDRAS NEGRAS (SAN VICENTE DO MAR)**

Depths in Metres

## Approach and entrance

Shape a course to round Punta Miranda – the southern extremity of the Peninsula del Grove – at least 600m off to enter the wide Ensenada de la Lanzada. From this position the yellow post marking the Lobeiras de Fuera rocks should be clearly visible bearing 065° or thereabouts, with the other two outer beacons lined up behind it. If in doubt continue east until they become clear.

Alter course for the marina when the breakwater end bears approximately 320° to pass equidistant between the port and starboard hand posts marking Pedra Seca and Sinal de Balea rocks respectively. The entrance itself is relatively narrow and the dark green starboard hand post (which marks a rock opposite the breakwater head rather than the inner breakwater) difficult to see until close in. Round the breakwater close to, to avoid a single rock on the channel side of the dark green beacon, and at slow speed as there is little space to manoeuvre once inside.

## Berthing

The three pontoons, all with individual fingers, provide some 135 berths of which 12 are reserved for visitors. As yet the harbour is relatively empty and new arrivals can berth wherever they wish, with depths of 3–4m at the outer pontoon. Each pontoon has a (noisy) security gate with card access. In 1999 the high season rate for a visiting yacht of just under 12m was 2,700 ptas (16·23 euros) per night inclusive.

## Facilities

*Travel-lift* 35 tonne capacity, apparently belonging to the *club náutico*.
*Water* On the pontoons.
*Showers* Behind the marina office.
*Electricity* On the pontoons.

*Fuel* Diesel and petrol from pumps on a floating pontoon below the marina office, said to carry at least 2m at low water.
*Club náutico* The Club Náutico San Vicente do Mar overlooking the marina is in fact a completely separate concern.
*Shops/provisioning* Small supermarket serving the holiday complex and local campsite, but little else.
*Cafés & restaurants* A few, including the *club náutico*.

### Communications

*Post office* In San Vicente do Mar.
*Public telephone* At the marina office.
*Car hire/taxis* Arrange via the marina office.
*Buses* Occasional buses to the mainland.

### Anchorages

In the right conditions it would be possible to anchor almost anywhere along the Playa de la Lanzada, protected from fetch from north around to east, although the low-lying isthmus would give little shelter from the wind. The sandy beach shoals gradually to the 10m line and beyond.

# Ría de Pontevedra (Ría de Marín)

### Tides

*Reference port* Lisbon
*Mean time differences* (at Marín)
HW: +60 minutes ±10; LW: +85 minutes ±5
(the above allows for the difference in time zones)
*Heights in metres*

| MHWS | MHWN | MLWN | MLWS |
|------|------|------|------|
| 3·3 | 2·6 | 1·2 | 0·5 |

### Charts

| | Approach | Ría |
|---|---|---|
| Admiralty | 3633 | 1758 |
| Spanish | 41B, 416, 925, 9250 | 416A, 9251 |

### Lights

*Approach*
1796 **Isla Sálvora** 42°27'·9N 9°00'·8W
Fl(3+1)20s38m21M 217°-clear-126°
Fl(3)20s 126°-dangerous-160°
White octagonal tower, red band 16m
1846 **Isla Ons** 42°22'·9N 8°56'·2W
Fl(4)24s125m25M Octagonal tower 12m
1884 **Monte del Faro** 42°12'·8N 8°54'·9W
Fl(2)8s185m22M Obscd 315°-016·5° over
Bajos de Los Castros and Forcados
Round tower 10m
*Ría north entrance*
buoy **Bajo Fagilda** 42°24'·9N 8°53'·7W
Q.R.6M Red pillar buoy
1850 **Bajo Picamillo** 42°24'·3N 8°53'·4W
Fl.G.5s10m8M Beacon tower 13m
1848 **Bajo Los Camoucos** 42°23'·8N 8°54'·7W
Fl(3)R.18s10m8M Beacon tower 13m
*Ría south entrance*
1873 **Punta Couso** 42°18'·6N 8°51'·3W
Fl(3)WG.10·5s18m10/8M 060°-G-096°-W-190°-G-000° Round masonry tower 5m

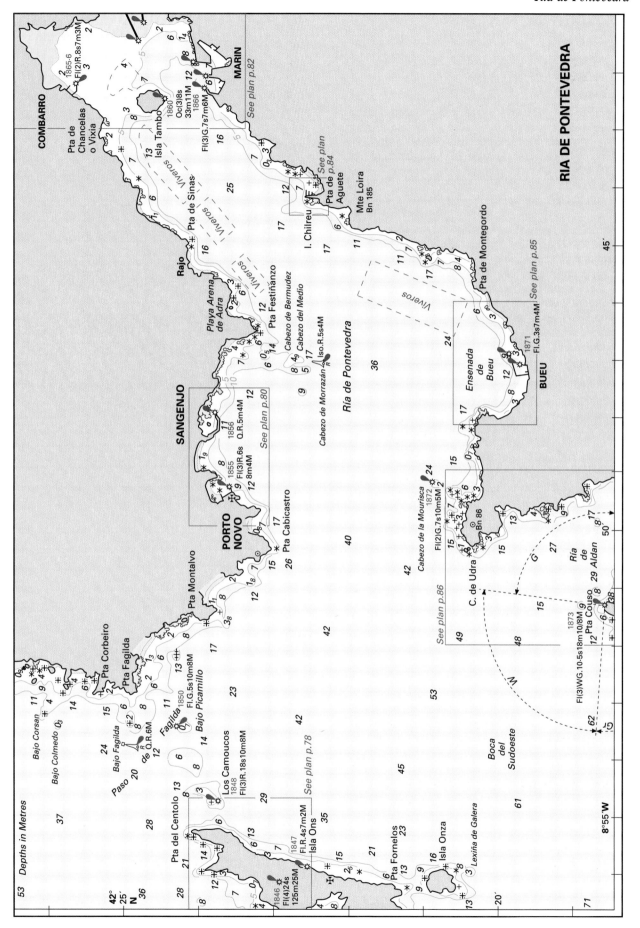

# RIA DE PONTEVEDRA

COMBARRO

Pta de
Chancelas
o Vixia

MARIN

See plan p.82

1865-6
Fl(2)R.8s7m3M

Isla Tambo

1860
Oc(3)8s
33m11M

1866
Fl(3)G.7s7m6M

Pta de Sinas

Rajo

Viveros

Viveros

Viveros

Playa Arena
de Adra

Pta Festiñanzo

Cabezo de Bermudez

Cabezo del Medio

Cabezo de Morrazán

Iso.R.5s4M

Ría de Pontevedra

I. Chilreu

Pta de
Aguete

See plan
p.84

Mte Loira
Bn 185

Pta de Montegordo

See plan p.85

1871
Fl.G.3s7m4M

BUEU

Ensenada
de
Bueu

SANGENJO

1856
Q.R.5m4M

See plan p.80

1855
Fl(3)R.6s

8m4M

PORTO
NOVO

Pta Cabicastro

Pta Montalvo

Pta Corbeiro

Pta Fagilda

Fl.G.5s10m8M

1850
Fl.G.5s10m8M

Bajo
Picamillo

Fagilda

Q.R.6M

Pta del Centolo

Los Camoucos

1848
Fl(3)R.18s10m8M

See plan p.78

1847
Fl.R.4s7m2M

Isla Ons

1846
Fl(4)24s
125m25M

Bajo Corsan

Bajo Colmedo

Paso

Bajo Fagilda

Pta Fornelos

Isla Onza

Lexiña de Galera

Cabezo de la Mourisca

1872
Fl(2)G.7s10m5M

Bn 86

See plan p.86

C. de Udra

Ría
de
Aldan

1873
Fl(3)WG.10.5s18m10/8M

Pta Couso

Boca
del
Sudoeste

Depths in Metres

42°
25'
N

1872 **Cabezo de la Mourisca** 42°20'·9N 8°49'·2W
   Fl(2)G.7s10m5M Beacon tower
*Ría*
buoy **Cabezo de Morrazán** 42°22'·5N 8°46'·9W
   Iso.R.5s4M Red pillar buoy

## General

The Ría de Pontevedra has only recently offered secure berthing to visiting yachts, either in the large all-weather marina at Sangenjo on the north coast or, in south or west winds, on one of the Real Club de Mar pontoons at Aguete.

It is not so interesting as the *rías* further north but Combarro, on the northern shore near the head of the *ría*, has remained largely unspoilt and is well worth a visit. It is also possible to reach the old city of Pontevedra by dinghy or small yacht, though for many the 12m air height would be the limiting factor. Landing is not permitted on Isla Tambo, which is a military restricted area with an unusual but conspicuous lighthouse. The Spanish Naval College has its home at Marín, a commercial and fishing harbour which offers scant welcome to yachts.

### Approach

Unless stopping at the Isla Ons, the entrance to the *ría* proper lies between the unmarked Punta Cabicastro, which has a rock off it, and Cabo de Udra, which is surrounded by foul ground.

From the north, give a good berth to Isla Sálvora[1796] which has off-lying reefs to the southwest. There are reefs and banks between the north end of Isla Ons and Punta Fagilda on the mainland, but other than Fagilda rock north of Bajo Picamillo[1850] and marked by a red can buoy these would not worry a yacht except in rough weather. They are easily avoided either by taking the channel west of Los Camoucos tower[1848] (Canal de los Camoucos), or by passing up to 0·5M either side of Picamillo tower, which itself is at the northeast end of a small 3m patch about 150m long. Continue southeast and the entrance opens to the east.

From the southwest, take a line midway between Isla Onza and the north end of the Islas Cíes. There are banks off the former and, more dangerously, rocks and banks up to 1·2M off Islas Cíes. Passing between the islands in the green sector of Punta Couso[1873] on a heading of 040° clears these dangers, plus those off Punta Couso and Cabo de Udra (note that Punta Couso light is not visible south of its green sector). The entrance to the *ría* is clear of dangers when Cabezo de la Mourisca[1872] bears east.

From Ría de Vigo, keep more than 400m off the coast between Cabo del Home and Punta Couso. When past Punta Couso, give Cabo de Udra at least 500m clearance and continue until Cabezo de la Mourisca bears east.

# Isla Ons

42°23'N 8°55'W

## Charts

|  | *Island* |
|---|---|
| Admiralty | *1758* |
| Spanish | *9251* |

## Lights
### Approach
1796 **Isla Sálvora** 42°27'·9N 9°00'·8W
   Fl(3+1)20s38m21M 217°-clear-126°
   Fl(3)20s 126°-dangerous-160°
   White octagonal tower, red band 16m
1884 **Monte del Faro** 42°12'·8N 8°54'·9W
   Fl(2)8s185m22M
   Obscd 315°-016·5° over Bajos de Los Castros and Forcados Round tower 10m
1848 **Bajo Los Camoucos** 42°23'·8N 8°54'·7W
   Fl(3)R.18s10m8M Beacon tower 13m
### Island
1846 **Isla Ons** 42°22'·9N 8°56'·2W
   Fl(4)24s125m25M Octagonal tower 12m
1847 **Almacén mole** 42°22'·6N 8°55'·9W
   Fl.R.4s7m2M Red round tower 5m

## General

A rugged and attractive island with relatively few permanent inhabitants though much visited by campers in the summer using ferries from Porto Novo and Bueu to the jetty at Almacén[1847]. A pleasant day visit can be made to the east coast though shelter is slender. There are no anchorages on the west coast.

The small southern island of Onza (or Onceta) is a bird sanctuary where landing is forbidden.

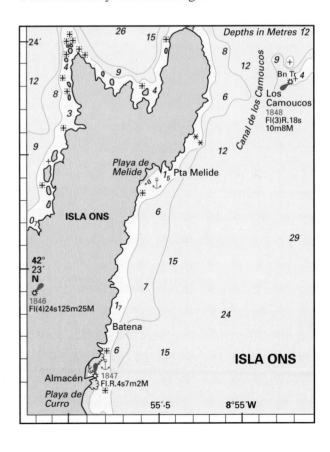

The recently-extended mole at Almacén on the Isla Ons, looking northwest, with the island's powerful lighthouse on the skyline.

## Approach

As for Ría de Pontevedra, opposite.

## Anchorages

1. Yachts sometimes go alongside the Almacén mole[1847] at the Playa del Curro, but it is not a good place to lie. There is little room and the ferries have first claim on the available space. There are reefs extending north and south of the entrance and also off-lying rocks, but it is possible to anchor east-northeast of the molehead in 12m or more over rock and weed.

   In 1999 a number of visitors' buoys were in position either side of the molehead. It is understood that they are maintained by the Casa Checko, to whom payment should presumably be made, but holding capacity, etc is not known. Further information on this point would be welcome.

2. The Playa de Melide, almost 1M north of the Almacén mole. Anchor in 4m over sand, rock and weed. The anchorage is sheltered from north through west to southwest but, like all the possible anchorages on Isla Ons, it would have to be vacated smartly if the wind gained an easterly component. The beach is favoured by nudists.

3. Another short-stay possibility in a light northerly is the small bay between Punta Fedorento and Punta Rabo d'Egua on the south coast.

## Facilities

There are bars and restaurants in Almacén, very welcome after a hot walk from the north of the island.

## Communications

Ferries from Almacén to Bueu and Porto Novo.

# Porto Novo

42°24'N 8°49'W

## Charts

|  | *Harbour* |
|---|---|
| Admiralty | *1758* |
| Spanish | *9251, 4161* |

## Lights

### Harbour

1855 **Breakwater** 42°23'·6N 8°49'W
   Fl(3)R.6s8m4M Red column 6m

## General

Porto Novo is a busy, and quite picturesque, fishing village which is growing as a holiday resort – enough to merit a morning craft market along the west side of the harbour. Though once an anchorage offering reasonable shelter, it is now packed with yacht and smallcraft moorings and anchoring inside the harbour is no longer possible.

The snug – and rather scenic – bay at Porto Novo, looking northwest. Sadly little room now remains for visitors.

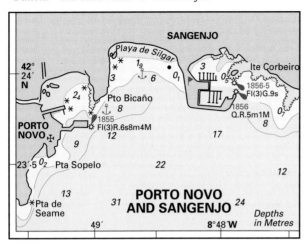

## Approach

No hazards, though headlands should be given an offing of at least 200m – in particular Punta Cabicastro which has an off-lying rock, and Punta Bicaño, northeast of the molehead, which has a reef with a rock (Laxe) off it less than 200m from the mole.

## Anchorage

Plans to build yachts pontoons running south from the inner mole have not materialised, and while out of season it may be possible to borrow a mooring via the Club Náutico de Porto Novo, ☎ 986 723266, this is unlikely in July or August. It is possible to anchor off the entrance in 5–8m over sand, taking care not to impede fishing boats or the Isla Ons ferries which berth on the inner end of the breakwater, but this position would offer no protection from east through to southwest.

## Facilities

Water from the fishermen's cooperative on the quay plus the usual shops, cafés and restaurants, but nothing specifically for yachts. The *club náutico* – which is listed as an official supplier of Spanish charts – has an office on the first floor of a somewhat anonymous building (though notable for its yellow awnings) shared with the fishermen's cooperative and other harbour concerns.

## Communications

Post office and telephones. Taxis, and buses to Pontevedra and beyond.

# Sangenjo (Sanxenxo)

42°24'N 8°48'W

## Charts

|  | *Harbour* |
|---|---|
| Admiralty | *1758* |
| Spanish | *9251, 4161* |

## Lights

Harbour
1856 **Breakwater** 42°23'·9N 8°47'·9W
   Q.R.5m1M Post with red lantern
1856·5 **Starboard beacon** 42°23'·9N 8°47'·9W
   Fl(3)G.9s4m2M Green beacon, ▲ topmark

## Marina radio

*Portomar Sangenjo* VHF Ch 09.

## General

Until very recently a crowded holiday resort with a small and equally crowded harbour, in 1999 the finishing touches were being put to an impressive marina which will eventually contain some 700 berths. Having displaced local fishermen from their previous place on the mole, a new harbour was planned for them to the northeast (though work had yet to begin).

Portomar Sangenjo in September 1999, before it was fully completed – when finished it will berth around 700 yachts. Seen here from almost due south.

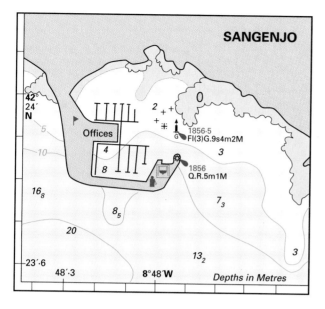

Sangenjo cannot claim to be an attractive town, and such is its popularity as a lively tourist resort with disco action through the small hours that the northern part of the marina may be noisy at night. However visitors are much more likely to be berthed in the quieter area to the south.

A *fiesta* in honour of San Ginés is held on 25 August, and a procession to the nearby Praia de La Lanzada takes place on the last Sunday in that month.

## Approach

No hazards, though headlands should be given an offing of at least 200m – in particular Punta Cabicastro which has an off-lying rock. There are rocks northeast of the relatively narrow entrance, but these are well buoyed.

## Berthing

On arrival yachts should secure anywhere in the central pool (see plan) prior to being allocated a berth. Only 300 of the planned 700 berths were installed by July 1999 – completion is anticipated by 2001 – but even so the marina was a long way from full. However a few yachts of considerable size were in place and it is claimed that when finished the marina will be able to accommodate yachts of up to 50m. Currently 30 berths are reserved specifically for visitors, but this will have increased to 70 by completion. All berths have individual finger pontoons.

The marina staff are friendly and helpful and good English is spoken in the office, ☎ 986 720517 *Fax* 986 720578. In 1999 the high season rate for a visiting yacht of just under 12m was 3,898 ptas (23·43 euros) per night, with an additional charge of 700 ptas (4·20 euros) per night for electricity and 300 ptas (1·80 euros) per night for water.

## Facilities

*Boatyard, engineers, electronic & radio repairs* Expected to be operational with workshops at the end of the breakwater by 2000 or 2001.

*Travel-lift* 70 tonne capacity, with no shortage of hardstanding.

*Sailmaker/sail repairs* Arrange via the marina office.

*Chandlery* In the town – may move to the marina complex in due course.

*Charts* In Vigo.

*Water* On the pontoons.

*Showers* In the marina building.

*Launderette* In the town.

*Electricity* On the pontoons.

*Fuel* Pumps due to be installed near the travel-lift by summer 2000.

*Bottled gas* Camping Gaz available in the town, or arrange via the marina office.

*Ice* At the marina office.

*Club náutico* The pleasant and distinctly upmarket Real Club Náutico de Sangenjo has premises on the root of the breakwater, including a smart upstairs restaurant with excellent views. It is not connected with the marina development.

*Weather forecast* Daily at the marina office.

*Banks* In the town, with card facilities.

*Shops/provisioning* Several supermarkets, including one opposite the root of the mole.

*Produce market* In the town.

*Cafés, restaurants & hotels* Thousands! A restaurant is planned for the upper floor of the marina building, probably by summer 2000.

*Medical services* In the town.

### Communications

*Post office* In the town.

*Mailing address*
  c/o **Portomar Sanxenxo**, Avda Augusto González Besada s/n, 36960 Sanxenxo, Pontevedra, España. *Fax service* 986 720578

*Public telephones* At the marina office and elsewhere.

*Car hire/taxis* In the town, or arrange via the marina office.

*Buses* To Pontevedra and beyond.

### Alternative anchorages

1. Off Playa de Silgar, a sandy beach some 750m in length between Porto Novo and Sangenjo. Anchor in 5m or less over sand with patches of weed and rock. The Playa de Silgar is a popular bathing beach backed by a long promenade, with a floating boom some distance from the beach to protect swimmers from water-skiers, etc.

2. 2M southeast of Sangenjo off Playa Arena de Adra (42°24'N 8°46'W), close east of Punta Festiñanzo, or in the next bay eastwards off the village of Rajó (Raxo), where a few fishing boats lie on moorings and there is a short stone quay.

   There are shallow patches up to 600m southwest of Punta Festiñanzo, but these are so amply cleared by Cabezo de Morrazán port hand buoy that a yacht can safely pass about halfway between the buoy and the shore. Both anchorages are exposed from east around to south, and would probably feel a southwesterly swell.

Looking north across the new breakwater at Combarro, one of Galicia's most attractive old harbour villages.

# Combarro

42°26'N 8°42'W

## Charts

|  | Harbour |
|---|---|
| Admiralty | 1758 |
| Spanish | 4162, 9251 |

## Lights

*Harbour*

1865·6 **Breakwater** 42° 25'·7N 8°42'·3W
  Fl(2)R.8s7m3M Red over grey tower 6m
  (the old north mole is no longer lit)

## General

Combarro claims to be the only Galician fishing village still left unspoiled, and though this is not strictly true as there has been considerable development away from the water's edge, it is undoubtedly worth visiting if conditions permit. At first the heavily restored older section, where stone houses with balconies supported by granite pillars crowd onto narrow flagged passages, may strike one as somewhat over sanitised, but this is unfair – Combarro is still very much alive and the majority of buildings are homes rather than tourist shops or restaurants (though there is no shortage of either). Not surprisingly Combarro features high on the Galician coach tour circuit, and a visit is best planned for mid-week.

Although it is possible to take a motorboat or small yacht up to Pontevedra itself – see Upriver, below – an alternative plan would be to leave the boat at Combarro and explore the upper reaches of the *ría* by dinghy.

## Approach

Best approach lies close around the south side of Isla Tambo as depths shoal to 1·5m between the island and the shore, where *viveros* may also be positioned.

## Anchorage

In 1997 a new breakwater was built about 300m southwest of the old, relatively short, mole, giving

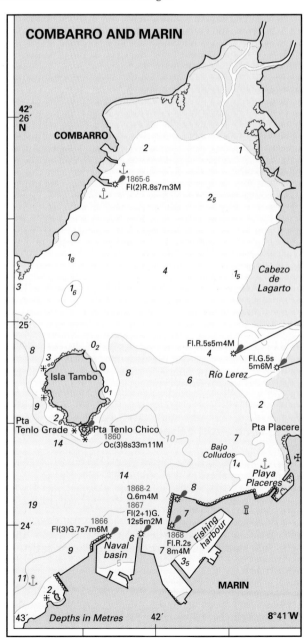

much improved protection from the southwest. It is possible to anchor between the two in 2–2·5m, or south of the new breakwater in around 3m. Depths shoal rapidly once northeast of the old mole. Thick weed can prove a problem while getting the anchor to set, but once it has worked through into the mud below holding is excellent and several yachts report sitting out gales at Combarro without problem.

It may be possible to lie alongside the new breakwater for short periods, though it is in fairly constant use by local mussel boats. Dinghies are best left at the steps on the northeast side of the old mole (which in any case gives closer access to the village).

## Facilities

Several supermarkets, banks, hardware store, etc, plus a mornings-only fruit market in the square. Many cafés and restaurants on the waterfront and in the old section, though due to its tourist appeal prices tend to be well above the local average.

## Communications

Post office and telephones. Frequent buses to Pontevedra and thence to Vigo or Santiago de Compostela.

## Upriver

Pontevedra is the capital of the province and an interesting old city with good shopping. There is a small marina on the river near the old town, but access height is limited to 12m by an electricity cable and two bridges. Training walls (Fl.R.5s 5m4M and Fl.G.5s5m6M) with markers define the channel, which is shallow on the south side – for best water keep to the northern third. There is an underwater obstruction carrying no more than 1m at low water springs in the centre of the channel between the electricity cable and the new bridge.

The *fiesta* of San Benito takes place at Pontevedra on 11 July.

# Marin

42°24'N 8°42'W

## Charts

| | *Harbour* |
|---|---|
| Admiralty | *1758* |
| Spanish | *9251, 4162* |

## Lights

### *Approach*
buoy **Outfall** 42°24'·4N 8°42'·9W
 Fl(4)Y Yellow conical buoy, × topmark
1860 **Punta Tenlo Chico, Isla Tambo** 42°24'·5N 8°42'·5W
 Oc(3)8s33m11M
 Concrete tower, round over conical

### *Harbour*
1866 **West breakwater** 42°23'·9N 8°42'·3W
 Fl(3)G.7s7m6M
 Round green column on square white base 6m
1867 **Commercial mole** 42°24'N 8°42'·1W
 Fl(2+1)G.12s5m2M
 Green round column on square base, red band 4m
1868 **NE wharf, SW corner** 42°24'·1N 8°41'·8W
 Fl.R.2s8m4M Octagonal masonry tower 4m
1868·2 **NE wharf, NW corner** 42°24'·2N 8°41'·8W
 Q.6m4M
 Black round tower on square yellow base 5m

## Port radio

*Marín Prácticos* VHF Ch 12, 16.

## General

The site of the Spanish Naval College, and a busy commercial and fishing port also engaged in shipbuilding, Marín is unsuitable for yachts (though included in these pages as a possible port of refuge). The west basin and the off-lying Isla Tambo are restricted military areas and there is a particularly noxious paper factory to the northeast of the town emitting sulphurous smells. The Naval College has its own basin for yachts and other small craft, but it is not available to visitors.

The large commercial harbour at Marin, seen from the west.

In 1999 a pair of small basins behind inner and outer moles were under construction close northeast of the main harbour. However judging by size and approach depths these are intended solely for local dinghies and smallcraft and hold no possibilities for visiting yachts.

### Approach

Head for Punta Tenlo Chico[1860] until the entrance is open.

### Anchorages

1. East of the northeast wharf, off the Playa Placeres where a smallcraft basin was under construction in 1999 (see above). Depths shoal some distance offshore, with less than 2m over Bajo Colludos.
2. West of the west mole, but very exposed to the southwest and west and likely to be uncomfortable.

### Facilities

Food and other shops. Ship repair facilities geared to fishermen and coasters.

### Communications

Post office and telephones. Buses and trains to Pontevedra. Taxis.

# Aguete

42°23'N 8°44'W

### Charts

|  | Harbour |
|---|---|
| Admiralty | 1758 |
| Spanish | 9251 |

### Lights

An olive green column some 7m in height has been in place at the end of the mole for several years, but as of March 2000 it remained unlit.

The pontoons of the Real Club de Mar Aguete, tucked behind the headland of that name on the south coast of the Ría de Pontevedra and seen here from the southwest.

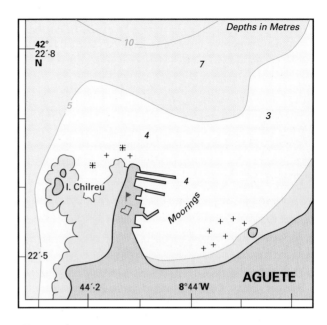

### General

Work started in the early 1990s to create a small marina in the open bay east of Punta de Aguete, protected from the west behind a wide mole but open to the north. By 1999 it was still incomplete and further work was not anticipated for several years. The surroundings are attractive and unspoilt, but it is a steep 1km walk from the harbour up to the village on the main Bueu–Marín road so it would be wise to arrive with the yacht already stocked up. The pontoons are administered by the Real Club de Mar Aguete, ☎ 986 702373/703205 *Fax* 986 702708, which has a large clubhouse – built to resemble a ship's bridge – overlooking the harbour.

Aguete is one of many harbours in Galicia to celebrate the *fiesta* of the Virgen del Carmen on 16 July with a waterborne procession. A lifesize statue of the Virgin is carried down to the harbour, loaded carefully aboard the club launch and taken for a tour of the harbour and beyond. Local craft of every size, all decked out with flags and bunting, provide a colourful escort.

### Approach

Straightforward from within the *ría*. There are rocks close north and west of Punta de Aguete – keep an offing of at least 350m until the mole (with the prominent white clubhouse) bears west of south. Rocks also fringe the northeast end of the beach.

### Berthing

In 1999 three pontoons ran eastwards from the wide mole, with small motorboats on the furthest in, a few yachts alongside the central one in 4–5m depths, and the outer one – understood to be a wave-break pontoon, though provided with cleats – completely empty. The bay itself was full of smallcraft moorings. Eventual plans are for bows-to berthing for about 100 boats with ten or twelve slots reserved for visitors. Other than the scant protection provided by the outer pontoon, both anchorage and moorings are fully exposed to winds and swell from the northern quadrant. In 1999 the high season rate for a visiting yacht of just under 12m was 1,740 ptas (10·46 euros) per night inclusive.

## Facilities

*Travel-lift* A slot has been built into the wide mole, but as of September 1999 there was no travel-lift to fill it.

*Water* On the pontoons.

*Showers* At the Real Club de Mar.

*Electricity* On the pontoons.

*Fuel* Diesel and petrol both available.

*Club náutico* The pleasant and welcoming Real Club de Mar Aguete has a terrace bar overlooking the harbour and a good restaurant.

*Banks* In the village on the main road about 1km away.

*Shops/provisioning* A few shops in the village, but it would be a tedious walk.

*Cafés & restaurants* The most convenient is undoubtedly at the Real Club de Mar.

## Communications

*Post office* On the main road.

*Mailing address*
c/o **Real Club de Mar Augete**, Avda Gago de Mendoza, Aguete 167 (Seixo), Apdo Correos 75, Marin, Pontevedra, España.
*Fax service* 986 702708.

*Public telephones* At the Real Club de Mar.

*Car hire/taxis* Arrange via the Real Club de Mar.

*Buses* Buses along the main road, north to Marín and Pontevedra and south to Cangas and Vigo.

# Bueu
42°19'·5N 8°47'W

## Charts

|           | *Harbour*  |
|-----------|------------|
| Admiralty | *1758, 2548* |
| Spanish   | *9251, 4163* |

## Lights

*Harbour*
1871 **Breakwater** 42°19'·8N 8°47'W
  Fl.G.3s7m4M Aluminium post 8m
1870 **Inner mole** 42°19'·7N 8°47'·1W
  Fl(2)R.6s7m4M Red framework tower 6m

## General

Bueu (pronounced 'bwayo') is a small fishing and market town with good beaches, which is developing into a minor tourist resort. The breakwater was extended in the late 1990s.

A separate west harbour marked on some editions of Spanish chart *9251* does not exist.

## Approach

Viveros are anchored off the Bueu shore but a wide north/south fairway has been left for the approach to the beach and the harbour, used by fishing boats and ferries.

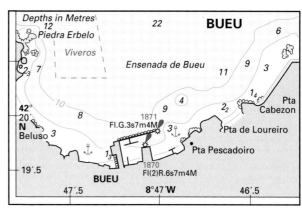

## Anchorage

The inner harbour is reserved for fishing boats, but it may be possible to lie alongside the outside wall of the inner mole, clear of the steps at its outer end which are used by local ferries. Failing this, anchor off the beach clear of the smallcraft moorings in 4–6m over mud. There is a small pontoon with a hammerhead a little way down the beach to the east where one might land by dinghy.

Alternatively, anchor west of the harbour in 3–5m over sand and mud, a spot which is reported to suffer surprisingly little swell in spite of being open from northwest through to northeast.

## Facilities

Supermarkets and other shops as well as the inevitable cafés and restaurants, but nothing specifically for yachts.

## Communications

Post office and telephones. Buses north to Marín and Pontevedra and south to Cangas and Vigo. Ferries to Isla Ons.

## Alternative anchorage

The Ría de Aldán (42°17'N 8°49'W), between Punta Couso and Cabo de Udra, is more a large bay

Bueu harbour, looking southwest. The outer breakwater has recently been extended.

than a full-scale *ría* and is entirely exposed to the north and northwest. However it is quiet and rather pretty, and worth a visit in suitable conditions for its rocky shores and small secluded beaches. There are good walks through the woods on the peninsula up ancient, steep, stone-paved tracks.

Anchorage is feasible in several of the small bays on the west side of the *ría* (though note the various off-lying rocks) protected from southeast through west to northwest, or near its head amongst the smallcraft moorings, with shelter from all directions other than northwest and north. There are numerous *viveros* lining the west side of the *ría* but space should be found inside them. The eastern side of the bay is deeper and somewhat prone to swell.

There is a short mole (Fl(2)R.10s5m5M Red round tower 8m) on the east shore near the head of the *ría*, backed by a quay and shellfish processing plant, where it might be possible to lie alongside briefly in calm conditions. However it appears relatively shallow – prospect first by dinghy. The village of Aldán offers basic facilities including shops and restaurants.

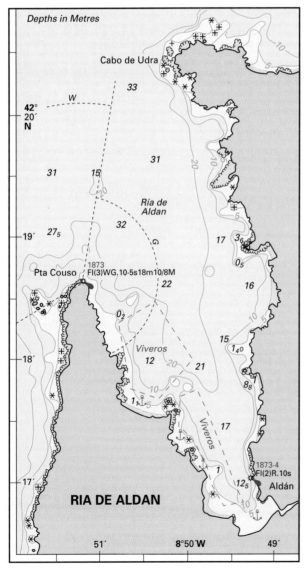

# Ría de Vigo

## Tides
*Reference port* Lisbon
*Mean time differences* (at Vigo)
HW: +50 minutes ±10; LW: +75 minutes ±10
(the above allows for the difference in time zones)
*Heights in metres*

| MHWS | MHWN | MLWN | MLWS |
|------|------|------|------|
| 3·4 | 2·7 | 1·3 | 0·5 |

## Charts

| | Approach | Ría |
|---|---|---|
| Admiralty | 3633 | 2548 |
| Spanish | 41B, 416, 417, 416B, 924, 925 | 4165, 4166 |
| Imray | C18 | C18 |

## Lights
### Approach
1846 **Isla Ons** 42°22'·9N 8°56'·2W
Fl(4)24s125m25M Octagonal tower 12m
1884 **Monte del Faro** 42°12'·8N 8°54'·9W
Fl(2)8s185m22M
Obscd 315°-016·5° over Bajos de Los Castros and Forcados
Round tower 10m
1916 **Cabo Silleiro Aeromarine** 42°06'·2N 8°53'·8W
Fl(2+1)15s83m24M
White tower, red bands, on white building 30m
Siren Mo(S)30s 900m NNW Old light tower
*0935* Radiobeacon *RO* 293·5kHz 100M
(Reliable sector 020°-145°)
### Ría north entrance
1873 **Punta Couso** 42°18'·6N 8°51'·3W
Fl(3)WG.10·5s18m10/8M
060°-G-096°-W-190°-G-000°
Round masonry tower 5m
1876 **Cabo del Home Ldg Lts on 129°** 42°15'·2N 8°52'·4W
*Front* Fl.3s36m9M 090°-vis-180°
White round tower 18m
1876·1 *Rear* **Punta Subrido,** 815m from front,
Oc.6s51m11M 090°-vis-180°
White round tower 13m
1874 **Punta Robaleira** 42°15'N 8°52'·4W
Fl(2)WR.7·5s25m11/9M Red tower 6m
300·5°-W-321·5°-R-090°, 115·5°-R-170·5°
1882 **Punta Monte Agudo, Islas Cíes** 42°14'·6N 8°54'·2W
Fl.G.5s23m9M 146·5°-vis-334° White tower 5m
buoy **Punta Subrido, *No.2*** 42°14'·5N 8°51'·8W
Fl(4)R.10s5M Red can buoy
### Ría middle entrance
1884 **Monte del Faro** 42°12'·8N 8°54'·9W
Fl(2)8s185m22M
Obscd 315°-016·5° over Bajos de Los Castros and Forcados
Round tower 10m
1886 **Punta Canabal** 42°12'·7N 8°54'·8W
Fl(3)20s63m9M White tower 10m
### Ría south entrance
1889 **Islote Boeiro** 42°10'·7N 8°54'·6W
Fl(2)R.8s21m6M
White conical beacon tower 6m
1888 **Cabo Vicos, Isla de San Martin** 42°11'·5N 8°53'·5W
Fl(3)R.9s92m7M 210·5°-vis-108°
White tower 7m

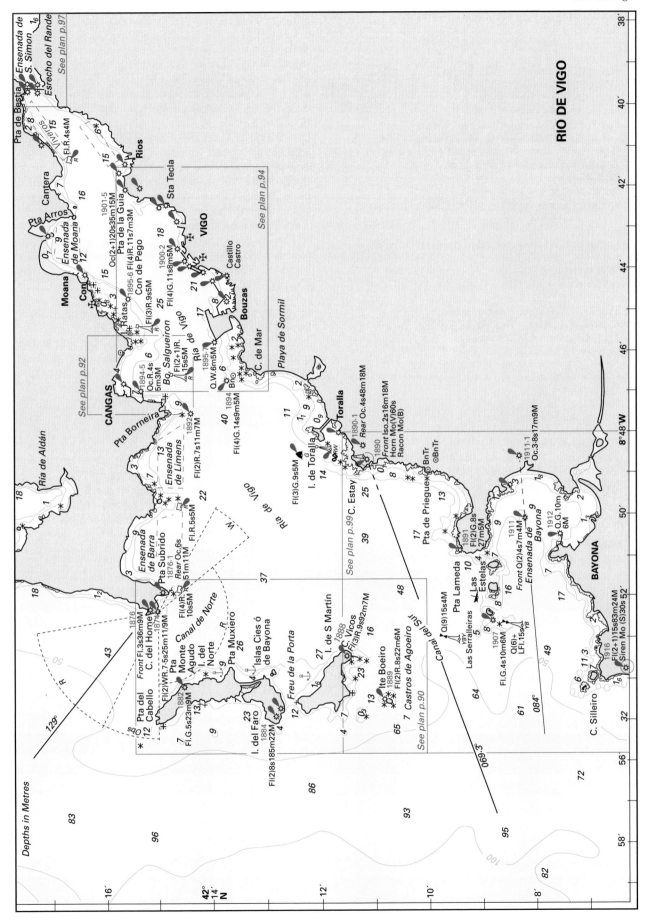

RIO DE VIGO

Depths in Metres

Ría de Aldán

Pta de Bestia
Ensenada de S. Simón
*Estrecho del Rande*
See plan p.97

Fl.R.4s4M

Pta Cantera

Rios

Pta Arros

Moana
Ensenada de Moana
Con
Ratas
1901·5 Oc(2+1)20s35m15M
Pta de la Guia
Con de Pego
1895·6 Fl(4)R.11s7m3M
Fl(3)R.9s5M
VIGO
Sta Tecla

CANGAS
See plan p.92
1894·5 Oc.R.4s 5m3M
Bq. Salguerron
Fl(2+1)R. 15s5M
1895· Q.W.6m5M
Bñ
Fl(4)G.11s8m5M
1900·2
Castillo Castro
Bouzas
Playa de Sormil
C. de Mar
See plan p.94

Pta Borneira
1892 Fl(2)R.7s11m7M
Ensenada de Limens
40 1894 Fl(4)G.14s9m5M
Toralla
1890·1 Rear Oc.4s48m18M
Front Iso.2s16m18M
Horn Mo(V)60s
Racon Mo(B)

Fl(3)G.9s5M
I. de Toralla
Fl(2)R.7s11m7M
1890
C. Estay
Pta de Priegue
BnTr
BnTr
See plan p.99

Ensenada de Barra
Pta Subrido
Rear Oc.6s 51m11M
1876·1
Fl.R.5s5M
Ría de Vigo

Canal de Norte
Fl(4)R. 10s5M
1876
Front Fl.3s36m9M
C. del Home 1874
Pta del Cabello
Fl(2)WR.7.5s25m11/9M
Pta Monte Agudo
I. del Norte
Pta Muxieiro
Islas Cíes ó de Bayona
1882 Fl.G.5s23m9M
13

Freu de la Porta
I. de S Martin
1888
C. Vicos
Fl(3)R.9s92m7M
tte Boeiro
1889 Fl(2)R.8s22m6M
Castros de Agoeiro
See plan p.90

I. del Faro
1884 Fl(2)8s185m22M
Fl.G.5s23m9M

069·3

084°

Canal del Sur
Q(9)15s4M
Pta Lameda
Las Serralleiras
Las Estelas
1891 Fl(2)G.8s
1907 Fl.G.4s10m6M
Q(6)+ LFl.15s
Front Q(2)4s7m4M
1911 O.Q.10m 6M
1912
Ensenada de Bayona
1911·1 Oc.3·8s17m9M

BAYONA

C. Silleiro
1916 Fl(2+1)15s83m24M
Siren Mo (Sl)30s 52'

1890 **Cabo Estay Ldg Lts on 069·3°** 42°11'·1N
8°48'·9W
*Front* Iso.2s16m18M 066·3°-vis-072·3°
Red pyramidal tower, white bands 8m
Horn Mo(V)60s 27m ENE. Racon Mo(B) 22M
*0933* Radiobeacon *VS* 312·5kHz 50M
1890·1 *Rear*, 660m from front,
Oc.4s48m18M 066·3°-vis-072·3°
Red pyramidal tower, white bands 7m
buoy **Las Serralleiras north** 42°09'·4N 8°53'·1N
Q(9)15s4M West cardinal buoy, ⚑ topmark
1907 **Las Serralleiras** 42°08'·8N 8°52'·6W
Fl.G.4s9m6M
White conical beacon tower 6m
1891 **Punta Lameda** 42°09'·4N 8°51'W
Fl(2)G.8s27m5M White tower 4m
*Ria*
buoy **Punta Corbeiro (Salaiño, No.4)** 42°14'·6N
8°49'·7W
Fl.R.5s5M Red can buoy
buoy **Isla de Toralla (Bajo Bondaña, No.1)**
42°12'·4N 8°48'·5W
Fl(3)G.9s5M Green conical buoy
1892 **Bajo Borneira, No.6** 42°14'·4N 8°47'·5W
Fl(2)R.7s11m7M White tower, red top 11m
1894 **Bajo Tofiño, No.3** 42°13'·7N 8°46'·7W
Fl(4)G.14s9m5M White tower, green top
buoy **Bajo Salguerión, No.8** 42°14'·6N 8°46'·6W
Fl(2+1)R.15s5M
Red pillar buoy, ■ topmark
buoy **Bajo Rodeira, No.10** 42°15'·1N 8°45'·5W
Fl(3)R.9s5M Red pillar buoy
1895·6 **Con de Pego** 42°15'·5N 8°44'·9W
Fl(4)R.11s7m3M Red round beacon tower 4m
1901·5 **Punta de la Guia** 42°15'·6N 8°42'·1W
Oc(2+1)20s35m15M
White round masonry tower 21m
*Note* There are sound signals on Cabo Silleiro[1917] and
Cabo Estay[1890].

## General

From a cruising point of view most would agree that this is the least attractive of the *rías*. Although the setting is fine, it is dominated by Vigo with its very extensive and busy docks and factories, its surrounding suburbs, dormitory towns and holiday developments. Practically all requirements, ship and domestic, can be met by the city.

However, despite its dominance it is still possible to escape Vigo and there are other interesting places to visit. The giant Rande suspension bridge spans the *ría* at its narrowest point, just east of the city, with the attractive Ensenada de San Simón and town of Redondela beyond, while the anchorages off the Islas Cíes are some of the most attractive in all the *rías*.

Legend has it that a fleet of treasure galleons laden with silver foundered in the *ría* in 1702, but no trace has yet been found.

## Approach

The northern entrance (Canal del Norte) lies between the northernmost island of the Cíes group, named both Isla del Norte and de Monte Agudo, and the Cabo del Home. It presents no problems in clear weather provided a good berth is given to the dangers which extend from the north end of the Isla del Norte. These are cleared if Punta Couso[1873] bears more than 060° (the green sector of the light). Steer for Cabo del Home on a heading of 129° until the leading marks[1876] can be identified. Steer on them until it is possible to turn down the centre of the channel on a heading of about 160° towards the distinctive peak of Monte Ferro (at night towards the light on Punta Lameda[1891]. When Punta Robaleira[1874] bears northeast, turn up the marked channel towards the prominent Castillo del Castro overlooking Vigo, passing south of the port hand buoy *No.2* off Punta Subrido. If using this entrance on a fine afternoon, the tower block on Isla de Toralla may be visible from well out to sea.

The middle entrance, immediately south of Monte del Faro[1884], is feasible in calm conditions provided that one heads for the centre of the channel and maintains a centre line all the way through. It should not be attempted at night or in rough weather or poor visibility without good local knowledge.

The southern entrance (Canal del Sur), is the main shipping channel and lies between the Islote de Boeiro[1889], off Isla de San Martín, the southernmost of the Islas Cíes, and Punta Lameda[1891], northeast of Cabo Silleiro[1916], which itself lies at the foot of Monte Ferro, a distinctive rounded hill 140m high at the end of an isthmus. If approaching the Canal del Sur from the north, give Islote Boeiro a least clearance of 0·8M to avoid a 4m patch to the south. Rocks surround the island closer inshore.

If approaching inshore from the south, once past Cabo Silleiro (which has rocks awash up to 0·7M to the northwest) the Ensenada de Bayona opens up. The north side of this bay is formed by a group of low islands, Las Estelas, which at first will appear below Monte Ferro. The western island, Las Serralleiras, (a group of rocks, some awash) is lit[1907], as well as being marked by north and south cardinal pillar buoys. From Cabo Silleiro, head towards Cabo Vicos[1888] on Isla de San Martín until Las Serralleiras has been passed, then turn into the *ría* and follow the coast not less than 1M offshore until the starboard hand channel buoy *No.1* off Isla de Toralla, with its prominent block of flats, can be cleared.

From further offshore to the southwest, follow the leading marks of Cabo Estay[1890].

In fog, particularly if navigating without GPS or radar, use the south entrance for the benefit of the sound signals and radio aids on Cabo Silleiro and Cabo Estay.

# Islas Cíes

42°13'N 8°54'W

## Charts

|  | Islands |
|---|---|
| Admiralty | 2548 |
| Spanish | 416B, 9250 |

## Lights

### Approach

1882 **Punta Monte Agudo** 42°14'·6N 8°54'·2W
Fl.G.5s23m9M 146·5°-vis-334° White tower 5m

1884 **Monte del Faro** 42°12'·8N 8°54'·9W
Fl(2)8s185m22M Obscd 315°-016·5° over Bajos de
Los Castros and Forcados
Round tower 10m

1886 **Punta Canabal** 42°12'·7N 8°54'·8W
Fl(3)20s63m9M White tower 10m

1888 **Cabo Vicos, Isla de San Martín** 42°11'·5N
8°53'·5W
Fl(3)R.9s92m7M 210·5°-vis-108°
White tower 7m

1889 **Islote Boeiro** 42°10'·7N 8°54'·6W
Fl(2)R.8s22m6M
White conical beacon tower 6m

## General

The Islas Cíes are mountainous, wooded and very attractive. The whole area is a Nature Park, and in addition a large part of Isla del Norte, Isla del Faro and all of Isla de San Martín are bird sanctuaries – mostly herring gulls, lesser black-backed gulls and shags, plus a few guillemots – where access is forbidden. However there are good tracks on Isla del Norte and Isla del Faro, which are linked by a narrow sandy isthmus, and it is worth studying the map displayed at the northern end of Playa Arena das Rodas.

There are no cars on the islands and few permanent inhabitants, but in summer many campers and day visitors come by ferry from Vigo, Bayona and Cangas to enjoy the clean sandy beaches – time a visit for midweek if possible. In terms of their surroundings the anchorages, which are on the east side of the islands, are amongst the best in the *rías*, but all are open to the east.

## Approach

The approaches to the islands from seaward are the same as those for the Ría de Vigo, opposite.

For Playa Arena das Rodas, if coming from the north, pass Monte Agudo[1882] keeping 500m offshore until rounding Punta Muxieiro and its square white daymark. Beware the rock off Punta Muxieiro.

From the mid-reaches of the *ría*, Monte del Faro[1884] is easily identified, standing on the highest point of the central island, Isla del Faro, as is the long beach lining the isthmus between Isla del Faro and Isla del Norte. Make for the square white daymark on Punta Muxieiro at the north end of the beach. From Bayona the daymark is framed by a channel in the Estelas group and, once through them, there is clear water apart from a 3·2m rocky patch, Bajo Carrumeiro, 600m east of the light on Cabo Vicos[1888].

Yachts anchored off the Playa Arena das Rodas at Islas Cíes, looking southwest. The white daymark on Punta Muxiero (see text) shows clearly at right.

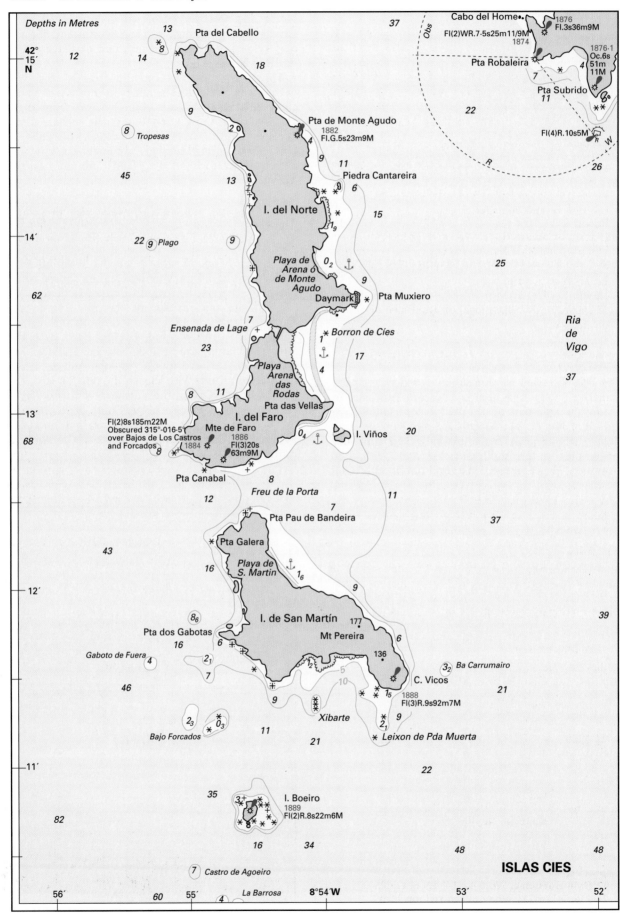

Depths in Metres

**42°
15′
N**

13
12

Pta del Cabello

*8

14

18

37

Cabo del Home●
Fl(2)WR.7·5s25m11/9M    1876
Fl.3s36m9M
1874
Pta Robaleira    1876·1
Oc.6s
4    51m
7    11M
Pta Subrido
11

8  *Tropesas*

2  0

Pta de Monte Agudo
1882
4    Fl.G.5s23m9M

9

45

13

9    11

Piedra Cantareira

6

22

I. del Norte

15

Fl(4)R.10s5M
W
R
26

**14′**

22  9  *Plago*

9

1 9

62

Playa de
Arena ó
de Monte
Agudo

0 2

25

9

Ria
de
Vigo

Daymark    Pta Muxiero

Ensenada de Lage    7

*Borron de Cíes*

23

1

17

37

Playa
Arena
das
Rodas

4

**13′**

8    11

Pta das Vellas

I. del Faro

I. Viños    20

68

Fl(2)8s185m22M
Obscured 315°-016·5°
over Bajos de Los Castros
and Forcados    1884
8

Mte de Faro
1886
Fl(3)20s
63m9M

0 4

Pta Canabal

8    *Freu de la Porta*

12    7

11

Pta Pau de Bandeira

37

Pta Galera

*Playa de
S. Martin*

**12′**

43

16

1 6

9

8 6

I. de San Martín    177
Mt Pereira

Pta dos Gabotas
16    6

6

136

3 2  *Ba Carrumairo*

39

*Gaboto de Fuera*  4

2 1

7

1 2    5
10

1 5

C. Vicos
1888
Fl(3)R.9s92m7M

21

46

9

*Xibarte*

9
2 1

*Leixon de Pda Muerta*

2 3    0 3

11    21

22

*Bajo Forcados*

**11′**

82

35

3 +
8

I. Boeiro
1889
Fl(2)R.8s22m6M

16    34

48    48

7  *Castro de Agoeiro*

**ISLAS CIES**

56′    60    55′    4    *La Barrosa*    **8°54′W**    53′    52′

## Anchorages

1. Off Playa Arena das Rodas. Anchor over sand, rock and weed towards the middle of the beach as depth allows. Borron de Cíes, a submerged rock some 20m across, lies about 200m south of the stone mole. It shows at low water and is usually detectable up to half tide. A second smaller rock, which is always covered, lies about 25m further southwest. Avoid anchoring too close to the mole, which is in constant use by tourist ferries. It is possible for a shallow-draught boat to anchor inshore of the rocks, once they have been identified, though in summer the beach itself is buoyed-off for swimming.

   Good anchorage, clear of both rocks and ferries, is to be found with the western white tower on Cap del Home framed in the centre of a cleft in the rocks at the end of Punta Muxeiro. Holding is good in sand.

2. In southerlies, anchor in the bay north of Punta Muxieiro and its daymark, off the Playa de Arena de Felgueiras.

3. In south to northwest conditions, better anchorage is to be had on the north coast of Isla de San Martín off the Playa de San Martín, in 3–5m over rock and sand. This is a particularly quiet and attractive spot although without access to facilities of any kind. The island is a bird sanctuary where landing is forbidden.

4. In east winds some shelter may be found in a small bay on the south coast of the Isla del Faro immediately west, and in the lee, of Isla Viños. It is occasionally used by fishing boats and there is not much room. The Monte Faro jetty some 600m to the west is used by fishing boats and the occasional ferry, and yachts are not welcome.

## Facilities

Apart from a beach bar, the only facilities available are near the campsite behind Playa Arena das Rodas on Isla del Faro, where a small supermarket and a couple of restaurants will be found. Prices tend to be high.

## Communications

Telephone box at the campsite. Ferries to Vigo, Bayona and Cangas from Playa Arena das Rodas and the Monte Faro jetty.

# Cangas

42°15'·5N 8°47'W

## Charts

|  | *Harbour* |
|---|---|
| Admiralty | *2548, 1757* (Playa de Cangas anchorage only) |
| Spanish | *4166* |

## Lights

*Approach*
1892 **Bajo Borneira, *No.6*** 42°14'·4N 8°47'·5W
 Fl(2)R.7s11m7M White tower, red top 11m

buoy **Bajo Salguerión, *No.8*** 42°14'·6N 8°46'·6W
 Fl(2+1)R.15s5M
 Red pillar buoy, ▪ topmark
buoy **Bajo Rodeira, *No.10*** 42°15'·1N 8°45'·5W
 Fl(3)R.9s5M Red pillar buoy
*Entrance*
1894·5 **South breakwater** 42°15'·4N 8°47'W
 Oc.R.4s5m3M Red round tower 5m
1895 **Main breakwater** 42°15'·6N 8°46'·9W
 Fl(2+1)R.12s8m3M Red round tower 6m
1895·4 **Inner mole** 42°15'·6N 8°46'·9W
 Q.RG.8m3M 065°-R-245°-G-065°
 White and red square tower 7m

## General

A fishing and industrial town used also as a dormitory area by many workers in Vigo. The old part of the town is quite attractive, and although hardly worth a special visit the port is useful as an alternative night stop to Vigo after a day in the city. A market is held on the seafront every Friday.

There is a fish-freezing plant (Frigorificos del Morrazo) close south of the harbour, where large trawlers berth to unload.

## Approach

The Ensenada de Cangas is entered between, on the port hand, the beacon tower off Punta Borneira[1892] and on the starboard hand Bajo Rodeira buoy *No.10*, which marks the foul ground extending south from Punta Rodeira. The line from buoy *No.10* to Cangas main breakwater only narrowly clears the shoals so, if coming from the east, pass 200–300m west of the buoy before turning towards the breakwater. Bajo Salguerión buoy *No.8* (marking a 3m bank to the north) can be left on either side.

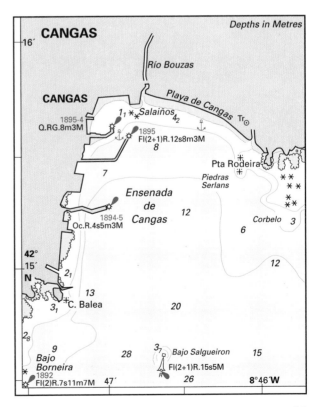

## Anchorage

There is sheltered anchorage for a few vessels between the inner mole and the main breakwater in 5–6m over mud. There is a smallcraft pontoon and a dozen or so local yachts lie bows-on to the main breakwater. Both sides of the inner mole are lined with fishing boats. The area between the main and south moles gives access to the refrigeration plant – anchoring would be unwise and may well be forbidden.

There is a quieter and more pleasant, though less sheltered, anchorage about 500m to the east off the Playa de Cangas in 5–6m over sand. Keep clear of the Piedras Serlans reef at the east end of the beach, as well as the Salaiños rocks off the end of the short mole to the west.

## Facilities

Cangas is a sizeable town with good shopping, plus banks (with card facility), restaurants and bars. Diesel may be available from a pump on the north side of the inner mole, otherwise by can from a filling station near the root of the breakwater.

Showers are available at the Club Náutico de Cangas, opposite the root of the breakwater. Frequent ferries cross the *ría* to Vigo, carrying both commuters and tourists.

## Communications

Post office and telephones. Buses and taxis, plus frequent ferries to Vigo and daily to the Islas Cíes.

## Alternative anchorages

1. Off the beach in the Ensenada de Barra about 3M to the west, sheltered to the west by Punta de Subrido but exposed from southwest to east. Attractive, unspoilt (with good walking in the dunes and pine scrub behind the beach) – and another favourite with naturists. Anchor in 6m or less with good holding over sand and weed. Outside the 10m line there is more rock and the holding poor.
2. At Con, 1·5M east of Cangas. There is little water in the harbour at Con which is, in any case, given over to fishing boats. It would be possible to anchor off in settled conditions, but shelter is poor.
3. In the Ensenada de Moaña, inside the *viveros*. Again the area between the two moles is both shallow and very full. Moaña has a reputation for particularly good seafood but the town is not pretty.
4. Off the Playa Borna, between the Cantera shipyard and Punta Borna, itself directly opposite Vigo. This is an unexpectedly quiet and attractive anchorage about 2·5M northeast of the city, well sheltered except from the southwest. Anchor between the *viveros* and the beach in 6–8m over sand, mud and weed.

Looking north-northeast over the three breakwaters at Cangas, with the prominent white fish-freezing plant at left.

# Vigo

42°14'·5N 8°43'W

## Charts

|  | *Harbour* |
|---|---|
| Admiralty | *2548, 1757* |
| Spanish | *416B* |

## Lights

*Approach*
**1890 Cabo Estay Ldg Lts on 069·3°** 42°11'·1N
  8°48'·9W
  *Front* Iso.2s16m18M 066·3°-vis-072·3°
  Red pyramidal tower, white bands 8m
  Horn Mo(V)60s 27m ENE. Racon Mo(B) 22M
*0933* Radiobeacon *VS* 312·5kHz 50M
**1890·1** *Rear*, 660m from front,
  Oc.4s48m18M 066·3°-vis-072·3°
  Red pyramidal tower, white bands 7m
buoy **Isla de Toralla (Bajo Bondaña, *No.1*)**
  42°12'·4N 8°48'·5W
  Fl(3)G.9s5M Green conical buoy
**1894 Bajo Tofiño, *No.3*** 42°13'·7N 8°46'·7W
  Fl(4)G.14s9m5M White tower, green top
buoy **Bajo Salguerión, *No.8*** 42°14'·6N 8°46'·6W
  Fl(2+1)R.15s5M
  Red pillar buoy, ▪ topmark

*Harbour*
**1895·7 Bouzas wharf, NW corner** 42°13'·9N 8°45'·7W
  Q.6m5M North cardinal column, ⇞ topmark
**1895·8 Bouzas wharf, NE corner** 42°14'·1N 8°45'W
  Fl.G.4s8m4M 113°-vis-336·5°
  Green square tower 4m
**1896 Dársena de Bouzas, W side** 42°14'N 8°44'·3W
  Fl(2)G.7s8m3M Green column 5m
**1897 Dársena de Bouzas, E side (Muelle del**
  **Berbés, SW end)** 42°14'N 8°44'·3W
  Fl(2)R.5s8m3M
  Silver framework tower 5m
**1898 Muelle del Berbés, NE end** 42°14'·4N 8°44'W
  Oc(3)G.12s8m4M Round green tower 6m
**1900 Muelle de Transatlánticos, SW end** 42°14'·4N
  8°43'·9W
  Fl(2)R.7s8m5M Masonry column 6m
**1900·2 Muelle de Transatlánticos, NE end** 42°14'·6N
  8°43'·5W
  Fl(4)G.11s8m5M Masonry column 6m
**1900·5 Marina north mole** 42°14'·6N 8°43'·4W
  Q.R.8m5M Red tower 7m
**1900·4 Marina south mole** 42°14'·6N 8°43'·4W
  Q.G.8m5M Green tower 7m
**1901 Muelle Transversal, NE corner** 42°14'·7N
  8°42'·9W
  F.G.5s9m4M Green column 5m
**1901·2 Muelle del Guixar, NW corner** 42°15'·1N
  8°42'·5W
  Fl(3)R.9s8m5M Red tower 6m
**1901·5 Punta de la Guia** 42°15'·6N 8°42'·1W
  Oc(2+1)20s35m15M
  White round masonry tower 21m
Plus many other lights in the harbour area.

## Coast radio station and weather/navigational services

**Vigo** (42°10'N 8°41'W) (24 hours) Remotely controlled
  from CCR Coruña – see page 25 – call *Coruña Radio*
  **VHF** Ch 16[1], 20, 62[2], 70[3].

*Weather messages*: Ch 10 at 0015, 0415, 0815, 1215,
  1615, 2015, in Spanish and English. Ch 20 at 0950,
  1150, 2150, 24 hour forecast for coastal waters.
*Navigational warnings*: Ch 10 at 0215, 0615, 1015, 1415,
  1815, 2215 in Spanish and English; and Ch 20 on
  receipt and at 0803, 1503 in Spanish for coastal waters
  of Rías de Pontevedra and Vigo.
1. Continuous watch is NOT maintained on VHF Ch 16.
   Vessels should call direct on Ch 20.
2. Reserved for Autolink (see Marine weather information by
   telephone, page 16.
3. Digital Selective Calling (DSC) distress and safety traffic.

## Marina and port radio

*Real Club Náutico de Vigo* VHF Ch 06.
*Vigo Prácticos* VHF Ch 12, 14, 16.

## General

Vigo is a lively and modern city with an ancient
history and strong maritime connections. A new
cargo terminal was constructed in the 1980s and
Vigo's capacity for handling cargoes, building
coasters and fishing boats, as well as landing fish, is
considerable. Its wharves now stretch well over 2M
along the coast, though the western section is
technically the harbour of Bouzas. In spite of losing
its transatlantic passenger business, Vigo retains the
outgoing attitude of an international port together
with the facilities of such a centre.

There are two marinas in the city, both of which
accept visiting yachts if space is available. One is
situated close east of the Muelle Transatlánticos and
administered by the old-established Real Club
Náutico de Vigo, the other is in the Dársena de
Bouzas and the responsibility of the much smaller
Liceo Marítimo.

## Approach

Once inside the Ría de Vigo there are no particular
problems provided one keeps roughly up the centre
of the *ría* within the marked channel (which at its
narrowest is about 1M wide). A useful guide is the
white hermitage on the summit of Monte de la
Guia, a rounded, wooded hill 122m high on the
south shore which appears beyond Vigo but before
the suspension bridge. At night, if in doubt, cross
the *ría* northwards and pick up Punta de la Guia[1901·5]
between 062° and 072°.

If unwilling to rely entirely on GPS in thick
weather, keep to the southeast shore but stay outside
the 20m line. Cabo Estay[1890] has a sound signal. The
next prominent mark is a tower block on Isla de
Toralla which can be seen for miles in clear weather
– *No.1* buoy lies about 0·5M off this island
(connected to the shore by a tall bridge), with Bajo
Tofiño[1894] about 2M to the northeast.

The first serious port activity is at the Bouzas
wharf[1895·7 & 1895·8], developed on a large quadrangle of
reclaimed ground in front of the once separate
village of Bouzas. After this the land falls away into
the Ensenada de Bouzas, protected by a long mole
and further reclaimed areas, where shipbuilding
takes place to the west while the east is given over to
the fishing harbour. The entrance is lit[1896 & 1897],
forming the approach to the Liceo Marítimo marina
in the far southwest corner.

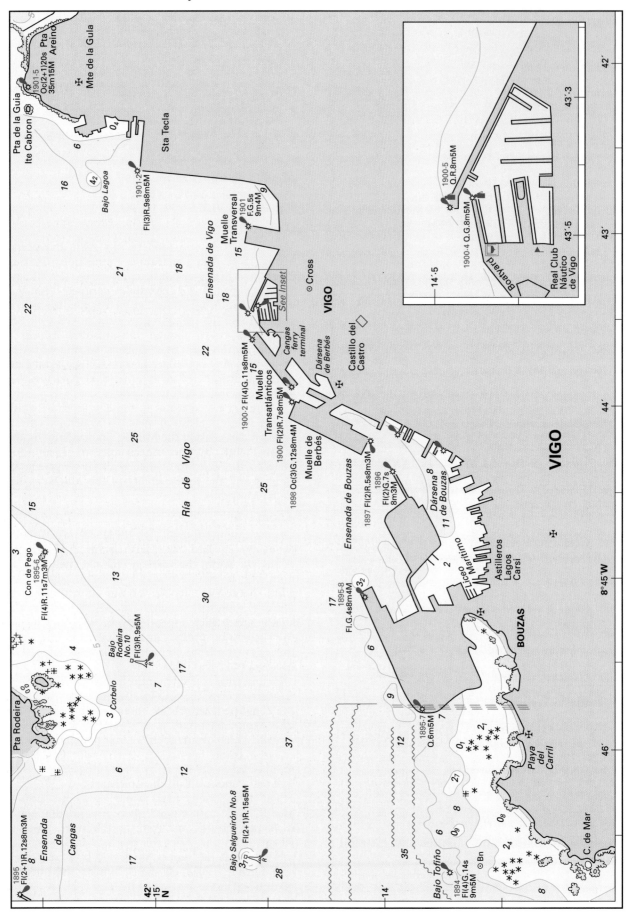

Pta de la Guia
Ite Cabron

1901·5
Oc(2+1)20s Pta
35m15M Areiño

Mte de la Gula

0·4

6

Bajo Lagoa

16

4·2

1901·2
Fl(3)R.9s8m5M

Sta Tecla

Ensenada de Vigo

Muelle
Transversal

21

18

15

1901
F.G.5s
9m4M

15

18

22

Ensenada de Vigo

See Inset

⊙ Cross

22

**VIGO**

1900·2 Fl(4)G.11s8m5M

Muelle
Transatlánticos

15

Cangas
ferry
terminal

Dársena
de Berbés

Castillo del
Castro

25

1900 Fl(2)R.7s8m5M

1898 Oc(3)G.12s8m4M

Muelle de
Berbés

25

Ría de Vigo

Ensenada de Bouzas

1897 Fl(2)R.5s8m3M

1896

Dársena
8

11 de Bouzas

15

1895·6
Fl(4)R.11s7m3M

Con de Pego

3

7

Liceo
Marítimo

**VIGO**

13

Bajo
Rodeira
No.10
Fl(3)R.9s5M

Corbelo

17

R

2

Astilleros
Lagos
Carsi

30

7

3

17

Pta Rodeira

4

5

37

17

6

12

**BOUZAS**

Playa del
Carril

1895·7
Q.6m5M

7

12

1895-8
F.l.G.4s8m4M

3₂

6

9

35

1894
Fl(4)G.14s
9m5M

Bajo Tofiño

⊙ Bn

6

8

0₈

C. de Mar

Bajo Salgueirón No.8
Fl(2+1)R.15s5M

28

R

1895
Fl(2+1)R.12s8m3M

Ensenada
de
Cangas

17

8

**42°**
**15′**
**N**

14′

46′

8°45′W

44′

## Inset (top right):

42′

43′·3

1900·5
Q.R.8m5M

43′·5

43′

1900·6
Q.G.8m5M

Boatyard

1900·4 Q.G.8m5M

14′·5

Real Club
Náutico
de Vigo

Beyond the Ensenada de Bouzas the shoreline trends north again towards the Muelle de Berbés and the entrance to the Dársena de Berbés, lit[1898 & 1900]. The Muelle de Transatlánticos beyond, with its large terminal buildings, was built when Vigo was a major port for Atlantic passengers.

If heading for the marina run by the Real Club Náutico de Vigo, when north of the northeast corner of the Muelle de Transatlánticos[1900·2] turn to clear the end of it by about 150m. The marina north mole[1900·5] lies about 350m beyond on 130°, with the south mole[1900·4] opposite. The entrance is narrow – 30m or less – and doglegged, making it somewhat blind.

Keep well clear of the entrance to the Dársena de Lage, which lies between the Muelle de Transatlánticos and the yacht basin, as this is the terminal for the frequent, noisy and turbulent Cangas ferries. The old *club náutico* resembles the superstructure of a passenger liner seen broadside, and is visible from some distance.

## Berthing

### 1. Real Club Náutico
☎ 986 449694 *Fax* 986 449695

The 420 berth marina, is usually very full, with little room to manoeuvre once inside and no places specifically reserved for visitors – a berth should be booked in advance if at all possible.

New arrivals should secure to the reception/fuel pontoon on the starboard side of the entrance and await instructions. Mooring is mainly by the standard bows-on, haul off line tailed to the pontoon method, though a few (almost certainly private) berths have individual fingers. In the short term (and particularly for multihulls) it may be possible to secure alongside the eastern mole outside the short spur (and thus subject to wash from the Cangas ferries). It is a very long walk to the marina office from this position.

The Real Club Náutico de Vigo has two separate clubhouses, that at the root of the mole being distinctly formal while the older building on the centre mole of the marina houses the berthing office – on the 'bridge' of the landbound vessel – with a dinghy store below. In 1999 the overnight rate for a visiting yacht of just under 12m at any time of year was 2,820 ptas (16·95 euros) during the first week, dropping to 1,397 ptas (8·40 euros) thereafter, both inclusive of water, electricity and tax.

### 2. Liceo Marítimo
☎ 986 232442 *Fax* 986 239955

The four pontoons of this small 'club' marina are mostly taken up with small motorboats, but there is space for a few larger yachts including the occasional visitor. The marina lies directly

The marina of the Real Club Náutico de Vigo, seen from almost due north with the city blocks of Vigo behind.

Looking northeast along Vigo's Dársena del Bouzas, with the pontoons of the small Liceo Marítimo marina in the foreground.

opposite a ship repair yard, so tending to be noisy and sometimes dirty. It is some distance from the nearest shops – and even further from the city centre – and has no real facilities on site other than the ubiquitous bar/restaurant in the clubhouse. In 1999 the overnight rate for a visiting yacht of just under 12m was only 575 ptas (3·46 euros) including tax, but with water (including showers) and electricity extra.

The two pontoons in the outer part of the Dársena de Bouzas, running southwest from the Muelle de Reparaciones, are owned by the R Andrade and Ronautica workshops respectively and do not accept visitors.

## Facilities

*Boatyard, engineers* Adolfo Galleo Guerrero, ☎ 986 433422 *Fax* 986 415035, at the Real Club Náutico marina handles minor repairs in GRP and timber, painting, etc. For major work contact:
**Astilleros Lagos**, Avda de Eduardo Cabello 2, Vigo 36208, España
☎ 986 232626 *Fax* 986 291833
This long-established boatyard has an excellent reputation and is situated at the east end of the Ensenada de Bouzas. The very helpful owner and his sons speak good English.

*Travel-lift* 25 tonne capacity lift at the Real Club Náutico marina, but somewhat limited hardstanding.

*Sailmaker/sail repairs* Arrange via either the RCN marina office or Astilleros Lagos.

*Chandlery* Several in the city, including RoNautica a block or two from the Real Club Náutico (mainly fancy items, but some hardware, rope, etc), and Yatesport at La Guia, about 1·5km northeast of the RCN marina.

*Charts*
**Orio y Cia SL**, Calle Orillamar 49, Apartado 618
☎ 986 293292 *Fax* 986 202253
are official suppliers of Spanish charts.

*Water* On the pontoons in both marinas.

*Showers* At both marinas (those at the RCN are situated in the 'old' building).

*Launderettes* In the city.

*Electricity* On the pontoons in both marinas.

*Fuel* Diesel and petrol at the RCN marina.

*Bottled gas* Camping Gaz available in the city.

*Club náuticos* As described above. The formal restaurant on the first floor of the Real Club Náutico de Vigo building is reputed to be excellent, with a more relaxed bar/restaurant downstairs.

*Weather forecast* Posted daily at the RCN marina.

*Banks* Many in the city.

The southern of the two Islas de San Simón seen from the west, with their offlying rocks clearly visible at right. Two yachts have worked behind the island for additional protection.

*Shops/provisioning* A large department store/ supermarket of the El Corte Ingles chain within walking distance of the RCN marina, or take a taxi to the Alcampo hypermarket. The variety of other shopping reflects Vigo's position as one of the leading cities of Galicia.

*Produce market* The A Pedra market is worth visiting, particularly for local seafood.

*Cafés, restaurants & hotels* Hundreds, to suit all tastes and pockets.

*Medical services* In the city.

## Communications

*Post offices* In the city.

*Mailing address*
   c/o **Puerto Deportivo del Real Club Náutico de Vigo**, Las Avenidas s/n, Vigo, Galicia, España.
   *Fax service* 986 449695

*Public telephones* At the RCN and in the city.

*Car hire/taxis* In the city.

*Buses* To Bayona and elsewhere, plus express coach service to Santiago de Compostela.

*Ferries* Frequent ferries to Cangas from a terminal close west of the RCN marina.

*Air services* Santiago de Compostela airport is about 80km distant via the excellent new motorway.

## Anchorages

There are several possible anchorages in the Ensenada de San Simón, east of the 38·8m suspension bridge which carries the motorway, all best suited to yachts with modest draught or able to take the ground:

1. On the western shore of the *ensenada* in the long bay between Punta San Adrián and Punta Pereiro, where there are smallcraft pontoons (note the awash rock, Islote Pedro, directly off the pontoons). Depths in the bay are variable, but seldom more than 2–3m – approach cautiously with an eye to the echo-sounder. Restaurants and basic shopping will be found ashore.

2. On the south shore of the *ensenada*, off Punta Soutelo in 3–4m. Beware of the sandbanks east of this anchorage which extend off the mouth of the Río de Redondela, itself defined by training walls which cover at half tide.

3. South of the reef which extends south from the Islas de San Simón (two islands linked by a distinctive bridge, and once used as a leper colony). The reef itself is marked by a beacon. Anchor clear of the latter and outside moored small craft in 2–3m. Alternatively it may be possible to work inside the island, but there is little depth. There is a restaurant on the spit of beach and food shops in Cesantes, about 1km up a steep hill.

The pontoons at Punta Pereiro in the Ensenada de San Simón, with Islote Pedro in the foreground.

97

# Bayona (Baiona)

42°07'N 8°51'W

## Tides

*Reference port* Lisbon
*Mean time differences*
HW: +45 minutes ±10; LW: +70 minutes ±10
(the above allows for the difference in time zones)

*Heights in metres*

| MHWS | MHWN | MLWN | MLWS |
|------|------|------|------|
| 3·5  | 2·7  | 1·3  | 0·5  |

## Charts

|           | *Harbour* |
|-----------|-----------|
| Admiralty | *2548*    |
| Spanish   | *4167*    |
| Imray     | *C19*     |

## Lights

### *Approach*

1876 **Cabo del Home** 42°15'·2N 8°52'·4W
 Fl.3s36m9M 090°-vis-180°
 White round tower 18m

1884 **Monte del Faro** 42°12'·8N 8°54'·9W
 Fl(2)8s185m22M Obscd 315°-016·5° over Bajos de
 Los Castros and Forcados
 Round tower 10m

1916 **Cabo Silleiro Aeromarine** 42°06'·2N 8°53'·8W
 Fl(2+1)15s83m24M
 White tower, red bands, on white building 30m
 Siren Mo(S)30s 900m NNW Old light tower

*0935* Radiobeacon *RO* 293·5kHz 100M
(Reliable sector 020°-145°)

### *Entrance*

1889 **Islote Boeiro** 42°10'·7N 8°54'·6W
 Fl(2)R.8s22m6M White conical beacon tower 6m

1891 **Punta Lameda** 42°09'·4N 8°51'W
 Fl(2)G.8s27m5M White tower 4m

1907 **Las Serralleiras** 42°08'·8N 8°52'·6W
 Fl.G.4s10m6M White conical tower 6m

buoy **Bajo Los Carollones** 42°08'·3N 8°52'·8W
 Q(6)+LFl.15s South cardinal buoy, ⍒ topmark

1911 **Cabezo de San Juan Ldg Lts on 084°** 42°08'·3N
 8°50'·1W
 *Front* Q(2)4s7m4M White conical tower

1911·1 *Rear* **Playa de Panjón**, 1780m from front,
 Oc.3·8s17m9M
 White tower on octagonal white base 9m

Looking northeast across the crowded harbour at Bayona, with the marina of the Monte-Real Club de Yates at centre and the anchorage on the right.

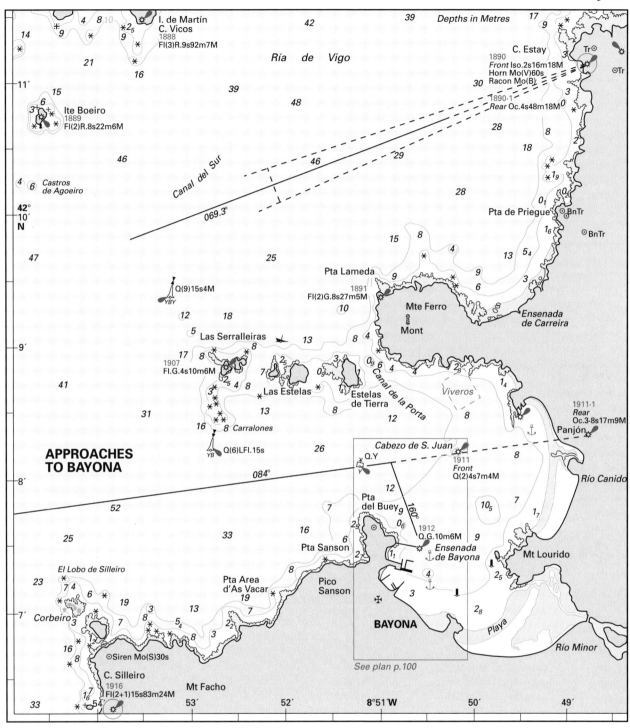

**APPROACHES TO BAYONA**

**BAYONA**

*See plan p.100*

buoy **Yellow buoy** 42°08'·2N 8°51'·2W
 Q.Y Can buoy, × topmark
*Harbour*
1912 **Breakwater** 42°07'·6N 8°50'·5W
 Q.G.10m6M
 Black and white chequered round tower 9m
*Note* There is a sound signal on Cabo Silleiro[1917].

## Marina radio

*Monte-Real Club de Yates* VHF Ch 06.

## General

Long a favourite harbour with British yachtsmen, Bayona is easily approached by day or night. It is well sheltered other than from strong winds with an easterly component which are rare in summer. The facilities of the imposing Monte-Real Club de Yates are made available to visiting yachtsmen who berth in their marina or use their moorings, but not to those who anchor (membership of a recognized foreign yacht club appearing to make no difference).

The town is attractive and thriving as a tourist resort, with well protected beaches and a secure place in history as Columbus' first mainland landfall in 1493 after returning from the New World – commemorated by a replica of the *Pinta* permanently berthed in the harbour. Perhaps more genuine is the old part of the town, surprisingly uncommercialised compared to the tourist shops along the front and a cool place to take a leisurely stroll on a hot day. Medieval walls surround the Parador Conde do Gondomar on the northern headland, commanding the harbour and its approaches, and there are pleasant walks among the pine forests beyond, where stands the enormous statue of the Virgen de la Roca.

### Approach from seaward

See the approach to the Ría de Vigo, page 88.

If coming from the north inside Islas Cíes, pass Cabo del Home[1876] and head for Punta Lameda[1891] below Monte Ferro, bearing about 160°. The shortest route then lies through the Canal de la Porta, between Monte Ferro and the easternmost of the three Estelas islands, Estela de Tierra. There is a 0·9m patch in the middle of this channel – keep to the west side.

Alternatively, to reach the main entrance of the Ensenada de Bayona, pass west of Las Serralleiras[1907] together with its cardinal buoys and continue south until the leading marks of Cabezo de San Juan[1911] and Panjón[1911·1] align on 083°. A yellow can buoy (lit) lies close to the leading line about 1M west of Cabezo de San Juan – it marks a pipeline and can be left either side. Alter course for the breakwater[1912] when it bears at least 160°.

If entering between Islas Cíes and Cabo Silleiro[1916] via the Canal del Sur, once past the off-lying dangers of Islote Boeiro[1889] remain on 145° until turning on the Bayona leading marks[1911].

From the south, round Cabo Silleiro (which has rocks awash up to 0·7M to the northwest) and head towards Las Serralleiras until turning onto the Bayona leading marks.

### Approach from the *ria*

Follow the coast southwestwards towards Monte Ferro, keeping at least 1M offshore. Then take the Canal de la Porto or the outside route as described above.

### Berthing and moorings

The 170 berth marina is owned and run by the Monte-Real Club de Yates, ☎ 986 355234/355576 *Fax* 986 355061, with some 50 berths reserved for visitors, mostly on the northeast pontoon. It is able to take one or two yachts of up to 35m and has many berths suitable for 12–15m LOA.

On arrival secure to the fuel/reception berth on the south side of the marina mole (though note that parts carry no more than 1·5m at low water) to be allocated a berth – even when apparently full a slot can usually be found. If there is no sign of life at the fuelling berth, the marina office will be found in the

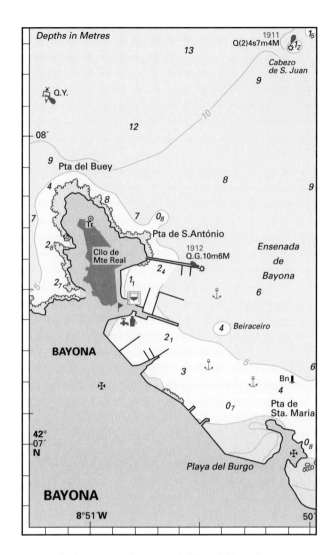

'tunnel' beyond the travel-lift. Office hours are 0900–1300 and 1600–1900 daily and good English is spoken. Security to the club as a whole, including the marina, is excellent, making Bayona one of the relatively few places in Galicia where a yacht could be left without undue worry during a visit to the UK or elsewhere.

The Monte-Real Club de Yates also owns a number of moorings, most of which are rented out to members. As of 1999 a few moorings were available for visitors, though it was anticipated that this might not be the case much longer. In 1999 the high season rate for a visiting yacht of just under 12m was 2,000 ptas (12·02 euros) per night inclusive, whether in the marina or on a buoy.

### Anchorage

Anchor outside the moorings, keeping well clear of the fairway to the south mole which is used by fishing boats. Alternatively choose a spot further south, between the mole and the red and black banded beacon with ⁞ topmark. Holding varies from very good indeed over sand and mud, to poor in the large patches of weed.

*Note* Though efficient and welcoming to those paying for a berth or mooring, the Monte-Real Club de Yates has long had a reputation for being unfriendly towards those not paying to use their facilities – crews attempting to land at the marina have been told their dinghies would be either confiscated or cast adrift, while others have been denied the chance to buy fuel or water.

As of 1999 the situation appeared to have improved, and while stressing that yachts at anchor 'are nothing to do with us', overt hostility is no longer in evidence. One very major improvement is that the MRCY office will now hold mail for yachts at anchor as well as for those in the marina.

## Facilities

*Boatyard* Repairs (but not major work) can be handed at the MRCY.

*Travel-lift* 17 tonne capacity lift at the MRCY.

*Engineers, electronic & radio repairs* Arrange via the MRCY.

*Sailmaker/sail repairs* In Vigo – arrange via the MRCY.

*Chandleries* Estelas on the front beyond the south mole, but small and slanted towards sports fishing, or the more businesslike Automar a short distance beyond.

*Charts* Spanish charts of local waters are available from Estelas or from the MRCY, with a full-scale chart agent in Vigo.

*Water* On the marina pontoons, plus public tap opposite the root of the south mole. Yachts at anchor can fill containers at the MRCY on payment of a small fee (apparently a set amount however much is used).

*Showers* At the MRCY. It may be possible for those not otherwise using MRCY facilities to pay for showers.

*Launderette* On the front between the two chandleries.

*Electricity* On the marina pontoons.

*Fuel* Diesel and petrol at the MRCY fuel berth (note the caution regarding depth).

*Bottled gas* Camping Gaz available in the town.

*Ice* At the MRCY.

*Club náutico* The Monte-Real Club de Yates is distinctly formal, and a reasonable standard of dress is expected in the dining room and grounds (from which there are excellent views over the harbour).

*Weather forecast* Posted daily outside the marina office.

*Banks* In the town (with card facilities).

*Shops/provisioning* Several small supermarkets, plus all the other shops to be expected in a town of medium size. Anything which cannot be found in Bayona will almost certainly be available in Vigo.

*Produce market* Good fish and produce market in the older (northern) part of the town.

*Cafés, restaurants & hotels* No shortage, from pavement cafés to the excellent restaurants at the MRCY and the Parador Conde do Gondomar (the latter open to non-residents). It has been reported that somewhat over-zealous security at the MRCY sometimes prevents the crews of visiting yachts (including those berthed in the marina) from dining there.

*Medical services* Clinic just south of the Estelas chandlery.

*Tourist office* Local maps and information available from a small booth near the gates to the parador.

## Communications

*Post office* In the old part of the town.

*Mailing address*
c/o **Monte-Real Club de Yates**, Recinto del Parador s/n, 36300 Bayona, Galicia, España.
*Fax service* 986 355061

*Public telephones* At the MRCY, plus kiosks near tourist office and elsewhere in the town. The MRCY also has telephone sockets into which modems can be plugged in order to send and receive e-mail.

*Car hire/taxis* In the town.

*Buses* Frequent service to Vigo and thence to Santiago de Compostela.

*Ferries* Tourist ferries to the Islas Cíes.

*Air services* International airport at Santiago de Compostela, about 90 minutes by road (as is Porto airport in northern Portugal).

## Alternative anchorage

In settled or easterly conditions it is possible to anchor off the small town of Panjón (Panxón) on the eastern side of the Ensenada de Bayona, with some protection from northwest round to south. The short stone mole (Fl(2)R.10s12m5M Red column 7m) shelters a small harbour packed with moorings, but it provides convenient steps while the Club Náutico de Panjón at its root has showers, a restaurant and bar. South of the harbour is a long sandy beach, the Playa de América. Basic shopping is available in the town, which is dominated by a spectacular church.

Looking north over the short mole at Panjón, on the east side of the Ensenada de Bayona, with the long Playa de América running away to the right.

# La Guardia (A Guarda)

41°54'N 8°53'W

## Tides

*Reference port* Lisbon
*Mean time differences*
HW: +50 minutes ±10; LW: +75 minutes ±10
(the above allows for the difference in time zones)
*Heights in metres*

| MHWS | MHWN | MLWN | MLWS |
|------|------|------|------|
| 3·3 | 2·6 | 1·2 | 0·4 |

## Charts

|  | Approach | Harbour |
|------|----------|---------|
| Admiralty | *3633* | |
| Spanish | *41B, 417, 924* | *417* |

## Lights

### Approach

1916 **Cabo Silleiro Aeromarine** 42°06'·2N 8°53'·8W
Fl(2+1)15s83m24M
White tower, red bands, on white building 30m
Siren Mo(S)30s 900m NNW Old light tower
*0935* Radiobeacon *RO* 293·5kHz 100M
(Reliable sector 020°–145°)

2008 **Montedor** 41°44'·9N 8°52'·4W
Fl(2)9·5s101m22M Horn Mo(S)25s 800m WSW
Square tower and building 28m
*0945* Radiobeacon *MR* 290kHz 150M (1 & 4 in
sequence)

### Harbour

1920·5 **North breakwater** 41°54'N 8°52'·9W
Fl.R.5s11m5M Siren Mo(L)30s3M
Round red column 3m

1921 **South breakwater** 41°54'N 8°52'·8W
Fl.G.3s11m5M Square green tower, white bands 3m

## Coast radio station and weather/navigational services

**La Guardia** (41°53'N 8°52'W) (24 hours) (Remotely
controlled from CCR Coruña – see page 25 – call
*Coruña Radio*
**VHF** Ch 16[1], 70[2], 82.
*Weather messages:* Ch 82 at 0950, 1150, 2150, 24 hour
forecast for coastal waters.
*Navigational warnings:* Ch 82 on receipt and at 0903,
1603 in Spanish for coastal waters.
1. Continuous watch is NOT maintained on VHF Ch 16.
Vessels should call direct on Ch 82.
2. Digital Selective Calling (DSC) distress and safety traffic.

The small, exposed harbour at La Guardia, looking east. Once again, no provision is made for visiting yachts.

## General

A border town and centre of seafood gastronomy in an attractive setting, La Guardia has more shops, restaurants, hotels and banks than might be expected. It is a busy fishing port with little prospect of anchoring in the harbour, and despite a mole partially closing the entrance from the north, heavy swells from the west can still set in. A visit in settled conditions can be rewarding, but be prepared to leave at once if conditions deteriorate.

Monte de Santa Tecla, which rises steeply behind the town, repays the effort of the 350m climb. Near the summit is a remarkable Roman-Celtic hut settlement, though somewhat over-restored, and beyond this a series of large stone crosses leads to a tiny church, a restaurant and a hotel. In clear weather there are magnificent views south to the Río Miño and as far north as the Islas Cíes.

Several *fiesta*s take place in La Guardia during the course of the year, including that of the Virgen del Carmen on 16 July, and those of Monte de Santa Tecla during the second week of August.

## Approach

Approaching from the north, beware of rocks awash up to 0·7M to the northwest of Cabo Silleiro[1916], and more rocks off the cliffs between it and the mouth of the Río Miño. Keep at least 1M offshore until La Guardia has been identified close north of Monte de Santa Tecla. It is the only town on this sector of the coast and has a church and clock tower, both conspicuous.

From the south, conical Monte de Santa Tecla stands out prominently, with a clutch of stone buildings and radio aerials on its summit and a factory with two tall chimneys at its Atlantic base.

Do not approach La Guardia at night, in thick weather, or if there is any noticeable swell.

## Entrance

The gap between the two moleheads is no more than 70m wide – enter on approximately 105°, staying near the centre as neither wall goes down sheer. Favour the north side of the harbour once inside, and keep well outside a line drawn from the molehead to the corner of the inner wharf in order to clear Barquiña, a rocky shoal some 20m outside this line.

Depths shoal from 8m at the entrance to 0·5m off the quay at the head of the harbour, and on either side it shoals rapidly.

## Anchorage and mooring

Very little space remains in which to anchor, as the centre of the harbour is taken up by closely packed fishing boat moorings, while to the south the fairway to the quay must not be obstructed. North of the moorings the water is shallow with an uneven, rocky floor likely to foul an anchor – should it hold at all.

The only real hope lies in enlisting the help of local fishermen, who may be able to advise if a mooring is free. It is essential to ask – preferably attempting some Spanish – rather than to help

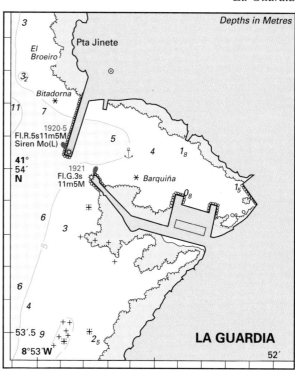

oneself, which will almost certainly result in a swift call to move on. It is reported that the fishermen are more likely to be cooperative if weather conditions, such as thickening fog, make it difficult for a yacht to depart.

## Facilities

Restaurants and cafés at the head of the harbour, plus shops, banks, etc in the town.

## Communications

Post office and telephones. A few taxis. Buses to Tuy (worth a visit to the old town, as is Valença on the Portuguese side) and Bayona, and from both to Vigo.

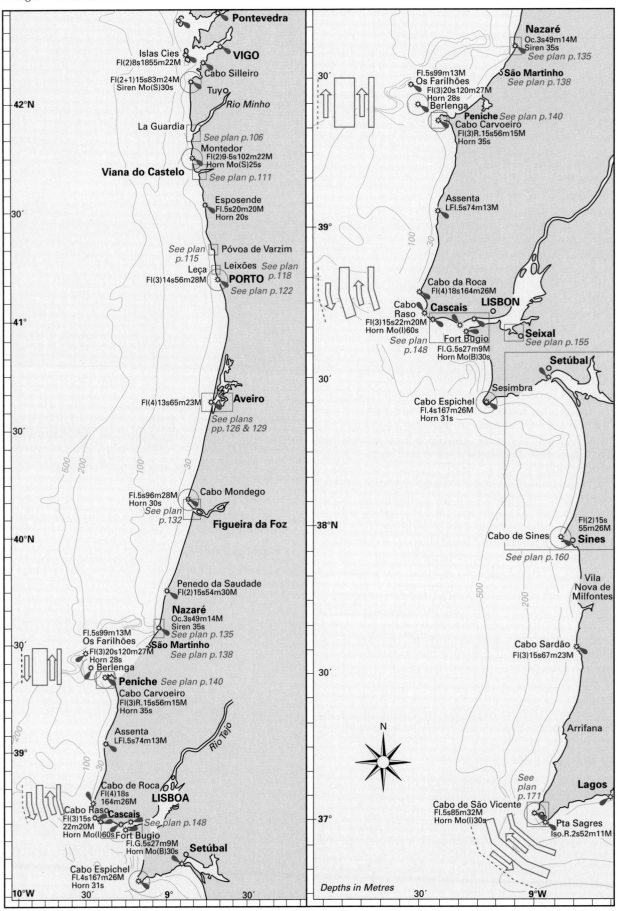

**Pontevedra**

Islas Cies
Fl(2)8s185m22M

**VIGO**

Cabo Silleiro
Fl(2+1)15s83m24M
Siren Mo(S)30s

Tuyo

*Rio Minho*

La Guardia

*See plan p.106*

Montedor
Fl(2)9·5s102m22M
Horn Mo(S)25s

**Viana do Castelo**

*See plan p.111*

Esposende
Fl.5s20m20M
Horn 20s

*See plan p.115*

Póvoa de Varzim

Leça
Fl(3)14s56m28M

Leixões *See plan p.118*

**PORTO**

*See plan p.122*

Fl(4)13s65m23M

**Aveiro**

*See plans pp.126 & 129*

Fl.5s96m28M
Horn 30s

Cabo Mondego

*See plan p.132*

**Figueira da Foz**

Penedo da Saudade
Fl(2)15s54m30M

**Nazaré**
Oc.3s49m14M
Siren 35s
*See plan p.135*

Fl.5s99m13M
Os Farilhões

Fl(3)20s120m27M
Horn 28s

**São Martinho**
*See plan p.138*

Berlenga

**Peniche** *See plan p.140*

Cabo Carvoeiro
Fl(3)R.15s56m15M
Horn 35s

Assenta
LFl.5s74m13M

*Rio Tejo*

Cabo de Roca
Fl(4)18s
164m26M

**LISBOA**

Cabo Raso
Fl(3)15s
22m20M
Horn Mo(I)60s

**Cascais**

*See plan p.148*

Fort Bugio
Fl.G.5s27m9M
Horn Mo(B)30s

**Setúbal**

Cabo Espichel
Fl.4s167m26M
Horn 31s

**Nazaré**
Oc.3s49m14M
Siren 35s
*See plan p.135*

**São Martinho**
*See plan p.138*

Fl.5s99m13M
Os Farilhões
Fl(3)20s120m27M
Horn 28s
Berlenga

**Peniche** *See plan p.140*
Cabo Carvoeiro
Fl(3)R.15s56m15M
Horn 35s

Assenta
LFl.5s74m13M

Cabo da Roca
Fl(4)18s164m26M

**Cascais**

**LISBON**

Cabo
Raso
Fl(3)15s22m20M
Horn Mo(I)60s

Fort Bugio
Fl.G.5s27m9M
Horn Mo(B)30s

*See plan p.148*

**Seixal**
*See plan p.155*

**Setúbal**

Sesimbra

Cabo Espichel
Fl.4s167m26M
Horn 31s

Fl(2)15s
55m26M

Cabo de Sines

**Sines**

*See plan p.160*

Vila
Nova de
Milfontes

Cabo Sardão
Fl(3)15s67m23M

Arrifana

*See plan p.171*

**Lagos**

Cabo de São Vicente
Fl.5s85m32M
Horn Mo(I)30s

Pta Sagres
Iso.R.2s52m11M

N

*Depths in Metres*

42°N

30′

41°

30′

40°N

30′

39°

30′

10°W    30′    9°    30′

30′

39°

30′

38°N

30′

37°

30′    9°W

# Portugal – the west coast

## Foz do Minho to Cabo de São Vicente

The Portuguese coast is not a cruising person's paradise, but it offers some remarkable places to visit – particularly Porto and Lisbon for their history, and Aveiro and the Rio Sado for their sandbanks and swamps. The coast itself is on the whole low – the hills are inland and in summer may be lost in the haze – and in places there are miles of featureless beach.

Only recently have the majority of harbours started to make provision for yachts, with marinas which accept visitors now operating at nine ports along the Atlantic coast in addition to those on the Algarve. Of these, five – Póvoa de Varzim, Nazaré, Peniche, Cascais and Sines – have opened since the previous (1995) edition of this book. Several of the older marinas – at Viana do Castelo, Leixões, Figueira da Foz and in Lisbon – either have had or are due to undergo facelifts, and visitors' berthing in Lisbon has become considerably more organised since the Administração do Porto de Lisboa took over running four of the city's six marinas.

A few harbours have hazards of one sort or another on their approach, most commonly a bar which alters with the winter storms and can be dangerous if there is a swell running, particularly if running across an ebbing tidal stream. Even though most river mouths are now dredged and no longer pose a threat in terms of depth – those of the Rio Minho in the north and Vila Nova de Milfontes in the south being notable exceptions – all can be dangerous in heavy weather, and on average at least one yacht is lost (or at least capsized) each year while attempting to enter harbour on the Portuguese Atlantic coast.

An excellent source of regularly updated information (in addition to any supplements which may be produced for this edition of *Atlantic Spain & Portugal*) is the website maintained by Viana do Castelo resident David Lumby at www.manorhouses.com/ports. As of March 2000 its 162 pages covered nearly all possible harbours and anchorages on the coast of Portugal, both Atlantic and Algarve, and yachtsmen without internet access should make every effort to get a friend to print them out a copy before departure. Needless to say, David's help was instrumental in updating the entire Portuguese section of the current volume.

### Hazards – lobster and fish pots

Clusters of fish pots may be met with at intervals along the Portuguese coast, particularly in the northern part and often around the approaches to harbours. Others are laid well out to sea in surprising depths, and although most are reasonably well marked with flags, a minority rely on dark coloured plastic containers or even branches. A few years ago a yacht had to be freed by the authorities at Viana do Castelo having become entangled, at night and in 30 knots of wind, with a pot float marked by a BLACK flag. Beware!

### Swell

Swell along this coast originates well offshore and as a result is seldom absent. In many ways it poses a greater danger than the wind, not least because it is extremely easy to underestimate its extent while still in deep water and to be taken by surprise by its height and power on closing the coast. In winter it can come from anywhere between southwest and northwest; in summer it is more likely to come from northwest, with heavy swell occurring about 10% of the time.

### Winds

In April the prevailing northerly Portuguese trades begin to set in, generally blowing at around 15–25 knots (force 4–6), and becoming more firmly established from north to south as the season advances. In winter, fronts and occasionally secondary depressions may cross the area. Summer gales are unusual – in winter, onshore gales can close some harbours for days.

Particular mention should be made of the strength of the afternoon sea breezes. From early summer onwards these start to blow at around 1200 each day, regularly reaching 25 knots (force 6) and occasionally 30 knots (force 7) and continuing to blow until sundown. Typically they pick up from the east, swinging north and increasing during the afternoon. For this reason passages north, particularly in smaller yachts or if lightly crewed, are

Portugal - the west coast

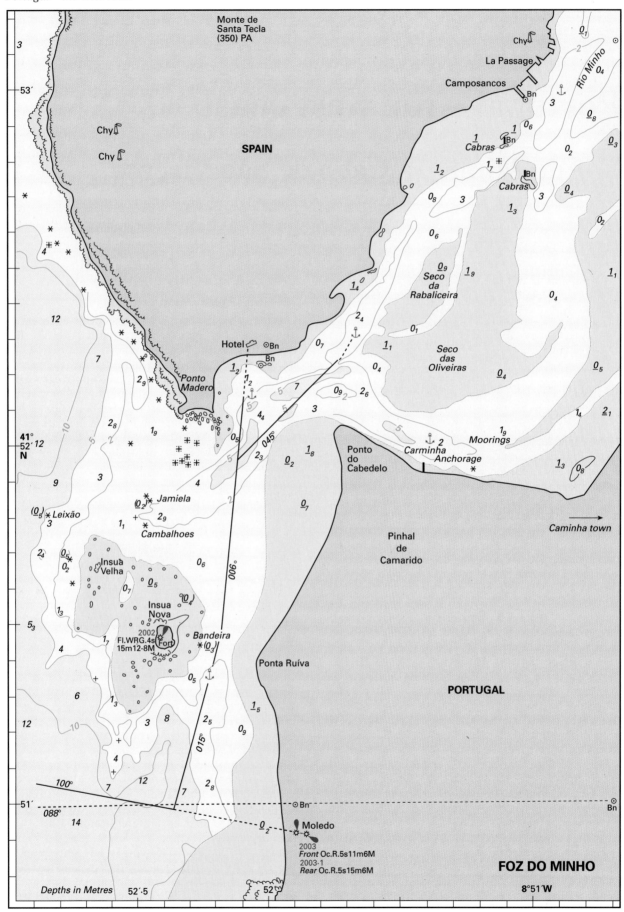

most easily made in short daily hops between dawn and midday with afternoons spent in harbour.

However it should be stressed that while these are the typical conditions, others can and do override them from time to time. In September 1999 southwesterly winds gusting to 35 knots (force 8) blew without respite for more than a week, closing harbours and causing several fatalities. Local yachtsmen agreed that they were most unusual that early in the year, but not unknown.

Winds are frequently stronger in river mouths and in the lee of headlands (due to the katabatic effects) and allowance should be made for this if entering under sail.

## Visibility

Poor visibility (less than 2M) can occur any time of year but there is a steep increase in its incidence (from 3% to 10%) 60M either side of Lisbon in July and an increase of approximately the same order further north in August and September. By October, all areas have returned to the 2%–4% level. Coastal fog can occur at any time but generally comes with light onshore winds.

## Shelter

Many Portuguese harbours provide excellent shelter once inside, but in strong onshore winds only Leixões, Nazaré, Peniche, Cascais, Lisbon and Sines are likely to be safe to enter. In really strong winds even the entrance to the Rio Tejo (Lisbon) can be dangerous.

## Currents

The set of the current depends upon the recent dominant wind, but the basic trend is from north to south. Its speed averages about 0·5 knot, though this can double in summer when the *nortada* (or Portuguese trade wind) has been blowing for some time.

## Tides

Tidal predictions throughout Portugal use Lisbon as the Standard Port. If tide tables are not available, as a very rough guide high water Lisbon occurs at approximately 0410 and 1630 at springs ±30 minutes, and 0920 and 2230 at neaps ±1hour 10 minutes.

The mean tidal range at Lisbon is 3·3m at springs and 1·6m at neaps, but both height and time of tide along the coast can be affected by wind. Offshore tidal streams are very weak and surprisingly little is known about them – at Cabo Carvoeiro it is said to flood to the southeast, roughly the opposite to the stream off Galicia, but it is not known where the change takes place.

## Climate

Rain occurs mainly between November and March, with cloud following the same pattern. Cool in winter, warm in summer, cooler in the north, warmer in the south. July averages for Lisbon are 14–36°C with 57% humidity; in January 3–16°C with 75% humidity.

## Coast radio stations and weather/navigational services

Many Portuguese coast radio stations and those broadcasting weather and navigational information are situated between, rather than at, ports or harbours. Details will be found under the nearest harbour to the station. All coast radio stations are remotely controlled from Lisbon, ☎ 214 190098 *Fax* 214 199900.

Broadcast times are quoted in UT unless otherwise specified.

## Marine weather information by telephone

In Portugal, recorded marine weather bulletins are available, in Portuguese, on the following numbers:
*Spanish border to Lisbon*
Inshore ☎ 0601 123 123; offshore ☎ 0601 123 140
*Lisbon to Cabo de São Vicente*
Inshore ☎ 0601 123 124; offshore ☎ 0601 123 141.

# Foz do Minho

41°52'N 8°52'W

## Tides

*Reference port* Lisbon
*Mean time differences* (at La Guardia)
HW: −10 minutes ±10; LW: +15 minutes ±10

*Heights in metres*

| MHWS | MHWN | MLWN | MLWS |
|------|------|------|------|
| 3·3  | 2·6  | 1·2  | 0·4  |

## Charts

|  | Approach | Entrance/river |
|---|---|---|
| Admiralty | *3633* | |
| Portuguese (old series) | *1* | *51* |
| Portuguese (new series) | *23201, 24201* | *26301* |
| Spanish | *417* | |

## Lights

### Approach
1916 **Cabo Silleiro Aeromarine** 42°06'·2N 8°53'·8W
Fl(2+1)15s83m24M
White tower, red bands, on white building 30m
Siren Mo(S)30s 900m NNW Old light tower
*0935* Radiobeacon *RO* 293·5kHz 100M
(Reliable sector 020°–145°)
2008 **Montedor** 41°44'·9N 8°52'·4W
Fl(2)9·5s102m22M Horn Mo(S)25s 800m WSW
Square masonry tower and building 28m
*0945* Radiobeacon *MR* 290kHz 150M (1 & 4 in sequence)
### Entrance
2002 **Insua Nova** 41°51'·4N 8°52'·5W
Fl.WRG.4s15m12·8M
204°-G-270°-R-357°-W-204°
White conical tower on square base 7m
2003 **Ldg Lts on 100°** 41°50'·9N 8°51'·9W
*Front* **Moledo** Oc.R.5s11m6M
White hexagonal column, red stripes, on beach 3m
*2003·1* *Rear*, 25m from front, Oc.R.5s15m6M
White hexagonal column, red stripes, on beach 7m

## Coast radio station

**Arga** (41°48'N 8°41'W) (24 hours) Remotely controlled from Lisbon
**VHF** Ch 16, 25, 28, 83.

## Port radio

*Capimarcaminha* VHF Ch 11, 16, (0900–1200, 1400–1700 Mon–Fri)

## General

The Rio Minho (or Río Miño to those further north) forms part of the boundary between Spain and Portugal. It gives its name to Portugal's northern province, where the hilly landscape with its numerous villages and their vines, eucalyptus and fruit trees is as pretty as its produce is good.

The Minho valley itself is particularly attractive and, with local knowledge and a current large-scale chart or plan, a yacht of modest draught can navigate a considerable distance up the river. Dinghies, multihulls and monohulls able to take the ground can penetrate as far as Valença on the Portuguese shore (where there are bridges with an estimated clearance 15m) or Túy (Tui) on the Spanish side.

The shallow river mouth (*foz*) is continually changing in shape, particularly regarding the position of the deep channel. For current information check David Lumby's website (see page 105).

## Approach

Between La Guardia and the mouth (*foz*) of the river is the 350m Monte de Santa Tecla, topped by grey stone buildings and an aerial. At its base is a conspicuous factory with two tall chimneys. In the middle of the entrance is the low-lying Insua Nova with its fort[2002]. South of the entrance a narrow strip of land fronted by a sandy beach separates the sea from hills which rise to some 700m about 8km inland.

## Entrance

The entrance is difficult and can be dangerous, and as recently as 1995 a yacht was capsized while attempting entry. It should therefore be considered only in calm weather with little or no swell. There are a mass of rocks, shoals and banks in the approaches and the river itself, the sands shift, and the currents run hard in the narrow entrance particularly after rain. Once in the channel there are no buoys or other channel markers. With any swell or westerly winds the bar is dangerous and a yacht can be trapped inside for some days, though well protected. In theory it is possible to pass either north or south of Insua Nova, but the northern passage should not be attempted without local knowledge.

If possible enter at about half flood, when Bandeira rock, 150m east of Insua Nova, will be visible.

If coming from the north keep at least 0·5M off Insua Nova and continue south until, by turning onto the Moledo leading line[2003] on 100°, one passes south of its fort by some 0·5M. If in doubt there is good water to the south. If coming from the south keep a good 0·5M offshore until able to turn onto 100°, as above. Although the Moledo leading marks are lit, night approach is out of the question. The nearby pair of beacons on 088° – see plan – may also be useful but the rear beacon, nearly a mile inland, is difficult to identify.

The mouth of the Rio Minho, with Insua Nova in the foreground, viewed from the southwest.

Insua Nova and the mouth of the Rio Minho, looking almost due south from the heights of Monte de Santa Tecla. No question as to why the northern passage is not recommended!

When the east side of Insua Nova bears 000°, turn onto approximately 015° to pass as close to the island as Bandeira rock allows – the sandbank off Ponta Ruíva opposite has extended westwards by some 150m since the previous edition of this book was researched and there appears no obvious reason for this growth to stop. If feasible, anchor about 250m southeast of the fort and reconnoitre by dinghy before pushing on. After leaving Bandeira rock close to port head straight for the conspicuous hotel on the Spanish shore on a bearing of approximately 006°, ignoring the leading marks to the east of the hotel. Just south of the latitude of the rocky shoal south of Ponto Madero turn northeast, parallel to the Spanish shore. South of the point depths shoal quickly inside the 5m contour.

If heading towards Caminha town, the channel lies approximately 200m off the southern shore. It shoals after the shore turns northeast towards Caminha.

If continuing north-northeast, keep close to the north shore and near the La Passage shipyard. Keep to the middle of the gap between the two Cabras (goat) rocks, awash at high tide but both marked by posts. More substantial lit beacons indicate the ferry channel between the small towns of Camposancos and Caminha.

**Anchorages near the Foz**

1. As already mentioned, temporary anchorage is possible 250m southeast of the fort on Insua Nova from which one can check out the next section by dinghy. Holding is good over clean sand, protected from west through north to southeast, but it is too exposed for an overnight stay.
2. South of the hotel on the Spanish side of the entrance, protected from the west by Ponto Madero, in 2–3m.
3. Between the Seco das Oliveiras sandbank and the Spanish shore in 2–3m.
4. Off the southern shore east of Ponta do Cabedelo (known as the Caminha anchorage in spite of being some way from the town).
5. Abeam of the La Passage shipyard, but keeping clear of the dredged ferry channel.

Looking southeast across the Rio Minho from Monte de Santa Tecla, with (Spanish) Camposancos in the foreground and (Portuguese) Caminha across the river.

## Formalities

A military patrol vessel is stationed at the jetty at Caminha anchorage, and there is a *capitania* near the Caminha ferry berth, open 0900–1230 and 1400–1800 weekdays, which should be visited if anchored in the vicinity. *Alfândega* (customs) buildings at both Caminha and Camposancos indicate a former interest in international traffic, but there has been no official activity for a number of years.

## Facilities

On the Portuguese shore a restaurant and a campsite with a small general store will be found near anchorage *No.3* above. Caminha itself (within walking distance) has shops, a market, banks and restaurants.

On the Spanish side there is a shipyard building trawlers at La Passage and a few buildings near the ferry landing at Goyan, but otherwise little between La Guardia and Túy.

## Communications

On the Spanish side a taxi can be organised via the shipyard. Caminha has taxis, plus buses and trains to Valença, Vigo and Porto, as well as post office and telephones.

## Additional anchorage

Ancora, with its small stone fort and miniature harbour, lies some 3M south of Foz de Minho. There is no room to seek protection inside the tiny harbour – even local craft are hauled high up a wide concrete apron – but in the right conditions anchoring is possible in 2–3m just off the breakwater. However, even if the morning breeze is offshore, by lunchtime the *nortada* may well make the anchorage untenable and the yacht should never be left unattended.

If intent on exploration remain at least 0·5M offshore until the harbour has been identified, then pick up the leading marks on 071° (two red and white posts on white pyramid bases). The cross on the hill above is almost in line.

The town has shops and restaurants.

# Viana do Castelo

41°41'N 8°50'W

## Tides

*Reference port* Lisbon
*Mean time differences*
HW: −10 minutes ±10; LW: +15 minutes ±5
*Heights in metres*

| MHWS | MHWN | MLWN | MLWS |
|------|------|------|------|
| 3·5 | 2·7 | 1·4 | 0·5 |

## Charts

|  | Approach | Harbour |
|---|---|---|
| Admiralty | 3633, 3634 | 3254 |
| Portuguese (old series) | 1 | 53 |
| Portuguese (new series) | 23201, 24201 | 26401 |
| Spanish | 41B | |
| Imray | C19 | C19 |

The entrance to Viana do Castelo from the south-southwest. Buoy No.2, a red pillar, can just be made out in the centre.

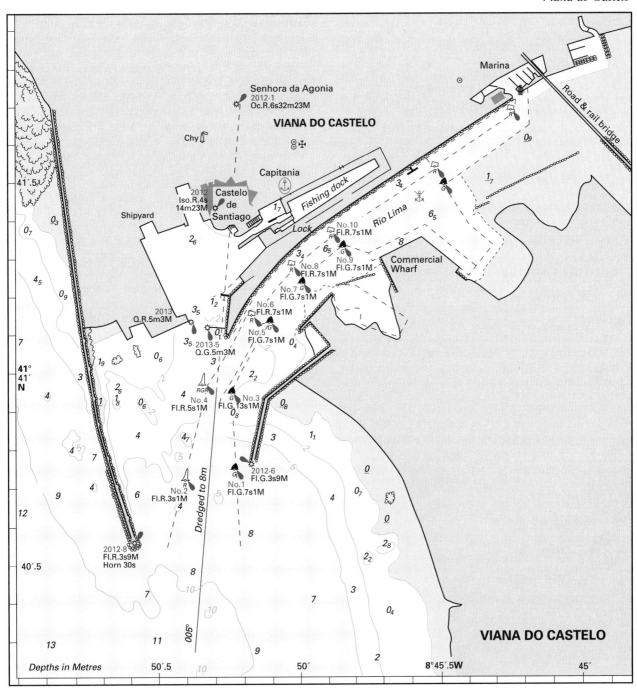

Viana do Castelo

## Lights

### Approach

2008 **Montedor** 41°44'·9N 8°52'·4W
  Fl(2)9·5s102m22M Horn Mo(S)25s 800m WSW
  Square masonry tower and building 28m

*0945* Radiobeacon *MR* 290kHz 150M (1 & 4 in
  sequence)

2016 **Esposende** 41°32'·5N 8°47'·4W
  Fl.5s20m20M Horn 20s 100m S
  Red round tower and building 15m

### Harbour

2012·8 **Outer breakwater** 41°40'·5N 8°50'·6W
  Fl.R.3s9M Horn 30s
  White round tower, red bands 10m

2012 **Fishing dock Ldg Lts on 012·5°** 41°41'·4N
  8°50'·3W

*Front* **Castelo de Santiago** Iso.R.4s14m23M
  241°-vis-151°
  Red round tower, narrow white stripes and lantern
  6m

2012·1 *Rear* **Senhora da Agonia**, 500m from front,
  Oc.R.6s32m23M 005°-vis-020°
  Red round tower, narrow white stripes and lantern
  9m

*Note* The above leading lights apply to the fishing
  harbour only and should NOT be followed through
  the entrance itself

2012·6 **East (inner) breakwater** 41°40'·7N 8°50'·2W
  Fl.G.3s9M
  White round tower, green bands 6m

buoy *No.2* 41°40'·6N 8°50'·4W
  Fl.R.3s1M Red pillar buoy

buoy **No.1** 41°40'·7N 8°50'·2W
  Fl.G.7s1M Green conical buoy
buoy **No.3** 41°40'·9N 8°50'·2W
  Fl.G.13s1M Green conical buoy
buoy **No.4** 41°40'·9N 8°50'·3W
  Fl.R.5s1M Red pillar buoy, green band
2013 **Fishing dock, port side** 41°41'·1N 8°50'·4W
  Q.R.5m3M White column, red bands
2013·5 **Fishing dock, starboard side** 41°41'·1N
  8°50'·3W
  Q.G.5m3M White column, green bands
buoy **No.6** 41°41'·1N 8°50'·1W
  Fl.R.7s1M Red can buoy
buoy **No.5** 41°41'·1N 8°50'·1W
  Fl.G.7s1M Green conical buoy
Seven further lit buoys mark the approach to the marina.

## Marina and port radio

*VianaMarina* VHF Ch 62, 16 (0900–1900 daily)
*Capimarviana* VHF Ch 11, 16 (0900–1200, 1400–1700
  Mon–Fri)
*Pilotosviana* VHF Ch 16, 14.

## General

Near the mouth of the Rio Lima, Viana do Castelo will provide a welcome break if slogging north and a fine introduction to Portugal if heading south. In the 16th century the town grew rich from trade with Brazil and from cod fishing on the Newfoundland Banks, where the Portuguese swapped local fortified wine for nets brought out by fishermen from England's West Country. This returned to England as 'Portuguese wine' later abbreviated to 'Port wine'. English merchants came to Viana do Castelo to develop the trade, which moved to Vila Nova de Gaia on the Rio Douro, opposite Porto, when the harbour at Viana silted up. In the meantime the town's citizens had built the beautiful grey granite and white stucco houses which make the old town attractive today. It still has a fishing fleet, some industry and is an active port.

In 1992 a small marina was opened about 1·5M upriver, just short of the two-tier road and rail bridge (designed by Gustaf Eiffel of Tower fame). The town is a short walk away through pleasant public gardens. There are plans to replace the marina with a larger facility, probably located in the fishing dock and possibly part of a larger 'maritime complex' containing a museum, etc, but as of 1999 no firm date had been set.

One of the major *festas* of the Minho area is the *romaria* dedicated to Nossa Senhora da Agonía which takes place in Viana do Castelo over the weekend nearest to 20 August. And at any time of year the energetic will enjoy the steep walk up to the Basílica on Monte de Santa Luzia, which commands superb views over the town.

VianaMarina, with Monsieur Eiffel's two-tier bridge in the foreground looking west (downriver).

## Approach

Both north and south of Viana the coast has hazards close offshore – for peace of mind keep outside the 20m line. The major lights are Montedor[2008] to the north, Senhora da Agonia[2012·1] at Viana itself, and Esposende[2016]. There are a pair of leading lights at Neiva, 3·5M to the south, which are not relevant to Viana.

The entrance is dredged regularly, making it safe in all but the severest weather or swell.

## Entrance

From the north, take a wide swing eastwards at least 500m south of the outer breakwater. Ignore the front leading light[2012], instead steering 005° on the rear light[2012·1] to pass up the centre of the buoyed channel.

From the south, head in from the 20m line with the radio aerial on Faro de Anha bearing around 080° until the rear leading light[2012·1] bears 005°, then proceed as above.

Leaving the entrance to the fishing dock to port, follow the buoyed channel northeast past the commercial wharf to the marina entrance on the north bank, just short of the bridge and marked by a tall signal mast (on which white over red lights may be displayed). A total of nine buoys line the channel between the fishing dock and marina entrance (only four of which are currently shown on Admiralty *3254*), all lit red or green and all with periods of 7 seconds.

The main channel is dredged to 8m as far as the commercial wharf, the marina and its approach channel both to 3m, though an obstruction has been reported in the entrance to the marina reducing it to 2·5m at low water springs. Beware strong crosscurrents at the marina entrance on both the flood and the ebb. Anchoring in the river is prohibited.

## Berthing

The small VianaMarina, ☎ 258 359546 *Fax* 258 359535, contains some 150 berths of which around 30 are reserved for visiting yachts of up to 14m. In addition there is a single berth capable of taking a 20m vessel.

Visitors berth in the eastern section of the marina, bow or stern-to against the westernmost of four pontoons. There is no reception pontoon – choose any suitable berth unless otherwise directed. A pickup line is provided. The management are considering fitting finger pontoons, but are aware that this would decrease the number of visiting yachts the marina could accept.

In 1999 the high season (15/5–15/9) rate for a visiting yacht of just under 12m was 2,716 escudos (13·55 euros) per night, inclusive of water, electricity and tax.

## Formalities

The marina office, currently located in a portacabin at the east end of the basin, is open 0900–1900 daily. Although for many yachts this will be their first (or last) Portuguese harbour, formalities are straightforward with the marina computer producing forms for automatic distribution to the various officials. The usual passports, ship's papers and insurance documents will be required. Normally no other offices need be visited, though owners of non-EU registered yachts, or with non–EU nationals amongst their crew, should check current requirements. Yachts which arrive outside office hours may be visited by a member of the *brigada fiscal*.

Should one need to visit the *capitania* it will be found on the north side of the road which parallels the fishing dock.

## Facilities

*Boatyard* No boatyard at the marina, but extensive shipyards west of the fishing dock where commercial vessels, as well as GRP and timber fishing boats, are built. In an emergency there is little doubt that yacht repairs in most materials could be undertaken. Enquire at the marina office.

*Travel-lift* Not as such, but the marina can arrange 40 and 28 tonne mobile port cranes.

*Engineers* Costa & Rego, situated at the end of the car parks between the river and the old commercial dock, are precision engineers and machinists. They can arrange engine repairs and will copy any unobtainable metal parts.

*Electronic & radio repairs* Arrange through the marina office, though more accustomed to fishing vessels.

*Sailmaker/sail repairs* Peres de Lima runs a sail loft near Porto airport. Minor repairs may be done locally – enquire at the marina office.

*Chandlery* A good range will be found at Angelo Silva Lda overlooking the fishing boat basin. On the opposite side of the road just short of the chandlery is a shop stocking Hempel marine paints. There is a smaller chandlery (and Mariner outboard agent) near the market.

*Water* On the pontoons.

*Showers* New showers near the marina office should be operational for the 2000 season.

*Launderette* Opposite the Hotel Park, near the marina entrance.

*Electricity* On the pontoons.

*Fuel* Diesel and petrol at the fuelling pontoon on the starboard side just inside the marina entrance.

*Bottled gas* Camping Gaz is readily available, but if needing to get Calor or other bottles filled (though see page 8) try Angelo de Silva Lda (see Chandlery above). Allow at least 24 hours.

*Clube náutico* Small *clube náutico* at the east end of the marina basin, which visiting yachtsmen are welcome to use.

*Weather forecast* At the marina office.

*Banks* In the town.

*Shops/provisioning* Good shopping of all kinds in the town, including several supermarkets, with a hypermarket about 1·5km inland.

*Produce market* Fish and produce market daily, plus open-air general market on Friday near the Castelo de Santiago at the seaward end of the town.

*Cafés, restaurants & hotels* Plenty in and around the town. The *clube náutico* has a bar overlooking the marina which also serves light meals.

*Medical services* Hospital, etc in the town.

## Communications

*Post office* In the town.

*Mailing address*
    c/o **Instituto Portuário do Norte**,
    Doca de Recreio/Marina, Rua da Lima,
    4900 Viana do Castelo, Portugal.
    *Fax service* 258 359535

*Public telephones* In the entrance to the *clube náutico* and elsewhere.

*Car hire/taxis* In the town. Taxis can be called from the marina office.

*Buses & trains* To Porto, Vigo and beyond.

*Air services* International airport at Porto some 50km away.

## Not feasible

Esposende, just under 10M south of Viana do Castelo, should be mentioned in passing – literally. A long sandbank blocks the mouth of the Rio Cávado, leaving a very shallow entrance some 50m wide which gives onto an equally shallow lagoon where a few small boats are moored. Shoals and isolated rocks (the Cavalos de Fão and Baixo da Foz) extend up to 1·5M offshore opposite the lighthouse[2016]. Give it a wide berth.

# Póvoa de Varzim

41°22'N 8°46'W

## Tides

*Reference port* Lisbon
*Mean time differences*
HW: −10 minutes ±10; LW: +15 minutes ±5
*Heights in metres*

| MHWS | MHWN | MLWN | MLWS |
|------|------|------|------|
| 3·5  | 2·7  | 1·4  | 0·5  |

## Charts

|                        | Approach | Harbour |
|------------------------|----------|---------|
| Admiralty              | 3634     |         |
| Portuguese (old series)| 1        |         |
| Portuguese (new series)|          | 27501   |

## Lights

### Approach

2016 **Esposende** 41°32'·5N 8°47'·4W
    Fl.5s20m20M Horn 20s 100m S
    Red round tower and building 15m

2020 **Póvoa (Regufe)** 41°22'·4N 8°45'·2W
    Iso.6s29m15M Red round tower on tripod 22m

2032 **Leça** 41°12'·1N 8°42'·6W Fl(3)14s56m28M
    White tower, narrow grey bands, red lantern 46m
    Seven F.R on chimneys 1M northwards

0949 Radiobeacon *LC* 290kHz 100M (2 & 4 in sequence)

### Harbour

2020·4 **North breakwater** 41°22'·2N 8°46'·2W
    Fl.R.3s14m12M Red tower, white bands 5m
    Siren 40s

*Note* The breakwater projects some distance beyond the light structure

2020·6 **South breakwater** 41°22'·2N 8°46'W
    LFl.G.6s13m4M Green post 4m

Póvoa de Varzim seen from almost due south, with the new marina in the foreground. A great deal of development has taken place over the last few years in both town and harbour.

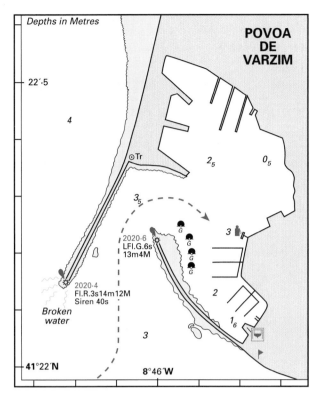

## Radio weather/navigational services

### Apúlia

*Storm warnings*: 2657kHz on receipt and at 0735, 2335 in Portuguese and English for coastal waters of Portugal up to 50M offshore.

*Weather messages*: 2657kHz at 0735, 2335 gale warnings, synopsis and forecast in Portuguese and English for coastal waters of Portugal up to 50M offshore.

*Navigational warnings*: 2657kHz on receipt and at 0735, 2335 in Portuguese and English for coastal waters of Portugal up to 50M offshore.

## Marina and port radio

*Marina da Póvoa* VHF Ch 62.

*Capimarvarzim* VHF Ch 11, 16 (0900–1200, 1400–1700 Mon–Fri).

## General

Coming in from the sea the view of Póvoa de Varzim has been described as 'like a miniature Manhattan' – though considerably less interesting. High-rise hotels line the beach, while the port is surrounded by a wire fence, inside which are assorted quays and jetties, and outside, a busy road. The town lives mainly by its tourists and its casino, though there is still an active fishing fleet.

The harbour is well protected from the northwest, but the entrance may be rough if the swell is heavy and even in moderate conditions breaking water can be expected off the breakwater end. After several years' work the new Marina da Póvoa opened at the end of June 1999, providing the harbour's first dedicated yacht facility.

## Approach

Between Viana do Castelo and Esposende[2016] the coast has off-lying dangers and should be given 2M clearance; south of Esposende there are sandy beaches and rocks with further off-lying hazards – for relaxed sailing keep outside the 20m contour.

The major light to the south is Leça[2032]. Again, the coast between has off-lying hazards and it is wise to keep outside the 20m contour.

A distinctive white apartment block stands a short distance north of the harbour. The latter may be identified by its tower – reminiscent of an airport control tower – which also serves as an excellent landmark. A range of fish-handling buildings stand behind it.

## Entrance

If approaching from the north swing wide of the breakwater end[2020·4] and its associated breaking water, and note that it is also foul up to 30m off on the south side. Approach heading north-northeast towards the spur which projects at right angles from the north breakwater, giving the latter a 50m offing. When the southern breakwater head[2020·6] has been cleared, turn to starboard for the marina or anchorage leaving the line of small green buoys (which mark shoals on the inside of the breakwater) well to starboard. There is about 3·5m in the entrance.

## Berthing

As mentioned above, the new Marina da Póvoa, ☎ 252 688121 *Fax* 252 688123, was up and running for the 1999 season, complete with two large buildings in addition to the nearby *clube naval*. It offers 241 berths on its six pontoons, about a third of which can accommodate yachts of 10m or more in depths of at least 2·4m – the four largest berths, for yachts of up to 18m, carry at least 3m at all times. Around 40 berths are reserved for visitors.

The marina lies in the shelter of the south breakwater, and even in gale force west-northwesterlies experiences remarkably little movement inside. All berths are provided with finger pontoons of appropriate length.

On arrival yachts should berth on the short hammerhead by the marina office (which in due course will double as the fuel pontoon). Office hours are 0900–1230 and 1400–1930, but a night watchman provides 24 hour security. When visited in September 1999 the marina officials were notably helpful and friendly, and good English was spoken.

In its first year of operation the overnight charge including VAT at 16% for a visiting yacht of just under 12m was 1,972 escudos (9·48 euros), or 2,320 escudos (11·57 euros) if her beam exceeded 3·7m, inclusive of water and electricity. Multihulls were subject to a 50% surcharge.

## Anchorage

As of 1999 anchoring in the harbour was still permitted, provided neither the marina approach nor the many fishing boat movements to and from the north breakwater were impeded. The most obvious spot is in the northeast of the harbour, clear of the yacht and smallcraft moorings, in about 3m over mud and sand. Depths shoals gradually at some distance from the shore.

## Formalities

If berthed in the marina visit the office taking passports, ship's papers and insurance documents. A single form (in quintuplicate, but on self-carbonated paper) must be completed, copies of which are then circulated by the marina to the *brigada fiscal*, *alfândega* and *policia maritima*. This procedure must be observed whether entering Portugal for the first time or arriving from elsewhere within the country. If not berthed in the marina it will be necessary to seek out the various officials at their offices in the town.

## Facilities

*Boatyard* Not currently envisaged.

*Travel-lift* 36 tonne capacity hoist and 6·3 tonne crane to be installed in January 2000 (the travel-lift dock is already in place). There is a large area of open space fronting the marina, part of which is designated for use as hardstanding. A small covered workshop has been provided in the central marina building, next to the main gate.

*Engineers, electronic & radio repairs* All skills available amongst those who service the fishing fleet – enquire at the marina office. A professional diver is also available.

*Water* On the pontoons.

*Showers* In the central marina building.

*Launderette* In the central marina building.

*Electricity* At every berth.

*Fuel* Diesel and pumps are due to be installed by June 2000. They will be sited ashore near the marina office and provided with long hoses to reach yachts berthed on the hammerhead.

*Bottled gas* Camping Gaz available in the town.

*Clube náutico* The Clube Naval Povoense has large premises overlooking the south breakwater, where members' dinghies and jet-skis are stored on the ground floor with a bar and restaurant above. Visiting yachtsmen are made welcome.

*Weather forecast* Posted daily at the marina office.

*Banks* In the town, about ten minutes' walk.

*Shops/provisioning* Good range in the town, with a large supermarket about 2km distant.

*Produce market* In the town.

*Cafés, restaurants & hotels* Wide variety in the town, as well as a restaurant at the *clube naval*.

*Medical services* Well equipped first aid post at the marina's central building, with doctors and a hospital in the town.

## Communications

*Post offices* In the town.

*Mailing address*
> c/o **Clube Naval Povoense**, Rua da Ponte 2,
> 4490 Póvoa de Varzim, Portugal
> *Fax service* 252 688123

*Public telephones* Two cabins are to be installed at the marina office, for coins and cards respectively.

*Car hire/taxis* In the town. A taxi can be called from the marina office.

*Buses & trains* To Porto, Viana do Castelo, etc.

*Air services* International airport at Porto some 20km away.

# Vila do Conde
41°20'N 8°45'W

## Tides

See Póvoa de Varzim, page 114

## Charts

|  | Approach | Harbour |
|---|---|---|
| Admiralty | *3634* | |
| Portuguese (old series) | *1, 22* | |
| Portuguese (new series) | | *27501* |

## Lights

### Approach
2016 **Esposende** 41°32'·5N 8°47'·4W
Fl.5s20m20M Horn 20s 100m S
Red round tower and building 15m
2020 **Póvoa (Regufe)** 41°22'·4N 8°45'·2W
Iso.6s29m15M Red round tower on tripod 22m
2032 **Leça** 41°12'·1N 8°42'·6W Fl(3)14s56m28M
White tower, narrow grey bands, red lantern 46m
Seven F.R on chimneys 1M northwards
*0949* Radiobeacon *LC* 290kHz 100M (2 & 4 in sequence)

### Harbour
2023·7 **Northwest breakwater** 41°20'·3N 8°45'·1W
Fl.R.4s8m9M Siren 30s
Red column, white bands 8m
2023 **Outer Ldg Lts on 079°** 41°20'·1N 8°44'·4W
*Front* **Azurara** Iso.G.4s9m6M
White post, red bands 7m, on the beach
2023·1 *Rear*, 370m from front, Iso.G.4s26m6M
White ▲ on white building, red bands 6m
2024 **Inner Ldg Lts on 000°** 41°20'·4N 8°44'·8W
*Front* **Barra** Oc.R.3s7m6M
White column, red bands 5m
2024·1 *Rear*, 130m from front, Oc.R.3s11m6M
White column, red bands 5m

## Port radio

*Capimarviconde* VHF Ch 11, 16 (0900–1200, 1400–1700 Mon–Fri).

## General

A small and difficult harbour only suitable for entry in calm weather, in daylight and towards high tide. The town has a thriving tourist industry and is known for its lace-making. A crafts fair is held over the last week of July and first week of August.

The village at the entrance, Azurara, has a Manueline fortified church, a small stone fort and an attractive rocky beach where, until very recently, seaweed was still collected for removal by horse-drawn sleds.

In 1999 it was said that 'something for yachts' was planned for Vila do Conde, probably close east of the small chapel where the inner leading lights intersect with the shore. However exactly what this might be, and when work might start, was not known.

## Approach

The entrance lies at the southern end of the line of high-rise blocks strung out along the beach between Póvoa and Vila do Conde. The northwest (seaward) mole[2023·7] of some 350m has a small chapel dedicated to Senhora da Guia at its root.

## Entrance

The first set of leading marks[2023], on 079°, clears the mole. The next set[2024], on 000°, leads over the bar – which may shoal to 0·5m at low water springs – but as the bar shifts these do not always indicate best water. In the mid-1990s the channel was marked by pairs of very small plastic buoys – red to port and white to starboard – but these were not in place in September 1999. Once round the eastern (inner) mole the channel swings to pass south of a small, L-shaped sandbank.

Tidal streams in the relatively narrow entrance can run strongly on both ebb and flood.

## Anchorage

Continue upriver to anchor just short of the road bridge in 3–4m, between a fortified church with a distinctive white dome and a vast, square convent building. Traces of the old shipyard which operated on the north bank until a few years ago can still be seen, opposite an almost equally derelict (but currently still functioning) boatbuilding concern to the south. The cleanliness of the water may leave something to be desired.

## Facilities

Reasonable food shops, banks and restaurants, plus Friday market.

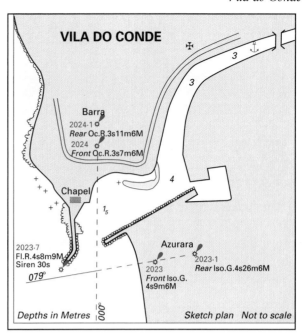

**VILA DO CONDE**

Barra
2024·1 ☼
*Rear* Oc.R.3s11m6M
2024 ☼
*Front* Oc.R.3s7m6M

Chapel

2023·7
Fl.R.4s8m9M
Siren 30s
079°

Azurara
2023·1
*Rear* Iso.G.4s26m6M
2023
*Front* Iso.G.
4s9m6M

*Depths in Metres*          *Sketch plan   Not to scale*

## Communications

Post office and telephones. Trains and buses to Porto, etc.

The narrow, dog-legged entrance to Vila do Conde, seen from the southwest.

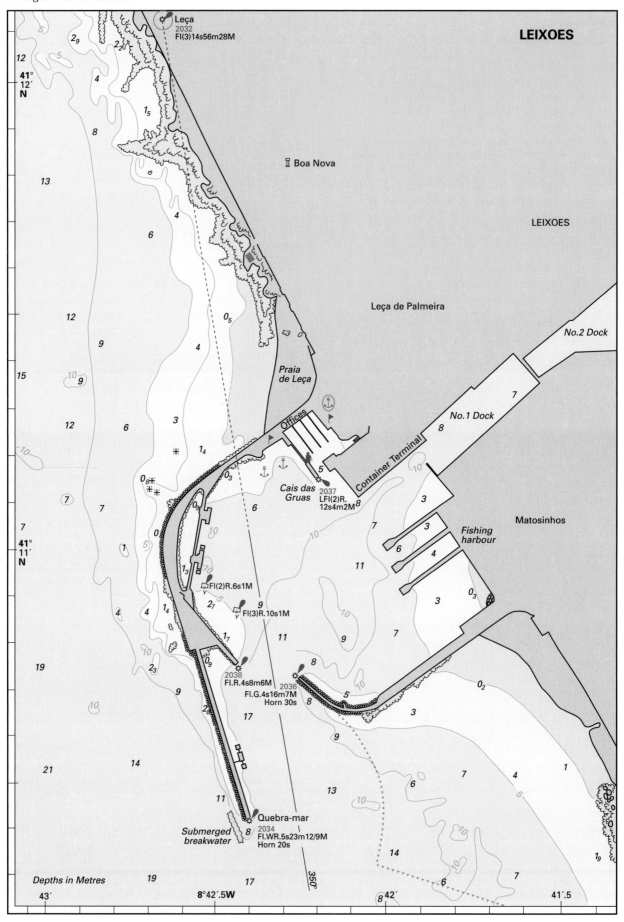

**LEIXOES**

Leça
2032
Fl(3)14s56m28M

♨ Boa Nova

LEIXOES

Leça de Palmeira

No.2 Dock

No.1 Dock

*Praia de Leça*

Offices

Container Terminal

7

8

Matosinhos

*Cais das Gruas*

2037
LFl(2)R.
12s4m2M

*Fishing harbour*

Fl(2)R.6s1M
Y

Fl(3)R.10s1M
Y

2038
Fl.R.4s8m6M

2036
Fl.G.4s16m7M
Horn 30s

*Quebra-mar*

*Submerged breakwater*

2034
Fl.WR.5s23m12/9M
Horn 20s

*Depths in Metres*

41°
12´
N

41°
11´
N

43´

8°42´.5W

350°

8° 42´

41´.5

118

# Leixões

41°11'N 8°42'W

## Tides

*Reference port* Lisbon
*Mean time differences*
HW: −15 minutes ±10; LW: +05 minutes ±5
*Heights in metres*

| MHWS | MHWN | MLWN | MLWS |
|------|------|------|------|
| 3·5 | 2·7 | 1·3 | 0·5 |

## Charts

|  | Approach | Harbour |
|---|---|---|
| Admiralty | *3634* | *254* |
| Portuguese (old series) | *1, 2, 16, 22* | *58* |
| Portuguese (new series) | *23202, 24201* | *26402* |

## Lights

### Approach

*0947* **Pedras Rubras (Porto) aerobeacon** 41°19'·1N
8°42'W
Aerobeacon *POR* 327kHz 250M
*2031* **Pedras Rubras (Porto) airport** 41°14'·3N
8°40'·4W
Aero Al.Fl.WG.10s84m Control tower 16m
*2032* **Leça** 41°12'·1N 8°42'·6W Fl(3)14s56m28M
White tower, narrow grey bands, red lantern 46m
Seven F.R on chimneys 1M northwards
*0949* Radiobeacon *LC* 290kHz 100M (2 & 4 in
sequence)
buoy **M1 (outfall)** 41°12'·5N 8°44'·7W
Fl.Y.4s6M Horn 30s Yellow spherical buoy
buoy **Tanker discharge** 41°12'·2N 8°45'W
Mo(U)15s6M Horn Mo(U)30s Yellow superbuoy

### Harbour

*2034* **West breakwater, head** 41°10'·4N 8°42'·4W
Fl.WR.5s23m12/9M 001°-R-180°-W-001°
Horn 20s Round grey tower 10m
*2038* **West breakwater, spur** 41°10'·7N 8°42'·4W
Fl.R.4s8m6M Red lantern 4m
*2036* **South breakwater** 41°10'·7N 8°42'·3W
Fl.G.4s16m7M 328°-vis-285° Horn 30s
Hexagonal tower, green lantern 10m
buoy **Breakwater south** 41°10'·9N 8°42'·4W
Fl(3)R.10s1M Yellow pillar buoy
buoy **Breakwater north** 41°10'·9N 8°42'·5W
Fl(2)R.6s1M Yellow pillar buoy
*2037* **Marina mole** 41°11'·1N 8°42'·2W
LFl(2)R.12s4m2M White post, red bands 3m

## Radio weather/navigational services

### Leixões

*Weather messages*: VHF Ch 11 at 1030, 1630 gale
warnings and forecast in Portuguese for Porto de
Leixões.
*Navigational warnings*: VHF Ch 11 at 1030, 1630 in
Portuguese for Porto de Leixões.

## Marina and port radio

*Marina Porto Atlântico* VHF Ch 62 (0900–1230 &
1400–2000 daily 16/6–15/9; otherwise 0900–1230 &
1400–1830 Monday–Saturday).
*Postradleixões & Estação Rada de Leixões* VHF Ch 01, 04,
09, 10, 11, 12, 13, 14, 16, 18, 19, 20, 60, 61, 63, 67,
68, 69, 71, 79, 80, 84; 2182, 2484, 2657kHz (24
hours).
*Pilotosleixões* VHF Ch 14, 16.
(radar station) VHF Ch 12, 16.

## General

Leixões, with its wide entrance, is by far the best
port of refuge on this stretch of the coast and can be
entered in almost any weather. The busy
commercial port is centred on oil, fishing and
general trade, while the Marina Porto Atlântico in
its northwest corner was one of the first yacht
harbours to be established on the Portuguese
Atlantic coast. The marina provides reasonable
shelter and facilities, and is an excellent base from
which to explore the fascinating city of Porto, easily
accessible by bus or taxi. The facilities available,
with the exception of provisions, are much better
than those on offer in Porto, but the nearby towns of
Leça de Palmeira and Matosinhos cannot compete
with the older city in terms of shopping, historical
interest and tourist sights.

Perhaps inevitably, bearing in mind its position in
the corner of a commercial harbour, the marina has
gained a reputation among yachtsmen for very dirty
water, particularly in southwesterly winds.
Yachtsmen (and women) who sat out a gale there in
autumn 1999 spoke with varying degrees of humour
of a dead rat which floated around the marina for at
least three days, ignored by the marina staff who
were otherwise praised as being helpful and
efficient. Not a place to investigate one's propeller!

Looking west of north into the large commercial harbour of Leixões. A fair-sized ship lies against the west breakwater, while a fleet of
racing dinghies makes its way in, probably heading for one of the *clube náuticos* in the northeast corner.

## Approach

Compared to the coastline further north, the area around Leixões is somewhat featureless. The oil refinery 1·5M north is a good mark by day or night, with the powerful Leça light[2032] lying between it and the harbour. If in the vicinity after dark note that both the yellow buoys listed under Approach Lights have been reported unlit at times during the past two years, and other unlit yellow buoys have been seen nearby. A prohibited zone extends 1000m in all directions from the superbuoy, which is located about 1·5M offshore and well outside the 20m depth contour.

Harbour regulations state that vessels must give the outside of the west breakwater a berth of at least 1M, but few fishing boats appear to observe this. There are, however, shoals up to 200m off the seaward side of this breakwater as well as obstructions off its end.

There are fewer obstructions if approaching from the south, though several lit yellow buoys may be encountered within 1M of the shore. The massed buildings of Porto can be seen from a good distance, with the entrance to Leixões 2M northwest.

## Entrance

The breakwater light may be difficult to identify against shore lights, but from south of the harbour Leça light[2032] on 350° leads between the breakwater spur and the south breakwater, after which the marina will become visible. During westerly gales the swell at the entrance may be heavy, but it decreases rapidly once inside. Floating debris can be a real hazard when crossing the harbour, and it is also best to avoid entry in the early evening when the many fishing trawlers are heading out to sea. The marina mole was extended by 30m a few years ago and is now lit[2037].

The Marina Porto Atlântico at Leixões, looking a little south of east. The marina offices are housed in the red-roofed buildings in the centre foreground.

## Berthing

The three yacht clubs and the Marina Porto Atlântico, ☎ 229 964895 *Fax* 229 964899, are all located around the old fishing harbour at the northwest of the main harbour, behind a short mole (the Cais das Gruas). The narrow entrance (less than 50m wide) faces southeast, but even so considerable swell may work in during strong southwesterlies. Boats berthed near the entrance will obviously bear the brunt.

The marina, which has been dredged to 5m and can berth about 240 boats, is crowded with local craft but space for a visitor can generally be found. It claims to be able to accommodate one or two yachts of up to 30m, though it is difficult to see where. Secure to the reception pontoon (to port on entry) and visit the marina office on the ground floor of the building at the root of the marina mole. Office hours are 0900–1230 and 1400–2000 daily from 16/6 until 15/9, closing at 1830 and all day Sunday outside the high season. Berthing is alongside narrow finger pontoons.

In 1999 the rate for a visiting yacht of just under 12m at any time of year was 3,569 escudos (17·80 euros) per night, inclusive of water, electricity and tax. Multihulls paid a 50% surcharge.

## Anchorage

Although in theory anchoring within the harbour is prohibited (and very occasionally anchored yachts will be moved on by the harbour authorities), in practice good anchorage will be found just outside the marina in the angle formed by the marina mole and the breakwater in 5m or more. Holding, particularly near the mole, is reported to be good over mud. There are several ladders at which dinghies can be left (though note the 3m spring range), including one giving directly onto the premises of the Yate Clube de Porto.

## Formalities

Visit the marina office taking passports, ship's papers and insurance documents, whether berthed in the marina or anchored off. A single form (in quintuplicate, but on self-carbonated paper) must be completed, copies of which are then circulated by the marina to the *brigada fiscal*, *alfândega* and *policia maritima*. This procedure must be observed whether entering the country for the first time or arriving from elsewhere within it. There is no charge, and though a departure date must be stated there is no need for formal outward clearance.

## Facilities

*Boatyard* A number of boatyards and independent contractors are able to handle repairs in GRP, wood, steel and aluminium. Ask at the marina office for recommendations.

*Travel-lift* No travel lift, but 6·5 tonne capacity crane at the marina.

*Engineers, electronic & radio repairs* Inboard and outboard engine specialists, and electrical and electronic workshops, are all available, though geared more to fishing vessels than yachts. Ask for directions at the marina office.

*Sailmaker* Peres de Lima, a taxi-ride away near the airport. Ask at the office for directions.

*Chandlery* Loja Náutica, ☎ 229 967889, near the marina office carry reasonably wide stocks, with more at their headquarters at Avenida de Liberdade 44, Leça da Palmeira ☎ 229 961224, ☎/*Fax* 229 951463, a few km northeast.

*Charts* Portuguese charts and other publications may be available from
‘Sailing’, Traversa des Laranjeiras 34, Foz do Douro, 4100 Porto
☎ 226 179936 *Fax* 226 103716.

*Water* On the pontoons.

*Showers* At the marina – free if occupying a berth, but charged for if anchored off. Not available 24 hours – check the door (next to the marina office) for opening times. The Yate Clube de Porto also has showers, which it may be possible to use by arrangement.

*Launderettes* In the town.

*Electricity* On the pontoons.

*Fuel* At the reception pontoon, to port just inside the entrance. Available 0900–1200 and 1400–1700 weekdays, 0900–1200 Saturday, closed Sunday.

*Bottled gas* Camping Gaz available in Leça da Palmeira.

*Clube náuticos* The Yate Clube de Porto, the Clube Vela Atlântico and the Clube Náutico de Leça overlook the harbour and the marina respectively

*Weather forecast* Posted daily at the marina office.

*Banks* In Leça da Palmeira, Matosinhos and Porto.

*Shops/provisioning* Good shopping locally, and a very wide choice in Porto.

*Produce market* In Matosinhos, a taxi-ride distant – or at least for the return, if heavily laden.

*Cafés, restaurants & hotels* Numerous in Leça da Palmeira and Porto, but all at some distance from the harbour. However the Yate Clube de Porto has a formal restaurant as well as a very pleasant terrace bar.

*Medical services* In Leça da Palmeira, with a large modern hospital in Porto.

## Communications

*Post offices* In Leça da Palmeira, Matosinhos and Porto.

*Mailing address*
c/o **Marina Porto Atlântico**, Molhe Norte,
Leça da Palmeira, 4450 Matosinhos, Portugal
*Fax service* 229 964899

*Public telephones* At the marina and elsewhere.

*Car hire/taxis* Both can be arranged via the marina office, though there is a good chance of flagging down a taxi on the main road outside the harbour gates.

*Buses* Numbers 44 and 76 both run into Porto (a city not to be missed). A convenient bus stop will be found on the main road just outside the harbour gates.

*Trains* Stations at Leça da Palmeira and Porto, both of which can be reached by bus.

*Air services* Porto International Airport lies about 6km northeast of the harbour.

# Porto and the Rio Douro
41°09'N 8°40'W

## Tides
*Reference port* Lisbon
*Mean time differences* (at entrance)
HW: 00 minutes ±10; LW: +20 minutes ±5
*Heights in metres*

| MHWS | MHWN | MLWN | MLWS |
|---|---|---|---|
| 3·2 | 2·5 | 1·3 | 0·5 |

*Mean time differences* (at Porto)
HW: 00 minutes; LW: +40 minutes
*Heights in metres*

| MHWS | MHWN | MLWN | MLWS |
|---|---|---|---|
| 3·3 | 2·6 | 1·3 | 0·5 |

## Charts

| | Approach | River |
|---|---|---|
| Admiralty | 3634 | 3254 |
| Portuguese (old series) | 1, 2, 16, 22 | 61, 62 |
| Portuguese (new series) | 23202, 24201 | 26402 |

## Lights
### Approach
*0947* **Pedras Rubras (Porto) aerobeacon** 41°19'·1N 8°42'W
Aerobeacon *POR* 327kHz 250M
2031 **Pedras Rubras (Porto) airport** 41°14'·3N 8°40'·4W
Aero Al.Fl.WG.10s84m Control tower 16m
2032 **Leça** 41°12'·1N 8°42'·6W Fl(3)14s56m28M
White tower, narrow grey bands, red lantern 46m
Seven F.R on chimneys 1M northwards
*0949* Radiobeacon *LC* 290kHz 100M (2 & 4 in sequence)
### River
2046 **Felgueiras (north breakwater)** 41°08'·9N 8°40'·6W
Fl.R.5s16m9M 265°-vis-134°
Siren 30s Hexagonal tower, red lantern 11m
2048 **Bar Ldg Lts on 079°** 41°08'·9N 8°39'·9W
*Front* **Cantareira** Oc.R.6s11m9M
White column, red bands and lantern 6m
2048·1 *Rear* **Sobreiras**, 562m from front, Oc.R.6s32m9M
Red and white banded square on wall 4m
(Difficult to identify even when one knows where to look)
buoy *No.4* 41°08'·8N 8°39'·8W
Fl.R.2s3M Red can buoy
buoy *No.1* 41°08'·8N 8°39'·5W
Fl.G.2s3M Green conical buoy
Buoy *No.4A* 41°08'·8N 8°39'·3W
(Unlit) Red can buoy
buoy *No.3* 41°08'·8N 8°39'·2W
Fl.G.3s3M Green conical buoy
buoy *No.6* 41°08'·9N 8°39'W
Fl.R.3s3M Red can buoy

## Port radio
*Capimardouro* VHF Ch 11, 16 (0900–1200, 1400–1700 Mon–Fri).
*Pilotosleixões* VHF Ch 14, 16.

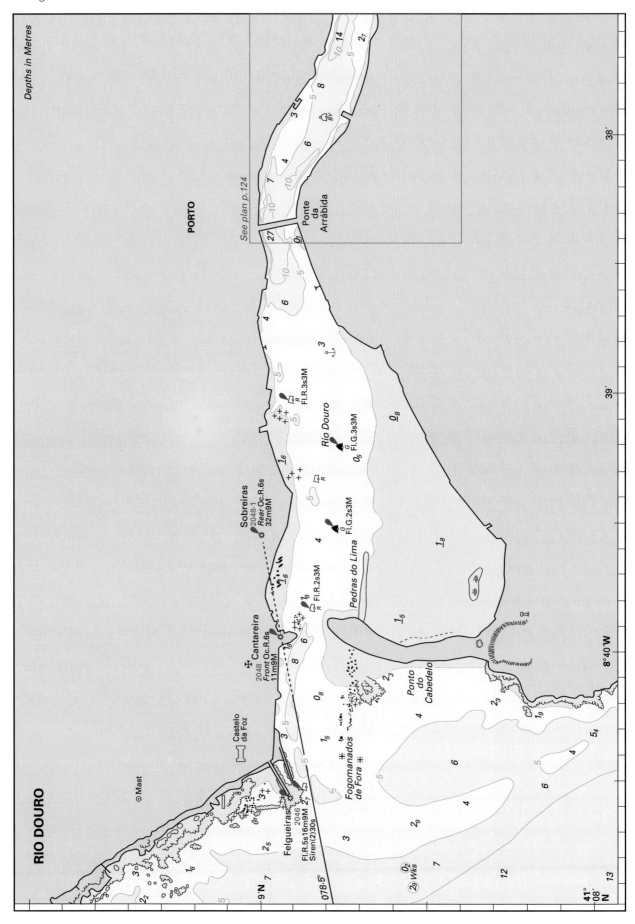

RIO DOURO

## General

The second city of Portugal, Porto's historic involvement with the rest of Europe, the Americas and the East makes fascinating reading – see Appendix II, *Further Reading*, for suggestions. The reverberations remain in its architecture, its customs and its behaviour as well as in its present commercial life, all of which makes for a vibrant city, full of contrasts and well worth exploring. For a microcosm of recent history, visit one of the port warehouses at Vila Nova de Guia on the south bank opposite the Cais da Estiva – all offer tours and tastings to visitors.

The entrance to the river is dangerous in strong winds or when there is heavy swell, with a 6–7 knot current on the ebb which may be even stronger after rain. In winter, storms may close the entrance for weeks. To add to the challenge the red can buoy previously positioned south of Felgueiras breakwater[2046] was removed in 1997, and the entrance – both the narrows and the 'bag' inside – are frequently crowded with dozens of small, open boats lying at anchor whilst their owners fish. It hardly needs saying that entry should only be attempted in daylight and settled weather.

A plan has been put forward to build two new moles at the entrance to the Rio Douro, with one or even two marinas in their shelter, but as of September 1999 no start had been made and local opinion doubted that it ever would be. In any case, being berthed at the entrance rather than in the river itself would seem to defeat much of the object of bringing one's yacht to Porto – the fine views of the city and the short walk into its historic centre. (Another school of thought holds that the marina will be built on the north bank of the river near the Cais de Estiva, which certainly seems a more logical position. Any feedback would be most welcome.)

## Approach

The low hills along the coast between Leixões and Porto extend south beyond the mouth (*foz*) of the Rio Douro. From some distance offshore the entrance shows up well as a cleft. Further south the foreshore is flat, with sandy beaches and marshes behind. From the south the buildings on the hill immediately north of the Rio Douro are conspicuous. Felgueiras breakwater and light structure[2046], together with a short inner mole, mark the north side of the entrance.

## Entrance

Ideally, identify the leading lights on 079° while still at least 0·5M offshore and follow them in towards the short mole at Cantareira[2048]. However they are notoriously difficult to identify even in ideal conditions, in which case (while avoiding the two

The entrance to the Rio Douro looking along the 078·5° leading line. The extensive foul ground off the north (Felgueiras) breakwater shows clearly, as does the rocky shoal of Fogomanados de Fora.

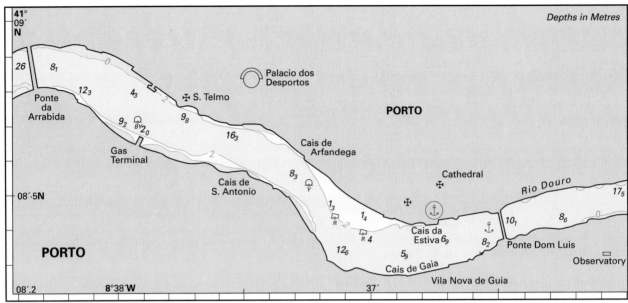

wrecks near 41°08'·6N 8°40'·9W), head due east for a position some 200m south of Felgueiras light[2046], alter onto approximately 070°, and favour the northern shore towards Cantareira[2048]. As of 1999 the bar had a least depth of more than 3m at MLWS, but this figure fluctuates from year to year. Cantareira mole has a rocky shoal off its southeast tip marked by a port hand buoy – skirt this buoy closely to keep well clear of the opposing Ponta do Cabadelo, a long sandspit which has extended first north and then east over the past decade.

Once in the Rio Douro, the channel as far as the Ponte de Arrábida (68m clearance) is well buoyed and should present no problems. Beyond the bridge there are only four more buoys, but at least 3m should be found in mid-channel up to the Ponte Dom Luís I (7·8m).

If, having dropped downstream on the ebb one then wishes to wait for a little more water over the bar, one experienced cruising couple recommend anchoring on the south side of the fairway, east of buoy *No.3* and clear of fishing boat moorings and the nearby quay. They report the holding to be reasonably good in 3–4m over a mixed bottom which shoals fairly quickly nearer the land.

### Berthing and anchorage

Probably the best berth, if space is available, is alongside the rather high and sometimes dirty wall of the Cais da Estiva (warehouse quay) on the north bank about 400m downstream of the Ponte Dom Luís I. The situation appears to fluctuate, but in September 1999 berthing was said to be on a 'first come, first served' basis, and though the quay was busy with hotel and tourist boats those yachts which found room alongside when they arrived were normally allowed to stay. If rafting up outside, bear in mind the tidal current which may reach 5–6 knots at springs or after heavy rain.

It may also be possible to find room at the Cais de Gaia on the south bank of the river about 700m below the bridge – very convenient if visiting the nearby port warehouses at Vila Nova de Guia – but the area is extensively used by cruise boats. The quay has an overhanging ledge under which it would be possible for a yacht's gunwale to get caught on the rising tide – one solution is to set a breast anchor with a bridle fore and aft to hold the yacht off, then use the dinghy to get ashore.

Security on the Cais de Guia is excellent, with a permanent guard posted at the gate to the street. The Cais da Estiva is far more accessible from the city, and although overlooked by a *brigada fiscal* office has no out-of-hours cover. Having to shift position up and down either quay at frequent intervals appears routine, making it difficult to leave the boat unattended for any length of time. One couple reported being moved repeatedly during their short visit, in spite (or possibly because?) of being the only yacht in the site.

A possible alternative, though discouraged by the authorities, is to anchor just below the bridge – only

The handsome Ponte Dom Luís I seen from the Cais da Estiva. A German yacht is anchored in midstream.

feasible in settled weather around neap tides and when there has been no recent rain further up the valley. Use heavy ground tackle with plenty of scope, but allow a full swinging circle. The ebb runs hard and a fresh breeze against it can cause a very nasty lop, dangerous for a small dinghy. The yacht should not be left unattended in these conditions (or some would say at all).

## Caution

Little secret is made of the fact that the Rio Douro carries much of Porto's raw sewage out to sea, and several crews have become ill after handling lines which have been in the water. Scrupulous washing is obviously essential.

## Formalities

Passports and ship's papers should be presented at the *brigada fiscal* office overlooking the Cais da Estiva where, in 1999, a set charge of 462 escudos (2·30 euros) was made for clearance, irrespective of the planned length of stay. The *policia maritima* sometimes visit yachts at either Cais to check that clearance has been obtained – necessary, even if coming from elsewhere in Portugal. In 1999 very little English was spoken.

## Facilities

Few facilities other than a café or two on the Cais de Estiva and a good range of general shops, restaurants, banks, etc within walking distance. Fresh water is difficult to obtain, although showers and laundry facilities are reported to be available in a communal services building about 100m upstream from the *capitania*.

Repairs or any other work are much better undertaken at the Marina Porto Atlântico in Leixões.

## Communications

Post office, plus several telephone offices from which faxes may also be sent. International and national air, rail and bus connections, plus the usual taxis and car rental.

## Upriver

Motorboats, or yachts with masts capable of being lowered, can explore as far as Barca de Alva, 200km upstream, following cruise boats into the large locks. The approaches require care and 6 knots of boat speed in some conditions, while it may take a week to work through the inevitable red tape before departure.

The upper reaches of the Rio Douro are particularly attractive, and if unable to venture by yacht it could be worth jumping ship to spend a few days aboard one of the many local hotel-boats which ply the river.

## Not feasible

The Lagoa de Esmoriz, close south of Espinho and some 11M south of Porto, bears more than a passing resemblance to Esposende – see page 114 – but on an even smaller scale. Sail on by.

# Ria de Aveiro

40°39'N 8°45'W

## Tides

*Reference port* Lisbon
*Mean time differences* (at entrance)
HW: +05 minutes ±5; LW: +10 minutes ±5
*Heights in metres*

| MHWS | MHWN | MLWN | MLWS |
|------|------|------|------|
| 3·2 | 2·6 | 1·4 | 0·7 |

## Charts

| | Approach | River |
|---|---|---|
| Admiralty | 3634 | 3253 |
| Portuguese (old series) | 2, 22, 33 | 59 |
| Portuguese (new series) | 23202, 24201, 24202 | 26403 |

## Lights

### Approach

2056 **Aveiro aeromarine** 40°38'·6N 8°44'·8W
Fl(4)13s65m23M
Round red tower, white bands, and building 62m
*Note* In September 1999 the tower was badly in need of repainting, and appeared a combination of pink and dirty grey
*0955* Radiobeacon *AV* 290kHz 100M (3 & 6 in sequence)

### River

2057 **North breakwater** 40°38'·6N 8°45'·7W
Fl.R.3s11m8M Horn 15s
*Note* In September 1999 work was in progress on the north breakwater (see photograph page 127).
2058 **South breakwater** 40°38'·5N 8°45'·4W
Fl.G.3s17m9M White tower, green bands 12m (situated 20m from outer end)
**Ldg Lts on 085·4°** *Front,* **South breakwater** (²⁰⁵⁸above)
*Rear,* 850m from front, Fl.G.4s53m9M
065·4°-vis-105·4°
Situated on tower of **Aveiro aeromarine** (²⁰⁵⁶above)
2058·55 **Entrance channel, north side** 40°38'·9N 8°44'·4W Fl.R.2s6m3M Red tower 4m
2056·2 **Ldg Lts on 065°** 40°38'·9N 8°44'·9W
*Front* Oc.R.3s7m9M 060·6°-vis-070·6°
Red round column 4m
2056·21 *Rear,* 440m from front
Oc.R.6s15m9M 060·6°-vis-070·6°
Red round column 13m
2058·5 **Central (inner) mole** 40°38'·6N 8°44'·9W
LFl.G.5s8m3M
White round tower, green bands 4m
2059 **Triangle – west angle** 40°38'·7N 8°44'·5W
Fl(2+1)G.6s7m6M
Green round tower, red band 4m
**Ldg Lts on 089·5°** *Front,* **Triangle – west angle** (²⁰⁵⁹above)
2059·1 *Rear,* **Fort de Barra**, 870m from front,
Fl.G.3s20m6M 084·5°-vis-094·5° White tower 19m
2059·2 **Triangle – north angle** 40°38'·8N 8°44'W
Fl.G.3s4m7M White round tower, green bands 4m
2059·35 **Praia do Porto** 40°38'·9N 8°44'W
Q(2+1)G.6s7m3M
Green round tower, red band 4m
2059·37 **São Jacinto, south mole**
40°39'·2N 8°44'W
F.R.6m4M White round tower, red bands 4m

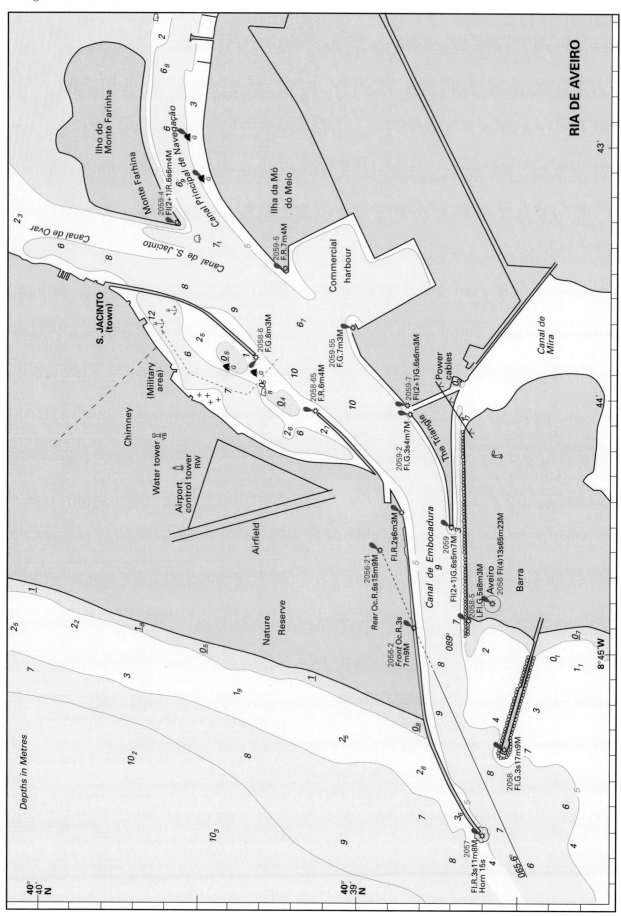

RIA DE AVEIRO

**2059·36 São Jacinto, north mole**
40°39'·4N 8°43'·8W F.G.6m3M
White round tower, green bands 4m

**2059·55 Commercial harbour, southwest**
40°39'N 8°43'·7W F.G.7m3M
White masonry tower, green bands 4m

**2059·5 Commercial harbour, northeast**
40°39'·2N 8°43'·6W F.R.7m4M
White masonry tower, red bands 4m

**2059·6 Monte Farinha** 40°39'·5N 8°43'·4W
Q(2+1)R.6s6m4M
Red round tower, green band 4m

Plus numerous lit and unlit buoys on the Canal Principal de Navegação, leading to the Canal das Pirâmides lock – see plan page 129.

## Coast radio station

**Arestal** (40°46'N 8°21'W) (24 hours) Remotely controlled from Lisbon
**VHF** Ch 16, 24, 26, 85.

## Port radio

*Capimaraveiro* VHF Ch 11, 16 (0900–1200, 1400–1700 Mon–Fri).
*Pilotosaveiro* VHF Ch 14, 16.

## General

The region is one of salt marshes and sand spits, low lying and often deceptive. The *ria* has been developed as an oil, timber and general port but it is possible to escape into unspoilt, almost desolate, surroundings. There are strong tidal streams and the entrance can be dangerous on the ebb, in spite of having been dredged to a reported 10m or more. In September 1999 a yacht was lost while attempting to enter at night in a 3m swell which doubtless increased to many times this in the entrance.

The town of Aveiro, some 12km from the entrance, prospered from trade with the New World until a storm in the 16th century closed the entrance. It was re-opened early in the 19th century and Aveiro recovered its prosperity. Today it combines modern business and industry with reminders of the past, and is one of the more attractive towns along the coast. The *Festa da Ria* takes place during the last two weeks of August.

Much work has been done to improve the port commercially and to channel the river, though many of the dyked areas shown as dry land on Admiralty *3253* – including some reclaimed salt-pans – are now back underwater. There are no specific facilities for yachts and the so-called Marina da Barra, shown on some plans inside the long sandbank which forms the southern lip of the entrance, did not exist as of September 1999. Even if built, access would be severely restricted by the medium tension power cables which cross the Canal de Mira at its northern end, with an estimated air height of 8–10m.

## Approach

Between the Rio Douro and Espinho, 9M to the south, the coast is backed by low hills some 7km inland and has isolated rocks inshore. From Espinho to Cabo Mondego, some 51M with the Barra de Aveiro rather less than halfway along, the coast is a continuous beach backed by lagoons or low-lying land. Inshore there are no particular fixed hazards, but winter storms may build sandbanks and it is prudent to keep outside the 20m line.

If approaching from the south it is equally necessary to keep a good distance off. A shoal patch carrying 1·5m at datum has been reported nearly 1M from the shore exactly 1M south-southwest of the entrance, and a dangerous wreck with a mast showing lies just over 2M southwest of the entrance at approximately 40°36'N 8°47'W.

The mouth of the Ria de Aveiro, looking from a little south of west. When the photograph was taken in September 1999 work was in progress on the outer end of the north breakwater. The amount of broken water – even on a relatively calm day – is remarkable.

### Entrance

As stated above, the potential dangers of the entrance should not be underestimated. Winds from between northwest and southwest can quickly produce a vicious sea, at its worst on the ebb tide – which may reach 8 knots in the entrance at springs following heavy rain. The ebb runs for about seven hours and the flood for five, the best time to enter or leave being shortly before high water.

If coming from the north give the end of the north breakwater a wide berth, as shoals south of its tip cause broken water in all but the calmest weather – see the photograph on page 127, taken about an hour before high water on a day with median tides. Elsewhere around 15m should be found in the outer entrance, but where this shoals to 10m (level with the outer end of the south breakwater) standing waves may form, particularly on the ebb.

There are two leading lines for the outer entrance. The northern line, on 085·4°, consists of the south breakwater light structure[2058] in line with Aveiro lighthouse[2056] and should be visible from some distance offshore. The southern line, on 065·6° and consisting of two red columns[2056·2 & 2056·21], is much harder to pick out and, even if identified, calmer water is likely to be found further south. A third leading line, on 089·5°, has been established inside the entrance, but is intended mainly for commercial traffic heading for the Canal de Mira.

Once the protection of the river mouth is gained, while the tide may still run strongly there should never be less than 7m depths. Leave the Triângulo[2059] to starboard and continue up the Canal de Embocadura. In contrast to some Portuguese harbours the channel buoys appear to be well maintained, with both buoys and shore marks corresponding to their published descriptions.

### Anchorages and berthing

1. In the Baia de São Jacinto, about 1·5M northeast of the river mouth. The entrance is shallow although there are good depths once inside, and it is essential to observe the buoyage – currently red and green buoys to port and starboard on entering, with a further green buoy marking the western edge of the north shoal. However the buoyage pattern appears to change from year to year, with a red and white chequered affair (also left to starboard on entry) in place in 1998. The outer moles are both lit (F.R and F.G), but movement after dark is not recommended.

If the third buoy is not in place and the *brigada fiscal* launch is not on hand to offer a lead in (as often happens), after passing between the entrance buoys head for a conspicuous yellow and black water tower on approximately 330°. Remain on this bearing until past the shallowest part of the bar (0·5–1m at datum).

When the base pier (often with small military craft alongside) bears 015° head in towards it, following the shore in 5–6m towards the ferry pier. Anchor between the pier and the outer mole in 10–12m. The bottom is somewhat uneven, with holding poor in places and excellent in others – in September 1999 one small yacht reported holding absolutely firm while laid over by gusts exceeding 50 knots. There are a few moorings at the north end of the bay, behind which are steps and a broad slipway.

São Jacinto is very much a holiday town, with numerous cafés and restaurants but nothing specifically for yachts, though a small shipyard lies just to the north. There is a nature reserve along the beach to the west but the large military area, including the airfield, is off limits to the public.

Aveiro's large, artificial Baia de São Jacinto, on the north side not far inside the *ria* entrance.

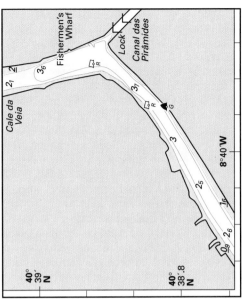

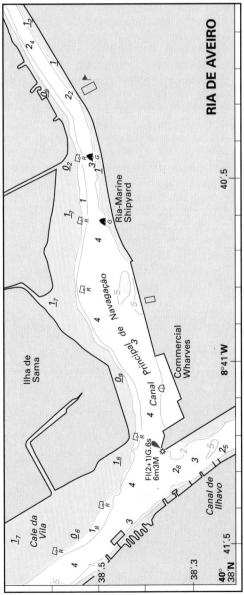

**RIA DE AVEIRO**

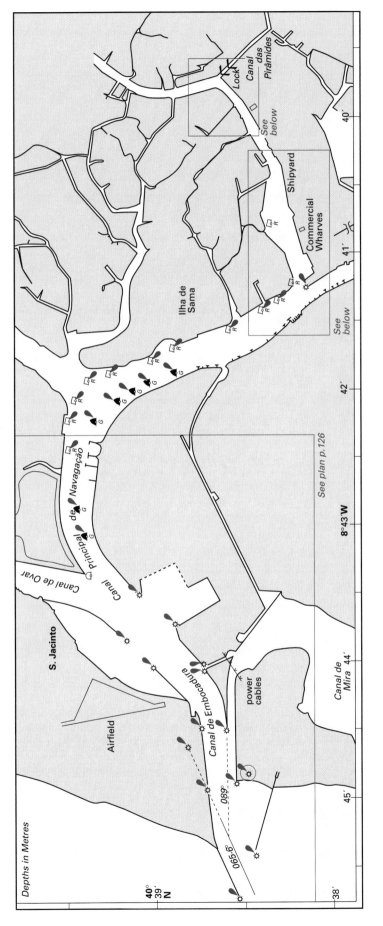

*Depths in Metres*

2. Further north in the Canal de Ovar, a lagoon separated from the sea by a sandbank carrying the access road to São Jacinto. Though relatively shallow (2·5–3m) where the Canal is wide, the narrow stretches contain pools with 5–7m. The currents in the Canal de Ovar weaken beyond São Jacinto and anchoring is practicable. If very shoal or able to take the ground it is possible to work a good distance up the channel.

3. At or near the smallcraft marina at the Clube de Vela Costa Nova on the Canal Mira, but air height is restricted to an estimated 8–10m by the power cables already mentioned, and depths are no more than 0·5m at datum. The channel is indicated by buoys and posts.

4. In the Canal Principal de Navegação, a buoyed channel carrying 2–3m and leading to the town of Aveiro. Tidal currents are strong and it may be difficult to find swinging room without impeding local traffic. Berthing at the Porto de Pesca (fish quay) is strongly discouraged and berthing at the Cais Comerçial (commercial wharf) is likely to be impracticable for yachts. The Clube Naval de Aveiro and neighbouring Sporting Clube de Aveiro have no more than 1m at their quays – local smallcraft are craned ashore when not in use. However for short periods it may be possible to lie alongside the jetty at the Ria–Marine shipyard – see under Facilities, below.

5. In the Canal das Pirâmides close to the town of Aveiro itself, where yachts moor to piles a couple of metres off either bank. Although the owners of shallow draft yachts have enjoyed visiting this unusual spot for many years, in 1999 there was considerable doubt as to whether they were still welcome, the lock-keeper stating that they were not. The Canal is administered by the Associação Turistica Vigilância – Amigos da Ria, Rue São Gabriel, 49 Ilhavo, from whom permission should in theory be sought. The alternative is simply to turn up and hope.

Until quite recently, traditional *moliceiros* were used to collect and transport seaweed up the shallow creeks reaching inland, where it was much in demand as fertiliser. In the background is a less than scenic sand and cement works.

The lock, which is on the southeast side of the Canal Principal de Navegação, is reported to open for one hour either side of high water and on demand at other times. Strong tidal eddies may be encountered at the entrance. Dimensions are 18m by 5m with a claimed 5·5m on the cill. Some sources attribute depth of 2·5m to the Canal, occasionally dropping to 2m, though others put it at no more than 1·3m.

**Formalities**

The *brigada fiscal* and possibly the *policia maritima* will visit if anchored in the Baia de São Jacinto or moored in the Canal das Pirâmides.

**Facilities**

Water by can from the *clube naval* or the *sporting clube*. Diesel by can from a filling station in Aveiro, where there are also shops, banks, restaurants and hotels. Portuguese charts and other publications may be available from Bolivar, on Rua da Aviação Naval 51, 3810 Aveiro.

The large Ria–Marine Estaleiro Naval Lda, ☎ 234 384049/426686, near the *clube naval* is capable of hauling yachts of all sizes and carrying out repairs in GRP, wood and steel. The standard of workmanship appears to be good, though the untidy state of the yard may at first be off-putting. Little or no English is spoken by the workforce. In the mid 1990s the yard was given responsibility for rebuilding Portugal's last East Indiaman, the *D Fernando II e Glória*, for the Lisbon Maritime Museum, a commission which they carried out to a high standard.

**Communications**

Post office, taxis, buses and trains at Aveiro.

The Canal das Pirâmides, which gives access to the old town of Aveiro. As of 1999 there was some doubt as to whether visiting yachts were still allowed access (via the lock at centre left).

# Figueira da Foz

40°09'N 8°52'W

## Tides

*Reference port* Lisbon
*Mean time differences*
HW: −10 minutes ±10; LW: +15 minutes ±5

*Heights in metres*

| MHWS | MHWN | MLWN | MLWS |
|------|------|------|------|
| 3·5 | 2·6 | 1·3 | 0·6 |

## Charts

| | Approach | Harbour |
|---|---|---|
| Admiralty | *3634, 3635* | *3253* |
| Portuguese (old series) | *2, 22, 34* | *64* |
| Portuguese (new series) | *23202, 24202* | *26404* |
| Imray | *C19* | *C19* |

## Lights

### Approach
2060 **Cabo Mondego** 40°11'·4N 8°54'·2W
Fl.5s96m28M Horn 30s
White square tower and building 15m
*0957* Radiobeacon *MD* 287·5kHz 150M (1 & 4 in
sequence)
*0958* **Monte Real aerobeacon** 39°54'·5N 8°52·9'W
Aerobeacon *MTL* 336kHz 150M
2062 **Buarcos** 40°09'·9N 8°52'·4W
Iso.GWR.6s11m9-5M 004°-G-028°-W-048°-R-086°
Round tower, red and white bands 7m
2072 **Penedo da Saudade** 39°45'·8N 9°01'·8W
Fl(2)15s54m30M
Square masonry tower and building 32m

### Harbour
2066 **North breakwater** 40°08'·8N 8°52'·4W
Fl.R.6s14m9M Horn 35s
White tower, red bands 7m
2068 **South breakwater** 40°08'·7N 8°52'·3W
Fl.G.6s13m7M
White tower, green bands 7m (situated 15m from
outer end)

2069 **Ldg Lts on 081·5°** 40°08'·7N 8°51'·2W
*Front* Iso.R.5s8m8M White column, red bands 3m
2069·1 *Rear*, 245m from front, Oc.R.6s12m8M
White column, red bands 3m
2069·4 **North inner mole** 40°09'N 8°52'W
Fl.R.3s9m4M Red tower, white bands 4m
2069·5 **South inner mole** 40°08'·8N 8°52'W
Fl.G.3s8m4M Green tower, white bands 4m
2069·6 **Marina, west mole** 40°08'·9N 8°51'·5W
F.R.6m2M Red column 3m
2069·7 **Marina, east mole** 40°08'·9N 8°51'·4W
F.G.6m2M Green column 3m
2069·8 **Confluência** 40°08'·8N 8°51'·3W
Fl(3)G.8s7m4M
Green tower, red band 4m

## Marina and port radio

*Marina da Figueira da Foz* VHF Ch 08, 16.
*Capimarfoz* VHF Ch 11, 16 (0900–1200, 1400–1700
Mon–Fri).
*Pilotosfigueira* VHF Ch 14, 16.

## General

Figueira da Foz is on the north bank of the longest
river to rise in Portugal, and although a modern
town with good facilities depending largely on
shipbuilding and tourism for its income, a large part
of the attractive old town remains. The city of
Coimbra, some 48km upstream, is worth visiting by
bus or train. The university, transferred there from
Lisbon in 1320, is partially disfigured by some
unsightly modern faculty blocks but the old city,
including the crenellated 12th century cathedral, is
memorable.

Although the 135 berth marina run by the Junta
Autónima do Porto da Figueira da Foz, ☎ 233
402910 *Fax* 233 402920, has been in place since the
early 1990s it still has a strangely unfinished look –
possibly the reason why there is nearly always space
available for visitors.

Figueira da Foz from the northwest, taken on a very hazy afternoon. The marina can be seen on the far left.

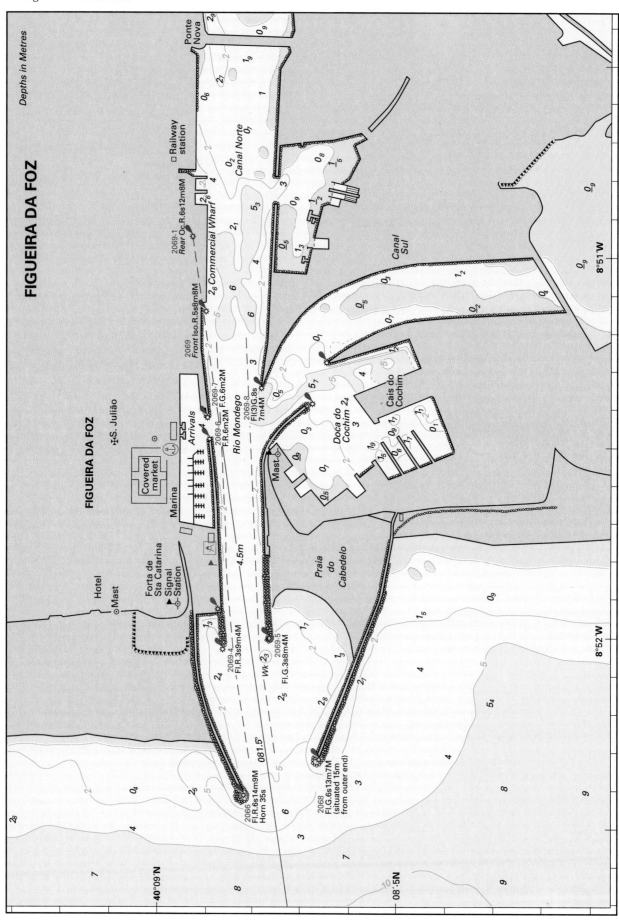

FIGUEIRA DA FOZ

*Depths in Metres*

FIGUEIRA DA FOZ

⚓S. Julião

Hotel
⊙ Mast

Forta de
Sta Catarina
▲ Signal
⊙ Station

Covered
market

Marina

Arrivals

Rio Mondego

Praia
do
Cabedelo

Ponte
Nova

□ Railway
station

2069·1
*Rear* Oc.R.6s12m8M

2069
*Front* Iso.R.5s8m8M

2·6 *Commercial Wharf*

2069·7
F.G.6m2M

2069·6
F.R.6m2M

2069·8
Fl(3)G.8s
7m4M

2069·4
Fl.R.3s9m4M

Wk

2069·5
Fl.G.3s8m4M

Mast

Canal Norte

Canal
Sul

Cais do
Cochim

Doca do
Cochim

2066
Fl.R.6s14m9M
Horn 35s

081·5°

4·5m

2068
Fl.G.6s13m7M
(situated 15m
from outer end)

40°09'N

8°52'W

8°51'W

08·5N

10·5N

## Approach

Figueira da Foz lies 2·5M south of Cabo Mondego[2060] which at a distance, from both north and south, can be mistaken for an island. The shore to the south of the town forms a continuous low, sandy beach backed by one of the largest coniferous forests in Europe. The major mark to the south is Penedo da Saudade[2072], 25M distant.

The pale grey suspension bridge 1·5M upriver from the entrance is conspicuous from offshore.

## Entrance

Regular dredging of the previously shallow bar has greatly improved the entrance and a minimum of 5m should be found at all times. However in strong onshore winds it can still be dangerous – a British yacht was lost in 1997, and waves were breaking all the way across the gap when visited in September 1999. At springs the ebb can run at up to 7 knots, particularly if there has been heavy rain inland, though this rate is unlikely to be reached during the summer.

Danger signals are displayed if necessary from Forte de Santa Catarina (on the north side of the entrance) as follows: black ball or vertical green, red, green lights – entrance closed; black ball at half-mast or vertical green, flashing red, green lights –

entrance dangerous. These signals – which are near some strong sodium lights and are difficult to see from offshore – are mandatory and instructions may also be given by radio. If no signals are displayed the entrance is considered to be safe – at least for large commercial vessels.

## Berthing

The entrance to the Marina da Figueira da Foz lies on the port hand about 0·7M inside the river mouth – beware of cross-currents, particularly on the ebb. Secure to the arrival pontoon opposite the entrance, and call at the building on the quay behind to visit the *policia maritima* and *brigada fiscal*. Although the word 'Reception' is prominently displayed this is somewhat misleading, as there is no marina office in the building. Instead the berthing master will be summoned from his portacabin near the marina security gate to allocate a berth.

The marina consists of a single long pontoon from which seven spurs run southward. All are fitted with individual finger pontoons and the two easternmost – some thirty berths – are reserved for visitors. Though easy of access, both eastern spurs are reported to suffer from strong cross-currents and swell on the ebb. This area is nominally dredged to 4·5m and able to take yachts of up to 25m LOA, though some would consider this optimistic.

Figueira da Foz marina, looking northwest into the entrance. Cabo Mondego can be seen on the skyline, with the town's long, golden beach below.

In 1999 the high season (1/5–30/9) rate for a visiting yacht of just under 12m was 2,650 escudos (13·22 euros) per night inclusive of water, electricity and tax, with a modest increase for beamy yachts.

## Formalities

Call at the *brigada fiscal* and *policia maritima* offices on arrival, bearing the usual passports and ship's papers. As of 1999 Figueira da Foz had not reached 'single form' status (see page 6), but at least the offices are all to hand.

The marina office itself is housed in a small portacabin at the west end of the basin, next to the pontoon security gate. In 1999 the hope was expressed that new buildings would be taking shape before too long – just as it had been five years previously.

## Facilities

*Boatyard* Not as such, though there are several concerns which could handle minor work. Papiro, ☎ 233 411849, at the west end of the basin advertises GRP work, including osmosis treatment, but appears fairly small.

There is a concrete slipway in the southwest corner of the basin where yachts of medium draft can dry out for scrubbing. A pressure washer (with operator) can be hired – enquire at the marina office. As with all such facilities it would plainly be wise to inspect thoroughly at low water before committing oneself.

*Engineers, electronic & radio repairs* Try KPM at the west end of the basin. If beyond their scope they should be able to advise.

*Sailmaker/sail repairs* Sails in need of repair are normally sent to Lisbon for attention – ask at the marina office.

*Chandlery* Limited stocks at Marés at the west end of the basin. Papiro (see above) stocks a full range of International Paints including Gelshield, antifouling, thinners, etc.

*Water* On the pontoons, with a generous number of long hoses.

*Showers* Currently in a portacabin near the security gate (and sometimes distinctly unpleasant), but due to be replaced by a new building within the next few years.

*Launderette* In the 'reception' building.

*Electricity* On the pontoons.

*Fuel* It is hoped that fuel pumps will be installed – probably at the east end of the basin – in time for the 2000 season. Pending this one must still use the commercial pump on the Cais do Cochim (not easy for a small yacht).

*Bottled gas* Camping Gaz available in the town.

*Ice* From the filling station opposite the office of the Junta Autónima do Porto da Figueira da Foz (the large building to the northwest of the marina basin).

*Clube náutico* The Clube Náutico de Figueira da Foz and the Associação Naval Figueira da Foz both have premises west of the harbour, but appear functional rather than social.

*Weather forecast* Posted daily on the noticeboard near the marina security gate.

*Banks* In the town.

*Shops/provisioning* Good shopping of all types in the town. The nearest supermarket will be found across the road and slightly west from the marina gate, up a small side street.

*Produce market* Covered market within a quadrangle of shops facing the yacht basin.

*Cafés, restaurants & hotels* Nothing on site, other than a café/bar in the 'Reception' building, but several restaurants across the road from the marina entrance with dozens more in the town proper.

*Medical services* In the town.

## Communications

*Post office* Just off the square of public gardens which face the yacht basin.

*Mailing address*
c/o **Instituto Portuário do Centro**, AP 2008–3080, Figueira da Foz, Portugal.
*Fax service* 233 402920
The marina office will receive faxes for yachts, but they must be sent from the post office.

*Public telephones* At the post office.

*Car hire/taxis* In the town.

*Buses & trains* In the town. The station is less than 0·5km east of the marina.


# Nazaré

39°35'N 9°05'W

## Tides

*Reference port* Lisbon
*Mean time differences*
HW: −20 minutes ±10; LW: 00 minutes ±5
*Heights in metres*

| MHWS | MHWN | MLWN | MLWS |
|------|------|------|------|
| 3·3  | 2·6  | 1·3  | 0·6  |

## Charts

|                         | Approach | Harbour |
|-------------------------|----------|---------|
| Admiralty               | 3635     |         |
| Portuguese (old series) | 22, 34, 3565 | |
| Portuguese (new series) | 23202, 24202, 24203 26302 | |

## Lights

### Approach

2072 **Penedo da Saudade** 39°45'·8N 9°01'·8W
Fl(2)15s54m30M
Square masonry tower and building 32m

2074 **Pontal da Nazaré** 39°36'·4N 9°05'W
Oc.3s49m14M 282°-vis-192° Siren 35s
Red lantern on SW corner of fort 8m

2076 **São Martinho (Ponta de Santo Antonío)**
39°30'·5N 9°08'·5W
Iso.R.6s33m9M Siren 60s
White round tower, red bands
Obscd on a bearing of more than 165°

2088 **Cabo Carvoeiro** 39°21'·5N 9°24'·4W
Fl(3)R.15s56m15M Horn 35s
White square tower and buildings 27m

*0961* Radiobeacon *CV* 287·5kHz 150M (2 & 5 in sequence)
(also transmitting experimentally on 301·5kHz)

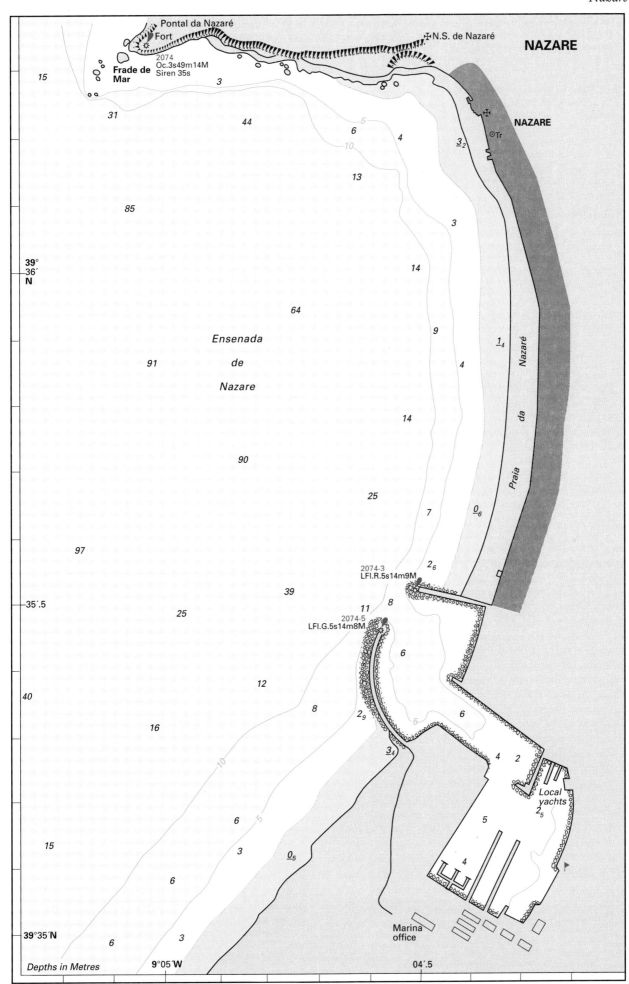

**NAZARE**

Pontal da Nazaré
Fort
✠ N.S. de Nazaré

2074
Oc.3s49m14M
Siren 35s

**Frade de Mar**

**NAZARE**

⊙Tr

15

31

3

44

5

6

4

$\underline{3}_2$

10

13

3

85

**39°
36′
N**

14

64

9

$\underline{1}_4$

*Ensenada*

91          *de*

4

*Nazare*

14

90

*Praia da Nazaré*

25

7

$\underline{0}_6$

97

$2_6$

2074-3
LFl.R.5s14m9M

39

8

35′.5

11
2074-5
LFl.G.5s14m8M

25

6

12

8

6

40

$2_9$

6

16

$\underline{3}_4$

4       2

*Local
yachts*

$2_5$

5

6

5

4

15

3       $\underline{0}_5$

6

**39°35′N**

6

3

Marina
office

*Depths in Metres*

**9°05′W**

04′.5

2086 **Ilha Berlenga summit** 39°25'N 9°30'·5W
  Fl(3)20s120m27M Horn 28s at N end of island
  White square tower and buildings 29m
*0959* Radiobeacon *IB* 287·3kHz 200M (3 & 6 in
  sequence)
2084 **Ilhéu Farilhão Grande** 39°28'·6N 9°32'·6W
  Fl.5s99m13M Red round tower 6m
*Harbour*
2074·3 **North breakwater** 39°35'·4N 9°04'·5W
  LFl.R.5s14m9M
  Red round tower, white bands 7m
2074·5 **South breakwater** 39°35'·3N 9°04'·6W
  LFl.G.5s14m8M
  Green round tower, white bands 7m

## Port radio

*Capimarnazaré* VHF Ch 11, 16 (0900–1200, 1400–1700
  Mon–Fri). Neither marina monitors VHF.

## General

Old Nazaré (O Sítio), whose citizens have a claim to
Phoenician origin, occupies a fine position looking
south over the beach that provided – and still
provides – the shelter needed for its prosperity. The
town now relies largely on tourism for its prosperity,
but the lower town on the beach keeps some of its
old atmosphere.

The harbour is a purpose built, well sheltered
fishing port with no hazards on the approach –
indeed it is claimed that Nazaré's harbour is never
closed, even in conditions in which it would be
foolhardy to attempt any of those further north
(other than Leixões). This is due to the Canhão da
Nazaré, a deep trench which runs close offshore and
markedly reduces swell, doubtless aided by the
protective headlands to north and south.

However, though useful as a port of refuge and
sheltering a small but friendly marina, many would
claim that the harbour itself is somewhat bleak, as
well as being more than 2km from the town itself,
though there is a bus service. (The surroundings are
very flat, however, and Nazaré is one of these places
where folding bicycles are at a premium). More than
one yachtsman has also remarked less than politely
on the siren which signals the return of a fishing boat
(and so a catch to be auctioned), though it seldom
sounds after midnight.

Possibly the most compelling reason to visit
Nazaré is as a base from which to visit a number of
Portugal's most famous places, including Fatima,
Alcobaça and Caldas da Rainha, all of which can be
reached by public transport. However the top 'must
see' is undoubtedly the early 15th century abbey of
Batalha – literally Battle Abbey – built to
commemorate Dom João I's victory over the
Spanish in *1385*. As well as being a masterpiece of
Manueline architecture it contains the tomb of
Prince Henry the Navigator, younger son of Dom
João and his English wife Philippa of Lancaster. The
slightly tortuous 90 minute bus journey via Leiria
will be amply rewarded.

## Approach

The low-lying beach which reaches from Figueira da
Foz to the light at Penedo da Saudade gives way to
a more broken coastline backed by low hills leading
south to the Pontal da Nazaré, with a light[2074] on the
wall of its fort, São Miguel. The point has rocks
200m offshore to the southwest, but within a further
60m the bottom drops to 50m or more.

The coast 4M south of Nazaré loses its sand
dunes and becomes rocky. South of São
Martinho[2076], towards the Lagoa de Obidos, there is
a rugged stretch of higher coast. South of this the
coast is again a sandy beach, here backed by cliffs,
as far as Cabo Carvoeiro[2088]. Fishing nets may be laid
on a line parallel to and up to 2M off this stretch of
shore.

On final approach from the south, particularly in
thick weather, note that the Canhão da Nazaré
underwater canyon trends north of east into the
Enseada da Nazaré, and that its 100m line comes
within 600m of the shore.

## Entrance

Straightforward, between the moles.

## Berthing

There are two marinas in the harbour, both small.
Visiting yachts should head for the three pontoons
in the southwest corner, administered by the Junta
Autónoma dos Portos do Centro, ☎ 262 561401
*Fax* 262 561402. Of the 52 berths, fourteen are
reserved for visitors (though more can be
accommodated by rafting up). There is no formal
reception area, but unless directed otherwise arrivals
normally secure to the centre hammerhead until
allocated a berth. Depths are said to be at least
4–5m throughout and the marina is capable of
taking one yacht of up to 25m (though this may
displace two or three smaller ones). All berthing is
alongside either main or finger pontoons.

Security is excellent, with a watchman
permanently on duty and access to the marina and
to the shower/laundry area via electronic card.
Outside office hours (0830–1900) a key can be
obtained from the kiosk at the main port gate,
except from 1230–1400 when the guard is at lunch.
There are plans to extend the marina, possibly by
dredging part of the large empty area between the
marina and the office – it is, after all, only sand – but
as of 1999 no date had been set.

In 1999 the high season (July–August) rate for a
visiting yacht of just under 12m was 3,510 escudos
(17·51 euros) for the first two nights dropping to
2,808 escudos (13·98 euros) for the third and
subsequent nights. Mid season (April–June and
September) rates were 2,246 (11·20 euros) escudos
dropping to 2,106 escudos (10·50 euros), with
1,404 escudos (7 euros) and 1,264 escudos (6·30
euros) in the low season. All were inclusive of water,
electricity and tax. Multihulls paid a 50% surcharge.

A pair of (private) pontoons have been in place in
the northeast corner for some years, occupied
mainly by local yachts and smallcraft though space
may occasionally be found for a visitor or two. They
are administered by the Clube Naval de Nazaré,
which has premises on the east side of the harbour.

## Anchorage

Anchoring is no longer allowed in the harbour or its approaches. However in settled weather it is possible to anchor anywhere along the beach off the lower town, protected from the prevailing northerlies by the Pontal da Nazaré. Holding is good over sand.

## Formalities

Nazaré does not yet have the 'single form' system (see page 6), but there is a *brigada fiscal* office in the same building as the marina office and normally no other officials need be seen.

## Facilities

Celtic Marine Services, run by retired Master Mariner/RYA Yachtmaster Instructor Mike Hadley, *Mobile* 968 074254 *Fax* 262 561412, *e-mail* celticmarine@sapo.pt, is one of those 'can do' companies willing to organise and oversee almost anything from major repair work by local contractors through yacht deliveries to hiring out bicycles. Invaluable, particularly to those without fluent Portuguese!

*Boatyard* Navalnazaré, ☎ 262 562244 *Fax* 262 562328, operate from premises near the main gate. In addition to building traditional wooden fishing craft they can handle repairs to yachts in GRP and steel, painting, etc.

*Travel-lift* Small travel-lift at Navalnazaré, but a crane is normally hired in to lift heavier yachts.

*Engineers, electronic & radio repairs* At Navalnazaré, who are also agents for a number of outboard manufacturers.

*Sailmaker/sail repairs* The nearest sailmaker is in Lisbon – enquire at the marina office.

*Chandlery* Some chandlery at Navalnazaré, with more general items at the nearby fishermen's cooperative. In late 1999 it was reported that a third chandlery had also opened.

*Water* On the pontoons.

*Showers* In the main building, with access via a key system (see Berthing, opposite).

*Launderette* Washing machine in the shower block, but no dryer.

*Electricity* On the pontoons.

*Fuel* Order via the marina officials, who will arrange for a road tanker to call. The whole process should take less than 30 minutes if reasonable notice is given. (Note that you pay for the quantity ordered rather than that actually taken aboard, so don't over-estimate!).

*Bottled gas* Camping Gaz available in the town.

*Ice* At the main gate.

*Clube náutico* The small Clube Náutico de Nazaré has premises on the east side of the harbour.

*Weather forecast* Posted daily in the large room below the marina office (and spare a glance for the fine display of fishing boat models).

*Banks* In the town.

*Shops/provisioning* Small mini-market below the marina office, with good general shopping in Nazaré itself.

*Produce market* Good market in the town.

*Cafés, restaurants & hotels* Café/bar at the mini-market, with a wide choice in the thriving holiday resort.

*Medical services* In Nazaré.

## Communications

*Post offices* In the town, though stamped mail can be left at the marina office for posting.

*Mailing address*
c/o **Instituto Portuário do Centro**,
Porto da Nazaré, 2450 Nazaré, Portugal.
*Fax service* 262 561402

*Public telephone* Kiosk near the marina security gate.

*Car hire/taxis* In the town (or can be arranged via the marina office).

*Buses* Buses into Nazaré approximately every two hours. A timetable is displayed on a door near the mini-market.

The well-designed harbour at Nazaré, which locals claim never experiences swell and is never closed. In this view, looking southeast, the small marina is on the far right.

# São Martinho do Porto

39°30'N 9°08'W

## Tides

See Nazaré, page 134

## Charts

|  | Approach | Harbour |
|---|---|---|
| Admiralty | *3635* | |
| Portuguese (old series) | *22, 34, 35* | *34* |
| Portuguese (new series) | *23202, 24202, 24203* | *27501* |

## Lights

### Approach

2072 **Penedo da Saudade** 39°45'·8N 9°01'·8W
  Fl(2)15s54m30M
  Square masonry tower and building 32m

2074 **Pontal da Nazaré** 39°36'·4N 9°05'W
  Oc.3s49m14M 282°-vis-192° Siren 35s
  Red lantern on SW corner of fort 8m

2076 **São Martinho (Ponta de Santo Antonío)**
  39°30'·5N 9°08'·5W
  Iso.R.6s33m9M Siren 60s
  White round tower, red bands, and building
  Obscd on a bearing of more than 165°

2088 **Cabo Carvoeiro** 39°21'·5N 9°24'·4W
  Fl(3)R.15s56m15M Horn 35s
  White square tower and buildings 27m

*0961* Radiobeacon *CV* 287·5kHz 150M (2 & 5 in
  sequence)
  (also transmitting experimentally on 301·5kHz)

2086 **Ilha Berlenga summit** 39°25'N 9°30'·5W
  Fl(3)20s120m27M Horn 28s at N end of island
  White square tower and buildings 29m

The narrow entrance to São Martinho do Porto's semicircular bay, looking south over Ponta do Facho.

*0959* Radiobeacon *IB* 287·3kHz 200M (3 & 6 in
  sequence)

2084 **Ilhéu Farilhão Grande** 39°28'·6N 9°32'·6W
  Fl.5s99m13M Red round tower 6m

### Harbour

2078 **Ldg Lts on 145°** 39°30'·1N 9°08'·3W
  *Front* **Carreira do Sul** Iso.R.1·5s9m9M
  White column, red bands 6m

2078·1 *Rear*, 127m from front, Oc.R.6s11m9M
  White column, red bands, on square white base 8m

## General

Once a small fishing port but now a town with a considerable tourist influence, São Martinho do Porto has a most attractive setting. The sea has widened a breach in the hard cliffs and excavated a crescent-shaped bay out of the softer rock behind. A foot tunnel has been driven through the cliff just short of the Ponta de Santo António, debouching onto a rocky shore where the unwary can get soaked.

Even though many of the buildings are new and most along the seafront are of four or five storeys, the town is surprisingly attractive with an almost Mediterranean feel to its architecture and the pavement cafés and tourist shops to match. The shallow, sheltered waters of the bay ensure a warmer than average swimming temperature.

The bay is shallow and should only be entered in calm settled weather. Once inside there is no swell even when breaking crests fill the entrance, but leaving in such weather would plainly be impossible.

## Approach

As for Nazaré, page 136.

Keep outside the headlands off São Martinho until the entrance is clearly seen. In particular, beware the rocks 300m off the unlit Ponta do Facho. This point, if one is close inshore to the northeast, masks Ponta do Santo António and its light[2076], 0·5M to the south.

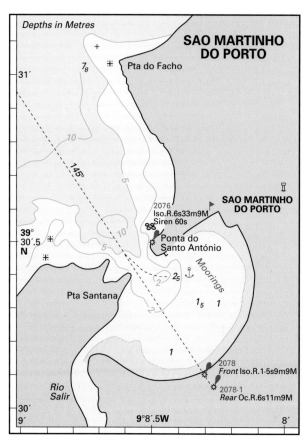

## Entrance

The leading marks[2078], on 145°, consist of two red and white banded columns 9m and 11m in height, which may be difficult to pick out against the sand and scrub background. Use them for the approach, but enter midway between Ponta do Santo António and Ponta Santana. Several dozen small white buoys are scattered across and just inside the entrance, presumably marking fish pots but posing an obvious hazard to propellers.

## Anchorage

Anchor outside the moorings in the northeast part of the harbour in 2–2·5m over sand. The quay leading round from Ponta de Santo António has about 2m at HWS at its head, but has projecting underwater ashlars and shoals towards the town.

In even moderate weather, though the anchorage may be tenable a boat can be trapped by the swell at the exit. If you do not have access to a local forecast, watch if the fishermen move en masse.

## Formalities

Call at the *policia maritima* office (easily identified by its mast and lights) with passports and ship's papers.

## Facilities

The small Clube Náutico de São Martinho do Porto, ☎ 262 980290, has premises on the north quay, with a larger building planned. Water would doubtless be available for the asking, but it is largely dinghy orientated and there is no fuel available.

The town has reasonable shopping, banks, restaurants, bars, etc.

## Communications

Post office and telephones. Taxis, buses and trains (a branch line between Lisbon and Coimbra).

## Not feasible

The Lagoa de Obidos, just south of Foz de Arelho and about halfway between São Martinho do Porto and Cabo Carvoeiro, may appear on glancing at Admiralty *3635* as a possibility. However the mouth is almost totally blocked by sandbars and the tide runs swiftly through the gaps. Unlike the rather similar Esposende there are no off-lying hazards.

# Peniche

39°21'N 9°22'W

## Tides

*Reference port* Lisbon
*Mean time differences*
HW: −25 minutes ±10; LW: 00 minutes ±5

*Heights in metres*

| MHWS | MHWN | MLWN | MLWS |
|------|------|------|------|
| 3·5 | 2·7 | 1·3 | 0·6 |

## Charts

| | Approach | Harbour |
|---|---|---|
| Admiralty | 3635 | |
| Portuguese (old series) | 22, 35, 36 | 35, 69 |
| Portuguese (new series) | 23202, 24202, 24203 | 26405 |

## Lights

### Approach

2084 **Ilhéu Farilhão Grande** 39°28'·6N 9°32'·6W
Fl.5s99m13M Red round tower 6m

2086 **Ilha Berlenga summit** 39°25'N 9°30'·5W
Fl(3)20s120m27M Horn 28s at N end of island
White square tower and buildings 29m

*0959* Radiobeacon *IB* 287·3kHz 200M (3 & 6 in sequence)

2088 **Cabo Carvoeiro** 39°21'·5N 9°24'·4W
Fl(3)R.15s56m15M Horn 35s
White square tower and buildings 27m

*0961* Radiobeacon *CV* 287·5kHz 150M (2 & 5 in sequence)
(also transmitting experimentally on 301·5kHz)

2102 **Assenta** 39°03'·4N 9°24'·8W
LFl.5s74m13M
White hut on conical base 4m

*0962* **Sintra aerobeacon** 38°52'·9N 9°24'W
Aerobeacon *STR* 371kHz 50M

2108 **Cabo da Roca** 38°46'·8N 9°29'·8W
Fl(4)18s164m26M Siren 20s
White square tower and buildings, red lantern 22m

### Harbour

2094 **West breakwater** 39°20'·8N 9°22'·4W
Fl.R.3s13m9M Siren 120s
White conical tower, red bands 8m

2096 **East breakwater** 39°20'·9N 9°22'·4W
Fl.G.3s13m9M
White conical tower, green bands 8m

## Coast radio station

**Montejunto** (39°10'N 9°03'W) (24 hours) Remotely controlled from Lisbon
**VHF** Ch 16, 23, 27, 87.

## Marina and port radio

*Marina da Ribeira* VHF Ch 16 (0930–1200, 1500–1800).
*Capimarpeniche* VHF Ch 11, 16 (0900–1200, 1400–1700 Mon–Fri).

## General

Possibly settled by Phoenicians and the scene of a landing in 1589 by an English force, Peniche today is an important fishing port with a large harbour. The town is of greater interest than many along this coast and the museum in the 16th century Citadel, later converted into a prison, is particularly recommended. Until the 15th century Peniche was an island, and the defensive walls which protected its shoreward side still run unbroken from north to south.

The port is large and well sheltered from the prevailing northerlies with an easy entrance, but it is not picturesque, though the comings and goings of the fishing fleet certainly add interest (and wash), as do the Isla Berlenga tourist ferries. The festival of *Nossa Senhora da Boa Viagem* takes place over the first weekend in August and includes harbour processions and blessing of the fishing fleet.

The small (140 berth) Marina da Ribeira, run by the Junta Autónoma dos Portos do Centro is now operating in the shelter of the west breakwater, but plans exist for a much larger affair, possibly on the east side of the harbour and with up to 1600 berths. However it is not known when – or even if and where – work is likely to start.

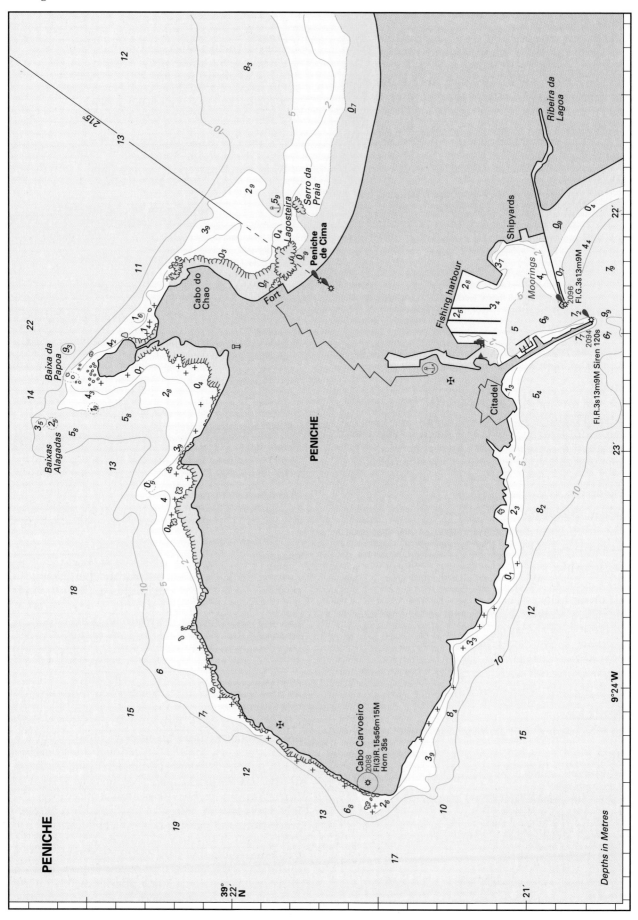

**PENICHE**

## Approach

From the north, the approach cuts a line drawn from Cabo Carvoeiro[2088] through Ilha Berlenga[2086] to Os Farilhões[2084] (10M offshore). Although the channel between Os Farilhões and Ilha Berlenga and its off-lying rocks is about 3M wide, care is needed as the current sets onto Ilha Berlenga. The better channel is that between Ilha Berlenga and Cabo Carvoeiro, though tidal streams between the islands and the mainland may make for a rough passage. From a distance the peninsula of Peniche can be mistaken for the island it once was.

From Cabo Carvoeiro to Cabo da Roca[2108], 33M south, the coast has steep cliffs with the occasional beach. The major light en route is Assenta[2102], 1M south of Ponta da Lamparoeira.

There are Traffic Separation Zones outside Os Farilhões and Ilha Berlenga and off Cabo da Roca, with minimum distances from the mainland of 15M and 10M respectively.

## Entrance

On final approach from the west around Cabo Carvoeiro, the east breakwater light[2096] appears to the north of the west breakwater light[2094]. Round the west breakwater about 50m off but beware of departing fishing boats, often in convoys.

## Berthing

Visiting yachts should secure to the long outer pontoon which shelters the marina proper, choosing a berth as space allows. As yet it is seldom full. Five or six trots can form against the pontoon, depending on overall length, with another six or eight yachts inside. At least 5m should be found throughout. After securing, await the arrival of a marina official or security guard, who amongst other things will issue a card to work the electronic gate. *Brigada fiscal* and *policia maritima* officials are also likely to visit. Anchoring is no longer allowed in the harbour.

The marina office, ☎ 261 783331 *Fax* 261 784225, shares premises at the root of the breakwater with the Ilha Berlenga ferry booking office – to place them nearer the end of the breakwater would be courting damage from winter storms. Office hours are 0930–1200 and 1500–1800 daily (though it may sometimes be closed for short periods at other times), but in addition a security guard is on duty from 0000–0015, 0700–0745, 0930–1200 and 1600–1730 weekdays, and 0000–0015 and 0800–1000 at weekends.

The marina itself is reasonably well protected, particularly at its northern end, though may suffer from swell in winds out of the south. More of a problem is the constant wash from fishing boats approaching and leaving their three long jetties to the northeast, at all hours of the day and night and almost invariably at speed. Generous fendering is essential, and care should be taken that masts are staggered to avoid rigging becoming entangled should two boats roll together.

In 1999 the high season (July–August) rate for a visiting yacht of just under 12m was 3,510 escudos (17·51 euros) for the first two nights dropping to 2,808 escudos (13·98 euros) for the third and subsequent nights. Mid season (April–June and September) rates were 2,246 (11·20 euros) escudos dropping to 2,106 escudos (10·50 euros), with 1,404 escudos (7 euros) and 1264 escudos (6·30 euros) in the low season. All were inclusive of water, electricity and tax. Multihulls paid a 50% surcharge.

Peniche harbour, looking northeast across the narrow isthmus towards Isla de Fora. The small new marina, on the inside of the west breakwater, appears fairly full with visiting yachts rafted alongside the further pontoon.

## Facilities

*Boatyard* Several boatyards with marine railways near the root of the east breakwater, backed by mechanical, electrical and electronic engineering workshops. Though more accustomed to fishing boats, in an emergency yachts can also be handled.

*Chandlery* Small chandlery on Rua José Estêvão, two streets back from the head of the harbour, with another some 3km away (ask at the marina office for directions).

*Water* On the pontoons.

*Showers* Two spotless loo/shower cubicles behind the marina office.

*Launderette* Next to the above.

*Electricity* On the pontoons.

*Fuel* On a short jetty opposite the marina office, and currently tidal. A pontoon is to be added so that it can be used at all states of the tide.

*Bottled gas* Camping Gaz available in the town.

*Clube náutico* The Clube Naval de Peniche has premises on the small crenellated area near the root of the west breakwater, beyond the red-doored lifeboat house.

*Weather forecast* Posted daily at the marina office, in Portuguese and English. In 1999 a black ball was also displayed on the harbour flagstaff to indicate winds in excess of 30 knots.

*Banks* In the town.

*Shops/provisioning* Good provisioning and general shopping, including a large supermarket in a new housing development northeast of the harbour.

*Produce market* In the town.

*Cafés, restaurants & hotels* Many. Harbourside restaurants specialise in sardines and other fish grilled on charcoal braziers by the roadside, a culinary experience not to be missed (and with a sadly limited life in view of EU hygiene regulations).

*Medical services* Hospital, etc in the town.

## Communications

*Post office* In the town.

The small, exposed harbour at Ericeira, looking southeast. Extensive storm damage to the breakwater reminds one that only one thing separates Ericeira from America – sea!

*Mailing address*
   c/o **Instituto Portuário do Centro**, Porto de Pesca de Peniche, 2520 Peniche, Portugal.
   *Fax service* 261 784225

*Public telephones* Kiosks on the root of the breakwater and elsewhere.

*Car hire/taxis* In the town. Taxis can be ordered via the marina office.

*Buses* Regular bus service to Lisbon (about 1hour 45 minutes) and elsewhere – a visit to the mediaeval walled town of Obidos is particularly recommended. Timetables are available from the marina office.

*Ferries* Tourist ferries to Isla Berlenga.

*Air services* International airport at Lisbon.

## Additional anchorages

1. *Ilha Berlenga* (39°25'N 9°30'W) – just under 6M northwest of Cabo Carvoeiro (shown in detail on an inset on Portuguese 'new series' chart *24203*). The island, together with its off-lying rocks and the seabed out to the 3m contour, is a nature reserve frequented by seabirds including gulls, puffins and cormorants. For this reason parts of the island are off-limits to visitors.

   Approach from the south, in order to avoid off-liers which fringe the island in all other directions, to anchor in a cove on the southeast coast under the lighthouse in 15m, avoiding the scattering of mooring buoys. A small yacht may be able to work into the inlet where the ferry berths, 500m north of the Forte de São João Baptista, but avoid anchoring near the fort itself. The latter, built by monks after repeated pirate raids, now houses a summer restaurant. There is also a small shop selling basic provisions.

   The Ilhéus Farilhões, some 4M north-northeast of Ilha Berlenga, offer no feasible anchorages.

2. *Peniche de Cima* (39°22'N 9°22'W) – on the north side of the peninsula southeast of Cabo de Chao. There are leading marks on 215° (LFl.7s10/14m8/7M, red column 7m and, 60m away, red lantern on gable of building 10m), but

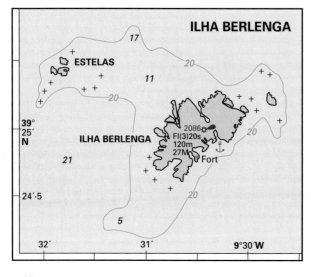

they appear to lead straight onto a rocky shoal. Keep well east, sounding in to anchor in 3–5m over sand. The entire bay is open to the north, and any northwesterly swell will also work in.

3. *Ericeira* (38°58'N 9°25'W) – 6M south of Assenta light and 11·5M north of Cabo da Roca, offers a possible stopping point in settled calm weather. However the single breakwater provides absolutely no shelter from onshore winds or swell, and local craft are kept ashore on the wide slipway. Though lit, night approach would be most unwise.

Keep well clear of the breakwater head – it lost its outer section in winter storms a few years ago and, although the outer block shows at all states of the tide, underwater rubble lies scattered in all directions. Best anchorage is to be found in the entrance to the bay, south of the breakwater head, in 5–6m over rock and sand. There is little depth off the small quay. A plan of the area is included on Portuguese 'new series' chart *27501*.

The clifftop village has retained much of its character and is renowned for its shellfish, kept fresh in pools at the foot of the cliffs. Portugal's

last king, Dom Manuel II, took passage from Ericeira in 1910 after a military revolt and following the assassination of his father and elder brother. The area is a popular destination for surfers from all over Europe.

# Cascais
38°42'N 9°25'W

### Tides
*Reference port* Lisbon
*Mean time differences*
HW: −35 minutes ±10; LW: −10 minutes ±5
*Heights in metres*

| MHWS | MHWN | MLWN | MLWS |
|------|------|------|------|
| 3·5 | 2·7 | 1·5 | 0·7 |

### Charts

| | Approach | Harbour |
|---|---|---|
| Admiralty | 3635 | 3263 |
| Portuguese (old series) | 22, 37, 23202 | 45 |
| Portuguese (new series) | 23203, 24203, 24204, 26406 | 26303 |
| Spanish | 42B | 4310 |

The large new Marina de Cascais, seen from south-southwest. When photographed in September 1999 it had been open for only a couple of weeks and had yet to fill up – there is little doubt that it will.

## Lights

### Approach

*0962* **Sintra aerobeacon** 38°52'·9N 9°24'W
Aerobeacon *STR* 371kHz 50M

2110 **Cabo Raso, Forte de São Brás** 38°42'·5N
9°29'·1W
Fl(3)15s22m20M 324°-vis-189°
Horn Mo(I)60s Red round tower 13m

2114 **Nossa Senhora de Guia** 38°41'·6N 9°26'·7W
Iso.WR.2s57m19/16M 326°-W-092°, 278°-R-292°
White octagonal tower and building 28m

2118 **Santa Marta** 38°41'·3N 9°25'·2W
Oc.WR.6s24m18/14M 233°-R-334°-W-098°
Horn 10s
White square tower, two blue bands, red lantern 20m

buoy **Fairway 'Tejo'** 38°36'·4N 9°23'·6W
Mo(A)10s12M Horn 30s Racon Mo(C)
Red and white pillar buoy, red • topmark 6m

buoy **Fairway No.2, Cabeza do Pato** 38°37'·2N
9°23'·2W
Fl.R.10s7M Red pillar buoy, ■ topmark

2124 **Forte de São Julião** 38°40'·4N 9°19'·4W
Oc.R.5s38m14M Grey square tower, red lantern 24m

### Harbour

buoy **MC1** 38°41'·2N 9°25'W
VQ(6)+LFl.10s South cardinal buoy, ▼ topmark

buoy **MC2** 38°41'·3N 9°24'·9W
VQ(6)+LFl.10s South cardinal buoy, ▼ topmark

buoy **MC3** 38°41'·4N 9°24'·8W
VQ(6)+LFl.10s South cardinal buoy, ▼ topmark

buoy **Port hand** 38°41'·5N 9°24'·7W
Fl.R.4s3M Red can buoy

2121 **Praia da Ribeira** 38°41'·7N 9°25'·1W
Oc.R.4s6m6M 251°-vis-309°
White metal column, red bands 5m

2122 **Albatroz** 38°41'·9N 9°24'·9W
Oc.R.6s12m5M
Lantern on roof of Hotel Albatroz verandah 6m

2119 **Marina east breakwater** 38°41'·5N 9°24'·8W
Fl(3)R.4s8m6M
Red column, white bands, on concrete base 4m

2119·1 **Marina north mole** 38°41'·5N 9°24'·9W
Fl(2)G.4s8m3M
Green column, white bands 4m

During 1999 eight more lit buoys were laid south and
east of Cascais, those Fl.Y. and with × topmarks
designating submarine outlets and those Fl and with
cardinal topmarks a prohibited area.

## Navtex

**Monsanto** Identification letter 'R'
*Transmits*: 518kHz in English.

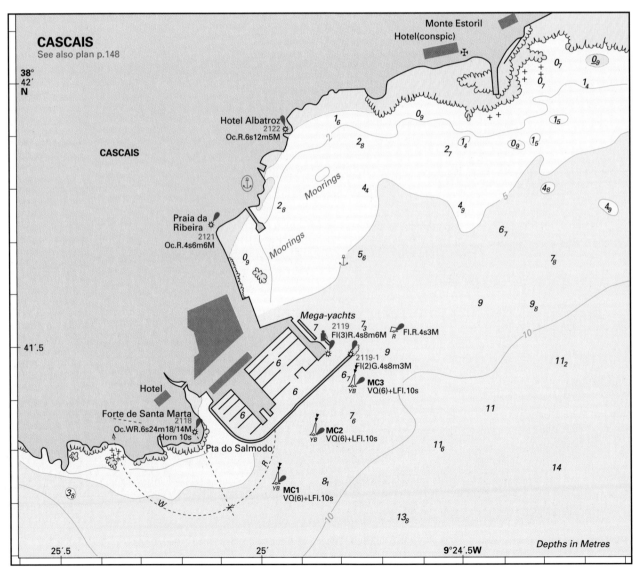

*Storm warnings*: on receipt for coastal waters of Portugal.
*Weather messages/navigational warnings*: 0250, 0650, 1050, 1450, 1850, 2250 for coastal waters of Portugal.

## Radio weather/navigational services

### Monsanto/Algés

*Storm warnings*: 2657kHz on receipt and at 0805, 2005 in Portuguese for coastal waters of Portugal up to 50M offshore.

*Weather messages*: 2657kHz at 0805, 2005 gale warnings, synopsis and forecast in Portuguese for coastal waters of Portugal up to 50M offshore.

*Navigational warnings*: 2657kHz at 0805, 2005 in Portuguese for coastal waters of Portugal up to 200M offshore. Important warnings are repeated in English.

*Weather messages*: VHF Ch 11 at 1000, 1630 gale warnings and forecast in Portuguese for Algés.

*Navigational warnings*: VHF Ch 11 at 1000, 1700 local warnings in Portuguese.

## Marina radio

*Marina de Cascais* VHF Ch 16, 62.

## General

There is no denying that Cascais is a pretty town, especially when seen from offshore and, being effectively a suburb of Lisbon, it has most of the facilities a visiting yachtsman might require – not least quick (and remarkably cheap) access to the city centre.

After many years of discussion, the large and very impressive Marina de Cascais, ☎ 214 824800 *Fax* 214 824899, finally opened in August 1999, and though many of the buildings were yet to be finished when visited the following month there is little doubt that it will become a favourite port of call for cruising yachtsmen. The complex, which is spacious and well-designed both afloat and ashore, is owned by a company which already boasts several large Mediterranean marinas – and this experience shows.

An unusual bonus is the very pleasant leafy park right opposite the marina's landward gates, complete with children's playground and mini-zoo. However it is a good ten minutes' walk into the town centre.

In January 2000 it was announced that a new marina was under development at Oeiras, about halfway between Cascais and Lisbon. When completed, hopefully in 2003, it should provide berthing for 235 yachts and 94 smallcraft of under 6m.

## Approach

From the north, keep 1M off the high cliffs of Cabo da Roca and the lower headland of Cabo Raso[2110], off which there is a Traffic Separation Zone. Between Cabo da Roca and Santa Marta[2118] there are steep rocky cliffs and fishing nets may be laid at least 0·5M offshore.

From the south, the track between Cabo Espichel and Cascais lies along 331°, leaving the red pillar buoy *No.2* about 1M to port. Further north, marking the entrance of the Rio Tejo and both well on the starboard hand if en route to Cascais, are Forte Bugio on a sandbank in the middle of the Tejo estuary and São Julião[2124] on the northern shore. The light on São Julião will probably be picked up before that on Santa Marta.

When approaching at night, shore lights tend to hide fishing boats which often do not display navigation lights.

See also plan page 148.

## Entrance

The bay is entered between the Cidadela de Cascais, prominently situated on the headland 300m behind the Marina de Cascais, and the Forte de Santo António da Barra, 1·5M to the east. Three south cardinal buoys and a single red can buoy are positioned some 100m from the marina's main breakwater, supposedly keeping yachts off a second, submerged wall which lies some distance outside the visible one. Tempting though it is to cut the corner this could be unwise.

The marina entrance faces northeast with a fetch of no more than 0·4M, and for a yacht with a reasonably powerful engine (there is little protection from strong south or southwest winds until inside) should remain feasible in almost all conditions. If entering at night, note that the east breakwater has a rubble extension at low level well beyond the light itself. Allow generous clearance.

The anchorage and town of Cascais, looking northwest. The marina entrance is on the left, with the fuel and mega-yacht pontoons outside.

## Berthing

A reception berth will be found on the starboard hand on entry, immediately below the marina office. Hours are 0800–2000 from May to September inclusive, 0900–1900 during the rest of the year. Mega-yachts – those over 40m or so – have a dedicated pontoon outside the north mole, west of the fuel pontoon, with a least depth of 7m. All 650 berths inside the marina are provided with finger pontoons (with thoughtfully rounded ends), with access to each main walkway controlled by the usual card-operated electronic gate. Depths throughout the marina are in excess of 6m.

On arrival, berth at the reception pontoon on the starboard side under the windows of the marina office. It is intended that the three outermost pontoons – containing around 125 berths – will be reserved for visiting yachts. Their crews are guaranteed plenty of exercise, particularly if the convenient shortcut through the premises of the Clube Naval de Cascais is closed off.

The rates set after opening in 1999 will remain in force throughout 2000 and possibly beyond. The high season (1 June–30 September) charge for a visiting yacht of just under 12m was 7,605 escudos (37·93 euros) per night – making it by far the most expensive marina in Portugal – and the mid season (1 April–31 May and 1 October–30 November) rate 4,563 escudos (22·76 euros). The monthly mid-season rate for a yacht of similar size was 114,122 escudos (569·24 euros), dropping to 76,073 escudos (379·45 euros) in the low season, with discounts available for longer periods. Charges were inclusive of water and electricity, and though quoted by the marina ex-IVA (the equivalent of VAT) at 17%, this has been added to the above figures for easy comparison with other harbours. Multihulls were charged at double the standard rate.

## Anchorage

It is still possible to anchor in Cascais bay, though the area occupied by smallcraft moorings is increasing steadily. However the marina provides some additional protection from the southwest to compensate. Pick any spot outside the moorings so long as it does not impede the fairway to the fishermen's quay or the marina entrance. Holding is generally good in sand and light mud, but the bay is frequently rolly and there may be downdrafts off the surrounding hills. It would be possible to land by dinghy on the rather dirty town beach or, by arrangement, at the Clube Naval de Cascais close north the marina. Note, however, that the *Clube Naval's* gates are locked at around 1900 each evening.

## Formalities

All formalities will be handled in the reception block, initially in the marina office where the standard multipart form must be completed. The *brigada fiscal*, *policia maritima* and possibly *alfândega* will also have offices in the building, and may choose to inspect a yacht either while she lies at the reception pontoon or after a berth is allocated.

Those anchored in the bay should also visit the authorities at their offices in the marina reception building.

## Facilities

*Boatyard, engineers, electronic & radio repairs, sail repairs* To be established on the centre quay, with all work done by approved contractors.

*Travel-lift* 70 tonne capacity lift already operational.

*Chandlery* Not anticipated at present.

*Water* On all pontoons.

*Showers* Three shower blocks, two in the central part of the complex and one at the reception building.

*Launderette* Will be provided in the marina complex.

*Electricity* On all pontoons.

*Fuel* Fuel pontoon (diesel and petrol) outside the north mole.

*Bottled gas* Camping Gaz available in Cascais.

*Ice* At the marina office.

*Clube naval* The Clube Naval de Cascais has premises immediately north of the marina. Although there is (currently) direct pedestrian access from the marina, it would probably be tactful to make an initial approach from the landward side.

*Weather forecast* Posted daily in the marina office.

*Banks* At least one automatic card machine in the marina complex, with banks in Cascais.

*Shops/provisioning* Small supermarket in the marina complex, with excellent grocery and other shopping in Cascais itself.

*Produce market* In Cascais. A general market is held every Wednesday, plus a fish market on the beach in the late afternoon.

*Cafés, restaurants & hotels* Several cafés and restaurants already operating in the marina complex, with dozens more of all three in the town.

*Medical services* First aid centre at the marina office, with full medical facilities (including English-speaking doctors) in the town.

## Communications

*Post office* In Cascais.

*Mailing address*
c/o **Marina de Cascais,** Edificio Controle, 2750–800 Cascais, Portugal

*Fax service* 214 824899

*Public telephones* Kiosks around the marina complex as well as in the town. An e-mail connection point is planned for the marina office.

*Car hire/taxis* Can be arranged through the marina office.

*Buses* Buses into Cascais from outside the main entrance.

*Trains* Frequent trains from Cascais to Lisbon's Cais do Sodré station, close to the city centre. The journey, via Estoril and Belém, takes about 30 minutes.

*Air services* Lisbon International Airport is less than an hour away by train and taxi.

# Lisbon and the Río Tejo

38°40'N 9°18'W

## Tides

Lisbon is a Standard Port

*Heights in metres*

| MHWS | MHWN | MLWN | MLWS |
|------|------|------|------|
| 3·8 | 3·0 | 1·4 | 0·5 |

## Charts

| | *Approach* | *Entrance/ estuary* |
|---|---|---|
| Admiralty | 3635 | 3263, 3264 |
| Portuguese (old series) | 22, 37 | |
| Portuguese (new series) | 23202, 23203, 24203, 24204, 26406 | 26303, 26304, 26305, 26306, 26307, 26406 |
| Spanish | | 4310 |
| Imray | C19 | C19 |

## Lights

### Approach

*0962* **Sintra aerobeacon** 38°52'·9N 9°24'W
  Aerobeacon *STR* 371kHz 50M
2108 **Cabo da Roca** 38°46'·8N 9°29'·8W
  Fl(4)18s164m26M Siren 20s
  White square tower and buildings, red lantern 22m
2110 **Cabo Raso, Forte de São Brás** 38°42'·5N
  9°29'·1W
  Fl(3)15s22m20M 324°-vis-189°
  Horn Mo(I)60s Red round tower 13m
2114 **Nossa Senhora de Guia** 38°41'·6N 9°26'·7W
  Iso.WR.2s57m19/16M 326°-W-092°, 278°-R-292°
  White octagonal tower and building 28m
2118 **Barra do Norte Ldg Lts on 285°** 38°41'·3N
  9°25'·2W
  *Front* **Santa Marta** Oc.WR.6s24m18/14M
  233°-R-334°-W-098° Horn 10s
  White square tower, two blue bands, red lantern 20m
2114 *Rear* **Nossa Senhora de Guia**, as above
buoy **Fairway 'Tejo'** 38°36'·2N 9°23'·6W
  Mo(A)10s12M Horn 30s
  Red and white pillar buoy, ● topmark 6m
  Racon Mo(C)
buoy **Fairway *No.2*, Cabeza do Pato** 38°37'·2N
  9°23'·2W
  Fl.R.10s7M Red pillar buoy, ■ topmark
2124 **Forte de São Julião** 38°40'·4N 9°19'·4W
  Oc.R.5s38m14M Grey square tower, red lantern 24m
2127 **Barra do Sul Ldg Lts on 047°** 38°41'·8N
  9°15'·9W
  *Front* **Gibalta** Oc.R.3s30m21M 039·5°-vis-054·5°
  White round tower, red cupola and ribs,
  illuminated by red fluorescent light 21m
2127·1 *Rear* **Esteiro**, 760m from front,
  Oc.R.6s81m21M 039·5°-vis-054·5°
  White square tower, two central red bands 15m
  Racon Mo(Q) 15M
2127·15 *Extreme Rear* **Mama Sul** 38°43'·7N 9°13'·6W
  Iso.6s153m21M 045·5°-vis-048·5°
  Platform (labelled MAMA 5m below summit)
2126 **Forte Bugio** 38°39'·7N 9°17'·9W
  Fl.G.5s27m9M Horn Mo(B)30s
  Round tower on centre of fortress, red lantern 14m
2138 **Chibata** 38°38'·5N 9°13'W (occas)
  F.R.15M Lantern on water tower
*0967* **Caparica aerobeacon** 38°38'·6N 9°13'·2W
  Aerobeacon *CP* 389kHz 250M

2139 **Cabo Espichel** 38°24'·8N 9°12'·9W
  Fl.4s167m26M Horn 31s 460m SW
  White hexagonal tower and building 32m
*0969* Radiobeacon *PI* 308kHz 50M (3 & 4 in sequence)
  (out of service until further notice)

### River

buoy **Channel *No.1*** 38°39'·5N 9°18'·7W
  Fl.G.2s3M Green conical buoy, ▲ topmark
buoy **Channel *No.3*** 38°39'·9N 9°18'·2W
  Fl.G.3s3M Green conical buoy, ▲ topmark
buoy **Channel *No.5*** 38°40'·3N 9°17'·6W
  Fl.G.4s3M Green conical buoy, ▲ topmark
buoy **Channel *No.7*** 38°40'·6N 9°16'·8W
  Fl.G.5s3M Green conical buoy
buoy ***No.9* Calhau do Mar** 38°40'·5N 9°14'·5W
  Fl.G.6s Green conical buoy
2127·4 **Doca de Pedroucos, west mole** 38°41'·5N
  9°13'·5W
  Fl.R.6s12m2M Metal mast 7m
2127·6 **Doca de Pedroucos, east mole** 38°41'·5N
  9°13'·4W
  F.G.12m4M Metal mast 7m
2130·4/5 **Ponte 25 de Abril, north pillar** 38°41'·5N
  9°10'·6W
  *NW & NE sides*: Fl(3)G.9s7m6M
  Round green column 2m
  *SW & SE sides*: Fl(3)R.9s7m6M
  Round red column 2m
  *W side*: Horn (2)25s
  *Top*: Fl.R.10s189m Summit of pillar
2130·6/7 **Ponte 25 de Abril, south pillar** 38°41'N
  9°10'·5W
  *NW & NE sides*: Fl(3)G.9s7m6M
  Round green column 2m
  *SW & SE sides*: Fl(3)R.9s7m6M
  Round red column 2m
  *W side*: Horn 25s
  *Top*: Iso.R.2s189m Summit of pillar
buoy **Canal do Alfeite, *No.1A*** 38°40'·9N 9°07'·8W
  Q(3)10s4M East cardinal pillar, ◊ topmark
2132 **Doca da Marinha, W side** 38°42'·3N 9°07'·8W
  F.R.10m2M Metal post 7m
2132·2 **Doca da Marinha, E side** 38°42'·4N 9°07'·7W
  F.G.10m2M Metal post 7m

### Canal do Cabo Ruivo (for MarinaExpo)

buoy ***CR1*** 38°43'·5N 9°05'·8W
  Fl.G.3s3M Green conical buoy
buoy ***CR2*** 38°43'·5N 9°05'·9W
  Fl.R.3s3M Red can buoy
buoy ***CR3*** 38°44'·3N 9°05'·6W
  Fl(2)G.6s3M Green conical buoy
buoy ***CR4*** 38°44'·4N 9°05'·6W
  Fl(2)R.6s3M Red can buoy
buoy ***CR5*** 38°45'·1N 9°05'·3W
  Fl(3)G.9s3M Green conical buoy
buoy ***CR6*** 38°45'·1N 9°05'·4W
  Fl(3)R.9s3M Red can buoy
Plus many other lights further upriver.

## Coast radio station

**Lisbon** (38°44'N 9°14'W) (24 hours)
*Transmits*: 2182, 2578, 2640, 2691, 2693, 2778, 2781, 3607kHz
*Receives*: 2182kHz
*Traffic lists*: 2693kHz at 0005, 0205, 0405, 0605, 0805, 1005, 1205, 1405, 1605, 1805, 2005, 2205
**VHF** Ch 16, 23, 25, 26, 27, 28
*Weather messages*: Ch 11 at 1030, 1700 gale warnings and forecast in Portuguese for Porto de Lisboa

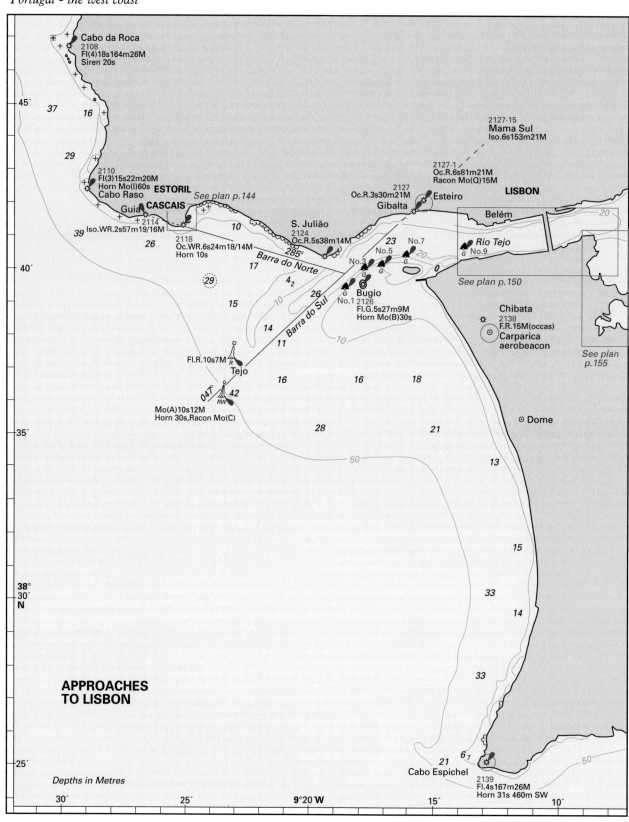

Cabo da Roca
2108
Fl(4)18s164m26M
Siren 20s

45′

37    16

29

2110
Fl(3)15s22m20M
Horn Mo(I)60s
Cabo Raso    **ESTORIL**    *See plan p.144*

Guia    **CASCAIS**

39    +2114
Iso.WR.2s57m19/16M

26    2118
Oc.WR.6s24m18/14M
Horn 10s

285°

S. Julião
2124
Oc.R.5s38m14M

*Barra do Norte*

2127·15
**Mama Sul**
Iso.6s153m21M

2127·1
Oc.R.6s81m21M
Racon Mo(Q)15M

2127
Oc.R.3s30m21M    Esteiro    **LISBON**
Gibalta

Belém

*Rio Tejo*

G  No.9

No.7

23

No.5

No.3

G    G    G

40′

17

4  2

15    26    Bugio
No.1  2126
G    Fl.G.5s27m9M
Horn Mo(B)30s

14

11    *Barra do Sul*

Fl.R.10s7M
Tejo

047°    42

Mo(A)10s12M
Horn 30s,Racon Mo(C)

28

16    16    18

21

Chibata
2138
F.R.15M(occas)
Carparica
aerobeacon

*See plan p.150*

⊙ Dome

13

*See plan p.155*

35′

15

**38°
30′
N**

33

14

33

**APPROACHES
TO LISBON**

25′

*Depths in Metres*

21    6  7
Cabo Espichel
2139
Fl.4s167m26M
Horn 31s 460m SW

30′    25′    9°20′W    15′    10′

---

*Navigational warnings*: Ch 11 at 1030, 1700 in Portuguese
for Porto de Lisboa

### Marina and port radio

*MarinaExpo* VHF Ch 12, transferring to Ch 62.
*Lisboa Port Control (Administração do Porto de Lisboa)* VHF
Ch 12, 13, 16, 61, 64.

*Pilotoslisboa* VHF Ch 09, 10, 14, 16.
*Ponte de Doca de Alcântara* (when operating – see page
152) VHF Ch 05, 12.

## General

A capital city remarkable for its slightly dilapidated beauty and the reverberations of its maritime past – its people, its way of life and its architecture all show influences far removed from Europe. In medieval times it was one of Europe's busiest ports, and can trace its roots back to the Romans and very probably the Phoenicians. Much of the city was rebuilt after a serious earthquake and fire in November 1755 in which more than 40,000 people died.

Amidst enough sights to occupy a month, perhaps the most memorable are the Belém area to the west of the city, which includes the fairytale Tôrre de Belém and the Museu de Marinha (maritime museum) housed in the western wing of the impressive Mosterio dos Jerónimos, and the old Alfama district on its hill to the east, dominated by the Moorish Castelo de São Jorge. A guidebook is almost a necessity.

In a guide for yachtsmen the Museu de Marinha deserves special mention. Its model collection is particularly fascinating, covering traditional sailing craft as well as yachts and naval vessels. There is also a comprehensive collection of navigational instruments and much attention to Portugal's great age of maritime discoveries. In the western hall an assortment of royal barges, sailing dinghies and seaplanes are on display – with everything labelled clearly in English as well as Portuguese. Allow three hours minimum. The museum is open 1000–1800 in summer and 1000–1700 in winter, the latter starting Tuesday of the week which includes 1 October. All public buildings in the Belém area are closed on Mondays.

## Approach

For the outer approaches to the Rio Tejo see Cascais, page 145.

## Entrance

The Rio Tejo is entered between Fort São Julião on the northern shore and Fort Bugio to the southeast. With any swell running it is safest to approach via the Barra do Sul (Barra Grande), first picking up the Tejo Fairway buoy (bearing 145° from Cabo Raso

Lisbon is a most attractive city to approach by water. Staying close to the northern shore one passes the 16th century Tôrre de Belém, the entrance to the Doca do Bom Sucesso, the Padrão dos Descobrimentos (Monument to the Discoveries) and the entrance to the Doca de Belém, with the Mosterio dos Jerónimos forming a backdrop to the whole.

*149*

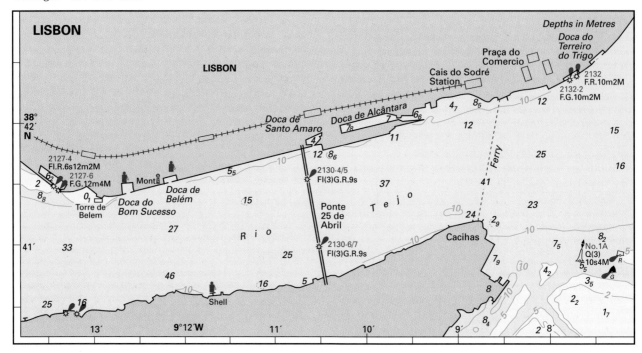

and 325° from Cabo Espichel, so that if sailing a direct course between the two one should, in theory, hit it!). The Barra do Sul leading lights on 047° then take one midway between Forte de São Julião[2124] and Forte Bugio[2126]. The limits of the shoal surrounding Forte Bugio are marked by a series of green conical buoys with ▲ topmarks. Tidal streams in the Barra do Sul can attain 3 knots at springs – more on the ebb after heavy rain – which in strong southwesterlies can create rollers on the offshore bar.

If coming from Cascais or beyond in conditions of flat sea but limited visibility the Barra do Norte, close under Forte de São Julião, may be preferable. A back bearing of Santa Marta[2118] and Nossa Senhora de Guia[2114] on 285° leads about 350m off the shore through a channel carrying a least depth of 5·2m. However, watch out for fishing vessels using the transit to exit the river. Alternatively, keeping the coast in view at about 0·5M distance until Forte de São Julião comes into sight, and then closing it to 350m, achieves the same end. Even if one should stray too far south the banks have a least charted depth of 4·2m. The Barra do Norte joins the Barra do Sul opposite Forte Bugio.

From midway between Forte de São Julião and Forte Bugio keep on the leading line as traffic dictates until well up to Gibalta[2127] before turning upriver. Again, tidal streams reach 2 or 3 knots either way at springs, not always running parallel to the shore, but are somewhat less powerful near the northern bank. This should be given an offing of at least 300m until the unmistakeable Tôrre de Belém has been passed, but beyond that can be approached within 100m in good depths. The Ponte 25 de Abril suspension bridge has a clearance of 70m – unlikely to worry any yacht! – but spare a glance for the towering statue of Christ near its southern end.

## Berthing

Six marinas exist on the north bank of the Rio Tejo, five of them in old, stone-walled basins. The exception, and the furthest upstream, is the new MarinaExpo built for Lisbon's much publicised Expo 98. Note that the current in the river is swift and that, with the possible exception of the Doca de Alcântara, all can have awkward crosscurrents at the entrance. Not only will these set the yacht sideways, but they may also tend to slew her round during those seconds when the bow is in the calm water of the entrance and the stern still in the moving river.

Of the five older marinas, the first four to be encountered are all run by the Administração do Porto de Lisboa (APL) and thus share characteristics such as good security with card-operated access gates, and similar working hours and price structure. Though all are popular with local yachtsmen, space for a visitor will normally be found somewhere – for peace of mind contact before arrival, ☎ 213 922011 *Fax* 213 922038, for instructions on which basin to approach. (Although it is possible to talk to the Administração do Porto de Lisboa on VHF Ch 12, the four APL marinas are not individually equipped with VHF and advice on berthing cannot be given over the radio.) Standard office hours are 0900–1300 and 1400–1800 Monday to Friday, closing one hour later at weekends. The only exception is the Doca de Belém, open 0800–1300 and 1400–2000 daily. Fluent English is spoken at both the main office and the individual marina offices. APL maintains an interesting website (in Portuguese and English) at www:porto-de-lisboa.pt.

In 1999 the rate for a visiting yacht of just under 12m at any time of year was 2,761 escudos (13·77 euros) per night if her beam was less than 3·3m, 3,220 escudos (16·06 euros) if it was more. The monthly rates for yachts of similar dimensions were 37,199 escudos (185·55 euros) and 45,557 escudos (227·24 euros) respectively. Charges are inclusive of water, electricity and tax. As of 1999 any multihull – regardless of length – with a beam exceeding 5m was charged a massive 10,477 escudos (52·26 euros) per night. However local officials hoped that this would shortly be reduced to a more reasonable 100% surcharge on the equivalent monohull rate.

Heading upstream the six marinas are:

1. **Doca do Bom Sucesso (APL)** – a short distance upstream from the (floodlit) Tôrre de Belém. Previously the marina to which foreign yachts were directed, it is now crowded with local yachts and unlikely to have space for visitors. The 161 berths (all with finger pontoons) are limited to 12m LOA, but recent dredging has increased depths to 3·5m. Fuel is available, the fuel pontoon being in the northeast corner of the basin with the office and showers nearby. However there is very little room to manoeuvre. The entrance is no longer lit.

2. **Doca de Belém (APL)** – 700m east of the Doca do Bom Sucesso and immediately beyond the prominent Padrão dos Descobrimentos (Monument to the Discoveries) which resembles a ship's prow. Again the 198 berths are reserved for residents and there is most unlikely to be room for a visiting yacht. Mooring is via haul-off lines tailed to the pontoon. Currently much of the marina is silted to less than 2m, but a 3m access channel has been dredged to the fuel pontoon on the rear wall directly opposite the entrance. Further dredging, to give 3·5m throughout, should take place before the 2000 season. New buildings are also planned, to house the marina office and showers and to increase the covered space available to the APL-administered boatyard next door. Again, the entrance is no longer lit.

3. **Doca de Santo Amaro (APL)** – 150m beyond the suspension bridge and dredged to a nominal 4m (though currently reported to carry considerably less than this over a very soft bottom). Currently the biggest of the four APL

Lisbon's Doca de Santo Amaro (left) and Doca de Alcântara (centre and right), with part of the massive Ponte 25 de Abril bridge in the foreground. Several more yacht pontoons have been placed in the Doca de Alcântara since this photograph was taken a few years ago.
*Penaguião & Burnay Lda, Lisbon*

marinas, with 331 berths all equipped with finger pontoons, it is crowded with local craft though a visiting yacht can sometimes be squeezed in. The entrance is narrow and unlit, but there is a convenient pontoon just inside on the port hand (though short on mooring cleats as it is not technically a reception pontoon but the property of the local rowing club). Alternatively use any unoccupied berth on a temporary basis. The marina office, labelled APL Docas de Recreio, is at the northeast end of the basin, with showers next door. There is no fuel available.

The only real drawback to the Doca de Santo Amaro – should space be available at all – is that it is not quiet. Traffic passing over the bridge sounds like a swarm of bees and could become irritating in time, but more importantly the area has become a popular centre for Lisbon nightlife with the bars and restaurants overlooking the basin remaining lively until 0400 or beyond. Of course more energetic crews may well consider this a plus...

4. **Doca de Alcântara (APL)** – a much larger basin than any of the others, entered about 1M upstream of the suspension bridge via an entry channel and a swing bridge. Currently this bridge (constructed around the turn of the century) is permanently open, but if operation is restarted will probably return to its previous schedule of opening at 0700, 0815, 0915, 1015, 1115, 1315, 1500, 1630 and 1800 daily, and then remaining open from 0000 to 0800, seven days a week. Surprisingly, the entrance is unlit.

Until fairly recently the Doca de Alcântara was purely a commercial basin and it is still used by ships of considerable size. For this reason it can sometimes be oily. The marina, which currently contains 254 berths, is at the far (western) end of the basin, which is more than 0·5M long. It remains the most likely spot for a visiting yacht of any size to find space, while very large yachts – in the 35m to 45m size range – can normally lie alongside the wall. Depths are considerable.

Plans are in hand to enlarge the marina to around 500 berths, though this will probably be done in stages. More immediately the two sections, currently reached by two separate gates, are to be joined together, with a new office/shower block beside a single entrance on the landward side. There is no reception pontoon as such, but visitors are normally berthed on the easternmost of the five pontoons where there are haul-off lines rather than fingers. Occasional thefts have been reported, but these are as likely to be the work of other yachtsmen as of local people. There is no fuel available.

Currently the surroundings to the Doca de Alcântara are largely commercial and relatively quiet, certainly at night. However it is anticipated that, within the next few years, shops and restaurants will be built on the spacious wharves nearby. The restored Portuguese East Indiaman *D Fernando II e Glória* (see page 130), is often berthed in the basin and open to the public.

5. **Doca do Terreiro do Trigo** – although the domain of APORVELA, ☎ 218 876854 *Fax* 218 873885, the Associação Portuguesa de Treino de Vela (sail training association), there is occasionally room for visitors. However when visited at low water springs in September 1999 silt was drying to 0·25m throughout much of the basin, and it would obviously not be wise to attempt entry until it has been confirmed that dredging has taken place. Office hours are 0930–1130 and 1400–1730.

To reach the Doca do Terreiro do Trigo (literally the 'wheat yard'), continue upriver past the ferry and railway terminals, the Praça do Comercio (which has a prominent equestrian statue facing the river) and a second ferry terminal. Immediately upstream are a pair of dock basins about 500m apart. The westernmost (the Doca da Marinha) is reserved for the navy, with the Doca do Terreiro do Trigo just beyond. A strong crosscurrent should be anticipated at the entrance, and wash from ferries and other river traffic may work in. The pontoons are equipped with longish fingers, and though no water or electricity are laid on the former can be had from the fuel berth at the head of the basin. The immediate surroundings are unexciting, but it is only a short walk to the historic and fascinating Alfama district.

6. **MarinaExpo** ☎ 218 985000 *Fax* 218 985008
   *e-mail* marinaexpo@mail.telepac.pt
   Lisbon's newest marina is situated some 7M upstream from the Tôrre de Belém and about 1·5M short of the new and impressive Vasco da Gama bridge. The approach up the Canal de Cabo Ruivo is straightforward, skirting container wharves for 1·5M after passing the Doca do Terreiro do Trigo before picking up the two buoys *CR1* and *CR2* (though a yacht can safely cut inside them). About 0·5M further upriver one passes the old Doca do Poço do Bispo with buoys *CR3* and *CR4* just upstream and the pair *CR5*

Lisbon occupies the north bank of the Rio Tejo, itself spanned by the massive Ponte 25 de Abril suspension bridge. The Doca de Santo Amaro (left) and Doca de Alcântara (centre) can just be made out, with the entrance to the latter's long, narrow basin visible to the right of the bridge support.

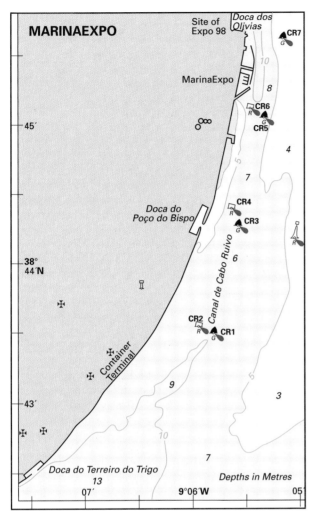

**MARINAEXPO**

and *CR6* some 0·7M beyond. From *CR6* it is under 300m to the unlit marina entrance.

Only the southern of the two basins was fully operational by September 1999, with 520 berths planned on completion including a few for vessels of up to 50m. Changes and improvements are already being made, notably the building of a solid breakwater to replace the floating barrier at the downstream end, in an effort to reduce the strong currents which flow through the marina – allow for these when manoeuvring or, ideally, time arrival and departure for slack water.

There is a reception pontoon below the square blue marina office, but if wind and/or tide make securing to it difficult it is also acceptable to use any free berth (all are provided with fingers). There is a single gate to the pontoons, controlled by the usual electronic card which also gives access to the showers and launderette.

The Expo 98 site, a few minutes' walk distant, makes for interesting wandering – some of the attractions, including the giant aquarium, remain open and there is no shortage of space for young crewmembers to work off excess energy. Admission to the area is free.

In 1999 the high season (1/6–30/9) rate for a visiting yacht of just under 12m was 3,650 escudos (18·21 euros) per night if her beam was

less than 3·3m, 3,978 escudos (19·84 euros) if it was more. The low season rates for yachts of similar dimensions were 1,451 escudos (7·24 euros) and 1,638 escudos (8·17 euros) respectively. The monthly low season rates were 39,312 escudos (196·09 euros) and 43,992 escudos (219·43 euros), with further discounts available for longer periods. Multihulls are charged the higher of the two monohull rates. Charges are inclusive of water and electricity, and though quoted by the marina ex-IVA (the equivalent of VAT) at 17%, this has been added to the above figures for easy comparison with other harbours.

### Formalities

At the Administração do Porto de Lisboa marinas it is only necessary to complete a standard form at the office, copies of which are distributed to the *brigada fiscal*, *policia maritima* and *alfândega* (customs).

Whether any or all choose to visit will be based on the yacht and crew's nationalities and her last port of call.

Much the same systems prevails at MarinaExpo, with copies of a multipart form passed to the various authorities. All three have offices in the reception building, but though skippers of non-EU registered yachts may have to visit the *alfândega* in person, other officials will come to the yacht only if they feel it necessary.

### Facilities

*Boatyard* Next to the Doca de Belém, and administered by APL, with all work carried out by sub-contractors who have to satisfy APL of their competence. There is a reasonable amount of hardstanding, with yachts in cradles or well supported with wooden shores.

A new boatyard, capable of handling yachts to 30m and at least 70 tonnes is planned for the Algés area west of the Tôrre de Belém. Again it will be overseen by APL, with work done by individual contractors. It is hoped that it will be functioning by the end of 2000. Meanwhile a yard at Seixal (see page 156) can handle larger yachts. A large, full-service boatyard is also planned for the MarinaExpo site.

A final possibility would be to contact Port Partner, ☎ 213 473606 Fax 213 473833, a yacht and ship agent which claims to be able to organise and/or oversee almost anything from major repairs to sightseeing trips. Good English is spoken.

*Travel-lift* 30 tonne capacity lift (up to 4·5m beam) at the Doca de Belém boatyard operated by Técniates Yacht Services, ☎ 213 623362 Fax 213 623367, the owner of which speaks good English. 30 tonne capacity lift also planned for the MarinaExpo boatyard.

*Engineers, electronic & radio repairs* At or via the Doca de Belém boatyard.

*Sailmaker/sail repairs* Two sailmakers in the Belém area – enquire at any of the marina offices.

*Chandlery* Conveniently, two of Lisbon's largest chandleries are virtually next door to each other (though neither is very clearly marked), both opposite the Cais do Sodré station east of the Doca de Alcântara.

**J Garraio & Ca Lda**, Avenida 24 de Julho 2 – 1° – Dt°, 1200 Lisboa

☎ 213 473081 *Fax* 213 428950

*e-mail* j.garraio@mail.telepac.pt

0900–1230 and 1400–1900, 0900–1230 Saturday

**Luiz Godinho Lda**, Rua de Pedrouços 89A, 1400 Lisboa

☎ 213 421001 *Fax* 213 016658

0900–1900, 0900–1300 Saturday.

Godinho is a conventional yacht chandler with good stocks of rope, chain, rigging wire and terminals (plus a swage machine) and other hardware, but few electronics and no books. Garraio displays a wide range of books in both Portuguese and English as well as some electronics, and has much more in their stores. If what you need is not on display, ask (some English is spoken in both shops).

Closer to the Doca de Santo Amaro/Alcântara complex with premises right under the suspension bridge is the smaller

**Marítima**

Doca de Santo Amaro,

1350–353 Lisboa

☎ 213 979598 *Fax* 213 979572

Finally overlooking the east end of the Doca Alcântara (on the south side near the swing bridge) is

**Azimute Lda**, Avenida Gomes de Araújo 11 – A – r/c, Edifício Bartolomeu Dias, Doca de Alcântara, 1350 Lisbon

☎ 213 920730 *Fax* 213 974494,

*e-mail* azimute@ip.pt

*Charts* J Garraio & Ca Lda are agents for both Portuguese and Admiralty charts and will deliver free to any of the APL marinas.

Portuguese charts are also available from Azimute (see above), or direct from

**Instituto Hidrográfico**,

Rua des Trinas 49, 1296 Lisboa

☎ 213 955119 *Fax* 213 960515

*e-mail* mail@hidrografico.pt

*website* www.hidrografico.pt

1000–1230 and 1430–1630 weekdays

a short walk northeast from the Doca de Alcântara.

*Water* On the pontoons in all the APL marinas and MarinaExpo.

*Showers* At the APL marinas and MarinaExpo. At present those at the Doca de Alcântara, though clean and well kept, are insufficient for the number of berths, but a new reception/shower block is planned.

*Launderette* None at the APL marinas, but many in the surrounding city. Opposite the pontoon access gate at MarinaExpo.

*Electricity* On the pontoons in all the APL marinas and MarinaExpo.

*Fuel* In the Doca do Bom Sucesso and Doca de Belém (0700–2100), and at MarinaExpo (0900–1900). If intending to fuel at either of the first two (and berthed in an APL marina) it would be worth arranging a time with the marina office, who will contact the fuel berth. That at the Doca de Belém is more easily accessible, with a channel dredged to at least 3m.

Yachts taking on large quantities might also investigate the Shell wharf on the south bank about 1M below the suspension bridge. Although primarily a commercial facility they are willing to serve yachts.

*Bottled gas* Camping Gaz exchanges at the Marítima chandlery (see above) and elsewhere; exchanges and other bottles refilled via the filling station behind MarinaExpo (though see page 8).

*Ice* From the filling station near MarinaExpo.

*Clube náutico* The Associação Naval de Lisboa has premises next to the Doca de Belém, where visiting yachtsmen are made welcome. APORVELA, the Portuguese Sail Training Association, have their headquarters at the Doca do Terreiro do Trigo.

*Weather forecast* Posted daily at all the APL marina offices and MarinaExpo.

*Banks* All over Lisbon. Particularly convenient are the card machine next to the Marítima chandlery overlooking the Doca de Santo Amaro, and the one in the Vasco de Gama shopping centre near MarinaExpo. Banks are normally open 0830–1200 and 1345–1430, weekdays only.

*Shops/provisioning* Absolutely everything available, as befits a capital city. Most convenient for provisioning if in the Doca de Santo Amaro/Alcântara complex is the large Pingo Doce supermarket reached via a pedestrian tunnel (ask at the marina office for directions). From the MarinaExpo the brand new Vasco de Gama shopping centre will answer most needs, but is neither very close nor cheap.

*Produce market* Excellent produce/fish market almost opposite the Cais do Sodré station east of the Doca de Alcântara (and thus very close to the Garraio and Godinho chandleries). The large two-storey building is surmounted by a most distinctive dome.

*Cafés, restaurants & hotels* Many and varied, at all prices. Some bars and restaurants feature live *fado* singing.

*Medical services* If berthed in one of the APL marinas one has access to the Administração do Porto de Lisboa's own Medical Centre, close to the Doca de Santo Amaro/Alcântara complex. Otherwise full medical services of all kinds are to be found in the city.

## Communications

*Post office* Large post office just west of the Praça Comérçio, plus many others. There is a post office in the Vasco de Gama shopping centre, and mail can also left at the MarinaExpo office.

*Mailing address* Mail for a yacht hoping to stay in one of the APL marinas is best sent to the head office:

**Administração do Porto de Lisboa,**
Nautica de Recreio, Doca de Santo Amaro,
1399–012 Lisboa, Portugal
*Fax service* 213 922038
MarinaExpo will also hold mail for visiting yachts
c/o **MarinaExpo**, Edificio da Administração, Passeio
de Neptuno, 1998–193 Lisboa Expo, Portugal.
*Fax service* 218 985008
Alternatively there is an entire building adjacent to the
main post office given over to nothing but *poste restante*.
See also the note on page 10.
*Public telephones* Kiosks handy to all marinas, plus
many throughout the city.
*Car hire* Many companies in the city, plus APL
receive a discount from AVIS which they pass on
to the hirer. But be warned – the normally easy-
going Portuguese appear to suffer a character
change behind the wheel, and some city driving is
manic.

*Taxis* No shortage.
*Buses/trams* The city's well-organised bus and tram
service is particularly useful near the waterfront
(many originate from the Praça Comerçio),
linking all six marinas with the city centre. A ride
in one of the small, pre-war trams is a Lisbon
'must'. A city centre bus route parallels the river
from close to MarinaExpo.
*Trains & Metro* Regular and frequent rail service
from the Cais do Sodré station to Cascais and
other points west. Most other trains depart from
Rossio station at the south end of the Avenida da
Liberdade.

Lisbon's *metro* had a facelift for the 1998 Expo,
making it the quickest way to reach city
destinations away from the waterfront. However
finding a city centre station can be a real
challenge – they tend to be very poorly signed.

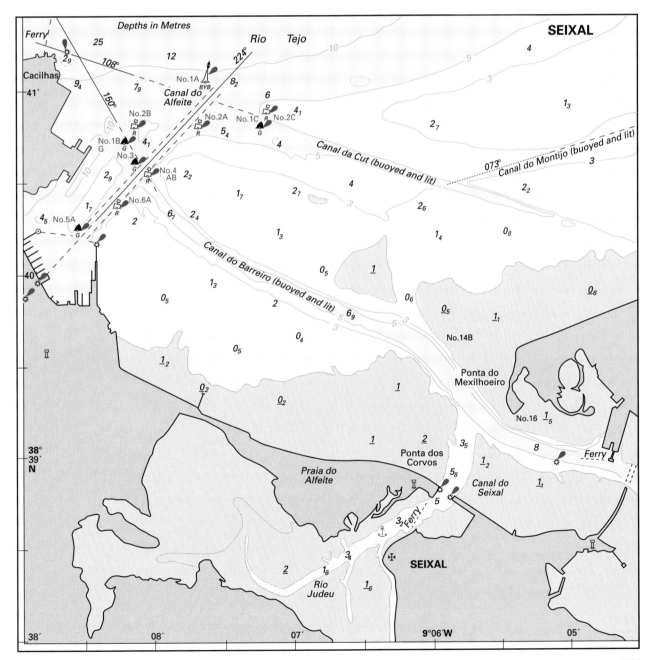

MarinaExpo's nearest metro station, the Gare do Oriente, is a good 20 minute walk from the marina.

*Ferries* Frequent ferries across the Rio Tejo to Cacilhas, from which one can get a bus up to the prominent statue of Christ near the south end of the 25 de Abril suspension bridge.

*Air services* International airport in the northeast part of the city, with regular flights to the UK, America, etc.

### Anchorages

There is no yacht anchorage convenient to Lisbon itself, though there are a number of possibilities further upriver where it widens into the Mar de Palha (literally 'Sea of Straw', or reeds), for which large-scale Portuguese charts will be required. In addition, the channels extending south from the Rio Tejo offer several good anchorages.

## Seixal

38°39'N 9°06'W

Round Ponta de Cacilhas, on the south bank of the Rio Tejo 1·5M east of the suspension bridge, and head 150° past the prominent Lisnave shipyard to cross the Canal do Alfeite near buoys *No.3* and *No.4*. Continue down the Canal do Barreiro, which is well buoyed but has quite heavy ferry traffic, some of it at high speeds. Buoy *No.13* (possibly now replaced by a beacon) marks the junction of the Canal do Seixal with the Canal Do Barreiro, from which can be seen the piers of the Canal do Seixal/Rio Judeu bridge. Pass between the piers to anchor opposite the village, as near the north bank as soundings allow to keep clear of traffic.

Seixal has a pretty waterfront and good shelter, and the lie of the land hides most of the heavy industrial development. Its river, the Rio Judeu, has several boatyards one of which deals mostly with yachts. There are restaurants, etc and basic shopping is available, but there is no yacht fuel. The ferry to Lisbon runs every 30 minutes between 0500 and 2330, alternatively take a bus to Cacilhas and the ferry from there.

## Canal do Montijo

38°41'N 9°02'W

Round Ponta de Cacilhas and head 108° into the buoyed Canal da CUF (Companhia União Fabril). The Canal do Montijo (also buoyed) leads off at 073° just over 1M from the entrance of the Canal da CUF. At high water it appears to be a large bay, but at low water mud and sandbanks define the channel accurately. The airfield on the low headland to the northeast is military, and landing is prohibited.

Montijo itself is not attractive and has little room, but there are pleasant anchorages to be found by soundings along the channel or its offshoots. There are no facilities.

## Sesimbra

38°26'·5N 9°07'W

### Tides

*Reference port* Lisbon
*Mean time differences*
HW: −35 minutes ±10; LW: −15 minutes ±5

*Heights in metres*

| MHWS | MHWN | MLWN | MLWS |
|------|------|------|------|
| 3·4 | 2·6 | 1·4 | 0·6 |

### Charts

| | Approach | Harbour |
|---|---|---|
| Admiralty | 3635, 3636 | |
| Portuguese (old series) | 22, 37, 38 | 79 |
| Portuguese (new series) | 23202, 23203, 24204 | 26407 |

Long breakwater at Sesimbra, looking northwest. The yacht pontoons on the left are crowded with local boats and visitors normally compete for space with the fishing boats.

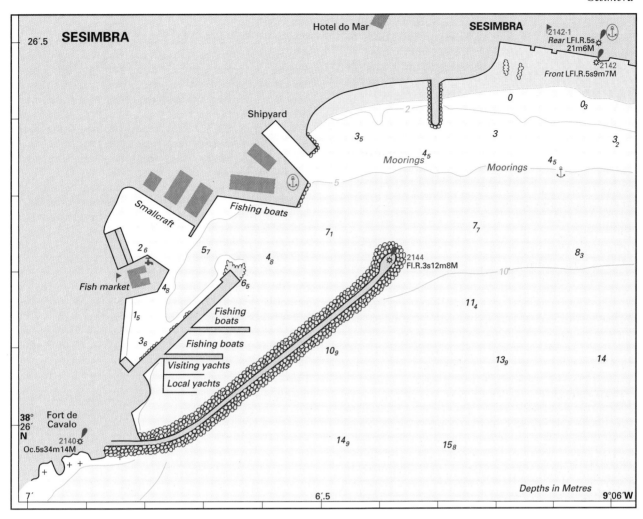

## Lights

### Approach

2139 **Cabo Espichel** 38°24'·8N 9°12'·9W
Fl.4s167m26M Horn 31s 460m SW
White hexagonal tower and building 32m

0969 Radiobeacon *PI* 308kHz 50M (3 & 4 in sequence)
(out of service until further notice)

2140 **Forte do Cavalo** 38°26'N 9°06'·9W
Oc.5s34m14M Red round tower 7m

2150·22 **Lightbeacon No.2** 38°27'·1N 8°58'·4W
Fl(2)R.10s13m9M Red post and platform
Racon Mo(B) 360° 15M

2142 **Ldg Lts on 003·5°** 38°26'·5N 9°06'W
*Front* LFl.R.5s9m7M W turret of fortress 10m

2142·1 *Rear*, 34m from front, LFl.R.5s21m6M
NW corner of fortress 17m

*Note* These lights do not lead to the harbour but to a
point on the shore about 0·5M to the east. Two sets
of three lights in line (Fl.R and Fl.) close east of
Sesimbra mark a submarine cable area and are NOT
leading lights.

### Harbour

2144 **Breakwater** 38°26'·2N 9°06'·4W
Fl.R.3s12m8M White tower, red bands 7m

*Note* Three outfalls lie within a 0·5M radius of the
breakwater head. Each is marked by a 3m yellow post
with × topmark and nearby yellow spherical buoy with
a similar topmark. The pairs are lit, Fl.Y.8s3M,
Fl.Y.6s3M and Fl.Y.4s3M respectively.

## Port radio

*Delegmarsesimbra* VHF Ch 11, 16 (0900–1200,
1400–1700 Mon–Fri).

## General

The town of Sesimbra lies 2km from its harbour, the
whole dominated by a large Moorish castle from
which there are wonderful views. Its economy is
based on fishing and tourism but is also becoming a
dormitory for Lisbon. The old town and the harbour
area are both attractive, the latter very much a
working port with brightly painted boats clustered
around a wharf complete with busy fish and shellfish
market (wholesale and retail).

The harbour is well protected by a 900m
breakwater and, despite having no specific facilities
for visiting yachts, makes an interesting port of call
for those not overly concerned about a lack of
marina comforts.

## Approach

The major mark from north or south is Cabo
Espichel[2139]. Forte do Cavalo[2140], 6·5M east of Cabo
Espichel, marks the landward end of the outer
harbour mole. The coast between the two should be
given an offing of at least 0·5M and after rounding
Cabo Espichel there is still some southing to be
made to get round Ponta da Pombeira.

The bluff trending east from Cabo Espichel rises from 160m near the cape to 500m towards Setúbal. Running up the hillside immediately east of Sesimbra are two sets of three lights in line: both sets flash 2·5s front, 3s centre, 3·5s rear, with a range of 2M; the western set on 030° flashes red and the eastern, on 000°, white. They mark submarine cables and anchoring within their limits is prohibited.

## Entrance

The entrance is straightforward, though it would be unwise to cut the outer molehead too closely in case of fishing vessels exiting at speed.

## Berthing

On arrival, visiting yachts normally secure to the south side of the southern of the two long jetties occupied mainly by fishing boats. This can cause problems, particularly for smaller yachts, as the high jetties are raised on concrete piles making fendering difficult, and unless berthed beside a ladder access may also be a problem. Some of these will be overcome by berthing alongside a fishing boat – call at the *clube naval*'s premises opposite the fish market for advice. There are no facilities, but neither is any charge made.

The two pontoons tucked between the jetties and the breakwater are administered by the Clube Naval de Sesimbra, ☎ 212 233451 *Fax* 212 281039, and are normally fully occupied by their members. However a space may sometimes be available, in which case the 1999 high season (1/5–30/9) rate for a visiting yacht of just under 12m was 3,500 escudos (17·46 euros) per night, dropping to 1,600 escudos (7·98 euros) outside these months.

## Anchorage

Sesimbra is an extremely busy fishing port and there is nowhere in the harbour itself that a yacht can anchor without being in somebody's way. Local yachts and smallcraft lie on moorings off the beach between the shipyard and the short east mole, and the only possible anchorage is to the east of them in 5–6m, exposed to the south and southeast. Holding is variable over kelp and rock with sand patches – the excellent sandy beach fronting the harbour and town is at least partially man-made.

Sesimbra has a deserved reputation for strong local northerlies which get up in the late afternoon and die in the small hours – lay ground tackle accordingly.

## Formalities

There is a *policia maritima* office in the new fishing port and a *brigada fiscal* in the town. In theory it is the skipper's duty to seek them out immediately on arrival, but in view of the walk involved it would be worth checking at the *clube naval* whether this is still considered necessary. Alternatively one or both may come to the yacht.

## Facilities

Water can be carried from a tap on the fishermen's wharf, as can diesel from a nearby pump intended primarily for lorries (though the hose is reported to be long enough to reach a yacht's tank). There is a small shipyard building fishing vessels opposite the breakwater end, the obvious place to start should engineering or other work be necessary, and a diving school at the root of the inner mole. A weather forecast is displayed outside the *clube naval*'s small building opposite the fish market – they also have more formal premises on the seafront near the fort.

The very attractive anchorage at Portinho de Arrábida, between Sesimbra and Setúbal, looking north.

Good shopping will be found in the town, together with a market, banks, hotels and restaurants specialising in seafood.

## Communications

Post office and telephone kiosks in the town, though apparently no public telephone near the fish market. Taxis. Bus station near the market (Lisbon 45 minutes).

## Additional anchorages

1. A bay 1·5M east of Cabo de Ares, in sand off a pleasant beach. The bottom shoals steadily towards the shore at the west end of the beach. Cabo de Ares has an off-lying rock – keep at least 0·5M clear all along the coast.
2. Portinho de Arrábida, a wooded bay backed by high cliffs some 6M east of Sesimbra, and one of the most dramatic – and scenic – anchorages in all Portugal. Although fully open to the south a surprising number of smallcraft lie on summer moorings in the western part of the bay (see photograph). There is usually some swell.

The approach from the west is complicated by a drying sandbank, the Baixo de Alpertuche, off Forte Arrábida. Keep 0·4M offshore until lightbeacon *No.2*²¹⁵⁰·²² bears 090°, before altering to 033° to clear Forte Arrábida by 150–200m. This should give a least depth of 2·4m at low water springs but the bank may grow and/or move. Admiralty chart *3270* will be found useful. Anchor outside the moorings in weed and hard sand – there are rocks and a small off-lying island at the east end of the bay.

There are no facilities other than a telephone kiosk behind the beach, together with several restaurants, and an oceanographic museum in Forte Arrábida on the western headland.

# Setúbal and the Rio Sado

38°27'N 8°58'W (entrance)

## Tides

*Reference port* Lisbon
*Mean time differences*
HW: −15 minutes ±5; LW: 00 minutes ±5
*Heights in metres*

| MHWS | MHWN | MLWN | MLWS |
|------|------|------|------|
| 3·4 | 2·7 | 1·3 | 0·5 |

## Charts

| | *Approach* | *Entrance/ estuary* |
|---|---|---|
| Admiralty | *3635, 3636* | *3270* |
| Portuguese (old series) | *22, 38* | *82* |
| Portuguese (new series) | *23202, 23203, 24204* | *26308, 26309, 26407* |

## Lights

### Approach
2139 **Cabo Espichel** 38°24'·8N 9°12'·9W
  Fl.4s167m26M Horn 31s 460m SW
  White hexagonal tower and building 32m
*0969* Radiobeacon *PI* 308kHz 50M (3 & 4 in sequence)
  (out of service until further notice)

2140 **Forte do Cavalo** 38°26'N 9°06'·9W
  Oc.5s34m14M Red round tower 7m
2150·22 **Lightbeacon *No.2*** 38°27'·3N 8°58'·4W
  Fl(2)R.10s13m9M Red post and platform
  Racon Mo(B) 360° 15M
2158 **Pinheiro da Cruz** 38°15'·6N 8°46'·2W
  Fl.3s66m11M White round column, red stripes
2160 **Cabo de Sines** 37°57'·5N 8°52'·7W
  Fl(2)15s55m26M
  White round tower and building 22m
  Obscd 001°–003° and 004°–007° within 17M
*Note* Numerous nearby red lights mark chimneys, radio masts, etc
*0971* Radiobeacon *SN* 308kHz 100M (5 & 6 in sequence)

### Entrance
2151 **Ldg Lts on 040°** 38°31'·2N 8°53'·9W
  *Front* **Fishing harbour E jetty** Oc.R.3s12m14M
  Red and white striped metal structure 10m
2151·1 *Rear* **Azêda**, 1·7M from front,
  Iso.R.6s60m20M 038·3°-vis-041·3°
  White round tower, red bands 31m
  (Reported difficult to distinguish against the lights of the city)
buoy *No.1* 38°27'·1N 8°58'·1W
  Fl.G.3s5M Green pillar buoy, ▲ topmark
2150·26 **Lightbeacon *No.4*** 38°28'N 8°57'·6W
  Fl.R.4s13m4M Red and white chequered column 5m
buoy *No.3* 38°28'·4N 8°56'·7W
  Fl.G.3s4M Green pillar buoy, ▲ topmark
2150 **Forte de Outão** 38°29'·4N 8°56'W
  Oc.R.6s33m12M
  Red hexagonal tower and lantern 11m
2150·28 **Lightbeacon *No.5*** 38°29'·3N 8°55'·3W
  Fl.G.4s13m4M Black post and platform 5m
2150·4 **Forte de Albarquel** 38°30'·7N 8°54'·7W
  Iso.R.2s15m6M Red lantern on S corner of fort
buoy **Bóia João Farto** 38°30'·4N 8°54'·4W
  Q(9)15s3M West cardinal buoy, ⻓ topmark
2152·1 **Anunciada** 38°31'·4N 8°54'W
  Iso.R.4s22m5M Red lantern
2152 **Algarve Exportador** 38°31'·3N 8°53'·6W
  Oc.R.4s15m5M Red lantern

## Radio weather/navigational services

**Setúbal** (38°26'N 8°58'W)
*Weather messages*: VHF Ch 11 at 1030, 1630 gale warnings and forecast in Portuguese for Porto de Setúbal.
*Navigational warnings*: VHF Ch 11 at 1030, 1630¹ in Portuguese for Porto de Setúbal.
1. Not Saturday or Sunday.

## Marina and port radio

*Doca de Recreio das Fontainhas* VHF Ch 12.
*Postradsetúbal* VHF Ch 11, 16 (24 hours); 2182, 2252, 2657kHz.
*Pilotossetúbal* VHF Ch 14, 16.

## General

The town of Setúbal lies more than 1M inside the entrance to the Rio Sado, but its associated industries start with the cement works at the narrows and extend to the large shipyard and ore wharf 5M upstream. It is the country's third largest port and cannot claim to be attractive. However it is possible to get well away from the town, and though large areas dry there is a navigable channel as far as

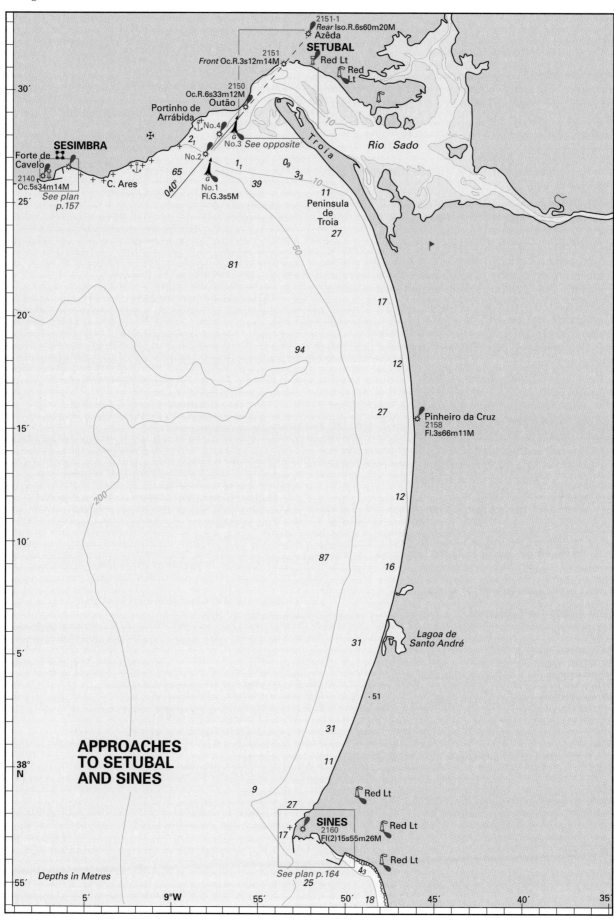

2151·1
*Rear* Iso.R.6s60m20M
✷ Azêda

2151
*Front* Oc.R.3s12m14M  **SETUBAL**
🚩 Red Lt

🚩 Red
Lt

2150
Oc.R.6s33m12M
Outão

Portinho de
Arrábida

No.4

No.3 *See opposite*

Troia

*Rio   Sado*

**SESIMBRA**

Forte de
Cavelo
2140
Oc.5s34m14M

*See plan
p.157*

C. Ares

2₁

No.2

040°

65

No.1
Fl.G.3s5M

1₁

39

0₉

3₃

10

11

Peninsula
de
Troia

27

81

50

17

12

94

27

Pinheiro da Cruz
2158
Fl.3s66m11M

200

12

87

16

31

Lagoa de
Santo André

· 51

31

**APPROACHES
TO SETUBAL
AND SINES**

11

9

Red Lt

27

Red Lt

**SINES**
2160
Fl(2)15s55m26M

17

Red Lt

*Depths in Metres*

*See plan p.164*

25

4₃

Red Lt

18

30′

25′

20′

15′

10′

5′

38°
N

55′

5′          9°W          55′          50′          45′          40′          35′

Alcacer do Sal, 24M upstream – or at least to the railway bridge below it.

There are Roman remains at California on the Península de Tróia. Despite being overlooked by the tower blocks of the tourist development to the north, the inlet still has an oddly haunted feel.

The entrance channel is narrow but well marked. Even so it should not be attempted except in fine weather and on the flood, and certainly not in an onshore wind. Once inside, the smallcraft basins are crowded and a visiting yacht is in competition with the residents, the fishing boats and the Península de Tróia ferries.

**Approach**

Lightbeacon *No.2*[2150·22] marks the southwest end of the approach channel. If coming from Sesimbra note that Cabo de Ares has an off-lying rock – keep

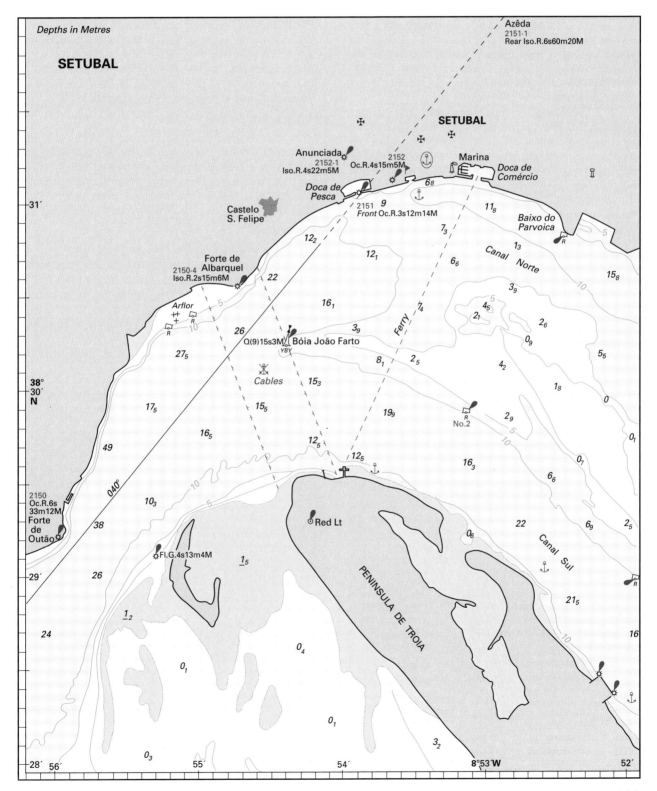

at least 0·5M clear all along the coast. From the south, the course from Cabo de Sines[2160] of 353° stands away from the unbroken low sand hills of the Tróia shore.

## Entrance

The entrance channel lies between lightbeacon *No.2* to the northwest and buoy *No.1* about 600m to the southeast. There are leading lights[2151] on 040°, and a daytime transit consisting of a beacon 200m northwest of Forte de Outão in line with the corner of Castelo São Filipe on 036·5°. It is essential to stay within the channel as there are shoals and drying banks on either side. Favour the north side of the channel on approaching Forte de Outão[2150] as the extensive sands to the south now extend well north of lightbeacon *No.5*[2150·28].

Before reaching Forte de Albarquel[2150·4] the estuary opens up to the southeast. 800m southeast of the fort the Cabeça do João Farto west cardinal buoy marks the western end of an extensive middle ground. Leave it to starboard for Setúbal or well to port to run up the east side of the Península de Tróia. Most of the north shore west of the town is lined with moorings.

## Berthing

There are three small basins – from east to west the Doca de Pesca (fish dock), that of the Clube Náutico de Setúbal, and the Doca de Comércio (commercial dock) which now contains a marina in addition to fishing boats and the embarkation point for the small car ferries to the Península de Tróia. Yachts are not welcome at the fish dock, the *clube náutico* harbour is tiny and very crowded, and the marina reserves only three berths for visitors (though a couple more can usually be fitted in).

The marina, or Doca de Recreio das Fontaínhas, is run by the Administração dos Portos de Sesimbra e Setúbal, ☎ 265 534095 *Fax* 265 230992, *website* www.cidadevirtual.pt/porto-setubal/index.html (in Portuguese and English). It occupies the western half of the basin and provides berthing for some 150 yachts and smallcraft as well as a few of the old double-ended trading vessels typical of the Sado estuary. All berths on the three long pontoons are alongside fingers and depths are said to be 3–3·5m throughout. One visiting yacht of up to 15m can normally be fitted in, but a smaller yacht clearly has a better chance of finding a berth. Security is excellent, with uniformed guards in addition to the usual electronic gate, and when visited in September 1999 the water appeared surprisingly clean, bearing in mind that the basin is shared with fishing boats and ferries.

On arrival secure to the centre hammerhead (it may be necessary to raft up) and walk up to the small office near the security gate. Hours are 0900–2100 from May to October, 0900–1900 at other times.

In 1999 the rate for a visiting yacht of just under 12m at any time of year was 2,185 escudos (10·90 euros) per night if her beam was less than 3·3m,

2,548 escudos (12·71 euros) if it was more. The monthly low season rates for yachts of similar dimensions were 29,438 escudos (146·84 euros) and 36,054 escudos (179·84 euros) respectively. Charges are inclusive of water, electricity and tax.

## Anchorages

There is a designated fishing and smallcraft anchorage southeast of the conspicuous Castelo de São Felipe in 10–12m, but it is some distance from all facilities. Alternatively it is possible to anchor off the *clube náutico* basin, convenient for shopping and where a dinghy can be left. Both these positions are exposed to the southern quadrant – should the wind shift into the south or southwest (unlikely in summer) move to the east side of the ferry landing stage at Punta do Adoxe on the Península de Tróia.

## Formalities

The *brigada fiscal* and *alfândega* have offices near the *capitania*, on the north side of the road which runs west from the marina basin, with the *policia maritima* behind. Being a major commercial harbour – and a somewhat 'unreconstructed' one at that – it is likely that the full run of offices will need to be visited.

## Facilities

*Boatyard* A yard at the western end of the town carries out work on yachts as well as fishing boats and local ferries.

*Travel-lift* Several marine railways of different capacities as the above.

*Water* On the marina pontoons, or by can from the *clube náutico*.

*Showers* Shower block near the marina office, with card access.

*Launderette* In the city.

*Electricity* On the marina pontoons.

*Fuel* None at the marina, but available by can from a filling station right opposite.

*Bottled gas* Camping Gas available in the city.

*Clube náutico* The Clube Náutico de Setúbal has premises overlooking the small basin west of the marina, with the usual bar and restaurant.

*Weather forecast* Displayed daily at the marina office.

Looking north-northwest over Setúbal's Doca de Recreio das Fontaínhas, which occupies the western end of the old Doca de Comércio. Directly opposite the entrance are the loading berths for the Península de Tróia car ferries.

*Banks* In the city.

*Shops/provisioning* Large supermarket one road inland from the *clube náutico*, and doubtless many others, as well as good general shopping in the city proper.

*Produce market* Fish and produce market next door to the supermarket above.

*Cafés, restaurants & hotels* Many throughout the city, including a restaurant above the shower block and several waterside restaurants in the nearby public gardens.

*Medical services* In the city.

## Communications

*Post office* In the city.

*Mailing address*
  c/o **Administração do Porto de Setúbal**,
  Praça da República, 2904–508 Setúbal, Portugal
  The marina office does not provide a fax service.

*Car hire/taxis* In the city.

*Public telephones* Outside the shower block.

*Buses & trains* Services to Lisbon and elsewhere.

*Ferries* Frequent service the Península de Tróia.

*Air services* Lisbon airport is some 35km distant.

## Alternative anchorages

1. In the shallow bay west of Forte de Albarquel, if space can be found amongst the moorings. Beware the double rock, Arflor, to the west, though this is now buoyed.

2. Along the eastern shore of the Península de Tróia, the northern 3M of which is quite steep-to. Almost no facilities other than a tourist development near the ferry landing.

3. Among the rice fields on the upper Rio Sado, well beyond the commercial wharves and shipyards. A large-scale Portuguese chart (best obtained in Lisbon – see page 154), a reliable echo sounder and plenty of time are all desirable.

# Sines

37°56'N 8°51'W

## Tides

*Reference port* Lisbon
*Mean time differences*
HW: −40 minutes ±10; LW: −15 minutes ±5
*Heights in metres*

| MHWS | MHWN | MLWN | MLWS |
|------|------|------|------|
| 3·3 | 2·6 | 1·3 | 0·6 |

## Charts

| | Approach | Harbour |
|---|---|---|
| Admiralty | 3636 | 3276 |
| Portuguese (old series) | 39 | 84 |
| Portuguese (new series) | 23202, 23203, 24204, 24205 | 26408 |
| Spanish | | 4311 |

## Lights

### Approach

2139 **Cabo Espichel** 38°24'·8N 9°12'·9W
  Fl.4s167m26M Horn 31s 460m SW
  White hexagonal tower and building 32m

*0969* Radiobeacon *PI* 308kHz 50M (3 & 4 in sequence)
  (out of service until further notice)

2160 **Cabo de Sines** 37°57'·5N 8°52'·7W
  Fl(2)15s55m26M
  White round tower and building 22m
  Obscd 001°-003° and 004°-007° within 17M

*Note* Numerous nearby red lights mark chimneys, radio masts, etc

*0971* Radiobeacon *SN* 308kHz 100M (5 & 6 in sequence)

2162 **Milfontes (Rio Mira)** 37°43'·1N 8°47'·3W
  Fl.3s22m10M Turret on white building 5m

2164 **Cabo Sardão** 37°35'·8N 8°48'·9W
  Fl(3)15s67m23M
  White square tower and building 17m

### Harbour

2160·16 **West breakwater** 37°56'·4N 8°53'·3W
  Fl.3s20m12M White tower, red bands 8m

*Note* Situated about 500m SHORT of the breakwater end, which is marked by a buoy

buoy **Breakwater end** 37°56'N 8°53'·2W
  Fl.R.3s6M Red pillar buoy, ■ topmark

2160·3 **Terminal Ldg Lts on 358°** 37°56'·7N 8°52'·9W
  *Front* Iso.R.6s17m5M Post 6m

2160·31 *Rear*, 580m from front,
  Oc.R.5·6s28m3M Post 20m

2160·38 **Resguardo** 37°57'·2N 8°52'·3W
  Oc.R.5s3M White GRP tower, red bands 3m

2160·36 **Fishing harbour (NW) mole**
  37°57'N 8°52'·1W Fl.R.6s6M
  White concrete tower, red bands 4m

2160·37 **Marina (SE) mole** 37°57'N 8°52'W
  Fl.G.4s4M White concrete tower, green bands 5m

2160·08 **East breakwater, NW corner**
  37°56'·2N 8°51'·9W LFl.G.8s16m6M
  Green column, white bands 7m

2160·12 **East breakwater, SE elbow**
  37°55'·9N 8°51'·3W LFl.Y.8s16m9M
  Yellow column 7m

Other lights exist within the commercial harbour.

## Coast radio station

**Atalaia** (38°10'N 8°38'W) (24 hours) Remotely controlled from Lisbon
**VHF** Ch 16, 24, 26, 85.

## Marina and port radio

*Marina de Sines* VHF Ch 12, 16 (24 hours).

*Controlportosines* VHF Ch 01, 04, 09, 10, 11, 12, 16, 18, 20, 63, 67, 68, 69, 81, 84 (24 hours)

*Capimarsines* VHF Ch 09, 10, 11, 12, 13, 16, 69 (24 hours).

*Pilotossines* VHF Ch 12, 14.

## General

Birthplace of Vasco da Gama and until 1971 a relatively quiet fishing port, Sines can now handle 500,000 tonne tankers and has heavy industry as well as petrochemicals supporting its economy. However, although it can be identified from well offshore by its many chimneys, many either lit or smoking, once in the anchorage or marina the industrial areas are masked behind the attractive old town and are soon forgotten.

The new Marina de Sines, which lies behind a substantial stone mole southeast of the fishing harbour, has received a unanimous thumbs up from all who have reported on it since it opened in 1997 – a surprisingly rare accolade.

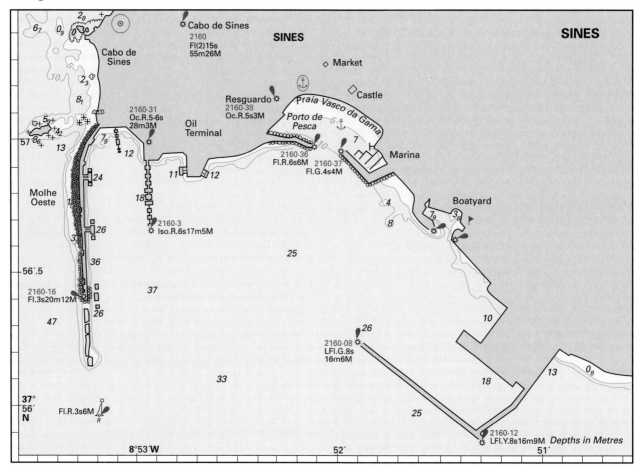

## Approach

Sines is most conveniently placed, being the only all-weather harbour between Lisbon, some 50M to the north, and Cabo de São Vicente, nearly 60M to the south.

For 35M north of Cabo de Sines the coast is an unbroken line of low sand hills – one long beach. The theoretical ranges of Cabo Espichel[2139] and Cabo de Sines[2160] lights overlap, but there are no other major lights in between. Cabo de Sines has off-lying rocks and islands but 0·5M provides safe clearance.

From the south, the last major light is Cabo Sardão[2164] 13M distant, with a less powerful light Vila Nova de Milfontes[2162]. The coast between Cabo Sardão and Sines is rocky with cliffs, though there are sandy beaches around Vila Nova de Milfontes and Porto Covo (the latter about 7M southeast of Sines and identifiable by its water tower).

## Entrance

The entrance to Sines lies 1·5M south of Cabo de Sines and is protected by a long breakwater, the southern end of which has been in ruins for some years and is partially submerged – note that the breakwater light[2160·16] is situated almost 500m SHORT of the breakwater end, which is marked by a (lit) red pillar buoy. DO NOT CUT INSIDE this buoy.

From the south the entrance is wide and should present no problems, though ships en route to the commercial terminals in the southeastern part of the harbour must be given ample space to manoeuvre.

## Berthing

The Marina de Sines is administered by the Administração do Porto do Sines, ☎ 269 860612 *Fax* 269 860691, *e-mail* dcom@portodesines.pt, *website* www.portodesines.pt/ (in Portuguese and English). On arrival yachts should secure to the hammerhead below the rocky outcrop, which also serves as a fuelling pontoon. The marina office – currently a white portacabin – is some distance away up a steep flight of steps and is manned around the clock by notably helpful staff. In place of the more usual gated pontoons the entire marina area is fenced off, with security guards making regular patrols.

Fifteen or so of the 230 berths are reserved for yachts in transit, normally on the northwestern pontoon (the approach to which can be exciting when the *nortada* is blowing). This is the first part of the marina to be affected by swell and storm surge, when visitors will be moved further in if space allows. (In October 1999 the outermost pontoon was being dismantled for winter storage ashore, though there was still plenty of space for both local and visiting yachts.) Depths vary from 3–8m, with 5m or more throughout the visitors' area, and all berths are alongside finger pontoons. The marina layout has changed several times over the past two years, and in normal conditions at least one 20m yacht can be accommodated.

The small marina at Sines looking east, with the southern end of the long Praia Vasco Da Gama on the left.

In 1999 the high season rate for a visiting yacht of just under 12m was 1,638 escudos (8·17 euros) per night if her beam was less than 3·3m, 1,901 escudos (9·48 euros) if it was more. The monthly low season rates for yachts of similar dimensions were 21,645 escudos (107·96 euros) and 28,956 escudos (144·43 euros) respectively, all inclusive of water, electricity and tax. As of 1999 there was no surcharge for multihulls.

There is a project to develop some of the land east of the marina with shops, restaurants, a chandlery and a (larger) launderette. Work is expected to start by autumn 2000.

### Anchorage

Yachts are still permitted to anchor off the Praia Vasco da Gama, in 3–5m over sand and a little weed, provided they keep well clear of both fishing vessels and the marina approach. Being open to the southwest the anchorage is seldom without a slight roll, but the marina could not be closer should the wind shift onshore. Dinghies can be landed on the beach, which is cleaned and raked daily and is very popular with local residents.

### Formalities

Whether at anchor or marina-berthed, take passports and ship's papers to the marina office to complete the usual form, copies of which are then circulated to the *brigada fiscal*, *alfândega* and *policia maritima*. The *brigada fiscal*, who operate from the small wooden hut near the slipway, may visit the yacht, particularly if there are non-EU nationals aboard.

### Facilities

*Boatyard* In the fishing and commercial areas, but as yet nothing specifically for yachts.

*Travel-lift* None as of September 1999, though the dock is in place. The marina's 6·3 tonne static crane can be supplemented by hiring in a more powerful mobile crane as necessary.

*Engineers, electronic & radio repairs* In the fishing and commercial areas – enquire at the marina office.

*Chandlery* Behind the fishing harbour, though it is hoped that one will be built near the marina within the next few years.

*Water* On the pontoons.

*Showers* In the office building.

*Launderette* Single washing machine at the marina office, with more planned (see Berthing, opposite).

The port of Sines, looking just north of east. The destroyed – but still highly dangerous – breakwater extension shows clearly, as do both the oil terminal and, more distantly, the small marina.
*Courtesy Administração do Porto de Sines SA*

*Electricity* On the pontoons.

*Fuel* Diesel and petrol at the hammerhead pontoon.

*Bottled gas* Camping Gaz available in the town.

*Clube náutico* Small *clube náutico* some distance southeast of the marina.

*Weather forecast* Posted daily at the marina office.

*Banks* In the town.

*Shops/provisioning* Good selection in the town, some 2km from the marina (though a lot less if the dinghy is used, when nearly all the carrying will be downhill). No shops at all near the marina, though see Berthing, page 164.

*Produce market* In the old town.

*Cafés, restaurants & hotels* Small bar next to the marina office, which may eventually expand. In the meantime the old town is well supplied with restaurants and hotels.

*Medical services* In the town.

## Communications

*Post office* In the town.

*Mailing address*

c/o **Administração do Porto do Sines**, Porto de Recreio, Apartado 16, 7520–953 Sines, Portugal

*Fax service* 269 860891

Faxes can be received at the marina office, but not sent.

*Public telephones* At the marina office and in the town.

*Car hire/taxis* In the town, or can be arranged via the marina office.

*Buses* Local buses, with a long-distance service to Lisbon (just under 3 hours) and elsewhere.

*Trains* Sines no longer has a passenger rail service.

# Vila Nova de Milfontes

37°43'N 8°47'W

## Tides

*Reference port* Lisbon

*Mean time differences* Milfontes

HW: −35 minutes ±5; LW: No data

*Heights in metres* Milfontes

| MHWS | MHWN | MLWN | MLWS |
|------|------|------|------|
| 3·7  | 2·9  | 1·5  | 0·7  |

## Charts

|                           | Approach      | River |
|---------------------------|---------------|-------|
| Admiralty                 | 3636          |       |
| Portuguese (old series)   | 39            |       |
| Portuguese (new series)   | 23203, 24205  | 27501 |

## Lights

### Approach

2160 **Cabo de Sines** 37°57'·5N 8°52'·7W
Fl(2)15s55m26M
White round tower and building 22m
Obscd 001°-003° and 004°-007° within 17M

*Note* Numerous nearby red lights mark chimneys, radio masts, etc

0971 Radiobeacon *SN* 308kHz 100M (5 & 6 in sequence)

2164 **Cabo Sardão** 37°35'·8N 8°48'·9W
Fl(3)15s67m23M
White square tower and building 17m

### River

2162 **Milfontes (Rio Mira)** 37°43'·1N 8°47'·3W
Fl.3s22m10M Turret on white building 5m

*Note* A pair of leading lights (Fl.R and Oc.R on 075°) 1M north of Vila Nova de Milfontes lead into the rocky cove at Portinho do Canal and should be ignored.

## General

Reputedly used by Hannibal and once rich enough to be sacked by Algerian pirates, pretty little Vila Nova de Milfontes on the Rio Mira shows scant evidence of its former importance. Despite much recent holiday development the white and tile village on the north bank has retained its character and mercifully escaped the high-rise blocks which mar so many resorts further north. Its peace and relative unspoiltness are a real treat – if only you can get in.

Though viable for a keelboat in the right conditions the Rio Mira is shallow and, in common with many other Portuguese rivers, has a bar with a reported depth of no more than 1m at datum – considerably less if any swell is running. Once inside protection is excellent but flat weather, and particularly an absence of swell, are essential for both entry and departure. About a mile from the entrance there is a road bridge with a clearance of some 12m, but it is possible to explore the river by dinghy for many kilometres beyond.

## Approach

The coast between Cabo de Sines[2160] to the north and Cabo Sardão[2164] to the south consists of rocky cliffs. There is a sandy beach at Porto Covo about 8M to the north, identifiable by its water tower.

## Entrance

Since Vila Nova de Milfontes calls for careful eyeball pilotage, enter only in calm weather on a rising tide, preferably in the afternoon with the sun behind the boat. The entrance is marked by the Rio Mira light[2162], shown from the corner of a square white building with a tiled roof on the north side of the entrance.

Approach to about 600m with the light bearing 050° and, with luck, a local fisherman will lead the way across the bar. Failing this, turn east and keep the reef which extends southwards from the light about 60m off on the port hand. Although part is exposed it extends for some distance underwater as a brownish–purple area – be guided by the colour of the water.

Once in the entrance best water is found relatively close under the light – see photograph – but past the light there is an unmarked middle ground below and downstream from the fort. Keep well south of centre for the deep channel, as the middle ground (which dries at low water springs) is V-shaped with its apex pointing upstream and it would be only too easy to find oneself in a blind alley. Floating (buoyed) fishing nets are sometimes laid inside the river.

## Anchorage

There is plenty of room to anchor in the river, either in the northwest bight just inside the mouth (depths are shallow), or further upstream off the fishermen's quay in 4m or more. The ebb tide runs at up to 3 knots and if there is any wind consider setting two anchors.

## Formalities

The arrival of a foreign yacht in the river is a sufficiently rare event that it would almost certainly attract a visit from the authorities. Failing that there is a *brigada fiscal* office up the steps at the downstream end of the quay.

## Facilities

Quay with small wooden jetty for dinghy landing with a café/restaurant ashore. Public tap opposite the jetty.

Most shops from supermarkets to souvenirs, banks, restaurants, etc. Superb beaches both inside and outside the entrance.

## Communications

Post office. Telephone kiosks. Buses.

## Other anchorages

1. *Arrifana* (37°17'·4N 8°52'W), a bay surrounded by dramatic cliffs giving shelter from north and east, lies 26M south of Vila Nova de Milfontes and 18M north of Cabo de São Vicente. Though isolated and remote it can be a useful passage anchorage, particularly if beating into the prevailing *nortada*. However with any swell rolling in the surfing community arrive in force...

   The coast is rocky and steep-to with off-lying stacks and islands. There is an old fort on the cliff to the north and a cairn, Pedra da Agulha, to the south. Beneath both are rocky islets – those under the fort are lumpy while those under the cairn have needle-like angularity. Approaching from the southwest, the islets off the fort stand out from the land and the white cottages behind the sandy beach become plain. Pots or net floats may be encountered anywhere in the bay. Anchor towards the north in 10–12m, but do not attempt to approach the short stone mole which is surrounded by off-lying rocks.

   A café/restaurant overlooks the beach, with a public telephone about 50m up the steep cobbled road to the village. Other than dramatic views and a few more restaurants there is little to justify the climb.

2. Although a quick glance at the chart might also suggest the bay at Carrapateira (37°11'·3N 8°54'·8W), 6·5M south of Arrifana and 11M north of Cabo de São Vicente as a possible anchorage in northeasterly winds, shelter is considerably poorer than at Arrifana and there are numerous rocks both in the approach and off the beach.

The Rio Mira, with Vila Nova de Milfontes on the north bank, looking east-northeast. Note the 'fishhook' sandbank directly below the small jetty – the channel runs on its southern side. The road bridge behind the town aids identification from offshore.

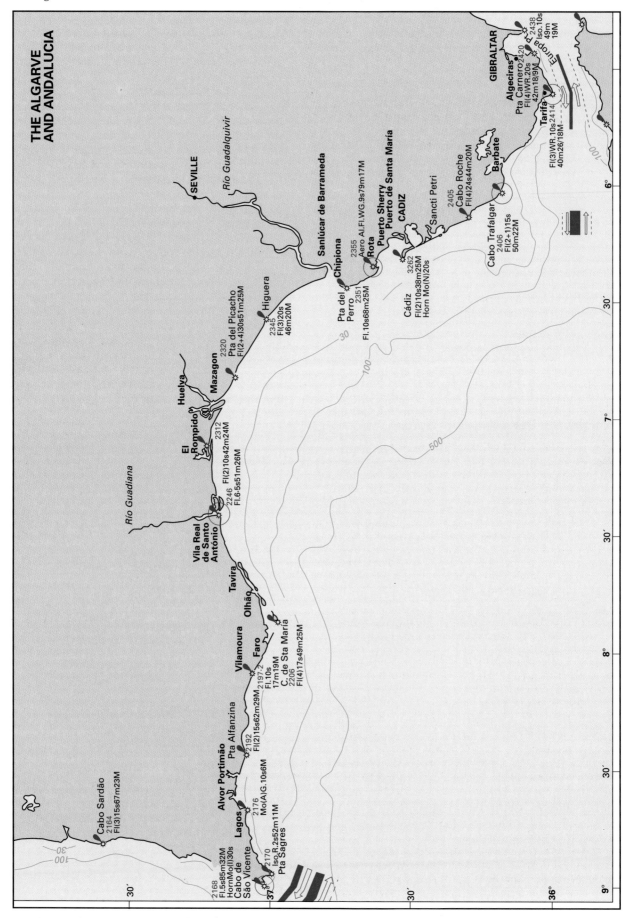

THE ALGARVE
AND ANDALUCIA

Cabo Sardão
2164
Fl(3)15s67m23M

2168
Fl.5s85m32M
HornMo(I)30s
Cabo de
São Vicente

2170
Iso.R.2s52m11M
Pta Sagres

Lagos

2176
Mo(A)G.10s6M

Alvor Portimão

2192
Fl(2)15s62m29M
Pta Alfanzina

Vilamoura

2197.2
Fl.10s
17m19M
Faro

2206
Fl(4)17s49m25M
C. de Sta Maria

Olhão

Tavira

Vila Real
de Santo
António

2246   Fl(2)10s42m24M
Fl.6-5s51m26M

Río Guadiana

El
Rompido

2312

Huelva

Mazagon

2320
Pta del Picacho
Fl(2+4)30s51m25M

2345
Fl(3)20s
46m20M

Higuera

SEVILLE

Río Guadalquivir

Sanlúcar de Barrameda

Chipiona

Pta del
Perro

2351
Fl.10s68m25M

2355
Aero Al.Fl.WG.9s79m17M
Rota

Puerto Sherry
Puerto de Santa Maria
CADIZ

Sancti Petri

Cádiz
3262
Fl(2)10s38m25M
Horn Mo(N)20s

2405
Cabo Roche
Fl(4)24s44m20M

Barbate

Cabo Trafalgar
2406
Fl(2+1)15s
50m22M

GIBRALTAR

Algeciras
Pta Carnero 2420
Fl(4)WR.20s
42m18/9M

Europa

2438
Iso.10s
49m
19M

Tarifa

Fl(3)WR.10s2414
40m26/18M

36°

30'

9°

37°

30'

8°

30'

7°

30'

6°

30

100

30

100

500

168

# The Algarve & Andalucia

## Cabo de São Vicente to Gibraltar

Both ends of this section have spectacular scenery with impressive cliffs. In the middle, these give way to sandy beaches often backed by lagoons – staging posts for migrant birds – with the Río Guadalquivir, the Coto de Doñana nature reserve, and the ancient cities of Seville and Cádiz. To the west, the Algarve has been intensively developed for the tourist and the shoreline is littered with high-rise blocks and time-share estates. In contrast, the country 10km inland has been left largely untouched. In Spain, the stretch east of Cádiz is the least developed piece of coast between Portugal and Mediterranean France.

The coastline covered in this section is more suited to cruising than that of the previous section. Having rounded the corner at São Vicente, the influences of the Mediterranean and the Moor begin to show and despite the tourist overlay on the Algarve, the lesser harbours are more attractive as well as being more frequent. Also, with a couple of exceptions, the entrances are easier.

From São Vicente to the Guadalquivir the bottom is sand. From Cádiz onwards it is usually mud, often glutinous, providing good holding but needing a deck pump (or mop and bucket) when the anchor is brought in. Anchoring off any beach is possible in fine, settled weather when there is no swell.

### Hazards – fishing nets and artificial reefs

During the summer *almadrabas* or tunny (tuna) nets tough enough to foul the screw of a freighter can be a considerable hazard, and may reach several miles offshore. It is not advisable to sail over one, and officially vessels should not pass between the inner end of a net and the shore (though local fishermen habitually do so). At one time tunny nets were set as far west as Vilamoura, but over the past decade only four have been laid annually, all in the 30M between Cabo Roche and Tarifa. However if the fish return elsewhere doubtless the nets will too. Further details of dates, locations and buoyage will be found under the notes for the nearest harbour, and annual positions are often displayed on marina notice boards. Note that the cardinal buoys used to mark the nets are frequently very undersized – sometimes less than 2m in height, including topmark – and should not be relied upon, particularly at night.

More prevalent though less worrying are the nets laid for other fish – less worrying because they generally lie too far beneath the surface to bother a yacht. When first laid they are inspected and must be correctly marked – two red or orange flags at the western end (anywhere from south-southwest to north) and a single green flag at the eastern end (north to south-southeast). In addition, white flags should be set at 1M intervals. At night each flag should be replaced by a yellow light (so two lights at the western end). However with the passage of time both lights and flags may disappear, to be replaced at random if at all.

In recent years a number of artificial reefs have been constructed off the coast to provide fish havens, reducing the charted depth by up to 2·5m (though even so, few will cause concern to yachts). Most are buoyed, often with yellow buoys and lights, and positions are indicated on current Admiralty and other charts.

### Swell

Less marked than along the west-facing coast, but heavy swell can be produced both by an Atlantic disturbance or by a *levanter* blowing through the Strait of Gibraltar.

### Winds

In summer north and northeast winds predominate in the west, but the further offshore the more variable they become. Further east, the influence of the Portuguese trade winds gradually dies away. Like the Atlantic coast, the Algarve is also subject to stiff afternoon sea breezes. From early summer onwards these start to blow at around 1400, regularly reaching force 6 and occasionally force 7 (25 or 30 knots) within an hour and continuing until sundown. Typically they pick up from the southwest, moving through west to west-northwest or northwest by evening.

East of Cádiz, the effect of the Strait becomes increasingly marked with 80% of winds in the Strait from either west (*poniente*) or east-northeast (*levante*). Gales are unlikely in the height of summer but *levanters* with winds of 50–60 knots are not unknown, visibility dropping to 1M or less. They are not seasonal, generally last for two to three days, and blow up with little or no warning from the barometer – though sometimes a deep purple bank of haze in the morning or a sudden fast steep swell may give a clue. The *poniente* is generally less strong than the *levanter* but may last five days or more. Squalls can occur at any time in the Bay of Gibraltar if the wind is between northeast and southeast.

### Visibility

Poor visibility, less than 2M, is more common (2–5%) in summer than in winter. Fog is infrequent but not unknown – the Algarve experienced two days with visibility of less than 200m in August 1995. The Cádiz area has a reputation for fog in certain conditions associated with a *levanter*.

### Shelter

In a *levanter* (easterly) shelter in the Strait is limited to the Cádiz complex, west of the Tarifa causeway, and Gibraltar. In a *poniente* (westerly) it is limited to the Cádiz complex, Tarifa itself, and Gibraltar.

### Currents

Along the Algarve coast the set is predominantly east of southeast, running at about 0·5 knot. By the time it reaches the Strait it is running east at 1–1·5 knots, compensating for water lost from the Mediterranean through evaporation. However this pattern can be upset by the wind – a southeasterly gale in the south of the area can produce a west-going stream along the coast as far as Cabo de São Vicente, while persistent strong westerlies, coupled with the regular current, can produce an easterly set of 4 knots.

### Tides

Tidal predictions for the Algarve use Lisbon as the Standard Port; those for Andalucia use either Lisbon, Cádiz or Gibraltar. When calculating Spanish tides using Lisbon data, note that allowance has already been made for the difference in time zones (Spanish time being UT+1, Portuguese time UT, both advanced one hour in summer – see page 10.)

If the necessary tide tables are not available, as a very rough guide high water at Lisbon occurs at approximately 0410 and 1630 at springs ±30 minutes, and 0920 and 2230 at neaps ±1hour 10 minutes; at Cádiz at approximately 0425 and 1640 ±25 minutes, and 0955 and 2240 ±1hour 30 minutes; and at Gibraltar at approximately 0415 and 1640 ±25 minutes, and 0955 and 2230 ±1hour 30 minutes.

Tidal range decreases eastward, from 2·8m at springs and 1·2m at neaps at Lagos, to 0·9m and 0·4m respectively at Gibraltar – see individual harbours.

There is no reliable information about tidal streams along the coast, though 2–3 knots has been reported in some places, notably around Faro and Olhão. In the centre of the Strait the east-going stream starts shortly after HW Gibraltar and the west-going stream about six hours later, though the closer inshore, the earlier the change takes place – see diagram page 245. In addition a great deal of detailed, practical advice on how best to tackle the Strait of Gibraltar – including unusually clear current and tidal flow diagrams – will be found in Colin Thomas's *Straits Sailing Handbook* – see Further reading, page 263.

### Climate

Most rain falls between the end of October and the beginning of April with virtually none in July and August. Cool in winter, hot in summer, Lagos has a mean of 36°C in July with Gibraltar capable of 40°C in a *levanter*. Sea temperatures at Gibraltar range from 21°C in summer to 14°C in winter.

### Coast radio stations

Many Portuguese coast radio stations and those broadcasting weather and navigational information are situated between, rather than at, ports or harbours. Details will be found under the nearest harbour to the station. All coast radio stations are remotely controlled from Lisbon, ☎ 214 190098 *Fax* 214 199900.

All coast radio stations in Andalucía are remotely controlled from CCR Málaga, ☎ 952 139307 *Fax* 952 214730.

Broadcast times are quoted in UT unless otherwise specified.

### Marine weather information by telephone

Recorded marine weather bulletins for Cabo de São Vincente to the Spanish border are available, in Portuguese, on the following numbers: inshore ☎ 0601 123 125; offshore ☎ 0601 123 142.

A recorded marine weather bulletin, ☎ 906 365373 (see also plan page 5), is provided by the *Instituto Nacional de Meteorología* for Andalucía and beyond. The service is only available within Spain, but can be accessed by vessels equipped with Autolink. The bulletin is read in Spanish.

*High Seas Bulletin* for São Vicente, Cádiz, etc.
*Coastal Waters Bulletin* for the coasts of Huelva, Cádiz, etc.

## Cabo de São Vicente and Ponta de Sagres
37°01'N 9°00'W & 37°00'N 8°57'W

### Tides

*Reference port* Lisbon
*Mean time differences* (at Enseada de Belixe)
HW: −40 minutes ±10; LW: −15 minutes ±5
*Heights in metres*

| MHWS | MHWN | MLWN | MLWS |
|------|------|------|------|
| 4·1 | 3·2 | 1·7 | 0·8 |

### Charts

| | Approach | Anchorages |
|---|---|---|
| Admiralty | 3636, 89, 92 | |
| Portuguese (old series) | 7, 24, 40 | 40 |
| Portuguese (new series) | 23203, 23204, 24205, 24206 | 27502 |

## Lights

### Approach

2164 **Cabo Sardão** 37°35'·8N 8°48'·9W
Fl(3)15s67m23M
White square tower and building 17m

2168 **Cabo de São Vicente** 37°01'·3N 8°59'·7W
Fl.5s85m32M Horn Mo(I)30s
Off-white round tower, red lantern, and building 28m

0973 Radiobeacon *VC* 305·5kHz 200M (1 & 2 in sequence)

2170 **Ponta de Sagres** 36°59'·6N 8°56'·9W
Iso.R.2s52m11M
White square tower and building 13m
F.R lights on posts 1M northwards

2174 **Ponta da Piedade** 37°04'·8N 8°40'·1W
Fl.7s50m20M
Yellow square tower on building 5m

## Coast radio station

**Picos** (37°18'N 8°39'W) (24 hours) Remotely controlled from Lisbon
**VHF** Ch 16, 23, 27, 85.

## Radio weather/navigational services

**Sagres** (37°N 8°57'W)

*Storm warnings*: 2657kHz on receipt and at 0835, 2035 in Portuguese and English for coastal waters of Portugal up to 50M offshore.

*Weather messages*: 2657kHz at 0835, 2035 gale warnings and forecast in Portuguese and English for coastal waters of Portugal up to 50M offshore.

*Navigational warnings*: 2657kHz on receipt and at 0835, 2035 in Portuguese and English for coastal waters of Portugal up to 50M offshore.

*Weather messages*: VHF Ch 11 at 1030, 1630 gale warnings and forecast in Portuguese for Ponta de Sagres.

*Navigational warnings*: VHF Ch 11 at 1030, 1630 in Portuguese for Ponta de Sagres.

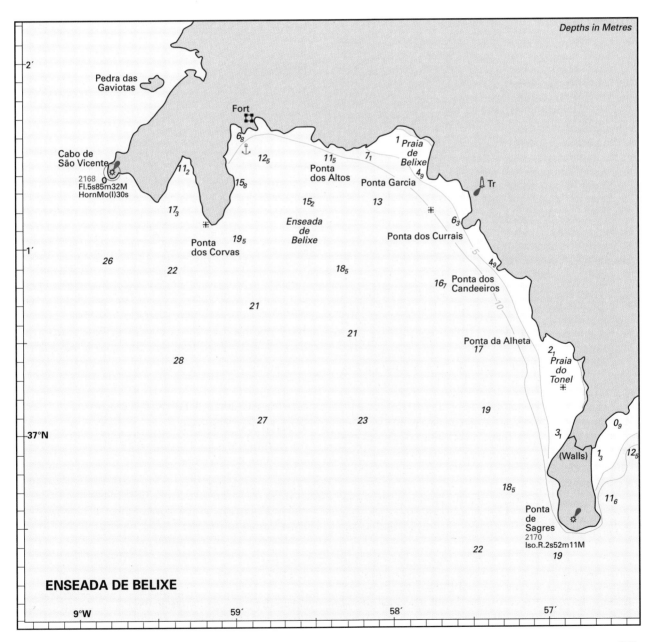

ENSEADA DE BELIXE

## General

Cabo de São Vicente and Ponta de Sagres make a formidable pair, wild and windswept, sometimes seen for miles but, even in summer, sometimes heard before seen.

Navigators will wish to visit the site of Prince Henry of that ilk's 'school of navigation' on the cliffs at Ponta de Sagres – complete with an acre or so of (allegedly) 15th century *rosa dos ventos* (wind compass) in the courtyard – but may be disappointed that, with the exception of a small chapel and the northern wall, little else remains. (Sadly Sir Francis Drake must take a share of the blame, though the final havoc was wrought by the 1755 earthquake and subsequent tidal wave). Over the past few years an 'interpretative centre' has been set up within the vast Fortaleza, but inevitably the information presented (in several languages) is aimed at a very broad public. Sadly the buildings are ugly and do not add to the general ambience.

## Approach

From the north the last major light is Cabo Sardão[2164] and from the east, Ponta da Piedade[2174] south of Lagos. The 36M of coast between Cabo Sardão and São Vicente is rocky and steep, and trends west of south. The 15M between Ponta de Sagres and Ponta da Piedade is also rocky and steep, but trending northeast.

If on passage southwards in the prevailing *nortada*, both wind and waves are likely to increase noticeably on approaching Cabo de São Vicente, a combination of gusts off the cliffs and reflected swell. Both Cabo de São Vicente and Ponta de Sagres should be allowed a generous 2M clearance in these conditions, though much flatter water will generally be found east of Ponta de Baleeira. Equally, yachts heading west and north may expect to encounter rapidly deteriorating conditions on rounding Ponta de Baleeira, and should be prepared accordingly. It may be necessary to stay 2M or more offshore until 5–6M north of Cabo de São Vicente in order to avoid the worst. By far the best time to make the passage is early in the morning before the *nortada* reaches its full strength, especially if heading north.

There is a Traffic Separation Zone to the southwest of the two headlands extending from 5M to 14M offshore, and a fish farm about 1M off the coast some 4M northeast of Ponta de Sagres, a potential hazard if on passage to or from Lagos or beyond – see page 174.

## Anchorages

The anchorages in the Enseada de Belixe and the Enseada de Sagres can be useful if waiting for the usual strong afternoon *nortada* to die before heading north around the cape – both are spectacular, the latter giving the best protection. If winds from the south make the beach anchorages impracticable, Baleeira (see opposite) offers more protection from this sector.

1. *Enseada de Belixe* (37°01'N 8°58'W), wide open to the west and south. Entry is straightforward day or night using the loom of Cabo de São Vicente light. If coming from the north pass outside the tall rock off the headland and continue beyond the first, small, wedge-shaped bay until Enseada de Belixe opens up round Ponta dos Corvos.

   Anchor in the western part of the bay in 14m, or for more shelter in the cove under the old fort where there is good holding in 9m about 100m from the shore. However beware the tidal rock some 200m south of the east end of the Praia de Belixe, which rises almost sheer out of 9m to show only at low water. Very little will be found ashore.

2. *Enseada de Sagres* (37°N 8°56'W), open to the southeast with easy entry and excellent shelter from west through north to northeast. Anchor off the beach in good holding over sand. There is a growing tourist development at the top of the hill with supermarkets, shops, banks and restaurants.

# Baleeira

37°01'N 8°55'W

## Tides

*Reference port* Lisbon
*Mean time differences* (at Enseada de Belixe)
HW: −40 minutes ±10; LW: −15 minutes ±5
*Heights in metres*

| MHWS | MHWN | MLWN | MLWS |
|------|------|------|------|
| 4·1 | 3·2 | 1·7 | 0·8 |

## Charts

| | Approach | Harbour |
|---|---|---|
| Admiralty | 3636, 89, 92 | |
| Portuguese (old series) | 7, 24, 40 | 40, 86 |
| Portuguese (new series) | 23203, 23204, 24205, 24206 | 27502 |

## Lights

### Approach

2168 **Cabo de São Vicente** 37°01'·3N 8°59'·7W
Fl.5s85m32M Horn Mo(I)30s
Off-white round tower, red lantern, and building 28m

0973 Radiobeacon *VC* 305·5kHz 200M (1 & 2 in sequence)

2170 **Ponta de Sagres** 36°59'·6N 8°56'·9W
Iso.R.2s52m11M
White square tower and building 13m
F.R lights on posts 1M northwards

2174 **Ponta da Piedade** 37°04'·8N 8°40'·1W
Fl.7s50m20M
Yellow square tower on building 5m

### Harbour

2171 **Breakwater** 37°00'·7N 8°55'·4W
Fl.WR.4s12m14/11M 254°-W-355°-R-254°
White tower, red bands 6m

## General

A relatively undeveloped harbour overlooked by a growing tourist resort, Baleeira's name gives it away as a former whaling centre. Today a small fishing fleet operates from the two central jetties, along with a number of tourist boats. The beach close north of the harbour can be dirty, but Praia do Martinhal a little further east is well up to the Algarve's usual high standard.

Once the steep walk up into the town has been achieved, Prince Henry the Navigator's fortress at Sagres is no more than 3km away. The energetic may also fancy the tramp as far as Cabo de São Vicente to watch the sun set (though the walk itself is somewhat boring).

## Approach and entrance

Outer approach as for Cabo de São Vicente and Ponta de Sagres – see opposite.

The harbour itself is sheltered by a high breakwater some 400m in length running northeast from Ponta da Baleeira, leaving it open to the east and with a fetch of nearly 1M to the northeast. The breakwater light[2171] is sectored, with its red area covering the Ilhotes do Martinhal, a group of large rocks some 500m to the northeast. Although it is possible to pass between the islands and the shore

In previous centuries the lighthouse at Cabo de São Vicente must have been a lonely place to live and work. Now most of it is open to the public even though its essential function remains unchanged.

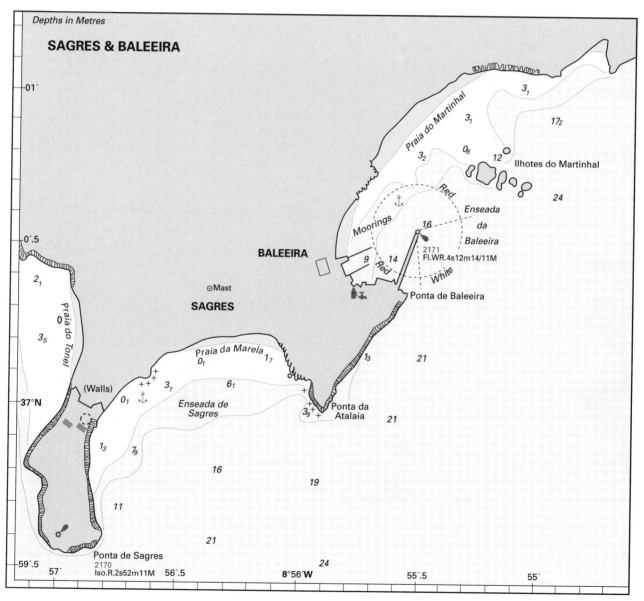

*Depths in Metres*

## SAGRES & BALEEIRA

Praia do Martinhal

Ilhotes do Martinhal

Red

Moorings

Enseada da Baleeira

16

2171
Fl.WR.4s12m14/11M

White

BALEEIRA

9  14  Red

⊙Mast

Ponta de Baleeira

SAGRES

Praia do Tonel

Praia da Marela

(Walls)

Enseada de Sagres

Ponta da Atalaia

Ponta de Sagres
2170
Iso.R.2s52m11M

the area is littered with rocks and strictly a case for eyeball navigation.

A fish farm has been set up about 1M off the coast some 2·5M northeast of the harbour, a potential hazard if on passage to or from Lagos or beyond. The long nets lie at a slight angle to the shore and are marked by two lit yellow buoys (powered by solar panels) and supported by yellow floats. The nets are not connected to the shore and, with due care, yachts can pass on either side. A great many other buoys marking shorter nets or individual fish pots will also be encountered in the area.

### Anchorage

Anchor outside the moorings, northwest or north of the breakwater head, in 6–10m. The bottom is mostly rock and reported to be very foul – a tripline is recommended (though in an emergency the Ilhas do Martinhal Dive Centre is said to be very helpful). The position can be distinctly rolly.

If possible avoid going ashore at low water, as the bottoms of the ladders are seriously dilapidated and the lower part of the ramp very slippery. There is little prospect of lying alongside other than very briefly – prospect first by dinghy.

Looking northeast across Baleeira harbour towards the Ilhotes do Martinhal. The concrete-piled jetties – and the many fishing boats – make lying alongside extremely difficult.

### Formalities

The *policia maritima* maintain an obvious presence around the harbour, doubtless in an effort to dissuade drug traffickers, and may well intercept the skipper and crew as they come ashore. The *brigada fiscal* are also likely to check on any foreign flag yacht.

The fishing harbour at Baleeira looking north, with several yachts anchored off.

### Facilities

Diesel and water (for which a small charge is made) on the fishermen's quay, 0900–1200 and 1500–1930 weekdays, 1100–1200 Saturday, closed Sunday. It is necessary to pay first at the *junta do porto* building up the slope at the head of the harbour. There is an old style boatyard just north of the jetties where fishing boats are brought ashore for work, but the (elderly) cradle would not suit most yachts. However engineering and other skills may well be available.

The tourist development at the top of the steep road has shops (including several supermarkets), banks and innumerable cafés, restaurants and hotels.

### Communications

Post office and telephones (including a kiosk near the *junta* building). Taxis. Bus service to Lagos and beyond.


# Lagos

37°06'N 8°40'W

### Tides

*Reference port* Lisbon
*Mean time differences*
HW: −25 minutes ±10; LW: −30 minutes ±5

*Heights in metres*

| MHWS | MHWN | MLWN | MLWS |
|------|------|------|------|
| 3·3  | 2·6  | 1·3  | 0·6  |

### Charts

|  | Approach | Harbour |
|---|---|---|
| Admiralty | 3636, 89, 92 | |
| Portuguese (old series) | 7, 24, 40 | 88 |
| Portuguese (new series) | 23203, 23204, 24205, 24206 | 27502 |
| Imray | C19 | C19 |

### Lights

#### Approach

2168 **Cabo de São Vicente** 37°01'·3N 8°59'·7W
Fl.5s85m32M Horn Mo(I)30s
Off-white round tower, red lantern, and building 28m

*0973* Radiobeacon *VC* 305·5kHz 200M (1 & 2 in sequence)

2170 **Ponta de Sagres** 36°59'·6N 8°56'·9W
Iso.R.2s52m11M
White square tower and building 13m
F.R lights on posts 1M northwards

2174 **Ponta da Piedade** 37°04'·8N 8°40'·1W
Fl.7s50m20M
Yellow square tower on building 5m

2178 **Ponta do Altar** 37°06'·4N 8°31'·1W
LFl.R.5s31m14M 290°-vis-170°
White square tower and building 10m

2192 **Ponta de Alfanzina** 37°05'·1N 8°26'·5W
Fl(2)15s62m29M
White square tower and building 23m

#### Harbour

2175 **West breakwater** 37°05'·8N 8°39'·9W
Fl.R.6s5M White square tower, red bands 7m

2176 **East breakwater** 37°05'·8N 8°39'·9W
Mo(A)G.10s6M
White square tower, green bands 6m

*Note* In 1998 actual range was reported as considerably less than this.
Long surface nets, lit or unlit, may be laid in the bay near the entrance to the harbour.

### Marina and port radio

*Marina de Lagos* VHF Ch 62 (0800–2200 1 June–15 Sept; 0900–1900 16 Sept–31 May).
*Capimarlagos* VHF Ch 11, 16 (0900–1200, 1400–1700 Mon–Fri).

### General

Lagos, on the banks of the Rio Bensafrim, is a crowded and active trading, tourist and fishing town. Its fairs, held on 16–17 August and 12–14 October, are lively events. It once had the only slave market in Portugal, and still has many notable buildings as well as an interesting museum and good nightlife.

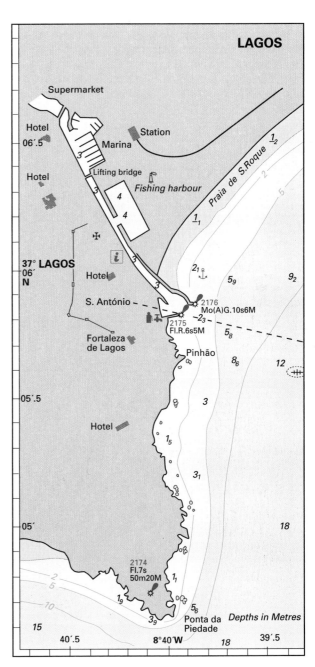

The large marina was opened in July 1994, and has since been awarded both the European Blue Flag and Eumarina Anchor Award. It is a safe and popular place to leave a yacht brought south during the summer before a late autumn passage to the Canaries or beyond, since facilities are good and security excellent. For those in transit there is also the option of anchoring off, and the Meia Praia, one of the Algarve's finest beaches, lies close east of the harbour.

## Approach

Lagos is 1·5M north of Ponta da Piedade[2174], 17M from Cabo de São Vicente[2168] and 7M from Portimão. Southwest of Ponta da Piedade the coast is rocky with cliffs and caves. Between Lagos and Portimão there are beaches, which towards Portimão are backed by cliffs. Lights to the east include Ponta do Altar (Portimão)[2178] and Ponta de Alfanzina[2192].

If coming from the west, the 5m line runs about 400m from the coast north of Ponta da Piedade to the breakwaters, which are lit[2175, 2176]. From the east, if on the wind, the line between the west breakwater and the church of Santo António, 282°, is a good mean.

## Entrance

Entrance between the twin breakwaters is straightforward, though in March 2000 it was reported that a bar carrying 2·3m above datum had built up some 200m southeast of the breakwater heads. Once through the entrance the channel has a least depth of 3m, as does the marina.

## Berthing

The impressive Marina de Lagos, ☎ 282 770210 *Fax* 282 770219, *e-mail* marlagos@mail.telepac.pt, *website* www.marlagos.pt, lies about 0·7M inside the entrance. Secure to the 80m reception pontoon, close downstream of the lifting pedestrian bridge, to arrange a berth and complete formalities. Otherwise the bridge normally opens on demand (VHF Ch 62) 0800–2200 between 1 June and 15 September, and 0900–1900 at other times. Times (which correspond with office hours) are the same at weekends. When a train is due to depart or arrive – the station lies just behind the marina – the bridge remains closed for 15 minutes before or after, respectively. There is a speed limit of 3 knots in the channel, and multihull owners should note that the bridge has a limiting width of 11m.

The marina can take 462 yachts of up to 30m LOA, with room always found for visitors. All berths are alongside finger pontoons, with exceptionally

A short distance up the Río Bensafrim lies the popular Marina de Lagos, seen here from the southeast. The rocky coastline south and west of the entrance is a favourite with cruising yachts and tourist boats alike.

The Marina de Lagos looking northeast. The reception / fuel pontoon can be seen on the right, near the pedestrian bridge and white marina offices.

large yachts occupying the seven hammerheads. The marina has been popular with British yachtsmen ever since it opened, and has a small but growing (and very loyal) band of long-term residents. The staff – all of whom appear to speak some English – are particularly helpful.

In 1999 the high season (1/6–15/9) rate for a visiting yacht of just under 12m was 4,797 escudos (23·93 euros) per night if her beam was less than 3.7m, 5,148 escudos (25·68 euros) if it was more. The monthly low season rates for yachts of similar dimensions were 50,310 escudos (250·95 euros) and 57,330 escudos (285·96 euros) respectively. Further discounts are available for longer periods. Charges are inclusive of water and electricity, and though quoted by the marina ex-IVA (the equivalent of VAT) at 17%, this has been added to the above figures for easy comparison with other harbours. Members of a number of British yacht clubs and class associations qualify for discounts on production of a membership card.

### Anchorage

Anchor outside, northeast of the east breakwater in 5–6m over good holding in hard sand. The corridor off the beach a little further east, indicated by a number of small yellow buoys, serves the local windsurfing centre and should be left clear. Inevitably this spot is very exposed to south and east, and a southwesterly swell may come around Ponta da Piedade. Land on the beach in the small western harbour, near the Clube de Vela de Lagos.

There is no space to anchor in the fishing harbour. The few yachts visible on moorings are either locally owned or have negotiated long-term lets from local mooring owners.

### Formalities

The *brigada fiscal*, *policia maritima* and *alfândega* all have offices in the marina reception building – enquire on first arrival whether or not it is necessary to visit them. If anchored off, the skipper should call at all three offices with ship's papers, passports, etc.

### Facilities

*Boatyard* José d'Abreu Pimenta & Fls Lda, ☎ 282 762839 *Fax* 282 767249, in the fishing harbour, with hydraulic cradle, scrubbing grid, pressure washer, etc. Good English is spoken and all the usual repair and maintenance services are available (owners are also allowed to do their own work), but security is poor. A marina boatyard has been planned for several years but as of late 1999 nothing had actually materialised.

A wide range of other services is offered by various long-term marina residents and local people – consult the noticeboard in marina reception.

*Travel-lift* Hydraulic cradle capable of hauling boats of up to 14 tonnes or 15m LOA at the boatyard.

*Engineers* At the boatyard, which is agent for a number of international manufacturers.

*Electronic & radio repairs* At the boatyard and also at Bluewater Yacht Services Lda, see below.

*Sailmaker/sail repairs* Enquire at the marina office.

*Chandleries* José d'Abreu Pimenta & Fls Lda (see above, who will also order from Lisbon if necessary), Nautilagos Lda in the line of fish and shellfish shops towards the fishing harbour, and Bluewater Yacht Services Lda on the upper deck of the marina's café/shop complex, who are agents for a number of international manufacturers. There is a fourth, more general, ironmonger/chandlery across the footbridge in the old part of the town.

*Charts* Limited range of both Portuguese and Admiralty charts available at the marina office (but not, of course, corrected to date).

*Water* At all berths. Yachts anchored off may be able to get water in the small western harbour (but check depths in advance).

*Showers* Single block at the north end of the marina's café/shops complex. A second block is planned. Crews of yachts anchored off may be able to shower at the *clube de vela* (see below).

*Launderette* At the north end of the marina's café/shops complex. Tokens are available at the marina office.

*Electricity* At all berths, with a variety of voltages available.

*Fuel* Petrol and diesel pumps on the reception pontoon below the bridge, available during office hours only. Credit cards are not accepted for fuel, although they are for berthing.

*Bottled gas* Camping Gaz exchanges at a hardware shop near the bus station, and possibly at the reception/fuel pontoon and the Nautilagos chandlery. Calor Gas and other cylinders cannot normally be refilled.

*Ice* At the fuel pontoon, or may be available at the north quay of the fish dock (where fish and shellfish can also be purchased).

*Clube náutico* The friendly Clube de Vela de Lagos, ☎ 282 762256 *Fax* 282 764277, is situated near the root of the west breakwater.

*Weather forecast* Posted daily at the marina reception.

*Banks* Bank, with card facility, in the marina's café/shops complex, plus many more in the town.

*Shops/provisioning* Several large supermarkets, including an enormous *Pingo Doce* near the road bridge north of the marina (trolleys can be wheeled back and left at one of several designated 'trolley areas' for collection). Good general shopping in the older town on the west bank (direct access over the pedestrian bridge). Limited shopping in the marina complex.

*Produce market* Produce and fish market near the west breakwater.

*Cafés, restaurants & hotels* Dozens if not hundreds, including several cafés and restaurants overlooking the marina itself.

*Medical services* In the town, including the private MedLagos Hospital, ☎ 282 760181, which also deals with dental problems.

## Communications

*Post office* In the town.

*Mailing address*
c/o **Marina de Lagos**, Apartado 18, 8600 Lagos, Portugal.
*Fax service* 282 770219

*Public telephones* Several around the marina complex.

*Car hire/taxis* Can be arranged via the marina office or in the town.

*Trains* Station just behind the marina complex, the western end of the (distinctly slow) Algarve coastal line.

*Air services* Faro international airport is about 50 minutes by taxi or, at a fraction of the taxi fare, 90 minutes by train (though a taxi will still be needed between the station and the airport).

## Alternative anchorages

1. Off the beach at Senhora da Luz (37°05'N 8°44'W), 3·5M west of Ponta da Piedade. Reported to be a pleasant anchorage in settled conditions off a small slipway, but fully exposed to the south.
2. Close east of Ponta da Piedade (37°05'N 8°40'W), and a good spot from which to explore the maritime caves and blow holes. If paddling ashore by inflatable, beware the high-speed tourist ferries which appear to hold their course regardless.

# Alvor

37°07'N 8°37'W

## Tides

See Lagos, page 175

## Charts

|  | Approach | Harbour |
|---|---|---|
| Admiralty | 3636, 89, 92 |  |
| Portuguese (old series) | 6, 24, 41, 23203 | 88 |
| Portuguese (new series) | 23203, 23204, 24205, 24206 | 27502 |

## Lights

### Approach

2174 **Ponta da Piedade** 37°04'·8N 8°40'·1W
Fl.7s50m20M
Yellow square tower on building 5m

2177·1 **Alvor** 37°08'·1N 8°36'·6W
LFl.R.6s31m7M
Red metal column, white bands 4m

2178 **Ponta do Altar** 37°06'·4N 8°31'·1W
LFl.R.5s31m14M 290°-vis-170°
White square tower and building 10m

2192 **Ponta de Alfanzina** 37°05'·1N 8°26'·5W
Fl(2)15s62m29M
White square tower and building 23m

### Estuary

2176·2 **West breakwater** 37°07'N 8°37'·1W
Fl.R.4s8m7M White tower, red bands 4m

2176·4 **East breakwater** 37°07'N 8°37'W
Fl.G.4s8m7M White tower, green bands 4m

The entrance to the Rio Alvor, only recently 'discovered' by cruising yachtsmen. This photograph looks northwest at about half flood, with the channel to the town leading out of picture to the right.

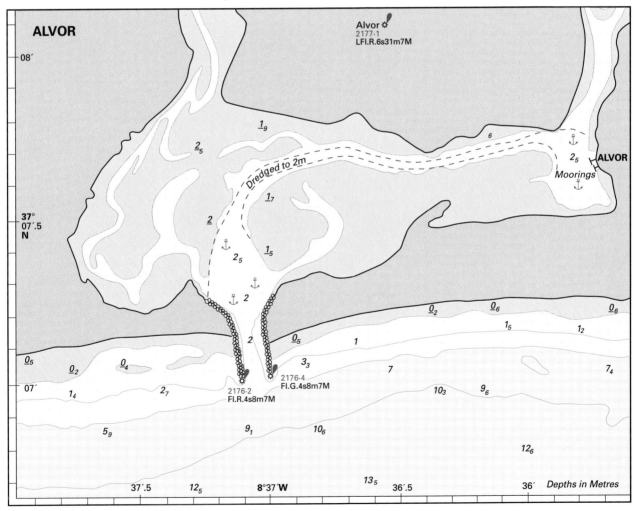

## General

Until the early 1990s a shallow sandy lagoon leading to a fishing village almost inaccessible to yachts, the construction of twin breakwaters at the entrance allied to extensive dredging within has opened the Rio Alvor to the cruising yachtsman. However care is still required, and Alvor should not be attempted when swell is running, in onshore winds, on the ebb tide or at night.

In 1996 it was reported that pontoons were to be installed for visiting yachts – apparently at the instigation of local fishermen who complained that they were having trouble reaching the fishing quay – but as of September 1999 no pontoons were in evidence and visiting yachts were still swinging happily to their own anchors. However it was reported that the project had not been abandoned, though no completion date could be given.

The town is touristy but attractive, with some good shops and cafés, and the anchorage a pleasant change from fishing harbours and marinas – and a paradise for birdwatchers. Construction work has been taking place along the waterfront, a more solid rock fronting being added to the existing sand. Should the red door to the lifeboat house be open, take the opportunity to admire the village's old rowing and sailing lifeboat, preserved there in pristine condition.

## Approach

Alvor lies 2·6M east of Lagos and 4·4M west of Portimão, surrounded by sandy beaches – the Meia Praia, one of the Algarve's finest beaches, lies between Lagos and Alvor. Closest major lights are Ponta da Piedade[2174], west of Lagos, and Ponta do Altar[2178] near Portimão. Alvor's own light[2177·1] is situated some distance inland.

High man-made sand dunes (created from dredged material) stand close each side of the entrance with conspicuous high-rise apartments further east.

## Entrance

Parallel breakwaters[2176·2, 2176·4] bracket the entrance, which was originally dredged to a nominal 4m.

The anchorage off Alvor town, seen from the southwest over its protective sandbank.

However considerable silting is reported to have taken place and by 1999 it was reported to carry no more than 2m at MLWS. Enter on the half flood, or sooner if conditions permit, keeping to the middle of the narrow channel on a bearing of approximately 352°. A sand bar has built up around the inner end of the east breakwater. Once inside, the estuary opens out and it is possible to anchor in the pool just inside the entrance, where at least 2m should be found at all times, or in slightly greater depths some 350m further north.

The narrow, dredged, but unmarked channel leading up to the basin off the town is most easily followed just after low water when the fringing sandbanks are uncovered. Again both channel and basin carry a nominal 2m at MLWS, but if in doubt the dinghy could be sent ahead to recce.

The fairway from the fishermen's quay to the main channel is marked by three pairs of (very small) red and green buoys, possibly as a response to the fishermen's complaint outlined above. On no account impede this fairway.

### Anchorage

Anchor near the entrance, as described above, or off the village outside local moored boats. In summer this area may become very crowded. Shelter in the basin is excellent and holding good over muddy sand. There are two pontoons with floating hammerheads where a dinghy might be left.

### Facilities

Water by can from a tap in the waterfront fish market. Supermarkets and general shopping plus many restaurants. The local shellfish is reputed to be particularly good.

### Communications

Post office. Taxis and buses (at the roundabout). Trains at Portimão about 3M away.

# Portimão

37°07'N 8°31'W

### Tides

*Reference port* Lisbon
*Mean time differences*
HW: −25 minutes ±10; LW: −30 minutes ±5

*Heights in metres*

| MHWS | MHWN | MLWN | MLWS |
|------|------|------|------|
| 3·3  | 2·6  | 1·4  | 0·7  |

### Charts

|                         | *Approach*      | *Harbour* |
|-------------------------|-----------------|-----------|
| Admiralty               | 3636, 89, 92    | 83        |
| Portuguese (old series) | 7, 8, 24        | 88        |
| Portuguese (new series) | 23203, 23204, 24206 | 26310 |

### Lights

#### Approach
2174 **Ponta da Piedade** 37°04'·8N 8°40'·1W
 Fl.7s50m20M
 Yellow square tower on building 5m

2178 **Ponta do Altar** 37°06'·4N 8°31'·1W
 LFl.R.5s31m14M 290°-vis-170°
 White square tower and building 10m
2188 **Praia de Carvoeiro** 37°05'·7N 8°28'·2W
 LFl.R.7s10m6M Mast 8m
2192 **Ponta de Alfanzina** 37°05'·1N 8°26'·5W
 Fl(2)15s62m29M
 White square tower and building 23m
*Harbour*
2181 **Ldg Lts on 021°** 37°07'·3N 8°31'·2W
 *Front* **Ferragudo** Oc.R.5s18m8M
 White tower, red bands
2181·1 *Rear*, 90m from front, Oc.R.7s33m8M
 White tower, red bands
2179 **West breakwater** 37°06'·4N 8°31'·7W
 Fl.R.5s9m7M
 White tower, red bands 7m
 F.R light on obstruction 0·9M northwards
2179·2 **East breakwater** 37°06'·4N 8°31'·5W
 Fl.G.5s9m7M
 White tower, green bands 7m
buoy *No.2* 37°07'N 8°31'·4W
 Fl.R.4s6M Red pillar buoy, ■ topmark
 buoy *No.4* 37°07'·4N 8°31'·4W
 Fl(2)R.6s6M Red pillar buoy, ■ topmark
 buoy *No.1* 37°07'·4 8°31'·4W
 Fl.G.4s5M Green pillar buoy, ▲ topmark

### Marina and port radio

*Marina de Portimão* VHF Ch 62 (anticipated).
*Postradportimão* VHF Ch 11, 16 (0900–1200, 1400–1700 Mon–Fri), 2252, 2182, 2657kHz.
*Pilotosportimão* VHF Ch 14, 16.

### General

Portimão on the Rio Arade has long been a busy fishing harbour, also handling small naval and commercial vessels. However in 1999 the waterfront on the west side was being transformed. In addition to the large Marina de Portimão taking shape near the entrance (technically in the suburb of Praia da Rocha), a yacht and smallcraft basin was in the early stages of construction further up the river opposite the fishermen's dock, and a brand new smallcraft pontoon was in position north of the road bridge. Somewhat surprisingly, the old yacht pontoon just below the bridge was also still in position and accepting visitors. From being one of those harbours where transients rafted four or five abreast and few facilities were available, Portimão will shortly rival Lagos or Vilamoura in its provision of berths and other services for visiting yachts.

The town of Portimão, on the west bank nearly 2M from the harbour mouth, is old and agreeable but undistinguished, while many yachtsmen will consider the seaside resort of Praia da Rocha verging on the unpleasant. The region's undoubted gem is the waterside village of Ferragudo on the east side of the estuary. If berthed in the marina make the effort to launch the dinghy, cross the river, and enjoy a lunch of *sardinas* grilled on a charcoal brazier on the tiny quay with seagulls wheeling overhead. A stroll through the village's steep cobbled alleys (mostly impassable to cars) will work off any resulting somnolence.

## Approach

The entrance is marked by the Ponta do Altar[2178] and is bracketed by Ponta da Piedade[2174] in the west and Ponta de Alfanzina[2192] in the east.

Between Lagos and Portimão the coast consists of sandy beaches with hills behind. East of Portimão there are a few small sandy beaches but the shore is mainly rocky with cliffs.

## Entrance

The ends of the breakwaters are lit[2179, 2179·2] – these lights in line bear 097° for those coming from Lagos. The leading line to enter the harbour itself is 021° (two red and white striped posts close east of Ferragudo church[2181]), which leaves the first port hand buoy, *No.2*, close to port before either making for the marina reception pontoon or following the channel north towards the upstream basin or the old yacht pontoon. If the latter, the buoyage is straightforward with a pair of lit buoys and then two unlit starboard hand buoys. The channel as far as Ponta São Francisco has a least depth of around 7m, decreasing to 2·5m off the yacht pontoon, but depths shoal rapidly outside the buoyed channel.

## Berthing

As mentioned above, there are already two berthing choices for visiting yachts and there may shortly be a third. There is no doubt that the Marina de Portimão will, when finished, provide excellent shelter and services on a par with the Algarve's other large marinas. However those who prefer more character in their surroundings (and a much lower daily charge) may still favour the upriver site.

## Marina de Portimão

In September 1999 the south basin of the Marina de Portimão, ☎/*Fax* 282 484842, was effectively complete, with a considerable proportion of the berths (all on individual fingers) occupied. It was hoped that the north basin, including the outer reception pontoon, would be in use by March 2000. The marina will eventually provide berthing for 642 yachts of up to 30m LOA, with 4m depths at the larger berths.

When visited the marina office was located in the walls below the Forte Santa Catarina, but in due course a purpose-built office will be located on the north arm at the root of the reception pontoon.

The wide entrance to Portimão looking northeast, with the new Marina de Portimão taking shape on the left.

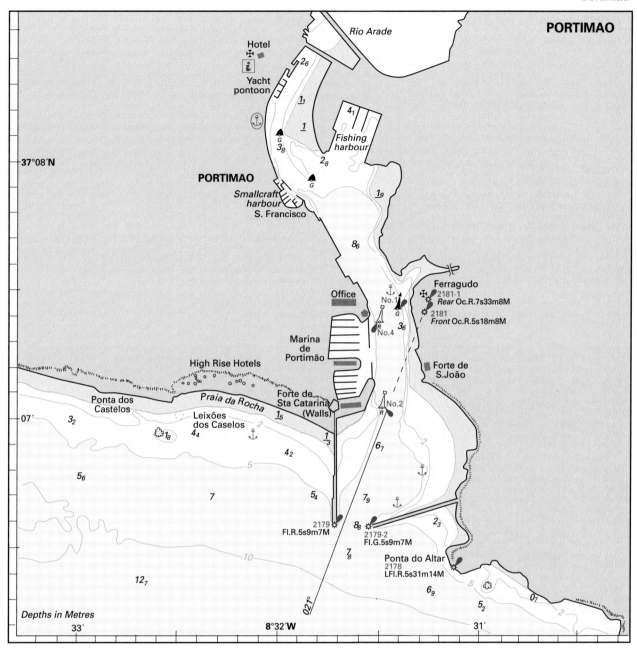

**PORTIMAO**

*Rio Arade*

Hotel

Yacht pontoon

37°08′N

PORTIMAO

*Smallcraft harbour*
S. Francisco

Fishing harbour

Office

Ferragudo
2181·1
*Rear* Oc.R.7s33m8M
2181
*Front* Oc.R.5s18m8M

Marina
de
Portimão

No.1

No.4

Forte de
S.João

High Rise Hotels

Ponta dos
Castelos

*Praia da Rocha*

Leixões
dos Caselos

Forte de
Sta Catarina
(Walls)

No.2

07′

2179
Fl.R.5s9m7M

2179·2
Fl.G.5s9m7M

Ponta do Altar
2178
LFl.R.5s31m14M

*Depths in Metres*

33′                        8°32′W                        31′

Though the buildings to the south were taking shape by September 1999 – see photograph – those to the north are expected to take considerably longer. In due course the Marina de Portimão should form an almost self-sufficient marina village, with facilities including some 30 shops, a variety of bars and restaurants and even a seawater swimming pool. Security is excellent, with two guards patrolling at all times in addition to card access gates.

In 1999 the high season (1/6–30/9) rate for a visiting yacht of just under 12m was 4,200 escudos (20·95 euros) per night if her beam was less than 3·3m, 4,600 escudos (22·94 euros) if it was more. The monthly low season rates for a yacht of similar size were 44,000 escudos (219·47 euros) and 49,000 escudos (244·41 euros) respectively, all inclusive of water, electricity and tax.

**Upriver**

As of September 1999 visiting yachts could still use the outside of a T-shaped floating pontoon on the port hand below the bridge. Most of the 55 more sheltered inner berths are occupied by locally owned boats, but the 36m outside length is reserved for transients. Strong tidal streams run through the berths, particularly on the ebb – manoeuvre and secure accordingly.

The pontoons are administered by the Junta Autonoma dos Portos de Barlevento (JAPBA), with offices next to the much larger *capitania* building 50m or so downstream. Access from the land is via a security gate for which a card is needed, and as both the above offices are open on weekdays only, 0900–1200 and 1400–1600, arrival outside office hours or at weekends would present problems (one option would be to go by dinghy to the Associação Naval pontoon beyond).

In 1999 the high season (16/6–15/9) rate for a visiting yacht of just under 12m was 1,960 escudos (9·78 euros) per night if her beam was less than 3·3m, 2,150 escudos (10·72 euros) if it was more. The mid season (16/3–15/6 and 16/9–15/11) rates were 1,370 escudos (6·83 euros) and 1,570 escudos (7·83 euros) respectively, all inclusive of water, electricity and tax. These somewhat exposed river pontoons are not a suitable place to leave a yacht unattended for long periods.

As mentioned above, work was just starting on a yacht and smallcraft harbour opposite the fishermen's basin and about 0·4M downstream from the pontoon, but no completion date could be given. Although intended to provide 300 berths of various sizes, it is possible that it will not accept visiting yachts but will be reserved entirely for local boats. Again it falls under the jurisdiction of the Junta Autonoma dos Portos de Barlevento.

## Anchorage

The anchorage inside the east breakwater is secure with very good holding in sand, though sometime affected by swell and/or wash. It would be a safe choice if arriving by night, but note that the bottom shelves steeply between the 5m and 2m contours.

Alternatively anchor off Ferragudo near the fishing boat moorings, in 3–4m over mud. North of the creek mouth holding is reported to be poor. Be sure to leave the marked channel clear as the fishing fleet appears to leave en masse in the hours before daybreak (if the throb of diesel engines in unison does not wake you, the wash will).

## Formalities

The marina office is equipped with multi-part forms – see page 6. If at anchor or berthed upriver enquire at the Junta Autonoma dos Portos de Barlevento for current requirements.

When photographed in September 1999 the Marina de Portimão was already accepting yachts, though far from finished. It will present a very different sight in a year or two's time.

Fish are landed, cleaned, cooked and eaten on the quayside at Ferragudo, across the river from Portimão. Researching a cruising guide does have its compensations. . .

## Facilities

*Boatyard* A boatyard geared to yachts is planned for the east side of the river near the road bridge. Currently the only working yards are beyond the bridge on the west side, where traditional fishing boats and other motor vessels are built and repaired.

*Travel-lift* Planned for the boatyard, but nothing at present.

*Engineers, electronic & radio repairs, sail repairs* Enquire at the marina office. If berthed in the marina only companies holding the appropriate concession will be permitted to work on yachts.

*Chandlery* A chandlery is planned for the marina complex, but nothing existed as of September 1999.

*Charts* The marina office intends to stock a limited range of local charts.

*Water* On the marina pontoons and the upriver pontoon.

*Showers* At the marina. Currently near the office under the old walls, but at least two shower blocks will be incorporated in the new buildings.

*Launderette* To be included in the new marina buildings.

*Electricity* On the marina pontoons and the upriver pontoon.

*Fuel* The marina reception pontoon will incorporate a fuel berth. Until then diesel is available at the south side of the fishing harbour quay – being intended for fishing boats, black tyres are used as fenders against the concrete block wall.

*Bottled gas* Camping Gaz available in Portimão.

*Ice* Likely to be available in the marina complex.

*Clube náutico* The Associação Naval Infante Sagres have premises near the upriver pontoon.

*Weather forecast* Posted daily at the marina, and sometimes at the *capitania*.

*Banks* In Praia da Rocha and Portimão.

*Shops/provisioning* In Praia da Rocha and Portimão, though considerably better (and cheaper) in the latter. Limited shopping in Ferragudo. A shopping centre is planned for the southern range of marina buildings.

*Produce markets* In Portimão and Ferragudo.

*Cafés, restaurants & hotels* Every second building, if not even more.

*Medical services* In Praia da Rocha and Portimão.

## Communications

*Post offices* In Praia da Rocha and Portimão.

*Mailing address*
c/o **Marina de Portimão**, Praia da Rocha, 8500 Portimão, Portugal.
☎/*Fax service* 282 484842.

*Public telephones* Kiosks are planned for the marina, and will be found in both towns as well as in Ferragudo.

*Car hire/taxis* No shortage.

*Buses* Frequent if slow.

*Trains* Station north of Portimão.

*Air services* Faro International Airport is some 55km distant.

## Alternative anchorages

1. Off Praia da Rocha, west of Portimão's west breakwater. A shoal patch carrying less than 2m extends 70m southeast from the southernmost of the two rocks off Ponta dos Castelos, itself 0·7M west of the breakwater. Suitable for daytime use only, and open to the south.

2. Off Praia de Carvoeiro (37°06'N 8°28'W), 3M east of Portimão and identified by a red light (LFl.R.7s) on an 8m post. Again a daytime anchorage open to the south.

3. Albufeira (37°05'N 8°15'W), 13M east of Portimão, was once a fishing village but has now grown into a considerable holiday resort ringed by unattractive apartment buildings. The wide bay is open to the south and the shore on either side is rocky. Anchor as draft permits, clear of the smallcraft moorings and the short jetty, which is used by tourist ferries.

   There are several secluded coves to the west of the town where anchorage may be found in calm weather, but there is little room to swing. A plan of the area is included on Portuguese 'new series' chart *27503*.

   In January 2000 plans were announced for a new marina in the bay, to be known as Praia da Baleeira (not to be confused with the Baleeira close west of Cabo de São Vicente). It was stated that it would contain 474 berths, surrounded by apartments, villas, shops restaurants and bars. It was expected to be operational within four years.

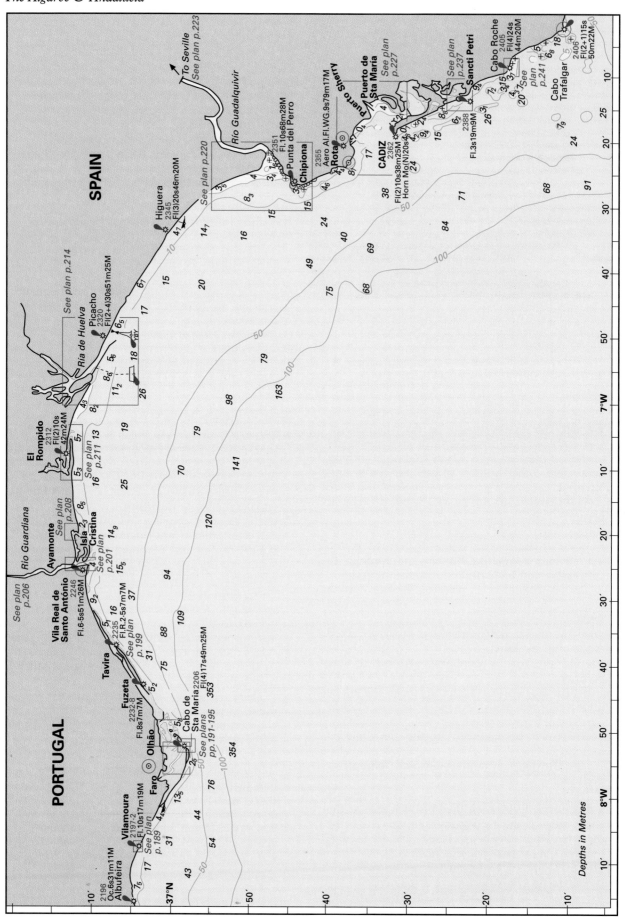

**PORTUGAL**

**SPAIN**

*To Seville*
*See plan p.223*

*See plan p.206*

*Rio Guadiana*

**Ayamonte**
*See plan p.208*

**Vila Real de Santo António**
2246
Fl.6·5s51m26M

*See plan p.201*

**Isla**
**Cristina**

**Vilamoura**
2197·2
Fl.10s17m19M

**Faro**

**Albufeira**
2196
Oc.6s31m11M

*See plan p.189*

**Tavira**
2235
Fl.R.2·5s7m7M

**Fuzeta**
2232·8
Fl.8s7m7M

*See plan p.199*

**Olhão**

**Cabo de Sta Maria** 2206
Fl(4)17s49m25M

*See plans pp.191-195*

**El Rompido**
2312
Fl(2)10s 42m24M

*See plan p.211*

**Picacho**
2320
Fl(2+4)30s51m25M

*Ria de Huelva*

*See plan p.214*

*Rio Guadalquivir*

**Higuera**
2345
Fl(3)20s46m20M

*See plan p.220*

**Punta del Perro**
2351
Fl.10s68m28M

**Chipiona**

2355
**Rota**
Aero Al.Fl.WG.9s79m17M

2362
**Puerto Sherry**

**Puerto de Sta Maria**

*See plan p.227*

**CADIZ**
Fl(2)10s38m25M
Horn Mo(N)20s

2388
Fl.3s19m9M

**Sancti Petri**

*See plan p.237*

**Cabo Roche**
2405
Fl(4)24s 44m20M

*See plan p.241*

2406
Fl(2+1)15s 50m22M

**Cabo Trafalgar**

*Depths in Metres*

# Vilamoura

37°04'N 8°07'W

## Tides

*Reference port* Lisbon
*Mean time differences* (at Albufeira)
HW: −10 minutes ±25; LW: 00 minutes ±5

*Heights in metres*

| MHWS | MHWN | MLWN | MLWS |
|------|------|------|------|
| 3·6 | 2·8 | 1·5 | 0·7 |

## Charts

| | Approach | Harbour |
|---|---|---|
| Admiralty | 89, 92 | |
| Portuguese (old series) | 7, 8, 24 | |
| Portuguese (new series) | 23203, 23204, 24206 | 27503 |

## Lights

### Approach

2192 **Ponta de Alfanzina** 37°05'·1N 8°26'·5W
Fl(2)15s62m29M
White square tower and building 23m

2197·2 **Vilamoura** 37°04'·4N 8°07'·3W
Fl.10s17m19M
Red framework on cream and red control tower 16m

2206 **Cabo de Santa María** 36°58'·4N 7°51'·8W
Fl(4)17s49m25M
White round tower and building 46m

*0979* Radiobeacon *SM* 305·5kHz 50M (3 & 4 in
sequence)

### Harbour

2197·3 **West breakwater** 37°04'·1N 8°07'·4W
Fl.R.4s13m5M
White tower, red bands 7m

2197·4 **East breakwater** 37°04'·1N 8°07'·3W
Fl.G.4s13m5M
White tower, green bands 7m

## Marina radio

*Vilamoura radio* VHF Ch 62 (24 hours); VHF Ch 16, calling and emergencies (office hours only, when Ch 62 may also operate at seriously reduced range).

*Weather information* in Portuguese and English is broadcast daily on VHF Ch 20 at 1000.

## General

Marina de Vilamoura, established in 1974, ☎ 289 310560 *Fax* 289 310580, *e-mail* marinavilamoura@lusotur.pt is the longest-established marina on the Algarve and the second-oldest west of the Mediterranean (Sheppard's Marina in Gibraltar opened its doors back in 1961). The benefits of this are seen in the excellent on-site facilities, the downside in that some of the fixtures and fittings are beginning to look a little worn (though upgrading is planned for the near future).

The marina, which boasts around 1,300 berths for vessels of up to 24m, is surrounded by a large tourist complex which includes four golf courses, a casino and countless hotels, and offers a wide choice of open-air cafés, boutiques, souvenir shops, etc. In contrast, a serious effort is being made to establish a

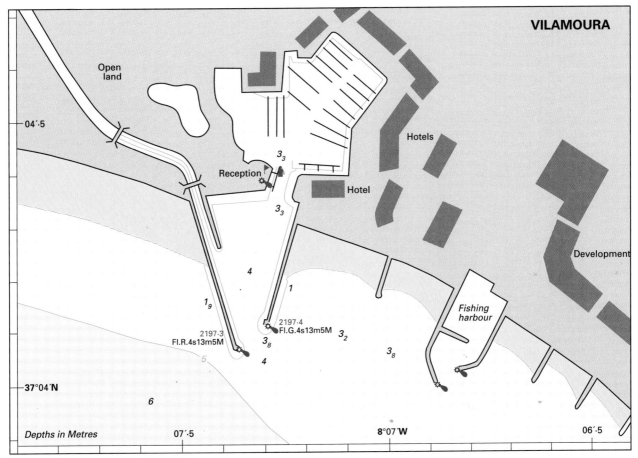

200 hectare Environmental Park just west of the marina to preserve the wetland home of many species of birds. There are also Roman ruins close by, together with a small museum.

There is a good beach within a short dinghy ride, or in walking distance if berthed on the west side of the basin. A commercial water-taxi, ☎ 289 313622, serves the marina, useful for those without dinghies.

Vilamoura is a popular and reasonably secure place to leave a yacht, either long-term or for a few months – perhaps between a summer passage southwards and the late autumn passage to Madeira, the Canaries and beyond – in which case its proximity to Faro airport is an obvious advantage.

## Approach

Vilamoura is marked by its own major light[2197·2] and is bracketed by Ponta de Alfanzina[2192] to the west and Cabo de Santa María[2206] to the southeast.

The coast is low and rocky and the breakwaters may be difficult to pick out, but the marina is surrounded by conspicuous tower blocks, particularly to the east where a large pale pink hotel stands close to the entrance. A small fishing harbour

(nearing completion in November 1999) lies a few hundred metres east of the entrance, with the tower blocks of Quarteira beyond.

## Entrance

The entrance is about 100m wide, between breakwaters[2197·3, 2197·4] stretching 500m from the shore, and can be dangerous in strong southerly winds (true of nearly all Algarve harbours). At present the outer basin is congested with moored fishing boats, but by spring 2000 they should have moved en masse to the new fishing harbour a few hundred metres further east.

Head for the 60m wide entrance to the inner basin and secure to the long reception pontoon beneath the control tower and offices. Depths in the outer harbour are approximately 4m, decreasing to 3·3m off the reception pontoon and in the southern part of the basin and 2m in the northeast section.

In 1998 it was reported that depths at datum in the entrance were no more than 1·6m (2·3m at low water springs), but dredging to at least 4m is due to take place before the start of the 2000 season.

The approach to the long-established Marina de Vilamoura, looking north-northeast. By 2000 the moored fishing vessels should have moved to their own purpose-built harbour a few hundred metres further east.

## Berthing

The Marina de Vilamoura has around 1,000 berths and can take vessels of up to 45 metre length. On arrival secure to the reception pontoon until clearance procedures have been completed and a berth allocated. If arriving outside office hours – 0830–2130 1/6–15/9; 0830–1930 1/4–31/5 and 16/9–31/10; 0830–1800 1/11–31/3 – it will be necessary to remain there until the offices open in the morning. Water and electricity are both available on the reception pontoon.

In 1999 the high season (1/6–30/9) rate for a visiting yacht of just under 12m was 4,914 escudos (24·51 euros) per night if her beam was less than 3·3m, 5,382 escudos (26·85 euros) if it was between 3·3m and 4m. The monthly low season rates for yachts of similar dimensions were 51,480 escudos (256·78 euros) and 57,330 escudos (285·96 euros) respectively. Further discounts are available for longer periods. Charges are inclusive of water and electricity, and though quoted by the marina ex-IVA (the equivalent of VAT) at 17%, this has been added to the above figures for easy comparison with other harbours. Yachts of over 12m may be charged extra for electricity, measured by meter, and it has been reported that, when a berth of the correct size is not available and a visiting yacht occupies a berth able to take a larger boat, the owner will be charged accordingly. Various major credit cards, including *VISA*, are accepted.

Pontoon security is assured by frequent patrols and monitored videos, rather than by locked security gates as in most marinas.

## Formalities

For many years the Marina de Vilamoura had a reputation for over-zealous officialdom, but by 1998 this appeared to have been resolved even though a careful if discreet watch was still kept on the movement of all yachts on the Algarve coast due to the activities of drug smugglers from North Africa.

In 1999 a few visiting skippers again reported problems and/or delays, mostly due to the fact that although the usual multiple-part form (for which ship's papers, passports and evidence of insurance are needed) was completed at the reception desk, the skipper was required to take the copies to the *alfândega* (customs) and *imigração* (immigration) offices in person. Although all three offices are in the same building the process could still be time-consuming, with long waits in busy periods.

As of 2000 the requirement to visit the *alfândega* office is generally to be waived, though skippers of non-EU registered yachts or with non-EU crew aboard will still be required to call at the *imigração* office on arrival and departure, as will those arriving from or departing for a non-EU country (including Gibraltar).

The *alfândega* office is nominally open 0830–2200 in summer and 0900–1700 in winter; the *imigração* office 0800–1930 throughout the year. Both are manned seven days a week. If planning to leave early in the morning clearance procedures are best dealt with the previous evening.

## Facilities

*Boatyard* Services are provided by a range of different contractors, or owners can do their own work. Contractors currently include Rui Figueiredo Pinto, ☎ 289 398767 (boatbuilding in timber); Fibramar Lda, *Mobile* 917 235150 (GRP repairs); Lacomar Lda, ☎ 289 312471 (osmosis treatment and painting); and Heitmann Yacht Service Lda, ☎ 289 360610, plus a number of individuals offering carpentry, general maintenance and caretaking.

*Travel-lifts* 30 and 60 tonne capacity hoists, plus two smaller cranes. The concreted hardstanding has good security but occasionally there is a shortage of space. There is also a tidal grid for boats drawing less than 2m.

*Engineers* Tecni-Marine, ☎ 289 301070 (Volvo agents); Murtanáutica Lda, ☎ 289 323936 (Yanmar agents); Emiliano Nunes, ☎ 289 321793; and Automourense Lda, ☎ 289 301020. All have workshops in the boatyard area. Jorge Ramela Costa, ☎ 289 366293, handles welding and mechanical work.

*Electrical and cooling systems* Marine Power Lda, ☎ 289 380979, *Mobile* 969 022344, (who also handle electronic & radio repairs) and Janusz Oszczepalski, ☎ 289 388762

*Sailmaker/sail repairs* J P Velas, ☎ 289 321155 and Carlos Gil Domingues, *Mobile* 9628 01463. A major sailmaker plans to open a loft for the 2000 season.

*Chandlery* A branch of Capitalcar, ☎ 289 314764, overlooks the boatyard area – well-stocked and carrying a good range of maintenance materials. Other chandleries exist around the marina basin, but tending towards the decorative rather than the practical.

Branches of Harken Chandlery, ☎ 289 310560, and Pinmar, Spain's leading yacht paint supplier, are due to open in the boatyard area during the 2000 season.

*Charts* Both Admiralty and Portuguese charts can be ordered from Lisbon via the marina office.

*Water* At all berths and the reception/fuel pontoon.

*Showers* Behind the marina office (effectively in the boatyard compound) plus three more blocks around the marina basin, all with card access.

*Launderettes* One on each side of the marina basin.

*Electricity* At all berths and the reception/fuel pontoon.

*Fuel* Diesel and petrol pumps at the north end of the reception pontoon.

*Bottled gas* At the chandlery, with Camping Gaz exchanges and other butane cylinders refilled (though see page 8).

*Ice* At the supermarkets, chandlery and filling station.

*Clube náutico* Next to the marina office, with bar and restaurant, ☎ 289 322734, overlooking the reception pontoon. Crews of visiting yachts have automatic membership.

*Weather forecast* Surface charts and a weather forecast for the entire Portuguese coast are displayed in the marina office, updated daily. In addition, weather information in Portuguese and English is broadcast daily on VHF Ch 20 at 1000.

*Banks* Several around the marina complex.

*Shops/provisioning* Several small supermarkets, mostly a street or two back from the marina, which meet daily needs but are inadequate for serious passage provisioning. For serious stocking-up the best bet would be the big Modelo supermarket about 15 minutes away by car (ask at the marina office for directions). Dozens of tourist and general shops overlook the marina basin.

*Produce market* Well-stocked markets in Quarteira and Lidl.

*Cafés, restaurants & hotels* Seemingly dozens of the former right beside the marina, with lots more (including several luxury hotels) within walking distance.

*Medical services* Medical centre, ☎ 289 314243, with dental and other services in the tourist complex, hospital in Faro.

## Communications

*Post Office* In the Vilamoura tourist complex, though stamps can be bought at any shop displaying the green *correio* sign.

*Mailing address*
    c/o **Marina de Vilamoura**, 8125–409 Quarteira, Algarve, Portugal
    *Fax service* 289 310580

*Public telephones* Several around the marina complex, including one beside the reception quay and another in the boatyard compound.

*Taxis/car hire* In the commercial area, or via the marina office. Note that sign-posting within the tourist complex is poor – allow for a few wrong turnings if hiring a car to catch a plane, etc.

*Buses* Bus service to Faro (about 40 minutes) and elsewhere.

*Air services* Faro international airport is about 20 minutes by taxi, 40 minutes by bus. There is also a small airport at Vilamoura itself.

# Faro and Olhão

36°58'N 7°52'W (at entrance)

## Tides

*Reference port* Lisbon
*Mean time differences* (at Cabo de Santa María)
HW: −40 minutes ±10; LW: −10 minutes ±5

*Heights in metres*

| MHWS | MHWN | MLWN | MLWS |
|------|------|------|------|
| 3·4 | 2·6 | 1·3 | 0·6 |

## Charts

| Faro | Approach | Channels |
|------|----------|----------|
| Admiralty | 89, 92 | 83 |
| Portuguese (old series) | 8, 24 | 91, 92 |
| Portuguese (new series) | 23204, 24206 | 26311 |
| Spanish | 44B | |

| Olhão | | |
|-------|---------|--------|
| Admiralty | 89, 92 | 83 |
| Portuguese | 8, 24, 41, 42 | 91, 92 |
| Spanish | 44A, 44B | |

## Lights

### Approach

2197·2 **Vilamoura** 37°04'·4N 8°07'·3W
  Fl.10s17m19M
  Red framework on cream and red control tower 16m

2200 **Faro airport** 37°01'·1N 7°58'·2W
  Aero Al.Fl.WG.10s35m Control tower 29m

*0978* **Faro aerobeacon** 37°00'·4N 7°55'·5W
  Aerobeacon *FAR* 332kHz 50M

2206 **Cabo de Santa María** 36°58'·6N 7°51'·8W
  Fl(4)17s49m25M
  White round tower and building 46m

*0979* Radiobeacon *SM* 305·5kHz 50M (3 & 4 in sequence)

2246 **Vila Real de Santo António** 37°11'·1N 7°24'·9W
  Fl.6·5s51m26M
  White round tower, very narrow black rings, red lantern 46m

*0981* Radiobeacon *VR* 305·5kHz 100M (5 & 6 in sequence)

### Entrance

2208 **West breakwater** 36°57'·9N 7°52'·2W
  Fl.R.4s9m6M White tower, red bands 5m

2209 **East breakwater** 36°57'·9N 7°52'·1W
  Fl.G.4s9m6M White tower, green bands 5m

2206·1 **Ldg Lts on 021°** 36°58'·3N 7°51'·9W
  *Front* **Barra Nova** Oc.4s8m6M
  White column, red stripes

2206 *Rear* **Cabo de Santa María**, as above

buoy **Port hand** *No.2* 36°58'·1N 7°52'·1W
  Fl.R.3s3M Red pillar buoy, ■ topmark

buoy **Port hand** *No.4* 36°58'·3N 7°52'W
  Fl.R.6s3M Red pillar buoy, ■ topmark

buoy **Port hand** *No.6* 36°58'·5N 7°52'·1W
  Fl.R.6s3M Red pillar buoy, ■ topmark

2211 **Ilha de Cultra, training wall** 36°58'·5N 7°52'W
  Oc.G.5s6m3M Metal column on building 6m

### Canal de Faro

2212 **First Ldg Lts on 099°** 36°58'·6N 7°52'W
  *Note* Used as a back bearing if entering
  *Front* **Mar Santo** Oc.R.5s9m5M
  White column, red bands 5m

2206 *Rear* **Cabo de Santa María**, 244m from front, as above

buoy **Starboard hand** *No.1* 36°58'·6N 7°52'·3W
  Fl.G.3s3M Green conical buoy, ▲ topmark

buoy **Starboard hand** *No.3* 36°58'·7N 7°52'·6W
  Fl.G.6s3M Green conical buoy, ▲ topmark

buoy **Starboard hand** *No.5* 36°58'·8N 7°54'W
  Fl.G.3s3M Green conical buoy, ▲ topmark

2214 **Second Ldg Lts on 328°** 37°00'·9N 7°54'·9W
  *Front* **Casa Cubica** Iso.R.6s11m6M
  Lantern on south wall 5m

2214·1 *Rear*, 731m from front, Oc.R.6s63m6M
  Lantern on church tower 21m

### Canal de Olhão

2222 **Cais Farol** 36°58'·8N 7°51'·9W
  Fl.G.3s7m6M Green metal column 5m

2221 **First Ldg Lts on 219·5°** 36°58'·1N 7°52'·5W
  *Note* Used as a back bearing if entering
  *Front* **Golada** LFl.R.5s6m6M
  White column, red bands, on white base

2221·1 *Rear*, 447m from front, Oc.R.5s8m7M
  White column, red bands, on white base

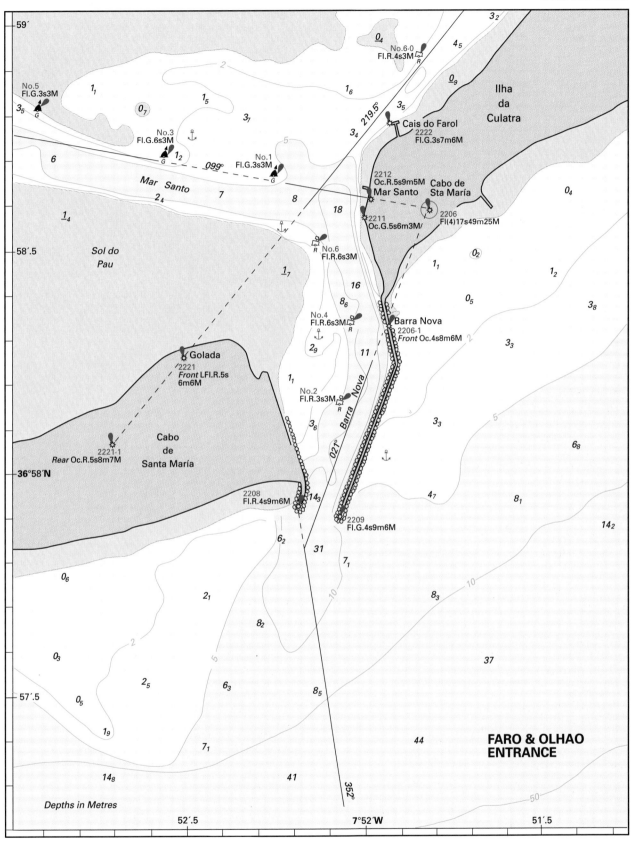

59′

No.6·0
Fl.R.4s3M
R

$0_4$

$3_2$

$4_5$

Ilha
da
Culatra

$0_9$

No.5
Fl.G.3s3M

$3_5$
G

$1_1$

$1_5$

$0_7$

$3_7$

2

$1_6$

$3_5$

Cais do Farol
2222
Fl.G.3s7m6M

219.5°

$3_4$

No.3
Fl.G.6s3M
$1_2$
G

Mar Santo

$2_4$

5

7

8

No.1
Fl.G.3s3M
G

6

099°

2212
Oc.R.5s9m5M
Mar Santo

Cabo de
Sta María

$0_4$

18

2211
Oc.G.5s6m3M

2206
Fl(4)17s49m25M

$1_1$

$0_2$

$1_2$

$3_8$

$1_4$

Sol do
Pau

58′.5

$1_7$

No.6
Fl.R.6s3M
R

16

$8_6$

$0_5$

$3_3$

No.4
Fl.R.6s3M
R

Barra Nova
2206·1
*Front* Oc.4s8m6M

2

Golada
2221
*Front* LFl.R.5s
6m6M

$2_9$

11

$1_1$

$3_3$

$6_8$

2221-1
*Rear* Oc.R.5s8m7M

Cabo
de
Santa María

$3_6$

No.2
Fl.R.3s3M
R

Barra Nova

021°

$3_3$

$5$

36°58′N

$14_3$

$4_7$

$8_1$

$14_2$

2208
Fl.R.4s9m6M

2209
Fl.G.4s9m6M

$6_2$

31

$7_1$

$0_6$

$2_1$

10

$8_3$

10

57′.5

$0_5$

$0_3$

$2_5$

$8_2$

2

$6_3$

$8_5$

37

50

$1_9$

$7_1$

44

**FARO & OLHAO
ENTRANCE**

$14_8$

41

352°

*Depths in Metres*

52′.5

7°52′W

51′.5

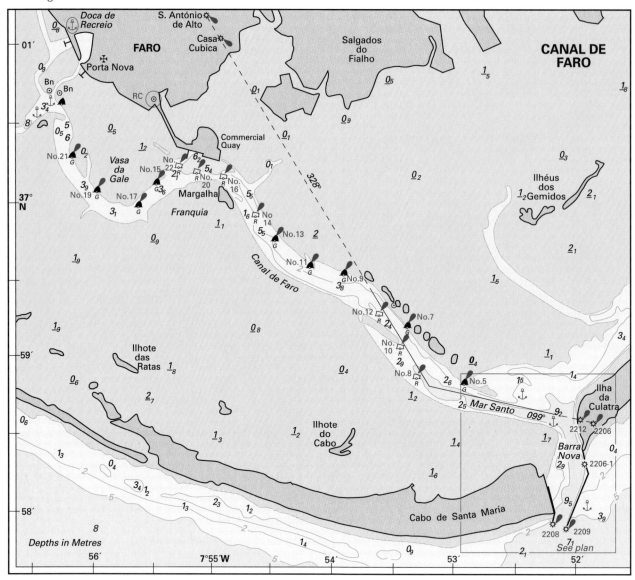

buoy **Port hand *No.6–0*** 36°58'·9N 7°51'·9W
  Fl.R.4s3M Red can buoy, ■ topmark
**2218 Ponte do Carvão, Ilha de Culatra** 36°59'·2N
  7°51'·2W
  Fl.5·5s6m6M Green column 4m
**2219 Ponte-Cais, Ilha de Culatra** 36°59'·7N
  7°50'·5W
  Oc.G.4s3m5M Green metal column
**2224 Second Ldg Lts on 124·5°** 36°59'·6N 7°50'·5W
  *Note* Used as a back bearing on entering
  *Front* **Arraiais** Iso.G.1·5s7m5M
  Black and white striped column with ▲ 5m
  (Reported difficult to identify)
**2224·1** *Rear*, 226m from front, Oc.G.3s13m5M
  Black and white striped column with ▲ 8m
**2225 Third Ldg Lts on 352·5°** 37°01'·5N 7°51'·7W
  *Front* **Murtinas** LFl.R.5s7m7M
  White column, red bands 4m
  (Reported difficult to identify)
**2225·1** *Rear*, 300m from front,
  Oc.R.5s13m7M White column, red bands 7m

**2226 Fourth Ldg Lts on 044°** 37°01'·5N 7°50'·5W
  *Front* **Cais de Olhão** Iso.R.6s8m7M
  White column, red bands 7m
  (Reported difficult to identify)
**2226·1** *Rear* **Igreja**, 360m from front,
  Oc.R.4s20m6M Church tower 12m
**2225·3 Fishing harbour, west mole** 37°01'·5N 7°50'W
  Fl.R.6s6M Octagonal metal post 5m
Many other lit buoys and beacons exist in the Canal de
Faro, Canal de Olhão and Canal da Assetia. However
none should be relied upon implicitly, and any or all
may be moved if the channels shift.

### Coast radio station

**Estoi** (37°10'N 7°50'W) (24 hours) Remotely controlled
  from Lisbon
**VHF** Ch 16, 24, 28, 86.

### Port radio

*Postradfaro* VHF Ch 11, 16 (24 hours); 2252, 2182,
  2657kHz.
*Pilotosfaro* VHF Ch 14, 16.
*Capimarolhão* VHF Ch 11, 16 (0900–1230, 1000–1730
  Mon–Fri).

## General

Both Faro and Olhão (pronounced 'Oh-le-ow') are considerable towns – and Olhão is an important fishing port with a pleasant, non-touristy atmosphere – but for many the greater appeal lies with the tidal lagoons which run along the coast for some 30M between the mainland and the sea. The whole off-lying islands form a *Parque Natural* where certain restrictions apply, and the bird life, including storks and various waders, is abundant. To take full advantage of the geography a sailing dinghy or a shoal-draught boat able to take the ground is needed, but there is water enough in the main channels for deep-draught yachts.

The entrance at Cabo de Santa María, shared by both channels, is well marked and the way through the sand defined by breakwaters. A stream of fishing boats may give a useful lead when they return with their catch in the early morning, but the bar – which is dredged from time to time – presents few problems in fine weather. Once inside, the channels are reasonably well buoyed, but if going to Olhão beware the wash of passing fishing boats. The ferries, too, are not over-considerate of yachts.

In Faro, the walled Cidade Velha (old town) right next to the Doca de Recreo should not be missed, providing welcome shade on a hot day and superb views over the estuary and town from the belltower of the Sé (cathedral). It is also a convenient spot for crew changes, due to the proximity of the airport.

One potential problem throughout the area is the prevalence of floating weed, which tends to clog engine water filters, and small crustaceans which take up residence in electronic log impellers. Both will need clearing regularly.

## Approach

The coast is very low-lying and currents of up to 3 knots may set along it. The 50m contour runs at 1M offshore at the point, further away on either side. The major light of Cabo de Santa María[2206] is on the sandspit about 1·3M northeast of the most southerly point of the cape and 0·7M north-northeast of the breakwaters. From a distance it looks like a needle on a sandy island.

Coming along the shore from the west, the beach starts a few miles east of Vilamoura and is backed by tourist villages. It becomes deserted to the southeast and 8M from Santa María the lagoon starts, with an occasional shallow entrance across the sand, and Faro airport behind. The 5m line runs 600–700m offshore, except southwest of the entrance where it turns south to a point, very steep-to (shoaling from 30m down to 5m within 50m or less) more than 0·5M offshore. A short distance west the 2m contour does much the same, extending to a point off which the water shoals from 15m down to 2m in little more than 100m. Either of these may cause a southwesterly swell to break. Maintain a distance of at least 0·7M offshore until the west breakwater bears 352°.

Cabo de Santa María at the entrance to the Faro and Olhão channels, seen from a little north of east.

The view south across the Faro reed-beds towards the open sea. In the foreground is the Quinta do Progresso boatyard (see text), with behind it the town channels and yacht anchorage.

To the east, the lagoon and its protecting banks extend 20M with some quite wide gaps. Opposite Fuzeta, 5M east of Olhão and identified by a distinctive church, the 50m line is about 2M offshore. In late 1999 it was reported that a tunny net had been laid south of Fuzeta (the first time for several years), its nearest point about 1M offshore. It was stated to lie within a square defined by the following positions: 37°01'·9N 7°43'·5W – 37°01'·9N 7°41'·8W – 37°00'·5N 7°41'·8W – 37°00'·5N 7°43'·5W. Although it is almost certainly buoyed the details have not been published.

### Entrance

The breakwaters are lit[2208, 2209], but are susceptible to storm damage. There can be a marked set across the entrance and it is important to remain on the leading line[2206·1]. The channel shifts from year to year.

From a point about 0·7M south of the entrance, steer 352° until the end of the east breakwater just opens to the east of a line with Santa María light[2206]. Watch for the set. Once inside, favour the east side. There are three port hand buoys before the channels to Faro and Olhão divide.

Though both channels are buoyed, the system is neither clear nor comprehensive and individual buoys are frequently out of position. The banks shift continually and yachts have reported grounding well within the marked channel. Enter only at half flood when most of the shoals are visible, and favour the outsides of bends. The tides run strongly and may reach 5 knots at springs.

*Note* Vessels drawing more than 2·5m may not use the channel at night (not recommended for the visitor, in any case). Vessels are forbidden to cross each other's bows at the junction of the channels –

those outward bound should remain outside the channel and let inward bound vessels pass.

### Anchorages

1. *Near the entrance* – outside, east of the east breakwater and south of Santa María light, or inside, either on the west side of the channel (see plan page 192), or in the Praça Larga inside Ilha da Culatra (see plan opposite). If using any of these anchorages after dark it is essential to display a riding light.

   Ponte-Cais caters for the tourist ferries from Olhão and has a small supermarket, several restaurants and bars, and a post office. The other anchorages call for total self-sufficiency.

2. *Faro* – the pool formed at the junction of the creeks, with the railway bridge covering the entrance to the Doca de Recreio bearing about 040°, is now largely occupied by moorings. However it is usually possible to find space in the channel leading southwest, where there is at least one deep pool, though two anchors (both from the bow and laid upstream and downstream respectively) may be required to limit the swinging room required.

   When approaching the junction, favour the port side of the channel past buoys *No.17*, *No.19* and *No.21*, switching to the starboard hand when the latter is 100m or so astern to avoid an extensive sandspit running out from the port bank (visible until mid-tide and sometimes marked by a small blue buoy). The deep channel here carries 4m or more depth but is a bare 15m wide.

   Land either at the Doca de Recreio, passing under the railway bridge (about 2m air draught at high water), or at the public jetty outside. In late

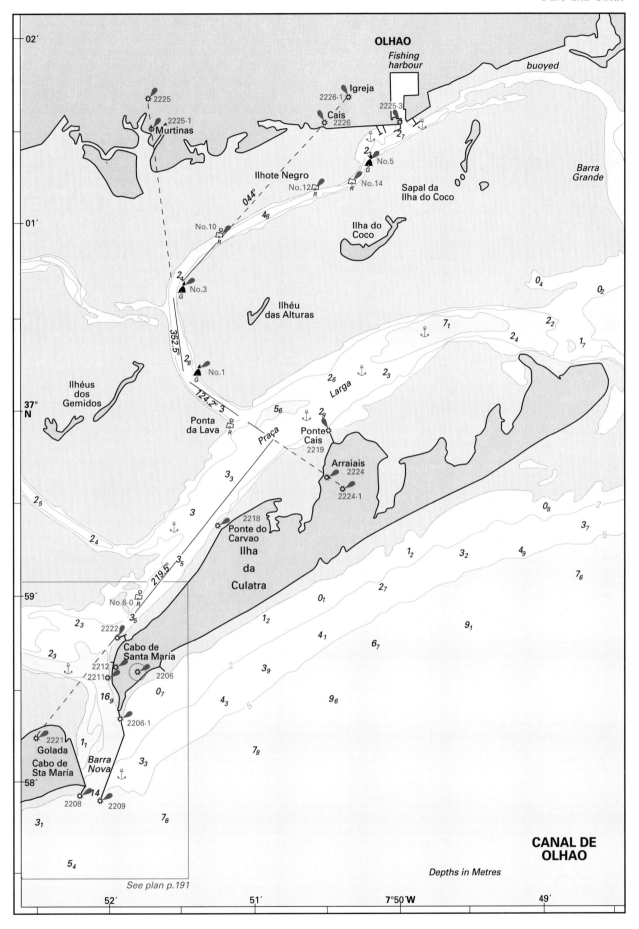

OLHAO

*Fishing harbour*

*buoyed*

2225

2225·1
☼Murtinas

Igreja
2226·1

Cais
2226

2225·3

2₇

Barra
Grande

2₃
No.5
G

Ilhote Negro

No.12
R

No.14
R

Sapal da
Ilha do Coco

044°

4₈

No.10
R

Ilha do
Coco

0₄

0₂

2₄
G
No.3

Ilhéu
das Alturas

7₁

2₂

1₇

352.5°

2₄

2₆
No.1
G

124.2°

Larga

2₆

2₃

5₆

2₉

0₈

2

Ilhéus
dos
Gemidos

37°
N

3₃

Praça

Ponta
da Lava
R

Ponte
Cais
2219

Arraiais
2224

2224·1

3₇

5

3

2₅

3

2218
Ponte do
Carvao

Ilha

da

Culatra

1₂

3₂

4₉

7₆

2₄

219.5°

3₅

No.6-0
R

2₇

0₁

9₁

59′

2₃

3₅

2222

1₂

4₁

6₇

2₃

2212
2211

Cabo de
Santa María

2206

16₉

0₇

3₉

9₆

4₃

2206·1

5

2221
Golada
Cabo de
Sta María

1₁

Barra
Nova

3₃

7₈

58′

14
2208

2209

7₆

**CANAL DE
OLHAO**

3₁

*Depths in Metres*

5₄

See plan p.191

52′          51′          7°50′W          49′

1999 dredging was taking place in the approaches to the latter. If landing in the basin note that the pontoons are closed off by individual security gates, and that the entire east side is reserved for fishermen. The office of the *capitania* overlooks the north end of the basin, sharing its premises with a small maritime museum. Both are open 0930–1200 and 1430–1700, Monday to Friday only.

Facilities include water from taps beside the slipway on the quay between the basin and the marshes, and the possibility of showers at the Ginásio Clube Navale next door (which also has a snack-bar and upstairs restaurant – the only thing it does not appear to have is much to do with sailing!). In the same building is Nautifaro, ☎ 289 801282, the larger of Faro's two chandleries, the other being 50m or so along the same quay.

Diesel is available by can from a filling station on the landward side of the basin, with a petrol pump also situated by the chandlery. Numerous engineering and other concerns advertise their services along the railings which line the basin's seaward side.

Faro is the regional capital and has facilities to match, including banks, shops of all kinds, wining and dining spots, and medical services. Communications include a post office and numerous telephone kiosks, taxis, car hire, buses, trains (the station is close north of the smallcraft basin), and of course Faro International Airport, a couple of kilometres northwest as the egret flies, though rather more by road. Perhaps surprisingly, the aircraft noise is barely noticeable and there appears to be almost no flying at night.

If wishing to haul out for work or dry storage it would be well worth investigating the Quinta do Progresso boatyard, *Mobile* ☎ 91931 7171, an unpretentious but seemingly well-run concern some distance north of the anchorage. 'Bruce',

the helpful Portuguese owner/manager, speaks English, French and some German. There are on-site workshops for engineering, spars and rigging, though owners are welcome to do their own work, and stout metal cradles are available, as is paint, etc. When visited in November 1999 a slightly elderly 24 tonne capacity travel-lift was in use, but a massive 100 tonne version able to handle up to 8m beam was on order for the 2000 season. Access is currently limited by draught (up to 2·5m at high tide, with pilotage available up the channel from the anchorage), but in spite of being surrounded by the Parque Natural it is hoped that permission to dredge will soon be granted.

3. *Olhão* – the small yacht basin run by the Grupo Naval de Olhão is filled with local motorboats, and yachts are not permitted in the fishing harbour. However good anchorage can be found close west of the ferry jetty, itself immediately west of the yacht basin. Alternatively choose a spot to the east of the fish dock entrance and the flatbed ferry jetty, where less wash should be experienced.

In either case work in as depth allows, and consider laying two anchors to avoid swinging too close inshore. When calculating minimum water depths allow for the suction and surge created by fishing boats passing at speed. Land on the steps at either ferry jetty or in the smallcraft basin, though note that all the pontoons in the latter are closed off by security gates.

Facilities include water by can from taps at the Grupo Naval, where there is also a café/restaurant, the possibility of showers and a petrol pump. Diesel must be carried from a filling station on the road behind the Grupo Naval. The office of the *capitania* is directly behind the Grupo Naval building, a few doors along from the Selcampo fishing tackle shop and chandlery. The smallcraft basin has a very sheltered drying

The large fishing harbour at Olhão with the much smaller yacht basin on the left, seen from almost due east. Visiting yachts lie at anchor on both sides of the entrance.

The maze of channels leading to Fuzeta are only suited to multihulls or other very shoal draught yachts, but once there it is sheltered in the extreme.

grid – apply to the Grupo Naval – and in an emergency the services of engineers and electricians would certainly be available at the fishing harbour. There is a large supermarket and produce market conveniently close to the western dinghy landings, plus the usual banks, restaurants, post office, telephones, taxis, etc.

There has been talk of building a full-scale marina at Olhão, probably sited west of the western jetty, but as of late 1999 nothing had been finalised.

### Additional anchorage

The inlet of Fuzeta (37°03'N 7°43'W), some 15M east of Cabo de Santa María and included on Portuguese 'new series' chart *27503*, might be described as a smaller version of Olhão tucked behind broadly similar banks. Though very appealing it is feasible only for shoal-draught yachts or multihulls able to enlist local assistance for the approach. The inner banks appear to be largely of sand, rather than the mixture of mud and sand encountered further west, making drying out much more pleasant. The small town has all the usual facilities, including fuel at the fishermen's quay (up the narrow inlet, now marked by prominent red/white and green/white banded towers), and nearby shops and produce market. A small and somewhat ramshackle boatyard lies near the head of the creek.

# Tavira
37°07'N 7°37'W

### Tides
See Río Guadiana, page 201

### Charts

|  | Approach | Harbour |
|---|---|---|
| Admiralty | *89, 92* | |
| Portuguese (old series) | *8, 24* | |
| Portuguese (new series) | *23204, 24206* | *27503* |
| Spanish | *44B* | |

### Lights
*Approach*
2206 **Cabo de Santa María** 36°58'·4N 7°51'·8W
  Fl(4)17s49m25M
  White round tower and building 46m
*0979* Radiobeacon *SM* 305·5kHz 50M (3 & 4 in sequence)
2246 **Vila Real de Santo António** 37°11'·1N 7°24'·9W
  Fl.6·5s51m26M
  White round tower, very narrow black rings, red lantern 46m
*0981* Radiobeacon *VR* 305·5kHz 100M (5 & 6 in sequence)
*Harbour*
2234 **Ldg Lts on 326°** 37°07·3N 7°37'·3W
  *Front* **Armação** Fl.R.3s6m5M
  Red and white banded post 5m

2234·1 *Rear*, 132m from front, Iso.R.6s9m5M
  Red and white banded post 5m
2235 **West breakwater** 37°07'N 7°36'·9W
  Fl.R.2·5s7m7M White column, red bands 4m
2235·2 **East breakwater** 37°07'N 7°36'·9W
  Fl.G.2·5s5m6M White column, green bands 5m

## General

An attractive and very old town – one of its bridges claims Roman origins, and the only Greek inscription to be found in Portugal was discovered in nearby Santa Luzia – Tavira is still heavily dependant on fishing and in spite of an ever-growing tourist trade has managed to retain much of its character. Some of its old walls and many of its tiled houses remain, with wrought iron balconies and original decoration, overlooked by floodlit churches and a ruined castle.

The anchorage is connected to the town by a 2km causeway flanked by salt pans, and by the Rio Gilão which at high tide is navigable by dinghy. Once in the anchorage there is good protection from the sea, though little from the wind, and the current runs strongly. Not surprisingly the birdwatching possibilities are excellent.

## Approach

Between the Faro/Olhão entrance and Tavira the coast comprises a low sandbank, broken east of Olhão and again off Fuzeta. Fishing nets may be laid up to 1·5M offshore along this stretch of the coast.

Identification from a distance may be aided by a square tower topped by a low spire, surrounded by a series of long, low buildings, which stands almost directly inside the entrance. In late 1999 considerable renovation was taking place on the site – previously owned by the Companhia de Pescarias do Algarve – with old buildings being re-roofed and foundations for a large new building excavated.

## Entrance

The entrance is dredged from time to time and is currently said to have a least depth of around 2·5m, though shoal patches have been reported well offshore in the vicinity and (growing) banks extend beyond the breakwater heads on both sides. Both breakwaters are lit[2235, 2235·2], but it is not an entrance to be attempted at night. There are leading lights[2234] on 325°, but they should not be relied upon as the channel shifts.

Do not enter before half tide or at all if the swell is heavy – if wind and/or swell are onshore conditions become rougher on the ebb. The best time for either entering or for leaving is about one hour before high water.

Approach keeping the east face of the west breakwater just open. When almost up to the east breakwater – and with depths beginning to shoal – cross to the other side and favour the western shore until the anchorage is reached. When taking the sharp turn to port into the anchorage keep a sharp lookout for tourist ferries leaving or approaching the jetty on the corner.

The entrance to Tavira looking west-northwest. Yachts can be seen anchored in the Ria Tavira, with the ferry jetty, smallcraft harbour and mouth of the Rio Gilão behind.

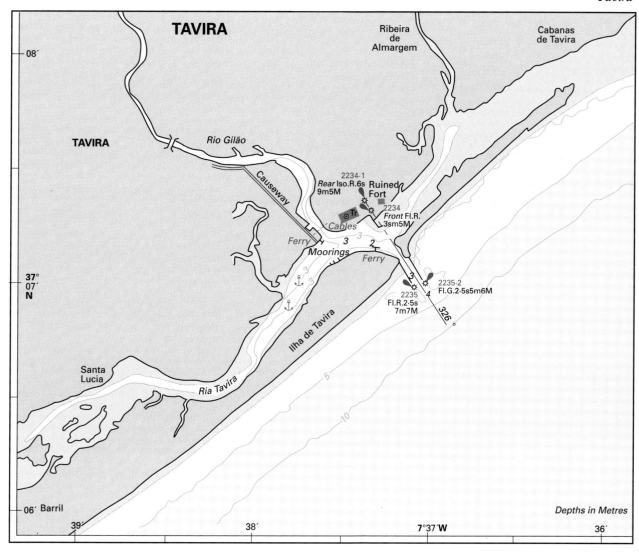

## Anchorage

The anchorage at Quatro Aguas ('four waters') south of the mainland ferry jetty, itself west of the Rio Gilão entrance, is now occupied by a scattering of moorings – see photo overleaf. Choose a spot beyond them, keeping well out of the channel. The bottom is foul in places and a trip line advised. Holding is good over sand, but the current runs strongly enough for most yachts to remain tide-rode even in contrary winds of 20 knots.

Alternatively continue southwest along the Ria Tavira towards Santa Lucia, again anchoring well clear of the fairway which is used by fishing boats day and night. Depths become shoal and it would be wise to prospect first by dinghy.

## Formalities

There is a manned *brigada fiscal* office next to the ferry jetty, but Tavira is not a port of entry/exit and passports cannot be stamped for departure (which in any case should only be necessary in the case of non-EU citizens). The *capitania* (open 0900–1230 and 1430–1800) is located in the town, close west of the fishing quay.

## Facilities

At the anchorage – water by can from the new Clube Náutico de Tavira, which also has showers and a small bar (seek permission before helping oneself to either of the former, as a small charge may be payable), plus several other bars and restaurants but no shops. The smallcraft harbour on the west bank just inside the Rio Gilão is too small, shallow and crowded to be feasible for a visiting yacht, and landing by dinghy at the single pontoon is impractical due to a locked security gate.

A square concrete barge lies on the beach immediately opposite the ferry jetty, against which it is possible to dry out to scrub, and in summer two or three seasonal cafés operate near the beach.

In the town – good shopping, banks, restaurants, hotels, etc. Diesel in cans from either the fishing quay or a filling station on the north bank of the river opposite the market. Some motorboat-orientated chandlery is to be found in an anonymous shop on the north bank of the river, one block northeast of the end of the cast-iron bridge.

The moorings and anchorage at Quatro Aguas on the Ria Tavira, looking north. The right-hand jetty serves the small ferries to the outer beaches, the left one belongs to the Clube Náutico de Tavira.

Looking across the shallow Rio Gilão at Tavira, one of the least spoiled towns on the Algarve coast.

## Communications

Post office and telephones in Tavira, as well as taxis, buses and trains. In summer a bus also runs down to the ferry jetty – check the noticeboard for times. Airport at Faro about 30km down the coast.

# Vila Real de Santo António, Ayamonte and the Río Guadiana

37°10'N 7°24'W

## Tides

*Reference port* Lisbon
*Mean time differences* (Portuguese time zone)
HW: −35 minutes ±20; LW: −20 minutes ±20

*Heights in metres*

| MHWS | MHWN | MLWN | MLWS |
|------|------|------|------|
| 3·2 | 2·5 | 1·3 | 0·5 |

## Charts

| | Approach | River |
|---|---|---|
| Admiralty | *89, 92* | |
| Portuguese (old series) | *8, 24* | *97* |
| Portuguese (new series) | *23204, 24206* | *26312* |
| Spanish | *44B, 441* | *441A* |

## Lights

### Approach

2246 **Vila Real de Santo António** 37°11'·1N 7°24'·9W
  Fl.6·5s51m26M
  White round tower, very narrow black rings, red
  lantern 46m

*0981* Radiobeacon *VR* 305·5kHz 100M (5 & 6 in
  sequence)

2312 **El Rompido** 37°13'·2N 7°07'·5W
  Fl(2)10s42m24M
  White round tower, pale grey bands 29m

### River

buoy **Starboard hand No.1** 37°09'N 7°23'·4W
  Q(3)G.6s4M Green pillar buoy, ▲ topmark

buoy **Port hand No.2** 37°09'·1N 7°23'·5W
  Fl.R.4s6M Red pillar buoy, ■ topmark

buoy **Port hand No.4** 37°09'·4N 7°23'·6W
  Fl.R.3s Red can buoy, ■ topmark

buoy **Starboard hand No.3** 37°09'·5N 7°23'·5W
  Q.G.4M Green pillar buoy, ▲ topmark

2249 **West breakwater** 37°09'·9N 7°23'·9W
  Fl.R.5s7m4M Red and white lattice tower 5m

2250 **East (submerged) training wall** 37°10'N
  7°23'·6W
  Fl.G.3s4M Concrete tower

2249·5 **Vila Real fish quay** 37°12'·2N 7°24'·8W
  F.R Red and white banded post 2m

2305 **Baluarte (Ayamonte)** 37°12'·8N 7°24'·6W
  Fl.G.3s3m3M
  Black and green framework tower, masonry base 6m

# Marina and port radio

*Doca de Recreio de Vila Real de Santo António* VHF Ch 12,
  16 & 20.
*Puerto Deportivo Ayamonte* VHF Ch 09.
*Capimarvireal* VHF Ch 11, 16 (0900–1200, 1400–1700
  Mon–Fri).

## General

The Río Guadiana forms part of the border between
Portugal and Spain. A suspension bridge spans the
river about 2M north of the twin towns of Vila Real
de Santo António and Ayamonte, though a
diminutive car ferry (which at first glance looks
more like a fishing boat) still carries local traffic
between the two towns. The river, which has strong
currents, is navigable to Pomarão some 25M
upstream and can make a pleasant change to
seafaring.

The bar can be rough on the ebb, particularly if
there is any swell running, and is hazardous in
onshore weather. When planning departure, take
into account the time taken to reach the bar and do
not be late.

Over the past few years facilities for yachts in the
river have improved dramatically, with a large new

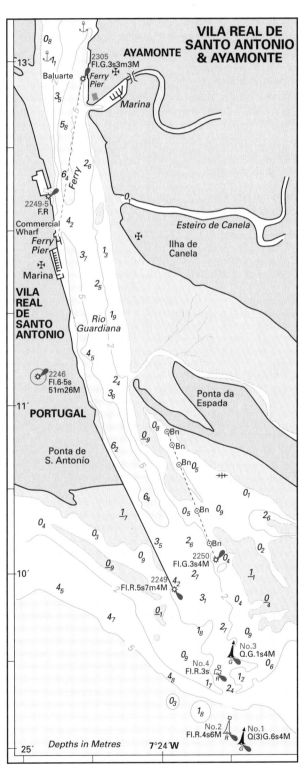

marina at Vila Real de Santo António on the Portuguese side and a smaller one, run by the Junta de Puertos de Andalucía, at Ayamonte on the Spanish side. In addition, facilities upstream have also improved, despite serious flood damage in 1997.

### Approach

Either side of the Río Guadiana the coast consists of a low sandbank broken by gaps giving access to the lagoons which run from west of Cabo de Santa María to 2M east of the Río Guadiana. Further east the sand continues unbroken for another 12M. Around the entrance to the Río Guadiana the 10m line lies about 2M offshore. Fishing nets may be laid up to 1·5M offshore.

Approaching from the west, two conspicuous marks are the high-rise buildings of Monte Gordo 2M west of the entrance and the tall Vila Real light[2246] (white with narrow black bands). From the east, the tower blocks of Isla Cristina stand out. The twin pillars of the suspension bridge are also conspicuous from offshore.

### Entrance

Do not attempt to enter other than at half flood or above (manoeuvring in the marina at Vila Real de Santo António is least traumatic at slack water), and be especially careful if there is any swell.

The river is canalised between a breakwater and a submerged training wall running 335°, their ends 550m apart and lit[2249, 2250]. Seaward of the walls are two pairs of port and starboard hand buoys, all lit (though the starboard hand buoys in particular have a reputation for unreliability and long periods off station).

Pass between the buoys and then head for the west breakwater, keeping it slightly open on the port bow. The east training wall is almost totally submerged, with a concrete tower[2250] marking its seaward end. Keep about 50m off the breakwater, remaining on the west side until off the town of Vila Real de Santo António.

The entrance to the Rio Guadiana looking north. Vila Real de Santo António (Portugal) lies on the left bank, with Ayamonte (Spain) a little beyond on the right. The twin towers of the suspension bridge can just be made out a few miles further upstream.

# Vila Real de Santo António (Portugal)

The town of Vila Real was largely rebuilt in the 18th century, following destruction in the 1755 earthquake and tidal wave which decimated Lisbon, and follows a strict grid plan with wide avenues and open squares. Even the much newer suburbs follow these lines – less interesting perhaps than the winding lanes of the older villages, but with considerably less scope for getting lost! All in all Vila Real is a pleasant town in which to wander, and has yet to be overtaken by serious tourism.

The new Doca de Recreio de Vila Real de Santo António, ☎/*Fax* 281 541571, was structurally complete by late 1997 and contains approximately 360 berths for yachts of up to 20m, all with finger pontoons. Depths of 4m or more will be found in the southern part of the basin, decreasing slightly to the north but with plenty throughout for the average cruising yacht. The marina office, open 0900–2000 daily in summer, and 0900–1400 and 1500–1830 daily in winter, currently occupies a portacabin at the north end of the basin but may move into the Associação Naval buildings at the other end when completed. The pontoons are protected by locked gates with the usual card access.

## Berthing

The narrow marina entrance – less than 20m wide – is situated at its downstream end, with a reception area just inside on the starboard hand. Both entrance and marina are subject to strong tidal cross-currents, making slack water by far the best time to manoeuvre, and once inside space is tight. Both sides of the entrance, as well as the upstream end of the fuel pontoon, are lit (Q.R, Q.G and Q.R respectively), but movement at night is to be avoided as it will be difficult to estimate and allow for the cross-current.

In 1999 the high season (16/6–15/9) rate for a visiting yacht of just under 12m was 1,700 escudos per night if her beam was less than 3·6m, 1,850 escudos if it was between 3·6m and 4m. The monthly low season (October–March) rates for yachts of similar dimensions were 29,250 escudos and 30,400 escudos respectively. Charges include water, but electricity is an additional 150 escudos per day or 2,500 escudos per month. Although quoted by the marina ex-VAT (at 17%), this has been added to the above figures for easy comparison with other harbours.

Yachts are no longer allowed to berth in the old Doca de Pesca about 0·5M upstream from the marina.

## Formalities

If the yacht is registered in the EU, and all her crew are EU nationals, completion of the usual multi-part form in the marina office is sufficient. Otherwise it will be necessary to visit the offices of the *policia maritima* and *imigração*, both of which are close by. Ask at the marina office for directions.

## Facilities

*Water* On the pontoons.
*Showers* Currently in portacabins next to the marina office, but likely to be found in the Associação Naval building when finished.
*Electricity* On the pontoons.
*Fuel* Diesel and petrol fuelling berth at the upstream end of the marina, but on the outer (ie. river) side.
*Clube náutico* The Associação Naval do Guadiana, previously situated next to the old fishing dock, will shortly move into new premises close south of the marina basin.
*Weather forecast* Posted daily at the marina office.
*Banks* In the town.
*Shops/provisioning/produce market* Good shopping of all kinds in the town.
*Cafés, restaurants & hotels* Several just across the road from the marina.
*Medical services* In the town.

## Communications

*Post office* In the town.
*Mailing address*
   c/o **Associação Naval do Guadiana**, Doca de Recreio, Avenida da República, 8900 Vila Real de Santo António, Algarve, Portugal
   ☎/*Fax service* 281 541571
*Public telephones* Several nearby.
*Car hire/taxis* In the town or via the marina office.
*Buses & trains* Both nearby – Vila Real is the eastern terminus of the Algarve coastal line.
*Ferries* Small but frequent passenger and car ferry to Ayamonte.
*Air services* Faro International Airport is some 60km distant by road or rail.

The new marina at Vila Real de Santo António (Portugal) looking northwest. The unusual grid plan of the town behind is unmistakeable.

## The Junta de Puertos de Andalucía marinas

One cannot cruise for very long on the Andalucían coast without encountering the string of yacht marinas and sport fishing harbours financed, built and run by the Junta de Puertos de Andalucía in Seville, ☎ 954 560744 *Fax* 954 561112, *e-mail* eppa@eppa.es. Currently there are eight yacht harbours on the Atlantic side, from Ayamonte on the Río Guadiana (the Portuguese/Spanish border), to Barbate, only 35M west of Gibraltar. Leaflets detailing the services available in each harbour, together with a small chart section showing the surrounding coastline and a plan of the marina itself, are available and it is worth collecting the entire set – Ayamonte, Isla Cristina, Mazagón, Chipiona, Rota, Puerto América (Cádiz), Sancti Petri and Barbate – at the first opportunity. The Junta de Puertos de Andalucía maintain a very useful website at www.puertosdeandalucia.com (versions in both Spanish and English) listing current berthing charges, etc.

Prices are standard for the entire chain in spite of widely differing facilities and appeal, but it appears that some discretion is allowed when it comes to charging for use of water and electricity. In 1999 a visiting yacht of just under 12m, with a beam of less than 4m, paid 2,915 ptas (17·52 euros) per night in the high season (1/6–30/9), or 1,457 ptas (8·76 euros) per night in the low season, decreasing slightly after the first three nights. A month in the low season for a yacht of similar size was 32,792 ptas (197·08 euros), payable in advance. Multihulls were charged 50% extra. Although quoted ex-VAT (at 16%), this has been added to the above figures for easy comparison with other harbours. *VISA* and other credit cards are accepted throughout the chain.

## Ayamonte (Spain)

The old fishermen's basin at Ayamonte now contains the westernmost of the string of yacht marinas and sport fishing harbours run by the Junta de Puertos de Andalucía – see text box. Though operational since April 1998 some facilities are still to be added and many would consider it overpriced for what is provided – and in the face of competition from across the river. However the town is attractive, and the marina well sheltered from the strong tidal currents which affect the Vila Real de Santo António facility.

The Puerto Deportivo Ayamonte, ☎/*Fax* 959 321694, *e-mail* ayamonted@eppa.es, currently consists of five pontoons containing 174 berths for (a few) yachts of up to 17m, with more pontoons planned. All berths are alongside fingers. Depths at the entrance are 4m or more, decreasing to 3m at the marina itself. Office hours are currently 0900–1400 and 1600–1900 (summer) and 0930–1400 and 1600–1800 (winter), and there is round-the-clock security in addition to electronic pontoon access gates.

### Berthing

The entrance is some 60m wide and suffers from strong cross-currents, but complete protection is gained once inside. Both sides of the entrance are lit (Q.G and Q.R), and in addition an unusual starboard hand beacon – a white lattice on a blue and cream base, with ▲ topmark – stands on the north side of the entrance.

Preferably call up before arrival on VHF Ch 09, otherwise secure to the westernmost hammerhead on first arrival, or failing that choose a suitable berth on the westernmost pontoon. Charges are at the standard Junta de Puertos de Andalucía rate – see text box.

### Formalities

As is usual in Spain formalities are very relaxed. After completing the usual paperwork in the marina office it is possible that an official may visit the yacht, though this is unlikely in the case of an EU yacht and crew.

### Facilities

*Engineers* Some mechanical skills available – enquire at the marina office.
*Chandlery* Not as such, but try the Camilo hardware store.
*Water* On the pontoons.
*Showers* In a portacabin next to the marina office.
*Launderette* On the north side of the marina basin.
*Electricity* On the pontoons
*Fuel* A detached pontoon has been positioned near the entrance to the basin and it is hoped that fuel pumps will be installed and functioning by 2000 or 2001.
*Bottled gas* Camping Gaz available in the town.
*Ice* At the marina office.
*Weather forecast* Posted daily outside the marina office.
*Banks* In the town.
*Shops/provisioning* Good shopping in the town, with a supermarket opposite the marina gates.
*Produce market* In the town.
*Cafés, restaurants & hotels* Plenty in the town, but as yet nothing at the marina itself.
*Medical services* In the town.

### Communications

*Post office* In the town.
*Mailing address*
c/o Puerto Deportivo Ayamonte, 21400 Ayamonte, Huelva, España
☎/*Fax service* 959 321694
*Public telephones* Beside the marina office and elsewhere.
*Car hire/taxis/buses* In the town.

*Ferries* Small but frequent passenger and car ferry to Vila Real de Santo António.

*Air services* Faro International Airport is some 65km distant by road, Seville approximately twice as far.

**Upriver** (see plan overleaf)

After passing under the rather elegant suspension bridge mentioned previously (clearance thought to be about 20m at high water, 22m at low water) the Río Guadiana is quiet, pretty and deep but has a current to be reckoned with – with the aid of the flood it is possible to make the 20M or so up to Portuguese Alcoutim and Spanish Sanlúcar de Guadiana on one tide. The river is not buoyed, other than a single red buoy marking shallows just downstream from the bridge, but is deep in the centre and on the outside of bends.

Although it could be unwise to venture upstream immediately after heavy rain further inland, which can send large items of floating debris such as branches, bamboo canes, etc careering downstream, there is general agreement that the upper reaches of the Río Guadiana are not to be missed. Claire

James, who plainly knows her birds, states that: 'White storks can regularly be seen on the lower reaches of the river above Ayamonte, and other interesting birds include cattle egrets, black-winged stilts and kingfishers. Red-rumped swallows, hoopoes, golden orioles and bee-eaters may be seen further upriver, and a flock of azure-winged magpies live close upstream of Alcoutim/Sanlúcar.'

The Spanish side is sparsely inhabited as far as Sanlúcar, but there are five small villages on the Portuguese side before reaching Alcoutim, including Foz de Odeleite, Guerreiros do Rio and Laranjeiras. In November 1997 a flash flood caused serious damage along the length of the river (it is rumoured that, due to lack of consultation, sluice gates were opened on both Portuguese and Spanish sides simultaneously) and many yachts were wrecked. The short pontoon at Foz de Odeleite was amongst the casualties but has since been rebuilt with water and electricity laid on – a small charge (less than 1000 escudos) is made for berthing. Free visitors' moorings have been positioned off all three villages.

The pontoons at Alcoutim and Sanlúcar also fell victim to the 1997 flood, though both have now

The new Junta de Puertos de Andalucía marina at Ayamonte (Spain) looking northwest, with the tall suspension bridge beyond. There are plans to extend the marina into the western part of the old fishermen's basin in due course.

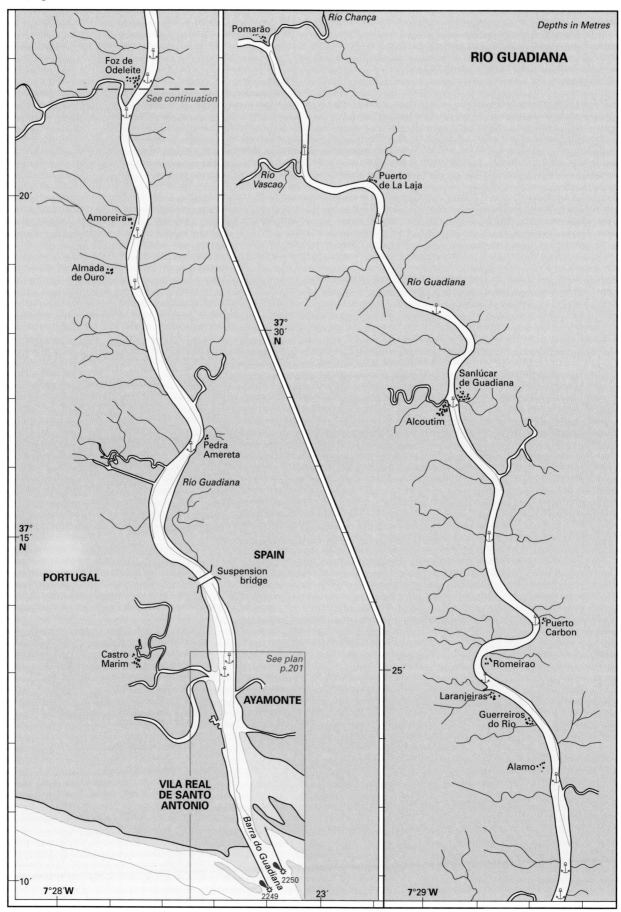

Depths in Metres

**RIO GUADIANA**

Río Chança

Pomarão

Foz de
Odeleite

*See continuation*

Río
Vascao

Puerto
de La Laja

20′

Amoreira

Almada
de Ouro

Río Guadiana

37°
30′
N

Sanlúcar
de Guadiana

Alcoutim

Pedra
Amereta

Río Guadiana

37°
15′
N

SPAIN

PORTUGAL

Suspension
bridge

25′

Puerto
Carbon

Castro
Marim

*See plan
p.201*

**AYAMONTE**

Romeirao

Laranjeiras

Guerreiros
do Rio

**VILA REAL
DE SANTO
ANTONIO**

Alamo

Barra do Guadiana

2250

2249

10′

7°28′W

23′

7°29′W

206

The attractive town of Alcoutim, some 20M up the Río Guadiana on the Portuguese side, with a few yachts alongside and others using the visitors' mooring buoys provided.

*Chris Knight*

been repaired with water and electricity again installed. Eight or so mooring buoys are provided on the Portuguese side, or it is possible to anchor off in 6m or more. Adjacent to the Sanlúcar pontoon are purpose-built showers and toilets for the use of berth-holders (key from the nearby *capitania*). Again, a small charge is made for berthing on either side of the river, whilst lying to the buoys is free. Both towns have basic shopping, cafés and bars, with a pedestrian ferry linking the two, but most agree that of the two Alcoutim is the more lively. Each has an impressive castle, but that of Sanlúcar dominates the scene.

A mudbank runs out from the west bank just north of Alcoutim – local advice is to keep well to starboard of the line of mooring buoys if heading upriver. With persistence most yachts can get as far as Pomarão, on the Portuguese side about 7M upstream of Alcoutim. This takes one past disused mine workings and derelict piers, once used by sizeable ore-carriers, but the river narrows and has silted in places (best water will generally be found on the eastern side). Particular caution should be exercised in the approach to Pomarão, which has numerous off-lying rocks and boulders as well as wreckage dating back to the 1997 flood. Two short pontoons, both provided with water and electricity, lie close under the town though the old facility on the far (south) side of the river is derelict. Charges are understood to be on a par with those further downstream

Intrepid owners may wish to continue beyond Pomarão towards Mertola, a sizeable Portuguese town, though as of 1999 a sand and shingle bar halted yachts a few miles downstream of the town, not even allowing sufficient depth to proceed by dinghy. This last stretch of the river runs between stony cliffs and is totally unspoilt. However rocks and sandbanks abound, the latter most often around the mouths of small tributary creeks, and navigation is strictly visual. The water comes straight off the mountains and is clear but very cold.

# Isla Cristina

37°11'N 7°20'W

## Tides

See Río Guadiana, page 201

## Charts

|  | Approach | River |
|---|---|---|
| Admiralty | 89, 92 | |
| Spanish | 44B, 441 | 441A |

## Lights

### Approach

2246 **Vila Real de Santo António** 37°11'·1N 7°24'·9W
Fl.6·5s51m26M
White round tower, very narrow black rings, red lantern 46m

0981 Radiobeacon *VR* 305·5kHz 100M (5 & 6 in sequence)

2312 **El Rompido** 37°13'·2N 7°07'·5W
Fl(2)10s42m24M
White round tower, pale grey bands 29m

### River and marina

2308 **Ldg Lts on 313°** 37°11'·6N 7°20'·4W
*Front* Q.8m5M Aluminium framework tower 7m

2308·1 *Rear*, 100m from front, Fl.4s13m5M
Aluminium framework tower 12m

buoy **Landfall buoy** 37°10'·6N 7°19'·4W
Fl.10s5M Pillar buoy, • topmark

*Note* In 1999 several (unlisted) port and starboard hand buoys were placed between the landfall buoy and the breakwater extremes

2307 **West breakwater** 37°10'·9N 7°19'·6W
VQ(2)R.5s7m4M Red framework tower 4m

buoy **Starboard hand** *No.3* 37°11'N 7°19'·5W
Fl.G.6s3M Green pillar buoy, ▲ topmark

*Note* Replaces beacon marking end of east breakwater

buoy **Starboard hand** *No.5* 37°11'·5N 7°20'·2W
Fl(3)G.9s Green conical buoy

buoy **Starboard hand** *No.6* 37°11'·6N 7°20'·2W
Fl(4)G.11s4M Green pillar buoy

buoy **Starboard hand** *No.7* 37°11'·7N 7°20'·1W
Fl.G.5s Green conical buoy

buoy **Port hand** *No.8* 37°11'·8N 7°19'·8W
Fl(2)R.8s4M Red can buoy

buoy **Port hand** *No.9* 37°11'·9N 7°19'·7W
Q.R.4M Red pillar buoy

2310 **Marina, south mole** 37°11'·9N 7°19'·6W
Q.G.5m2M Green column 2m

2311 **Marina, north mole** 37°11'·9N 7°19'·6W
Q.R.5m2M Red column 2m

pontoon **Marina wavebreak pontoon** 37°11'·9N 7°19'·6W
Fl.Or Red over green drum on post

*Note* The tall white building on Punta del Caimán just south of the marina entrance is NOT a light structure but an apartment block.

## Marina radio

*Puerto Deportivo Isla Cristina* VHF Ch 09.

## General

Once purely a fishing port, Isla Cristina on its long sandspit to the east of the Ría de la Higuerita is rapidly being developed for tourism – much of it Spanish – and its marina was one of the first built by the Junta de Puertos de Andalucía – see page 204. Even so, few of the buildings surrounding it are either complete or occupied, and there are relatively few facilities on site. However the old town a short walk away is attractive and the waterfront interesting, particularly the thriving fishing harbour.

The marina is approached up a sinuous, shoal and changing channel flanked on one side by marsh and on the other by abandoned and beached fishing boats; it is best tackled in calm weather, in daylight and at half or three-quarter flood.

### Approach

The entrance to the Ría de la Higuerita is 3·6M east of the entrance to the Guadiana[2246] and 9·5M west of the light at El Rompido[2312]. The water between the Guadiana and the *ría* is shoal and the 5m line lies more than 1·5M off Isla Canela, the low-lying land immediately to the east of the Guadiana.

Although both Isla Canela and Isla Cristina are low-lying, tower blocks on both sides of the entrance show up well from seaward. Near the southwest corner of Punta del Caimán will be seen a tall beige building complete with domed superstructure, looking for all the world like a rather fancy lighthouse. In fact it is yet another apartment block – but a fine daymark. An older tower, the Torre Catalán, lies halfway between Isla Cristina and Rompido.

A fish haven has been established about 2·5M southeast of the entrance.

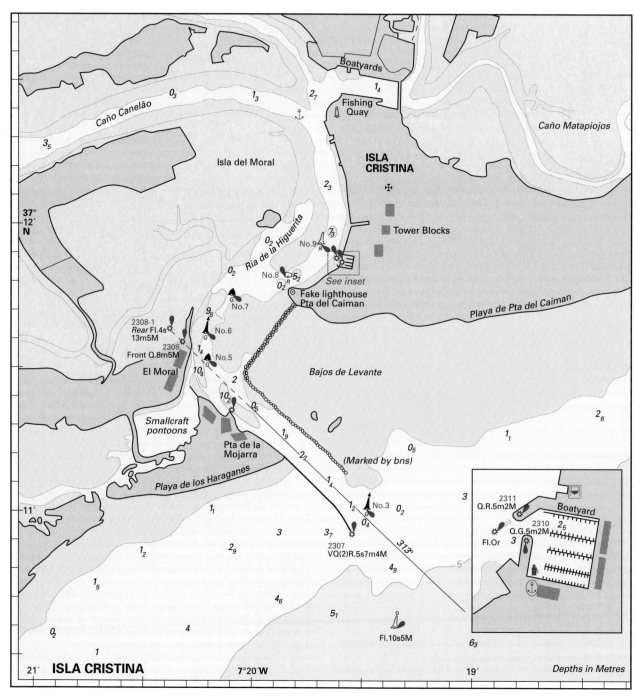

ISLA CRISTINA

*Depths in Metres*

The entrance to the Ría de la Higuerita – which gives access to Isla Cristina – looking northwest. The tall white apartment block mentioned in the text stands on the right, looking for all the world like a major lighthouse.

## Entrance

Approach from the south, preferably at between half and three-quarter flood, and turn in to run parallel with the west breakwater. The deeper water is on the western side of the channel. Follow the leading marks[2308] on 313° – the grey framework towers resemble electricity pylons and can be difficult to distinguish from offshore.

The channel bends to starboard, with a drying middle ground marked by a starboard hand buoy which must not be ignored. Similarly a port hand buoy almost opposite the marina entrance marks a second sandbank. In 1998 a low wavebreak pontoon was laid off the marina entrance – desperately needed since few fishing boats take any notice of the 4 knot speed limit.

## Berthing

The relatively narrow entrance to Puerto Deportivo Isla Cristina, ☎/*Fax* 959 343501, *e-mail* islacristinad@eppa.es, lies inside the wavebreak pontoon described above, with squat red and green

Puerto Deportivo Isla Cristina from the southwest, showing the low wavebreak pontoon which has recently be installed to protect the entrance from fishing boat wash.

structures[2310] on either side. Depth at the entrance is 3m, with 2–2·5m inside. Secure to the reception/fuel pontoon immediately to starboard to be allocated a berth – preferably having already called up on VHF Ch 09. Larger yachts are usually placed in the northern part of the harbour, and most of the 203 berths have finger pontoons. As of late 1999 the pontoons were not fitted with electronic gates, though these were due to be installed.

Office hours vary from summer to winter, being 0930–1400 and 1600–1800 daily in the latter and longer in the former. There is 24 hour security throughout the year.

In late 1999 a smallcraft harbour was under construction on the west bank of the river near the Isla Canela development (itself close to the root of the west breakwater). However it is understood to be a private facility for the apartment owners, and in any case the finger pontoons are too short, and the basin almost certainly too shallow, to accept a cruising yacht of any size.

### Anchorage

It is possible to anchor further up the river, almost opposite the Doca de Pescuero at the junction with the Caño Canelão, as far west as water permits. However the area is subject to wash from the quite heavy traffic – which, like that at many busy ports, tends to make its approach and departure at full speed.

### Formalities

Whether arriving from Spain or Portugal a single-sheet form is completed at the marina office, a copy of which is automatically passed to the authorities. Nothing further needs to be done, though if the yacht is non-EU registered or there are non-EU nationals aboard one or more sets of officials may visit.

### Facilities

*Boatyard* An area of gated hardstanding near the travel-lift enables owners to do their own maintenance or to call in one of the individual concessions set up in the area. These include Nautica Levante SYS, ☎ 959 332730 *Fax* 959 332797, which advertises a wide range of services including maintenance and repairs to GRP, timber and steel; and Y.LEC, ☎/*Fax* 959 343259, also specialising in general yacht maintenance.

For more serious work it would be worth contacting Astilleros Conrado Moreno SL, ☎/*Fax* 959 331795, a large building and repair yard on the north side of the fishing harbour. Fishing vessels of considerable size are moulded in GRP, though work can also be carried out in timber and steel. One of the several marine railways would be capable of handling all but the very largest yachts.

*Travel-lift* 32 tonne capacity lift at the marina.

*Engineers* Nautica Levante SYS (see above), and Onumar Nautica SL in the same area, agent for various popular makes of engine.

*Electronic & radio repairs* Worth trying Nautica Levante SYS, otherwise Astilleros Conrado Moreno SL install and service sophisticated electronics.

*Sailmaker/sail repairs* Nautica Levante SYS (see above), who can also handle rigging.

*Chandlery* Nothing at the marina, but at least two fishing-orientated chandlers near the fishing harbour plus various ironmongers, etc.

*Water* On the pontoons.

*Showers* At the rear of the marina complex.

*Launderette* In the town.

*Electricity* On the pontoons.

*Fuel* Diesel and petrol available at the fuel/reception berth.

*Bottled gas* Camping Gaz available in the town.

*Ice* At the marina office.

*Club náutico* The *club náutico* overlooking the marina closed in October 1999. It is not yet known if anything will replace it.

*Weather forecast* Posted daily at the marina office.

*Banks* In the town.

*Shops/provisioning* All usual shops in the town, but a long walk. Nothing – not even a bakery – nearby.

*Cafés, restaurants & hotels* Single café/bar overlooking the marina, but no restaurant. Both are easily found in the older part of the town, with hotels mainly centred in the newer beachside areas.

*Medical services* In the town.

### Communications

*Post office* In the town.

*Mailing address*
    c/o **Puerto Deportivo Isla Cristina**, Officina del Puerto, 21410 Isla Cristina, Huelva, España.
    *Fax service* 959 345501

*Public telephones* Kiosk near the marina office, with others in the town.

*Car hire/taxis* Available in the town or via the marina office.

*Buses* To Ayamonte, Huelva and beyond.

*Air services* International airports at Faro (Portugal) and Seville (Spain).

## El Rompido
37°13'N 7°07'W

### Tides
See Mazagón, page 215

### Charts

| | Approach | River |
|---|---|---|
| Admiralty | 89, 90, 92 | |
| Spanish | 44B, 441 | 441B |

### Lights

#### Approach
2246 **Vila Real de Santo António** 37°11'·1N 7°24'·9W
    Fl.6·5s51m26M
    White round tower, very narrow black rings, red lantern 46m
0981 Radiobeacon VR 305·5kHz 100M (5 & 6 in sequence)

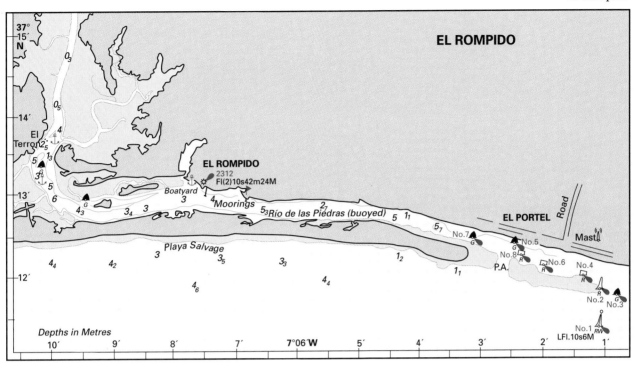

2312 **El Rompido** 37°13'·2N 7°07'·5W
  Fl(2)10s42m24M
  White round tower, page grey bands 29m
2320 **Picacho** 37°08'·2N 6°49'·5W
  Fl(2+4)30s51m25M
  White tower with brick corners, as has building, 25m

### River

Situation as of November 1999, but see also Entrance below.
buoy **Fairway No.1** 37°11'·5N 7°01'·1W
  LFl.10s6M
*Listed* Red and white vertical striped pillar buoy, •
  topmark
*Actual* In November 1999 this buoy was a large can
  rather than a true pillar, covered with a peeling
  rainbow of red, yellow, green and white paint. It had
  been in a similar state when seen two years
  previously.
buoy **Starboard hand No.3** 37°11'·9N 7°00'·9W
  Fl.G.5s3M Green conical buoy
buoy **Port hand No.2** 37°12'N 7°01'·1W
  Fl.R.5s3M Red pillar buoy
buoy **Port hand No.4** 37°12'·1N 7°01'·3W
  Fl(2)R.10s3M Red can buoy
buoy **Port hand No.6** 37°12'·4N 7°01'·9W
  Fl(3)R.15s3M Red can buoy
buoy **Port hand No.8** 37°12'·5N 7°02'·4W
  Fl(4)R.20s3M Red can buoy
buoy **Starboard hand No.5** 37°12'·3N 7°02'·5W
  Fl(2)G.10s2M Green conical buoy
buoy **Starboard hand No.7** 37°12'·4N 7°03'·1W
  Fl(3)R.15s3M Green conical buoy
Further buoys mark the channel, but all – including the
above – are moved from time to time as the channel and
its surrounding sandbanks shift. The main entrance has
migrated nearly 1M eastwards over the past five years.

### Boatyard and yacht club radio

*Varadero Río Piedras* and *Club Náutico Río Piedras* VHF Ch
  09. Neither maintain set listening hours.

### General

Most cruising yachtsmen would agree that El
Rompido offers one of the most attractive
anchorages along this stretch of the coast, but before
gaining its tranquil interior the difficult, twisting bar
must be negotiated – see Entrance, below. The
anchorage below the lighthouse is some 6M from
the entrance, and the river, separated from the sea
by a sand ridge steadily growing eastwards, seems
more like a lagoon than a river. The Club Náutico
Río Piedras is friendly though a little way from the
town proper, while the Varadero Río Piedras SA,
run by Wolfgang Michalsky, is highly recommended
for all yacht repairs as well as possible winter lay-up.
Otherwise shore facilities are limited but growing.

### Approach

From the west, the shoreline is unbroken between
Isla Cristina and El Rompido with a daymark, the
Torre Catalán, on the higher dunes west of the point
where the Río de las Piedras turns inland. From this
tower to the entrance – some 7M – the river runs
parallel to the shore behind a low sandbank, the
Playa Salvage.

To the east, the beach is backed by dunes rising
up to 40m and topped by umbrella pines. The
entrance, almost 6M east of El Rompido light,
currently lies about 1M east of a conspicuous
television mast close to a road running inland (the
markers for the entrance in 1995).

A fish haven centred on a spot about 3M south of
the entrance and measuring a good 2M square is
shown on Admiralty Charts *89*, *90* and *92*, but as
clearance over it is 5m+ it should not concern many
yachts.

The long sandspit at the entrance to the Río Piedras (El Rompido), looking northeast. The shallow bar extends a considerable distance further east, and as of 1999 the landfall buoy was positioned almost 2M from the end of the visible sand.

## Entrance

*Note* The buoyage detailed below was in place as of January 2000, but may have changed radically by later in the season. A secondary entrance carrying much the same depths had opened up well to the west of the buoyed entrance – see plan – and representations were being made to the authorities in Huelva to move the buoyage to this new gap. Yachtsmen are recommended to telephone Wolfgang Michalsky (who speaks fluent English) at the Varadero Río Piedras SA, ☎ 959 399026, for up-to-date information.

Currently the entrance is marked by a red and white striped buoy (though see Lights above), with eight or more channel buoys marking the entrance and river. All are moved around from time to time as the channel and its surrounding sandbanks shift. The shallowest part of the bar lies between the fairway buoy and the 'gate' formed by buoys *No.2* and *No.3*, and is said to carry a scant 1m at low water springs (though a generous 4m at high water).

Once over the bar the channel lies unnervingly close to the beach – watch out for swimmers! – for nearly 2M until through the second 'gate' of buoys, *No.8* and *No.5*, and approaching *No.7*. (If the western entrance replaces the current one this entire stretch will be avoided.) Once inside the end of the land proper the channel widens, though the buoys should still be observed.

While multihulls and other shallow-draft vessels should not encounter problems, owners of deep-keeled craft – particularly if attempting to enter in less than perfect conditions – may be able to arrange with Wolfgang to be 'talked in' (using either VHF Ch 09 or, increasingly, mobile phone) by an English-speaking member of his staff who has previously driven to the entrance. This service is free to those intending to use his boatyard, other yachts are charged a small fee.

## Anchorage and moorings

Anchor on the north side of the river as moorings and draught permit, or negotiate a mooring with Wolfgang Michalsky – the boatyard controls fifteen moorings of up to 3m draught, capable of holding 60–80 tonnes – though it may be necessary to book. The boatyard has a small floating jetty at which it is possible to land by dinghy. There are other moorings further downstream but nearly all are occupied by local craft.

Alternatively, continue upstream to anchor off the village of El Terron, where water and basic shopping are available. Holding is said to be good.

## Facilities

*Boatyard, engineers, electronic & radio repairs* Wolfgang Michalsky's Varadero Río Piedras SA, ☎ 959 399026 *Fax* 959 399034, *e-mail* michalsky@interbook.net, is situated just upstream of the long hammerhead jetty, almost directly below the lighthouse. It claims to be one of the largest private boatyards in southern Spain and has a reputation for helpfulness and efficiency.

Employees or subcontractors can handle repairs in timber, GRP and metals including stainless steel and aluminium. Alternatively owners can do their own work. There are on-site mechanical and electronics workshops, plus an agency for Volvo, Nautech and Lewmar. Michalsky himself speaks excellent English and is a Lloyds surveyor. The boatyard is also reported as a good place for winter lay-up, though space is limited.

*Travel-lift* The boatyard's marine railway can handle vessels of up to 100 tonnes and 6m beam.

*Sailmaker/sail repairs* Olivier Plisson, ☎ 959 399267, handles sail repairs and general canvaswork.

*Chandlery* Well-stocked chandlery at the boatyard.

*Water* By can from the boatyard or the Club Náutico de Río Piedras (where there is a coin-operated tap on the pontoon).

*Showers* At the boatyard (free to those using yard moorings, otherwise a small charge) or at the Club Náutico de Río Piedras.

*Launderette* Washing machine at the boatyard. Timing and fee negotiable.

*Fuel* At the hammerhead jetty east of the boatyard, which has separate pumps for fishing boat and yacht diesel.

*Ice* At the *club náutico*.

*Club náutico* The Club Náutico de Río Piedras, ☎ 959 399349 *Fax* 959 399217, occupies a slightly isolated site some distance downstream from the town and has its own hammerhead pontoon, plus a very pleasant terrace bar/restaurant.

*Weather forecast* May be available at the boatyard on request.

*Bank* In the town, including a cash machine at the west end of the old quarter.

*Shops/provisioning* Several small supermarkets.

*Produce market* On the main square.

*Cafés, restaurants* A profusion in the old part of the town, including restaurants serving excellent seafood. Hotels are mostly to be found in the newer area to the east.

*Medical services* In the town.

## Communications

*Post office* In the town.

*Mailing address* A yachtsman himself, Wolfgang Michalsky is willing to hold mail for visiting boats whether or not they will be using his facilities.
c/o **Varadero Río Piedras SA**, 21459 El Rompido, Cartaya/Huelva, España.

*Fax service* 959 399034 by arrangement

*Public telephones* Several throughout the town.

*Taxis* Best ordered by phone.

*Buses* To Huelva, for connection with trains to Seville, etc.

*Air services* International airports at Faro and Seville.

El Rompido, some 5M from the mouth of the Río Piedras, seen from the southeast. The fishermen's jetty and that of the Varadero Río Piedras are at upper left, that of the Club Náutico de Río Piedras inside the rows of moorings on the right.

# Punta Umbria

37°10'N 6°57'W

## Tides

See Mazagón, opposite

## Charts

|  | Approach | River |
|---|---|---|
| Admiralty | 90, 92 | 83 |
| Spanish | 44B, 441 | 441B, 4413 |

## Lights

### Approach

2312 **El Rompido** 37°13'·2N 7°07'·5W
  Fl(2)10s42m24M
  White round tower, pale grey bands 29m
2320 **Picacho** 37°08'·2N 6°49'·5W

Fl(2+4)30s51m25M
White tower with brick corners, as has building, 25m
2345 **Higuera** 37°00'·6N 6°34'·1W
  Fl(3)20s46m20M Masonry tower 24m

### River

buoy **Channel No.1** 37°09'·7N 6°57'·1W
  VQ(6)+LFl.10s5M
  South cardinal buoy, ⧩ topmark
2315 **Breakwater head** 37°09'·8N 6°56'·8W
  VQ(6)+LFl.10s9m5M
  Black tower, yellow top, ⧩ topmark 4m
buoy **No.2** 37°10'·4N 6°56'·6W
  Q.5M North cardinal buoy, ⧩ topmark
2316 **Yacht club jetty** 37°10'·5N 6°57'W
  Fl(3)G.15s6m3M Green post 3m
2317 **Ferry jetty** 37°10'·8N 6°57'·3W
  Fl(2)G.10s7m3M Green post 3m
Plus several more lights further upstream.

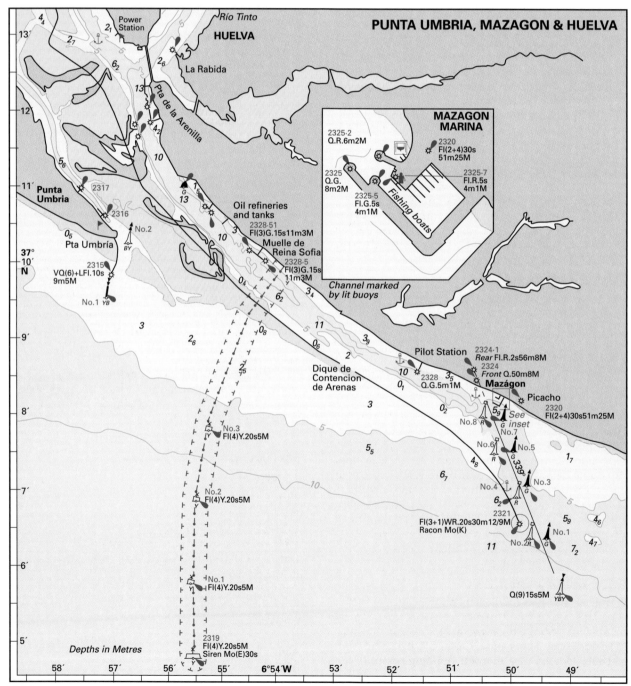

The long curved breakwater at Punta Umbría, looking northwest. The pontoons and moorings administered by the Club Marítimo de Tenis de Punta Umbría can be seen on the port side beyond several large apartment blocks.

## Marina radio

*Punta Umbría Club* VHF Ch 09.

## General

Once a small fishing village, of which there are still traces to be found upstream from the busy fishing quay, and with some elegant (and a few ostentatious) houses lining the riverbank, the bulk of Punta Umbría now consists of the inevitable high-rise flats. Its advantages include convenient shopping with several large supermarkets. However it may not prove as peaceful as expected, as the fishing fleet are reported to start leaving at 0430 and keep passing until dawn.

## Approach and entrance

The breakwater[2315] extends 0·5M offshore – see plan. At the time of writing best water was to be found close east of the breakwater, but the sandbanks frequently shift. The main channel carries no more than 1·5m at low water – enter at half flood. A restricted area containing a tanker loading berth and associated pipeline extends almost 5M offshore close east of the entrance.

In theory it is also possible to approach from the Huelva direction, via the Estero del Burro (which runs northwest from opposite the Real Club Marítimo de Huelva), the Estero del Burrillo and the Canal de Saltés. However there is an unmanned lifting bridge across the Estero del Burro with an estimated clearance of about 12m at high water when closed, and though the Huelva harbour pilots can arrange for it to be opened (24 hours' notice required), it is hard to believe that they would take very kindly to the request.

## Anchorage and moorings

The channel is largely occupied by moorings with very little space left in which to anchor. It may be possible to arrange for a mooring through the Club Marítimo de Tenis de Punta Umbría, ☎ 959 311899, located in a maroon building opposite the southernmost jetty, from which a pontoon extends upriver with a further detached pontoon outside it. It might also be possible to secure alongside for a short period if space is available. However in all cases allow for the strength of the ebb tide, which may reach 4–5 knots at springs even close in to the shore.

## Facilities

Water from a standpipe on the jetty of the *club maritimo*, which has the usual bar and restaurant.

Further upstream, past the ferry and fishing boat jetties, lie a cluster of workshops and several boatyards including the busy Nauticas Punta Umbría SA where many local yachts are wintered ashore. The yard is served by a good-sized marine railway, is able to handle most types of yacht and engine maintenance and has some chandlery available. Security – the variety with teeth – appears to be excellent. Their premises are shared by Shanty Sails, ☎ 959 310700, while close by is Nauti-Ria SL, specialising in engine repairs and an anonymous and slightly ramshackle yard building large wooden fishing boats. On the track behind is a large and cavernous supermarket.

# Mazagón

37°08'N 6°50'W

## Tides

*Reference port* Lisbon
*Mean time differences* (at Huelva bar)
HW: +10 minutes ±10; LW: +35 minutes ±5
(the above allows for the difference in time zones)
*Heights in metres*

| MHWS | MHWN | MLWN | MLWS |
| --- | --- | --- | --- |
| 3·2 | 2·5 | 1·2 | 0·4 |

## Charts

| | Approach | Harbour |
| --- | --- | --- |
| Admiralty | 90, 92 | 83 |
| Spanish | 44B, 441 | 4413 |

## Lights

### Approach
2312 **El Rompido** 37°13'·2N 7°07'·5W
 Fl(2)10s42m24M
 White round tower, pale grey bands 29m
2320 **Picacho** 37°08'·2N 6°49'·5W
 Fl(2+4)30s51m25M
 White tower with brick corners, as has building, 25m
2345 **Higuera** 37°00'·6N 6°34'·1W
 Fl(3)20s46m20M Masonry tower 24m

### Restricted area
2319 **Tanker loading berth** 37°04'·8N 6°55'·5W
 Fl(4)Y.20s8M Yellow superbuoy Siren Mo(E)30s
buoy **Pipeline marker No.1** 37°05'·6N 6°55'·3W
 Fl(4)Y.20s5M Yellow buoy, × topmark
buoy **Pipeline marker No.2** 37°06'·8N 6°55'·1W
 Fl(4)Y.20s5M Yellow buoy, × topmark
buoy **Pipeline marker No.3** 37°08'N 6°54'·8W
 Fl(4)Y.20s5M Yellow buoy, × topmark

### Rivermouth
2321 **Breakwater head** 37°06'·5N 6°49'·9W
 Fl(3+1)WR.20s30m12/9M 165°-W-100°-R-125°
 White round tower, red band 27m
 Racon Mo(K) 360° 12M
buoy **Channel** 37°05'·6N 6°49'·2W
 Q(9)15s5M West cardinal buoy, ⚡ topmark
2324 **Ldg Lts on 339°**
 37°08'·5N 6°50'·6W *Front* Q.50m8M
 Red square on red and white chequered tower 10m
2324·1 *Rear*, 158m from front, Fl.R.2s56m8M
 Red square on red and white chequered tower 11m
buoy **Port hand No.2** 37°06'·3N 6°49'·6W
 Fl.R.5s4M Red pillar buoy, ■ topmark
buoy **Starboard hand No.1** 37°06'·4N 6°49'·4W
 Fl.G.5s4M Green pillar buoy, ▲ topmark
buoy **Port hand No.4** 37°06'·9N 6°49'·9W
 Fl (2)R.10s3M Red pillar buoy, ■ topmark

buoy **Starboard hand No.3** 37°07'N 6°49'·7W
 Fl(2)G.10s3M Green pillar buoy, ▲ topmark
buoy **Port hand No.6** 37°07'·6N 6°50'·2W
 Fl(3)R.15s3M Red pillar buoy, ■ topmark
buoy **Starboard hand No.5** 37°07'·6N 6°50'W
 Fl(3)G.15s3M Green pillar buoy, ▲ topmark
buoy **Starboard hand No.7** 37°07'·9N 6°50'·2W
 Fl(4)G.20s4M Green pillar buoy, ▲ topmark
buoy **Port hand No.8** 37°07'·9N 6°50'·4W
 Fl(4)R.20s4M Red pillar buoy, ■ topmark

### Marina
2325 **Southwest breakwater head** 37°08'N 6°50'·1W
 Q.G.8m2M Grey framework on green base 4m
2325·2 **Northeast breakwater head** 37°08'N 6°50'W
 Q.R.6m2M Grey framework on red base 4m
2325·5 **Southwest breakwater spur** 37°08'N 6°50'W
 Fl.G.5s4m1M Grey framework on green base 4m
2325·7 **Reception quay** 37°08'N 6°49'·9W
 Fl.R.5s4m1M Grey framework on red base 3m

## Marina radio
*Puerto Deportivo Mazagón* VHF Ch 09.

## General
Another of the new harbours built and run by the Junta de Puertos de Andalucía – see page 204 – Puerto Deportivo Mazagón, ☎/Fax 959 376237, e-mail mazagond@eppa.es, is somewhat larger than most. It opened in July 1993, but even so building was still in progress six years later and, judging by the amount of empty space within the perimeter fence, this aspect of the project is still a long way from complete. There is an excellent (and surprisingly clean) beach right next to the marina, with a quiet and leafy town a steepish walk up the road.

Puerto Deportivo Mazagón at the entrance to the Ría de Huelva, see from the south.

## Approach and entrance

Pine-topped sand cliffs stretch from the light at El Rompido[2312] to the tower blocks at Punta Umbría. From this point, the last 6·5M of very low shore is backed by the breakwater – one of the longest in Europe – ending with the light[2321]. A restricted area containing a tanker loading berth and associated pipeline extends almost 5M offshore about 4·5M west of the rivermouth. Anchoring and fishing are banned in the vicinity, but vessels may pass inside the buoys.

To the east, for some 20M the shore is backed by sand dunes ending at the resort town of Matalascañas which has prominent radio aerials. A firing range – which is not marked on the Admiralty chart – exists inshore from about 5M southeast of Mazagón to near Matalascañas, a distance of some 12M. When active, a Range Safety Vessel will call up any craft straying into the area on VHF Ch 16 with instructions to keep clear.

On closer approach, Mazagón marina will be seen on the starboard hand about 1M inside the breakwater end[2321]. The entrance, which is lit[2325], carries at least 4·5m as far as the reception pontoon, which is on the port hand below the prominent tower housing the marina offices.

## Berthing

Berth alongside the reception pontoon, where diesel and petrol are available. If arriving outside office hours (which vary according to the time of year) the security staff will allocate a berth. Eight pontoons take yachts of up to 20m, with the larger to the south (in 3·5m or more) and smaller further north (2·5m or less). All pontoon berths are equipped with fingers. Yachts of between 20 and 30m LOA lie alongside the southwest breakwater, the outer part of which appears to have been colonised by fishing boats. Charges are at the standard Junta de Puertos de Andalucía rate – see page 204 – and, as at nearly all their marinas, security is excellent.

## Anchorages

See under Huelva, page 218.

## Facilities

*Boatyard* Not as such, though there is a large area of rather windswept hardstanding and several workshops run as individual enterprises, with more currently being built. Alternatively owners are welcome to do their own work.
*Travel-lift* 32 tonne capacity hoist.
*Engineers* Naupri and others, offering repairs and maintenance to both yachts and engines.
*Sailmaker/sail repairs* The marina office will contact Shanty Sails, ☎ 959 310700, in Punta Umbría.
*Chandlery* Two chandleries amongst the shops on the northwest quay, both small but reasonably well stocked.
*Charts* Spanish charts are available in Huelva from **Valnáutica SL – Idamar SA**, Avenida Enlace, 16 ☎ 959 250999 *Fax* 959 250214.
*Water* On the pontoons.
*Showers* At the rear of the shops near to the marina office.

*Launderette* Machines due for installation by 2000 – currently there are facilities for hand washing only.
*Electricity* On the pontoons.
*Fuel* Diesel and petrol at the reception/fuel berth.
*Ice* From either the marina office or one of the bars.
*Club náutico* The blue and white tiled Club Náutico de Mazagón looks strangely like an up-ended swimming pool (which it has, plus a tennis court, both available to visitors for a nominal fee). It also offers the more usual restaurant, etc.
*Weather forecast* Posted daily at the marina office.
*Banks* In the town.
*Shops/provisioning* Small general shop with some food and drink items in the marina complex, otherwise good shopping in the town (but some distance away).
*Cafés, restaurants & hotels* Several cafés and restaurants in the marina complex, with more in the town.
*Medical services* In the town.

### Communications

*Post office* In the town.
*Mailing address*
c/o **Oficina del Puerto**, Puerto Deportivo Mazagón, 21130 Mazagón, Palos de la Frontera, Huelva, España
*Fax service* 959 376237
*Public telephones* One in the marina complex with many more in the town.
*Car hire/taxis* Can be arranged via the marina office.
*Buses* In the town, connecting with trains at Huelva.
*Air services* About equidistant between Faro and Seville.

# Huelva

37°06'·5N 6°49'·9W

### Tides

*Reference port* Lisbon
*Mean time differences* (at Muelle de Fabrica)
HW: +15 minutes ±10; LW: +45 minutes ±5
(the above allows for the difference in time zones)
*Heights in metres*

| MHWS | MHWN | MLWN | MLWS |
|---|---|---|---|
| 3·5 | 2·7 | 1·2 | 0·5 |

### Charts

| | Approach | River |
|---|---|---|
| Admiralty | 90, 92 | 83 |
| Spanish | 44B, 441 | 4413 |

### Lights

***Approach*** – as for Mazagón
***River***
2328 **Muelle de la Barra** 37°08'·6N 6°51'·5W
Q.G.5m1M Green post
2328·5 **Muelle de Reina Sofia, SE end**
37°10'N 6°54'·2W Fl(3)G.15s11m3M
Green column on dolphin 7m
2328·51 **Muelle de Reina Sofia, NW end**
37°10'·1N 6°54'·4W Fl(3)G.15s11m3M
Green column on dolphin 7m

Ten pairs of lateral buoys (all lit) mark the deep channel of the Ría de Huelva. There are many more lit structures further upstream.

### Port radio

*Huelva Barra Prácticos/Huelva Puerto Prácticos* VHF Ch 06, 11, 12, 14, 16 (24 hours).

### General

Apart from a few buildings of interest, Huelva's main claim to a place in history is based on its links with Columbus, who prepared for his voyages here (possibly because he had relatives nearby with whom he could leave his son Diego). There is a large statue of Columbus near the confluence of the Ría de Huelva and the Río Tinto.

Otherwise Huelva is best described as a city of oil refineries and heavy industry such as minerals (the famous Río Tinto) and hydrocarbons, the smog from which can drift for miles out into the Atlantic. It is not generally a very salubrious port of call, though in recent years an obvious effort has been made by the city council to improve Huelva's appearance and also cut down on pollution.

### Approach and entrance

Approach as for Mazagón. A west cardinal buoy marks an 8m patch 1·2M southeast of the breakwater head[2321] but this is unlikely to worry yachts. Provided the buoyage is observed both the entrance and the Ría de Huelva itself present no problems. The Puerto Deportivo Mazagón (page 216) will be seen against the shore about 1·5M inside the breakwater end[2321].

### Anchorages

The tide runs strongly in the Ría de Huelva – heavy ground tackle is required – and it is essential to display a riding light as there is a considerable amount of fishing boat traffic at night as well as large freighters which pass each other in the channel.

1. Close north of the breakwater, about 400m in from the end. Considerable wash from passing traffic should be anticipated.
2. Northwest of the pilot station on the north shore about halfway up the buoyed channel, or northwest of the marina, well clear of the channel itself. Again both positions may be uncomfortable due to wash.
3. Off the Real Club Maritimo de Huelva, an angular white building just upstream of the Río Tinto bridge and the Columbus statue, and easily identified by two white chimneys with red and white bands around their tops which lie just behind. The *club maritimo* has a pontoon to which it might be possible to secure for a short period (even members are not permitted to lie alongside long-term) and extensive moorings, and it may be necessary to anchor to the west of the buoyed channel in order to maintain swinging room. The western bank is completely undeveloped, making a pleasant contrast to the industrial buildings of Huelva.

### Facilities

Water tap on the Club Maritimo pontoon, with the usual bar and restaurant ashore. Otherwise though Huelva is a busy industrial city with the usual shops, banks, restaurants, hotels, etc, all are a long way from the anchorages. Upstream will be found yards and workshops servicing both merchant ships and the fishing fleet, but they are not really tuned to the needs of yachts.

### Communications

Post office and telephones in the city, as well as taxis, buses and trains.

## Chipiona

36°45'N 6°26'W

### Tides

*Reference port* Lisbon
*Mean time differences* (at Río Guadalquivir bar)
HW: 00 minutes ±5; LW: +25 minutes ±5
(the above allows for the difference in time zones)
*Heights in metres*

| MHWS | MHWN | MLWN | MLWS |
|------|------|------|------|
| 3·2 | 2·5 | 1·3 | 0·4 |

### Charts

| | Approach | Harbour |
|---|---|---|
| Admiralty | 90, 92 | 85 |
| Spanish | 44B, 44C, 442 | 4421, 4422 II |

### Lights

*Approach*
2320 **Picacho** 37°08'·2N 6°49'·5W
    Fl(2+4)30s51m25M
    White tower with brick corners, as has building, 25m
2345 **Higuera** 37°00'·6N 6°34'·1W
    Fl(3)20s46m20M Masonry tower 24m
2351 **Punta del Perro (Chipiona)** 36°44'·3N 6°26'·4W
    Fl.10s68m25M
    Conical stone tower on building 62m
2350·4 **Bajo Salmedina** 36°44'·4N 6°28'·6W
    Q(9)15s9m5M West cardinal tower, ⵣ topmark
*Note* Destroyed by a storm in 1995 and not yet rebuilt (1999), although there is an unlit beacon tower on the shoal itself.
buoy **Salmedina** 36°44'·4N 6°28'·6W
    Q(9)15s5M West cardinal buoy, ⵣ topmark 4m
*Note* Currently replaces the destroyed lighthouse
*0990* **Rota aerobeacon** 36°38'·6N 6°19'W
    Aerobeacon *AOG* 267·6kHz 40M
2355 **Rota Aeromarine** 36°38'·2N 6°20'·8W
    Aero Al.Fl.WG.9s79m17M
    Red and white chequered spherical tank on 8 columns 49m
*0992* **Rota** 36°37'·7N 6°22'·8W
    Radiobeacon *D* 303kHz 80M
2362 **Cádiz, Castillo de San Sebastián** 36°31'·8N 6°18'·9W
    Fl(2)10s38m25M Horn Mo(N)20s
    Aluminium tower on castle 37m
    Q 1·5M to ESE, on 114m tower
*River entrance*
buoy *No.1*, **El Perro** 36°45'·8N 6°26'·9W
    LFl.10s5M Red and white pillar buoy, topmark
    Racon Mo(M) 10M

Puerto Deportivo Chipiona at the mouth of the Río Guadalquivir, looking east. The two red pillar buoys mentioned in the text can be seen opposite the entrance.

buoy *No.2*, **Picacho** 36°47'·5N 6°26'·7W
 Fl(9)15s5M West cardinal buoy, Ⅹ topmark
*Marina*
buoy *No.1* 36°45'·2N 6°25'·5W
 Fl(2)R.6s3M Red pillar buoy, ▪ topmark
buoy *No.2* 36°45'·1N 6°25'·4W
 Fl(4)R.11s2M Red pillar buoy, ▪ topmark
2352 **Outer breakwater head** 36°45'N 6°25'·7W
 Fl(2)G.10s5m5M Round green tower 5m
2354 **Inner breakwater** 36°44'·9N 6°25'·6W
 Fl(2)R.10s4m3M Round red tower 3m
2354·5 **Breakwater spur** 36°45'N 6°25'·7W
 Fl(3)G.9s4m1M Round green tower 3m

## Marina radio

*Puerto Deportivo Chipiona* VHF Ch 09.

## General

One of the first of the new harbours built by the Junta de Puertos de Andalucía – see page 204 – the Puerto Deportivo Chipiona, ☎ 956 373844 *Fax* 956 370037, *e-mail* chipionad@eppa.es, opened in 1992 and was formed by the extension of the old fishing harbour. The basin is now largely occupied by yachts, with local boats in the southwest basin and visitors to the northeast, while fishing vessels berth along the breakwater. Facilities are good and Chipiona is an obvious place to wait for a fair tide up the Río Guadalquivir, as well as to top up with fuel. The town is pleasant and shady with many restaurants, supermarkets and shopping precincts, and is well worth exploring.

If intending to venture up the Río Guadalquivir, note the paragraph on page 222 regarding Ricardo Franco's *La Navegación de Recreo por el Río de Sevilla* (Leisure Navigation on the River of Seville), which is understood to be available from the Chipiona marina office.

## Approach and entrance

Between Huelva and the Río Guadalquivir the first 20M of coast is backed by sand dunes, but southeast of the resort town of Matalascañas the coastline flattens. A firing range – which is not marked on the Admiralty chart – exists inshore from about 5M southeast of Mazagón to near Matalascañas, a distance of some 12M. When active, a Range Safety Vessel will call up any craft straying into the area on VHF Ch 16 with instructions to keep clear.

On approaching the mouth of the Río Guadalquivir shape a course for *No.2* buoy, a west cardinal guarding Bajo Pichaco rock. Though the buoy is sometimes difficult to see against the land, the wreck which has lain on the rock for the past six years or more is prominent by day or night. From half tide onwards it is possible for a yacht to cut inside the wreck, but without large-scale charts this is not recommended.

When coming from the west, if in any doubt make for Punta del Perro light[2351] on a safe bearing and pick up the fairway buoy *No.1*, which bears 345° from the light. A fish haven has been established north of the entrance to the Río Guadalquivir, but

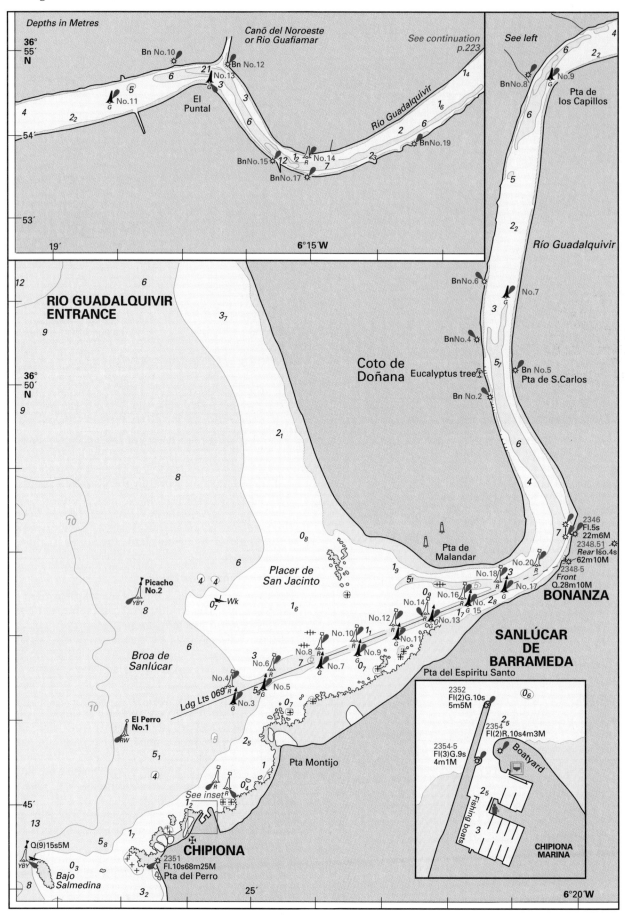

Depths in Metres

36° 55′ N

Bn No.10

Canõ del Noroeste or Rio Guafiamar

*See continuation p.223*

*See left*

Bn No.12

21

No.13

No.11

El Puntal

6

3

3

6

Río Guadalquivir

1₄

1₆

2

6

54′

2₂

4

BnNo.15  12

No.14

7

BnNo.17

BnNo.19

2₃

BnNo.8

No.9

Pta de los Capillos

6

53′

19′

6°15′W

36° 55′ N

4

6

2₂

Río Guadalquivir

5

2₂

12

6

BnNo.6

No.7

3

RIO GUADALQUIVIR ENTRANCE

3₇

9

BnNo.4

Coto de Doñana

Eucalyptus tree

5₇

Bn No.5

Pta de S.Carlos

36° 50′ N

9

Bn No.2

6

2₁

4

8

6

2346
Fl.5s
22m6M

2348.51
Rear Iso.4s
62m10M

7

Pta de Malandar

2348.5
Front
Q.28m10M

BONANZA

Picacho No.2

4    4

0₇  Wk

Placer de San Jacinto

6

0₈

1₉

5₁

No.20

No.18    3

No.16    No.17

SANLÚCAR DE BARRAMEDA

YBY

8

1₆

No.14    0₉

No.16

2₈

15

No.12    1₁

No.13    1₇

Broa de Sanlúcar

6

No.10    1₁

No.11

3    No.6

7    No.7

No.8

No.9

0₇

Pta del Espiritu Santo

No.4

5₉  No.5

Ldg Lts 069°

No.3

0₇

El Perro No.1

RW

2₅

5₁

4

1

Pta Montijo

2352
Fl(2)G.10s
5m5M

0₆

2354
Fl(2)R.10s4m3M

2₅

2354·5
Fl(3)G.9s
4m1M

Boatyard

0₄

See inset

1₂

2₅

45′

13

5₈

1₇

Fishing boats

3

CHIPIONA MARINA

Q(9)15s5M

5₈

0₃

2351
Fl.10s68m25M
Pta del Perro

CHIPIONA

YBY

Bajo Salmedina

8

3₂

25′

6°20′W

as minimum clearances are a good 4·5m at datum it can be ignored by most yachts. From the southeast, round Bajo Salmedina with its west cardinal buoy and again make for buoy *No.1*.

The marina lies 1·3M southeast of this buoy and 0·9M northeast of Punta del Perro[2351] – since the outer breakwater was extended a few years ago its entrance is hidden until very close in. Make for the breakwater head[2352] leaving the two red pillar buoys to port, finally swinging southwest to enter. The entrance, which is reported to have shoaled over the past few years, now carries around 2·5m as does most of the marina.

## Berthing

Secure to the reception pontoon at the head of the central mole – the Muelle de Espera – directly beneath the marina office. Visitors are normally berthed in the northeast basin, convenient for the shops and restaurants, with finger pontoons throughout. One or two seriously large yachts – up to 40m – can lie alongside the west side of the outer pontoon, but in many cases depth would be the limiting factor. There are 355 berths in total, with space always available for visitors.

Office hours in winter are 0900–1330 and 1530–1830 Monday to Saturday, 0900–1500 Sunday, staying open later during the summer.

Charges are at the standard Junta de Puertos de Andalucía rate – see page 204. As in most of their marinas security is via card-operated gates to the pontoons.

## Facilities

*Boatyard* On the northeast arm, with a generous area of concreted hardstanding behind a high security fence. Fishing boats are handled as well as yachts and work appears to be of a good standard.
*Travel-lift* 45 tonne capacity lift in the boatyard area.
*Engineers, electronic & radio repairs* Available through the boatyard.
*Chandlery* Two well-stocked chandleries near the boatyard area, plus F Medina Nautica opposite the root of the main breakwater.
*Water* On the pontoons.
*Showers* In the main block, with access via electronic card.
*Launderette* No launderette (or laundry) either in the marina complex or in the town as a whole.
*Electricity* On the pontoons.
*Fuel* Diesel and petrol at the reception pontoon.
*Bottled gas* Camping Gaz available in the town.
*Ice* At the marina office.
*Weather forecast* Posted daily at the marina office.
*Banks* In the town.
*Shops/provisioning/produce market* The nearest food shop of any kind is a supermarket some 300m distant, with plenty more in the town proper.
*Cafés, restaurants & hotels* A good range – Chipiona has long been a popular holiday resort among Spaniards – with several small café/restaurants overlooking the northeast basin.
*Medical services* In the town.

## Communications

*Post office* In the town.
*Mailing address*
   c/o **Oficina del Puerto**, Puerto Deportivo Chipiona, Avda Rocío Jurado s/n, 11550 Chipiona, Cádiz, España
   *Fax service* 956 370037
*Public telephones* Two in the marina complex, plus many in the town.
*Car hire/taxis* Best organised via the marina office.
*Buses* To Rota, Seville (about 2 hours), etc.
*Air services* International airport at Seville, national airport at Jerez for connections to Madrid, etc.

# Seville and the Río Guadalquivir

36°22'N 6°00'W

## Tides

*Reference port* Lisbon
*Mean time differences* (at Río Guadalquivir bar)
(the above allows for the difference in time zones)
HW: 00 minutes ±5; LW: +25 minutes ±5

*Heights in metres*
| MHWS | MHWN | MLWN | MLWS |
|---|---|---|---|
| 3·2 | 2·5 | 1·3 | 0·4 |

*Mean time differences* (at Bonanza)
HW: +30 minutes ±10; LW: +70 minutes ±10
(the above allows for the difference in time zones)

*Heights in metres*
| MHWS | MHWN | MLWN | MLWS |
|---|---|---|---|
| 3·0 | 2·4 | 1·1 | 0·5 |

*Mean time differences* (at Seville)
HW: +4 hrs 15 min ±15; LW: +5 hrs 30 min ±20
(the above allows for the difference in time zones)

*Heights in metres*
| MHWS | MHWN | MLWN | MLWS |
|---|---|---|---|
| 2·1 | 1·8 | 0·9 | 0·5 |

## Charts

| | Approach | River |
|---|---|---|
| Admiralty | 90, 92 | 85 |
| Spanish | 44B, 44C, 442 | 4421, 4422 II–XVIII |

## Lights

*Approach* – as for Chipiona
*Entrance*
2348·5 **Ldg Lts on 069°** 36°47'·9N 6°20'·2W
  *Front* Q.28m10M
  White structure with red and white chequers 22m
2348·51 *Rear*, 0·6M from front, Iso.4s62m10M
  White structure with red and white chequers 30m
buoy *No.1*, **El Perro** 36°45'·8N 6°26'·9W
  LFl.10s5M Red and white pillar buoy, • topmark
  Racon Mo(M) 10M
buoy *No.2*, **Picacho** 36°47'·5N 6°26'·7W
  Fl(9)15s5M West cardinal buoy, ⚡ topmark
*River*
Eight pairs of lit pillar buoys, plus one extra port hand buoy, mark the channel as far as Bonanza.
2346 **Bonanza** 36°48'·2N 6°20'·1W
  Fl.5s22m6M Red brick tower 20m
2349 **Bonanza, detached breakwater, S end**
  36°48'·2N 6°20'·2W Fl(2+1)G.21s6m5M
  Green column, red band, over diagonal stripes 2m

**2349·1 Bonanza, detached breakwater, N end**
  36°48'·4N 6°20'·2W
  Fl.G.5s6m5M Green column 2m
Many other lit buoys and beacons mark the Río
Guadalquivir up to Seville.

### Marina and port radio

*Puerto Gelves, Marina Yachting Sevilla* and *Club Náutico Sevilla* all VHF Ch 09.
*Chipiona Prácticos, Sanlúcar de Barrameda Prácticos* VHF Ch 09, 10, 12, 13, 14, 16.
*Bonanza Prácticos, Sevilla Prácticos* VHF Ch 09, 12, 14, 16, 20, 22.

### General

The Parque Nacional de Doñana on the west bank of the Guadalquivir is world famous for its birds and other wildlife and on the way up to Seville it should be possible to spot some of its residents. The city itself is fascinating and steeped in history, the old part appearing to have considerably more than its fair share of monuments and historic buildings, including a stunning cathedral and several royal palaces. A guide book and street plan are almost necessities. In common with most large cities Seville has a reputation for crimes such as bag snatching, muggings and vehicle theft, but a purposeful air, valuables tucked away out of sight and avoidance of secluded areas after dark should give reasonable protection.

A yacht provides a most convenient base for exploration, but as summer temperatures can rise above 40°C (102°F) the best time to visit is in spring or autumn – though Seville is also becoming an increasingly popular place to winter on board.

In early 2000 it was reported that Ricardo Franco, a master mariner and very experienced Guadalquivir pilot, had written a book entitled *La Navegación de Recreo por el Río de Sevilla* (Leisure Navigation on the River of Seville), which included large-scale charts of the river and text in both English and Spanish. Amongst the stockists listed was the marina office at Chipiona. Further information was to be found on the internet website www.eintec.es/riodesevilla/.

### Approach

As for Chipiona as far as buoy *No.1*, from which a bearing of 069° leads into the main channel.

### Entrance

The channel is wide and very well buoyed, but can become dangerously rough when strong west or southwest winds oppose the spring ebb and cause short steep seas to build. The 'service centre' for the Río Guadalquivir's buoyage is at Bonanza and, perhaps as a result, maintenance is generally excellent.

### The river

It is about 55M from the mouth to Seville. Starting an hour or so before the beginning of the flood (which a yacht can ride upriver for at least 9 hours – see Tides above) most yachts will be able to make it on one tide. To catch one's breath before heading upriver – and to top up with fuel – a stop in the marina at Chipiona would be convenient. Alternatively in light weather it is possible to anchor opposite Sanlúcar de Barrameda, where there is a large and stylish yacht club, a superb beach and, perhaps of greatest interest, the visitors' centre for the Parque Nacional de Doñana housed in the old ice factory – itself worth a visit for its imaginative tilework. However in November 1999 no trace could be found of the marina referred to in some Junta de Puertos de Andalucía literature, and it can only be assumed that the project came to nothing.

Little more than 1M further upriver lies Bonanza, where a yacht may be able to secure temporarily to the inside of the detached concrete breakwater – quite unmistakable with its downstream end painted in diagonal red and green stripes – while the fishing fleet is at sea. Other possibilities are to anchor north of the moorings well out of the powerful current, or on the west bank around the corner 1M above Bonanza, again well out of both the fairway and the current. Even at neaps the ebb may run at 3 knots in the centre of the channel, and is considerably stronger at springs. The flood never attains anything like the same rates.

After passing the tall, shining heaps of locally-produced salt just upstream of Bonanza the river winds through flat and somewhat featureless countryside – a passage described with feeling as 'very long and boring' – until close to Seville, progress best being marked by simply ticking off the buoys and beacons as they are passed. There is good water the whole way – 6,000 tonne freighters visit the city – but the channel is not always in the centre of the river. Where beacons run down one side they indicate the deeper water, seldom less than 5m. However the water carries such a heavy load of silt that echo-sounders are generally unable to cope, and typical performance is to give no sensible reading for tens of minutes, then briefly read the correct depth for a minute or two, and then go haywire again. Probably of more concern is the commercial traffic, with ships apparently maintaining full speed both day and night.

There are several possible anchorages to be found out of the fairway, but none are very convenient and the current can be strong.

Returning downstream, unless one can make at least 7 knots the passage will take more than one tide – since low water at Bonanza occurs nearly 4·5 hours earlier than at Seville, so for every mile made downstream the ebb will finish that much earlier. Leave Seville about 3·5 hours before local high water (45 minutes after HW at the bar) and after about 2·5 hours of foul tide pick up the ebb. If unable to make 7 knots it will be necessary either to push against the flood – though this seldom exceeds 2 knots even at springs – or to anchor en route.

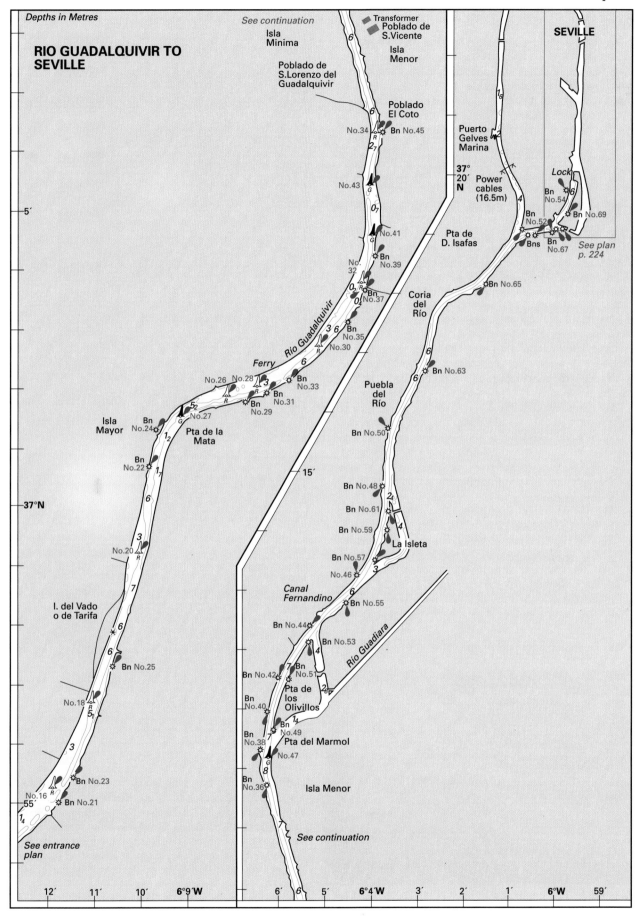

Depths in Metres

**RIO GUADALQUIVIR TO SEVILLE**

See continuation

Isla Minima

Transformer
Poblado de S.Vicente

Isla Menor

**SEVILLE**

Poblado de S.Lorenzo del Guadalquivir

6

Poblado El Coto

No.34 ☼ Bn No.45

R
2₇

No.43

G

Puerto Gelves Marina

**37° 20′ N**

Power cables (16.5m)

1₆

1₂

4

Lock

Bn No.54 ☼ 1₆

Bn No.52 ☼

Bn No.69

5′

0₇

No.41

G

No. 32

☼ Bn No.39

R
Bn No.37

Pta de D. Isafas

Coria del Río

Bns
Bn No.67

See plan p. 224

Bn No.65

*Río Guadalquivir*

0₂

0₄

3  6  ☼ Bn No.35

R
No.30

Ferry

6

6

Bn No.63

No.26  No.28  3  ☼ Bn No.33

R
Bn No.31

Bn No.29

Puebla del Río

Bn No.50

Isla Mayor

Bn No.24 ☼

G

5₂

1₂

Pta de la Mata

15′

Bn No.48

2₄

Bn No.22 ☼

1₇

Bn No.61

4

6

Bn No.59

37°N

La Isleta

Bn No.57

3

No.20 ☼

No.46

R

7

*Canal Fernandino*

6

Bn No.55

I. del Vado o de Tarifa

Bn No.44 ☼

*Río Guadiara*

6

Bn No.53

6

4

Bn No.25 ☼

7  Bn No.51

Bn No.42 ☼

2₄

No.18 ☼

R

Pta de los Olivillos

5₁

Bn No.40

1₄

3

Bn No.49

Pta del Marmol

Bn No.38

G

No.47

Bn No.23 ☼

8

No.16

R

Bn No.36

Isla Menor

55′  Bn No.21 ☼

1₄

See entrance plan

7

See continuation

12′    11′    10′    **6°9′W**    6′    5′    **6°4′W**    3′    2′    1′    **6°W**    59′

233

# Seville

The Río Guadalquivir divides on the southern outskirts of the city to form an island, the two branches rejoining some 6M further upstream. The western branch containing the Puerto Gelves marina is in fact artificial, and was created to enable the eastern, commercial branch to be canalised.

The eastern branch currently offers a choice of two possible places to berth since the Marina Sur, which made a brief appearance in 1996, is no longer functioning. To reach the Marina Yachting Seville and, further up, the Club Náutico Sevilla it is necessary to pass through the lock into the Canal Alfonso XIII, which also contains the city's surprisingly extensive cargo-handling wharves. The lock – which displays a green light when it is clear to enter – opens at 0100, 0400, 0700, 0900, 1100, 1300, 1600, 1900 and 2100 between April and October, at 0100, 0400, 0700, 0930, 1030, 1300, 1600, 1800 and 2000 from November to March, but it may be possible to double up with a freighter at other times. The lock-keepers monitor VHF Ch 12 and speak some English. There are no bollards inside the lock, though some loops of rope are provided at the upstream end or yachts may secure to the ladders.

Two double sets of power cables cross the river just downstream of the lock, continuing to the western branch below Puerto Gelves marina. Where the second (and lower) set cross the western branch the air height is given as 16·5m – air height at the lock is not specified but appears similar.

## 1. Puerto Gelves

☎ 955 761212/760728 *Fax* 955 761583

A small marina, , planned in conjunction with EXPO '92 but not completed for a further two years. Although conceived as a marina village with apartments surrounding the dredged basin, by late 1999 little building had actually taken place and it was difficult to believe that one was within a few miles of a major city. The river carries 4–5m other than very close to the banks, but the marina is effectively the limit of

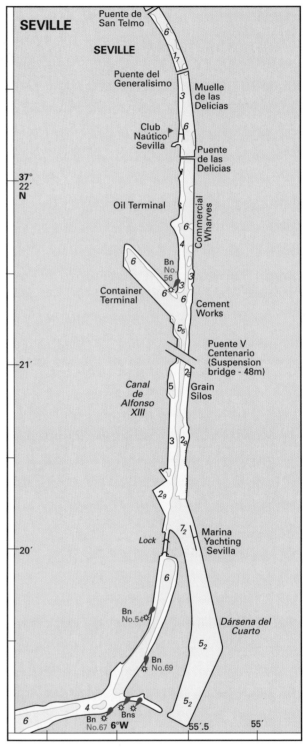

Puerto Gelves marina, on the western branch of the Río Guadalquivir at Seville, looking west across the 'soupy' river.

navigation for yachts as several low road and rail bridges cross the river less than a mile upstream.

The marina, which contains 150 pontoon berths for yachts of up to 16m plus many more smallcraft 'dry-sailed' from the boatyard area, has in the past suffered from chronic silting which has reduced low water depths in the basin to less than 2m (though the underlying mud is extremely soft). However the management have recently acquired their own small dredger so hope to keep abreast of the problem. The river water appears basically clean but distinctly soupy.

The single pontoon of Marina Yachting Sevilla, with the Canal Alfonso XIII access lock behind, looking a little south of west.

On arrival secure to the reception pontoon on the starboard side of the entrance – in spite of the marina's relatively small size it is claimed that space is always available for visitors – and call at the portacabin office to be allocated a berth. Several of the staff speak good English or other European languages. Hours are 0900–1430 and 1600–1930 weekdays, 0900–1400 Saturday, closed Sunday, though uniformed *marineros* are on duty at all times. Their presence comprises the only real security as the pontoons are not gated and sadly, but perhaps not surprisingly, some thefts have been reported. The entrance is lit, with appropriately painted beacons on either side, but navigating in the river after dark would be unwise.

In 1999 the charge for a visiting yacht of just under 12m was 1,020 ptas (6·13 euros) per night for the first three nights, dropping to 850 ptas (5·11 euros) per night thereafter – this did not vary throughout the year. The monthly charge for a yacht of similar size was 23,970 ptas (144·06 euros), again at any time of year, with discounts for longer periods. Charges were inclusive of water, electricity and tax, though multihulls paid a 50% surcharge.

It is also possible to anchor in the river just upstream of the marina entrance, where maximum tidal range is 1·6m and holding generally good in soft mud – but note that after heavy rain inland the current has been known to attain 8 knots! On payment of a small fee, those at anchor can use the marina's showers, launderette, etc.

2. **Marina Yachting Sevilla** – hard round to starboard from the lock amidst rural if somewhat bleak surroundings. Although established for some six or seven years it does not appear to have developed much in that time and facilities remain poor. Noise from the nearby shipyard, combined with the lock loudspeaker, can also be a problem. Its final disadvantage for visitors is that it is some

3·5km from the city centre, tucked behind an industrial area and far from either shops or public transport – though there is no reason why the enterprising crew should not commute into the city by dinghy. . .

The marina comprises a single pontoon with yachts berthed alongside. Depths range from 4–7m. Secure in any available space, and if an attendant does not appear seek out the main office, ☎ 954 230326 *Fax* 954 230172 (open 0900–1330 and 1600–1930), which is on the upper floor of a motorboat showroom a short distance up the road. Little English appears to be spoken.

Charges are calculated on a length x breadth basis and do not alter throughout the year. In 1999 the rate including VAT at 16% for a beamy monohull of just under 12m LOA was around 1,600 ptas (9·62 euros) per night or 44,640 ptas (268·29 euros) per month, inclusive of water and electricity.

3. **Club Náutico Sevilla** – There is no question that the Club Náutico Sevilla offers by far the most convenient berthing in the city as well as excellent shoreside facilities. To reach the club it is necessary to negotiate not only the lock but also the Puente de las Delicias lifting bridge (which replaces the old Puente Alfonso XIII, now dismantled). Between April and October the bridge opens at 1000 and 2000 on weekdays and 0830 and 2000 on weekends and public holidays; from November to March the evening opening is at 1700 rather than 2000. There are several jetties on the port side below the bridge where it may be possible to secure whilst waiting, but note that the bridge only opens if there is traffic – to make your requirements quite clear, be close to the bridge in mid-channel a good five to ten minutes before the listed opening time. It is also worth

Looking northwest across the Río Guadalquivir towards the pontoons and well-kept grounds of the Club Náutico Sevilla. The Puente de las Delicias can be seen at far left.

calling on VHF Ch 12, as even if this does not elicit a response it should alert the bridge-keepers to a yacht's presence.

The Club Náutico Sevilla, ☎ 954 454777 *Fax* 954 284693, lies on the west bank just upstream of the lifting bridge, backed by extensive and well-kept grounds containing tennis courts, mini-golf and several swimming pools. Berthing is stern-to off one of two long pontoons (haul-off lines are provided, tailed to the pontoon). With only 60 yacht-sized berths available it is advisable to book well in advance in the high season. Depths are a minimum of 3m, and one yacht of up to 45m can be fitted in. In the absence of other instructions choose any suitable spot and visit the berthing office (open 0900–1900 weekdays, 0900–1300 Saturday, closed Sunday), up the stairs in the main clubhouse a little south of the pontoons (the reception downstairs is for the club as a whole). The staff are helpful and some English is spoken.

Charges are calculated on a length x breadth basis and do not alter throughout the year (other than at the time of Seville's great April *feria*). In 1999 the rate for a beamy monohull of just under 12m LOA was around 2,964 ptas (17·81 euros) per night or 73,507 ptas (441·79 euros) per month inclusive of water, electricity and tax.

## Facilities

*Boatyard* Astilleros Magallanes, ☎/*Fax* 955 760545, at Puerto Gelves is run by the marina company and shares their portacabin office. The usual services are available plus osmosis treatment, steelwork, welding, etc, together with a good-sized area of secure hardstanding where owners are welcome to do their own work. The only facility of its kind in the area.

*Travel-lift* 25 tonne capacity hoist at Puerto Gelves.

*Engineers, electronic & radio repairs* At Astilleros Magallanes, Puerto Gelves. A mechanic is available at Marina Yachting Sevilla and repairs can be arranged through the office at the Club Náutico Sevilla.

*Sailmaker/sail repairs* A branch of Sun Sails at Puerto Gelves, open 1100–1400 and 1800–2100 weekdays and 1100–1400 Saturday during the summer only, or on request in winter. Their main loft is nearby – enquire at the marina office.

*Chandlery* Náutica Vergara at Puerto Gelves.

*Charts* Valnáutica, ☎ 954 617708, at Calle Castillo Constantina 17 –1°D, are an official stockist of Spanish charts.

*Water* On the pontoons at all three marinas.

*Showers* At all three marinas.

*Launderette* Washing machines in the shower blocks at both Puerto Gelves and Marina Yachting Sevilla. Surprisingly there are no laundry facilities at the Club Náutico Sevilla though the office can arrange for it to be done elsewhere.

*Electricity* On the pontoons at all three marinas.

*Fuel* Newly installed diesel and petrol pumps at Puerto Gelves, opposite the reception, which provide the only convenient source of yacht fuel in the city.

*Bottled gas* Camping Gaz exchanges via the Puerto Gelves office or at most hardware stores, but no chance of getting other cylinders refilled.

*Ice* Available at the bars overlooking Puerto Gelves marina.

*Clube náutico* The Club Náutico Sevilla is worth a visit even if not staying on its pontoons. A reasonable standard of dress is expected in the clubhouse.

*Weather forecast* Posted at the Puerto Gelves office at weekends – during the week it is necessary to ask. Not provided at Marina Yachting Sevilla or the Club Náutico Sevilla.

*Banks* Throughout the city and at Gelves.

*Shops/provisioning* Excellent in the city, as one would expect, but no shops anywhere near Marina Yachting Sevilla, and none actually on the Puerto Gelves site (though all the usual shops will be found in the nearby village). Several of the larger city supermarkets have delivery services.

*Produce markets* Near the river north of the bullring and on Calle Alfarería in the Triana district (about 20 minutes' walk from the Club Náutico Sevilla), plus weekly market at Gelves.

*Cafés, restaurants & hotels* Thousands, at all price levels, including a bar or restaurant at each of the three marinas. The Club Náutico Sevilla has a particularly pleasant terrace bar close to its yacht pontoons.

*Medical services* All aspects including major hospitals. Doctor and dentist at Gelves.

## Communications

*Post office* Throughout the city and at Gelves.

*Mailing addresses*
c/o **Puerto Gelves**, Autovía Sevilla – Coria, km 4·5, 41120 Gelves, Sevilla, España
*Fax service* 955 761583
c/o **Marina Yachting Sevilla SA**, Carretara del Copero s/n, Punta del Verde, 41012 Sevilla, España
*Fax service* 954 230172
c/o **Club Náutico Sevilla**, Avda Sanlúcar de Barrameda s/n, Apartado de Correos 1003, 41011 Sevilla, España.
*Fax service* 954 284693

*Public telephones* Next to the chandlery at Puerto Gelves, and several in the grounds of the Club Náutico Sevilla. Telephone in the bar at Marina Yachting Sevilla.

*Car hire/taxis* Readily available in the city (though the rush hour is even worse than most). The office staff at all three marinas are happy to telephone for taxis.

*Buses* Bus link every 20 minutes from just outside Puerto Gelves into the centre of Seville (about 15 minutes), and from near the Club Náutico Sevilla.

*Trains* Links throughout Spain (eg 2·5 hours to Madrid).

*Air services* International airport just outside the city.

# Cádiz Bay
## Approaches to Rota, Puerto Sherry, Santa Maria and Cádiz
36°34'N 6°21'W

## Charts

|  | *Approach* |
|---|---|
| Admiralty | *90, 92* |
| Spanish | *44B, 44C, 443, 443A, 443B* |
| Imray | *C19* |

## Lights
### *Approach*
2351 **Chipiona, Punta del Perro** 36°44'·3N 6°26'·4W
Fl.10s68m25M
Conical stone tower on building 62m
2350·4 **Bajo Salmedina** 36°44'·4N 6°28'·6W
Q(9)15s9m5M West cardinal tower, ⮙ topmark
*Note* Destroyed by a storm in 1995 and not yet rebuilt (1999), although there is an unlit beacon tower on the shoal itself.
buoy **Salmedina** 36°44'·4N 6°28'·6W
Q(9)15s5M West cardinal buoy, ⮙ topmark 4m
*Note* Currently replaces the destroyed lighthouse
*0992* Rota 36°37'·7N 6°22'·8W
Radiobeacon *D* 303kHz 80M

2355·2 **Rota old lighthouse** 36°37'N 6°21'·4W
Oc.4s33m13M
Off-white round tower, red band 28m
2355 **Rota Aeromarine** 36°38'·2N 6°20'·8W
Aero Al.Fl.WG.9s79m17M
Red and white chequered spherical tank on eight columns 49m
*0990* Rota aerobeacon 36°38'·6N 6°19'W
Aerobeacon *AOG* 267·6kHz 40M 423kHz 100M
2362 **Cádiz, Castillo de San Sebastián** 36°31'·8N 6°18'·9W
Fl(2)10s38m25M Horn Mo(N)20s
Aluminium tower on castle 37m
Obscd over the port by houses in the town
Q 1·5M to ESE, on 114m tower
2405 **Cabo Roche** 36°17'·8N 6°08'·3W
Fl(4)24s44m20M
Pale yellow square tower with silver lantern 20m
### *Entrance*
buoy **Bajo El Quemado** 36°36'N 6°23'·9W
Fl(2)R.9s6M Red pillar buoy
buoy **Las Cabezuelas** 36°35'·3N 6°19'·9W
Q(4)R.10s6M Red pillar buoy
buoy *No.1*, **Los Cochinos** 36°33'·2N 6°18'·9W
Fl.G.3s3M Green pillar buoy, ▲ topmark 7m
buoy **Punta del Sur** 36° 31'·4N 6°20'·3W
Q(9)15s6M West cardinal buoy, ⮙ topmark

Harbours and marinas – listed individually.

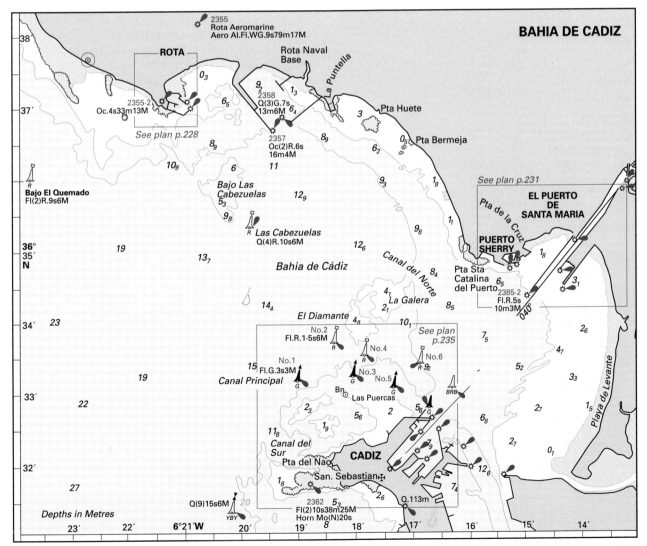

## Approach

The Bahía de Cádiz is some 7M wide and shelters the harbours of Rota, Puerto Sherry and Santa María as well as Cádiz itself.

Coming from the northwest, once the west cardinal beacon marking the Bajo Salmedina west of Chipiona is cleared an offing of 1M will be sufficient to clear the shoals off Punta Candor. If making for the Puerto Deportivo Rota this offing should be maintained until the south breakwater head[2355·4] bears no more than 030° before altering course northeastwards.

If coming from the south, an offing of at least 2M is necessary to clear the various offshore hazards. In particular, do not be tempted to take any short cuts around the peninsula of Cádiz itself – the reefs and shoals running westwards from the Castillo de San Sebastián[2362] have claimed many vessels over the years. Unless very confident it would be wise to come in on the west cardinal buoy about 1M southwest of the Castillo, from there shaping a course of 030° for Los Cochinos buoy *No.1* and so entering the Canal Principal.

There is a second passage into the southern part of the bay, which uses bearings on various buildings in Cádiz itself to plot a course between the isolated rocks and shoals. However this is definitely one for the experienced navigator possessing both fair weather and a current large-scale chart.

# Rota

36°37′N 6°21′W

## Tides

*Reference port* Cádiz
*Mean time differences*
HW: −10 minutes; LW: −15 minutes ±5
*Heights in metres*

| MHWS | MHWN | MLWN | MLWS |
|------|------|------|------|
| 3·1 | 2·4 | 1·1 | 0·4 |

## Charts

|  | *Harbour* |
|------|------|
| Admiralty | *86* |
| Spanish | *4433* |

## Lights

*Approach*
2355·2 **Rota old lighthouse** 36°37′N 6°21′·4W
  Oc.4s33m13M
  Off-white round tower, red band 28m
*Marina*
2355·4 **South breakwater** 36°36′·9N 6°21′W
  Fl(3)R.10s9m9M
  Red post on short concrete tower 3m
2355·5 **North breakwater** 36°37′N 6°21′W
  F.G Green metal post
  (Close to floodlit statue of the Virgin and Child).

## Marina radio

*Puerto Deportivo Rota* VHF Ch 09.

## General

An interesting old town with stone archways spanning its narrow streets, Rota is not improved by

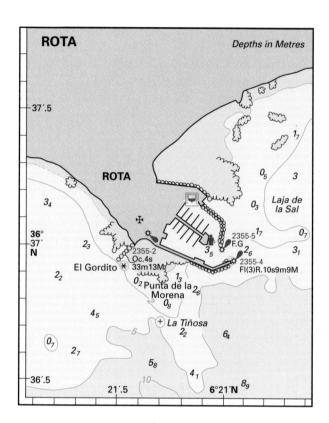

the proximity of the US Naval Base about 1M to the east. However excellent beaches fringe its harbour on both sides, and the tall slim lighthouse with its single red band which stands near the root of the south breakwater makes identification certain by day or night.

The harbour forms part of the chain run by the Junta de Puertos de Andalucía, and like Chipiona combines the functions of yacht and fishing harbours. It is occasionally referred to as Puerto Astaroth, but is more normally known by the less romantic but much more descriptive title of Puerto Deportivo Rota.

## Approach and entrance

From the west, shoal patches of less than 2m extend 1M offshore between Punta Candor and Rota, and even from Bajo El Quemado pillar buoy it is not possible to steer direct for the breakwater head. Continue southeast until the south breakwater head[2355·4] bears no more than 030° before altering course to round its end – the entrance itself faces northeast. The north breakwater is lit[2355·5], but the white statue of the Virgin and Child is more easily seen by day.

From the south or southeast the breakwater head can be approached direct. The entrance forms a dogleg and is relatively narrow, but otherwise presents no problems.

## Berthing

A reception/fuel pontoon lies against the central hammerhead with the marina office, ☎/*Fax* 956 813811, on the left. Currently only 27 of the 296 berths can take yachts of more than 12m, though when visited in November 1999 extra pontoons were being installed in the southern half of the harbour – previously reserved for fishing boats – and it was hoped that some of them would be for larger yachts. Depths vary from 2·5m to 3·5m.

Office hours in winter are 0930–1400 and 1600–1730 Monday to Saturday, 0930–1330 Sunday, staying open later during the summer. Charges are at the standard Junta de Puertos de Andalucía rate – see page 204.

### Facilities

*Boatyard* On the north side of the marina, with a large area of secure (but somewhat windy) hard standing.

*Travel-lift* 35 tonne capacity lift at the boatyard.

*Engineers, electronic & radio repairs* Available at or via the boatyard.

*Chandlery* Small chandlery, outboard repairs, etc at Náutica Pepito, ☎ 956 143353, by the entrance to the boatyard.

*Water* On the pontoons.

*Showers* In the anonymous cream building with grey doors near the root of the central mole. Entry requires the usual electronic card.

*Launderette* In the town.

*Electricity* On the pontoons.

*Fuel* Diesel and petrol at the reception pontoon on the central hammerhead.

*Bottled gas* Camping Gaz available in the town.

*Weather forecast* Posted daily outside the marina office.

*Banks* In the town.

*Shops/provisioning* Good shopping in the town only a short walk from the marina.

*Produce market* Directly opposite the marina.

*Cafés, restaurants & hotels* The usual holiday town variety, plus a small bar/restaurant near the root of the central mole.

*Medical services* In the town.

### Communications

*Post office* In the town.

*Mailing address*
c/o **Oficina del Puerto**, Puerto Deportivo Rota, Calle Higuereta 1, 11520 Rota, Cádiz, España ☎/*Fax service* 956 813811

*Public telephones* Several in the marina area.

*Car hire/taxis* Can be organised via the marina office.

*Buses* To Chipiona, El Puerto de Santa María, Seville, etc.

*Air services* International airport at Seville, national airport at Jerez for connections to Madrid, etc.

Puerto Deportivo Rota, also known as the Puerto Astaroth, looking east with the much larger Rota Naval Base in the background.

# Rota Naval Base

36°37'N 6°19'W

## Lights

### Harbour

2357 **West breakwater** 36°36'·7N 6°19'·5W
Oc(2)R.6s16m4M
Aluminium column and platform 4m

2358 **East breakwater** 36°36'·9N 6°19'·3W
Q(3)G.7s13m6M
Aluminium column and platform 4m

## General

This large harbour about 1M east of Rota marina
and fishing harbour is a restricted naval area and
forbidden to yachts.

# Puerto Sherry

36°35'N 6°15'W

## Tides

See El Puerto de Santa María, page 232

## Charts

|  | Harbour |
|---|---|
| Admiralty | 86 |
| Spanish | 4432, 4434 |

## Lights

### Final approach

2385·2 **Santa María, West training wall, head**
36°34'·4N 6°14'·9W
Fl.R.5s10m3M Red metal tower 6m

### Marina

2382 **Southwest breakwater** 36°34'·8N 6°15'·2W
Oc.R.4s4M
Wide cream tower with attached arches 15m

2382·3 **East mole, SE corner** 36°34'·8N 6°15'·1W
Oc.G.5s3M Green block on wall

2382·5 **Inner harbour, W side** 36°34'·8N 6°15'·1W
Q.R.1M Squat red structure 2m

2382·4 **Inner harbour, E side** 36°34'·8N 6°15'·1W
Q.G.1M Squat green structure 2m

## Marina radio

*Puerto Sherry* VHF Ch 09.

## General

Puerto Sherry is by far the largest, oldest and best
equipped marina on the Atlantic coast of Andalucía.
Planned as a true 'marina village' with construction
begun in 1985, many of the apartments and hotels
still remain unfinished fourteen years on. There is
no true village ashore, the marina complex being
backed by carefully landscaped villas and golf
courses. All visiting yachtsmen have free access to
the complex's swimming pools and saunas for the
first three days of their stay. Probably fewer will be
able to make use of the complex's private heliport.

## Approach and entrance

From north of west approach via Las Cabezuelas
buoy and the Canal del Norte, passing no more than
1M off Punta Santa Catalina del Puerto in order to
avoid the La Galera and El Diamante banks which
shoal to 2·1m.

The large and very well equipped Puerto Sherry seen from the southwest. In the distance are the training walls of the Río Guadalete
leading to El Puerto de Santa María.

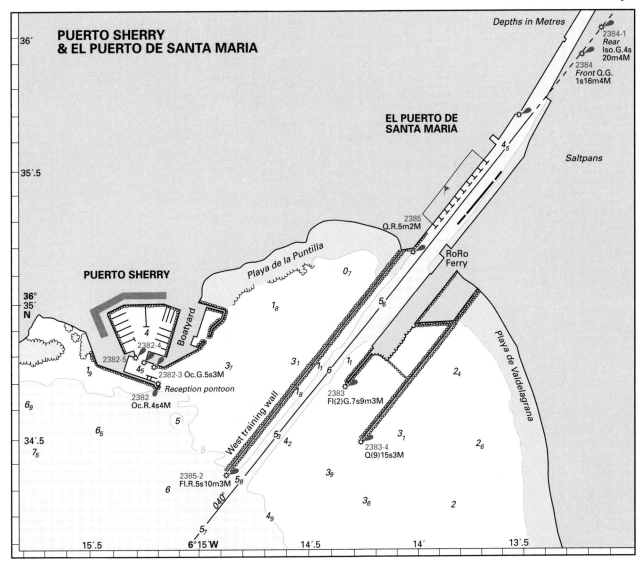

**PUERTO SHERRY
& EL PUERTO DE SANTA MARIA**

Depths in Metres

2384·1
Rear
Iso.G.4s
20m4M

2384
Front Q.G.
1s16m4M

**EL PUERTO DE
SANTA MARIA**

Saltpans

**PUERTO SHERRY**

Playa de la Puntilla

Boatyard

2382·4

2382·5

2382·3 Oc.G.5s3M

4₅

Reception pontoon

2382
Oc.R.4s4M

2385
Q.R.5m2M

RoRo
Ferry

Playa de Valdelagrana

West training wall

2383
Fl(2)G.7s9m3M

2383·4
Q(9)15s3M

2385·2
Fl.R.5s10m3M

040°

36°
35′
N

36°
35′

34′.5

36′

35′.5

15′.5

6°15′W

14′.5

14′

13′.5

From south of west, follow the directions for Cádiz – page 235 – diverging from the Canal Principal after passing El Diamante port hand buoy *No. 4*. From there a direct course of 063° leads to the marina entrance.

The entrance lies some 750m northwest of the end of the training wall of El Puerto de Santa María[2385·2], and faces southeast. There is a stated 4·5m in the channel and 3–3·5m throughout the rest of the marina.

**Berthing**

Puerto Sherry, ☎ 956 870303/870000 *Fax* 956 873902, contains nearly 800 berths for craft of up to 60m in totally sheltered conditions, with room always available for visitors. The reception pontoon is sited to port just inside the entrance, below the conspicuous cream 'lighthouse' building which houses the marina offices. All pontoons are equipped with fingers – those immediately overlooked by the two hotels are somewhat public, those to the south are quieter but entail a longer

walk. In fact the size of the complex is such that, if berthed on one of the western pontoons and needing to visit the boatyard area, it might well be worth launching the dinghy!

In 1999 the high season (1/6–15/9) rate for a visiting yacht of just under 12m was 4,026 ptas (24·20 euros) per night, with discounts available for stays of a week or more stays. The monthly low season rates for a yacht of similar dimensions was 36,242 ptas (217·82 euros). Charges are inclusive of water and electricity. Although quoted ex-VAT (at 16%), this has been added to the above figures for easy comparison with other harbours.

**Facilities**

*Boatyard, engineers, electronic & radio repairs* On the wide east mole, with several companies sharing the workload. Largest is probably Industria Nautica del Sur, ☎ 956 874000/01, handling general repairs, engine maintenance, osmosis treatment, painting, etc, followed by Puerto Nautica SL, ☎ 956 540878, and Tecninautica.

*Travel-lift* 50 tonne capacity lift, with a large area of secure hardstanding.

*Sailmaker/sail repairs* Velas Climent SL, ☎/Fax 956 870539, occupies a rather anonymous white building with blue trim in the boatyard area. They are a true sailmaker, as well as handling repairs and general canvaswork.

*Chandleries* Both Industria Nautica del Sur and Puerto Nautica SL have well-stocked chandleries.

*Charts* Can be ordered via the marina office.

*Water* On the pontoons.

*Showers* Several shower blocks around the marina complex.

*Launderette* Next to the hotel.

*Electricity* On the pontoons.

*Fuel* Petrol and diesel pumps on the west side of the entrance to the inner harbour.

*Bottled gas* Not available.

*Ice* Several machines around the marina complex.

*Club náutico* In theory, but more of a general sports/social club.

*Weather forecast* Posted daily at the marina office.

*Bank* Not only no bank, but no card machine in the entire complex.

*Shops/provisioning* Small supermarket below the hotel, but not a place for serious storing-up.

*Cafés, restaurants & hotels* Wide choice overlooking the marina, with more under construction.

*Medical services* First aid point in the marina, with more serious facilities in nearby Puerto de Santa María.

## Communications

*Post office* Not as such, but the photographic shop sells stamps and mail can be left at the marina office for posting.

*Mailing address*
c/o **Puerto Sherry**, Marina Puerto de Santa María SA, Apartado de Correos 106, El Puerto de Santa María, Cádiz, España.
*Fax service* 956 873902

*Public telephones* A generous number dotted around the marina complex.

*Car hire/taxis* Can be arranged via the marina office. The walk along the beach to El Puerto de Santa María should take well under half an hour.

*Air services* International airport at Seville, national airport at Jerez for connections to Madrid, etc.

## Anchorage

Yachts of modest draft can anchor off Playa de la Puntilla, east of Puerto Sherry marina and north of the Puerto de Santa María training wall, sheltered from all directions other than southwest. However depths at low water springs are no more than 1·5m unless very well out, shoaling towards the beach. Holding is good over sand and mud.

# El Puerto de Santa María
36°35'N 6°14'W

## Tides
*Reference port* Cádiz
*Mean time differences*
HW: −05 minutes ±10; LW: −05 minutes ±10
*Heights in metres*

| MHWS | MHWN | MLWN | MLWS |
|------|------|------|------|
| 3·2 | 2·6 | 1·1 | 0·4 |

## Charts

|  | *Harbour* |
|------|------|
| Admiralty | 86 |
| Spanish | *4432, 4434* |

## Lights
### Harbour
2384 **Ldg Lts on 040°** 36°35'·8N 6°13'·3W
*Front* Q.G.16m4M Aluminium framework tower 14m
2384·1 *Rear*, 235m from front, Iso.G.4s20m4M Aluminium framework tower 18m
2385·2 **West training wall, head** 36°34'·4N 6°14'·9W Fl.R.5s10m3M Red metal tower 6m
2383·4 **East outer breakwater** 36°34'·5N 6°14'·3W VQ(9)15s3M West cardinal tower 3m
2383 **East inner breakwater** 36°34'·7N 6°14'·3W Fl(2)G.7s9m3M Green metal tower 4m
2385 **West training wall, root** 36°35'·2N 6°14'W Q.R.5m2M Red tower 3m

## Marina radio
*Real Club Náutico de Santa María* VHF Ch 09.

## General
El Puerto – the Santa María was added relatively recently – is a pleasant town and a very old port which formerly handled all the produce of Jerez, brought down the Río Guadalete on barges. Whitewashed sherry *bodegas* (warehouses) still line parts of the river and most producers offer tours – check with the tourist office. In Elizabethan times, at least one planned attack on Cádiz went awry

The Real Club Náutico de El Puerto de Santa María, seen here from the southeast, offers one of the most attractive ports of call in Andalucía.

when English sailors on forays ashore discovered the stored liquor and drank themselves to a standstill.

The Real Club Náutico de El Puerto de Santa María prides itself on its friendly 'family' atmosphere, a welcome contrast to the somewhat impersonal feel of many marinas. In common with many Spanish yacht clubs it has a small but attractive garden and sports facilities including a gymnasium, tennis courts and swimming pool, which visiting yachtsmen are welcome to use.

The river, which is relatively narrow, still carries some commercial traffic and there is no space to anchor.

### Approach and entrance

From north of west approach via Las Cabezuelas buoy and the Canal del Norte, passing no more than 1M off Punta Santa Catalina del Puerto in order to avoid the La Galera and El Diamante banks which shoal to 2·1m.

From south of west, follow the directions for Cádiz – page 235 – diverging from the Canal Principal after passing El Diamante port hand buoy *No.4*. From there a direct course of 073° leads into the entrance channel, which itself runs 040°, parallel to the training wall which is lit[2385·2].

### Berthing

The beautifully kept Real Club Náutico, ☎ 956 852527/852861 *Fax* 956 874400, *e-mail* RCNPTO@teleline.es, administers an equally shipshape marina capable of berthing around 175 yachts and smallcraft, including a few vessels of up to 20m. Other than at the innermost berths, depths are generous at 5m or more. About 20 places are normally reserved for visitors, all of them on the ten hammerhead pontoons approached from the northwest bank – the three detached pontoons on the southeast side of the channel are reserved for club members.

Preferably call on VHF Ch 09 on approach – at least one of the office staff speaks excellent English – otherwise secure to any hammerhead and enquire at the white control tower or the office (near the road gate and turnstile) for a berth. The office is open 0830–2200 daily and (most unusually for Spain) does not close for *siesta*.

In 1999 the rate for a visiting yacht of just under 12m at any time of year was 2,000 ptas (12·02 euros) per night, or 50,000 ptas (300·51 euros) per month, inclusive.

### Facilities

*Boatyard* Small boatyard at the upstream end of the premises with limited hardstanding mostly occupied by members' yachts.
*Travel-lift* Not as such, but a 25 tonne marine railway and 5 tonne crane.
*Engineers* Some mechanical capabilities at the boatyard. For serious problems it may be necessary to go to Puerto Sherry.
*Water* On the pontoons.
*Showers* Spotless showers in the Real Club Náutico.

*Laundry/launderette* The office can arrange to have laundry collected, otherwise launderettes in the town.
*Electricity* On the pontoons.
*Fuel* No fuel as of 1999, but anticipated in the near future.
*Bottled gas* Camping Gaz available in the town.
*Ice* At the Real Club Náutico.
*Weather forecast* Available at the office on request.
*Banks* In the town.
*Shops/provisioning/produce market* In the town.
*Cafés, restaurants & hotels* Very pleasant restaurants at the Real Club Náutico, both terrace and indoor (the latter more formal), with plenty more in the town and along the beach.
*Medical services* In the town.

### Communications

*Post office* In the town.
*Mailing address*
c/o **Real Club Náutico de El Puerto de Santa María**, Avenida de la Bajamar 13, 11500 - El Puerto de Santa María, Cádiz, España
*Fax service* 956 874400
*Public telephones* Several on the Real Club Náutico premises.
*Car hire/taxis* In the town, or can be arranged via the office.
*Buses & trains* To Cádiz, Jerez, Seville and elsewhere.
*Ferries* Passenger ferries to Cádiz (not a bad way to visit that city).
*Air services* International airport at Seville, national airport at Jerez for connections to Madrid, etc.

## Cádiz

36°33'N 6°17'W

### Tides

Cádiz is a Standard Port

*Heights in metres*

| MHWS | MHWN | MLWN | MLWS |
|------|------|------|------|
| 3·3 | 2·5 | 1·2 | 0·5 |

### Charts

| | Harbour |
|---|---|
| Admiralty | 86 |
| Spanish | 4432, 4435 |

### Lights

#### Approach
2362 **Castillo de San Sebastián** 36°31'·8N 6°18'·9W
　　Fl(2)10s38m25M Horn Mo(N)20s
　　Aluminium tower on castle 37m
　　Obscd over the port by houses in the town
　　Q 1·5M to ESE, on 114m tower
buoy *No.1*, **Los Cochinos**
　　36°33'·2N 6°18'·9W
　　Fl.G.3s4M Green pillar buoy, ▲ topmark 7m
buoy **Port hand** *No.2* 36°33'·8N 6°18'·4W
　　Fl.R.1·5s6M Red pillar buoy, ■ topmark
buoy **Starboard hand** *No.3*
　　36°33'·3N 6°18'·1W
　　Fl.G.5s Green pillar buoy, ▲ topmark

buoy *No.4,* **El Diamante** 36°33'·6N 6°17'·8W
    Q(4)R.12s5M Red pillar buoy, ▪ topmark
buoy *No.5,* **El Fraile** 36°33'·5N 6°17'·3W
    Fl(3)G.13s4M Green pillar buoy, ▲ topmark
buoy *No.6,* **La Monja,** 36°33'·5N 6°17'·1W
    Fl(3)R.10s4M Red pillar buoy, ▪ topmark
buoy **Starboard hand** 36°32'·8N 6°16'·7W
    Q.G.3M Green pillar buoy
buoy **Port hand** 36°33'N 6°16'·2W
    Q(2)10s3M Black pillar buoy, red band
*Harbour*
2367 **North breakwater** 36°32'·6N 6°16'·7W
    Fl.G.3s12m5M Green triangular column 6m
2368 **East breakwater** 36°32'·5N 6°16'·5W
    Fl.R.2s11m5M Red triangular column 5m
2370 **Marina east mole** 36°32'·5N 6°16'·9W
    Fl(4)G.16s1M Green post 2·5m
2370·2 **Marina south mole** 36°32'·5N 6°16'·9W
    Fl(4)R.16s1M Red post 2·5m
Plus other lights both in the interior of the harbour and in the Caño de la Carraca.

## Coast radio station

**Cádiz** (36°30'N 6°20'W) (24 hours) Remotely controlled from CCR Malaga
**VHF** Ch 70[1].
1. Digital Selective Calling (DSC) distress and safety traffic.

## Port radio

*Puerto América* VHF Ch 09.
*Cádiz Prácticos* VHF Ch 11, 12, **14**, 16 (24 hours).

## General

Cádiz is one of the oldest cities in Spain, having been founded by the Phoenicians over 3,000 years ago. It has long been a major port, with a fine defensive position and good shelter, and for many years handled nearly all the lucrative trade with the New World. This led to great wealth, the results of which can still be seen in the scale of its public and private buildings, many of which date back to the 18th century. The commercial area extends along the peninsula to the southeast, less impressive architecturally but containing good shopping, restaurants and hotels.

Until the early 1990s Cádiz was a difficult city to visit by yacht, the docks devoted to fishing and commercial use and the small Real Club Náutico de Cádiz basin packed with local craft. The opening of the Puerto América marina has overcome this problem, and though set amidst bleak surroundings nearly 2km from the old city it offers reasonable shelter and security for the yacht whilst the crew explore elsewhere.

The wide entrance to the Commercial Basin at Cádiz, with Puerto América marina in the foreground. The purpose of the new breakwater stretching towards the camera is not yet clear.

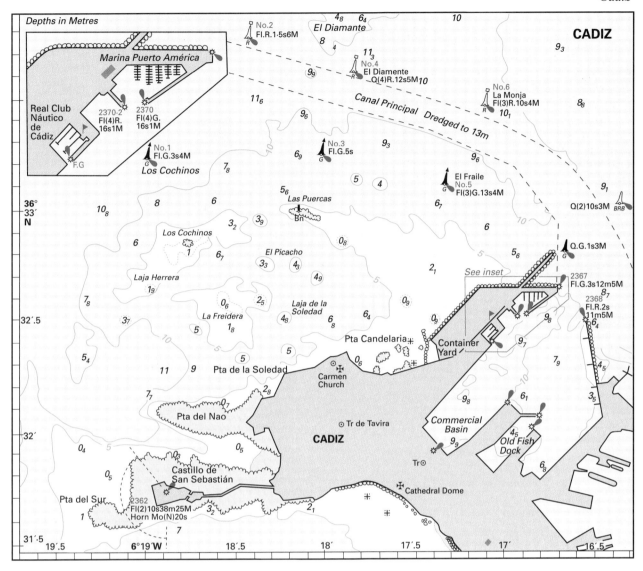

## Approach and entrance

The Canal Principal is well buoyed and lit, and may safely be used by day or night. After identifying Los Cochinos buoy *No.1*, in normal weather it is safe to make direct for buoy *No.5* (starboard hand) on 094°, passing close inside buoy *No.3* in a least depth of 5m. Do not, however, be tempted to cut much inside buoy *No.1* for fear of the unmarked Los Cochinos shoal. From buoy *No.5* a course of 115° leads outside the starboard hand buoy marking a recent – and still unlit – breakwater extension, around which the north breakwater head[2367], will be seen.

In heavy weather, or when a large swell is running, it would be wise to remain in the Canal Principal which has a dredged depth of 13m.

Once round the north breakwater the marina entrance[2370, 2370·2] is on the starboard hand some 400m to the southwest. There is no reception pontoon as such – on arrival secure either to the fuel pontoon on the port side of the entrance, or take any vacant berth on the westernmost pontoon (immediately opposite the entrance).

## Berthing

Another in the Junta de Puertos de Andalucía chain, even after five years Puerto América, ☎/*Fax* 956 224220, appears to be lagging somewhat behind its peers in terms of completion and facilities. The marina buildings, such as they exist, are housed in huts and portacabins and the lasting impression is of a vast, dusty, concrete wasteland, little changed since 1995.

Some 152 berths currently exist, though originally more were planned, and yachts lie on one of five pontoons, each berth provided with an individual finger. As mentioned above, visiting yachts normally occupy the westernmost pontoon, immediately opposite the entrance and broadside on to almost continuous wash from passing traffic (container ships, cruise ships and ferries all use the Commercial Basin). However the marina can accommodate yachts of up to 15m, is very deep and, perhaps due to its unappealing position, is seldom crowded.

Office hours are 0900–1400 and 1700–1900 Monday to Saturday, 0900–1400 Sundays, with security guards on duty at other times (there are no gates to the pontoons). Berthing charges are at the standard Junta de Puertos de Andalucía rate – see page 204.

## Facilities

*Boatyard* Various workshops on site (though the state of some of the yachts ashore does not inspire confidence). For major repairs Puerto Sherry would almost certainly be a better bet.

*Engineers, electronic & radio repairs* Enquire at the marina office.

*Charts*
**Instituto Hidrográfico de la Marina**, Plaza de San Severiano 3, DP 11007 Cádiz
☎ 956 599409 *Fax* 956 599396
Not geared to direct contact with the public. A better bet for Spanish charts would be either
**JL Gándara y Cia SA**, Calle La Línea de la Concepción 11
☎ 956 270443 *Fax* 956 272207
(in the Zona Franca industrial area) or
**Papelería D Manuel Pereira González**, Calle Pelota, 14 – bajo
☎ 956 286201 *Fax* 956 289612.

*Water* On the pontoons.

*Showers* In portacabins next to the marina office. A key is needed for access.

*Laundry* Can be arranged via the marina office.

*Electricity* On the pontoons.

*Fuel* Diesel and petrol at the fuelling pontoon on the west side of the entrance.

*Bottled gas* Camping Gaz available in the city.

*Ice* At the *club náutico*.

*Club náutico* The nearby Real Club Náutico de Cádiz, ☎ 956 228701/212991 *Fax* 956 253903, is friendly to reasonably well-dressed visitors, and has a pleasant terrace bar and restaurant.

*Weather forecast* Posted daily in the marina office.

*Banks* Many in the city.

*Shops/provisioning/market* Excellent shops and a good produce market, but all at some distance from the marina.

*Cafés, restaurants & hotels* Snack bar next to the marina office plus a small restaurant at the Real Club Náutico. For those with transport there is a wide choice in the old city.

*Medical services* In the city.

## Communications

*Post office* In the city.

*Mailing address*
c/o **Puerto América**, Punta de San Felipe s/n, Dársena Comercial de la Bahía, 11004 Cádiz, España
*Fax service* 956 224220

*Public telephone* Just inside the door to the portacabin office, otherwise a booth at the Real Club Náutico de Cadiz plus many in the city.

*Car hire/taxis* Can be organised via the marina office.

*Buses & trains* Links to Jerez, Seville, etc from the city, but no public transport near the marina.

*Ferries* Passenger ferries to El Puerto de Santa María – and to the Canaries!

*Air services* International airport at Seville. National airport at Jerez for connections to Madrid, etc.

# Sancti-Petri

36°23'N 6°13'W

## Tides
See Cádiz, page 233

## Charts

| | Approach | River |
|---|---|---|
| Admiralty | *90, 92* | |
| Spanish | *44B, 44C, 443, 443B* | *4438* |

## Lights

### Approach
2362 **Cádiz, Castillo de San Sebastián** 36°31'·8N 6°18'·9W
Fl(2)10s38m25M Horn Mo(N)20s
Aluminium tower on castle 37m
Obscd over the port by houses in the town
Q 1·5M to ESE, on 114m tower

2405 **Cabo Roche** 36°17'·8N 6°08'·3W
Fl(4)24s44m20M
Pale yellow square tower with silver lantern 20m

2406 **Cabo Trafalgar** 36°11'N 6°02'W
Fl(2+1)15s50m22M
White conical tower and building 34m

*0994* Radiobeacon *B* 297kHz 50M

### River
2387 **Punta del Arrecife** 36°23'·8N 6°13'·4W
Q(9)15s8m3M
West cardinal tower, ⚹ topmark

2388 **Castillo de Sancti-Petri** 36°22'·9N 6°13'·1W
Fl.3s19m9M Square tower 16m

2398 **Coto San José Ldg Lts on 050°** 36°23'N 6°12'·1W
*Front* Fl.5s13m6M
Aluminium framework tower 10m

2398·1 *Rear*, 50m from front, Oc(2)6s17m6M
Aluminium framework tower 10m

2404 **Batería de Urrutia Ldg Lts on 346·5°** 36°23'·7N 6°12'·9W
*Front* **Punta del Boquerón** Fl.5s12m6M
Aluminium framework tower 10m

2404·1 *Rear*, 60m from front, Oc(2)6s22m6M
Aluminium framework tower 10m

Looking northeast into the Caño de Sancti-Petri, with the island lighthouse in the foreground. The red and green entrance beacons can just be made out to the right of the breaking shoal.

# SANCTI-PETRI

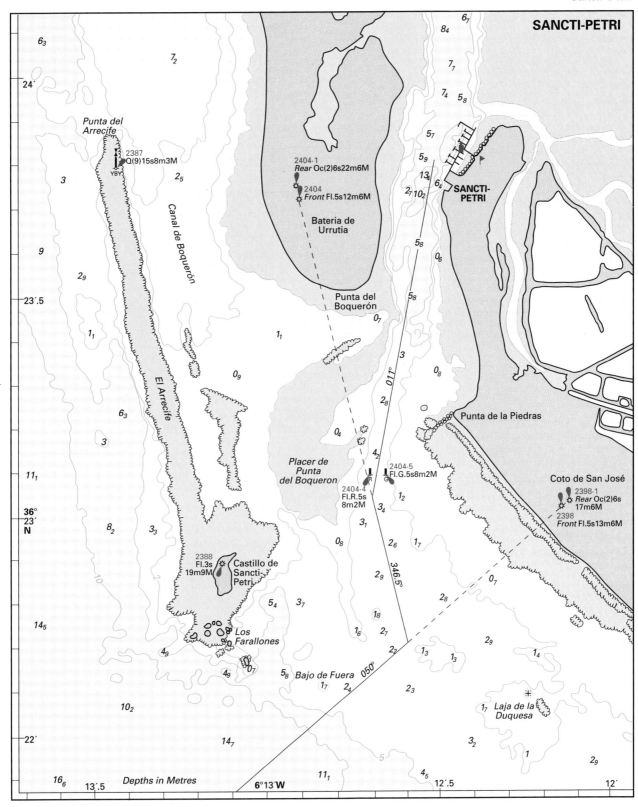

2404·4 **Bajo de Poniente** 36°23'·1N 6°12'·7W
Fl.R.5s8m2M Red column
2404·5 **Piedra Larga** 36°23'·1N 6°12'·6W
Fl.G.5s8m2M Green column

## Harbour radio

*Puerto Deportiv Sancti-Petri* and *Club Náutico de Sancti-Petri*, both VHF Ch 09.

## General

The sandy and windswept lagoon at Sancti-Petri provides a peaceful port of call for those confident of their pilotage and not too worried about facilities ashore. Other than an active and friendly *club náutico* and a few summer-only cafés the village which occupies the eastern peninsula is almost entirely deserted, though most buildings – the market, the school, the hotel – are clearly identifiable. The majority, including the boarded up church, still have their roofs; street lamps run down the cobbled streets; benches recline in the shade of palm trees around the square – only missing are the people.

History is unclear as to whether Sancti-Petri died after the tunny fishing company which provided nearly all its employment closed down, or whether it was forcibly emptied during the Franco years for use as a military training area. In July 1997 some of the houses in the southern part of the village were being renovated by Spanish families, one couple seemingly caretakers. Others houses appeared to be occupied by squatters. However two years later work had come to a halt, a situation which seems unlikely to last – try to get there before Sancti-Petri is rediscovered and 'developed' as bijou residences.

Facilities for yachts are improving, though still limited, with both pontoon berths and moorings available (although very crowded in summer). Alternatively it is possible to anchor further up the estuary where the bird life is a twitcher's dream. The small stone quay is used by fishing vessels and ferries, many running excursions out to the Isla de Sancti-Petri, a tiny, rocky island which has been inhabited since prehistoric times. It is claimed that the remains of a temple to Hercules can still be seen, along with more recent fortifications and the square-sided lighthouse.

## Approach

Approaching Sancti-Petri from Cádiz or other points north the coastline is low and somewhat featureless, consisting of marshes and saltpans. Remain outside the 10m line in order to avoid a small, unmarked, isolated rock about 2M north of Punta del Arrecife (itself marked by a west cardinal column with topmark[2387]), at the northern end of the Isla de Sancti-Petri. Give the island itself generous clearance until able to pick up the outer leading marks on 050° as detailed below.

Coming from the south, beware the long, rocky shoal which runs southwest from Cabo Trafalgar[2406], culminating in the dangerous Bajo Aceitera more than 1·5M offshore. In heavy weather the Placer de Meca bank, 3·2M to the west, may break and should also be avoided. A race can form up to 8M offshore in these conditions, particularly when east-going current and tidal stream oppose the *levanter*. North of the cape a direct course for Santi-Petri takes one uncomfortably close to the 1·2m shoal of Lajas de Conil – keep a good 2·5M offshore until approaching Cabo Roche[2405]. Once past the headland with its square lighthouse there are no hazards before the isolated Laja Bermeja about 1M south of the entrance – remain outside the 10m line until able to pick up the outer leading marks on 050° as detailed below. In onshore swell the 3·4m and 3·7m offshore banks may break, in which case any thoughts of entering Sancti-Petri should be forgotten.

## Entrance

Though protection once inside is good, the entrance should only be attempted on a rising tide, in fair weather and in good visibility. If in doubt wait for a local vessel to give a lead in. The bar is believed to carry 2·5m at low water springs, but an onshore swell can create very dangerous conditions and the surrounding sandbanks shift with every gale. The current runs strongly, with a good 2 knots on the flood and more on the ebb. Night approach is not recommended.

Make for the conspicuous Castillo de Sancti-Petri[2388] situated on rocks at the southern end of El Arrecife (literally, 'the reef'), the northern end of which is marked by a west cardinal column with topmark[2387]. On no account try to cut between the two, or between the cardinal and the mainland shore. South of the *castillo* pick up the Coto San José outer leading marks[2398] on 050° – the aluminium framework towers are not conspicuous and tend to blend in with the vegetation. Turn onto 346° when the Batería de Urrutia inner leading marks[2404] (also aluminium towers) come into line. Buoys are usually laid seasonally, being moved as the sandbanks shift, and if in place will mark the current channel.

Continue on 346° until about 100m short of the gate formed by Bajo de Poniente[2404·4] and Piedra Larga[2404·5] (identical red and green columns with lattice baskets surrounding their lights), turning slightly to starboard through the gap. Continue upriver on 011°, favouring the starboard side. At least 3m should be found throughout.

## Berthing and mooring

There are two sets of pontoons at Sancti-Petri, both so small as to hardly justify the name marina. Those further downstream form the Puerto Deportivo Sancti-Petri, by far the smallest affair in the Junta de Puertos de Andalucía chain, those beyond – together with the many moorings – are administered by the Club Náutico de Sancti-Petri.

The Puerto Deportivo Sancti-Petri, ☎/*Fax* 956 496169, comprises 87 berths for boats of up to 12m, of which 13 are reserved for visitors (though few of these are in the 10–12m band). All except the outermost are in less than 2m. Arrivals should secure to one of the three hammerheads and visit the portacabin office on the small quay (due to be replaced by a more solid structure). Charges are at the standard Junta de Puertos de Andalucía rate – see page 204 – and security via their usual electronic gates (though it is hard to imagine a safer place).

The Club Náutico de Sancti-Petri, ☎/*Fax* 956 495434, ☎ 956 495428, which occupies the only

Two sets of pontoons lie off the semi-derelict village, with further moorings out of frame on the left. Sancti-Petri is definitely for those happy to be self-sufficient.

two storey building on the waterfront, has a combination of berths and moorings able to take some 250–300 yachts in total. Again most alongside berths are shoal draft though the majority of the moorings carry 3m+. On arrival secure to the upstream hammerhead, if not already intercepted by the club boatman, and visit the office to be allocated a berth or mooring – hours are normally 1000–1300 and 1800–2100. In 1999 the rate for a visiting yacht of just under 12m at any time of year was 1,740 ptas (10·46 euros) inclusive of water, electricity and tax whether berthed or on a mooring. Dinghies may be left on the pontoons.

### Anchorage

It is possible to anchor almost anywhere in the estuary as depth permits over sand and mud – some 7–10m should be found north of the moorings – but note that in places the ebb can run at 3 knots or more. It is understood that 2m can be carried right up to the jetty at San Fernando, some 3M into the lagoon.

### Facilities

*Engineers* A mechanic is available through the *club náutico*.

*Chandlery* Small chandlery on the quay.

*Water* On both sets of pontoons – yachts on moorings may be able to lie alongside briefly to fill tanks.

*Showers* On the quay for puerto deportivo users, or in the *club náutico*.

*Electricity* On both sets of pontoons.

*Fuel* Diesel pump at the end of the *club náutico* jetty – check depths before venturing in. No petrol available.

*Ice* At the *club náutico*.

*Clube náutico* Small and friendly club, with few facilities but helpful members.

*Weather forecast* Posted daily at the puerto deportivo office.

*Banks* Several in Chiclana de la Frontera about 7km inland, and possibly in Costa Sancti–Petri 2km distant.

*Shops/provisioning/market* The nearest serious shopping is in Chiclana de la Frontera, though basic needs can be met in Costa Sancti–Petri.

*Cafés, restaurants & hotels* Bar/restaurant at the *club náutico*, plus other cafés and restaurants open only during summer.

*Medical services* Red Cross post operational in summer only, otherwise in Chiclana de la Frontera.

### Communications

*Post office* In Chiclana de la Frontera. No box either, though harbour staff may be willing to post stamped mail for visitors.

*Mailing addresses*
   c/o **Oficina del Puerto**, Puerto Deportivo
   Sancti-Petri, Poblado de Sancti-Petri,
   11139 Chiclana de la Frontera, Cádiz, España
   ☎/*Fax service* 956 496169
   c/o **Club Náutico de Sancti-Petri**, Apdo de
   Correos 118, Chiclana de la Frontera, Cádiz, España
   ☎/*Fax service* 956 495434

*Public telephones* On the quay and in the *club náutico*.

*Taxis* Organise via the marina office or the *club náutico*.

*Buses* About every two hours from a stop near the quay, or it may be possible to beg a lift.

# Puerto de Conil

36°18'N 6°08'W

### Tides

*Reference port* Cádiz
Mean time differences (at Cabo Trafalgar)
HW: +15 minutes ±10; LW: −05 minutes ±10

*Heights in metres*

| MHWS | MHWN | MLWN | MLWS |
|------|------|------|------|
| 2·4 | 1·9 | 0·9 | 0·4 |

### Charts

| | *Approach* |
|------|------|
| Admiralty | *90, 92* |
| Spanish | *44B, 44C, 105, 444* |

### Lights

#### Approach

2362 **Cádiz, Castillo de San Sebastián** 36°31'·8N
6°18'·9W
Fl(2)10s38m25M Horn Mo(N)20s
Aluminium tower on castle 37m
Obscd over the port by houses in the town
Q 1·5M to ESE, on 114m tower
2405 **Cabo Roche** 36°17'·8N 6°08'·3W
Fl(4)24s44m20M
Pale yellow square tower with silver lantern 20m
2406 **Cabo Trafalgar** 36°11'N 6°02'W
Fl(2+1)15s50m22M
White conical tower and building 34m
*0994* Radiobeacon *B* 297kHz 50M

#### Harbour

2405·4 **Southwest breakwater** 36°17'·6N 6°08'W
Fl.R.6s10m5M Red round tower 6m
2405·6 **Northeast mole** 36°17'·7N 6°08'·1W
LFl.G.7s7m3M Green round tower 3m
2405·8 **Inner mole** 36°17'·7N 6°08'·1W
Fl(2)R.8s8m2M Red round tower 4m

### General

Puerto de Conil lies tucked behind the headland of Cabo Roche[2405], almost midway between the Isla de Sancti-Petri and Cabo Trafalgar. A colourful, busy and obviously thriving fishing harbour – with all the associated smells and interest – there are no facilities other than a fishermen's bar and several water taps, and as the harbour is situated several kilometres from the town of the same name there is literally nothing outside the harbour gates other than miles of open heathland.

Hundreds of rusty fisherman anchors are stored behind the harbour, to be used when the tunny (tuna) nets are set. There is a major fossil bank near the root of the east mole.

### Approach

Approaching Cabo Roche from the northwards presents no particular hazards in fair weather, though in any swell the 3·4m and 3·7m offshore banks may well break. In such conditions it would be wise to stay well outside the 20m line and continue for Barbate or beyond.

The small fishing harbour of Puerto de Conil, looking northeast. Although the harbour itself is crowded, convenient anchorage is to be had just outside.

Coming from the south, rocky shoals run southwest from Cabo Trafalgar[2406] culminating in the dangerous Bajo Aceitera more than 1·5M offshore. In heavy weather the Placer de Meca bank, 3·2M to the west, may break and should also be avoided. A race can form up to 8M offshore in these conditions, particularly when east-going current and tidal stream oppose the *levanter*. An inside passage is used by fishermen, but it should not be attempted without local knowledge. Careful pilotage remains necessary after rounding the cape to pass either inside or outside the 1·2m Lajas de Conil – in this case the inside passage is more than a mile wide and carries 8m or more – but see also the Caution below.

In contrast, the final approach to Puerto de Conil is straightforward with the 10m line running within a few hundred metres of the shore.

### Caution

Several artificial reefs have been created southwest of Puerto de Conil, but none in depths to concern yachts. More to the point, an *almadraba* or tunny (tuna) net known as *El Palmar* is laid between March and September each year between Cabo Roche and Cabo Trafalgar. For the past four years it has been in roughly the same position, and in 1999 it was lit by four (small) cardinal buoys:

buoy **North** 36°15'·2N 6°06'·8W
   Q.3M North cardinal, ⬧ topmark
buoy **West** 36°14'·5N 6°08'·8W
   Q(9)15s3M West cardinal, ⬧ topmark
buoy **South** 36°14'·3N 6°08'W
   Q(6)+LFl.15s3M South cardinal, ⬧ topmark
buoy **East** 36°15'·1N 6°05'·3W
   Q(3)10s3M East cardinal, ⬧ topmark

### Berthing and anchorage

Until recently Puerto de Conil consisted only of a single short breakwater, but the addition of an angled extension plus a short opposing mole has much increased its size. Even so all the inner walls other than the fishing quay are rubble-fronted (dinghies and other smallcraft lie on haul-out

Cabo Trafalgar lighthouse at the end of its long sandy spit, looking east. For all its innocent appearance shoals run out more that 1·5M offshore.

moorings), and a yacht would almost certainly have to remain outside the entrance.

Anchor southeast of the small east mole in 3–5m over sand, protected from southwest through north to east but fully exposed to south and southeast. There is a reported 2·5m inside the harbour.

## Barbate
36°11'N 5°56'W

### Tides

*Reference port* Cádiz
*Mean time differences*
HW: +05 minutes ±0; LW: +15 minutes ±0
Heights in metres

| MHWS | MHWN | MLWN | MLWS |
|------|------|------|------|
| 1·9 | 1·5 | 1·0 | 0·6 |

### Charts

| | Approach | Harbour |
|---|---|---|
| Admiralty | 92, 142, 773 | |
| Spanish | 44C, 105, 444 | 4441 |
| Imray | C19 | |

### Lights

*Approach*
2406 **Cabo Trafalgar** 36°11'N 6°02'W
   Fl(2+1)15s50m22M
   White conical tower and building 34m
*0994* Radiobeacon *B* 297kHz 50M
2408 **Barbate** 36°11'·3N 5°55'·3W
   Fl(2)WR.7s22m10/7M 281°-W-015°-R-095°
   White round tower, dark red bands 18m
2411·5 **Punta de Gracia (Punta Camarinal)**
   36°05'·5N 5°48'·5N
   Oc(2)5s74m13M Masonry tower 20m
2412 **Punta Paloma** 36°04'N 5°43'·1N
   Oc.WR.5s44m10/7M 010°-W-340°-R-010°
   (over Bajo de Los Cabezos) Two-storey building 5m
2414 **Tarifa** 36°00'·1N 5°36'·5W
   Fl(3)WR.10s40m26/18M 089°-R-113°-W-089°
   White tower 33m
   Siren (3)60s Masonry structure 10m
   Racon Mo(C) 360° 20M
*0996* Radiobeacon *O* 299kHz 50M

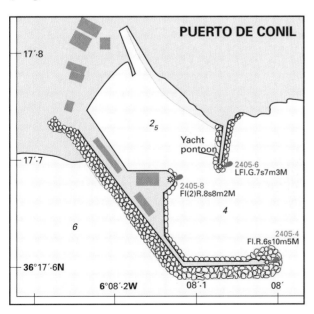

**PUERTO DE CONIL**

17'·8

2₅

Yacht pontoon

2405·6
LFl.G.7s7m3M

2405·8
Fl(2)R.8s8m2M

17'·7

4

6

2405·4
Fl.R.6s10m5M

36°17'·6N

6°08'·2W    08'·1    08'

### Marina

2409 **South breakwater** 36°10'·8N 5°55'·5W
  Fl(2)R.6s11m5M Red conical tower 2m
2409·2 **Ldg Lts on 297·5°** 36°11'N 5°55'·9W
  *Front* Q.2m1M 280·5°-vis-310·5° Concrete pillar 3m
2409·21 *Rear*, 385m from front,
  Q.7m1M 280·5°-vis-310·5°
  Concrete pillar on perimeter wall 6m
buoy **Port hand *No.2*** 36°10'·9N 5°55'·6W
  Fl(2)R.5s5M Red pillar buoy, ■ topmark
buoy **Starboard hand *No.1*** 36°10'·9N 5°55'·6W
  Fl.G.4s 5M Green pillar buoy, ▲ topmark
buoy **Starboard hand *No.3*** 36°11'N 5°55'·7W
  Fl(3)G.7s2M Green conical buoy
buoy **Port hand *No.4*** 36°11'N 5°55'·8W
  Fl(3)R.7s2M Red can buoy
2410 **East breakwater** 36°11'N 5°55'·8W
  Fl.G.3s7m2M Green masonry tower 2m
2411·25 **Marina, south mole** 36°11'·1N 5°55'·9W
  Fl(2)R.2M Red column 4m
2411·2 **Marina, north mole** 36°11'·2N 5°55'·9W
  Fl(2)G.2M Green column 4m
*Note* The leading lights on 058·5° close east of the
  marina entrance lead into the shallow Río Barbate.

### Marina radio

*Puerto Deportivo Barbate* VHF Ch 09.

### General

Formerly known as Barbate de Franco (pronounced
'Barbartay', with the 'de Franco' now dropped), the
old town has been swallowed up by new
development and has no great appeal, though the
marina is useful as a refuge from the strong winds
characteristic of the Straits. The harbour, in which
fishing boats berth to the east and yachts to the west,
covers a large area and is the easternmost (in the
Atlantic) of the string of harbours and marinas
financed, built and run by the Junta de Puertos de
Andalucía in Seville – see page 204.

The shallow Río Barbate about 0·4M to the east is
used by local boats, but the entrance is difficult and
depths within are less than 2·5m.

### Approach

Coming from the west, rocky shoals run southwest
from Cabo Trafalgar[2406] – which at only 20m or so
appears low-lying compared to the hills 2km to the
northeast – culminating in the dangerous Bajo
Aceitera more than 1·5M offshore. In heavy weather
the Placer de Meca bank, 3·2M to the west, may
break and should also be avoided. A race can form
up to 8M offshore in these conditions, particularly
when east-going current and tidal stream oppose the
*levanter*. An inside passage is used by fishermen, but
it should not be attempted without local knowledge.

From the southeast, Punta Camarinal cuts the
direct line from Tarifa (off which a race may also
form). Note the dangerous shoal, Bajo de Los
Cabezos, 5M west of Tarifa and 2M south of Punta
Paloma, on which waves break even in calm
weather. Between Punta Camarinal and Barbate the
coast is relatively steep-to.

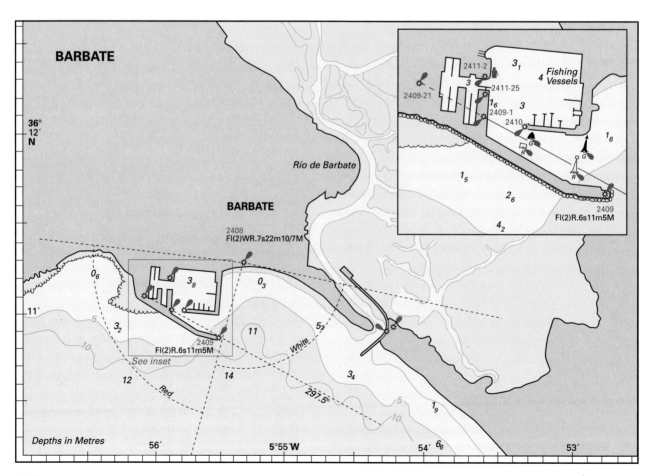

Puerto Deportivo Barbate, at the western end of the enormous harbour run by the Junta de Puertos de Andalucía, seen from the southwest.

## Caution

Two *almadrabas* or tunny (tuna) nets are laid annually near Barbate. *Ensenada de Barbate* is laid from March to September each year very close to the harbour entrance – it is stated that vessels should not pass between the inner end of the net and the shore, but the local fishermen habitually do so. For the past four years it has been set in roughly the same position, and in 1999 it was lit by four (small) cardinal buoys:

buoy **North** 36°10'·9N 5°55'·2W
   Q.3M North cardinal, ⬥ topmark
buoy **West** 36°09'·4N 5°55'·9W
   Q(9)10s3M West cardinal, ⲭ topmark
buoy **South** 36°09'N 5°56'·7W (March to June)
   36°08'·2N 5°54'·9W (June to September)
   Q(6)+LFl.12s3M South cardinal, ⬥ topmark
   (Why this buoy was moved in June is unclear)
buoy **East** 36°09'·1N 5°55'·3W
   Q(3)10s3M East cardinal, ⬥ topmark

*Almadraba Cabo Plato* is laid from March to August each year off the small village of Zahara some 4·5M southeast of Barbate. Again it appears to maintain much the same position, and in 1999 it was lit by three (small) cardinal buoys:

buoy **West No.1** 36°07'·6N 5°52'W
   Q(9)15s3M West cardinal, ⲭ topmark
buoy **West No.2** 36°06'·5N 5°52'W
   Q(9)15s3M West cardinal, ⲭ topmark
buoy **South** 36°06'·4N 5°50'·5W
   Q(6)+LFl.15s3M South cardinal, ⬥ topmark

For the past three winters (September–February) the *Ensenada de Barbate* net has been replaced by a floating fish cage some 270m by 60m, marked by two lit buoys which may be accompanied by marker boats:

buoy **East** 36°09'·2N 5°55'·5W
   Q(3)10s3M East cardinal, ⬥ topmark
buoy **West** 36°09'·3N 5°55'·8W
   Q(9)10s3M West cardinal, ⲭ topmark

## Entrance

Head north for Barbate light[2408], keeping it slightly open of the south breakwater[2409]. Turn in on 297° when the entrance is clear, using the leading lights[2409·2] if at night. The east breakwater remains hidden behind the eastern end of the south breakwater until well into the bay (see chart). Four buoys mark the channel within the harbour entrance, forming two relatively narrow 'gates'. The inner starboard hand buoy was not in place in November 1999. Depths in the entrance channel and throughout both fishing harbour and marina are claimed to be 3m, though shoaling has been reported close to the marina south mole.

The Puerto Deportivo Barbate, ☎ 956 431907 *Fax* 956 431918, *e-mail* barbated@eppa.es, is reached through a narrow entrance leading almost due west from the main harbour, with a reception pontoon on the port hand under the small office building. Winter office hours are 0900–1330 and 1600–1800 Monday to Saturday, 0900–1330 Sunday, remaining open later in summer.

The north side of the entrance is shielded from the shipyard beyond by a low yellow and black barrier with low green and red striped light support on its outer end.

## Berthing

The marina consists of two separate and almost completely enclosed bays, one leading out of the other, with pontoons laid around their perimeters and down the centre of the larger western basin. Currently there are 169 berths, but more may be laid in due course – there is certainly no shortage of space. Yachts of up to 25m can be accommodated, providing the 3m controlling depth is not a limitation, and all but the very largest have individual finger pontoons. There is always room for visitors, who are usually berthed near the marina office.

Berthing charges are at the standard Junta de Puertos de Andalucía rate – see page 204.

## Facilities

*Boatyard, engineers, electronic & radio repairs* Náutica Trafalgar, ☎ 956 434265, handle general and mechanical repairs from their workshops near the fuel pontoon. Other skills available at the trawler shipyards.

*Travel-lift* 32 tonne capacity lift handling both yachts and fishing boats, with fenced hardstanding.

*Chandlery* Small chandlery at Náutica Trafalgar.

*Water* On the pontoons.

*Showers* In the (new) office building.

*Launderette* Planned for 2000.

*Electricity* On the pontoons (but using non-standard plugs which are available from the marina office).

*Fuel* Available from 0830–1840 daily from the fuelling pontoon on the north side of the entrance.

*Bottled gas* Camping Gaz available in the town about 2km distant.

*Ice* At the marina café.

*Club náutico* Near the fishing harbour.

*Weather forecast* Posted daily at the marina office.

*Bank* In the town.

*Shops/provisioning* Good supermarket on the road behind the harbour, with more in the town, but no shops at all at the marina.

*Produce market* In the town.

*Cafés, restaurants & hotels* Small café/bar at the marina serving some food, but no restaurant. Plenty of all three in the town.

*Medical services* In the town.

## Communications

*Post office* In the town.

*Mailing address*
  c/o **Puerto Deportivo Barbate**,
  Oficina del Puerto, Avda del Generalisimo s/n,
  11160 Barbate, Cádiz, España
  *Fax service* 956 431918

*Public telephones* Several kiosks around the marina.

*Car hire/taxis* Book via the office.

*Buses* Bus service to Cádiz, Algeciras and La Línea.

*Air services* International airport at Gibraltar, a short walk across the border from La Línea. Alternatively Jerez or Seville.

# Surface flow in the Strait of Gibraltar

Surface water flow through the Strait is the product of a combination of current and tidal stream, the former dominant for at least eight hours out of the twelve.

A permanent, east-going current sets through the Straits, compensating for water lost from the Mediterranean through evaporation. Strength varies from 1 knot close to the northern shore to approaching 2 knots in the centre and southern part of the channel, with a decrease to 1·5 knots or less near the Moroccan shore. However this pattern can be upset by the wind, and persistent strong westerlies, coupled with the regular current, can produce an easterly set of up to 4 knots. Conversely, the entire flow may reverse after prolonged easterly winds, though in practice this seldom happens.

Tidal streams, though capable of exceeding 3 knots at springs and more off the major headlands, must be worked carefully if attempting to make progress westwards – riding the stream eastwards is generally not a problem unless faced with a strong *levanter*. Streams turn earlier near the coast – see plan opposite – but bear in mind that even then the current may prove stronger than the tide for a considerable part of the cycle. In the middle the tidal stream runs directly through the Strait, but inshore it tends to follow the coastline. Where, with a west-going tide, the boundary between east and west-moving water lies depends on the relative strengths of the two forces, and in stronger winds may be readily detectable by the sea state. Tidal races may form off Cabo Trafalgar, the Bajo de Los Cabezos west of Tarifa, and Isla de Tarifa itself, typically when east-going current and tidal stream oppose the *levanter*.

Over the course of the passage, particularly in a slower yacht or if beating, it may be possible to extend the duration of favourable tide available by moving from one tidal band into another. For example: leaving Gibraltar at HW +3hrs to head west, using the west-going stream inshore until it turns east at HW −3hrs, then moving offshore to gain a further three hours of west-going stream until HW Gibraltar (though it should be noted that this tactic will take a yacht from the Inshore Traffic Zone into the main west-going shipping channel).

A great deal of detailed, practical advice on how best to tackle the Straits of Gibraltar – including unusually clear current and tidal flow diagrams – will be found in Colin Thomas's highly recommended *Straits Sailing Handbook* – see Further reading, page 263.

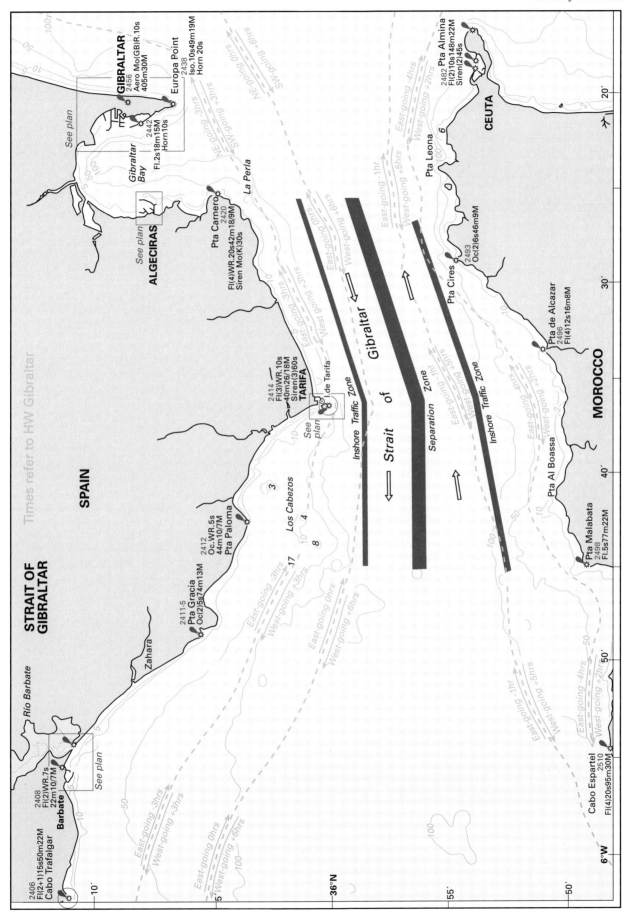

STRAIT OF GIBRALTAR

Times refer to HW Gibraltar

SPAIN

2406
Fl(2+1)15s50m22M
Cabo Trafalgar

*Rio Barbate*

Barbate
2408
Fl(2)WR.7s
22m10/7M

*See plan*

Zahara

2411·5
Pta Gracia
Oc(2)5s74m13M

2412
Oc.WR.5s
44m10/7M
Pta Paloma

*Los Cabezos*

3

4

10

8

17

*East-going -3hrs*
*West-going +3hrs*

*East-going 0hrs*
*West-going +6hrs*

ALGECIRAS

*See plan*

Pta Carnero
2420
Fl(4)WR.20s42m18/9M
Siren Mo(K)30s

*La Perla*

*Gibraltar Bay*

*See plan*

GIBRALTAR
2456
Aero Mo(GB)R.10s
405m30M

2442
Fl.2s18m15M
Horn10s

Europa Point
2438
Iso.10s49m19M
Horn 20s

2414
Fl(3)WR.10s
40m26/18M
Siren(3)60s

TARIFA
I.de Tarifa

*See plan*

Inshore Traffic Zone

*Strait*

*of*

*Gibraltar*

Separation Zone

Inshore Traffic Zone

*East-going 0hrs*
*West-going +6hrs*

*NE-going -3hrs*
*SW-going +3hrs*

*NE-going 0hrs*
*SW-going +6hrs*

*East-going +3hrs*
*West going -3hrs*

*East-going +3hrs*
*West-going +6hrs*

*East-going +5hrs*
*West-going -1hr*

*East-going -1hr*
*West-going +5hrs*

*East-going +2hrs*
*West-going +5hrs*

*East-going -4hrs*
*West-going +2hrs*

CEUTA

2482 Pta Almina
Fl(2)10s148m22M
Siren(2)45s

Pta Leona

6

2493
Oc(2)6s46m9M

Pta Cires

Pta de Alcazar
2496
Fl(4)12s16m8M

MOROCCO

Pta Al Boassa

Pta Malabata
2498
Fl.5s77m22M

*East-going -4hrs*
*West-going +2hrs*

*East-going +5hrs*
*West-going -1hr*

Cabo Espartel
2510
Fl(4)20s95m30M

*East-going +5hrs*
*West-going -1hr*

6°W

50'

40'

30'

20'

10'

55'

36°N

5'

50'

245

# Tarifa

36°00'N 5°36'·5W

## Tides

*Reference port* Gibraltar
*Mean time differences*
HW: −40 minutes; LW: −40 minutes

*Heights in metres*

| MHWS | MHWN | MLWN | MLWS |
|------|------|------|------|
| 1·4 | 1·0 | 0·6 | 0·3 |

## Charts

| | Approach | Harbour |
|---|---|---|
| Admiralty | 92, 142, 773 | 142 |
| Spanish | 44C, 105, 445, 445B | 4450 |
| Imray | C19 | |

## Lights

### Approach

2406 **Cabo Trafalgar** 36°11'N 6°02'W
  Fl(2+1)15s50m22M
  White conical tower and building 34m
*0994* Radiobeacon *B* 297kHz 50M
2411·5 **Punta de Gracia (Punta Camarinal)**
  36°05'·5N 5°48'·5N
  Oc(2)5s74m13M Masonry tower 20m
2412 **Punta Paloma** 36°04'N 5°43'·1N
  Oc.WR.5s44m10/7M
  010°-W-340°-R-010° (over Bajo de Los Cabezos)
  Two-storey building 5m
2414 **Tarifa** 36°00'·1N 5°36'·5W
  Fl(3)WR.10s40m26/18M 089°-R-113°-W-089°
  White tower 33m Racon Mo(C) 360° 20M
  Siren (3)60s Masonry structure 10m
*0996* Radiobeacon *O* 299kHz 50M
2420 **Punta Carnero** 36°04'·7N 5°25'·5W
  Fl(4)WR.20s42m18/9M 018°-W-325°-R-018°
  (Red sector covers La Perla and Las Bajas shoals)
  Siren Mo(K)30s
  Yellow round tower, green base, silver lantern 19m

### Harbour

2415 **Isla de Tarifa, NE** 36°00'·3N 5°36'·3W
  Fl.R.5s11m3M Red square tower 3m

2416 **East breakwater** 36°00'·5N 5°36'·1W
  Fl.G.5s10m5M 249°-vis-045° Green lattice tower 5m
  (Dwarfed by square stone pillar surmounted by
  statue of man, approximately 55m)
2418 **West (inner) mole** 36°00'·6N 5°36'·1W
  Fl(2)R.6s6m1M Red lantern on white hut 4m

## Navtex

**Tarifa** Identification letter 'G'
*Transmits*: 518kHz in English.
*Weather messages*: 0900, 2100 gale warnings, synopsis and
  forecast for areas 6–7 (see plan page 5).
*Navigational warnings*: 0100, 0500, 1300, 1700 for
  Navarea II and coastal waters.

## Radio weather/navigational services

**Tarifa** (36°03'N 5°33'W)
*Weather messages*: VHF Ch 10, 74 at 0015, 0215, 0415,
  0615, 0815, 1015, 1215, 1415, 1615, 1815, 2015,
  2215 in Spanish and English – actual wind and
  visibility at Tarifa followed by the forecast for the Strait
  of Gibraltar, Cádiz Bay and Alborán.
*Navigational warnings*: on receipt in Spanish and English
  for the Strait of Gibraltar between Cabo Espartel and
  Punta Almina.
*Visibility (fog) warnings*: VHF Ch 10, 74 at 0015, 0215,
  0415, 0615, 0815, 1015, 1215, 1415, 1615, 1815,
  2015, 2215 (more frequently when visibility falls below
  2M) in Spanish and English.

## Traffic Separation Zone

There is a Traffic Separation Zone in the Strait of
Gibraltar between 5°25'·5W and 5°45'W – see plan page
245. The Inshore Traffic Zone to the north is nowhere
less than 1·6M wide (off the Isla de Tarifa) and generally
more than 2M.

*Tarifa Traffic* monitors VHF Ch 16 and 10 and vessels are
advised to maintain a listening watch whilst in the area.
Information is broadcast at 15 minutes past the hour
(even hours only), more frequently in poor visibility.
Radar assistance may be available on request, together
with a weather forecast which is also broadcast every two
hours from 0100 on VHF Ch 10.

The entrance to Tarifa harbour looking northeast, with the east breakwater and its prominent statue on the right.

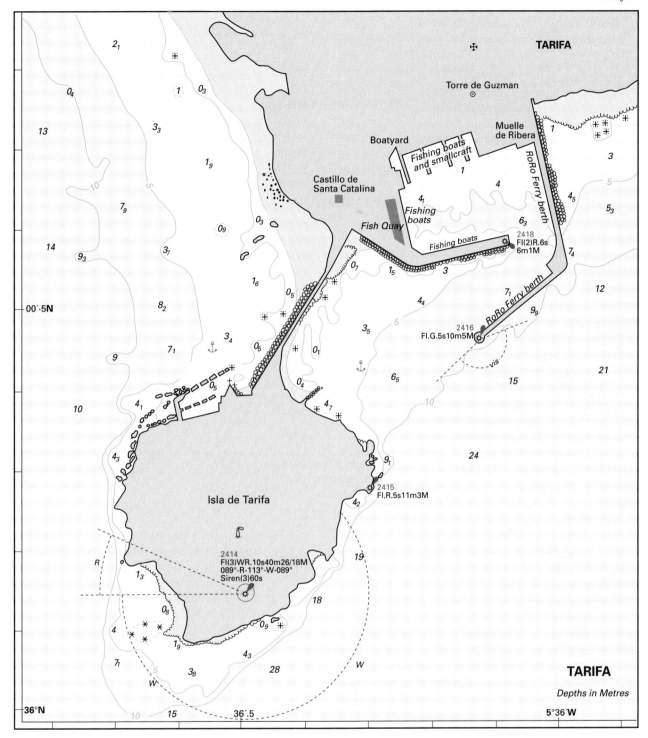

**TARIFA**

*Depths in Metres*

## General

Tarifa is the most southerly city of mainland Europe and, at barely 8M distant, considerably closer to North Africa than is Gibraltar. It is famous for its frequent strong winds, which together with excellent beaches have made it the boardsailing capital of Europe.

Reputedly where the Moors landed on their European invasion, the older part of the town still shows a strong North African influence, particularly in the well preserved streets around the harbour. It has an active (but not over-obtrusive) tourist industry and consequently is well provided with shops, restaurants and hotels. A diving school has been established just outside the harbour gates.

Unfortunately the Isla de Tarifa is a military area and closed to the public, as is the handsome old Castillo de Santa Catalina to the northwest, but the road between Tarifa and Algeciras is worth traversing if possible for its dramatic views of both Gibraltar and the Strait.

## Approach

From the west, Tarifa light[2414] stands on its promontory clear of the land. Chief danger is the Bajo de los Cabezos, 5M west of Tarifa and 3M south of Punta Paloma. The bank is marked by broken water even in calm weather, and several wrecks are reputed to lie close to the surface.

From the east, there are dangers up to 1M offshore between Punta Carnero[2420] and Punta de Cala Arenas, but once west of the latter the shore is generally steep to. There is a prominent windfarm on the hills northeast of the town.

A race may form off Isla de Tarifa when east-going current and tidal stream oppose the *levanter*.

## Caution

An *almadraba* or tunny (tuna) net known as *Lances de Tarifa* is laid between June and November each year northwest of Isla de Tarifa. For the past four years it has been set in roughly the same position, and in 1999 was lit by two (small) west cardinal buoys:

buoy **West No.1** 36°02'N 5°38'·3W
   Q(9)15s3M West cardinal, ⟨ topmark
buoy **West No.2** 36°01'·2N 5°38'·3W
   Q(9)15s3M West cardinal, ⟨ topmark

## Entrance

The harbour entrance faces southwest towards the Isla de Tarifa and its connecting causeway. Head for the conspicuous statue at the end of the east breakwater[2416], before making the dogleg into the harbour.

*Note* In a levanter this approach becomes a lee shore and it may be wiser to use the second of the anchorages mentioned below – or to press on for Barbate or beyond.

## Berthing

Tarifa is far from yacht-orientated, and it will be necessary to take pot-luck amongst the large

Fishing vessels in Tarifa harbour on a blowy Sunday afternoon, with the Torre de Guzman behind.

trawlers which berth against the east breakwater, avoiding the two Ro-Ro ferry berths. However there is little to secure to, and the high wall is poorly provided with ladders. If lying alongside is not feasible it may be possible to anchor stern-to, when a bower with heavy ground tackle and 30m or more of chain will allow the yacht to be hauled off in the event of increasing westerly winds. A trip-line is essential. Note that the extreme southwest end of the breakwater is reserved for the small naval vessels which patrol the Straits on the lookout for smuggling, etc.

Over the last couple of years the long, narrow naval pens in the north part of the harbour have been converted into stern-to berthing for the port's smaller fishing vessels and other assorted smallcraft. A number of the old dividing moles have been removed, together with the debris which used to litter the area, but no room remains for visitors. Similarly the fish quay is taken up entirely by the active fishing boats.

## Formalities

There is a *policia* portacabin at the root of the east breakwater, at which immigration formalities can be handled if arriving from outside Spain – most probably Gibraltar. However it appears to be manned only when a ferry is due.

A representative from the *capitania* is likely to visit, and a charge of around 2,500 ptas (15·03 euros) per night may be made for a visiting yacht of 11–12m despite the almost total lack of facilities.

## Facilities

Virtually nothing, other than water from taps behind the old naval pens and on the fishing quay. There is no yacht fuel and no possibility of getting electricity aboard. The small boatyard (with marine railway) in the northwest corner of the harbour is geared to fishing boats but could doubtless carry out minor yacht repairs if necessary.

A café/bar and public toilets will be found on the southwest arm, otherwise the town has shops of all kinds, a produce market, banks, restaurants and hotels.

## Communications

Post office in the old part of town, with telephones around the harbour, etc. Taxis in surprising numbers. Buses to Cádiz, Algeciras and La Línea, from which it is a short walk to the international airport at Gibraltar.

## Anchorages

1. In the clean sandy bay northeast of Isla de Tarifa, between the causeway and the harbour entrance, in 4–5m over sand. The area is popular with both divers and boardsailors, but a yacht may attract curiosity from the authorities.
2. Just north of a derelict mole on the northwest side of Isla de Tarifa, with shelter from easterly seas (though not the wind) given by the causeway. Good holding over sand in 3–4m.

# Algeciras

36°09'N 5°25'W

## Tides

*Reference port* Gibraltar
*Mean time differences*
HW: −10 minutes; LW: −10 minutes

*Heights in metres*

| MHWS | MHWN | MLWN | MLWS |
|------|------|------|------|
| 1·1 | 0·9 | 0·4 | 0·2 |

## Charts

| | *Approach* | *Harbour* |
|---|---|---|
| Admiralty | *92, 142, 773, 1448, 3578* | *1448* |
| Spanish | *44C, 105, 445, 445A, 453* | *4451* |
| Imray | *C19* | |

## Lights

### Approach

2420 **Punta Carnero** 36°04'·7N 5°25'·5W
  Fl(4)WR.20s42m18/9M 018°-W-325°-R-018°
  (Red sector covers La Perla and Las Bajas shoals)
  Siren Mo(K)30s
  Yellow round tower, green base, silver lantern 19m
buoy **East cardinal** 35°06'·8N 5°24'·7W
  Q(3)10s4M BYB pillar buoy, ♦ topmark, 4m
2456 **Gibraltar Aeromarine** 36°08'·7N 5°20'·5W
  Aero Mo(GB)R.10s405m30M
  Obscured on westerly bearings within 2M
2438 **Europa Point, Gibraltar** 36°06'·7N 5°20'·6W
  Iso.10s49m19M 197°-vis-042°, 067°-vis-125°
  Oc.R.10s15M and F.R.15M 042°-vis-067°
  (Red sector covers La Perla and Las Bajas shoals)
  Horn 20s White round tower, red band 19m

### Commercial Harbour

2424 **Northeast breakwater** 36°08'·9N 5°25'·6W
  Fl(2)R.6s11m8M Red metal post 5m

### Dársena del Saladillo (marina)

buoy **Port hand** 36°07'·2N 5°25'·6W
  Fl(2)R.7s5M Red pillar buoy

Looking south over the new marina at Algeciras (still unfinished in November 1999) with Punta Carnero running out to the left. In the far distance can be seen the mountains of Morocco.
*La Autoridad Portuaria de la Bahia de Algeciras*

buoy **Starboard hand** 36°07'·3N 5°25'·6W
  Fl(2)G.7s5M Green pillar buoy
buoy **Arrecife** 36°07'·3N 5°25'·9W
  Fl(3)G.9s3M Green pillar buoy, ▲ topmark
2423 **South breakwater** 36°07'·2N 5°26'W
  Fl(3)R.9s7m3M Red and white post 6m
2423·2 **North breakwater** 36°07'·2N 5°26'·1W
  Fl(4)G.11s2m3M
  Green light on small red support 1m
2423·1 **Inner (marina) mole** 36°07'·2N 5°26'·2W
  Fl(4)R.11s2m3M Red and white post on red base 2m

## Radio weather/navigational services

**Algeciras** (36°09'N 5°27'W)
*Weather messages*: VHF Ch 15, 74 at 0315, 0515, 0715, 1115, 1515, 1915, 2315 in Spanish and English.
*Navigational warnings*: on request in Spanish and English.

## Yacht club and port radio

*Real Club Náutico de Algeciras* VHF Ch 09, 16.
*Algeciras Prácticos* VHF Ch 09, 12, 13,16.

## General

An industrial and ferry port, not picturesque and not particularly clean. However it is very busy and handles a lot of guest-worker traffic returning to Africa with roof racks bending under their loads. There are hotels (one a ghost of one of the grander in Europe), shops and restaurants.

There is currently no room in the main harbour for visiting yachts – both the small municipal marina and the even smaller Real Club Náutico de Algeciras marina, ☎ 956 572503, are permanently full, even out of season. However a large new facility has been under construction for several years in the Dársena del Saladillo just south of the port, and when opened should considerably ease the berthing problem. The following approach and entrance instructions thus apply to the Dársena del Saladillo rather than to the commercial harbour.

## Approach

The approaches to Algeciras are extremely busy with commercial traffic of all sizes. In particular, a sharp watch needs to be kept for the many high-speed ferries, including hydrofoils, which run between Algeciras and Morocco. These are notorious for maintaining their course and speed at all times, presumably adhering to the 'might is right' principle.

Coming from the west, there are dangers up to 1M offshore between Punta de Cala Arenas and Punta Carnero[2420]. On rounding this headland the city and harbour will be seen some 3M to the north behind a mile-long breakwater terminating with a light[2424]. Various ledges run out from the headlands between Punta Carnero and the entrance to the Dársena del Saladillo (also lit). Yachts can safely cut inside the east cardinal buoy placed nearly a mile offshore, though an offing of at least 0·5M should be maintained. Further ledges lie both north and south of the entrance, and the three buoys marking the approach should under no circumstances be ignored.

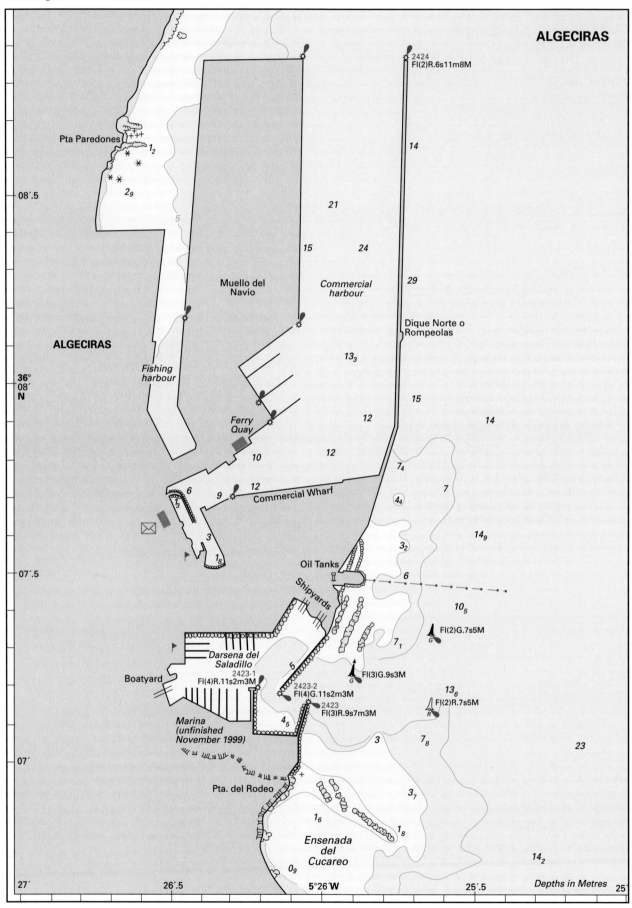

**ALGECIRAS**

Pta Paredones

$1_2$

$2_9$

08´.5

**ALGECIRAS**

Muello del
Navio

21

15

24

*Commercial
harbour*

14

29

*Fishing
harbour*

Dique Norte o
Rompeolas

2424
Fl(2)R.6s11m8M

36°
08´
N

$13_3$

15

12

14

*Ferry
Quay*

12

10

$7_4$

12

6

$1_3$

9

12

Commercial Wharf

$4_4$

7

3

$14_9$

$1_8$

$3_2$

Oil Tanks

07´.5

6

Shipyards

$10_5$

Fl(2)G.7s5M
G

$7_1$

Fl(3)G.9s3M
G

*Darsena del
Saladillo*

Boatyard

2423·1
Fl(4)R.11s2m3M

5

2423·2
Fl(4)G.11s2m3M

$13_6$
Fl(2)R.7s5M
R

2423
Fl(3)R.9s7m3M

*Marina
(unfinished
November 1999)*

$4_5$

3

$7_8$

23

07´

Pta. del Rodeo

$3_7$

$1_6$

$1_8$

*Ensenada
del
Cucareo*

$14_2$

$0_9$

27´

26´.5

5°26´W

25´.5

Depths in Metres

25´

If approaching from Gibraltar or other points east, the entrance to the Dársena del Saladillo should be easily seen south of the oil tanks on the commercial quay and it can be approached directly.

## Entrance

The dogleg entrance to the Dársena del Saladillo has been very well designed, such that when visited in a 30 knot easterly wind no swell at all was entering. As noted above, three buoys mark the final approach, after which the entrance itself is straightforward.

## Berthing

When visited in November 1999 the new marina appeared structurally almost complete – as it apparently had for at least two years. Seven long pontoons were in place on the south side of the bay, behind a solid mole with a short angled end, and some of the access roads were also complete. However no buildings had yet been started. Neither could any completion date be given, though 'one or two years' was suggested. The claim that it will hold some 800 berths looked entirely possible. There was no sign of finger pontoons, or fittings for them, so berthing is likely to be bow or stern-to with the usual haul-off ropes.

Although currently under the jurisdiction of the main port authority, it is understood that the marina will eventually be run by the Real Club Náutico de Algeciras, who will also have a new clubhouse on the site.

On the north side of the bay the premises of the Club Náutico Saladillo are already functioning, complete with three pontoons berthing craft to about 10m. However they are understood to be reserved entirely for the use of members and the three smallcraft pontoons further east are too small to take a visiting yacht. A shipyard building fishing trawlers and small commercial vessels occupies the far northeast corner, with a number of semi-submerged hulks in the approach.

## Facilities

It is safe to say that berths on the new marina are certain to be provided with water, showers and electricity, and that the new Real Club Náutico clubhouse will have a bar and restaurant. It has also been stated that the boatyard at the head of the harbour, now mostly dealing with wooden fishing boats, is to be adapted for yacht work.

Otherwise all the usual shops, banks, restaurants and hotels are to be found in the city, but at some distance. Spanish charts may be obtained from Valnáutica SL, ☎ 956 570677 *Fax* 956 285270, at Avenida 28 de Febrero 33.

## Communications

Post office and telephones in the town. Car hire and taxis; trains to many destinations including Madrid; buses to La Línea, from which it is a short walk to the international airport at Gibraltar.

# Gibraltar

36°09'N 5°21'W

## Tides

Gibraltar is a Standard Port

*Heights in metres*

| MHWS | MHWN | MLWN | MLWS |
|------|------|------|------|
| 1·0  | 0·7  | 0·3  | 0·1  |

## Charts

| | Approach | Harbour |
|---|---|---|
| Admiralty | 92, 142, 773, 1448, 3578 | 45, 144, 1448 |
| Spanish | 44C, 105, 445, 445A, 453 | 4452 |
| Imray | C19, M1 | C19 |

## Lights

### Approach

2420 **Punta Carnero** 36°04'·7N 5°25'·5W
Fl(4)WR.20s42m18/9M 018°-W-325°-R-018°
(Red sector covers La Perla and Las Bajas shoals)
Siren Mo(K)30s
Yellow round tower, green base, silver lantern 19m

2456 **Gibraltar Aeromarine** 36°08'·7N 5°20'·5W
Aero Mo(GB)R.10s405m30M
Obscured on westerly bearings within 2M

2438 **Europa Point, Gibraltar** 36°06'·7N 5°20'·6W
Iso.10s49m19M 197°-vis-042°, 067°-vis-125°
Oc.R.10s15M and F.R.15M 042°-vis-067°
(Red sector covers La Perla and Las Bajas shoals)
Horn 20s White round tower, red band 19m

### Harbour

2442 **South breakwater, north end (A Head)**
36°08'·1N 5°21'·8W Fl.2s18m15M Horn 10s
Grey round tower 15m

2445 **Detached breakwater, south end (B Head)**
36°08'·2N 5°21'·8W Q.R.9m5M
Metal structure on concrete building 11m

2451·2 **Queensway Quay Marina, south pontoon**
36°08'·1N 5°21'·3W 2F.G(vert) 5m

2451 **Queensway Quay Marina, west (detached) pontoon**
36°08'·2N 5°21'·3W 2F.R(vert)

2450·7 **Cormorant Camber, south end**
36°08'·3N 5°21'·3W 2F.R(vert) 5m

2451·5 **Coaling Island, north mole**
36°08'·5N 5°21'·5W 2F.G(vert)

2446 **Detached breakwater, north end (C Head)**
36°08'·6N 5°22'W Q.G.10m5M
Metal structure on concrete building 11m

2448 **North breakwater, southwest arm (D Head)**
36°08'·7N 5°21'·9W Q.R.18m5M Round tower 17m

2449·2 **North breakwater, northwest elbow (E Head)** 36°09'N 5°21'·9W F.R.28m5M Tower

2436·8 **La Linea, main breakwater** 36°09'·6N 5°22'W Fl(2)G.6s8m4M Round green and white tower 4m

Plus other lights in the interior of the harbour and to the north.

## Radio weather/navigational services

### Gibraltar Broadcasting Corporation

*Weather messages*: 91·3, 92·6, 100·5MHz and 1458kHz at 0610, 0930, 1030, 1230, 1300, 1530, 1715 Mon–Fri; 0930, 1030, 1230, 1300 Sat; 1030, 1230 Sun. Synopsis, situation, wind and sea states and visibility in English for waters to 50M from Gibraltar (1300 broadcast in Spanish).

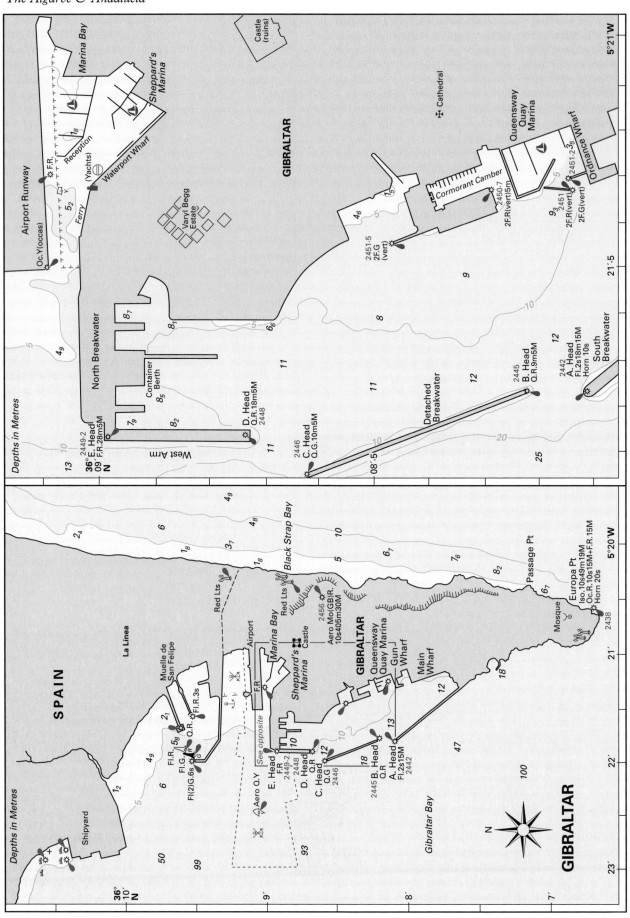

*Depths in Metres*

Marina Bay

Sheppard's Marina

Castle (ruins)

Airport Runway

F.R.

Reception

$1_8$

Oc.Y(occas)

$5_2$ Y

Ferry (Yachts)

Waterport Wharf

GIBRALTAR

✠ Cathedral

Varyl Begg Estate

Queensway Quay Marina

Cormorant Camber

Ordnance Wharf

2451·2·35

2F.R(vert)15m

$9_3$ 2451

2F.R(vert)

2F.G(vert)

2450·7

$4_6$

$5$

$5$

2451·5 2FG (vert)

$9$

$21'·5$

$10$

North Breakwater

$8_7$

$8_1$

$5$

$6_6$

$8$

Container Berth $8_5$

$8_2$

$7_9$

2449·2

**36°** E. Head

09 F.R.28m5M

**N**

West Arm

$11$

$13$

$10$

$5$

$4_9$

D. Head Q.R.18m5M 2448

$11$

C. Head Q.G.10m5M 2446

Detached Breakwater

$11$

$12$

$10$

$08'·5$

$20$

$25$

A. Head Fl.2s18m15M Horn 10s 2442

$12$

B. Head Q.R.9m5M 2445

South Breakwater

$5'21'W$

*Depths in Metres*

**SPAIN**

La Linea

Muelle de San Felipe

Shipyard

$1_2$

$2_1$

Fl.R. $5_8$

R

Fl.G. G

Fl(2)G.6s

Q.R.

Fl.R.3s

$4_9$

$6$

$5$

$50$

$99$

$93$

$100$

**36° 10' N**

Red Lts

Black Strap Bay

$4_9$

$4_8$

$6$

$1_8$

$3_7$

$1_8$

$5$

$10$

$2_4$

$6_7$

$7_6$

$8_2$

$6_7$

Passage Pt

Airport

F.R

Marina Bay

Sheppard's Marina

⚓

Castle

Red Lts

Aero Mo(GB)R. 10s405m30M

2456

*See opposite*

Aero Q.Y

E. Head F.R 2449·2 2448

D. Head Q.R

C. Head Q.G 2446

$10$

$12$

$18$

$10$

GIBRALTAR

Queensway Quay Marina

Gun Wharf

Main Wharf

2445 B. Head Q.R

A. Head Fl.2s15M 2442

$13$

$18$

$12$

$47$

$100$

Gibraltar Bay

Mosque

2438

Europa Pt Iso.10s49m19M Oc.R.10s15M+F.R.15M Horn 20s

$18$

$21'$

$22'$

$23'$

$9'$

$8'$

$5°20'W$

**N**

**GIBRALTAR**

*Weather messages and sailing forecast*: 91·3, 92·6, 100·5MHz and 1458kHz at 0630, 0730, 0830, 1130, 1740 Mon–Fri; 0630, 0730, 0830, 1130 Sat; 0730, 0830, 1130 Sun. Synopsis, situation, wind and sea states and visibility and sailing forecast for waters to 50M from Gibraltar.

### British Forces Broadcasting Service, Gibraltar

*Storm and gale warnings*: 93·5, 97·8MHz on receipt in English for the Gibraltar area.

*Weather messages*: 93·5, 97·8MHz at 0745, 0845, 1130, 1715, 2345 LT Mon–Fri; 0845, 0945, 1230 LT Sat–Sun. Shipping forecast: synopsis, situation, wind and sea states and visibility plus HW/LW times.

*Weather messages*: 93·5, 97·8MHz at every H+06 from 0706–2406 LT Mon–Fri; 0706, 0806, 0906, 1006, 1206, 1306, 1406 LT Sat–Sun. Synopsis, situation, wind and sea states and visibility plus HW/LW times for the Gibraltar area.

## Port radio

*Marina Bay* VHF Ch 71 (0830–2200 LT Summer, 0830–2030 LT Winter).

*Sheppard's Marina* VHF Ch 71 (0900–1800 LT Mon–Fri, 0900–1300 LT Sat).

*Queensway Quay Marina* VHF Ch 71 (0830–2145 LT Summer, 0830–2015 LT Winter).

*Queen's Harbour Master* VHF Ch 08 (0800–1630 LT Mon–Thu, 0800–1600 LT Fri).

*Gibraltar* VHF Ch 06, 12, 13, 14, 16 (24 hours).

*Windy* (Lloyds Gibraltar Radio) VHF Ch 08, 12, 14, 16 (24 hours).

## General

Gibraltar is a safe and convenient stopping point for yachts entering or leaving the Mediterranean, as well as being a duty-free port. All facilities are available for repairs and general maintenance, and both general and ship's stores of every kind can be obtained in Gibraltar or by air from England – for some items it may be cheaper, if more effort, to arrange for delivery from England 'For Yacht —— in Transit' and therefore duty free, rather than to buy off the shelf once there. Both the pound sterling and the Gibraltar pound (at parity) are legal tender.

Long popular with English-speaking yachtsmen, all the marinas are busy and it may be wise to book ahead. Two are close to the airport runway which is convenient for crew changes but can be noisy; the third, Queensway Quay Marina, is about 1M further south behind the outer breakwater, in an area previously known as the Auxiliary Camber. All suffer from swell in westerly winds and violent gusting in easterly *levanters*.

Unless in a tearing hurry a tour of the Rock itself must be *de rigeur*, and the museum – with displays of Gibraltar in prehistoric, Phoenician and Roman times – is also recommended. Transiting the border into Spain also is quick and easy on foot, though a passport should be carried, but another matter entirely by car. It is normal to queue in either

'The Rock' looking north, with Europa Point lighthouse at bottom right and near it – and very distinctive from the sea – the white-painted mosque with its tall minaret.

253

The view northwest from the Rock over the airport runway to the long, hooked breakwater at La Linea. At the time of writing it provided good anchorage but little else.

*Claire James*

direction, but while the wait to come in seldom exceeds ten minutes it is not unusual to queue for an hour or more to leave – considerably longer during the rush hour. A phone call to 42777 will give the current outward waiting time. If telephoning from Spain, by mobile phone in either country, it is necessary to include the Spanish access code of 956-7 – see page 11.

### Approach

By day the massive Rock is visible for many miles, though if approaching from the west it opens fully only after rounding Punta Carnero[2420] into Gibraltar Bay. Almost without exception the coastline is steep to, but beware of squalls and sudden windshifts in the bay, particularly during a *levanter*. Yachts must give way to naval and commercial vessels at all times. The west coast of Gibraltar is fringed with wrecks from all eras, many popular as dive sites – any vessel flying International Code Flag 'A' (white with a blue swallowtail) should be given generous clearance.

By night, Gibraltar advertises its presence by flashing its red symbol GB[2456] to the heavens and by

a lesser light[2438] at Europa Point. The precipitous east face is largely dark; the west, where the town and harbours lie, is like a Christmas tree. This can be confusing even in good visibility and make lights difficult to identify – apart from those mentioned above, the most conspicuous are likely to be those on the south breakwater's A Head[2442] and north breakwater's D Head[2448].

### Entrance and Formalities

If making for Marina Bay or Sheppard's Marina it is necessary to call first at Waterport, the customs and reporting station on the north mole opposite the western end of the runway. At night, after rounding north breakwater E Head[2449.2] the row of red lights at the end of the airport runway mark the north side of the channel leading to the customs berth and marinas. Normal particulars of vessel and crew will be required, but formalities are otherwise minimal.

If heading for Queensway Quay Marina, pass between south breakwater A Head[2442] and detached breakwater B Head[2445], after which the marina entrance[2451] is 0·4M to the east. The buildings overlooking the marina are floodlit.

**Berthing**

1. **Marina Bay**

    ☎ 73300 (☎ from Spain 956 7-73300) *Fax* 42656

    Northernmost of the three and largest, with about 200 berths able to take vessels of up to 70m or 4·5m draught, the marina was completed in 1981.

    Arrivals berth alongside the office, towards the outer end of the main pier, having first called at Waterport (see above) for inward clearance. Hours are 0830–2200 (summer), 0830–2030 (winter). Berthing is Mediterranean-style – bow or stern-to with a buoy and lazy-line provided to the pontoon – and prior booking is advised.

    In 1999 the high season (1/5–31/10) rate for a visiting yacht of less than 12m LOA was £6·25 per night, dropping to £4·70 in winter. The monthly low season rate for a yacht of similar size was £131·13 if paid in cash, though most credit cards are also accepted. Electricity and water were metered additional to the above, and a daily Government Levy of 47p per day was also payable. Multihulls paid a 50% surcharge.

2. **Sheppard's Marina**

    ☎ 75148/77183 (☎ from Spain 956-7 75148/77183) *Fax* 42535, *e-mail* sheppard@gibnet.gi

    (Established way back in 1961), Sheppard's is still very much a working boatyard, without the shopping complex aspect but with comprehensive repair and maintenance facilities. A convenient walkway has recently been created to give easy access to the Marina Bay shops, with the boatyard and pontoons behind a security fence with the usual electronic gate.

    Arrivals berth alongside the pontoon extending southwest from the main pier, having first called at Waterport (see above) for inward clearance. Office hours throughout the year are 0900–1800 Monday to Friday, 0900–1300 Saturday, closed Sunday. Berthing is a mixture of bow or stern-to and alongside, with most of the short-term visitors berths amongst the latter. Due to its sheltered position, Sheppard's is least plagued by surge of all Gibraltar's marinas.

    In 1999 the high season (1/6–31/11) rate for a visiting yacht of less than 12m LOA was £4·56 per night if stern-to, dropping to £3·84 in winter, or £8·40 per night throughout the year if alongside. Water was included but electricity was charged at 50p/day. There was no specified monthly rate, but discounts were available for six month stays if paid for in advance. Multihulls paid a 50% surcharge.

3. **Queensway Quay Marina**

    ☎ 44700 *Fax* 44699, *e-mail* qqmarina@gibnet.gi

    Around 100 berths including several for yachts of up to 35m and space for a few mega-yachts of up to 90m. The southernmost of the three pontoons, where short-term visitors are normally berthed, can be distinctly rolly even in an easterly. Berthing is Mediterranean-style – bow or stern-to with a buoy and lazy-line provided to the pontoon – and depths 3·5m throughout.

Queensway Quay has the advantage over the older marinas of greater distance from the dust and noise of the airport, and being barely five minutes from the town centre.

Arrivals should secure to the inside of the south pontoon to be allocated a berth. Customs formalities can be dealt with by fax from the marina office during office hours – 0830–2145 (summer) and 0830–2015 (winter). Access to the pontoons is via number-activated security gates.

In 1999 the high season (1/5–31/10) rate for a visiting yacht of less than 12m LOA was £6·95 per night, dropping to £5·95 in winter. The monthly low season rate for a similar sized yacht was £175·23 if paid in cash, though most credit cards are also accepted. Electricity and water were metered additional to the above. Multihulls paid a 50% surcharge.

**Anchorages**

Anchoring is permitted, though not encouraged, immediately north of the airport runway, northwest of Windsock Island – see plan. Holding is good in 4–5m over sand and it is possible to land by dinghy at the smallcraft pontoons off Western Beach. As this area is British territory it is first necessary to visit Waterport (see above) for inward clearance.

It is also possible to anchor further north in Spanish waters off La Linea (literally 'the line' – an allusion to its military role during the various sieges of the Rock). A long, hooked breakwater, lit[2436·8], encloses a large area of water, part of it dredged to 6·5m and much of the rest carrying 3–4m, with good holding over sand and shingle. However water quality can sometimes be poor (ie. polluted with raw sewage) making swimming unwise. Smallcraft pontoons – the aptly named 'Puerto Chico' – are positioned between the two short northeast moles, but depths are a scant 2m and there is no provision for visitors. It is understood that a full-scale marina may eventually be built near the root of the main breakwater, but work had not started as of November 1999. There is good shopping, including a large supermarket, conveniently close to the anchorage.

**Facilities**

It has been said that if you can't buy it or get it fixed in Gibraltar, you probably can't buy it or get it fixed anywhere. Though perhaps not totally true there is much in the remark and the following list is not, and cannot hope to be, comprehensive. If still searching, the advertisements in Colin Thomas's *Straits Sailing Handbook* – see Further reading, page 263 – would be a good place to start.

*Boatyard* Sizeable boatyard at Sheppard's Marina, with shipwrights and riggers on site. Painting, osmosis treatment and GRP repairs are handled by Calybre Ltd, ☎ 75869 *Fax* 40153. DIY work is also permitted. Mega-yacht capability at Cammell Laird Gibraltar, ☎ 40354 *Fax* 44404, at the southern end of the harbour.

*Travel-lift* 40 tonne capacity travel-lift plus 3 tonne crane at Sheppard's Marina.

*Engineers* Sheppard's can handle light engineering, welding, engine servicing and repairs (agents for Volvo Penta, Mercury and Suzuki). Also Marine Maintenance Ltd, ☎ 78954 *Fax* 74754, *e-mail* fred@gibnet.gi, (Perkins and Yanmar) and Scan-Gib Ltd, ☎/*Fax* 45722, at Marina Bay; and Medmarine Ltd, ☎ 48888 *Fax* 48889, (Yamaha) at Queensway Quay. Tempco Marina Engineering, ☎ 74657 *Fax* 76217, specialise in refrigeration, etc.

*Electronic & radio repairs* Sheppard's (as above) or ElectroMed, ☎ 77077 *Fax* 72051, *e-mail* mail@electro-med.com, at Marina Bay, who can supply and repair equipment from most major manufacturers.

*Sailmaker/sail repairs* As of February 2000 there was no sailmaker or repairer in Gibraltar itself, the nearest being Magnusson Sails, ☎ 952 791241 *Fax* 952 791241, about 35 miles away in Estapona, who may be willing to deliver/collect.

*Liferaft servicing* GV Undery & Son, ☎ 73107 *Fax* 46489 (who are also compass adjusters) and Yachting Gibraltar Ltd, ☎ 73736 *Fax* 350 75274, at Marina Bay.

*Chandleries* At all three marinas, that at Sheppard's being by far the largest with a wide range of electronics, etc. It is claimed that anything not in stock can be ordered from the UK – delivery takes between 3 days and 3 weeks on a speed = cost basis.

Yachting Gibraltar Ltd and Marine Maintenance Ltd (Plastimo agents) both have premises at Marina Bay, while Medmarine Ltd overlook Queensway Quay.

*Charts* Though prices are reported to be much higher than in the UK fully corrected Admiralty charts and other publications from **Gibraltar Chart Agency Ltd**, 11A Block 5 Watergardens ☎ 76293 *Fax* 77293

*Water* On the pontoons at all three marinas.

Looking west over Queensway Quay Marina from the top of the cable car, with the South breakwater ('A' Head) and Detatched breakwater ('B' Head) in the background.

*Showers* At all three marinas. Queensway Quay has particularly good disabled facilities.

*Launderettes* At Marina Bay and Queensway Quay, the latter incorporating a dry cleaners.

*Electricity* On the pontoons at all three marinas.

*Fuel* Diesel and petrol at the fuelling berth inshore of the customs berth (0800–1800 daily), or on the inside of the south pontoon at Queensway Quay. Paraffin from the filling station near Sheppard's Marina.

*Bottled gas* Camping Gaz from the Shell office at the fuel berth, Marine Maintenance Ltd at Marina Bay and elsewhere. Marine Maintenance may also be able to arrange refills of some types of cylinder, though not Calor Gas (see also page 8).

*Ice* From most filling stations.

*Yacht club* The old-established Royal Gibraltar Yacht Club (☎ 78897) welcomes visiting yachtsmen as honorary members while in port.

*Weather forecast* Posted daily at all three marinas.

*Banks* At *Marina Bay* and in the town.

*Shops/provisioning* Supermarkets (including Tesco) and other shops at Marina Bay with a smaller general store at Queensway Quay, but for serious storing–up most people descend on the vast Safeway on the Varyl Begg. Shops of all kinds in the town.

Duty-free stores are available at Waterport customs berth, or Albor Ltd, ☎/*Fax* 73283, at Marina Bay – which doubles as a newsagent and bookshop – can order almost anything in almost any quantity for a yacht in transit.

*Produce market* Excellent produce market over the border at La Línea.

*Cafés, restaurants & hotels* Bars and restaurants overlooking both Marina Bay and Queensway Quay, with many more in the town. Hotel accommodation on the Rock tends to be both limited and (compared with nearby Spain) expensive.

*Medical services* Health centre and chemist at Marina Bay, St Bernards Hospital, (casualty, ☎ 73941) in the town.

## Communications

*Post office* On Main Street, providing a quick and reliable service to/from the UK.

*Mailing addresses*
c/o **Marina Bay Complex Ltd**, Marina Bay,
PO Box 80, Gibraltar
*Fax service* 42656
c/o **H Sheppard & Co Ltd**, Waterport, Gibraltar
*Fax service* 42535
c/o **Queensway Quay Marina**, PO Box 19,
Ragged Staff Wharf, Gibraltar.
*Fax service* 44699

*Public telephones* Covenient to all three marinas, and in the town. Some marina berths have telephone points.

*Car hire/taxis* No shortage of taxis and rental cars (which may be taken into Spain).

*Buses & trains* Buses to La Línea for connection with the Spanish bus service.

*Ferries* Twice weekly ferry to Tangier.

*Air services* Frequent air services to several UK destinations, Tangier, Casablanca and Marrakesh – but no flights to Spain.

A family of Barbary Apes at home on the Rock.

# Appendix

## I. Charts

Charts are listed in the same order in which islands and harbours are described in the text. They and other publications may be updated annually by reference to the Admiralty *List of Lights and Fog Signals Volume D (NP 77)* or weekly via Admiralty or other *Notices to Mariners*. See also page 3.

British Admiralty charts and publications, are available from:

**Imray Laurie Norie & Wilson Ltd**
Wych House St Ives Huntingdon
Cambridgeshire PE27 5BT England
☎ 01480 462114; *Fax* 01480 496109
*e-mail* ilnw@imray.com

*Note* Large-scale charts are only shown on index diagrams where the scale permits.

### British Admiralty

| Chart | Title | Scale |
|---|---|---|
| 45 | Gibraltar harbour | 3,600 |
| 83 | Ports on the south coasts of Portugal and Spain | |
| | Porto de Portimão | 20,000 |
| | Approaches to Faro and Olhão | |
| | Puerto de Huelva | 25,000 |
| | Approaches to Puerto de Huelva | 60,000 |
| 85 | Río Guadalquivir | 40,000 |
| | Puerto de Sevilla | 15,000 |
| | Barra del Río Guadalquivir | 20,000 |
| 86 | Bahia de Cádiz | 25,000 |
| 87 | Cabo Finisterre to the Strait of Gibraltar | 1,000,000 |
| 89 | Cabo de São Vicente to Río de Las Piedras | 175,000 |
| 90 | Río de Las Piedras to Cabo Trafalgar | 175,000 |
| 92 | Cabo de São Vicente to the Strait of Gibraltar | 400,000 |
| 142 | Strait of Gibraltar | 100,000 |
| | Tarifa | 25,000 |
| 144 | Gibraltar | 10,000 |
| 773 | Strait of Gibraltar to Isla de Alborán | 300,000 |
| 1108 | Gijon to Punta Candelaria | 200,000 |
| 1111 | Punta de la Estaca de Bares to Cabo Finisterre | 200,000 |
| 1113 | Harbours on the northwest coast of Spain | |
| | Ría de Camariñas | 30,000 |
| | Ría de Corme y Lage | 40,000 |
| 1114 | Ría de Ares, Betanzos and la Coruña | 25,000 |
| | Puerto de la Coruña | 15,000 |
| 1115 | Ría de el Ferrol del Caudillo | 15,000 |
| | Punta de San Carlos to Castillo de la Palma | 7,500 |
| 1448 | Gibraltar Bay | 25,000 |
| | Algeciras | 12,500 |
| 1756 | Ría de Muros | 40,000 |

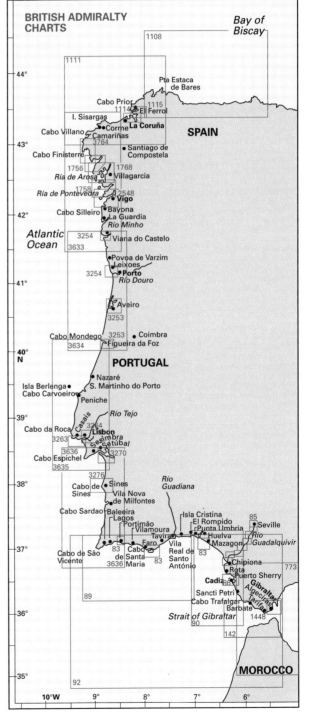

| Chart | Title | Scale |
|---|---|---|
| 1757 | Harbours on the west coast of Spain | |
| | Vigo | 15,000 |
| | Villagarcía de Arosa | 20,000 |
| 1758 | Ría de Pontevedra | 40,000 |
| | Marin | 20,000 |
| 1768 | Ría de Arosa | 40,000 |
| 2548 | Ría de Vigo | 42,000 |
| 3253 | Aveiro and Figueira da Foz | |
| | Aveiro | 15,000 |
| | Figueira da Foz | 15,000 |
| 3254 | Viana do Castelo, Leixões and Río Douro | |
| | Porto de Leixões and Río Douro | 12,500 |
| | Viana do Castelo | 15,000 |
| 3263 | Approaches to Lisboa | 25,000 |
| 3264 | Port of Lisboa | 25,500 |
| | Canal do Alfeite | 12,500 |
| 3270 | Porto de Setúbal | 25,000 |
| 3276 | Porto de Sines | 10,000 |
| | Approaches to Sines | 60,000 |
| 3578 | Eastern Approaches to the Strait of Gibraltar | 150,000 |
| 3633 | Islas Sisargas to Montedor | 200,000 |
| 3634 | Montedor to Cabo Mondego | 200,000 |
| 3635 | Cabo Mondego to Cabo Espichel | 200,000 |
| 3636 | Cabo Espichel to Cabo de São Vicente | 200,000 |
| 3764 | Cabo Toriñana to Punta Carreiro | 40,000 |

**Spanish Hydrographic Institute**

| Chart | Title | Scale |
|---|---|---|
| 41 | De Cabo de la Estaca de Bares a Río Lima | 350,000 |
| 41A | De Puerto de San Ciprián a Cabo Finisterre | 200,000 |
| 41B | De Cabo Villano a Esposende | 175,000 |
| 42 | De Cabo Corrubedo a Cabo Carvoeiro | 350,000 |
| 43 | De Cabo Carvoeiro a Cabo de San Vicente | 350,000 |
| 44 | De Cabo de San Vicente al Estrecho de Gibraltar | 350,000 |
| 44B | De Cabo de Santa María a Cabo Trafalgar | 175,000 |
| 44C | Costa Sur de España y Norte de Marruecos. De broa de Sanlúcar a Estepona y de Larache a Cabo Mazarí | 175,000 |
| 45 | Estrecho de Gibraltar y Mar de Alborán | 350,000 |
| 105 | Estrecho de Gibraltar. De Cabo Roche a punta de la Chullera y de Cabo Espartel a Cabo Negro | 100,000 |
| 412A | Rías de El Ferrol, Ares, Betanzos y La Coruña | 25,000 |
| 415B | Aproches de la Ría de Arosa y Corrubedo | 25,000 |
| | Isla Sálvora | 25,000 |
| 415C | Ría de Arosa | 25,000 |
| 416 | De la Península del Grove a Cabo Silleiro | 60,000 |
| 416A | Ría de Pontevedra | 25,000 |
| 416B | Ría de Vigo | 25,000 |
| 417 | De Islas Cies a Río Miño | 60,000 |
| | Plano inserto Puerto de la Guardia | 5,000 |
| 441 | De Río Guadiana a la Ría de Huelva | 50,000 |
| 441A | Desembocadura del Río Guadiana y Ría de Isla Cristina | 20,000 |
| 441B | Río de las Piedras | 25,000 |
| 442 | De punta del Picacho a Rota | 60,000 |

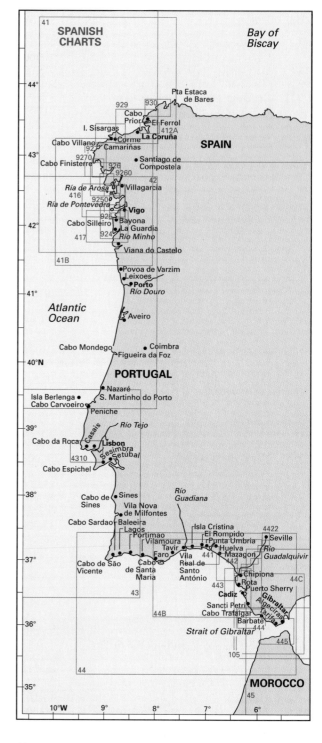

| Chart | Title | Scale |
|---|---|---|
| 443 | De Chipiona a Cabo Roche | 50,000 |
| 443A | Aproches del Puerto de Cádiz – Zona Norte | 25,000 |
| 443B | Aproches del Puerto de Cádiz – Zona Sur | 25,000 |
| 444 | De Cabo Roche a punta Camarinal | 50,000 |
| 445 | Estrecho de Gibraltar. De punta Camarinal a punta Europa y de Cabo Espartel a punta Almina | 60,000 |
| 445A | Bahía de Algeciras | 25,000 |
| 445B | Bajo de los Cabezos e Isla de Tarifa | 25,000 |

| Chart | Title | Scale |
|-------|-------|-------|
| 453 | De punta Europa a la Torre de las Bóvedas | 50,000 |
| 924 | De Islas Cíes a Río Miño | 50,000 |
| 925 | De Cabo Corrubedo a Cabo Silleiro | 50,000 |
| 926 | De Cabo de la Nave a la Isla Sálvora | 50,000 |
| 927 | De Cabo Villano a Monte Louro | 50,000 |
| 928 | De las Islas Sisargas a Cabo Villano | 50,000 |
|  | Plano inserto Fondeadero de las Islas Sisargas | 15,000 |
| 929 | De punta Frouseira a las Islas Sisargas, con las Rías de El Ferrol, Ares, Betanzos y La Coruña | 55,000 |
| 4122 | Acceso a la Ría de El Ferrol | 10,000 |
| 4123 | Puerto de El Ferrol | 10,000 |
| 4125 | Rías de Ares y Betanzos | 10,000 |
| 4126 | Ría y Puerto de La Coruña | 10,000 |
| 4152 | Puerto de Santa Eugenia de Riveira | 7,500 |
|  | Puerto de la Puebla del Caramiñal | 7,500 |
|  | Puertos de Villaneuva y San Julián de Arosa | 10,000 |
|  | Puertos de Cambados y San Martin del Grove | 10,000 |
|  | El Grove | 10,000 |
|  | La Toja, Espigón | 10,000 |
| 4153 | Puerto de Villagarcía de Arosa y Villajuan | 7,500 |
| 4161 | Puerto de Portonovo y Sangenjo | 7,500 |
| 4162 | Puerto de Marín | 5,000 |
| 4163 | Puerto de Bueu | 7,500 |
| 4165 | Ría de Vigo (Hoja I) | 7,500 |
| 4166 | Ría de Vigo (Hoja II) | 7,500 |
| 4167 | Puertos de Panjón y Bayona | 10,000 |
| 4219 | Puerto de Aveiro | 10,000 |
| 4310 | Desembocadura del Río Tejo y Puerto de Lisboa | 40,000 |
| 4311 | Puerto de Sines | 10,000 |
| 4413 | Barra y Puerto de Huelva | 25,000 |
| 4421 | Broa de Sanlúcar de Barrameda y fondeadero de Bonanza | 12,500 |
| 4422 | Río Guadalquivir. De la Broa de Sanlúcar a Sevilla | |
|  | Hoja I – Indice gráfico del Río Guadalquivir | 200,00 |
|  | Hoja II – Broa de Sanlúcar y fondeadero de Bonanza | 25,000 |
|  | Hoja III – Barra del Río Guadalquivir (Fifteen further sheets, Hojas IV to XVIII, cover the Río Guadalquivir as far as Puerto de Sevilla) | 12,500 |
|  |  | 12,500 |
| 4432 | Puertos de Cádiz, Base Naval de Rota y El Puerto de Santa María | 15,000 |
| 4433 | Puerto de la Base Naval de Rota | 5,000 |
| 4434 | Puerto de El Puerto de Santa María | 5,000 |
| 4435 | Puerto de Cádiz (Hoja I) | 5,000 |
| 4436 | Puerto de Cádiz (Hoja II) | 5,000 |
| 4437 | Arsenal de La Carraca y accesos al mismo | 5,000 |
| 4438 | Barra de Sancti-Petri | 5,000 |
| 4441 | Puerto de Barbate | 10,000 |
| 4450 | Puerto de Tarifa | 7,500 |
| 4451 | Bahía de Algeciras – Zona Oeste | 10,000 |
| 4452 | Bahía de Algeciras – Zona Este | 10,000 |
|  | Bahía y Puerto de Tánger | 4,360 |
| 9250 | De Isla Sálvora a las Islas Cíes | 30,000 |
| 9251 | Ría de Pontevedra | 20,000 |
| 9260 | De Monte Louro a la Isla Sálvora | 30,000 |
| 9261 | Ría de Arosa | 30,000 |

| Chart | Title | Scale |
|-------|-------|-------|
| 9263 | Ría de Arosa (Hoja II) Ensenadas de Santa Eugenia de Riveira, Puebla del Caramiñal, Rianjo, Carril y Villagarcía | 20,000 |
| 9264 | Ría de Muros y Noya | 20,000 |
| 9270 | De Cabo de la Nave a Monte Louro | 30,000 |
| 9271 | Seno de Corcubión | 15,000 |
| 9272 | Ría de Camariñas | 12,500 |
| 9280 | Ría de Corme y Lage | 15,000 |

**Portuguese Hydrographic Institute**
(New series – see page 3)

| | | |
|---|---|---|
| 23201 | Vigo a Leixões | 200,000 |
| 23202 | Leixões a Lisboa | 300,000 |

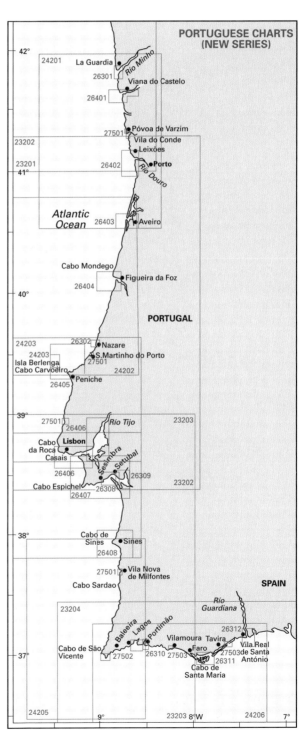

| Chart | Title | Scale |
|---|---|---|
| 23203 | Lisboa a Cabo de São Vicente | 300,000 |
| 23204 | Cabo de São Vicente ao | |
| | Estreito de Gibraltar | 350,000 |
| 24201 | Carminha a Aveiro | 150,000 |
| 24202 | Aveiro a Peniche | 150,000 |
| 24203 | Nazaré a Lisboa | 150,000 |
| | Plano Ilha Berlenga | |
| 24204 | Cabo da Roca ao Cabo de Sines | 150,000 |
| 24205 | Cabo de Sines a Lagos | 150,000 |
| 24206 | Cabo de São Vicente à Foz do | |
| | Guadiana | 150,000 |
| 26301 | Barra e Porto de Caminha | 10,000 |
| 26302 | Porto da Nazaré | 7,500 |

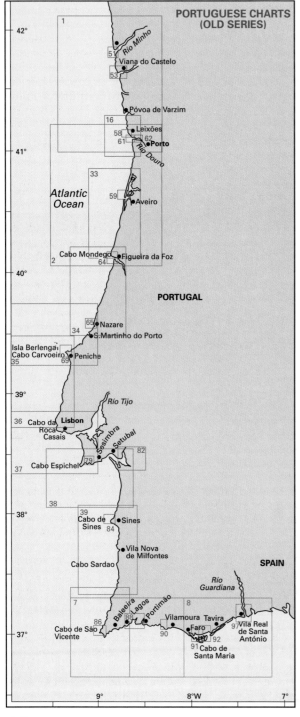

| Chart | Title | Scale |
|---|---|---|
| 26303 | Barras do Porto de Lisboa e | |
| | Baia de Cascais | 15,000 |
| 26304 | Porto de Lisboa (de Paço de Arcos ao | |
| | Terreiro do Trigo) | 15,000 |
| 26305 | Porto de Lisboa (de Alcântra à | |
| | Cala do Montijo | 15,000 |
| 26306 | Porto de Lisboa (do Terreiro do Trigo | |
| | a Sacavém) | 15,000 |
| 26307 | Rio Tejo (de Sacavém a Vila Franca | |
| | de Xira) | 15,000 |
| 26308 | Barra e Porto de Setúbal | 15,000 |
| 26309 | Porto de Setúbal (da Carraca à | |
| | Ilha do Cavalo) | 15,000 |
| 26310 | Barra e Porto de Portimão | 7,500 |
| 26311 | Barra e Portos de Faro e Olhão | 15,000 |
| 26312 | Barra e Portos de Vila Real de | |
| | Santo António e Ayamonte | 15,000 |
| 26401 | Aproximações a Viana do Castelo; | |
| | Barra e Porto de Viana do Castelo | 30,000 |
| 26402 | Aproximações a Leixões; Porto de Leixões | |
| | e Barra do Rio Douro | 30,000 |
| 26403 | Aproximações a Aveiro; Barra e | |
| | Porto de Aveiro | 30,000 |
| 26404 | Aproximações à Figueira da Foz; | |
| | Barra e Porto da Figueira da Foz | 30,000 |
| 26405 | Aproximações às Berlengas e a Peniche; | |
| | Porto de Peniche | 30,000 |
| 26406 | Cascais a Vila Franca de Xira; | |
| | Barras do Porto de Lisboa | 50,000 |
| 26407 | Cabo Espichel ao Porto do Setúbal; | |
| | Porto de Sesimbra; Barra do | |
| | Porto de Setúbal | 50,000 |
| 26408 | Aproximações a Sines; Porto de Sines | 30,000 |
| 27501 | Portos da Costa Oeste: Barra e Porto de | |
| | Esposende; Porto de Póvoa de Varzim; | |
| | Porto de Vila do Conde; Baia de São | |
| | Martinho do Porto; Porto de Ericeira; | |
| | Barra de Vila Nova de Milfontes | 7,500 |
| 27502 | Ponta de Piedade à Praia do Vau (inc Lagos); | |
| | Enseadas de Belixe, Sagres e Baleeira | 15,000 |
| 27503 | Portos da Costa Sul: Enseada de Albufeira; | |
| | Vilamoura; Barra de Tavira | 10,000 |

## Portuguese Hydrographic Institute

(Old series – see page 3)

| Chart | Title | Scale |
|---|---|---|
| 1 | Rio Minho à Espinho | 150,000 |
| 2 | Espinho ao Cabo Mondego | 150,000 |
| 7 | Cabo de São Vicente à Albufeira | 150,000 |
| 8 | Albufeira ao Rio Guadiana | 15,000 |
| 16 | Aproximações de Leixões (Vila Chã | |
| | à Espinho) | 50,000 |
| 22 | Leixões à Lisboa | 300,000 |
| 24 | Cabo de São Vicente ao Estreito de | 350,000 |
| | Gibraltar | |
| 33 | Furadouro ao Cabo Mondego | |
| | (aproximações de Aveiro) | 75,000 |
| 34 | Cabo Mondego à Nazaré | 75,000 |
| | Plano São Martinho do Porto | |
| 35 | Nazaré ao Cabo Carvoeiro | 75,000 |
| | Planos Isla Berlenga, Ilhéus Farilhões | |
| 36 | Cabo Carvoeiro ao Cabo da Roca | 75,000 |
| | Plano Ericeira | |
| 37 | Cabo da Roca ao Cabo Espichel | |
| | (aproximações de Lisboa) | 75,000 |
| 38 | Cabo Espichel à Lagoa de Sto André | |

| Chart | Title | Scale |
|---|---|---|
| | (aproximações de Setúbal) | 75,000 |
| 39 | Lagoa de Sto André ao Cabo Sardão | |
| | (aproximações de Sines) | 75,000 |
| 40 | Ponta da Atalaia à Ponta da Piedade | 75,000 |
| 51 | Barra e Porto de Caminha | 10,000 |
| 53 | Barra e Porto de Viana do Castelo | 5,000 |
| 58 | Porto de Leixões | 7,500 |
| 59 | Porto de Aveiro | 10,000 |
| 61 | Rio Douro – Foz a Gaia | 7,500 |
| 62 | Rio Douro – Gaia ao Esteiro | 7,500 |
| 64 | Barra e Porto da Figueira da Foz | 10,000 |
| 65 | Enseada da Nazaré | 7,500 |
| | Plano Porto da Nazaré | |
| 69 | Peninsula de Peniche | 20,000 |
| 79 | Enseada de Sesimbra | 10,000 |
| 82 | Rio Sado | 25,000 |
| 84 | Porto de Sines | 7,500 |
| 86 | Enseada de Belixe, Sagres e Baleeira | 20,000 |
| 88 | Lagos à Portimão | 20,000 |
| 90 | Enseada de Albufeira | 10,000 |
| 91 | Barra e Ria de Faro | 15,000 |
| 92 | Barra e Ria de Olhão | 15,000 |
| 97 | Barra e Portos de Vila Real de Santo António e Ayamonte | 15,000 |

## Imray charts

| Chart | Title | Scale |
|---|---|---|
| C18 | Biscay Passage Chart | |
| | Falmouth to Vigo | 686,000 |
| | Plans La Coruña, Approaches to Vigo | |
| C19 | Portuguese Coast Passage Chart | |
| | Cabo Finisterre to Gibraltar | 758,800 |
| | Plans Bayona, Viana do Castelo, Figueira da Foz, Approaches to Lisbon, Lagos, Bahía de Cádiz, Strait of Gibraltar, Gibraltar | |
| M1 | Southeast Spain | |
| | Gibraltar to Cabo San António | 685,000 |
| | Plans Strait of Gibraltar, etc | |

## II. FURTHER READING

### Pilot books, almanacs and yachtsmen's guides – general

This volume is currently the only UK-published guide to the area written primarily for yachtsmen. However details of principal harbours and some interesting background information appear in the British Admiralty Hydrographic Department's *NP 67: West Coasts of Spain and Portugal Pilot* (7th edition, 1999). The American equivalent is the US Defense Mapping Agency's *Pub 143 : Sailing Directions for the West Coast of Europe and North West Africa*, which covers Iberia in somewhat sparser detail.

Some useful information may also be found in the *Guía del Navegante España y Portugal*, also known as the *Yachtsman's Guide to Spain and Portugal*, published annually by PubliNáutic, with text in English and Spanish. This directory of marinas and services covers the entire Atlantic and Mediterranean coasts of Iberia as well as the Balearic Islands – towards which it is heavily slanted – but is no substitute for a detailed cruising guide.

The same may be said of both the *Cruising Association Handbook* and the *Macmillan Reeds Nautical Almanac*, each of which covers major harbours on the Atlantic coasts of Spain and Portugal as far as Gibraltar. In both books the text is backed up by clear, four-coloured plans, but while a great deal better than nothing for a yacht on passage, neither can provide the detailed information required for a leisurely cruise. All are available from UK chandleries and sailing bookshops.

### Pilot books, almanacs and yachtsmen's guides – area specific

If cruising the *rias* it would be worth keeping an eye open for a copy of *Portos de Galicia*, published in the mid-1990s by the Xunta de Galicia and covering the coast from Ribadeo in the north to La Guardia in the south. The first part is taken up with plans and eye-catching photographs (many of them aerial shots), accompanied by text in Castilian Spanish and Galego, with the English text in its own section near the back. Reproductions of sixteen medium-scale Spanish charts conclude the book. Though distinctly lacking in navigational detail the photos alone justify its purchase.

Two recently published guides, with a third due shortly, are those produced by the Portuguese Instituto Hidrográfico. The series title is *The Yachtsmen's Guide to the Coast of Portugal*, with *Lisbon and Ports of the Central Zone* and *Southern West Coast and Algarve* available so far. The final volume will presumably cover the stretch from the Rio Minho south to Nazaré. Written in very passable English with all plans and photographs in full colour, these attractive little guides would deserve a slot on any yacht's bookshelf – if they can be located. The best bet if not actually in Lisbon would probably be to order through either the Portuguese Instituto Hidrográfico de la Marina, J Garraio & Ca Lda or Azimute Lda (see page 154 for contact details).

Of interest if cruising the Algarve, though by now extremely out of date, is the *Roteiro da Costa do Algarve* published by the Portuguese Instituto Hidrográfico in 1984. Little of the text (in Portuguese, French and English) is of practical use, but some of the photography is excellent.

As yet unseen in the UK, is *La Navegación de Recreo por el Río de Sevilla* (*Leisure Navigation on the River of Seville*) by Ricardo Franco. Written by a master mariner and very experienced Guadalquivir pilot and published early in 2000, this book includes large-scale charts of the river with text in English and Spanish. Further information can be found on the internet at www.eintec.es/riodesevilla/, with the marina office at Chipiona amongst the stockists listed.

Finally, any skipper planning to continue east through the Strait of Gibraltar is strongly recommended to purchase a copy of Colin Thomas's excellent *Straits Sailing Handbook*. This A5-sized book, ring-bound between soft covers, is published annually and includes some useful advertising. It is available from Imray Laurie Norie & Wilson Ltd or can be ordered directly from the author at Straits Sailing, 6 The Square, Marina Bay, Gibraltar, ☎ 51372, *Fax* 51373, *e-mail* straits.sail@gibnynex.gi. In addition to very clear current and tidal flow diagrams the 2000 edition contains Lisbon and Gibraltar tide tables, weather information, and passage and port data covering the stretch between Chipiona and Benalmadena, including several harbours on the Moroccan coast.

## Travel guides

Travel guides appear to rival cookery books in the sheer quantity published, with different series aimed at various sectors of the market. There are the predominantly practical, the strictly erudite and sunshine holiday hoppers, and final choice must be down to personal preference. However unless intending to pass through in an unseeing rush, there should be a place for several of the following on the yacht's bookshelf:

*AA Explorer series*; *APA Insight Guides*; *Baedeker's Guides* (AA Publishing); *Berlitz Pocket Guides* and *Berlitz Travellers Guides*; *Blue Guides* (Black); *Cadogan Guides*; *Eyewitness Travel Guides* (Dorling Kindersley); *Fodor's Guides*; *Independent Traveller's Guides* (Harper Collins); *Let's Go: Spain and Portugal* (Let's Go Inc./Macmillan); *Lonely Planet Guides*; *Michelin Guides*; *Spain & Portugal in Your Pocket* (Pocket Travellers); *Sunflower Landscapes*; *Rough Guides*; *Time Out Guides* (Penguin Books).

## General or specialised

*AA Essential Food and Drink: Spain* (AA Publications).

*Backwards out of the Big World*, Paul Hyland (Harper Collins). A fascinating account of travelling in Portugal interspersed with historical sidelights.

*Living in Portugal*, Susan Thackeray (Robert Hale). Useful for anyone considering laying up or living aboard.

*Moors in Spain and Portugal, The*, Jan Read. (Arnold). A history and a cultural account.

*Portuguese: the land and its people, The*, Marion Kaplan (Penguin).

*Rock of Contention*, George Hills (Robert Hale). An interesting account of Gibraltar from prehistoric times until 1973.

*Self Catering in Portugal*, Carol Wright (Croom, Helm).

*Self Catering in Spain*, Carole Stewart and Chris Stewart (Croom, Helm).

*Spain*, Jan Morris (Faber & Faber and Penguin).

*Spain*, Sacheverell Sitwell (Batsford).

*Spanish Civil War, The*, Hugh Thomas (Eyre & Spottiswood).

*Spanish Journeys: A Portrait of Spain*, Adam Hopkins. History, travel and a good deal about art and architecture in one readable paperback.

*Unknown Portugal*, George Pillement (Johnson).

*Yachtsman's Ten Language Dictionary, The*, Barbara Webb and Michael Manton; Adlard Coles Nautical.

## III. Glossary

A more complete glossary is given in the *Yachtsman's Ten Language Dictionary* compiled by Barbara Webb and Michael Manton with the Cruising Association (Adlard Coles Nautical). Terms related to meteorology and sea state follow at the end of each section.

### General and chartwork terms

| English | Spanish | Portuguese |
| --- | --- | --- |
| anchor, to | fondear | fundear |
| anchorage | fondeadero, ancladero | fundeadouro, ancoradouro |
| basin, dock | dársena | doca |
| bay | bahía, ensenada | baía, enseada |
| beach | playa | praia |
| beacon | baliza | baliza |
| beam | manga | largura, boca |
| berth | atracar | atracar |
| black | negro | preto |
| blue | azul | azul |
| boatbuilder | astillero | estaleiro |
| bottled gas | cilindro de gas, carga de gas | cilindro de gás, bilha de gás |
| breakwater | rompeolas, muelle | quebra-mar, molhe |
| buoy | boya | bóia |
| bus | autobús | autocarro |
| cape | cabo | cabo |
| car hire | aquilar coche | alugar automóvel |
| chandlery (shop) | efectos navales, apetrachamento | fornecedore de barcos, aprestos |
| channel | canal | canal |
| charts | cartas náuticas | cartas hidrográficas |
| church | iglesia | igreja |
| crane | grua | guindaste |
| creek | estero | esteiro |
| Customs | Aduana | Alfândega |
| deep | profundo | profundo |
| depth | sonda, profundidad | profundidade |
| diesel | gasoil | gasoleo |
| draught | calado | calado |
| dredged | dragado | dragado |
| dyke, pier | dique | dique |
| east | este | este |
| eastern | levante, oriental | levante, do este |
| electricity | electricidad | electricidade |
| engineer, mechanic | ingeniero, mecánico | engenheiro, técnico |
| entrance | boca, entrada | bôca, entrada |
| factory | fábrica | fábrica |
| foul, dirty | sucio | sujo |
| gravel | cascajo | burgau |
| green | verde | verde |
| harbourmaster | diretor do porto | capitán de puerto |
| height, clearance | altura | altura |
| high tide | pleamar, marea alta | preia-mar, maré alta |
| high | alto/a | alto/a |
| ice | hielo | gelo |
| inlet, cove | ensenada | enseada |
| island | isla | ilha, ilhéu |
| islet, skerry | islote | ilhota |
| isthmus | istmo | istmo |
| jetty, pier | malecón | quebra-mar |
| knots | nudos | nós |
| lake | lago | lago |
| laundry, launderette | lavandería, automática | lavanderia, automática |
| leading line, transit | enfilación | enfiamento |

| English | Spanish | Portuguese |
|---|---|---|
| leeward | sotavento | sotavento |
| length overall | eslora total | comprimento |
| lighthouse | faro | farol |
| lock | esclusa | esclusa |
| low tide | bajamar, marea baja | baixa-mar, maré baixa |
| mailing address | dirección de correo | endereço para correio |
| marina, yacht harbour | puerto deportivo, dársena de yates | porto desportivo, doca de recreio |
| medical services | servicios médiocos | serviços médicas |
| mud | fango | lôdo |
| mussel rafts | viveros | viveiros |
| narrows | estrecho | estreito |
| north | norte | norte |
| orange | anaranjado | alaranjado |
| owner | propietario | propietário |
| paraffin | parafina | petróleo para iluminãçao |
| petrol | gasolina | gasolina |
| pier, quay, dock | muelle | molhe |
| point | punta | ponta |
| pontoon | pantalán | pontáo |
| port (side) | babor | bombordo |
| Port of Registry | Puerto de Matrícula | Porto de Registo |
| port office | capitanía | capitania |
| post office | oficina de correos | agência do correio |
| quay | muelle | molhe, cais |
| ramp | rampa | rampa |
| range (tidal) | repunte | amplitude |
| red | rojo | vermelho |
| reef | arrecife | recife |
| reef, spit | restinga | restinga |
| registration number | matricula | número registo |
| repairs | reparacións | reparações |
| rock, stone | roca, piedra | laxe, pedra |
| root (eg. of mole) | raíz | raiz |
| sailing boat | barca de vela | barco à vela |
| sailmaker, sail repairs | velero, reparacións velas | veleiro, reparações velas |
| saltpans | salinas | salinas |
| sand | arena | areia |
| sea | mar | mar |
| seal, to | precintar | fechar |
| shoal, low | bajo | baixo |
| shops | tiendas, almacéns | lojas |
| shore, edge | orilla | margem |
| showers (washing) | duchas | duches |
| slab, flat rock | laja | laje |
| slack water, tidal stand | repunte | águas paradas |
| slipway | varadero | rampa |
| small | pequeño | pequeno |
| south | sur | sul |
| southern | meridional | do sul |
| starboard | estribor | estibordo |
| strait | estrecho | estreito |
| supermarket | supermercado | supermercado |
| tower | torre | tôrre |
| travel-lift | grua giratoria, pórtico elevador | e pórtico, pórtico elevador, içar |
| water (drinking) | agua potable | água potável |
| weather forecast | previsión/boletin metereológico | previsão de tempo, boletim meteorológico |

| English | Spanish | Portuguese |
|---|---|---|
| weed | alga | alga |
| weight | peso | pêso |
| west | oeste | oeste |
| western | occidental | do oeste |
| white | blanco | branco |
| windward | barlovento | barlavento |
| works (building) | obras | obras |
| yacht (sailing) | barca de vela | barco à vela |
| yacht club | club náutico | clube náutico, clube naval |
| yellow | amarillo | amarelo |

**Meteorology and sea state**

| English | Spanish | Portuguese |
|---|---|---|
| calm (force 0, 0–1 kts) | calma | calma |
| light airs (force 1, 1–3 kts) | ventolina | aragem |
| light breeze (force 2, 4–6 kts) | flojito | vento fraco, brisa |
| gentle breeze (force 3, 7–10 kts) | flojo | vento bonançoso, brisa suave |
| moderate breeze (force 4, 11–16 kts) | bonancible | vento moderado, brisa moderado |
| fresh breeze (force 5, 17–21 kts) | fresquito | vento fresco, brisa fresca |
| strong breeze (force 6, 22–27 kts) | fresco | vento muito fresco, brisa forte |
| near gale (force 7, 28–33 kts) | frescachón, ventania moderada | vento forte, |
| gale (force 8, 34–40 kts) | duro | vento muito forte, ventania fresca |
| severe gale (force 9, 41–47 kts) | muy duro | vento tempestuoso, ventania forte |
| storm (force 10, 48–55 kts) | temporal | temporal, ventania total |
| violent storm (force 11, 56–63 kts) | borrasca, tempestad | temporal desfieto, tempestade |
| hurricane (force 12, 64+ kts) | huracán | furacão, ciclone |
| breakers | rompientes | arrebentação |
| cloudy | nubloso | nublado |
| depression (low) | depresión | depressão |
| fog | niebla | nevoeiro |
| gust | racha | rajada |
| hail | granizada | saraiva |
| mist | neblina | neblina |
| overfalls, tide race | escarceos | bailadeiras |
| rain | lluvia | chuva |
| ridge (high) | dorsal | crista |
| rough sea | mar gruesa | mar bravo |
| short, steep sea | mar corta | mar cavado |
| shower | aguacero | aguaceiro |
| slight sea | marejadilla | mar chão |
| squall | turbonada | borrasca |
| swell | mar de leva | ondulação |
| thunderstorm | tempestad | trovoada |

*Atlantic Spain and Portugal*

## General and chartwork terms

| Spanish | English | Portuguese |
|---|---|---|
| Aduana | Customs | Alfândega |
| agua potable | water (drinking) | água potável |
| alga | weed | alga |
| almacéns | shops | lojas |
| alto/a | high | alto/a |
| altura | height, clearance | altura |
| amarillo | yellow | amarelo |
| anaranjado | orange | alaranjado |
| ancladero | anchorage | fundeadouro, ancoradouro |
| apetrachamento | chandlery (shop) | fornecedore de barcos, aprestos |
| aquilar coche | car hire | alugar automóvel |
| arena | sand | areia |
| arrecife | reef | recife |
| astillero | boatbuilder | estaleiro |
| atracar | berth | atracar |
| autobús | bus | autocarro |
| azul | blue | azul |
| babor | port (side) | bombordo |
| bahía | bay | baía, enseada |
| bajamar | low tide | baixa-mar, maré baixa |
| bajo | shoal, low | baixo |
| baliza | beacon | baliza |
| barca de vela | sailing boat, yacht | barco à vela |
| barlovento | windward | barlavento |
| blanco | white | branco |
| boca | entrance | bôca, entrada |
| boya | buoy | bóia |
| cabo | cape | cabo |
| calado | draught | calado |
| canal | channel | canal |
| capitanía | port office | capitania |
| carga de gas | bottled gas | cilindro de gás, bilha de gás |
| cartas náuticas hidrográficas | charts | cartas |
| cascajo | gravel | burgau |
| cilindro de gas | bottled gas | cilindro de gás, bilha de gás |
| club náutico | yacht club | clube náutico, clube naval |
| dársena de yates | marina, yacht harbour | porto desportivo, doca de recreio |
| dársena | basin, dock | doca |
| dique | dyke, pier | dique |
| direcçión de correo | mailing address | endereço para correio |
| diretor do porto | harbourmaster | capitán de puerto |
| dragado | dredged | dragado |
| duchas | showers (washing) | duches |
| efectos navales | chandlery (shop) | fornecedore de barcos, aprestos |
| electricidad | electricity | electricidade |
| enfilación | leading line, transit | enfiamento |
| ensenada | bay, inlet, cove | baía, enseada |
| entrada | entrance | bôca, entrada |
| esclusa | lock | esclusa |
| eslora total | length overall | comprimento |
| este | east | este |
| estero | creek | esteiro |
| estrecho | narrows, strait | estreito |
| estribor | starboard | estibordo |
| fábrica | factory | fábrica |
| fango | mud | lôdo |
| faro | lighthouse | farol |
| fondeadero | anchorage | fundeadouro, ancoradouro |
| fondear | anchor, to | fundear |
| gasoil | diesel | gasoleo |
| gasolina | petrol | gasolina |
| grua giratoria | travel-lift | e pórtico, pórtico elevador, içar |
| grua | crane | guindaste |
| hielo | ice | gelo |
| iglesia | church | igreja |
| ingeniero, mecánico | engineer, mechanic | engenheiro, técnico |
| isla | island | ilha, ilhéu |
| islote | islet, skerry | ilhota |
| istmo | isthmus | istmo |
| lago | lake | lago |
| laja | slab, flat rock | laje |
| lavandería, l. automática | laundry, launderette | lavanderia, l.automática |
| levante | eastern | levante, do este |
| malecón | jetty, pier | quebra-mar |
| manga | beam | largura, boca |
| mar | sea | mar |
| marea alta | high tide | preia-mar, maré alta |
| marea baja | low tide | baixa-mar, maré baixa |
| matricula | registration number | número registo |
| meridional | southern | do sul |
| muelle | breakwater, pier, | quebra-mar, |
| molhe, | quay, dock | cais |
| negro | black | preto |
| norte | north | norte |
| nudos | knots | nós |
| obras | works (building) | obras |
| occidental | western | do oeste |
| oeste | west | oeste |
| oficina de correos | post office | agência do correio |
| oriental | eastern | levante, do este |
| orilla | shore, edge | margem |
| pantalán | pontoon | pontão |
| parafina | paraffin | petróleo para iluminãçao |
| pequeño | small | pequeno |
| peso | weight | pêso |
| piedra | rock, stone | pedra |
| playa | beach | praia |
| pleamar | high tide | preia-mar, maré alta |
| pórtico elevador | travel-lift | e pórtico, pórtico elevador, içar |
| precintar | seal, to | fechar |
| previsión/boletin metereológico | weather forecast | previsão de tempo, boletim meteorológico |
| profundidad | depth | profundidade |
| profundo | deep | profundo |
| propietario | owner | propietário |
| Puerto de Matrícula | Port of Registry | Porto de Registo |

| Spanish | English | Portuguese |
|---|---|---|
| puerto deportivo | marina, yacht harbour | porto desportivo, doca de recreio |
| punta | point | ponta |
| raíz | root (eg. of mole) | raiz |
| rampa | ramp | rampa |
| reparacións | repairs | reparações |
| repunte | tidal range, stand, slack water | águas paradas, amplitude |
| restinga | reef, spit | restinga |
| roca | rock | laxe |
| rojo | red | vermelho |
| rompeolas | breakwater | quebra-mar, molhe |
| salinas | saltpans | salinas |
| servicios médiocos | medical services | serviços médicas |
| sonda | depth | profundidade |
| sotavento | leeward | sotavento |
| sucio | foul, dirty | sujo |
| supermercado | supermarket | supermercado |
| sur | south | sul |
| tiendas | shops | lojas |
| torre | tower | tôrre |
| varadero | slipway | rampa |
| velero, reparacións velas | sailmaker, sail repairs | veleiro, reparações velas |
| verde | green | verde |
| viveros | mussel rafts | viveiros |

## Meteorology and sea state

| Spanish | English | Portuguese |
|---|---|---|
| calma | calm (force 0, 0–1 kts) | calma |
| ventolina | light airs (force 1, 1–3 kts) | aragem |
| flojito | light breeze (force 2, 4–6 kts) | vento fraco, brisa |
| flojo | gentle breeze (force 3, 7–10 kts) | vento bonançoso, brisa suave |
| bonancible | moderate breeze (force 4, 11–16 kts) | vento moderado, brisa moderado |
| fresquito | fresh breeze (force 5, 17–21 kts) | vento frêsco, brisa fresca |
| frêsco | strong breeze (force 6, 22–27 kts) | vento muito fresco, brisa forte |
| frescachón | near gale (force 7, 28–33 kts) | vento forte, ventania moderada |
| duro | gale (force 8, 34–40 kts) | vento muito forte, ventania fresca |
| muy duro | severe gale (force 9, 41–47 kts) | vento tempestuoso, ventania forte |
| temporal | storm (force 10, 48–55 kts) | temporal, ventania total |
| borrasca, tempestad | violent storm (force 11, 56–63 kts) | temporal desfieto, tempestade |
| huracán | hurricane (force 12, 64+ kts) | furacão, ciclone |
| aguacero | shower | aguaceiro |
| depresión | depression (low) | depressão |
| dorsal | ridge (high) | crista |
| escarceos | overfalls, tiderace | bailadeiras |
| granizada | hail | saraiva |
| lluvia | rain | chuva |
| mar corta | short, steep sea | mar cavado |
| mar de leva | swell | ondulação |
| mar gruesa | rough sea | mar bravo |

| Spanish | English | Portuguese |
|---|---|---|
| marejadilla | slight sea | mar chão |
| neblina | mist | neblina |
| niebla | fog | nevoeiro |
| nubloso | cloudy | nublado |
| racha | gust | rajada |
| rompientes | breakers | arrebentação |
| tempestad | thunderstorm | trovoada |
| turbonada | squall | borrasca |

## General and chartwork terms

| Portuguese | English | Spanish |
|---|---|---|
| agência do correio | post office | oficina de correos |
| água potável | water (drinking) | agua potable |
| águas paradas, amplitude | tidal range, stand, slack water | repunte repute |
| alaranjado | orange | anaranjado |
| alfândega | customs | aduana |
| alga | weed | alga |
| alto/a | high | alto/a |
| altura | height, clearance | altura |
| alugar automóvel | car hire | aquilar coche |
| amarelo | yellow | amarillo |
| areia | sand | arena |
| atracar | berth | atracar |
| autocarro | bus | autobús |
| azul | blue | azul |
| baía, enseada | bay, inlet, cove | bahía, ensenada |
| baixa-mar, maré baixa | low tide | bajamar, marea baja |
| baixo | shoal, low | bajo |
| baliza | beacon | baliza |
| barco à vela | sailing boat, yacht | barca de vela |
| barlavento | windward | barlovento |
| bôca, entrada | entrance | boca, entrada |
| bóia | buoy | boya |
| bombordo | port (side) | babor |
| branco | white | blanco |
| burgau | gravel | cascajo |
| cabo | cape | cabo |
| calado | draught | calado |
| canal | channel | canal |
| capitán de puerto | harbourmaster | diretor do porto |
| capitania | port office | capitanía |
| cartas hidrográficas | charts | cartas náuticas |
| cilindro de gás, bilha de gás | bottled gas | carga de gas, cilindro de gas |
| clube náutico, clube naval | yacht club | club náutico |
| comprimento | length overall | eslora total |
| dique | dyke, pier | dique |
| do oeste | western | occidental |
| do sul | southern | meridional |
| doca | basin, dock | dársena |
| dragado | dredged | dragado |
| duches | showers (washing) | duchas |
| e pórtico, pórtico elevador, içar | travel-lift | grua giratoria, pórtico elevador |
| electricidade | electricity | electricidad |
| endereço para correio | mailing address | dirección de correio |
| enfiamento | leading line, transit | enfilación |
| engenheiro, técnico | engineer, mechanic | ingeniero, mecánico |
| esclusa | lock | esclusa |

| Portuguese | English | Spanish |
|---|---|---|
| estaleiro | boatbuilder | astillero |
| este | east | este |
| esteiro | creek | estero |
| estibordo | starboard | estribor |
| estreito | narrows, strait | estrecho |
| fábrica | factory | fábrica |
| farol | lighthouse | faro |
| fechar | seal, to | precintar |
| fornecedore de barcos, aprestos | chandlery (shop) | apetrachamento, efectos navales |
| fundeadouro, ancoradouro | anchorage | fondeadero, ancladero |
| fundear | anchor, to | fondear |
| gasoleo | diesel | gasoil |
| gasolina | petrol | gasolina |
| gelo | ice | hielo |
| guindaste | crane | grua |
| igreja | church | iglesia |
| ilha, ilhéu | island | isla |
| ilhota | islet, skerry | islote |
| istmo | isthmus | istmo |
| lago | lake | lago |
| laje | slab, flat rock | laja |
| largura, boca | beam | manga |
| lavanderia, l. automática | laundry, launderette | lavandería, l. automática |
| laxe | rock | roca |
| levante, do este | eastern | levante, oriental |
| lôdo | mud | fango |
| lojas | shops | almacéns, tiendas |
| mar | sea | mar |
| margem | shore, edge | orilla |
| norte | north | norte |
| nós | knots | nudos |
| número registo | registration number | matricula |
| obras | works (building) | obras |
| oeste | west | oeste |
| pedra | rock, stone | piedra |
| pequeno | small | pequeño |
| pêso | weight | peso |
| petróleo para iluminãçao | paraffin | parafina |
| ponta | point | punta |
| pontáo | pontoon | pantalán |
| Porto de Registo | Port of Registry | Puerto de Matrícula |
| porto desportivo, doca de recreio | marina, yacht harbour | puerto deportivo, dársena de yates |
| praia | beach | playa |
| preia-mar, maré alta | high tide | pleamar, marea alta |
| preto | black | negro |
| previsão de tempo, boletim meteorológico | weather forecast | previsión/boletin metereológico |
| profundidade | depth | profundidad, sonda |
| profundo | deep | profundo |
| propietário | owner | propietario |
| quebra-mar | jetty, pier | malecón |
| quebra-mar, molhe, | breakwater, pier, quay, dock | muelle, rompeolas cais |
| raiz | root (eg. of mole) | raíz |
| rampa | ramp, slipway | rampa, varadero |
| recife | reef | arrecife |

| Portuguese | English | Spanish |
|---|---|---|
| reparações | repairs | reparacións |
| restinga | reef, spit | restinga |
| salinas | saltpans | salinas |
| serviços médicas | medical services | servicios médiocos |
| sotavento | leeward | sotavento |
| sujo | foul, dirty | sucio |
| sul | south | sur |
| supermercado | supermarket | supermercado |
| tôrre | tower | torre |
| veleiro, reparações velas | sailmaker, sail repairs | velero, reparacións velas |
| verde | green | verde |
| vermelho | red | rojo |
| viveiros | mussel rafts | viveros |

**Meteorology and sea state**

| Portuguese | English | Spanish |
|---|---|---|
| calma | calm (force 0, 0–1 kts) | calma |
| aragem | light airs (force 1, 1–3 kts) | ventolina |
| vento fraco, brisa | light breeze (force 2, 4–6 kts) | flojito |
| vento bonançoso, brisa suave | gentle breeze (force 3, 7–10 kts) | flojo |
| vento moderado, brisa moderado | moderate breeze (force 4, 11–16 kts) | bonancible |
| vento fresco, brisa fresca | fresh breeze (force 5, 17–21 kts) | fresquito |
| vento muito fresco, brisa forte | strong breeze (force 6, 22–27 kts) | fresco |
| vento forte, ventania moderada | near gale (force 7, 28–33 kts) | frescachón |
| vento muito forte, ventania fresca | gale (force 8, 34–40 kts) | duro |
| vento tempestuoso, ventania forte | severe gale (force 9, 41–47 kts) | muy duro |
| temporal, ventania total | storm (force 10, 48–55 kts) | temporal |
| temporal desfieto, tempestade | violent storm (force 11, 56–63 kts) | borrasca, tempestad |
| furacão, ciclone | hurricane (force 12, 64+ kts) | huracán |
| aguaceiro | shower | aguacero |
| arrebentação | breakers | rompientes |
| bailadeiras | overfalls, tide race | escarceos |
| borrasca | squall | turbonada |
| chuva | rain | lluvia |
| crista | ridge (high) | dorsal |
| depressão | depression (low) | depresión |
| mar bravo | rough sea | mar gruesa |
| mar cavado | short, steep sea | mar corta |
| mar chão | slight sea | marejadilla |
| neblina | mist | neblina |
| nevoeiro | fog | niebla |
| nublado | cloudy | nubloso |
| ondulação | swell | mar de leva |
| rajada | gust | racha |
| saraiva | hail | granizada |
| trovoada | thunderstorm | tempestad |

## IV. Abbreviations used on charts

| Spanish | Portuguese | Meaning |
| --- | --- | --- |
| F. | F. | Fixed |
| D. | Rl. | Flashing |
| Gp.D. | Rl.Agr. | Group flashing |
| F.D. | F.Rl. | Fixed and flashing |
| F.Gp.D. | F.Rl.Agr. | Fixed and group flashing |
| Ct. | Ct | Quick flashing |
| Gp.Ct. | Ct int | Interrupted quick flashing |
| Oc. | Oc. | Occulting |
| Gp.Oc. | Oc.Agr. | Group occulting |
| Iso | Is. | Isophase |
| Mo. | Morse | Morse |

**Colours**

| Spanish | Portuguese | Meaning |
| --- | --- | --- |
| am. | am. | Yellow |
| az. | azul | Blue |
| b. | br. | White |
| n. | pr. | Black |
| r. | vm. | Red |
| v. | vd. | Green |

**Seabed**

| | | |
| --- | --- | --- |
| A | A. | Sand |
| Al | Alg | Weed |
| R. | R. | Rock |
| F | L. | Mud |
| Co. | B. | Gravel |

# Index